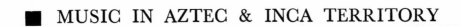

MUSIC IN AZTEC & INCA TERRITORY

Occidental culture: simultaneous performance of three-tubed flute and rattle. Field Collection, México.
Photo by Frederick Field *Courtesy of Charles L. Boilés*

MUSIC IN AZTEC & INCA TERRITORY

by Robert Stevenson

UNIVERSITY OF CALIFORNA PRESS □ BERKELEY, LOS ANGELES, LONDON

A. M. D. G.

University of California Press
Berkeley and Los Angeles, California
University of California Press, Ltd.
London, England
Copyright © 1968, 1976 by The Regents of the University of California
California Library Reprint Series Edition, 1976
ISBN: 0–520–03169–5
Library of Congress Catalog Card Number: 67–22715
Printed in the United States of America
Designed by Hans Wehrli

This is the first book in any language to juxtapose the musics of the two high American cultures. Since Indian musical life did not collapse all at once with the execution of Cuauhtémoc or Atahuallpa, this volume includes not only chapters describing music in Aztec and Inca areas at the moment of the first invasion, but also running summaries of the pre-1800 events in Mesoamerica and in the Andean highlands which directly expressed or affected Indian musical life.

Cathedral music in the Americas before 1800 does not enter the present scheme, even though abundant evidence survives to show that Indians monopolized instrumental music in Spanish-American cathedrals. On the other hand, the sections on postcontact musical life do stress those elements in the European tradition which can be proved to have affected great hordes of Indians—such as the fourteen music publications at Mexico City during 1556–1604 which were designed for Indian use. The apex of Indian musical culture awaited the seventeenth century when two exceptional Indian composers flourished whose works still survive to attest their merits, Don Juan de Lienas, active at Mexico City before 1650, and Juan Matías, maestro de capilla at Oaxaca *ca.* 1655–1667.

Several recent books in Spanish contain abundant iconography. I refer among others to the publications of Samuel Martí and Arturo Jiménez Borja (see bibliography). The 1925 two-volume study of Inca music by the d'Harcourt team (in French) still remains invaluable for its luxurious illustrations, not to mention the store of musical examples. Their *La musique des Aymara sur les hauts plateaux boliviens* (Paris: Société des Américanistes, 1959) boasts 17 excellent photographs and 104 musical examples.

The generosity of Rodolfo Barbacci—the erudite Maecenas whose Casa Mozart in Lima (formerly at Jirón Arequipa 184) published Rodolfo Holzmann's epochal 120-page *Panorama de la Música Tradicional del Perú* (Lima: Ministerio de Educación Pública, Escuela Nacional de Música y Danzas Folklóricas, 1966)—made possible the addition of a 31-page *Suplemento Ilustrativo* filled with fine photographs of indigenous players and instruments. Apart from such richly illustrated books as those of the d'Harcourts, Jiménez Borja, Martí, and now Holzmann, a considerable number of more specialized studies dealing with only one or two instruments from a limited area became available in the 1960's to augment the iconography of pre-Cortesian music. By way of example, I can mention Javier Romero Quiroz's two lavish booklets, *El Huehuetl de Malinalco* and *El Teponaztli de Malinalco* (Toluca: Universidad Autónoma del Estado de México, 1958 [70 pages] and 1964 [33 pages]), or Charles Lafayette Boilés' two brilliant articles, "La Flauta Triple de Tenenexpan" and "El Arco Musical, ¿Una Pervivencia?" in *La Palabra y el Hombre: Revista de la Universidad Veracruzana,* II Época/34 (April–June, 1965), 213–222, and 39 (July–Sept., 1966), 383–403, each handsomely illustrated.

As if the numerous fine photographs already published by Boilés, E. Thomas Stanford, and José Raúl Hellmer were insufficient, they each held in reserve enough others to make a veritable atlas of pre-Cortesian organography. What did principally restrain me, however, from insisting that the 1968 printing of this book contain costly plates to compete with the books and articles mentioned above were then the announced plans of José Luis Franco Carrasco. In 1962 and again in 1967 he generously showed me a monumental array of photographs, many never previously published anywhere, which he wished to include in a picture book. To have attempted anticipating him, or for that matter Boilés, Stanford, and Hellmer, would have been to treat unkindly these former friends.

On the other hand, to have included only a few illustrations would have inevitably committed me to a few hackneyed favorites, such as the Malinalco *huehuetl* and the Tlaxcala *teponaztli* for central Mexico. These two already appear in every popular book on the Aztecs. And rightly so. They are always included because they are among the most picturesque specimens that survive. But being superb examples of the wood-carver's craft does not guarantee that they are the most important musically, any more than Louis XV legs augur better piano tone or a handsome face makes MacDowell a finer composer than Mozart. The solution adopted in 1968 was to forego all plates except a frontispiece; the solution in the present reissue has been to include a mere sampling culled with his kind permission from the works of Martí— who died at Tepotzlán on March 29, 1975.

Thanks are owing the Thomas Y. Crowell Company, New York City, for permission to repeat certain material first published in *Music in Mexico:*

A Historical Survey (1952) and to the Technical Unit of Music and Folklore, General Secretariat, OAS, Washington, D.C., for similar authorization to incorporate in revised and updated form three chapters from *The Music of Peru: Aboriginal and Viceroyal Epochs* (1960). The distinguished folklorist and collector, Henrietta Yurchenco, graciously granted permission to cite her results. Numerous other authorities generously aided me, as the testimony of my text and footnotes constantly reveals.

One further prefatory explanation: the greater space devoted to Meso-american music does not reflect my personal preferences but merely indexes the presently available literature on the subject. Two to three times as much work has been done since 1850 on pre- and postcontact cultures in Mexico as in Peru. To cite Germanic scholarship by way of example: for every Tschudi or Uhle in Peru there has been a Seler, a Beyer, a Schultze Jena, a Lehmann, a Berlin, a Krickeberg, or a Nowotny in Mesoamerica. A synthesis such as the present book (which seeks for its basis verified research results) can devote no more space to any one topic than the literature already published by experts in anthropology, ethnology, paleography, and philology will permit.

Why the disproportionate literature? For one explanation, Mexico has always been much more easily accessible to northern hemisphere visitors. But in the sixteenth, seventeenth, and eighteenth centuries, Peru eclipsed even Mexico in the eyes of the Spanish Crown; and it was to Peru that conspicuously successful viceroys were promoted after years of faithful service in Mexico. At the arrival in Lima of Antonio de Mendoza, the first of these viceroys rewarded with promotion from Mexico to Peru, Negroes— already prominent in the musical life of Peru—lined the reception route playing drums draped in scarlet (*Libros de Cabildos de Lima, Libro Cuarto (Años 1548–1553)*, transcribed by Bertram T. Lee [Lima: Torres Aguirre-Sanmartí y Cía., 1935], p. 434 [Act of August 31, 1551]). The musicians hired to play trumpets welcoming the next viceroy were Mexican Indians ("los yndios pedro de tapia y francisco y anton naturales de mexico," *Libros de Cabildos . . . Libro Quinto (Años 1553–1557)*, p. 482 [Act of July 10, 1556]).

Another viceroy promoted from Mexico to Peru, Melchor Antonio Portocarrero de la Vega (1636–1705), commissioned the first New World opera, Tomás de Torrejón y Velasco's *La Púrpura de la Rosa* (Lima, Oct. 19, 1701). Were this preface the place to do so, further data could be offered to prove that Peru was as prime a musical area as Mexico, despite the limited literature. A capital in which strains of Senegal drumming and of Aztec trumpeting could mix with the heritage of Inca and of European music so early as the 1550's obviously deserves more attention from the ethnomusicologist than it has as yet received. Perhaps some reader of the present book will feel inspired to follow in the wake of viceroys like Mendoza and the Conde de la Monclova, or in the footsteps of such prize musicians as the Aztec-blood Pedro de Tapia and his two trumpeter colleagues of the same lineage, who centuries ago started the trek from Mexico City to Lima.

R.S.

March 1967

CONTENTS

Part I: THE AZTEC AREA

Part II: THE INCA AREA

PART 1

THE
AZTEC
AREA

THE CHALLENGE OF AZTEC MUSIC

In the United States popular opinion has it that no one knew anything about the Aztecs until William H. Prescott wrote his *History of the Conquest of Mexico* (3 vols.; New York: Harper and Brothers, 1843). Accomplished prose stylist that he was, Prescott cared no more for ethnic or art music than did Emerson [1] and limited himself to three indexed mentions of music and one of song (I, 108, 170, 172, 194). In his chapter on the "Golden Age of Tezcuco" (= Texcoco), he dismissed music thus (I, 170):

Lastly, there was an extraordinary tribunal, called the council of music, but which, differing from the import of its name, was devoted to the encouragement of science and art. Works on astronomy, chronology, history, or any other science, were required to be submitted to its judgment, before they could be made public.

Further on, when summarizing what Alva Ixtlilxóchitl had to say of Nezahualcóyotl's leanings toward monotheism—a topic in which Prescott could take a more personal interest—he tarried to mention the nine-storied tower on which the Texcocan ruler

mingled with his reverence for the Supreme the astral worship which existed among the Toltecs. Various musical instruments were placed on the top of the tower, and the sound of them, accompanied by the ringing of a sonorous metal struck by a mallet, summoned the worshippers to prayers, at regular seasons.

[1] *The Letters of Ralph Waldo Emerson,* ed. Ralph L. Rusk (New York: Columbia University Press, 1939), IV, 84, 87. Emerson heard Chopin in London but could not appreciate him.

In his footnote Prescott speared not only a misinformed Englishman but also by inference anyone who would presume to dig deeper into the musical usages of preconquest Mexico: " 'This was evidently a gong,' says Mr. Ranking, who treads with enviable confidence over the 'suppositos cineres,' in the path of the antiquary. See his Historical Researches on the Conquest of Peru, Mexico, &c., (London, 1827) p. 310." For all his Peruvian and Mexican fantasies, John Ranking's 478 pages (against Prescott's 1,492 pages on the conquest of Mexico alone) at least provided him with sufficient space to hint that the Aztecs were not completely "music-less." Prescott could not mention even the palace dwarfs and clowns who entertained Moctezuma without calling them "hideous anomalies" (II, 119) and fearing that "they were in some cases the result of artificial means, employed by unnatural parents." For amusement Moctezuma "at other times . . . witnessed the graceful dances of his women, or took delight in listening to music,—if the rude minstrelsy of the Mexicans deserve that name" (II, 127). This marks Prescott's limit, so far as Aztec music goes. Even the addlepated Ranking does at least specify Moctezuma's *musique de table* as a combination of "flute, snail-shell, a kettle drum" (p. 344), and does make room for the "sorrowful song, and drums and flutes" with which the bodies of deceased Mexican and Tarascan royalty were carried to their temples (pp. 381–382).

But must one really continue these many decades after Prescott believing his report that nothing except a "rude minstrelsy scarcely deserving the name of music" preceded Cortés' advent? Certainly not, if the evidence that continues to be gathered by such competent field researchers as Boilés, Franco, and Hellmer is taken seriously. Such a triple flute as the Tenenexpan described by Boilés, or a quadruple from Teotihuacán in the Museo Nacional de Antropología, or any of several other multiple flutes in the Fred Field and other private collections, even makes possible the claim that three-part harmony sounded on Mexican soil half a millennium before the three-part *Benedicamus Domino* trope (*Congaudeant catholici*) found its way into the Codex Calixtinus. Simultaneously with their multiple flutes, Mexican instrument makers were fabricating clay ocarinas and flutes with a reedy tone reminiscent of the oboe, gained by deflecting the air stream through an "oscillating chamber," as José Luis Franco calls it.

Still other claims for a remarkable music culture flourishing as early as A.D. 500–800 in Maya and Totonac areas, as well as at Teotihuacán, have been recently advanced. Did the Toltecs and Aztecs who followed in the wake of the classical civilizations inherit the musical science mastered by their predecessors? This would be a more difficult thesis to sustain. Nonetheless, some enthusiastic investigators contend that the Aztecs (not to be confused with earlier tribes) consciously systematized modulation, worked out written schemes of rallentando-accelerando, crescendo-diminuendo, devised ostinato patterns, and hit on many other schemes that induce formal unity in music, long before the art had progressed thus far in Italy, France, Spain, or Germany.

These recent attempts at draping Aztec music with so many victory flags run the danger of overplaying the hand, just as does the libretto of the first opera produced in Germany on an Aztec theme. The opera—*Montezuma* with music by Carl Heinrich Graun (1701–1759) and with a libretto versified from Frederick the Great's prose original—was mounted January 6, 1755. In October, 1753, Frederick sent a prose draft of the libretto to Count Francesco Algarotti, warning him: "[Here is an opera called *Montezuma*.] I chose the subject and am now adapting it. I need hardly tell you in advance that I take Montezuma's side and make Cortez the tyrant." [2]

So indeed he does. Cortés descends to the coarsest brutality while Moctezuma rises serene—the kind of generous, hospitable, and liberal-minded ruler adored by the Age of Enlightenment. For a bedfellow Cortés picks none other than Narváez, and together the wicked twosome trap Moctezuma in his garden; not their valor but rather a fell clap of artillery flattens Mexico (as if it had been that easy). For the "love" theme, that soul of chastity, Moctezuma, woos a Tlaxcalan princess; together they share a touching *Celeste Aïda* moment. In one of her last outbursts she exclaims against the firing of the city.

No less party spirit has been shown in some recent accounts of Aztec music, especially when all the provable advances made during the classical horizon (in instrument making) become Aztec property also. To avoid getting caught in the cross fire, we shall for the present try to avoid passing value judgments on a music scarcely less difficult to reconstruct than classic Greek music. Our more limited aim will be to synopsize the extensive literature from the sixteenth century to the present on music as practiced in Aztec-dominated territory at the moment of first contact with Europe. For a sequel, we shall (on pages 154–240) survey the changes wrought in Mexico during the earliest decades of acculturation.

Amid the smoke of controversy, one fact does rise clear. As a concert-hall art leading a straitjacketed existence apart from other arts, "music" never came alive in pre-Cortesian Mexico. Just because it always remained a twin to ritualistic dance, in any fair estimate of "music" in the Aztec scheme the reader needs to be reminded constantly that Aztec concepts and usages are being passed through the colander of our own categories. Gertrude P. Kurath and Samuel Martí attempt to remedy the defects of a too rigid schematization when they conjointly discuss *Dances of Anáhuac: The Choreography and Music of Precortesian Dances* (New York: Wenner-Gren

[2] *Denkmäler deutscher Tonkunst*, 1. Folge, 15. Band, p. ix.

Foundation for Anthropological Research, 1964). Their valiant effort at bringing the arts under one compatible roof should prompt other synthetic studies in English.

One such study would begin with the question: In what specific ways did Aztec arts submit themselves to the control of their religious philosophy? Miguel León Portilla's *Los antiguos mexicanos a través de sus crónicas y cantares* (México: Fondo de Cultura Económica, 1961) moves in the desired direction. Quoting from the Náhuatl informants whose testimonies were gathered by Bernardino de Sahagún in the *Códice Matritense de la Real Academia de la Historia* (Madrid), folio 180v, he claims that the indigenous philosophers denied to such civic centers as Azcapotzalco, Culhuacán, and Xochimilco even lungs to breathe, until "song received its rules, drums were fashioned and music sounded. Then, only, did life begin to stir in those cities." Like some Prometheus bringing down divine fire to suffering mankind in Greek myth, so also the *tlamatini* bestowed fine arts on the bereft interior highlands of Mexico—whence, declared Sahagún's informants (fols. 191v–192), the tlamatinime departed for the Gulf Coast.

The knowledge-bringers were also there in Tamoanchan,[3] those who were reported to possess the codices. But they refused to prolong their stay. The wise ones departed thence carrying with them the writings and paintings in black and red, they left bearing away with them the arts of the Toltecs, the music of flutes. . . .

And when they left they wended their way toward the face of the Sun bearing with them the black and red ink, codices and paintings; they carried away wisdom and learning, they took everything with them, the books of songs and the music of flutes.[4]

The story of Quetzalcóatl, the culture hero who was "the greatest figure in the ancient history of the New World, with a code of ethics and

[3] Tamoanchan = "the house of descent, place of birth, mystic west where gods and men originated" (Laurette Séjourné, *Burning Water: Thought and Religion in Ancient Mexico* [London: Thames & Hudson, 1956], pp. 118, 123, fig. 37).

[4] León Portilla, *Los antiguos mexicanos a través de sus crónicas y cantares* (México: Fondo de Cultura Económica, 1961), pp. 37, 50. Donald Robertson, reviewing this work in *American Anthropologist*, 63/6 (Dec., 1961), 1375–1376, sees "the danger that sources, which seem to be reflections of the pre-Conquest past, will have important if not massive unrecognized components of Hispanic thought and influence." If so, the Náhuatl texts should at least be studied in the original tongue. These can be seen in the facsimile edition of the manuscript (Madrid: Fototipia de Hauser y Menet, 1907) published in Volume VIII of Bernardino de Sahagún's *Historia de las Cosas de Nueva España* (Library of Congress call number F1219.S1313), under the supervision of Francisco del Paso y Troncoso. Volume V of this edition contains color reproductions of the valuable plates in the Sahagún source known as the *Códice Florentino* (music instruments at Láminas 8.38, 11.17, 11.19, 16.57, 17.63, 23.16, 23.19, 32.91, 48.64, 48.68–70, 51.88, 55.31). These pictures are constantly referred to throughout the present book.

[unprecedented] love for the sciences and the arts," has long been among the most familiar of Aztec legends. According to Aztec expectation, Quetzalcóatl, having retreated toward the east, would return from the east. But if Quetzalcóatl's eastern migration is well known, no one seems to have tried correlating similar legends that deal with messengers carrying away the "music of flutes" to the east. Is it significant in the light of these legends that much more archaeological evidence for a flute-dominated organology now comes to light at Gulf Coast sites than was revealed by the Escalerillas Street findings in 1900 at Mexico City?

Within our own generation, panpipes, previously unknown in Mexico, were unearthed at Tres Zapotes, and multiple flutes obligatorily sounding several notes at once were found not only there but at other sites as far north along the Yucatán Peninsula as Jaína Island and along the coastal plain of Veracruz as Tajín. Also, it has been coastal sites in Tabasco and Veracruz which have yielded the first and finest examples of the "oscillating air chamber" flute that sounds reedy (after the breath is deflected through a "goiter" beneath the flute's mouth).[5] The paramountcy of Gulf Coast cultures will be demonstrated even more authoritatively when Charles L. Boilés publishes his eagerly awaited *Aerofonos precolombinos de Veracruz,* scheduled by the Universidad Veracruzana in Jalapa. As a sample of what he holds in store, Boilés published in 1965 his essay on the triple flute of Tenenexpan. Even without the further publications promised by Boilés, Franco, Hellmer, and Stanford, however, enough evidence has already reached print to make us believe that Sahagún's native informants were repeating not mere legend but were attesting history when they ruefully recalled those messengers who bore away the "music of flutes" from Tamoanchan to the Gulf Coast before the year 1000. Quetzalcóatl retreated to the east, and thence he seemed to be returning in the person of Cortés. The messengers who carried away the music of flutes to the east coast may also seem to have been returning when Cortés' entourage included the professionals whose music the indigenes seized like a long-lost personal possession.

Among the other lacunae awaiting competent Náhuatl scholarship is the Aztec god "of music"—if a god who also served so many other ritual

---

[5] An authoritative essay on "oscillating air chamber" ocarinas and flutes was published in the Sunday *Excelsior,* October 14, 1962, Sección B, pp. 5B (cols. 4–8) and 8B (cols. 7–8). Entitled "Instrumentos musicales prehispánicos," this article takes the form of an interview with José Luis Franco (conducted by Marcela del Río). Line drawings of five whistles, a three-note Veracruz ocarina (shaped like a bird's beak), and a "goiter" two-hole flute from Tabasco enhance the value of the article. See also Franco's report "Sobre un Grupo de Instrumentos Prehispánicos con Sistema Acústico no Conocido," published in *Actas y Memorias* of the XXXV Congreso Internacional de Americanistas [1962] (México: Editorial Libros de México, S.A., 1964), III, 369.

purposes as Xochipilli ("Flower Prince"), and whose alter ego in the pantheon was Macuilxóchitl ("Five Flower"), can correctly be called the god "of music." Justino Fernández made a foray into the field when he published as recently as 1959 "Una aproximación a Xochipilli" in *Estudios de Cultura Náhuatl* (I, 31–41). But, as befitted his title, he principally concerned himself with the extremely beautiful cross-legged statue of the Flower Prince dug up at frigid Tlamanalco, D.F., and not with the attributes of Xochipilli-Macuilxóchitl, which permitted Carlos Chávez' giving his Aztec evocation (premiered in New York in 1940) such a name.[6]

Other aspects of Aztec musical policy which invite thorough research include:

1) *The civil privileges, such as tribute exemption, which professional musicians enjoyed.* In a letter to Charles V, dated November 3, 1532, Sebastián Ramírez de Fuenleal, president of the Royal Audiencia at Mexico City, specified exemption from paying tribute as a concession offered both singers and painters under Aztec law, because of their service to the community in preserving the memory of past glories.[7] Only because the singers attached to the many Mexican temples passed easily into Christian service, did a ready-made public exist for the numerous Mexican music imprints antedating 1600. The issue, three years before Jamestown's founding, of so big a book, consisting entirely of music, as did Juan Navarro's 210-page *Liber in quo quatuor passiones . . . continentur* (Mexico City: Diego López Dávalos, 1604), reflects glory not merely on the Spaniard who compiled the music but also on the native tradition of choirs that created a public for such a book.

2) *The custom of marking the hours in Aztec temples with a musical fanfare.* Long before friars arrived, temple musicians at Tenochtitlan were already in the habit of calling the city to prayers at stated intervals. Five times nightly and four times daily was the rule for priests in the major temples.[8] Outside the capital, musical fanfares to mark the hours of prayer were just as much the rule. Take, for instance, Cholula, near present-day Puebla. Before Cortés, this town boasted "more than 40,000 inhabitants"

[6] *Time,* May 27, 1940, p. 65, describes the Museum of Modern Art concert in New York at which was premiered Chávez' "fanciful reconstruction—called Xochipilli-Macuilxóchitl after the Aztec god of music." Asked whether it was "the real stuff," *Time* replied that "it really sounded like an Aztec jam session. Flutes and pipes shrilled and wailed, a trombone (subbing for the snail shell) neighed an angular melody, to the spine-tingling thump-and-throb of drums, gourds, rattles."

[7] Printed in Henri Ternaux-Compans, *Voyages, relations et mémoires originaux* (Paris: Arthus Bertrand, 1840), XVI, 218–219. See also Henry R. Wagner, "Henri Ternaux-Compans: A Bibliography," *Inter-American Review of Bibliography,* VII/3 (1957), item 22, p. 245.

[8] Bernardino de Sahagún, *Florentine Codex: Book 2—The Ceremonies,* trans. Arthur J. O. Anderson and Charles E. Dibble (Santa Fe: School of American Research, 1951 [Monographs, 14/III]), p. 202.

and drew many pilgrims because it was center of the Quetzalcóatl cult. A large corps of professional musicians lived off temple revenue, and it was their duty to escort the processions, to play at nightfall, at midnight, and at daybreak, summoning the populace to prayer. Gabriel de Rojas, corregidor of this "holy" city in 1581, wrote a description, comparing it with Rome or Mecca "because of the similar veneration in which it was held" by the central highlanders of Mexico.

Next to the temple there was a large block in which a great number of trumpeters and drummers lived whose duty it was to play their instruments before the pontiffs when they sallied forth. Also the trumpeters had the duty of playing their trumpets as a universal call to prayer at sunset, midnight, and daybreak. At midnight the ministers in the temple rose, prayed, bathed, and incensed the idol. The common folk in their homes rose, bathed, and recited their prayers.[9]

3) *The slots occupied by tenure musical appointees to Aztec temples.* According to the authoritative sixteenth-century chronicler Diego Durán (*Historia de las Indias de Nueva-España y Islas de Tierra Firme* [Mexico: J. M. Andrade y F. Escalante, 1867], I, 160), every important Mexican temple before Cortés employed graded officials who exactly corresponded to the precentor, succentor, and choir of professional singers customary in major Spanish sixteenth-century cathedrals. If such a musical hierarchy existed, it is too profound a fact for the student of acculturation to continue ignoring.

With such facts as these in mind, we can better understand how the eight canonical hours introduced by Franciscans, Dominicans, and Augustinians were so immediately and so easily substituted for already established Mexican custom. Rising regularly during the night for penances, prayers, incense, and music was nothing new for them. Nor were priestly processions with perfume and music. The maintaining of a graded professional corps of temple musicians for all this ceremony supplies the backdrop needed to explain how so luxuriant a flowering of church music could so quickly have occurred in colonial Mexico.

Still other facets of Aztec musical usage deserving of intensive study will undoubtedly come to light as more and more attention is trained on such documents as the *Cantares en idioma mexicano* (containing numerous drum notations), as more and more attempts are made to understand Náhuatl poetics, and as more and more effort is expended on the different regional and social-strata differences exhibited in surviving Náhuatl songs. Since, however, at the moment a survey of the already published literature seemed the most needed foundation on which to build a better future understanding, all these higher ambitions have had to give way to a synopsis of what has

---

[9] Gabriel de Rojas, "Descripción de Cholula," *Revista Mexicana de Estudios Históricos,* I/6 (Nov.–Dec., 1927), 162.

already been published. To have pursued all the inviting avenues for further research would have meant writing a book too ponderous for publication in English.

The temptation to plow the field more thoroughly has not been easily resisted. A really painstaking essay on the paintings of musicians and their instruments in both pre- and postcontact codices is still sorely needed. According to Juan A. Vásquez (*América Indígena*, XXIV/3 [July, 1964], 273), more than fifty such codices survive: fifteen at the Paris Bibliothèque Nationale; five at the Bodleian Library, Oxford; four at the Vatican Library; and fourteen at the Museo Nacional de Antropología in Mexico City. Twelve of the "more than fifty" early codices antedate the Conquest; others, like the Codex Borbonicus in Paris, were painted so soon after 1520 as to have suffered practically no European influence. One prime codex recently attracted the attention of an ethnomusicologist when María del Carmen Sordo Sodi published "Los dioses de la música y de la danza en el Códice Borgia" in *Revista del Conservatorio,* VII (June, 1964), 8–10, thus whetting the appetite for other essays to follow. But as she would be the first to agree, one codex is only an earnest.

Pre-Hispanic or no, at least forty codices record material of interest to the ethnomusicologist. Even late picture books such as the Codex Azcatitlan (painted *ca.* 1550 in the northern part of the Valley of Mexico) can yield extremely useful documentation on precontact Aztec music. Take as only one typical instance plate 24 of this codex (facsimile in *Journal de la Société des Américanistes,* n.s., XXXVIII [1949], suppl.). Robert Barlow describes plate 24 thus (*ibid.,* pp. 129–130):

In the middle of the patio rises the temple of Huitzilopochtli and Tlaloc. Inside the temple sit two besieged chieftains, while a third topples dead down the stairs below. Two musicians—one playing the vertical drum [*huehuetl*] the other the horizontal [*teponaztli*]—stick by their instruments and continue drumming, despite death and destruction all about them. At their feet lie the head of one slain eagle-costumed warrior and the dead body of the tiger warrior. . . . This carnage and the struggle of the few native warriors still alive depicts the massacre at the feast of Toxcatl—ordered in Cortés's absence by his trigger-happy lieutenant Pedro de Alvarado.

The moral of such a painting for the music historian is clear. At any ceremonial or religious feast, the Aztec musician could no more think of flying from his post, however grave the danger, than could the beleaguered soldiers. It was his inescapable duty to continue playing until the last note of the preordained ritual, or until his own death.

Let us turn finally to two other large blocks of material crying out for closer attention: (1) the corpus of Aztec song: Daniel G. Brinton's grossly inaccurate translation from the Náhuatl of selected *Cantares en idioma mexicano (Ancient Nahuatl Poetry* [Philadelphia, 1890]) has never been superseded by a better translation in English; and (2) pre-1600 teponaztlis in Mexico, Guatemala, and El Salvador: no reliable inventory has yet been published, nor are the tunings for even the inventoried instruments to be trusted. These samples of uncompleted tasks show the roads up which the future investigator is invited, but which must now be left for others with more time to roam.

Because the focus here is primarily on music in Aztec-dominated territory, Tarascan music is neglected, even though Michoacán bordered Mexico. For the same reason, the music of the wild tribes to the north is scarcely mentioned. On the other hand, the *pipiles* living as far south as modern El Salvador fit into the scheme, both because they acknowledged Aztec supremacy and because of their kindred dialect. For a delimitation of the various terms that can be confusing—"Aztec," "Mexica," and "Tenochca" —Diego Durán's *The Aztecs* (New York: Orion Press, 1964, p. 333) may prove helpful. The curious fact that Durán's translators could make *The Aztecs* do for a title that, in Spanish, runs to a dozen words, *Historia de las Indias de Nueva-España y Islas de Tierra Firme*, illustrates what catchall service the word "Aztecs" now renders English readers.

To go back only a generation, George C. Vaillant's classic *Aztecs of Mexico* (1941; 2d ed., 1962) exemplified the same trend toward synecdoche.[10] Not only have the "Aztecs" become popularly confused with the whole of preconquest Mexico, but anything on the aborigines intended for a wide English-speaking audience must somehow bow to this confusion. Like Debussy's *Clair de lune*, known by all, to the detriment of the *Suite Bergamasque* from which it comes, the "Aztecs" have somehow succeeded in upstaging all other actors in Mexican history.

---

[10] In the latest revision, "Aztec" music still cuts a miserable figure (Garden City: Doubleday, 1962), p. 136. The sentence, "The two-tone and one-tone drums could emit sonorous rhythms, but the bone and clay flutes pipe pitifully and are not gauged to a fixed scale," combines misinformation (huehuetls were *not* "one-tone drums") with condescension ("pipe pitifully"). Frederick A. Peterson, *Ancient Mexico* (New York: G. P. Putnam's Sons, 1959), devotes a chapter instead of a paragraph to precontact music and dance (pp. 202–216) and gets to the heart of the problem when he protests against downgrading Mexican aboriginal music merely because it "was *different* from European music" (p. 216). As in any survey by a nonspecialist, errors creep in occasionally, but his attitude is sympathetic and he benefited from the advice of his illustrator, José Luis Franco.

2 AZTEC MUSIC AT CONTACT: A SURVEY OF EXISTING LITERATURE

REVIVING INTEREST IN PRECONTACT MUSIC

Before 1920 most Mexican writers on music were content either to repeat the strictures against Aztec music uttered by such early conquistadores as Bernal Díaz del Castillo (*ca.* 1492–*ca.* 1581), or to follow the authority of such later historians as the exiled Creole Jesuit, Francisco Javier Clavijero (1731–1787), who called Aztec music the poorest art of the preconquest natives.[1]

Bernal Díaz, because his astonishingly vivid accounts of the music played and sung by the Aztecs during their ritual sacrifices of Spanish prisoners of war were picturesque, was a favorite authority. Quite naturally Aztec music could have seemed to Díaz only dismal and horrible. He associated it always with the memory of his comrades-in-arms sacrificed on the altar stone of the war god Huitzilopochtli. Even the battle music, exciting though he admitted it to have been, could not have won any praise from Bernal Díaz, the "true

---

[1] *Storia antica del Messico* (Cesena: Gregorio Biasini, 1780), II, 179: "Il loro canto era duro, e nojoso all'orecchie europee; ma eglino ne prendevano tanto piacere, che solevano nelle lor feste passar cantando tutto il dì. *Questa finalmente fu l'arte, nella quale meno riuscirono i Messicani.*" Earlier in the volume he had thus decried Aztec battle music (II, 146): "La lor Musica militare, nella quale era più il rumore, che l'armonìa, si componeva di tamburelli, di cornette, e di certi lumaconi marini, *che rendevano un suono acutissimo.*" Clavijero's original Spanish omitted the italicized criticisms: "This was unquestionably the art in which the Mexicans were least successful" (*The History of Mexico*, trans. Charles Cullen [2d ed.; London: J. Johnson, 1807], I, 399) and "which made an extremely shrill sound" (I, 369). See *Historia antigua de México*, ed. Mariano Cuevas (México: Editorial Porrúa, 1945), II, 302, 257.

historian" of all that befell the conquerors. Locked in a life-and-death struggle with the Aztecs, the conquistadores could not easily have discerned esthetic virtues in the opposing culture, even had they wished to be broad-minded.

A modern historian comfortably remote from the scene can describe Aztec civilization in terms of "well-planned cities with towering pyramids and impressive temples," of "vast and brilliantly colored palaces with extensive apartments and terraces," of "huge market squares with continually moving caravans of traders," of "[a] monetary system using gold and copper for currency," of "[a] highly developed system of picture writing," and of "elaborate patronage of the arts, such as poetry, the ritual dance, and music";[2] but what Díaz, who was closer to the scene, could see of their patronage of the arts afforded him less cause for rejoicing. He was a soldier; and the references in his *Historia verdadera* occur oftenest in the midst of his battle descriptions. His musical references include mention of the large Aztec war drum (*tlalpanhuehuetl*), of the instruments made of animal and human bone (*chicahuaztli* and *omichicahuaztli*), of the conch shell and vertical trumpets (*tecciztli* and *tepuzquiquiztli*), of the flutes (*tlapitzalli*), and of certain other instruments that are now less easily identifiable.

The following extracts, which are given in Alfred P. Maudslay's translation, show the kind of contact Bernal Díaz had with Aztec music:

As we were retreating we heard the sound of trumpets from the great Cue (where stand the idols Huichilobos [= Huitzilopochtli] and Tezcatepuca [= Tezcatlipoca]), which from its height dominates the whole City, and also a drum, a most dismal sound indeed it was, like an instrument of demons, as it resounded so that one could hear it two leagues off, and with it many small tambourines and shell trumpets, horns, and whistles. At that moment as we afterward learnt, they were offering the hearts of ten of our comrades and much blood to the idols that I have mentioned.	como nos yvamos rretrayendo oymos tañer del cu mayor q̄s donde Estavan sus ydolos huichilobos y tezcatepuca q̄ señorea El altor del a toda la gran çibdad y tanbien vn atanbor El mas triste sonido En fin como ynstrumento de demonios, y rretunbava tanto q̄ se oyera dos leguas y juntam^te con el muchos atabalejos, y caracoles, y bozinas, y silbos Entonçes segun despues supimos estavan ofresçiendo diez coraçones, y mucha sangre A los ydolos q̄ dho tengo, de nros Conpañeros.
Again there was sounded the dismal drum of Huichilobos and many other shells and horns and things like trumpets and the sound of them	torno a sonar el atanbor muy doloroso del Huichilobos y otros muchos caracoles y cornetas y otras como tronpetas y todo el

[2] Laurence E. Schmeckebier, *Modern Mexican Art* (Minneapolis: University of Minnesota Press, 1939), p. 4.

all was terrifying, and we all looked towards the lofty Cue where they were being sounded, and saw our comrades whom they had captured when they defeated Cortés were being carried by force up the steps, and they were taking them to be sacrificed. When they got them up to a small square in [front of] the oratory, where their accursed idols were kept, we saw them place plumes on the heads of many of them and with things like fans [pitchforks] they forced them to dance before Huichilobos, and after they had danced they immediately placed them on their backs on some rather narrow stones which had been prepared as [places for] sacrifice, and with stone knives they sawed open their chests and drew out their palpitating hearts and offered them to the idols that were there, and they kicked the bodies down the steps, and Indian butchers who were below cut off the arms and feet and flayed [the skin off] the faces, and prepared it afterwards like glove leather with the beards on.

sonido de ellos espantable y mirabamos al alto cu En donde las tañian y vimos que llevavan por fuerça las gradas arriba a nros conpañeros que habian tomado en la derrota q̄ dieron a cortes que los llevavan a sacrificar, y desque ya los tuvieron arriba en vna plaçeta que se hazia en el adoratorio, donde estavan sus malditos ydolos vimos que a muchos dellos les ponian plumajes en las cabeças y con vnos como aventadores les hazian baylar delante del Huichilobos y desque avian baylado luego les ponian despaldas ençima de vnas piedras algo delgadas q̄ tenian hechas para sacrificar y con vnos navajones de pedernal los aserraban por los pechos y les sacaban los coraçones buyando y se los ofresçian a sus ydolos que alli presentes tenian y los cuerpos dabanles con los pies por las gradas abajo, y estaban aguardando abajo otros yndios carniçeros que les cortaban braços y pies y las caras desollaban y los adouaban despues como cuero de guantes y con sus barbas

The Mexicans offered great sacrifice and celebrated festivals every night at their great Cue at Tlatelolco and sounded their cursed drum, trumpets, kettle drums and shells, and uttered yells and howls, and kept many bonfires of burning wood going all night long. Then they sacrificed our comrades to their accursed Huichilobos and Tezcatepuca.[3]

los mexicanos cada noche hazian grandes sacrifiçios y fiestas En el Cu mayor del tatelulco y tañian su maldito atanbor y otras tronpas y atabales y caracoles y davan muchos gritos y alaridos y tenian toda la noche grandes luminarias de mucha leña Ençendida y Entonçes sacrificavan de nros conpañeros A su maldito huichilobos y tezcatepuca

[3] Bernal Díaz del Castillo, The True History of the Conquest of New Spain (London: Hakluyt Society, 1912), IV, 142, 149–150, 154. For Albert Idell's translation of the same passages, see The Bernal Díaz Chronicles (New York: Doubleday, 1957), pp. 364, 368–369, 373. The Spanish text is published in Genaro García's edition based on the original manuscript of Díaz's Historia verdadera de la conquista de la Nueva España (México: Secretaría de Fomento, 1904), II, 96, 102, 105.

It is too much to expect that the conquerors who fought with Cortés should have been able to have evaluated Aztec music dispassionately. The memory of their own battles must surely have been too immediate and overwhelming. On the other hand, certain sixteenth-century missionaries— the learned Franciscan, Bernardino de Sahagún, for instance, or the laborious Dominican, Diego Durán—heard Aztec music with different ears, and were therefore able to render a more sympathetic account of it. But the unfavorable comments of Bernal Díaz, rather than these favorable accounts, created the climate of opinion in which the older generation of Mexican music historians lived, until about 1920.

As late as 1917 a member of the National Conservatory of Music faculty, Alba Herrera y Ogazón, published (under the official auspices of the Dirección General de las Bellas Artes) a treatise on Mexican music entitled *El Arte Musical en México*, in which she vigorously condemned Aztec music. In her way of thinking, Aztec music, since it exactly expressed the soul of a cruel and barbarous people, was a degenerate expression, and therefore unsuited to the refined tastes of civilized Europeans. The following two sentences carry the main drift of her argument against Aztec music:

From the exemplars of Aztec instruments preserved in the National Museum of Mexico, we may infer that the music of that people during the preconquest era was as barbarous and frightful as were the ceremonies at which their music was heard.

The conch shell, the Mixtec tún, the teponaztli, the chicahuaztli, the rattle, the Zapotec chirimía, and the Yaqui drum, are not instruments capable of producing either alone, or in conjunction with each other, a grateful harmony: nor of evoking a spiritual response in conformity with presently accepted standards of behavior; what these depraved sounds do conjure up are instead scenes of unrelieved ferocity.[4]

The only indigenous music Herrera y Ogazón could praise was a Tarascan melody which fortuitously resembled a theme from the scherzo of Beethoven's Symphony, Opus 92. Her mentor, Gustavo E. Campa, a former head of the National Conservatory, had discovered the note-for-note resemblance of the Tarascan melody in question, and since it exactly duplicated a theme already admired by cultivated musicians, she too lauded it. But this tendency to admire nothing in indigenous art unless some chance resemblance to a recognized European masterpiece could be discovered in it

---

[4] Alba Herrera y Ogazón, *El Arte Musical en México* (México: Dirección General de las Bellas Artes, 1917), p. 9. Continuing in the same strain, she contended that the eerie light of the sacrificial fires, the color of freshly spilled human blood, the shrieks of the captives, and the frenzy of the diabolical priests must have combined to produce a truly terrifying spectacle during rites when hapless victims by the hundreds were cruelly offered to their gods. "The music for these ceremonies must undoubtedly have been as lugubrious, incoherent, and macabre as the passions that inspired it" (p. 10).

prevented her, as it deterred others in Mexico, from seeing the idiomatic virtues of aboriginal art.

After 1920, however, a change occurred. At a time when Stravinsky's "primitive" *Le sacre du printemps* and Prokofieff's "barbaric" *Suite scythe* were revolutionizing art concepts in Europe, the primitivism and barbarism of native art in Mexico began to win praise instead of censure. Within a decade after the publication of Herrera y Ogazón's text, *El Arte Musical en México,* so complete a reversal of opinion on the merits of indigenous expression had taken place that Aztec music, rather than being decried, was being held up for the first time as the worthiest music for Mexican composers to imitate. Qualities in indigenous music which only a few years before had been looked upon as basic defects suddenly began to be spoken of as merits. Carlos Chávez spoke for the newer generation when he said Mexicans must now learn to "reconstruct musically the atmosphere of primitive purity" because "the musical culture of the aborigines constitutes the most important stage in the history of Mexican music." [5]

THE "AZTEC" RENAISSANCE

In a lecture delivered under the auspices of the National University of Mexico in October, 1928, Chávez summarized the newer ideas on aboriginal music which were soon to become regnant. His pronunciamento, entitled *La Música Azteca,* advocated a return to preconquest musical ideals because pre-Hispanic music "expressed what is profoundest and deepest in the Mexican soul." Concerning the melodic system of the Aztecs, his theses may be summarized as follows:

The Aztecs showed a predilection for those intervals which we call the minor third and the perfect fifth; their use of other intervals was rare. This type of interval preference, which must undoubtedly be taken to indicate a deep-seated and intuitive yearning for the minor, found appropriate expression in modal melodies which entirely lacked the semitone. Aztec melodies might begin or end on any degree of the five-note series. In discussing their music one might therefore appropriately speak of five different melodic modes, each of them acknowledging a different tonic in the pentatonic series.

Since the fourth and seventh degrees of the major diatonic scale (as we know it) were completely absent from this music, the implications of our all-important leading tone were banished from Aztec melody. If it should seem that their particular pentatonic system excluded any possibility of "modulating," we reply that these aborigines avoided modulation (in our sense of the word) primarily because modulation was alien to the simple and straightforward spirit of the Indian.

[5] Otto Mayer-Serra, "Silvestre Revueltas and Musical Nationalism in Mexico," *Musical Quarterly,* XXVII/2 (April, 1941), 127.

For those whose ears have become conditioned by long familiarity with the European diatonic system, the "polymodality" of indigenous music inevitably sounds as if it were "polytonality." (Polytonality in music we might say is analogous to the absence of perspective which we encounter in aboriginal painting. The paintings of the preconquest codices show us what this absence of perspective means.)

It seems evident that either the aborigines possessed an aural predisposition, or that an ingrained habit of listening was developed among them, which we today do not possess. They were thus enabled to integrate into meaningful wholes the disparate planes of sound that (in the European way of thinking) clashed in their music.[6]

These excerpts are of value if for no other reason than that they show how completely Mexican musical opinion had reversed itself during the 1920's. Characteristics that previously had been looked upon as basic faults and crude distortions in the indigenous music of Mexico—its "minor quality," its "monotony," its "simultaneous sounding of different pentatonic melodies" that are out of tune with one another in our way of thinking, its fondness for "two or more rhythms the beats of which never coincide"—came now to be regarded as virtues.

Thus it happened that at the very hour Diego Rivera was praising what the preconquest natives had done in the visual arts and calling it an achievement superior to that of their conquerors,[7] Chávez was finding similar virtues in the music of the pre-Cortesian aborigines. If, when he first began summoning Mexican musicians to heed the Aztec past, his voice may have been crying in the wilderness, it did not long remain so. He was soon joined by so many others in his own generation that to list their names would be to list nearly every well-known Mexican composer of his epoch. Daniel Ayala, Francisco Domínguez, Blas Galindo, Raúl Guerrero, Eduardo Hernández Moncada, Candelario Huízar, Vicente Mendoza, Pablo Moncayo, and Luis Sandi all followed his lead in extolling the virtues of indigenous music, and in copying indigenous models wherever possible.

METHODS USED BY CONTEMPORARY SCHOLARS IN THE STUDY OF PRECONQUEST MUSIC

The three lines of investigation most fruitfully pursued by Mexican scholars who, in Chávez' time, have studied preconquest music have been (1) the

[6]Jesús C. Romero, *Música precortesiana* (México: Talleres Gráficos de la Editorial Stylo, 1947), pp. 252–253; also, "Causas que interrumpieron su tradición," *Orientación Musical: Revista Mensual,* II/23 (May, 1943), 17.

[7] Hubert Herring and Herbert Weinstock, eds., *Renascent Mexico* (New York: Covici-Friede, 1935), p. 234. Rivera wrote for this book a chapter entitled "Plastic Art in Pre-Conquest Mexico," in which he gave it as his opinion that most of the Spaniards

systematic study of musical instruments known to have been used by Aztecs, Mayas, Tarascans, and Zapotecs; (2) the assembling of opinions on Aztec music from sixteenth-century authors who were friendly to Indian cultures rather than opposed; (3) the collection of melodies from certain out-of-the-way Indian groups which even today, after the lapse of centuries, may still preserve some of the basic elements found in the pre-Cortesian system.

AZTEC MUSICAL INSTRUMENTS IN MUSEUMS AND CODICES

For more than a century the minute scrutiny of archaeological instruments has been a favorite method in the study of music from extinct cultures. F. J. Fétis (1784–1871) based his conclusions concerning ancient music on results obtained from the study of Egyptian flutes. Using Fétis' methods, such later investigators as F. W. Galpin (1858–1954) and Kathleen Schlesinger (1862–1953) studied the music of the ancient Sumerians and Babylonians, and of the classical Greeks. The use such Mexican investigators as Daniel Castañeda (b. 1898) and Vicente T. Mendoza (1894–1964) have made of archaeological instruments is therefore nothing new.

After prolonged investigation of preconquest instruments, Castañeda and Mendoza reached the following conclusions concerning the organography of the aborigines at the time Cortés arrived:

I. *A notable sameness prevailed in the types of instruments used.* Obviously enough, the same instrument was given different names in the different languages spoken in preconquest Mexico. But the Aztec huehuetl was the same instrument as the Maya *pax,* and the Aztec teponaztli the same instrument as the Maya *tunkul,* the Tarascan *cuiringua,* the Otomí *nobiuy,* and the Zapotec *nicàche.* Because the like of a teponaztli had never been seen by European eyes, a Spanish-Tarascan dictionary such as Maturino Gilberti's *Vocabulario en lengua de Mechuacan* (México: Juan Pablos, 1559) had to resort to *tañer teponaztli* to translate the Tarascan word *cuirinani.* This expedient at least guarantees that the Aztec and Tarascan instruments are identical. Similarly, Juan de Córdova's *Vocabvlario en lengva, çapoteca* ([México: Pedro Ocharte and Antonio Ricardo, 1578], fols. 43v, 399) vouches that the nicàche is the same as the teponaztli.

As for other instruments: the Aztec *tlapitzalli* was the same instrument as the Tarascan *cuiraxetaqua,* and the Aztec huehuetl the same as the Tarascan *tavenga.* Castañeda is his "Una flauta de la cultura tarasca" (*Revista Musical Mexicana,* 1/5 [March 7, 1942], 110–111) draws up a list of instruments

---

who invaded Mexico were "very close to living on the Neolithic level." The Spaniards were too "barbarous" to appreciate the advanced "mental development" of the race destroyed by them, according to Rivera.

in the two cultures, Aztec and Tarascan: *puuaqua* (Gilberti, *op. cit.*, 1901 ed., p. 241: "caracol grande de agua con que tañen") = *tecciztli* (Alonso de Molina, *Vocabvlario en lengva mexicana y castellana* [México: Antonio de Espinosa, 1571], fol. 93) = large conch trumpet; *pungacutaqua* (p. 92: "trompeta, o cosa assi") = *tepuzquiquiztli* (fol. 104) = vertical trumpet; *quirihpaqua* (Juan Baptista de Lagunas, *Dictionarito breve y compendioso en la lēgua de Michuacan* [México: Pedro Balli, 1574], p. 156: "vn instrumento musical de vna quixada, con que tañen, o hazen ruydo, quando representan el bayle de los Chichimecas &c") = *omichicahuaztli* = bone rasp.

Confirming Castañeda's thesis that the instruments were the same, but gathering his results by a sounder scientific method, E. Thomas Stanford—staff ethnomusicologist of the Museo Nacional de Antropología e Historia in Mexico City—has recently published not only an exhaustive comparison of Tarascan and Náhuatl terms but also has studied Mixtec vocabulary in his definitive article appearing at pages 101–159 of *Yearbook II*, Inter-American Institute for Musical Research (New Orleans: Tulane University, 1966), "A Linguistic Analysis of Music and Dance Terms from Three Sixteenth-Century Dictionaries of Mexican Indian Languages." Especially welcome is Stanford's convincing analysis of Tarascan terminology.

Try as they might, the warlike Aztecs never conquered the Tarascans. Instead, the Tarascans, as late as the reign of the Aztec king, Axayacatl (1469–1481), so roundly defeated his 24,000-strong army sent against them that he died soon after the eighty-day funeral ceremonies for his dead warriors.[8] Their independence, one of another, vetoes the possibility that the one group imposed its culture on the other by warlike means. Perhaps the identical organography of the Otomíes and Zapotecs can be so explained, since these and many other enclaves were absorbed into the expanding Aztec "empire," but for such unconquered tribes as the Tarascans, no such explanation holds.

II. *The organography of the Aztecs, despite their youthful exuberance, borrowed extensively from older cultures in the territory that they did conquer.* In 1946 a series of remarkably preserved Maya paintings was discovered on the walls of an eighth-century temple at Bonampak (located in what then rated as the most inaccessible jungle of Chiapas).[9] Interest-

---

[8] Nicolás León, *Los Tarascos: Notas históricas, étnicas y antropológicas* (México: Imp. del Museo Nacional, 1904), pp. 102–107 (quoting Diego Durán, *Historia de las Indias de Nueva-España,* chap. 37 = *The Aztecs* [New York: Orion Press, 1964], pp. 165–168).

[9] Sylvanus G. Morley found the date March 18, 692, inscribed on one of the Bonampak temple stones. See *Memorias y Revista de la Academia Nacional de Ciencias (antigua Sociedad Científica Antonio Alzate),* LVI/2–3 (1948), 349. For a popular account of the spectacular Bonampak discovery see Charles M. Wilson, "Open

ingly enough, the same instruments pictured on the Bonampak temple walls were still in use when Cortés arrived in the sixteenth century.[10] Examples of such instruments may be cited here (but with their Aztec, not with their Maya, names): the *ayacachtli* (a gourd or gourd-shaped rattle, similar to maracas, with attached handle); the *áyotl* (the shell of a turtle; when struck with a stag's antler each arm of the plastron sounded a different pitch); the *huehuetl* (an upright drum fashioned out of a hollowed tree trunk; stretched across the top of the drum was a jaguar skin that could be tightened or loosened to raise or lower the pitch; the player used his fingers rather than mallets).

III. *The precontact aborigines frequently inscribed their instruments with carvings that tell (symbolically) the purposes their instruments were intended to serve.* The significance of the hieratic carvings that Mixtec, Tlaxcalan, and Aztec instrument makers inscribed on such instruments as the teponaztli and huehuetl can be understood now only by scholars who can decipher the hieroglyphs used in their systems of picture writing.

The University of Berlin professor Eduard Seler (1849–1922) doubtless contributed more to our present-day understanding of the hieratic carvings inscribed on Aztec instruments than did any other scholar of his generation. In an article describing the most famous of surviving wooden drums, "Die holzgeschnitzte Pauke von *Malinalco* und das Zeichen *atl-tlachinolli*" (published at Vienna in *Mitteilungen der Anthropologischen Gesellschaft*, XXXIV/4–5 [Sept. 25, 1904], 222–274, and more accessibly in his *Gesammelte Abhandlungen*, III [Berlin: Behrend, 1908], 221–304), he explained the various carvings inscribed on a *tlalpanhuehuetl* in the museum at Toluca. According to Seler, the carvings on this yard-tall upright drum show a

---

Sesame to the Maya," *Bulletin of the Pan American Union*, LXXXII/7 (July, 1948), 376–384. *Excelsior,* the Mexico City daily that was the first to announce Giles Healey's stumbling on the temple (March 29, 1946) carried, on April 5, 1961, an interview with an Italian art expert, Francesco Pelessoni, prophesying the imminent ruin of the Bonampak paintings from exposure (*Katunob*, II/4 [Dec., 1961], 18–21).

[10] For a discussion of the Bonampak paintings as revelators of Mayan musical practices, see Karl Ruppert, J. Eric S. Thompson, and Tatiana Proskouriakoff, *Bonampak, Chiapas, Mexico* (Washington: Carnegie Institution, 1955), p. 60; also Vicente T. Mendoza, "Música indígena de México," *México en el Arte*, IX (1950), 58. Pages 59 and 62 of the latter show color reproductions of the instruments. Because of the inaccessibility of the Lacanha Valley (State of Chiapas) where the Bonampak temples are located, the Mexican government commissioned Agustín Villagra to execute full-scale color duplicates for the Instituto Nacional de Antropología at Mexico City.

The paintings inspired the *Ballet Bonampak*, music by Luis Sandi and libretto by Pedro Alvarado Lang. A four-movement suite derived from this ballet included "Xtabay, an authentic Maya theme, which accounts for much of the beauty of the work," wrote one of the Mexico City newspaper critics after premiere of the suite at the second Festival de Música Panamericana, August 2, 1963, José Serebrier conducting.

group of captured warriors being forced to dance to music of their own making, just prior to being sacrificed. These carvings on the Malinalco tlalpanhuehuetl recall a similar scene pictured in Diego Durán's *Atlas* (trat. 1°, lám. 19ª, cap. 54).

Because it can be readily understood (Durán's picture uses no glyphs), Seler reproduced this drawing as illustration 68 in his article (*Gesammelte Abhandlungen*, III, 279). The Durán drawing shows several captured warriors being forced to dance to their own music before being dragged off to the sacrificial stone. One captive shakes the ayacachtli while two others play the teponaztli and the huehuetl. Standing over them and forcing them to dance and play are two of the victorious captors who carry clubs edged with obsidian knives.

After calling attention to the Durán drawing, Seler demonstrates that the symbols and glyphs carved on the Malinalco tlalpanhuehuetl tell exactly the same story of warriors awaiting sacrifice.

The carvings on the Malinalco drum surround the upper half of it. The upper half is divided from the lower half by a carved band running completely around the middle of the drum. On this central encircling band is inscribed the hieroglyph of war, the *atl tlachinolli* sign, and also the sacrificial rope sign, repeated five times. The lower half is so cut that the drum stands on three legs, each of which is separately carved.

The upper half of the drum is on one side inscribed with a carved eagle and jaguar, representing warriors. The eagle and the jaguar carry sacrificial banners and face the likeness of the sun. The upper half of the drum is on the other side inscribed with a figure representing Xochipilli-Macuilxóchitl, god of music and dancing.

Xochipilli-Macuilxóchitl wears the feathers of the coxcoxtli bird. He holds in his left hand a flower and in his right hand a feather fan. Below his feet appears the glyph for music [*cuicatl*] in the shape of an ascending vapor. In close association with the glyph for music appears another glyph signifying "green jewel, costliness." He wears on his sandals the insignia of the god of dancing.

The three legs of the drum show two jaguars and an eagle. Like the jaguar and eagle on the upper half of the drum, they carry sacrificial banners. Again, as on the upper half, these signify warriors who are about to be sacrificed.

Seler's explanation (*Gesammelte Abhandlungen*, III, 274–279), presented here in abridged form, gives some idea of the complicated symbols Aztec instrument makers inscribed on their huehuetls. Their teponaztlis were often inscribed with hieratic carvings of equal complexity. In an important monograph (*The Wood-Carver's Art in Ancient Mexico* [New York: Museum of the American Indian, 1925], pp. 64–79), Marshall H. Saville cites at least a dozen instruments of the huehuetl or teponaztli class scattered in various museums which can today be profitably studied by those interested in the kinds of symbols ancient Mexican instrument makers inscribed on their instruments. Over and over he repeats that the carvings are like pages from the pre-Cortesian codices.

Depicting such things as "gods, houses, ceremonial objects, and dates," any given set of carvings may reveal such important details as the following: the exact time and place the instrument was to have been used; the part it was to have played in the ceremonial functions at which it was heard; the length of time it was to have been sounded; the persons who were supposed to play it.

So contended Saville. Nonetheless, experts may disagree on which "gods, houses, ceremonial objects, and dates" were intended by any given wood-carver. In a detailed study of *El Huehuetl de Malinalco* published a generation after Seler (Toluca: Ediciones de la Universidad Autónoma del Estado de México, 1958), Javier Romero Quiroz, for instance, accepted only the broad outlines of Seler's interpretation summarized above. At pages 68–69 of his lavishly illustrated seventy-page monograph, Romero Quiroz specified his areas of disagreement: (1) not Xochipilli-Macuilxóchitl but Tonatiuh = the Sun (whose alias is Huitzilopochtli) is the god carved on the drum; (2) the disguise is that of the cuauhtli = eagle, not of the coxcoxtli bird; (3) instead of dancing, as Seler supposed, Tonatiuh ascends on high accompanied by two Fire-Serpents. Apart from such differences in interpretation as these, Romero Quiroz does agree that the Malinalco drum carvings depict warriors who dance to its throbbing beats before having their own throbbing hearts cut out and waved aloft to sustain the Sun.

IV. *All Aztec instruments were either idiophones, aerophones, or membranophones. Stringed instruments were evidently unknown among any of the tribes conquered by Cortés.* Just as the Náhuatl language may surprise a beginning student because it lacked such consonants as *b, d, f, g, r,* and *v,* so Náhuatl music may surprise a beginning student because it eschewed string tone.

True, there remain some authorities [11] who maintain that the musical bow, though not used by the precontact Aztecs, was used by other tribes in

[11] José Raúl Hellmer wrote an important article for the *Toluca Gazette* of June 1, 1960, lauding the musical instruments in vogue among the pre-Aztec tribes of Mexico and taking issue with the received opinion that pre-Cortesian America knew no stringed instruments. "Several authorities on musical folklore have become convinced that simple forms of stringed instruments did exist before the arrival of the Spaniards among at least several ethnic groups: the Seris and Coras in western Mexico, the Chinantecos and Huaves in Oaxaca, and the Lacandones in Chiapas" (quoted in *Katunob,* II/1 [March, 1961], 73).

The Chinantecos came under missionary influence before 1560, to which year Joaquín García Icazbalceta assigns the publication at Mexico City of *Artes de los idiomas Chiapaneco, Zoque, Tzendal y Chinanteco (Bibliografía Mexicana del Siglo XVI,* new edition by Agustín Millares Carlo [México: Fondo de Cultura Económica,

Mexico. Convinced that the "third and highest class" of instruments is strings, these modern apologists appeal to such articles as Daniel G. Brinton's "Native American Stringed Musical Instruments" (*American Antiquarian,* XIX/1 [Jan., 1897], 19–20). For the first of four examples controverting the generally held opinion that "the American Indians at the time of discovery did not use anywhere on the continent a stringed instrument," Brinton cited "the *quijongo* of Central America," a monochord "made by fastening a wooden bow with a stretched cord, over the mouth of a gourd or jar which serves as a resonator."

Saville, in "A Primitive Maya Musical Instrument" (*American Anthropologist,* X/8 [Aug., 1897], 272–273) and "The Musical Bow in Ancient Mexico" *ibid.,* XI/9 [Sept., 1898], 280–284), supported Brinton. In the first of these articles Saville described a primitive stringed instrument which he had personally encountered in the winter of 1890–91 while exploring a cave on the Tabí hacienda in Yucatán. Some Mayas from "various small villages in the interior of the country, remote from Spanish influences," introduced him to a "primitive form of stringed instrument" called a *hool.* This instrument was made

---

1954], pp. 183–184). The compiler of this dictionary was the Spanish-born Dominican, Francisco de Cepeda (1532–1602).

Mentioned in Bk. IX, chap. 18, and Bk. XI, chaps. 14, 18, of Antonio de Remesal's *Historia de la Prouincia de S. Vicente de Chyapa y Guatemala* (Madrid: Francisco de Angulo, 1619), Cepeda excelled both as linguist and as musician. According to Remesal, Cepeda's musical skill greatly enhanced his missionary success (*Biblioteca "Goathemala,"* V [Guatemala: Tip. Nacional, 1932], 569: *entendía bien la música, que le importó para el tiempo que gastó entre los indios;* see also pp. 330, 544).

If all this was true of the first missionary to publish a dictionary in their language, the Chinantecos can scarcely be labeled a tribe that escaped acculturation. Claims for the purity of tribal music in any given area, no matter how inaccessible the enclave nowadays, require constant checking against surviving records of colonial missionary endeavor.

For data on the dissemination of the "music bow" among other relevant tribes, see Fritz Bose, "Die Musik der Chibcha und ihrer heutigen Nachkommen," *Internationales Archiv für Ethnographie,* XLVIII, pt. 2 (Leiden: E. J. Brill, 1958), pp. 159–160, 173–174. The importation of slaves (Negroes came to the New World with the conquistadores) accounts for the African influence to which Bose appropriately invites attention.

The latest literature on the problem, "El Arco Musical, ¿Una Pervivencia?" appearing in *La Palabra y el Hombre: Revista de la Universidad Veracruzana,* II Época/39 (July–Sept., 1966), 383–403, merits special consideration because of the many discoveries that can be credited to the author of the article, Charles L. Boilés—clay bongos and a clay mouthpiece for an apparently pre-Cortesian *caracol* in the Museo Nacional de Antropología, microtonic and transverse ocarinas from a late Olmec site (Fred Field Collection, Mexico City), and others. At page 393, Boilés comments on Saville's possible confusion of *hool* with *jul.* After citing terms for string instruments in fourteen native language dictionaries, he leaves the question of pre-Cortesian origins open for further study (p. 395).

. . . by stretching a piece of rope-like vine called *ohil*, between the two ends of a pliable piece of wood, making a bow about two feet in length. One end of this bow is placed near the face, about one-third of the distance from the end, so that the mouth covers but does not touch the string, forming a resonator. Between the string and the bow a piece of wood is placed in such a manner that it may be pressed against the string or relaxed at will. The tones are produced by tapping on the string, thus producing a sound somewhat resembling that made in playing a jews-harp, but more agreeable to the ear. The different tones are produced by the pressure or relaxation of the stick upon the string and by the opening and partial closing of the mouth over the same. This instrument is used by the Mayas for the *jaranas* [12] or native dances, the tune being a weird though not unpleasing one, and constantly repeated with but little variation during the evening. I found that it required considerable skill to manage the bow and much practice to play it, but many of the Indians were quite skillful in rendering the principal tune used.

A closer scholar than Brinton, Saville was the first to recognize that more clinching proof for the pre-Cortesian existence of stringed instruments was needed than any mere "survival" of a bow 373 years after the Spanish discovery of Yucatán, no matter how remote the hamlet nor apparently backward the tribesmen. His second article therefore appealed to the evidence of a pre-Columbian painted record brought from Puebla, Mexico, to Darmstadt by Philipp J. Becker and, after his death in 1896, purchased for the k. k. Naturhistorisches Hofmuseum at Vienna. Describing this codex, Saville wrote: ". . . it is made of deerskin, coated over with a slight surface of white paste, really stucco, upon which the ideographs and pictures have been painted in various colors, and, unlike many of the ancient codices, has been painted on but one side of the page." A reproduction of this codex had already been published in 1891 at Geneva by Henri de Saussure, who gave it the title *Le manuscrit du Cacique* because forty years earlier it had belonged to a Mixtec Indian (from the region of Oaxaca) claiming to be the descendant of *caciques*, or native chiefs. Little realizing its value, the Indian had parted with it, giving it to an attorney, Don Pascual Almazán, who in 1852 had helped him vindicate title to some hereditary possessions. Describing the upper third of pages 8 and 9 of this codex (Saussure's numbering), Saville

[12] Saville, misspelling the word, gives it as *jarandas*. Robert Redfield, *The Folk Culture of Yucatan* (Chicago: University of Chicago Press, 1941), pp. 273–274, describes the jarana as the "Yucatecan form of those Latin-American folk dances descended from the *jota* and its cousins of Spain." According to his now out-of-date observations, the jarana lasts from dusk to dawn, climaxes every fiesta of a patron saint, takes place on a wooden platform "to accentuate the beat of the dance steps," and requires brasses and drums for its accompaniment. An early printed example can be found in José Jacinto Cuevas, *Mosaico Yucateco* (1869; repr. 1951). Cuevas' jarana moves in eighth-notes, chooses ¾ time signature, and groups into four four-bar phrases, every first bar of a phrase going in tonic, every third and fourth bar in dominant.

. . . found a series of six figures, forming, so far as my knowledge goes, a unique representation of what may be called a pre-Columbian "orchestra." For the sake of convenience I have numbered them from 1 to 6. Figure 1 represents a seated person playing the horizontal wooden drum, *teponaztli,* a log hollowed out on the under side and having on the upper surface two tongues made by two long, lateral cuts separated in the center by a cross-cut. The two drumsticks, with ends covered with *ulli* (india-rubber) for beating these tongues, are well shown. This form of drum is still used in Mexico and Central America, in remote villages, on feast days, and in several museums are preserved specimens with beautifully carved symbolic pictures. Figure 2 shows a person standing on a low platform, playing the *huehuetl*—a vertical drum hollowed out of a log, the upper end covered with a skin, played by beating with the hands, as here shown. A magnificent carved *huehuetl* is preserved in the Toluca Museum, Mexico. . . . Figure 5 shows the rattle, with a curved handle [*ayacachtli*]. Figure 6, the last of the row, which most concerns us, represents a seated person with a bow held by the left hand, the string being pressed against the arm near the elbow, while in the left [*sic*] hand is held a forked stick, undoubtedly for use in twanging the tightened cord of the bow. These six musicians all face the same way, to the left, as is the case with the heads in the Mayan hieroglyphs.

This ensemble of musicians, in which the bow has a place, seems to be sufficient proof of the existence of the musical bow in ancient Oaxaca at a time anterior to the coming of the Spaniards.

The lucubrations of an armchair anthropologist like the surgeon Brinton (1837–1899), who never soiled his hands with fieldwork, could be dismissed by leading Mexicanists and his "Native American Stringed Musical Instruments" consigned to the limbo of his many other unfortunate guesses. But Saville (1867–1935), later to become president of the American Anthropological Association (1926–1928), belonged to a different breed. To multiply the mischief of Saville's articles, fashionable anthropology had not yet learned to be "skeptical of survivals" and, at the turn of the century, was still addicted to the opinion (now held erroneous) that folkloric survivals offer a reliable "guide to the past." [13]

It therefore required as great an authority as Seler, already recognized as the leading Mexicanist of pre–World War I Germany, to answer Saville. The son of a professional organist, Seler was well endowed not only paleographically and linguistically but also temperamentally for the task. As early as 1898 he had already published a highly suggestive article (in *Globus,*

---

[13] *Encyclopedia Americana* (1965 ed.), XI, 422f., conveniently summarizes presently accepted opinion. See also William Bascom, "The Main Problems of Stability and Change in Tradition," *Journal of the International Folk Music Council,* XI (1959), 7–12. Formerly, some scholars could claim that "primitive people lived in 'cultural strait jackets' which prevented change and, indeed, even individual variation in behaviour" (p. 8). But folklorists now agree that music and instruments of the most undeveloped peoples can change radically within a generation or so—even with no pressures from the outside.

LXXIV/6, pp. 85–93) on Mexican bone rattles, and was therefore merely pushing further into personally mapped territory when "Mittelamerikanische Musikinstrumente" appeared in *Globus* (LXXVI/7 [Aug. 19, 1899], 109–112).

Seler began with an examination of Saville's key evidence—the sixth of the Mixtec musicians pictures in the Codex Becker. At once he found that it had been tampered with. The figure in which Saville had placed blind faith had been hand-drawn for the Geneva 1891 "facsimile" publication by a Swiss naturalist who "restored" all those paintings in the original which were worn away by creasing or other hard use. A "true copy" of the orchestral players, made at Seler's request from the original codex, then reposing in the Natural History Museum at Vienna, revealed that it had been precisely the "restoration" of the dilapidated sixth figure in the orchestral panel that had deceived Saville.

According to Saville's interpretation, the sixth, the last of the persons represented here, holds the "music-bow" under his left arm and in his right hand a forked rod, which is intended for tapping the string. Since all the space between the alleged bow and its alleged string is painted blue, it is very hard for me to understand how Saville could come to see an instrument like that described above. Also the way in which the instrument is held has absolutely no connection with its interpretation as a "music-bow."

To forestall an appeal to other specialists, Seler ("Mittelamerikanische Musikinstrumente," p. 110 n. 7) mentioned corroborating verdicts already handed down by two Americans, Zelia Nuttall (1858–1933) and Edward S. Morse (1838–1925). Although Seler did not doubt that the sixth figure in the Mixtec group did indeed hold in his hands a musical instrument, he identified it as a tortoiseshell gong (called áyotl by the Aztecs).

In my opinion, the player clasps in his left arm the shell of a tortoise, and he holds in his right hand a stag's horn with which he belabors the tortoise shell, the under side of which is turned to the front and receives the drubbing. . . . Diego de Landa [*Relación de las cosas de Yucatán*, written *ca.* 1566, chap. 22 (México: Pedro Robredo, 1938), p. 109] mentions tortoise shells, the same as Mexican *áyotl*, as coming not only from Mexico, but also from Yucatán. The name *kayab*, "with which one sings," which was in use among the Mayas for the tortoise as symbol of the hieroglyph of the seventeenth *uinal* or period of 20 days, seems to refer to the musical use of its shell.[14] Among the ancient Mexicans the tortoise shell drum was a very commonly used instrument. It was beaten at the death feast, at the feast in honor of the rain-gods on the Etzalqualiztli, at the feast to

---

[14] J. Eric S. Thompson, *Maya Hieroglyphic Writing* (Norman: University of Oklahoma Press, 1960), pp. 116–117, agrees that Seler correctly identified *kayab*, glyph of the seventeenth month, as the head of a turtle. Inasmuch as the root *kai* means "to sing" and *ab* is an instrumental suffix, *kayab* could mean "with what one sings" (p. 117). The whole problem of derivation, however, still remains shrouded in ambiguities, according to Thompson.

the mountain-gods in the Atemoztli, at the dance of the women, the "leaps" at the feast of Toxcatl, and on other occasions.[15]

Seler in the same paragraph contended that only the underside of the tortoise carapace was beaten with the stag's horn. For proof, he appealed to the evidence of folio 60 in the codex at the Biblioteca Nazionale, Florence, cataloged as Magliabecchi XIII, 11, 3. Reproduced in full color shortly after Seler's article on the subject (Zelia Nuttall, *The Book of the Life of the Ancient Mexicans* [Berkeley: University of California Press, 1903]), this handsome painting pictures the feast celebrated eighty days after the death of an honored warrior, and once a year for four years thereafter. Two singers officiate, one accompanying himself on the drum (tlalpanhuehuetl), the other swinging a rattle with his right hand and beating the tortoiseshell (áyotl) with an antler held in his left hand. Before them sits a magnificently costumed mummy bundle wearing a wooden mask (painted black around the eyes and red around the mouth). Burned after the ceremony, this mummy bundle represents the happy warrior himself, whose spirit now mounts to the domain of the Rosy Morn.

Having disposed of Saville's Mixtec "string" player to the satisfaction of his own and succeeding generations, Seler left still untouched in his 1899 *Globus* article several questions of prime interest to present-day musical archaeologists: (1) On what occasion, and (2) for what purpose, did the Mixtec players pictured in the Codex Becker I assemble? (3) Who, precisely, were these players?

For answers, we turn to Karl A. Nowotny. In his preface to a new facsimile edition (*Codices Becker I/II* [Graz: Akademische Druck- u. Verlagsanstalt, 1961], p. 14), Nowotny summarizes his own findings and those of the Champollion of Mixtec studies, Alfonso Caso (1896——). The codex consists of three fragments (panels 1–3, 4–14, and 15–16) and depicts events belonging to the years 1047, 1048–1055, and 1066, respectively.

In 1047 died King 11 Wind ("Bloody Tiger"), ruler of the town of Xipe Bundle. Codex Becker I joins several other Mixtec genealogical codices in recounting the dynastic struggles that ensued after this king's death. Panels 8–9 of our codex show, in the upper strip, six players celebrating. One of these musicians is none other than the royal David of Mixtec annals, King 8 Deer (1011–1063), familiarly known as "Tiger Claw." [16] As befitted royal

---

[15] Bernardino de Sahagún, *Florentine Codex: Book 2—The Ceremonies*, trans. Arthur J. O. Anderson and Charles E. Dibble (Santa Fe: School of American Research, 1951 [no. 14, pt. iii]), pp. 72 (Toxcatl), 77 (Etzalqualiztli), 140 (Atemoztli).

[16] James Cooper Clark, *The Story of "Eight Deer" in Codex Colombino* (London: Taylor and Francis, 1912), was the first to publish a history of this heroic conqueror. See *Journal de la Société des Américanistes*, n.s., IX/2 (1912), 377, for a summary. "Certain of Cooper Clark's shrewd observations are still valid," remarks Alfonso Caso (*Interpretation of the Codex Bodley 2858* [Mexico City: Sociedad Mexicana de Antropología, 1960], p. 37). Caso's "Vida y aventuras de 4 Viento 'Serpiente de

dignity, he and his younger brother Prince 9 Flower [17] blow trumpets while Prince 12 Olin (= *ollin* = "movement") swings a gourd rattle and Lord 5 Movement beats the tortoiseshell.

The date of this paean is 1048, and the inspiration for it was the defeat, capture, and sacrifice of one of King 8 Deer's most potent rivals in the race for Xipe Bundle. The rival's body had been burned and 8 Deer had made his oblations in a temple (shown in upper left of panel 7, Codex Becker I). He thence emerges to join his confederate chieftains in the music making. Not yet done, however, with other contenders, 8 Deer must wait until the following year (1049) to make good his claims by capturing the town of Xipe Bundle itself.[18]

Were musical archaeology our prime concern, a table could profitably be drawn here listing all the musical paintings in precontact codices. Such a table would be more useful if it could be accompanied with reproductions from each of the approximately twenty such codices in European libraries. To date, two heavily illustrated and typographically splendid books have been published which might well have included such a catalogue raisonné—*Instrumentos musicales precortesianos* (México: Instituto Nacional de Antropología, 1955) and *Canto, danza y música precortesianos* (Fondo de Cultura Económica, 1961). Unfortunately, in neither book has a consistent attempt been made to secure accurate reproductions (cf. pp. 59 [1955] and 99 [1961]), nor are the illustrations always properly credited, even when reproduced luxuriously (the two singers on the right in the color plate opposite page 70 [1955] come from Magliabecchi XIII, 11, 3 at Florence, not Borbonicus at Paris). More important, the iconography from the authentically precontact codices is not sorted out nor arranged logically. However, since our overriding concern here is indigenous music as it existed at the moment of contact with European, rather than the long musical buildup preceding the founding of Tenochtitlan (Mexico City) by the Aztecs in 1325, fuller treatment of the precontact codical material must await a specialized monograph.

Among the various kinds of instrumental sound used by the Aztecs, which did they really prefer? Did their favored instruments reflect their other

Fuego'" (*Miscelánea de estudios dedicados a Fernando Ortiz* [Havana: Sociedad Económica de Amigos del País, 1955], I, 289–298) narrates later events in the life of "the great king of Tilantongo and Teozacoalco called 8 Deer," weaving them together from data supplied in the Bodley, Selden, and Zouche-Nuttall codices at Oxford and the Codex Becker I at Vienna.

[17] Born 1012, according to Nowotny, p. 10; but in 1015, according to Caso, *Interpretation of the Codex Bodley 2858*, p. 38 [7–v].

[18] Caso, "Vida y Aventuras de 4 Viento," p. 294. For another huehuetl player in Codex Becker I, differently colored, see panel 7, bottom left.

known spiritual interests? In *Mexico before Cortez* (New York: Doubleday, 1963), Ignacio Bernal divides the whole sweep of Mexican history from archaic peoples to Aztecs into seven sections, with the Aztecs coming at the close. If Shakespeare's "seven ages" applied (*As You Like It,* II, vii), the Aztecs, arriving during the "last scene of all, that ends this strange eventful history," ought to have been the least aggressive of the lot. Yet the opposite held true, and their favorite musical instruments faithfully reflect their bold, thrusting character. Whatever else may be argued, none can deny that the Aztecs forwent the luxury of languid legato and of long swooning sounds when they elected as their favorite instruments the teponaztli and the huehuetl.

The use of just these instruments as a twosome is everywhere attested in Sahagún, Durán, Motolinía, and in the other authentic source material that survives. Moreover, the teponaztli stresses 2 by being an instrument of two keys only. Among the numerous precontact songs in *Cantares en idioma mexicano,* a sixteenth-century collection edited by Antonio Peñafiel (México: Secretaría de Fomento, 1899), are many that emphasize the dual principle still further. Throughout this songbook in the Aztec language (Náhuatl), many cantares are headed by a kind of primitive music notation that consists of two vowels only, and of two consonants only. What is to be made of this predilection for twosomes?

Miguel León Portilla perhaps provides the best answer in his perceptive study, *La filosofía náhuatl estudiada en sus fuentes* (México: Instituto Indigenista Interamericano, 1956). He is interested not so much in the beliefs of the plebeian as in those of the wise man, the thinker, the controlling priest who devised ritual—the tlamatini (Molina's *Vocabvlario en lengva mexicana,* 1571, fol. 126). According to informants from whom Sahagún gained his data, the tlamatini believed personified duality to be the great "I am" at the heart of the universe. A father-mother pair, Ometecuhtli and Omecihuatl, engendered all other being.

The universal undergirding male-female principle is nowhere better proclaimed than in a certain Náhuatl text taken down by Sahagún from the lips of a native informant. This text appears in the Códice Matritense now at the Royal Academy of History in Madrid (for a facsimile of fol. 175*v,* see León Portilla, *op. cit.,* p. 161). Not only in this "philosophy" but elsewhere as well, the Aztecs emphasized 2, or 2 times 2. Such authorities as Seler, Caso, and others (listed by León Portilla, *op. cit.,* pp. 31–59) recognized duality as everywhere fundamentally important to the Aztec. Even the way the language was pronounced corroborates this obsession with 2 and with the male-female dichotomy. Alonso de Molina begins his *Arte de la lengua Mexicana* (México: Pedro Ocharte, 1571, fol. 5) with the warning that men and women pronounced so simple a word as that for the upright drum (huehuetl) differently. Men made four syllables of the word, women only two. In English phonetic equivalents, Molina is saying that men pronounced it "oo-ay-oo-aytl" but women made of it "way-waytl." [19]

If their very instruments had names that had to be pronounced in two different ways, will it seem strange that pairs of musicians—one playing the two-keyed teponaztli, the other the huehuetl—dominate all Aztec music? Just as European musicians in the Ars Antiqua period took the Trinity as inspiration for their mensural praxis, so Náhuatl conviction that duality controls the universe finds reflection in Aztec instruments and tunes.

ALPHABETICAL SYNOPSIS

In running through the following alphabetical list of Aztec instruments, the reader will do well to remember that he is the not so much surveying remains of a bygone art, as the sacred sound symbols of a now vanished cult. It was the cult that dictated what instruments were to be used, in which ceremonies they were to intervene, and how they were to be played.

No attempt has been made to include all instruments—only a representative set. For further specialized data on the names of instruments, and their relationships with dance and song, see E. Thomas Stanford, "A Linguistic Analysis of Music and Dance Terms from Three Sixteenth-Century Dictionaries of Mexican Indian Languages," in *Yearbook II* (1966) of the Inter-American Institute for Musical Research. Profiting from a dictionary of roots being written by Morris Swadesh, Stanford prepared a useful control and adjunct to the information supplied below, especially since terms found in dictionaries of three languages (Mixteco, Tarasco, Náhuatl) undergird his analysis, not simply those in Náhuatl.

Other pertinent literature that arrived too late for consideration, or remained still unpublished in early 1967, can be no more than briefly mentioned here. For the exhibition of autochthonous instruments shown during August and September, 1966, in the Museo del Palacio de Bellas Artes, María del Carmen Sordo Sodi—successor to Jesús Bal y Gay as chief of the musicology section in the Instituto Nacional de Bellas Artes—wrote the article "Instrumentos prehispánicos" included in the guide handed to visitors at the exhibition (some instruments are listed with their Mayan names). Favorable comments inspired by the exhibition appeared in "Un Pueblo Melódico," *Visión*, XXXI/10 (Sept. 30, 1966), 42–43; "Instrumentos Musicales," *Política*, VII/153 (Sept. 1, 1966), 59; "Instrumentos Musicales Mexicanos," *El Universal*, September 18, 1966 (Sunday pictorial supple-

---

[19] See facsimile (Madrid: Ediciones Cultura Hispánica, 1945), fol. 5: "Ytem los varones, no vsan de, v, consonante, aunque las mugeres Mexicanas, solamente, la vsen. Y assi dizen ellos veuetl, que es atabal, o tamborin, con quatro sillabas: y ellas dizen veuetl, con solas dos sillabas." See Joseph Haekel, "Zur Problematik des Obersten Goettlichen Paares im Alten Mexiko," *El México Antiguo* (Sociedad Alemana Mexicanista), IX (1959), 39–76, for the omnipresent role of duality in ancient Mexican religions.

ment), and "Interesante Exposición de Instrumentos," *El Universal*, August 28, 1966 [Miguel Bueno wrote both *El Universal* pieces]; and "Instrumentos Musicales en México," *Excelsior*, December 4, 1966 (Sunday supplement), pp. 6–7 [by Ignacio Rodríguez]. José Valderrama wrote "La Marimba y el Teponaztli Como 'Intrusos'" for *Novedades*, August 15, 1966, pp. 1, 8. Since the majority of the aboriginal instruments belonging to the sumptuous Museo Nacional de Antropología are now kept in storage, the catalog that Miss Sordo contemplates of the entire collection will be an eagerly awaited publishing event. Other authors with important monographs in preparation include not only Franco, Hellmer, and Boilés, but also Samuel Martí. Born in Chihuahua on May 18, 1906, a student of Manuel Gil in El Paso, a violinist in Chicago, and conductor of the Orquesta Sinfónica de Yucatán (after moving to Mérida in 1935), Martí later located in Mexico City, where he became, in the 1950's and 1960's, the most prolific author on Mexican ethnomusicological subjects. According to Boilés, the compendium of musical terms in all American Indian languages being prepared by Martí will inaugurate a new epoch.

One further observation before plunging into the list: Molina's 1571 spellings guide us even when he seemingly contradicts himself (*atecocoli* [*sic*] and *atecuculli*). For *tlalpan* he gives "ground"; but since he does not combine this with *huehuetl*, while other authors such as the knowledgeable Alvarado Tezozomoc spell the word either *tlapanhuehuetl* or *tlalpanhuehuetl*, as the mood strikes them (Hernando Alvarado Tezozomoc, *Crónica Mexicana*, ed. Manuel Orozco y Berra [México: Ireneo Paz, 1878], pp. 262, 279, 427, 449, 477, 515), both spellings can be defended from authority.

atecocoli = *atecuculli*

Both spellings for this ubiquitous instrument—the large perforated conch shell blown as a trumpet—appear in Molina's classic 1571 dictionary. The first turns up in the Spanish–Náhuatl section (fol. 24*v*, under "caracol muy grande que sirue de bozina, o de corneta"), the second in the Náhuatl–Spanish section (fol. 7*v*). Molina explains in his *Arte de la lengua Mexicana* (fol. 5), published the same year, that "native speakers make so little distinction between *o* and *u* that one or the other vowel can be written indifferently." The many other vagaries in the spelling of indigenous words in early documents show how hard it was to imprison distinctive native sounds within the walls of the conventional Spanish alphabet.[20]

[20] Moreover, native words were themselves pronounced differently from town to town, as Juan de Córdova emphasized in his *Arte en lengva Zapoteca* (México: Pedro Balli, 1578), fol. 68*v*. He defended this diversity "because in Spain it happens the same: in Old Castile they say *haçer*, *xugar*, *yerro*, *alagar*, while at Toledo they say *hazer*, *jugar*, *hierro*, *halagar*." Cf. Joaquín García Icazbalceta, *Bibliografía Mexicana del Siglo XVI*, rev. and aug. Agustín Millares Carlo (México: Fondo de Cultura Económica, 1954), p. 293.

In Tarascan, the conch trumpet = puuaqua (Gilberti, *op. cit.*, 1559 ed.), in Zapotec, *paatáotocuècheni* or *paaniçatàopáni;*[21] but the listing of names in the native languages quickly grows to unmanageable lengths because this was a basic instrument everywhere.

Although its name in the language of those who built the great pyramids of the Sun and the Moon at Teotihuacán thirteen or fourteen centuries ago can never be known, the conch shell was so much their favorite that it constantly inspired their designs. One Teotihuacán shell trumpet (illustrated in Martí, *Instrumentos musicales*, p. 48) has even served Laurette Séjourné as a sacred text in her recent survey of "thought and religion in ancient Mexico" (*Burning Water* [London: Thames & Hudson, 1956], pp. 138, 180.9). On it are incised hieroglyphs for the cycle of time and for the numbers 9 and 12. Just as the player's breath gives life to a shell that otherwise would forever slumber in silence, so also the Wind God Quetzalcóatl breathes life into a void. The shell is therefore the appropriate emblem for this man-become-god deity.

How many sounds can be extracted from any given archaeological conch trumpet is a question that ought to involve less speculation than the interpretation of hieroglyphs on a Teotihuacán artifact. In *Mexican Music* (New York: Museum of Modern Art, 1940, p. 8), Herbert Weinstock claimed the five notes of a D-major arpeggio, rising from the A below middle C to d^1 an eleventh above, as an easy possibility. Martí casts some doubt on this report when he laments (*Instrumentos musicales*, p. 53) that not even the ablest trumpeters in the Mexican Musicians' Union can now extract any such series from a *caracol*. He does, however, call attention to a conch trumpet from the Toltec period with four holes cut into the shell (and illustrates the Tepic museum exemplar, *ibid.*, p. 52). These holes can be stopped with the fingers, like the holes of a flute, thus providing the several pitches needed to transform the conch from a mere monotone signaling into a "musical" instrument. If clay mouthpieces such as the one discovered by Boilés at the Museo Nacional de Antropología were frequently inserted, then these too would have brought a wider range within the player's easy control.

Another even better word for "shell trumpet" than *atecocoli* is *tecciztli,* according to Molina's dictionary. It is this last word that now and then slips into Sahagún's Náhuatl text; he himself translates it *caracol.*[22] However,

---

[21] Juan de Córdova, *Vocabvlario en lengva çapoteca* (Mexico: Pedro Ocharte and Antonio Ricardo, 1578), fol. 72v. Zapotec abounded in synonyms and elegance demanded constant switching from one to another: "Y los Indios en sus platicas vsan por elegancia de todos, porque este es su modo de hablar" (Aviso III in Córdova's *Prefactio*).

[22] Cf. *Florentine Codex: Book 2—The Ceremonies*, p. 98: "Auh in tlamacazque, tenanamjquj tlapitztiuh, *tecciztli* in qujpitztiuh" = "And the priests, [who] attended them, went blowing horns, they blew shell trumpets as they went"; p. 138: "in petlatl,

much oftener than *tecciztli,* Sahagún's native informants used still another term for "shell trumpet"—*tlapitzalli.* Anderson and Dibble, translators of Sahagún's Náhuatl text into English, follow his lead;[23] but despite the example set by Sahagún this meaning (caracol) passes unnoticed in the only recent book dealing specifically with aboriginal instruments in Mexico—*Instrumentos musicales precortesianos* (1955)—pages 79–92 of which restrict the meaning of *tlapitzalli* to "flutes." This same book inspires another misconception when plate 57 from Sahagún's Florentine Codex is reproduced on page 49 with the caption: "A conch trumpet player performing at a funeral ceremony." The illustration, painted for Sahagún by a native Aztec artist, shows three figures: (1) the trumpeter, (2) a man asleep, (3) someone trying to awaken the man asleep by pouring water on him. The painting, very important for an understanding of the hour at which the conch trumpet always sounded, accompanies Sahagún's Book II, Appendix III.[24] Translated literally from Náhuatl into English, the accompanying text reads (Anderson and Dibble, *Book 2—The Ceremonies,* p. 192):

Thus was done the blowing of trumpets: when it was late at night, when it was already approaching midnight, the trumpets were sounded, that all the priests might offer blood. . . . Thus were men awakened: those known as the *beaters*

---

in *tecciztli,* in jcpalli" = "mats, shell trumpets, and seats." These passages appear in Sahagún's own translation of the original Náhuatl thus: "También los ministros . . . iban tañendo sus cornetas y sus caracoles" and "petates, cornetas, caracoles" (see Bk. II, chaps. 27 [51] and 34 [51] of his *Historia General de las Cosas de Nueva España,* ed. Ángel M. Garibay [México: Editorial Porrúa, 1956], I, 181, 213).

Hernando Alvarado Tezozomoc writes *tecziztli* for *tecciztli* in his *Crónica Mexicana* of 1598 (México: Editorial Leyenda, 1944), chap. 70, p. 331, when describing the dedication of the Great Temple in 1487. The ceremony ordered by Ahuizotl began with priests playing the *tecziztli = tecciztli,* "a large white shell trumpet the sound of which was enough to curdle the blood of those who heard it."

[23] Sample occurrences in *Book 2—The Ceremonies,* pp. 89, 136, 173, 192, 202, 205. Sahagún's translations: "cornetas y caracoles" (Garibay ed., I, 174 [18]); "cornetas y caracoles (I, 212 [42 and 44]); "trompetas" (I, 237 [42]); "caracoles y cornetas y trompetas" (I, 248 [36]); "caracoles y pitos y trompetas" (I, 253 [3]); "caracoles y pitos y trompetas" (I, 254 [8]).

Alluding to the Anderson and Dibble translation of Sahagún's Náhuatl, Charles L. Boilés warns us that "the translators were not careful of small but immensely important details which would profoundly affect conclusions drawn by investigators using their texts" (*Yearbook II* [1966] of the Inter-American Institute for Musical Research [Tulane University], p. 176). Throughout the present book, every effort has been made to heed Boilés' caveat, and to confirm their translations into English. Even Sahagún's Spanish bears misinterpretation, especially if read without thorough understanding of the musical terminology current in sixteenth-century Spain.

[24] Garibay ed., I, 248 [36 and 37]: "Todas las noches, un poco antes de la media noche, los ministros de los ídolos que tenían cargo de esto, tocaban los caracoles y cornetas y trompetas, y luego se levantaban todos a ofrecer sangre e incienso a los ídolos, en los *cúes* y en todas las casas particulares. . . . Los que no despertaban a aquella hora castigábanlos echando sobre ellos agua. . . ."

began the keeping of the watch; and if any did not awake, they poured water upon him.

The water being poured on him who sleeps through the conch trumpet's nightly call to prayer and penance—and not water being poured on a corpse—is the scene in plate 57.

Plate 60 of the series accompanying Sahagún's Book II pictures a pair blowing conch trumpets. An image of the Sun God separates the trumpeters. Four times each day, and five each night, incense and blood are needed to sustain the deities. At the ceremony here pictured not only do conch trumpets sound praises to the Sun God, but also two acolytes wave burning incense before his likeness. Meanwhile, a seated pair draw blood by passing straws through their ears.

The occasions thus far cited suggest that conches were primarily cult instruments. Even today, whenever the conch trumpet still sounds in remote indigenous villages, it remains a ritual instrument. Séjourné, in her *Supervivencias de un mundo mágico* (México: Fondo de Cultura Económica, 1953, pp. 55–56), tells of visiting the Zapotec village of Cuixtla. In the twilight she hears "the strange voice of the conch trumpet summoning the village to age-old rituals in honor of a magic herb brought back from a distant and difficult mountain."

However, plate 88 accompanying Sahagún's *Book 8—Kings and Lords* (chap. 17, par. 4) pictures a small ensemble playing for what can be called a "secular" event—the nightly dance of young warriors. The purpose of this dance was to warn Mexico's close-by neighbors that the flower of her youth remained ever alert against sneak attacks. The instruments portrayed include various rattles, the inevitable horizontal and upright drums— teponaztli and huehuetl, and the conch shell.

Since conch trumpets were so constantly needed, no one will be surprised to find that occasionally they had to be duplicated in clay. Evidently enough large seashells were not always available. In such an event ersatz pottery facsimiles filled the breach in Mexico, just as they frequently served as substitutes in pre-Hispanic Peru. Below, on page 256, attention is called to the six precontact clay trumpets shaped like conch shells now in the National Museum at Lima. Martí's *Instrumentos musicales precortesianos* (p. 51) shows an excellent photograph of a Mexican archaeological clay trumpet (private collection of José María Arreola).

Concerning the two vertical trumpets, purportedly of gourd, pictured at panel 9 of Codex Becker, which Vicente T. Mendoza in 1941 suggested calling *atecocolli*, see above, page 28, and below, page 78.

ayacachtli

Indispensable to the dance, gourd (or gourd-shaped) rattles appear in the Bonampak murals, Codex Becker I, the illustrations that accompany Sahagún's Florentine Codex, and frequently elsewhere. The Toltecs, whose last king, Huemac, was forced to flee their capital of Tula in 1168, raised artistic standards to a level that for centuries thereafter continued to be the despair of the Aztecs, their successors and emulators. They "were fine singers and while dancing or singing played drums and shook rattle sticks called *ayacachtli*," reports Sahagún (Bk. X, chap. 29 [Garibay ed., Vol. III, p. 188]).

Seler (*Gesammelte Abhandlungen, II, 677*) claims that the head of the rattle as pictured in the Florentine Codex (Bk. VIII, pl. 70) looks "flower-shaped." The native painting made for Sahagún does show the handle with its tassel clearly enough, but to call the head of it "flower-shaped" takes some imagination, unless we accept Sahagún's accompanying text, translated by Anderson and Dibble to read "rattles shaped like dried poppy heads" (*Florentine Codex: Book 8—Kings and Lords* [1954], p. 45). Molina (*Vocabvlario en lengva mexicana*, 1571, fol. 3) supports this translation of the Náhuatl text when he defines ayacachtli as "sonajas hechas a manera de dormideras" ("rattles looking like poppies"). Sahagún's Náhuatl informants assured him that, in the full bloom of the Aztec empire, ayacachtli made of gold were the rule for the royal dances (*Book 8—Kings and Lords* [1954], p. 28). But by the time he made his Spanish translation, Sahagún had to confess that all such gold *sonajas* had long since disappeared (*Historia General*, Bk. VIII, chap. 9 [Garibay ed., Vol. II, pp. 298–299]).

Nowadays this rattle—with beads, dried seeds, or pebbles inside its head—takes the name given it by sixteenth-century Brazilian Indians: *maraca*. In 1554 Hans Staden, while waiting to be roasted and eaten by the Tupinambá cannibals in southern Brazil, met it, and found that maracas were considered to be divinities.[25] In Part II, chapter 22, of his *Warhaftige Historia* (Marburg: Andres Kolben, 1557), he wrote a description translated by Malcolm Letts as follows:

It is hollow within, and they put a stick through it and cut a hole in it like a mouth, filling it with small stones so that it rattles. They shake it about when they sing and dance and call it maraca, and each man has his own. . . . After the Paygi (or wise men) have changed the rattles into gods, each man takes his rattle away, calling it his beloved son, and building a hut apart in which to place it, setting food before it, and praying to it for what he desires. These rattles are their gods.

[25] "Sie haben sunst auch der rasselen, Maraka genant, wie die andern Wilden, welche sie für götter halten, haben ire getrencke und däntze" ("They have their rattles called Maraka, like the other savages, which they look upon as their gods, and they have their own dances and drinking ceremonies") (*N. Federmanns und H. Stades Reisen in Südamerica 1529 bis 1555*, ed. Karl Klüpfel [Stuttgart, 1859], p. 171 = pt. ii, chap. 3). The word *maraca* appears in Brazilian documents dated 1561, 1578, 1587, and later. For comprehensive etymology, see Georg Friederici, *Amerikanistisches Wörterbuch* (Hamburg: Cram, De Gruyter, 1947), p. 392.

Staden, like other observers in Brazil, comments on the custom of forcing prisoners to dance, sing, and shake rattles before being killed and eaten. The same custom prevailed, of course, in Mexico.

To add local color to a Mexican dance in his three-act operatic master-piece, *Fernand Cortez ou La Conquête du Mexique* (Paris, Académie Impériale de Musique, Nov. 28, 1809), Gaspare Spontini (1774–1851) added ayacachtlis to the accompanying ensemble. Although numerous other operas introducing Cortés and Moctezuma had reached the boards in the preceding half century (Gian Francesco de Majo, 1765; Josef Mysliveček, 1771; Baldas-sare Galuppi, 1772; Giacomo Insanguine, 1780; Marcos António Portugal, 1798), Spontini pioneered in calling for an "indigenous" instrument. Scarcely less meticulous in his scoring than Meyerbeer, Spontini specified ayacachtli at page 271 of the full score published in 1817 by Erard: "Ce pas est accom-pagné avec l'instrument appellé Ajacatzily, que le danseur frappera ad libitum." The mixing of autochthonous with conventional European instru-ments was to become a commonplace in Mexican nationalist scores of the 1930's and 1940's.

áyotl

A tortoiseshell, the pair of prongs on the belly side of which were struck with antlers, the áyotl was a favorite instrument of the Mayas, who gave it the name of *kayab* (see above, p. 26). After the Bonampak murals, the Codex Becker I, Tezozomoc's description of the 1487 dedication of the Great Temple at Mexico City (*Crónica Mexicana* [1944 ed.], p. 331), and the references to it in Sahagún (Bk. II, chaps. 24, 25, 35), the ethos of the áyotl [26] becomes rather clear. Because of its frequent use at sacrificial and memorial events, it seems not to have been considered appropriate for light pastimes, nor is it included in the inventory of Moctezuma II's palace instruments. Sahagún (Bk. VIII, chap. 14, par. 7) excludes it from the *mixcoacalli*, "the gathering place of the professional singers and dancers, and the storeroom for all their musical instruments and dance costumes." [27]

But it was suited to the midnight funeral procession of the Tarascan king

[26] Further data on "Las conchas de tortuga como pequeños percutores" in *Anales del Museo Nacional de Arqueología, Historia y Etnografía*, 4ª época, VIII [1933], 549–555, with accompanying plates; in Seler, *Gesammelte Abhandlungen*, II [1904], 889–890; Martí, *Instrumentos*, pp. 33–34, *Canto*, pp. 99–102.

[27] Eduard Seler, *Gesammelte Abhandlungen*, II (Berlin: A. Asher, 1904), 676: "das *mixcouacalli* . . . das als Versammlungsort der professionellen Sänger und Tänzer und als Magazin für alles, was zum Tanze gehörte, Musikinstrumente und Tanzkostüme, diente." Sahagún may have omitted áyotl from the *mixco[u]acalli* inadvertently. In translating Bk. VIII, chap. 9 (*Historia General*, Garibay ed., II, 299), he included "golden tortoise carapaces" among the musical instruments played at royal *areitos* (dance festivals). Three votive clay tortoiseshells clearly intended as musical instru-ments came to light in the Escalerillas Street excavations at Mexico City on December 13, 1900 (Seler, II, 890).

(*cazonci*). The *Relación de las ceremonias y ritos y población y gobierno de los indios de la provincia de Michoacán* (1541), MS ç. IV.5. at El Escorial, tells how the dead ruler's chief drummer, along with the carpenter in charge of making the royal drums, marched in a funeral procession with forty other household officials. "Some alligator bones and tortoiseshells" [28] provided fitting music. At the close of the ceremony, wives and officials were clubbed to death, their bodies thrown into a heap, and all dumped into a common grave.

This description of Tarascan royal interments can be confirmed from such later writers as Juan de Torquemada and Alonso de la Rea (1615 and 1643).

cacalachtli

Apart from the ayacachtli, some other types of Aztec rattle have been collected in museums. José Alcina Franch discusses two of the less familiar types in his informed essay, "Sonajas rituales en la cerámica mejicana" ("Ritual Rattles in Mexican Pottery"), *Revista de Indias*, XIII/54 (Oct.–Dec., 1953), pages 527–538. The more important of the peculiarly "Mexican" rattle types discussed in this article is a tripod vase, the hollow legs of which contain clay pellets; these jingle when the jar is moved about. Of the approximately 1,500 precontact Mexican pottery jars studied by Alcina Franch—from Michoacán, Cholula, Pánuco, and Santiago Tuxtla (Veracruz), as well as from characteristically Aztec and Mixtec sites—22 percent, he found, stand on rattling legs. Less frequently, the handles of certain clay stamps, used to print designs on the skin, contain the same kind of rattling pellet. Alcina Franch contends that these rattles guarantee a ritual use. As soon as any apparently nonmusical object—be it jar, stamp, or whatever—betrays itself as a rattle (or as any other kind of instrument), one can be sure of its use in religious ceremonies, he asserts.

Although he offers no Aztec name for these clay rattles or jingling clay receptacles, Molina, in *Vocabvlario en lengva mexicana* (1571, fol. 10v), defines *cacalachtli* as "clay jingle" and *cacalaca* as to sound the clay jingle or any "clay receptacle with small stony pellets inside." Sahagún calls a clay incense ladle that rattles a *cacalachtli* in Appendix 3 to *Book 2—The Ceremonies* (Anderson and Dibble trans., p. 181).

chicahuaztli

Ayacachtli and cacalachtli by no means exhausted the types of Aztec rattling instruments. Chicahuaztli was a third type. Contrary to the ayacachtli,

---

[28] See the new edition by José Tudela and others (Madrid: Águilar, 1956), p. 22: "Iban tañendo delante, uno, unos huesos de caimanes; otros unas tortugas." In a footnote to line 11 of this page, the editor rightly insists that "Tarascan instruments were the same as Mexican."

the gourd rattle with short handle which was equally at home in cult or pastime musical ensembles, the chicahuaztli was a long rattle stick, ending usually in a jagged point, which could be shaken only in religious ceremonies.

Any profane use was apparently denied the chicahuaztli. The verb *chica[h]ua* itself means "to fortify, to make strong," and *chicahuaztli* rightly denotes an instrument "whereby something is made strong and powerful." The very name therefore helps explain the use to which these rattlesticks were put in worship and also their use as insignia of Xipe tótec [Our Lord the Flayed One], and of various earth, water, and rain deities.

So explained Seler (*GA*, II, 674–675), reinforcing his dicta with pictures excerpted from the Codex Borgia (49, Xipe tótec), and from the Sahagún, Durán, and Tovar manuscripts.

In chapter 27 of *Book 2—The Ceremonies* (trans. Anderson and Dibble, 1951, p. 99 = *Historia General de las Cosas de Nueva España*, 1938 ed., I, 165), Sahagún describes the chicahuaztli dangled in front of a woman captive who impersonates Xilónen (Young Corn Mother): "And when they had come to the place where Xilónen was to die, then the fire priest advanced to receive her; before her he carried the rattle board [*chicaoaztli* = *chicahuaztli*], rattling it." At the feast of the water gods described in chapter 25 of the same book (Anderson and Dibble, *op. cit.*, 1951, p. 77 = *Historia General*, 1938 ed., I, 146, 149), a priest marches along with an oversized chicahuaztli on his back. Its large size permits the stringing of several rattles on the *ayacachicahuaztli* ("mist rattle board"). These need only shaking to produce rain.

chichtli

Sahagún mentions this whistle flute when describing the sacrificial slaying of the merchants' slaves, Book IX, chapter 14 (Anderson and Dibble, *op. cit.*, 1959, p. 63).[29] The night before their death, the slaves had their hair pulled out. During this yanking, someone ran around blowing the *chichtli* to urge the sacrificers on. The whistling sound, *chich*, gave it its name, says the Náhuatl text. During this ceremony, the chichtli player carried a vessel into which the hair of the soon-to-die slaves was cast.

chililitli or caililiztli

Nezahualcóyotl (1402–1472), famous poet-king of Texcoco (the capital lying on the east edge of the lake), gained credit among certain Spanish chroniclers for having been a monotheist. Late in life he did build at Tezcotzinco a nine-story temple symbolizing the nine heavens. Above the

---

[29] Garibay ed. (1956), III, 52; Wigberto Jiménez Moreno ed. (México: Editorial Pedro Robredo, 1938), II, 381.

top story he reared a shrine to "the Lord of Creation," Tlachiuali = Tonaca-
tecutli = Tloque Nahuaque.[30] This shrine, whose outside walls were sprin-
kled with stars over a black background, and the inside with gold, jewels,
and featherwork, housed neither statue nor image of "the Lord of Creation,"
whom Nezahualcóyotl lauded as "unseen," "cause of causes," and "all-
powerful." [31] Four times daily the music of chililitli (copper disks), of
cornetts, flutes, conch shells, and of a metal gong struck with metal hammer,
sounded from the ninth story of this temple, calling the King to prayer. In
time, this whole temple to the "unseen god" came to be called chililitli in
honor of its tintinnabulation.[32]

Sahagún's informants knew the instrument, and mentioned its being
played during the feast of the water gods (Bk. II, chap. 25 [Anderson and
Dibble, 1951, p. 77; Garibay ed. of corresponding Spanish text, Vol. I, p.
164, par. 25]). At midnight the priests disrobed, bloodied themselves with
the pricking of maguey spines, then bathed themselves, blew tecciztli
(conch trumpets), and struck chililitli with pine mallets (Anderson and
Dibble, *op. cit.*, cued by Saldívar, *Historia de la música en México*, p. 21).

Sahagún himself rendered chililitli in this passage as "unos chiflos hechos
de barro cocido" (clay whistles). Following Sahagún, the popular modern
author Rubén M. Campos is content for *chilili[h]tli* to mean "clay fife" (*El
folklore y la música mexicana* [México: Secretaría de Educación Pública,
1928], pp. 24, 28). But in his uncertainty he is also willing for it to be an
"instrument like the ocarina." "Strike copper disks with pine [mallets]"
accords more with the sense of the Náhuatl *cohcouiloc chililitli* taken down
from the lips of Sahagún's native informants if, as Anderson and Dibble
opine, *cohcouiloc* derives from *ocouilia* > *ocotl* = "pine branch."

[30] Further details in Frances Gillmor's finely researched *Flute of the Smoking Mirror*
(Albuquerque: University of New Mexico Press, 1949), p. 157 n. 23.

[31] Fernando de Alva Ixtlilxóchitl, *Obras históricas* (México: Editora Nacional, 1952),
I, 253. Around 1600, Ixtlilxóchitl (*ca.* 1568–*ca.* 1648) wrote his "Relaciones históricas"
(Vol. I of the *Obras*) to glorify his Texcoco ancestors. Himself a graduate of the
mission school at Tlatelolco, he may be pardoned for seeking to clothe his forebears in
garments as Christian-looking as possible. Withal, his accounts are now taken seriously
by the best Mexicanists. See Walter Krickeberg, *Las antiguas culturas mexicanas*
(México: Fondo de Cultura Económica, 1961), p. 204: "Formerly he was considered
unreliable, but nowadays credence is allowed his narrative—based as it was on native
paintings in the official archives at Texcoco."

[32] Ixtlilxóchitl, *Obras*, II (*Historia Chichimeca*, chap. 45), 228. If Sahagún was right
in deriving *chichtli* from the sound it made (*chich*), perhaps *chililitli* is an onomato-
poeic word also. Juan de Córdova gave *quihuaquihuaquihua* ("keewahkee-
wahkeewah") as the Zapotec word for small bells, and *quamquamquam* or *tamtam-
chamcham* as the Zapotec for the sound of bell (*Vocabvlario*, fol. 69v). The word
chililitli, although Ixtlilxóchitl was writing his *Historia Chichimeca* between 1608 and
1616, escapes Molina, 1571 (Stanford does not list it at pages 134–135 of his article in
Yearbook II [1966]). Neither Rincón, 1595, nor Carochi, 1645, seems to have known it
either.

çoçoloctli

Molina's *Vocabvlario en lengva castellana* (1571, fol. 63) records three
Náhuatl words for flute, and çoçoloctli is last choice, the other two being
vilacapitztli (= *huilacapitztli*) and *tlapitzalli*. Yet, it is Molina's last choice,
the çoçoloctli, that Sahagún places in the mixcoacalli—the palace collection
of musical instruments (Bk. VIII, chap. 14, par. 7 [Anderson and Dibble,
op. cit., 1959, p. 45]). As for the other two types of flute, Sahagún does
frequently mention priests blowing tlapitzalli at solemn ceremonies. Another who played tlapitzalli was the Adonis who walked about the city in
perfect delight for an entire year impersonating the god Tezcatlipoca.
Crowned with flowers, hung with golden bracelets, married to four beautiful maidens, he enjoyed every favor. At the end of his allotted year, however, he had to mount the steps of a poor temple at the top of which he
would be thrown on his back and have his heart torn out. While ascending
the temple steps he would then break first the tlapitzalli, next the huilacapitztli (*Book 2—The Ceremonies*, p. 68 = Garibay ed., Bk. II, chap. 24, par.
23 [I, 155]). But not the çoçoloctli. Seler suggests that this last was a flute
made of reed (*Gesammelte Abhandlungen*, II, 677). For confirmation, he
cites the yellow color of the twin flutes shown in plate 70, painted by a
native artist to illustrate Sahagún's mention of the çoçoloctli in chapter 14 of
Book VIII. This painting shows the instruments stored in the mixcoacalli.
The twin four-hole flutes are each tied near the mouthpiece with what
look like ribbons. For these, various explanations have been advanced: (1)
the "ribbon" prevented air leakage from the cane tube; (2) the "ribbon"
protected the spider egg sac (stretched over a hole near the neck) which
was responsible for the buzzing sound made by the çoçoloctli; (3) the
"ribbon" served no musical purpose, but was simply royal insignia. José
Luis Franco offered the second explanation, Charles L. Boilés the third.
Luis Reyes, a native Náhuatl speaker now teaching at the Universidad
Veracruzana, identified the çoçoloctli as a buzzing-tone instrument (information from Boilés). Whatever the tone quality of the çoçoloctli, the
Aztec flutes described and handsomely photographed in Martí's *Instrumentos musicales precortesianos* (1955) at pages 81, 83, 85, and 89, are
clay specimens. These are the tlapitzalli that the handsome youth impersonating the god Tezcatlipoca could break one by one as he mounted the
temple steps after his year of perfect felicity.

coyolli

Jingles were made of various substances—clay, nutshells, dried fruit, as well
as gold and copper. Slit below and with a hard pellet inside, they were often
strung together and worn as dancers' necklaces, bracelets, and anklets.
Like Asenjo Barbieri, whose *Las castañuelas* (1878) reaches no less than
forty-six pages, a sufficiently erudite and witty scholar could no doubt

produce an essay of equal length on the *maichiles* of Peru, or the leg rattles, with various names, of Mexico. Jingles with dried seeds inside were called coyolli (= *cuyulli*) (*Anales del Museo Nacional de Arqueología, Historia y Etnografía,* 4ª época, VIII [1933], 572). The moon goddess Coyolxauqui, known to all tourists because of her colossal head in the Sala Mexica of the Museo Nacional de Antropología, wears on her cheeks the jingles that give her the name, "painted with bells."

huehuetl

A "venerable man" is a *huehue* in Náhuatl (= *veue* in Molina, fols. 117*v*, 157); and the most venerated of Mexican instruments was the *huehuetl.* So fundamental was it to Aztec musical culture that Daniel Castañeda and Vicente T. Mendoza could publish a superb 127-page essay adorned with 50 plates and numerous diagrams on the huehuetl family alone (*Anales del Museo,* 4ª época, VIII [1933], 287–310, 449–549, 661–662).

Commonly, the huehuetl was a cylindrical wooden drum sitting on three legs, the top of the drum stretched with animal hide, the bottom open. Beat on with the fingers and not mallets, it stood upright and could usually emit two well-defined tones—the higher by striking near the rim of the drumskin, the lower by moving toward the center. With the skin evenly stretched and of the same consistency throughout, these two tones sounded a fifth apart. Not only do early Spanish writers confirm this interval of a fifth, but also modern investigators working with experimentally constructed huehuetls (*Anales del Museo,* 4ª época, VIII, 280–281, 290). Castañeda and Mendoza did, however, manage to find one huehuetl, "probably pre-Cortesian," which emitted the interval of a fourth when struck near the rim and near the center of the drumhead (*ibid.,* pp. 661–662).

The frame could also be of clay. No less an authority than Alfonso Caso, then director of the National Museum, inserted into the main body of this Castañeda-Mendoza essay his analysis of a huehuetl, the clay frame of which survives in three fragments (*ibid.,* pp. 457–507). Stamped in the clay on one side of Caso's huehuetl can be seen the figure of Oçomatli (Howling Monkey). This is the eleventh-day sign in the twenty-day Aztec ritual month. It was claimed by Aztec diviners that all males born under this sign would be "singers or dancers or painters or learn some desirable art" (Sahagún, Bk. IV, chap. 21 [Garibay ed., I, 349.2]). The Oçomatli sign visible on Caso's huehuetl also places it under the patronage of Xochipilli (Flower Prince, God of Pleasure, Feasting, Frivolity), whose alter ego was Macuilxóchitl (Five Flower) (p. 454). As if the idea of adorning one side of this clay huehuetl with a Howling Monkey were not enough, Caso's monkey enjoys celestial company. He is surrounded by nine of the circumpolar constellations. The signs for these nine constellations fit into a broad belt encircling him (see fig. 16 after p. 576). Upon comparing a suitable map of the skies with the Oçomatli sign stamped into the clay (lámina 18), Caso concluded that the stamp itself had been fabricated in the year 747, during the Toltec period. The huehuetl could have been made any time later, but the Oçomatli sign refers to that one year only (p. 465). The elaborate astronomy known in Mexico before the year 900 has long been admired. Caso demonstrates that some of this heavenly lore found its way even into the decoration of a huehuetl.

Because decorations resist the passage of time, it is much easier for Seler in "Die holzgeschnitzte Pauke von *Malinalco*" (*Gesammelte Abhandlungen,* III, 221-304) and for Caso in his just-mentioned "Ensayo de interpretación del disco estelar que aparece en los tres fragmentos del huehuetl del Ozomatli" to dwell on the visible, and to neglect somewhat the music that once issued from these huehuetls. Can their symbolisms and decorations in any way help us conjure up anew what matters most to the present-day musician— "the sound that once through Moctezuma's halls"? Yes, even if these decorations do no more than make the ethnocentric musician of today pause before such superbly crafted instruments and agree with Vicente T. Mendoza that drums so finely wrought and so elaborately decorated can never have been drudges to a merely "simplistic" music.[33]

For the Aztec poet, the huehuetl captured every mood; but best of all it incited to sacrificial heroism. Take for example the twelfth item in *Cantares en idioma mexicano* (a song edited by Antonio Peñafiel, 1899, pp. 8-9, with the title "Xopan cuicatl," and later by Leonhard Schultze Jena in *Alt-Aztekische Gesänge* [Stuttgart: W. Kohlhammer Verlag, 1957], pp. 26-27). The poem starts: [34]

I am playing my huehuetl, I who hunt for songs to awaken and fire our friends whose hearts lie listless, for whom the day does not yet break—those who sleep in comas, those who glory in gloomy night when the flowering dawn already sings her song and when once again morn lightens the place where huehuetls play.

With equal appropriateness huehuetls hymn the triumphs when Mexico wins, or console the widows when Mexico loses the battle, as for instance when Tzitzicpandáquare leads the Tarascans to the slaughter of 20,000 Aztec warriors.[35]

---

[33] "La Música y la Danza," in Jorge R. Acosta and others, *Esplendor del México Antiguo* (México: Centro de Investigaciones Antropológicas, 1959), I, 323: "Puede asegurarse que a la llegada de los españoles, en el siglo XVI, la música de los mexicanos en Tenochtitlan no era de estructura simplista."

[34] For correct translations, see Schultze Jena's German, *Alt-Aztekische Gesänge*, p. 27, and Ángel M. Garibay's Spanish, *Poesía indígena de la altiplanicie* (2d ed.; México: Universidad Nacional Autónoma, 1952), p. 79 and notes on pp. 192-193. John H. Cornyn, *The Song of Quetzalcoatl* (2d ed.; Yellow Springs, Ohio: Antioch Press, 1931), pp. 149, 191, paraphrases and annotates the same *cantar*—uncritically, however.

[35] Nicolás León, *Los Tarascos*, p. 107; Diego Durán, *Historia de las Indias de Nueva-España* (Mexico: J. M. Andrade y F. Escalante, 1867), I, 295: "tomauan el atambor los

Because the huehuetl gloried in being the one indispensable instrument, the word *huehuetitlan*—meaning "place huehuetls are played"—became by metonymy any "gathering of singers and musicians." [36] The huehuetl indeed occupied so exalted a place in indigenous thought that poets could address it as "a book from which flowers bloom," [37] and could see it in imagination as "adorned with quetzal feathers and braided with flowers of gold." [38]

Cylindrical drums, the upper open end covered with cured skin, came in several sizes. Those called tlalpanhuehuetl rested on the ground and were usually so tall that a man had to stand while playing one. Only Alvarado Tezozomoc vouches for a tlalpanhuehuetl short enough so that the drummer could sit while playing it (*Crónica Mexicana* [1958], 1944 ed., ch. 53, p. 234: "un atambor bajo *tlapanhuehuetl*"). The huehuetls now in museums were made of a hollowed-out tree trunk or of a cylinder of clay. Nevertheless, huehuetls of precious metal may also have been known before cupidity turned them into coin. A preconquest Flower Song (part of the Chalca Trilogy = Song XXXV*b* of *Cantares en idioma mexicano* [Schultze Jena ed., 182, line 15]) alludes to a "huehuetl of gold." This may be mere poetry, but a huehuetl of precious metal is again mentioned so late as 1645 in Horacio Carochi's *Arte de la lengua mexicana* (1892 ed., p. 480: *teōcuitlahuēuētl*).

Oak, walnut, and a Mexican conifer called *ahuehuete,* especially the latter, were the favored trees for making huehuetls. The National Museum tlalpanhuehuetl known as the Tenango drum is of oak. But by far the best known of all drums—the Malinalco huehuetl first described by Seler and now photographed in every popular book on the Aztecs—is of ahuehuete (*Anales,* lám. 12 preceding p. 311). This tree resembling cypress "was the chief wood used for musical instruments; and was even called the 'drum-tree' growing beside the water (a-huehuetl)," according to William Gates, translator of *The de la Cruz-Badiano Aztec Herbal of 1552* (Baltimore: Maya Society, 1939, p. xxvii).

For the etymology of *ahuehuete* = *ahuehuetl,* Gates relies on Fray Francisco Ximénez, a lay Dominican (d. 1620) who in 1615 published at Mexico City *Quatro Libros de la Naturaleza, y Virtudes de las plantas, y Animales.* According to Ximénez, some misinformed Indians claimed that the ahuehuete tree takes its name from the distant drum-roll sound made when wind blows through its branches. Before 1579 Durán had heard the same folk etymology. "I asked why they called this tree the 'water-drum-tree,'" wrote Durán, "and they replied: 'because its roots grow into the water and because of the delicious sound made by the wind blowing through the

---

cantores y empeçauan á cantar cantares de luto y de la suciedad quel luto y lágrimas traen consigo." Also Durán's *Atlas,* trat. 1., lám. 12, cap. 38.

[36] Garibay, *Poesía indígena,* p. 203.

[37] Schultze Jena, *op. cit.,* p. 98 [70] = Garibay, *Historia de la Literatura Náhuatl* (México: Editorial Porrúa, 1953), I, 66: "Libro que brota flores es mi atabal." Book = die Bilderschrift = amoxtlin.

[38] Schultze Jena, *op. cit.,* p. 46 [lines 15–16] = Garibay, *Historia,* I, 18.

branches'" (*Historia*, 1867–1880 ed., II, 212). Ximénez discounted any "wind-through-the-branches-sounding-like-a-drum" origin for the tree name but does accept the "drum-tree-growing-beside-the-water" derivation (Francisco J. Santamaría, *Diccionario de Mejicanismos* [México: Ed. Porrúa, 1959], p. 45, col. 1). Whatever the roots of the word, *ahuehuetl* has continued from Ximénez' time to the present as the one bone of contention on which every etymologist feels obliged to sharpen his teeth (Anderson and Dibble, *Book 2—The Ceremonies*, p. 131.4).

The smallest huehuetls were portable. Itzcóatl, Aztec king 1427–1440, when leading his warriors into battle "played a small huehuetl hanging from his shoulder, and the sound of it excited the Mexicans to fight." [39] Nezahualcóyotl, his Texcoco ally, rushed into battle with a small golden huehuetl tied to his left shoulder.[40] Huehuetls ranging in size from the Malinalco exemplar—98 cm. tall, with a diameter varying between 41.5 cm. at the mouth and 48.5 at the middle bulge—to a stone one 41.8 cm. high are explained (with diagrams, dimensions, and photographs) in the classic study by Castañeda and Mendoza. Players tuned their huehuetls with exquisite precision, either tightening the drumhead or heating it. The pitches of so variably sized a drum family cannot be dogmatized; but Castañeda and Mendoza suggest that modern kettledrums inhabit ranges an octave or more lower than that of museum huehuetls.[41] These are of course cylindrical instruments with their resonance chamber open at the lower end. However, apart from open cylinder huehuetls, Mixtec codices picture occasional huehuetls with hemispherical shells, like modern kettledrums. When so shaped, they rest on a base and whether or not the resonance chamber was open below can only be guessed [Codex Becker I]. The Maya codices, Dresden and Troano,[42] picture sitting figures (human or animal) beating clay huehuetls of peculiar shape. These look like water jugs connected at their base. The mouth of one jug, slightly taller than the other, is stretched with skin.

Martí identifies the clay *kayum* stretched with skin drumhead as a direct descendant of the Mayan codical huehuetls (*Instrumentos*, pp. 33–34). In the explanatory guide for the exhibition of ancient instruments in August and Sep-

[39] Durán, *op. cit.*, I, 76 = *The Aztecs*, trans. by Doris Heyden and Fernando Horcasitas (New York: Orion Press, 1964), p. 58.

[40] *Anales del Museo*, p. 288 and plate after p. 310.

[41] *Ibid.*, p. 302. They calculated 479 vps = B flat above middle C for the fundamental of the Tenango huehuetl in the Museo Nacional (illustrated in plates 48 and 49 accompanying the article). Seler, in his "Die Tierbilder der mexikanischen und der Maya-Handschriften," *Zeitschrift für Ethnologie*, XLI (Berlin: Behrend, 1909), 820, explains the carvings of eagle and turkey-gobbler which appear on opposite sides of the Tenango huehuetl (fig. 591 on p. 824).

[42] Seler, *Gesammelte Abhandlungen*, II, 701–702 = *Globus*, LXXVI (1899), 111–112 (figs. 7 and 8). The Códice Troano cut (Abb. 8 in Seler) can be studied more profitably in the color reproduction (México: G. M. Echaniz, 1939), plate A. 20. Two clay huehuetls are being played in this scene, the one on the left by a man sitting on the ground. For the left huehuetl alone, which takes standard shape, see Martí, *Canto*, p. 81, fig. 37c.

tember, 1966, at the Museo del Palacio de Bellas Artes, María del Carmen Sordo Sodi finds the kayum to be one of the few autochthonous instruments of Mexico unparalleled anywhere else; also, she mentions the water inside the clay frame which helps regulate the pitch. Frans Blom sees a relation between the drumhead, made of the skin of the *baatz* = monkey, and Hun-Baatz, one of the twin deities of song, dance, and drama mentioned in the *Popol-Vuh* (*Popol-Vuh: The Sacred Book of the Ancient Quiché Maya*, English version by Delia Goetz and Sylvanus G. Morley [London: William Hodge & Co., 1951], pp. 126, 129–130 [p. 130: "they were invoked by musicians and singers . . . but were changed into animals and became monkeys because they became arrogant"]). The jug-shaped clay frame still survives among Maya-descended Indians in Chiapas.

However, among the Aztecs the cylindrical form was standard. The three legs with their sawtooth edges had indeed so standard an appearance that in making up a glyph for towns like Ahuehuepan, Ahuehuetzinco and Tehuehuetl, all the native artist needed do was to show a vertical drum standing on its sawtooth legs.[43]

Codex Laud, 34 (Bodleian Library) shows the young moon goddess Xochiquetzal.[44] Her right hand holds what looks like a two-pronged antler. This is her beater for a shallow huehuetl. With her left hand she swings a rattle. On two counts the Codex Laud music-making violates norms: (1) huehuetl players in the other precontact codices are men; (2) they beat it with their hands—not with an antler or a mallet. Sometimes they prove themselves ambidexterous with one hand on the drum, in the other a rattle. To cite examples from Mixtec records: both Codex Vaticanus B3773, 38, and Nuttall, 73,[45] picture the player pounding the drum with one hand and shaking the ayacachtli = rattle with the other. Or to cite an example from the Maya area: Thomas Gann in the late 1890's discovered a temple mural near the village of Corozal, British Honduras. This revealed a superbly costumed huehuetl player. With his right hand he beats the death drum. With his left he swings a large rattle.[46] In such earlier murals from the Maya area

[43] *Anales del Museo*, p. 292. According to Fernando Ortiz, "Instrumentos musicales indoamericanos," *Inter-American Review of Bibliography*, VII/4 (Oct.–Dec., 1957), 383, the sawtooth legs symbolize lightning. The huehuetl sits on three legs so that between them firebrands can easily be inserted to heat the leather, thus raising the drum pitch.

[44] Seler, *Codex Borgia* (Berlin, 1906), II, 188–189, discussed the Codex Laud 34 cut, and identified the gods. Xochiquetzal's feast continued to be celebrated on October 6 late into the sixteenth century. See Durán, *op. cit.*, II, 193. She was the "goddess of painters, embroiderers, weavers, and silversmiths."

[45] Seler, *Comentarios al Códice Borgia* (México: Fondo de Cultura Económica, 1963), I, 42, shows 4-Monkey playing the drum with his right hand, rattle in left. This cut, accredited to Nuttall, 73, reverses the hands used for playing in Codex Vaticanus 3773, 38 = Seler, *Gesammelte Abhandlungen*, II, 699 (Abb. 5) = Gabriel Saldívar, *Historia de la Música en México* (México: Editorial "Cultura," 1934), p. 18, fig. 42.

[46] Thomas Gann, "Mounds in Northern Honduras," *Nineteenth Annual Report of the Bureau of American Ethnology 1897–98*, pt. 2 (Washington: Government Printing Office, 1900), pl. xxxi after p. 670. The 9-foot section of the west wall from which this

as the Bonampak paintings, and in such Mixtec codices as Borgia (plate 60) the player uses both hands, however. Two hands are also the rule in the paintings accompanying Sahagún's Florentine Codex.

The most precise written instructions and notation that a trained ethnomusicologist can give today, telling how drums from the Guinea Coast of Africa should be played, do not help us very much unless we can ourselves hear them played, either live or in a recording.[47] How then can we expect any useful information to survive from the sixteenth century telling us what drum rhythms and pitches were the rule in precontact Mexico? Nevertheless, one series of Aztec songs did begin to be recorded in our Western alphabet only eleven years after Mexico City fell into Cortés' hands. The manuscript, now known as *Cantares en idioma mexicano*, "is one of the most valuable and authentic sources" of pre-Hispanic life and thought.[48]

---

plate was copied no longer exists. As soon as it was uncovered, Gann recognized it as "the best preserved wall in the entire building, the entire mural painting, from cornice to floor, being almost perfect" (p. 664). "Seven colors were employed in painting the stucco. . . . When first discovered the colors were very brilliant, but after exposure to the light for a day or two, a great deal of their luster was lost" (pp. 669–670). Worse yet was to befall the superb Santa Rita murals (so called because the mounds were found on the Santa Rita sugar plantation just outside Corozal). Before Gann could finish copying them, Maya Indians living nearby destroyed them all, ostensibly to make medicine but more probably "because the painted figures would come to life and harm the living" (J. Eric S. Thompson, *Maya Archaeologist* [Norman: University of Oklahoma Press, 1963], p. 226).

These frescoes are "distinctly Mexican, although the hieroglyphs and the subject matter are Maya," says Thompson, who dates them shortly before the Spanish conquest. Whether the muralist was Maya or Mexican, his style certainly did not please Gann when he copied the Santa Rita murals; nor did Gann like the "subject matter" either, a dance with severed heads. At the spring festival in the second month described by Sahagún in Bk. II, chap. 21 (Anderson and Dibble, *Book 2—The Ceremonies*, p. 53, lines 16–19 [Martí, *Canto*, p. 194, fig. 103]), the gladiatorial sacrifice culminated with the flaying of the captives. All the captors then severally "take with them the head of a captive, a sacrificial victim, and therewith dance; this is called 'the dance with severed heads.'" The grisly dancer in the Santa Rita mural grasps two severed heads, not just one. A skull decorates the death drum. Glyphs for music belch from between the teeth of this skull. The fingernails of the ecstatic masked drummer look like cat claws.

[47] Even so renowned an expert as A. M. Jones began his explanations of Central African drumming "with the help of gramophone recordings and by demonstrations." See *African Music Society Newsletter*, I/3 (July, 1950), 16–17, for details of the rebuffs he met when he "decided something ought to be done to put African music on the map in Britain."

[48] Garibay, *Historia de la Literatura Náhuatl*, I, 52. A facsimile of the manuscript was issued under Antonio Peñafiel's supervision in 1904. Five years earlier he had published a not altogether satisfactory transcript (Vol. II in his *Colección de Documentos para la Historia Mexicana* [México: Secretaría de Fomento, 1899]). The single facsimile in Martí, *Canto*, p. 142, fig. 73 = p. 106 (lines 4–32) in Peñafiel's 1899 transcript = pl. 6 (after p. 192) in Garibay's *Historia*, I.

The drummer [49] to whom we are indebted for the advice on how to beat the huehuetl that heads Song XIV of this collection came from Azcapotzalco, the Tepanec capital subdued by the closely neighboring Aztecs in 1427. As a youth this drummer studied in Tlatelolco. Each of his three dated songs in *Cantares en idioma mexicano,* at folios 7 (1551), 37*v* (1553), and 41 (1564), begins with notation for the drums. His name in the manuscript—Don Francisco Plácido—makes him seem a Spaniard. However, all the leading Indians of the century who learned to write in the Roman alphabet took Spanish names, sometimes dropping their native names entirely. Plácido had noble blood in his veins, and in 1563 governed the Otomí town of Xiquipilco. Legend descending through the mouths of Boturini (1746) and Beristaín (1819) makes him a composer of songs for the devotion denounced by Sahagún as a mere continuation of the old superstition of Tonantzin.[50]

Certainly he claimed nothing new for the rhythmic scheme explained at the beginning of Song XIV. Instead he claimed to be reviving the old way of beating drums for a "Huexotzinco" or Huejotzingo dance song.[51] Paraphrased and with a musical example added, his directions run thus:[52]

The huehuetl is played the following way. First, a peal that dies away, then another doing the same, then three drumbeats. What distinguishes the pattern is beginning with the single peals dying away. Next, comes a roll near the center of the drumhead. This breaks off, whereupon the pattern resumes—beginning with the single stroke at rim of the huehuetl.

[49] For Don Francisco Plácido's biography, see Rafael García Granados, *Diccionario Biográfico de Historia Antigua de Mejico* (México: Instituto de Historia [Publicaciones, primera série, núm. 23, III], 1953), III, 73 [item 4336], 177 [4884]; Garibay, *Historia,* II, 101–102, 104–105, 230, 264; Schultze Jena, *op. cit.,* pp. 33, 205, 225.

[50] García Icazbalceta, *Bibliografía Mexicana del Siglo XVI,* 1954 ed., p. 381: "se adoraba un ídolo que antiguamente se llamaba Tonantzin"; Sahagún, *Historia General,* Garibay ed. (1956), III, 352.7 = Bk. XI (Apéndice sobre supersticiones). According to Sahagún, Bk. I, chap. 6 (Garibay ed., I, 46.VI.3), Tonantzin "which means Our Mother" was but another name for the goddess Cihuacóatl. But see also George C. Vaillant, *Aztecs of Mexico* (Garden City: Doubleday, 1962), p. 146.

[51] Schultze Jena, *op. cit.,* p. 33: "Neuerdings ist dieser Singtanz noch einmal im Hause des Gouverneurs von Azcapotzalco, Diego de León (aufgeführt worden)"; p. 35: "Die am Schluss der Ankündigung gebrauchte Wendung *neuerdings noch einmal* beweist, dass es sich um einen alten Singtanz handelt, der im Jahre 1551 wieder an das Licht gezogen wurde."

[52] For Garibay's interpretation of Don Francisco Plácido's drumming instructions, see his *Historia* (1953), I, 168–169. Daniel G. Brinton, *Ancient Nahuatl Poetry* [Library of

The singer must come in at his proper place and will know where. This song-dance type was revived at Easter 1551 in the house of Diego de León, governor of Azcapotzalco, with Don Francisco Plácido beating the drums.[53]

The number of huehuetls needed to accompany any given song in this collection varies from one to ten. Song XLVIII,[54] for instance, requires one huehuetl for the first nine strophes, two huehuetls for the next three, three for the next six, four for the next four, and five for the next eight. This is a song of the Tlaxcalans—the tribe that engaged periodically in "flowery war" with the Aztecs and had the wit to throw in their lot with Cortés when he came marching through to victory. With any one huehuetl uttering two sounds a fifth apart, ten huehuetls must have given a rich accompaniment indeed to Song XLV.[55] There are sixty strophes in this *tombeau* memorializing Don Hernando de Guzmán, the renowned Indian manuscript illuminator who, shortly before his death, became ruler of Coyoacán (father's Náhuatl name was Itztlollinqui [56]). The first eight strophes require but one

Aboriginal American Literature, Number VII] (Philadelphia, 1887), p. 50, was the first to publish the passage in the original Náhuatl (as transcribed by Brasseur de Bourbourg). However, he refused to translate it. "Auh inic motzotzona huehuetl: cencamatl mocauhtiuh, auh yn oc cencamatl, ipan huetzi yetetl ti, auh in huelic ompehua, ca centetl ti; Auh inic mocuepa. quin iquac yticpa huetzi y huehuetl, çan mocemana in maitl. auh quin iquac ye inepantla oc ceppa itenco hualcholoa in huehuetl."

[53] As late as "La Música y la Danza," in *Esplendor del México Antiguo*, I (1959), p. 324, Vicente T. Mendoza continues preferring Garibay's translation of the Náhuatl (published in 1953) rather than Schultze Jena's (1956). After changing Garibay's *caen* into *cae en*, and nothing else, he decides that the sense is too obscure for the passage to be useful today. Gerdt Kutscher of Berlin was the first to attempt an English translation of this "obscure" passage. See "The Translation of the 'Cantares Mexicanos' by Leonhard Schultze Jena," *Proceedings of the Thirty-Second International Congress of Americanists* [1956] (Copenhagen: Munksgaard, 1958), p. 254. With so many translators at loggerheads, it would be foolhardy to shout Eureka for any specific rhythmic interpretation (such as that suggested by the quarter notes, triplet, and tremolo inserted in our English translation), or for the leap of a fifth down implied when the roll starts (measure 2 of the example).

[54] Schultze Jena, *op. cit.*, pp. 296–305 = Peñafiel, *Cantares en idioma mexicano* (México: Secretaría de Fomenta, 1899), pp. 134–136.

[55] Schultze Jena, *op. cit.*, pp. 272–287 = Peñafiel, *op. cit.*, pp. 77–82. Although both transcribe the sixth word in the title as "cacacuicatl," it should read "cococuicatl" according to Garibay (*Historia* [1954], II, 102), in which event it would mean "turtledove song." For Don Hernando de Guzmán's biography (he once governed Tlatelolco), see Garibay, II, 113, and García Granados, *Diccionario*, III, 83 (4406). According to Chimalpahin Quauhtlehuanitzin, *Annales* (trans. from Náhuatl by Rémi Siméon [Paris: Maisonneuve & Ch. Leclerc, 1889], p. 290), Don Hernando de Guzmán inherited the rule of Coyoacán in 1576 but died the same year during an epidemic. Martí makes of Song XLV a "nuptial song" and reads the deceased's name as Lerdo (should be Hernando). See *Canto*, p. 145, lines 4–7.

[56] Chimalpahin, *op. cit.*, p. 210: "Don Juan de Guzmán Itztlollinqui was son of Quauhpopocatzin, hereditary king of Coyoacán," and ruled forty-four years: 1526–1569.

huehuetl, the number of huehuetls rising progressively to ten for strophes 49–60.

To interest the listener further, the drumbeat pattern can change within any given group of strophes. In the last twelve of the sixty strophes of the song just mentioned (XLV), the seventeen-syllable drumbeat pattern for strophes 49–54 reads, for instance:

tocoto   coti quiti   tocoto   coti quiti   totiti

But strophes 55–60 exploit a still more complex pattern involving twenty-two syllables:

toco toco tiquiti   toco toco tiquiti   totiquiti   totiquiti

Complex rhythmic patterns like these betray Spanish influence, contends the eminent Americanist Karl A. Nowotny in his article on Aztec drumming, "Die Notation des *Tono* in den Aztekischen Cantares" (*Baessler-Archiv*, Neue Folge, IV/2 [XXIX. Band] [Dec., 1956], 186). As part of his admirable analysis, Nowotny tabulates each of the 758 drumbeat patterns recorded in the manuscript of *Cantares en idioma mexicano*. Without doubt, the earliest datable songs in the collection do always match the simplest drumbeat patterns. Nowotny also discovers another important fact: exactly the same drumming notation served for both the vertical and the horizontal types of Aztec drum—huehuetl (a membranophone) and teponaztli (an idiophone).

As another evidence of their notorious obsession with duality, Aztec drum notation constantly involves paired variables: (1) the two vowels *i* (as in machine) and *o*, and (2) the two consonants *t* and *c* (= *qu* or *k*). How shall the two vowels be interpreted? As pitch indicators? We recall the two pitches available to the huehuetl player by merely moving from the rim toward the middle of his drumskin; we remember also the two pitches that can be sounded on the two-keyed teponaztli by striking one key and then the other. Is it too daring to suppose that both huehuetl and teponaztli players allowed the *i* vowel to signal the higher note and *o* the lower? In any event, this can be accepted as a working hypothesis.[57] Less easily found, however, is an acceptable explanation of the consonants that begin each syllable of the drum notation: *t* and hard *c* (*k* = Spanish *qu* before *e* and *i*). The drum notation for the Don Hernando de Guzmán *planctus* has already proven that drum strokes can bundle together in anything from two strokes to seven.[58] However, the vast majority of these drumbeat groups, whatever the number of strokes in a group, begin with a *t* syllable rather than a *c* syllable. So overwhelming is this majority that Nowotny counts 636 of the 758 as beginning thus. What is more, no single drumbeat group ever

[57] Mendoza originated this explanation; see *Panorama de la Música Tradicional de México* (México: Imprenta Universitaria, 1956), p. 26: "es de lógica elemental percibir que la vocal *i* resulta más aguda que la *o*."

[58] Nowotny, "Die Notation," p. 188, breaks down the seven-syllable *tocotocotiquiti* into *zwei Doppelschläge und dreifacher Schlag* = *toco-toco-tiquiti*.

contains both *co* and *qui* (*ko* and *kee* in English sounds), nor for that matter two *co*'s or two *qui*'s, claims Nowotny (p. 186). Obviously, the *k* sound at the beginning of the drum syllable—whether *co* or *qui*—signaled a deed that the drummer might be allowed only once to a drumbeat group.

What was that "deed"? Nowotny suggests that the *k* signaled something akin to "downbeat." [59] Conductors of European music are nowadays expected to give but one downbeat in a bar. Can the analogy help us comprehend Aztec drumming? Whether the instrument was teponaztli or huehuetl, the Aztec drum syllables coalesce into groups of two to a bar (429 times in the *Cantares*), three to a bar (260 times), four to a bar (47 times), five to a bar (17 times), and six to a bar (2 times). Again: in none of these groups does the *k* drum syllable enter more than once.

No law decreed, however, that a group could not be formed without the *k* drum syllable in it. Reduced to a European analogy, this means that bars could be formed exclusively of upbeats. Nowotny counts 43 instances of *titi*, *toti*, or *toto*, 10 of *tititi*, 6 of *totototo*, 5 of *tototototo*, 3 of *titito*, and 2 each of *titotito*, *totititi*, and *titoti*. He even finds instances of *titititititi* and of *totototototo* (one each). In all, 73 groups containing nothing but *t* drum syllables appear, making a tenth of his 758 groups.

Just as Sahagún's role in compiling the *Cantares* has been contested,[60] so also Nowotny's *t*- and *k*-counts can be challenged by those who read the syllable groupings differently. Fortunately the facsimile of the manuscript rests on the shelves of most large university libraries; and any curious scholar can therefore test Nowotny's theses at will.

Despite the rigor of his method, Nowotny excludes from his count all those drum syllables that end in *n*. True, most instances of *tinco*, *ticon*, *tinti*, *tocon*, *tiquitin*, *tontiton*, *ticoton*, *tintinti*,[61] and *tocontin*[62] spring to view in

---

[59] Since the *Baessler-Archiv* is a specialized anthropological journal not easily accessible to the general reader, Nowotny's key sentences (p. 186) are quoted here: "Das erste Gesetz, welches sofort auffällt, ist, dass die Silben qui und co niemals in einem und demselben Trommelschlag öfter als je einmal vorkommen. Wenn diese Silben die kräftigen Schläge, im Gegensatz zu den leichten ti und to bezeichnen, so würde sich daraus ergeben, dass in jedem Trommelschlag nur ein kräftiger Teilschlag vorkommen darf."

Nowotny rightly warns against misleading European analogies (p. 189). Another danger looms: none of the presently available printed editions of the *Cantares* can be trusted blindly. The only remedy is a constant returning to the 1904 facsimile of the manuscript.

[60] Wigberto Jiménez Moreno, in his introduction to Sahagún's *Historia General de las Cosas de Nueva España* (México: Pedro Robredo, 1938), I, xxxv, summed up a heavily footnoted case against Sahagún's having collected the *cantares* published by Peñafiel: "this collection has been attributed to Sahagún but without any solid basis." Garibay countered in his *Historia de la Literatura Náhuatl*, I, 153–156. Mendoza accepts as irrefragable facts, dates and attributions merely suggested by Garibay.

[61] Peñafiel, *Cantares* (1899), pp. 104–105, 120, 128.

[62] The *tocontin* = *tocotin* welcomed the seventeenth viceroy, Diego López Pacheco

later leaves of the *Cantares,* and may therefore traduce precontact indigenous drumming techniques. However, this cannot be infallibly so. Already at
folio 37 of the manuscript *tonco* [63] appears. This is in Song XXXVI, the
pre-Hispanic origin of which cannot be disputed. Nowotny's list also lacks
any drum syllables with an *h* in them: *tihti* and *tocotihtoto,* [64] for instance.
Adding final *h* after a vowel lengthened and emphasized it, according to the
best grammarian at the end of the Conquest century. [65] The analogy from
speech suggests that the two drum strokes in *tihti* were related thus:

To return, however, to the question of initial consonants in drum syllables: Mendoza offers another explanation for the *t* and *k* (*c* or *qu*). His
findings first appeared in his widely hailed *Panorama de la Música Tradicional de México* (México: Imprenta Universitaria, 1956, pp. 20–26). Inasmuch as this book and the Nowotny article appeared the same year, neither
author is likely to have influenced the other. Did Mendoza eventually read
Nowotny? Perhaps, but if so he ignored him. As if to prove that he repented
of nothing written in 1956, two years later he republished, word for word,
pages 20–27 of the *Panorama* in a Festschrift sponsored by the 31st Congress of Americanists, *Miscellanea Paul Rivet octogenario dicata* (México:
Universidad Nacional Autónoma, 1958), II, 777–785. Nothing is new here,
not even the misleading title. As if one republication did not suffice, Mendoza the next year repeated himself, again word for word, in his essay "La
Música y la Danza" (*Esplendor del México Antiguo,* I, 323–329).

Having endorsed his own findings so fervently, Mendoza leaves us a
testimony that cannot be cast aside lightly. Since neither Nowotny nor he
writes haphazardly, comparison of their results ought to become more than

---

(Marqués de Villena), when he made his triumphal entry into Mexico City in 1640. To
the accompaniment of ayacachtlis and teponaztlis, it was danced in a "grave and
majestic" manner on November 18 (Cristóbal Gutiérrez de Medina, *Viage de Tierra, y
Mar* [1640], 1947 ed., p. 88). It was danced to the sound of tlapanhuehuetl, teponaztli,
omichicahuaztli, ayacachtli, and cuauhtlapitzalli, when Sigüenza y Góngora visited
Querétaro in 1675. Sor Juana Inés de la Cruz introduced the sung tocotin into her
Nolasco villancicos of 1677 and set it with Náhuatl text in her Assumption villancicos of
1687.

Since it descended into colonial times as a singularly solemn and pure dance, what
was its pre-Hispanic character? It appears as a "Huexotzinca dance-song" in the
Cantares (Peñafiel, 1899, p. 128). On the purity of the "glorious youth of Huexotzinco"
whose sacrifice inspired innumerable dance songs, see Sahagún, Bk. VI, chap. 21
(Garibay ed., II, 143.6–143.7).

[63] Schultze Jena, *op. cit.,* p. 201 (line 13).

[64] Peñafiel, 1899, p. 121 (bottom of the page).

[65] Antonio del Rincón, *Arte Mexicana* [México: Pedro Balli, 1595], ed. by Antonio
Peñafiel (México: Secretaría de Fomento, 1885), pp. 61–62. The Tlaxcalans so liked
the final aspirate *h* that introducing it tagged a speaker as a native of that area.

an exciting parlor game. Both choose the identical method: the counting and classification of the drummings labeled *tonos* in the *Cantares*. But their "numbers game" yields widely varying results. As if to warn us against placing too much faith in any mere statistics, important discrepancies turn up at once when their counts are compared. Mendoza reports 81 instances of *toco*, 60 of *tico*, 39 of *tiqui*, 38 of *coto*, and 29 of *quiti*. Nowotny's count for the same notations runs 140, 102, 49, 39, and 39. Similar divergencies in counting three-syllable notations shake one's confidence further; *tiquiti* (39 versus 50 in Nowotny), *tocoti* (36, 51), *tocoto* (21, 25), *titico* (20, 25); or, for the four-syllable, *titiquiti* (9, 11), *totototo* (5, 6).

Mendoza contends that not only do the vowels *o* and *i* designate pitches, but also the consonants *t* and *c*(= *qu*). In his view, *tiqui toco* may well have meant the following notes in descending order: c^1 *a g e*.[66] Martí esteems Mendoza's scheme highly (*Canto*, pp. 146–148), even though it will not work for such a notation as the *coto tiqui titi totocoto* that heads Song XLV (unless one drum can sound four pitches!). Another stronger argument against considering *t* and hard *c* as pitch indicators is the problem foreseen by Nowotny when he found that the drum syllables beginning with *c*(= *qu*) do not twice enter the same group of syllables. How does this affect Mendoza's theory? As just noted, he claims that the four syllables represent four different pitches. Interpreting them thus, the two pitches c^1 and *g* would become "busy" notes, available as many as six times in a row. On the other hand, the drummer would never be allowed to play *a* and *e* in the same group, nor to play each more than once in a group. Under such a regimen, the notes *a* and *e* (or whatever other pitches one wishes to assign *qui* and *co*) would turn into queen bees singularly jealous of their hives.

But to turn from the controversy stirred by *qui* and *co:* do the *Cantares en idioma mexicano* contain any dynamics or expression marks? Not until Domenico Mazzochi's madrigals of 1638 do signs for crescendo and diminuendo begin appearing in European music. Forte and piano indications were first introduced by Giovanni Gabrieli only a generation earlier.[67] If European notation was so tardy in accepting expression signs, the discovery that huehuetl players in Mexico knew them a century earlier would indeed be an intriguing facet of New World musical history. The handsomely illustrated *Canto, danza y música precortesianos* published by the Fondo de Cultura Económica in 1961 makes such a startling claim. On pages 143–146, nine instances of *ic on tlantiuh* or *yc on huehuetl* or simply *ic on* are adduced from folios 26*v*, 28*v*, 29 (twice), 54, 57*v* (twice), 68*v*, and 70*v* of *Cantares en idioma mexicano* to mean diminuendo.[68] Something is also

---

[66] *Panorama* (1956), p. 24 = *Esplendor*, p. 326 = Martí, *Canto*, p. 147.

[67] Cf. article on "Expression" in *Harvard Dictionary of Music*.

[68] Usually Martí's "rso." = verso and his "vso." = recto. The "expression marks" that he finds at fols. 26*v*, 28*v*, 29 (twice), 57*v* (twice), 68*v*, and 70*v* turn up in

found meaning crescendo and agitato. But confidence in these readings is not increased when the author translates *Xopan* as "spring" instead of "summer," substitutes *huey huehuetl* (translated "large drum" or "tlalpan-huehuetl") for *yey huehuetl* (meaning "three huehuetls") and *Lerdo* for *Hernando.*

None of the alleged diminuendos exists in the manuscript, as consultation with Schultze Jena's paleographically and linguistically competent *Alt-Aztekische Gesänge* at once discloses. The heading of Song XXVII reads, for instance, "Tico toco tocoto ic ontlantiuh ticoto ticoto." The words "ic ontlantiuh" mean "finishes with." What the superscription actually means is this: starting with the drumbeat pattern of "tico toco tocoto, finish with ticoto ticoto." At many other places in this collection the drummer is instructed to begin with one pattern and to close with another. Diminuendos are never suggested by these shifts in the drumbeat pattern.[69]

Among other significant errors, the heading of Song L is misread *Atequili cuicatl* (*recte, Atequilizcuicatl*) and is mistranslated to mean "without singing [i.e., an instrumental passage]." Garibay, whose competence in Náhuatl few would contest, discusses this very song at length in his *Historía de la Literatura Náhuatl* (II [1954], 102, 108–109). Literally, the title means "song of the work of the water." Despite its forbidding length, the poem deserves the scholar's best attention, if for no other reason than its numerous topical allusions. The tribute exacted in the supplying of water serves as the mere framework of an elaborate historical allegory. However, the interpretation of the title to mean "without singing [i.e., an instrumental passage]" comes no closer to *Atequilizcuicatl* than "mess of pottage" comes to *Hohe Messe.* Garibay summarizes his views on the role of voices and instruments on page 403 of this same volume when he states categorically: "*Cuicatl* always means instrumentally accompanied song. Song unaccompanied did

---

Schultze Jena, *op. cit.*, at pp. 138.2 (Song XXI), 148.23 (XXV), 152.16 (XXVII), 154.12 (XXVIII), 316.8 (L. 13), 322.14 (L. 43); and Peñafiel (1899), pp. 110, 112.

[69] However, the progressive growth of the accompanying instrumental ensemble from one to five, or even to ten, huehuetls does suggest that by the time the *Cantares* were compiled Aztec musicians prized climax highly enough to seek it consciously, in rising terraces of sound. The word transcribed as "huey" in *Canto, danza y música precortesianos,* pp. 144–146 ("yc huey huehuetl," four times), should read each time "yc yey huehuetl." This means "with three huehuetls," and the phrase always occurs as part of a rising series, "with two," "with three," "with four" huehuetls. The phrase "ic on tetl huehuetl" (*Canto,* p. 145) should read "ic ontetl huehuetl." This means "with two huehuetls." See Schultze Jena, *op. cit.,* p. 298.24; Molina, *Vocabvlario en lengua castellana y mexicana* (México: Antonio de Espinosa, 1571), fol. 119: "2 Dos. ontetl." Molina's discussion of Aztec methods of counting (fols. 118*v*–119*v*) might well be required reading for all those who constantly keep trying to correlate the Aztec world outlook with the European. Nothing is to be gained by refusing to accept the Aztecs (or any other New World tribe) on their own terms.

not exist and—vice versa—there was little instrumental music without singing."

huilacapitztli

Instrumentos musicales precortesianos (1955), invaluable for its numerous illustrations, identifies only one of the six ocarinas pictured in the chapter on huilacapitztli as Aztec. Front and rear views of a five-note clay specimen shaped like a human head (eyes closed, mouth wide open) appear on pages 72–73 to show what an Aztec ocarina in the Museo Nacional de Antropología looks like. The rest of the ocarinas illustrated in this chapter prove the popularity of the instrument in the Mayan and certain Gulf Coast cultures, but not in the Valley of Mexico.

This dispersal can scarcely startle the reader who already knows Raoul d'Harcourt's article, "Sifflets et ocarinas du Nicaragua et du Mexique" (*Journal de la Société des Américanistes*, n.s., XXXIII [1941], 165–172, with two plates). D'Harcourt agreed to write it after the Musée de l'Homme obtained in 1938 five exquisite ocarinas from the island of Ometepe in Lake Nicaragua. Such unusual features as their large size (ranging to 20 cm), their carefully executed mouthpieces, and their refined finger holes assured d'Harcourt that these newly acquired specimens deserved an article of their own, despite his having already, a decade earlier, devoted an essay to pre-Hispanic ocarinas found elsewhere in Central America and in Colombia.[70] Two of the newly obtained instruments from Ometepe emitted no less than eight pitches each. Found on the largest isle in the only lake anywhere which contains freshwater sharks, these ocarinas boast animal shapes no less weird than the sharks. In ascending order, the pitches emitted by ocarina D.38.19.24 in the Musée de l'Homme collection approximate a European major scale (the supertonic doubly sharped): $b\ d^1\natural\ d^1\sharp\ e^1\ f^1\sharp\ g^1\sharp\ a^1\sharp\ b^1$. The pitches of the other (D.38.19.23) spell all notes in an overtone series through three octaves (except the eleventh partial): $c^1\ g^1\ a^1\ b^1\flat\ b^1\natural\ c^2\ d^2\ e^2$.

So far as the rest of this Nicaraguan ocarina quintet is concerned, d'Harcourt found one uttering seven pitches, and the other two uttering six. With this evidence in hand, not even he could any longer defend the favorite thesis of those many Americanists who had heretofore straitjacketed all New World indigenous music within the confines of the pentatonic scale. Instead, he was forced to concur with E. M. von Hornbostel that wide variety did prevail in the choice of notes for New World fixed-pitch instruments, especially in areas where a fixed-pitch instrument such as the ocarina reached its apogee of public favor.[71]

---

[70] "L'ocarina à cinq sons dans l'Amérique préhispanique," *Journal de la Société des Américanistes*, n.s., XXII/2 (1930), 347–364, with six plates.

[71] Hornbostel also criticized d'Harcourt for trying to give every ocarina note a European scale name. In a letter dated April 19, 1928, Hornbostel explained what

Obviously, it reached its apex in what are now Costa Rica and Nicaragua.[72] The only two provably Mexican ocarinas at the Musée de l'Homme [73] which d'Harcourt found worth describing cannot compare with those from Central America in the same collection. More to the point, neither of the two "Mexican" ocarinas that he described can be Aztec. Nor is any ocarina an Aztec cultural artifact among those chosen for pitch analysis in *Instrumentos musicales precortesianos* (1955, pp. 163–164). The ocarinas described and illustrated in Frans Blom's *The Conquest of Yucatan* (Boston: Houghton Mifflin, 1936), page 136 and Plate VI, not only precede the Aztec invasion of the Valley of Mexico by a millennium, but also have nothing to do with Yucatan, the Ulúa River valley in northern Honduras having been the area where they came to light.

Under these circumstances, the idea must be surrendered that either the Aztecs themselves or their close allies took fondly to the ocarina—that is to say, the globular flute so often given anthropomorphic or zoomorphic shape in Central America. It is not even certain that the term *huilacapitztli*—translated to mean simply "flute or fife" in Molina's 1571 Náhuatl-Spanish dictionary [74]—should nowadays be applied to ocarinas. When *Canto, danza y música precortesianos* (p. 338) calls "bird-shaped ocarinas" *huilacapitztli*,[75] the author may be right, but Stanford's analysis of roots (*Yearbook II*, p. 111) makes "a cane or reed vertical flute" much the more probable sense.

The native painting that accompanies Sahagún's Book II, chapter 24 (Anderson and Dibble, *op. cit.*, 1951, illustration 17, after p. 102), shows no broken ocarinas. Yet the corresponding Náhuatl text distinctly specifies that

---

results were being obtained at Berlin by Curt Sachs, who was using a tonometer to record the exact frequencies of thirty ocarinas (*ibid.*, pp. 352–356): "Every day we see what errors arise from trying to assimilate the pitches of these instruments to the notes of the tempered scale," he warned. In reply, d'Harcourt contended that no native ever heard with the precision of a tonometer. At the close of this article, he unrepentantly added a *table analytique* of ocarina scales in old-fashioned European semitones (pp. 360–364).

[72] *Journal de la Société des Américanistes*, n.s., XXXIII, 170–171. Concerning a Costa Rica six-hole ocarina allegedly capable of emitting eighteen notes of a chromatic scale, see Martí, *Instrumentos*, pp. 106–108. Guillermo Águilar Machado called it the "Huetar ocarina" and assigned it to the Costa Rica National Museum (*ibid.*, p. 106).

[73] Cataloged M. H. 36.19.38 and 32.65.441, the first blows pitches equivalent to an ascending series of five black keys beginning on $f\sharp$ and the second yields $f\sharp a^1b^1e^2f\sharp a^2$. The latter ocarina looks like the "flauta antropomorfa doble" pictured in Martí, *Canto*, p. 337 (fig. 177, accredited by him to the Stavenhagen collection).

[74] *Vocabvlario en lengva mexicana*, fol. 157v: "Vilacapitztli, flauta, o pifaro."

[75] Martí consistently omits the *t* before *z* in this word, both in *Instrumentos* and *Canto*. Such suppression, unauthorized by ancient or modern authority, in itself vitiates confidence in his classification scheme. See Seler, *Globus*, LXXVI/7 (Aug. 19, 1899), 112 (col. 1); *Gesammelte Abhandlungen*, II (1904), 702.

the handsome youth broke first his tlapitzalli, then his huilacapitztli, as he ascended the temple steps to meet his doom. Anderson and Dibble here translate these two words as "flute, whistle" (p. 68). But when the plural of huilacapitztli recurs in chapter 35 of this same Book 2—The Ceremonies (p. 141), they are content to let it mean simply "flutes." For allowing it to signify "flutes" generically, they stand on Sahagún's own example. In his Spanish translation, he gave only *flautas*,[76] thereby discouraging any finer distinction.

Both tlapitzalli and huilacapitztli turn up in *Cantares en idioma mexicano*, frequently in poetical compounds. The combination *chalchiuhhui-lacapitztli* intrudes in the first strophe of a song (XXIII) subtitled "Huexotzincos come begging Moctezuma's aid against the Tlaxcalans" (1507).[77] This twenty-three-letter combination means "green jewel flute." Schultze Jena interprets another thirty-six-letter combination of morphs, *chalchiuh-huilacapitzhuehuetzcaticate*, to mean "they are trilling on the green jewel flute."[78]

omichicahuaztli

Seler devoted one of his more ambitious articles to the bone rasp when he published "Altmexikanische Knochenrasseln" (*Globus*, LXXIV/6 [Aug. 6, 1898], 85–93).[79] With it were included twenty reproductions of museum exemplars and codical paintings. As if so complete an article were still insufficient, the leading French anthropologist Joseph Louis Capitan (1854–1929) elected to discover for the Aztec bone rasp a prehistoric Gallic ancestor. However, "L'Omichicahuaztli [*sic*] mexicain et son ancêtre de l'époque du renne en Gaule" (*Verhandlungen des XVI. Internationalen Amerikanisten-Kongresses Wien . . . 1908* [Vienna: A. Hartleben's Verlag, 1910], pp. 107–109) does little more than prove that his knowledge of the omichicahuaztli was so slight as not even to permit his spelling the word correctly, either in his title or in his article. In contrast, Hermann Beyer (1880–1942) made a distinct contribution to knowledge six years later when he published "Una representación auténtica del uso del Omichicahuaztli" (*Memorias y Revista de la Sociedad Científica "Antonio Alzate,"* XXXIV/4–9 [June, 1916], 129–136, with four illustrations).

For data on the omichicahuaztli, probably the most quoted early authority is Hernando Alvarado Tezozomoc, grandson of the Aztec ruler when Cortés invaded Mexico, Moctezuma II.[80] Chapter 25 of his *Crónica Mexi-*

---

[76] *Historia General*, Garibay ed. (1956), I, 155.23 (= Bk. II, chap. 24); I, 215.10 (= Bk. II, chap. 35).

[77] *Alt-Aztekische Gesänge*, p. 144.12.

[78] *Ibid.*, p. 335, col. 2.

[79] Republished in *Gesammelte Abhandlungen*, II (1904), 672–694.

[80] García Granados, *Diccionario Biográfico de Historia Antigua de Méjico*, III, 208 (item 5058). His father was Diego de Alvarado Huanitzin, his mother Francisca Moteuczoma. His blood therefore contained no admixture of Spanish.

cana (*ca.* 1598) describes the funeral rites ordered by Moctezuma I (reigned 1440–1469) after a particularly bloody war with the Chalca.[81] Throughout the four-day mourning exercises, youths scraped dried, striated deer bones. Using a smaller bone piece for scraper, they made "very doleful" music. This, plus the din of "raucous flutes," accompanied an old folks' dance around the dressed mummy bundles set up in the great square fronting Huitzilopochtli's temple. After the four days, all these bundles were burned. Durán describes the same ceremonies in his chapter 18 (*Historia de las Indias*, I [1867 ed.], 155). Evidently the rituals throughout were extremely precise. Singing of responses especially composed for the ceremony and hand clapping to the rhythm of the drumbeats preceded the music of "bones with small teeth cut into them like ladder rungs."

However lugubrious the sound to European ears, the omichicahuaztli left so indelible an impression that Sahagún on his own initiative added it to the list of palace instruments he obtained from native informants—although of course it did not belong there.[82] By mistake, Tezozomoc also mentioned it in his chapter 80. The circumstances bear repeating: Ahuitzotl (reigned 1486–1502) forced his tributaries to build him a water conduit from Coyoacán, even though every omen had foretold disaster for the Aztecs if it was completed. At the dedication ceremonies, an officer disguised as the Goddess of Waters shook some *sonajas* just prior to jumping in the conduit. As a gloss, Tezozomoc adds that these sonajas were omichicahuaztli.[83] Durán corrects him, however (*Historia*, I, 388–389). The officer impersonating the Goddess of Waters carried "sonajas hechas a manera de tortugas," that is to say, tortoise-shaped rattles. The Náhuatl for this should be *áyotl*, not *omichicahuaztli*.

Tezozomoc's last much-quoted reference to omichicahuaztli comes in his

---

[81] Moctezuma I routed the Chalca in 1455 and inflicted worse defeat in 1465 (Chimalpahin Quauhtlehuanitzin, *Annales*, pp. 118, 124). Both Tezozomoc and Durán described the funeral music with bone rasps after the second of these defeats.

[82] Cf. Spanish description of the royal singers' storeroom in Bk. VIII, chap. 14, par. 7 (Garibay ed., II, 313.7.1) with the Náhuatl (Anderson and Dibble, *Florentine Codex, Book 8* [1954], p. 45, paragraph beginning "Mixcoacalli"). The Náhuatl omits any mention of *omichicahuaztli*. Seler remarks: "When translating this chapter into Spanish, Sahagún discovered that the musical instruments enumerated for the dance could not make a complete list, since the bone rasps so familiar to him were missing; so, on his own responsibility, he has added *omichicahuaztli*" (*Globus*, LXXIV/6 [1898], 87, col. 1). Durán, *Historia*, I, 155, vouched for its continuing widespread use in the 1570's as an instrument to accompany native dancing. Sahagún had therefore every right to know it familiarly.

[83] *Crónica Mexicana*, 1944 ed., pp. 382–383. Durán's corresponding chapter (XLIX) is translated into English on pp. 211–216 of *The Aztecs* (relevant passage on p. 212 following the quatrain). Tezozomoc returns to omichicahuaz[tli] on pp. 389, 406 (1944 ed.), but must be mistaken in both these instances, also. If Ahuitzotl dons the Xipe Totec disguise, as Tezozomoc avers on p. 389, then omichicahuaztli can only read *chicahuaztli*.

chapter telling the tale of the famous talking stone (chap. 102). Here once more the story leading up to mention of the instrument is important: Moctezuma II decides that the "sacrificial stone set up by his grandfather smacks too much of the small and cheap and that it fails to match the majesty of Mexico." [84] He therefore orders his stonemasons to scour his domains for a large enough rock. They find one and at last start moving it. More recalcitrant than Balaam's ass, the stone keeps muttering prophecies of doom as they drag it along. When they try getting it over a bridge, it falls, carrying many to death with it. Never afterward can it be budged. This dire portent convinces Moctezuma that the time has come for his stonemasons to carve his own likeness in Chapultepec rock. (The disfigured remains can still be seen in present-day Chapultepec Park.[85]) They carve him seated on his tiger-skin throne with his shield, but also, according to Tezozomoc, holding the one instrument that properly betokens his approaching end—the omitzicahuaz[tli].[86] Upon viewing his effigy in stone, Moctezuma bemoans invincible fate, then returns to the city to endure the arrival of the Spaniards, the fall of Mexico, and death.[87]

So absolute was the funerary character of the omichicahuaztli that Walter Krickeberg could decree that "it was used exclusively in the funeral rites of kings and of famous warriors." According to him, the gritty sounds, produced by scraping notched bone with a shell or bone plectrum, had their symbolical purpose. The discord of death tolerated no suave or "beautiful" sounds, only disagreeable scraping sounds at varying pitches.[88] If this imposes too much of a European interpretation, at least the codices bear him out in limiting the omichicahuaztli to exequies.

Hermann Beyer, who was later while a Tulane University professor to enjoy renown primarily as a Mayan expert, in 1916 published ample evidence for its having been considered the funeral instrument par excellence [89] long before Moctezuma I's time. For proof, he pointed to a scene in Codex Vindobonensis—the beautifully painted genealogical codex dispatched from Villa Rica July 10, 1519, as one of Cortés' earliest gifts to

[84] *The Aztecs*, p. 250 = Durán, *Historia*, I, 507 (chap. 66).

[85] See H. B. Nicholson, "The Chapultepec Cliff Sculpture of Motecuhzoma Xocoyotzin," *El México Antiguo*, IX (1959), 379–444, esp. pp. 382–383, 403–404.

[86] Both Nicholson and Ignacio Alcocer agree that the instrument should be chicahuaztli, however. Alcocer discovered in 1935 that "quite a substantial portion remains of the staff, the chicahuaztli, held in the right hand" (*ibid.*, pp. 396, 403). The statue under discussion was carved in 1519 when Moctezuma was fifty-two (*ibid.*, p. 410).

[87] Durán, *Historia*, I, 514 (chap. 66).

[88] *Altmexikanische Kulturen* (Berlin: Safari-Verlag, 1956), p. 245 (translated *Las antiguas culturas mexicanas* [México: Fondo de Cultura Económica, 1961], p. 166). He draws an analogy with the former "German custom of replacing bells during Holy Week with the racket of slappers and clappers."

[89] "Una representación auténtica del uso del Omichicahuaztli," *Memorias y Revista de la Sociedad Científica "Antonio Alzate,"* XXXIV/4–9 (June, 1916), 129–130, 136.

Charles V.[90] At 24 recto of this codex we see Quetzalcóatl scraping the omichicahuaztli during funeral ceremonies. Facing him sits Xochipilli,[91] and below them we see the mummy bundle ready for the fire. To increase its resonance Quetzalcóatl rests the notched bone on a skull. With one hand firmly grasping the notched femur, he rubs its grooves with a scraper held in his other hand.[92] "Meanwhile he sings the 'very sad song' mentioned by Tezozomoc, the *miccacuicatl*,[93] this threnody being symbolized by the glyph ascending from his open mouth." The Mixtec Codex elucidates Tezozomoc's chapter 25 in at least two ways: (1) by proving that the player scraped a notched bone laid above a resonator (Tezozomoc's resonator is a conch shell [94] instead of a skull); (2) in confirming that the omichicahuaztli did not sound alone but served as accompaniment for funeral singing.

To prove that several different tessituras can be produced by rubbing a single notched bone, Caso discovered at Monte Albán a whale rib incised with four different sets of grooves.[95] Obviously the omichicahuaztli belongs to no one tribe or epoch. Before Caso unearthed his Zapotec whale-rib rasp,[96] antedating the Spanish Conquest by a millennium, Carl Lumholtz and Frank Russell had already confirmed its use by Tarahumara and Pima

[90] Walter Lehmann, "Les peintures mixtéco-zapotèques et quelques documents apparentés," *Journal de la Société des Américanistes*, n.s., II/2 (Oct. 15, 1905), 267. The fifty-two leaves are of deerskin. Lehmann supervised facsimile publication of this codex in 1929.

[91] Karl A. Nowotny, "Erläuterungen zum Codex Vindobonensis (Vorderseite)," *Archiv für Völkerkunde*, III (Vienna: Wilhelm Braumüller, 1948), 192, identifies the one figure playing the omichicahuaztli as Quetzalcóatl, but does not accede to Beyer's identification of the other as the "solar deity Xochipilli" (*Memorias*, XXXIV, 131).

[92] The codical painting gives Quetzalcóatl two left hands; Beyer, *op. cit.*, explained this (p. 135).

[93] Beyer, *op. cit.*, p. 131, used the Náhuatl term defined by Molina, *Vocabvlario* (1571), fol. 55v: "obsequias de muerto."

[94] Tezozomoc, *op. cit.*, p. 95, reads "como un caracol." Beyer, *op. cit.* p. 132, corrected Tezozomoc's text from *como* to *con un;* "omichicahuaztli of hollow dried deerbone, *like* a conch shell" became in Beyer's emended reading "*with* a conch shell [resonator], which made it sound very doleful." Martí accepts Beyer's emendation (*Canto*, p. 372.71).

[95] Pictured in *Instrumentos musicales precortesianos*, p. 46 (National Museum of Anthropology collection); mentioned, *ibid.*, p. 44, and in *Canto*, p. 338, without supporting documentation.

[96] So spectacular were all the gold and jade ornaments found that Caso could entitle his article for *National Geographic Magazine*, LXII/4 (Oct., 1932), 487–512, "Monte Albán, Richest Archeological Find in America." However, Caso's *Las Exploraciones en Monte Albán* issued by the Instituto Panamericano de Geografía e Historia (Publications 7[1932], 18[1935]), his *Exploraciones en Oaxaca* (Publication 34), and his *Culturas Mixteca y Zapoteca* (1942) disappoint the reader interested in musical artifacts. He mentions finding copper jingles (*cascabeles de cobre*) at Mitla, a post– Monte Albán Zapotec site (see *Las Exploraciones*, 1935, pp. 28, 31), but in these publications fails to picture any Zapotec whale-bone rasp.

Indians in the present century (citations in Beyer, "Una representación," pp. 132–135).

quiquiztli

Molina (*Vocabvlario en lengva mexicana,* fol. 90) cites this instrument as a conch-shell trumpet. In the Spanish–Náhuatl section, however, he has already proffered two other names for the conch-shell trumpet—atecocoli (= atecuculli) and tecciztli.

Since Sahagún's informants could name both tecciztli and quiquiztli in the same breath, perhaps the natives did make some distinction. To cite four occasions when it was played: (1) The Florentine Codex, *Book 2—The Ceremonies,* chapter 21 (describing "The Flaying of Men" [Anderson and Dibble, p. 50]), tells how both tecciztli and quiquiztli blared forth while hapless victims were being dragged to the sacrificial stone, there to defend themselves with mere feather-edged pine clubs against their captors wielding obsidian-edged wooden swords. (2) So that no hour for prayer would pass without music in the priest's dwelling (*calmécac*), four professional players of quiquiztli, ayacachtli, áyotl, and teponaztli were required during ceremonies of the sixth month to remain behind while the populace gathered at the waterside to wade and babble like ducks (Bk. II, chap. 25 [Anderson and Dibble, *op. cit.,* p. 77]). (3) Quiquiztli blazoned royal orders on the battlefield (*Book 8—Kings and Lords,* chap. 12 [1954, p. 35]). (4) Toward sunset, just before the "bathed slaves" died, quiquiztli snarled an ominous warning from the top of Huitzilopochtli's temple (*Book 9—The Merchants,* chap. 14 [1959, p. 65]).

When himself translating these several passages into Spanish, Sahagún forwent anything more exact than "shell trumpet" for quiquiztli (=*caracoles mariscos*[97]). Seler in 1899 (*Globus,* LXXVI, 112) and two Mexican investigators[98] in 1953 identified it as *fasciolaria gigantea.* If gigantic size was its identifying characteristic, the Aztec quiquiztli matches the Inca *huayllaqquepa.*

Carrying size to an extreme, a shell trumpet grosser than the trunk of the meek musician playing it can be viewed in plate 23 [35] of the Codex Magliabecchi, XIII, 11, 3. Although this pictorial survey of precontact Mexican life was painted on European paper "of around 1562–1601" and Spanish explanatory notes cover pages facing the paintings, Codex Tudela from which it was copied bears the date 1553 when the memory of preconquest

---

[97] *Historia General,* Garibay ed., II, 304.28 (= Bk. VIII, chap. 12). See also I, 144.18, 164.30, and III, 54.15 (= Bk. II, chaps. 21, 25, and Bk. IX, chap. 14).

[98] Dibble and Anderson, *Book 9—The Merchants* (1959), p. 65 n. 8, cite Ignacio Ancona H. and Rafael Martín del Campo, "Malacología precortesiana," *Memoria del Congreso Científico Mexicano* (México: Universidad Nacional Autónoma, 1953), Vol. VII (Ciencias Biológicas), p. 16. These Mexican investigators found that the trumpets in the Museo Nacional de Antropología comprise seven different kinds of conch (p. 19).

custom was still authentic (Donald Robertson, *Mexican Manuscript Painting of the Early Colonial Period* [New Haven: Yale University Press, 1959],
p. 126).

tecciztli (= *tecziztli* = *tezizcatli*)

Otro caracol grande—"another large conch"—serves as Molina's succinct
definition (fol. 92). Such modern authorities as Seler, Ignacio Ancona H.,
and Rafael Martín del Campo ("Malacología precortesiana," p. 16) identify
it as a trumpet made of the *Strombus gigas*. According to *Book 2—The
Ceremonies,* it belonged in the calmécac, and was the priests' instrument
(chaps. 21, 27, 34; Anderson and Dibble [1951], pp. 50, 98, 138). Apparently
always needing company, it joins quiquiztli (50), teponaztli (98), and
other instruments in the passages just cited. Significantly, it finds no place
in the repertory of palace instruments (Bk. VIII, chap. 14, par. 7 [1954,
p. 45]). At the war captains' feast in the fifteenth month, young fighters
and priests chase each other. If the warriors catch a priest they rub him
with powdered maguey leaves until he burns and itches so violently that
his flesh creeps. If they succeed in breaking into a calmécac, they rob it
of mats, seats, and tecciztli. Sahagún here translates *tecciztli* as "cornetas,
caracoles." [99]

Tezozomoc tells of priests playing tecciztli at Ahuitzotl's monster dedication of the great temple in 1487. Twenty thousand captives [100] ascended the
sacrificial altar to the blasts of tecciztli "which alone were enough to curdle
the blood." According to him, tecciztli could be of either shell or bone.[101]

tecomapiloa

In contrast with other Aztec instruments, the tecomapiloa was a woman's
instrument, and sexual connotations can be read into its very shape. Sahagún records its use at both the feasts of the young corn (eighth month)
and of the ripe corn (eleventh month). In the first of these was slain the
maiden who impersonated Xilónen, goddess of tender maize (Sahagún,
Book 2—The Ceremonies, chap. 27 [102]). The word itself means "hanging
gourd" and combines *tecomatl* ("large clay cup") with *piloa* ("hang something up").[103] The gourd, hanging from a small teponaztli carried under her

[99] *Historia General,* Garibay ed., I, 213.51.

[100] Durán, *Historia,* I, 357 (chap. 44), says 80,400 were killed.

[101] *Crónica Mexicana,* chap. 70 (1944 ed., p. 331): "el *tecziztli* [*sic*], un caracol
grande o bocina de hueso blanco que atemorizaba las carnes al que la oía." It was
played in concert with teponaztli, tlalpanhuehuetl, ayacachtli, áyotl, and chicahuaztli.

[102] Anderson and Dibble translation, 1951, p. 98; Sahagún's Spanish (Garibay ed.,
1956), I, 180.48–181.49.

[103] Molina, *Vocabvlario en lengva mexicana,* fols. 93, 81v: "vaso de barro, como taça
honda"; "colgar alguna cosa de alto, assi como ropa, &c." Martí mentions the tecomapiloa in all his books: *Instrumentos musicales precortesianos,* pp. 11, 12, 19; *Canto, danza*

arm by each priestess during Xilónen's march to the place where she was to die, served as a resonator and "made it sound much better than the usual teponaztli."

While dancing in the circle that brings Xilónen into the presence of the fire priest (who beheads her and tears out her heart), the priestesses beat their "hanging gourd" drums with rubber-tipped sticks. Ahead of them go warriors dancing in a serpentine pattern. Locking arms, they keep time to a beat more like that of "old Castilian dances" than that of the usual Aztec festive dance, reports Sahagún in his *Historia General* (1938 ed., I, 165).

The eleventh month of the Aztec ritual calendar was Ochpaniztli (a name familiar to students of modern Mexican music because Candelario Huízar made it the title of a symphony premiered in 1936). At the feast of that month, an impersonator of the goddess Toci cuts open the breasts of four captives. Next a group of medicine women join some old priests in singing to the sound of the tecomapiloa—described in the Náhuatl text as a small teponaztli, "from which was hung a small water gourd." Upon their reaching the place of the skull frame, Toci throws down her huehuetl and stamps on it (Anderson and Dibble, *Book 2—The Ceremonies*, p. 114).

Gourd resonators hanging beneath wooden keys struck with rubber-tipped mallets are still today a familiar sight to anyone who knows the Guatemalan *marimba con tecomates*.[104] A congener for the tecomapiloa crops up in even so distant a land as the Congo, where a wooden key suspended over a gourd can be claimed as the kinsman of multikeyed marimbas con tecomates.[105]

y música precortesianos, pp. 312, 335; *Dances of Anáhuac* (Viking Fund Publications in Anthropology 38 [1964]), p. 174. However, he mispells the word. *Tecomapiloa* is the only correct form. The Náhuatl roots confirm the spelling; so do the Pedro Robredo ed. (1938 [I, 165]) and the Garibay ed. (1956 [I, 181.49]).

[104] Vida Chenoweth, *The Marimbas of Guatemala* (*Lexington: University of Kentucky Press*, 1964), chap. 3 (pp. 26–40). For information on gourd resonators, see pp. 27–29.

[105] *Ibid.*, p. 60. Further data in Olga Boone, "Les Xylophones du Congo Belge," *Annales du Musée du Congo Belge. Ethnographie-Série III. Notes analytiques sur les Collections*, III/2 ([Tervueren] Oct., 1936), 130–131. Figs. 114 and 115 picture a hanging gourd similar to the Aztec tecomapiloa.

Arthur Morelet's description of Guatemalan marimbas, especially those encountered in the island town of Flores (not taken by the Spaniards from the Itzás until 1697), still merits attention, although published in 1857 (*Voyage dans l'Amérique centrale* [Paris: Gide et J. Baudry], with appendix of ten native airs after II, 324; English translation: *Travels in Central America including accounts of some Regions Unexplored since the Conquest* [New York: Leypoldt, Holt & Williams, 1871], pp. 209–210, 212–215; native airs, including one called *Malinche*, at p. 214). Morelet opted for the Indian origin of the marimba.

Whatever its origin, as early as 1680 the marimba already enjoyed the reputation of being a typical instrument of the Guatemalan Indians. According to a contemporary account by Diego Félix de Carranza y Córdova (accessible in Domingo Juarros' *Compendio de la Historia de la Ciudad de Guatemala*, I [3d ed.; Guatemala City: Tipografía

teponaztli

Just as the huehuetl was the alpha of Aztec instruments, so the teponaztli was the omega. A hollowed-out wooden cylinder laid sideways, the teponaztli could produce two pitches. These were sounded by striking the two tongues of an ⌶ -shaped incision (cut laterally into the wood). Rubber-tipped mallets called *olmaitl* were always used. The interval formed by the two tongues varied from one teponaztli to another, anything from a major second to a perfect fifth being possible.

The wood-carver cut a rectangular opening into the opposite side of the cylinder from the two keys, giving him access to the interior while hollowing out the teponaztli. He needed great skill if he were to hollow out an interior of exactly the right size to reinforce the fundamentals sounded by the two wooden keys. After studying fourteen museum teponaztlis, Castañeda and Mendoza drew up a comprehensive table comparing the natural vibration periods of the resonance chambers with the fundamentals sounded by the two keys.[106] Their results confirm the Aztec wood-carvers' empirical mastery of the laws of acoustics. When an interior vibrates freely at 229 vps = slightly sharp A (third below middle C), as does the hollow inside the so-called Malinalco teponaztli (National Museum), Castañeda and Mendoza found the keys producing sounds of 448 and 672 vps,[107] very close approximations to the first and second overtones. The interior air column of the Tlaxcala teponaztli, often called the most beautiful piece of carved wood in the National Museum, vibrates slightly above concert pitch b^1b(479 vps); the right tongue sounds its closely approximate octave (949 vps), while the left utters a note a minor third lower.[108] When both tongues

---

Nacional, 1936], 245), the Indians celebrated on November 10, 1680, with "cajas, atabales, clarines, trompetas, marimbas y todos los instrumentos que usan los indios." Shortly after Guatemala Cathedral was raised to a metropolitan, Antonio de Paz y Salgado published an account of the festivities, *Las luces del cielo de la Iglesia Difundidas en el Emispherio de Guathemala* (México: María de Ribera, 1747), again mentioning the marimba as a typical instrument of the Guatemalan Indians (p. 28; see David Vela, *La Marimba: Estudio sobre el Instrumento Nacional* [Biblioteca Guatemalteca de Cultura Popular, LIV] [Guatemala City: Centro Editorial "José de Pineda Ibarra," 1962], pp. 104–106).

[106] "Los Teponaztlis en las Civilizaciones Precortesianos," *Anales del Museo Nacional de Arqueología, Historia y Etnografía,* 4ª época, VIII, fig. 3 (after p. 52).

[107] *Ibid.,* p. 56. Note that the A sounds 448 vps. Written notes in fig. 3 call for an 8va-sign above them.

[108] *Ibid.,* pp. 9 ("el ejemplar de talla más hermosa que posee el Museo Nacional") and 55. Black and white photographs in Antonio Peñafiel, *Monumentos del Arte Mexicano Antiguo* (Berlin: A. Asher, 1890), p. 122; Rubén M. Campos, *El folklore y la música mexicana* (México: Secretaría de Educación Pública, 1928), p. 23; and in many other books. For a partial list see Castañeda and Mendoza, *op. cit.,* p. 9. Martí, *Instrumentos,* p. 27, reproduces it again, but mistakenly infers (p. 28) that their fig. 3 refers to fifteen teponaztlis of which "seven produce a minor third."

cannot be fitted into the lower notes of an overtone series, Castañeda and Mendoza discover that at least one tongue usually can. Tone quality differs from teponaztli to teponaztli, depending on which keys most readily excite sympathetic vibrations in the interior air column.

In museum exemplars studied to date, the tongues emit notes a major second to a fifth apart. Which intervals, however, did the instrument makers prefer? Seconds? Fifths? So far as the fourteen teponaztlis tabulated by Castañeda and Mendoza are concerned, minor thirds prove the favorites. Six teponaztlis [109] in the group sound this interval, including the instrument reputedly used by the Tlaxcalans when they went into battle with Cortés against the Aztecs (bequeathed by him to the Mexico City Ayuntamiento). Three [110] each produce the interval of a fifth, and another trio [111] emit major seconds.

Only one teponaztli emits a major third and only one sounds a perfect fourth (Cipactli 4035-B).[112] Listed in the order just given, the fourteen [113] teponaztlis analyzed by Castañeda and Mendoza utter approximately the following pitches.

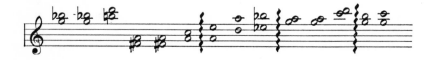

[109] Besides the Tlaxcala, this group includes those called Cabeza de Cipactli 7 (pp. 14, 57–58), Cuauhtli-Ocelotl (pp. 18–20, 59), Sellos Españoles (pp. 20, 59), Tercera Menor (pp. 21, 60–61), and 1040-B (pp. 21, 60).

[110] Malinalco (pp. 10–11, 56), Cabeza de Cipactli (pp. 12, 56–57), Dos Coatls (pp. 22–24, 61–62). The last of these departs from the usual type of teponaztli. Instead of an aperture below the keys, both ends of the cylinder are open. To play Dos Coatls, the drummer had to cover both ends with skin.

[111] Macuilxóchitl (pp. 12–14, 57), Rostros Mutilados (pp. 16–18, 58–59), Palo de Rosa (pp. 20–21, 60). The second of these, a Mixtec teponaztli, has been frequently photographed, despite the mutilation of the figures carved around it. Damage to the left key can be plainly seen in Castañeda and Mendoza, plate 9 (after p. 80).

[112] Because the keys of the Cipactli (= crocodile) 4035-B are crudely fashioned, the pitch was difficult to ascertain (pp. 15–16, 58). The stylized crocodile carved into the wood gives this teponaztli its name. The *tercera mayor* teponaztli, though devoid of any ornamentation (pp. 21–22, 61), shows finer workmanship in the parts that matter musically—keys and resonance chamber.

[113] Obviously a mere fourteen teponaztlis at the Museo Nacional in Mexico do not exhaust the list of surviving specimens. The Trocadero in Paris reported two that sound the interval of a major third and one that utters a major second (Castañeda and Mendoza, *op. cit.*, p. 657). But since foreign museums all together own not more than twenty, and since no consistent attempt has been made to register their pitches, they will all have to be left out of account for the present.

According to José Luis Franco Carrasco, the American Museum of Natural History in New York City (79th Street and Central Park West) "recently" acquired an excep-

The note pairs of the first, eighth, and last teponaztlis register an eighth to a quarter tone above the written notes, 440-A system. Exact vps for all fourteen teponaztlis—given by Castañeda and Mendoza on pages 55–62 of their monograph—confirmed them in the belief that, whatever the interval, the teponaztli makers always found a way to tune the two keys to adjacent notes in an overtone series. The fineness of workmanship can be better appreciated when one remembers the small size of such a teponaztli as the third in the above list, this being the Mixtec teponaztli known as Cuauhtli-Ocelotl (Eagle Jaguar [114]) which is only 35 cm long (exterior diameter, 10.4 cm; diameter of interior resonance chamber, 9.7 cm).

Anyone familiar with the marimba or xylophone knows that the length of the wooden keys diminishes as the scale ascends. Chenoweth found, for instance, that lengthwise the lowest and highest keys of the Ave Lira marimba (Antigua Guatemala) measured 29 and 6 inches, respectively.[115] In contrast, Aztec wood-carvers deliberately eschewed so facile a method of obtaining varying pitches from the two teponaztli keys. Whatever the shape of the tongues—and four different shapes were known [116]—the tongues obeyed a law of "equal length." [117] If the lengths of the two tongues in any given teponaztli do not differ, how then did the instrument makers obtain the desired interval between them? By thinning one tongue more than the other, was Castañeda and Mendoza's answer.

The carver thinned the tongues by cutting and scraping their inside surfaces or, more rarely, their outside surfaces. When the outside was thus cut, visible troughs resulted. If the cut was sufficiently sharp, the resulting "platform" may even have given a tongue the look of being divided into two separate keys. It of course remains true that the tongues of most of the teponaztlis discussed and photographed in *Anales del Museo* (4ª época, vol. VIII) look as smooth on top as a ballroom floor. However,

tionally interesting teponaztli, the first to enter a museum with the plank shutter for the nether opening still intact. Franco owns a photograph, which he plans to publish. This specimen may mean that such loose planks were regularly used as shutters. If so, the acoustical result would bear on the problem urged by Oviedo, who reported that the natives elsewhere in the Indies set the teponaztli on the ground to close the nether opening. See note 144 below.

[114] See Castañeda and Mendoza, *op. cit.*, pp. 18–20, lám. 5 and fot. 10 (after p. 80). Also, Martí, *Canto*, p. 102.

[115] *The Marimbas of Guatemala*, p. 12; the Ave Lira is a "typical" chromatic marimba.

[116] Castañeda and Mendoza, *op. cit.*, illustrate the four types (p. 64). Without their numerous diagrams, the technicalities of construction easily baffle the uninitiated.

[117] As an apparent exception to the rule of equal-length tongues, Nowotny cites the teponaztli in the Museum für Völkerkunde at Vienna (Philipp J. Becker collection, 59.894). Pictured in his article "Americana," *Archiv für Völkerkunde*, XVI (1961), Tafel VII, and described, pp. 123–128, the Vienna teponaztli is scarcely 10 inches long. The right tongue is broken, but "must have been somewhat longer than the left" (*ibid.*, p. 124). For other exceptions, see Castañeda and Mendoza, *op. cit.*, p. 65.

one in the Museo Nacional, dubbed Macuilxóchitl, and another in the Toluca Museum [118] prove exceptions; their tongues rise midway from "floor" to "platform." A casual glance at the line caused in even a good photograph by so abrupt a rise may delude the viewer into fancying that two keys replace the usual one tongue. The same optical delusion can easily deceive the unwary viewer into supposing that the teponaztli drawn in Durán's *Atlas* (trat. 1°, lám. 19°, cap° 54) is a four-keyed instrument. The player shown in the *Atlas* (trat° 2°, lám 6°, cap° 8°) seems to be crouching over a five-keyed instrument. The teponaztli painted by a native artist for Sahagún's Florentine Codex (Bk. VIII, chap. 14, pl. 70) out-Herods Herod with what appears to be a six-keyed teponaztli! However, Brinton's thesis that teponaztlis fathered a hybrid race of five- or six-keyed marimbas, the keys jutting out like teeth from the gums,[119] still lacks any confirmation in surviving museum exemplars. Until such proof is forthcoming, the marimba must continue to be regarded as an instrument of African origin.

But what about the article, "Los Antiguos Mexicanos y su Música," *Boletín Bibliográfico de la Secretaría de Hacienda y Crédito Público*, Año X, Época Segunda, no. 286 (Jan. 1, 1964), at page 15 of which was announced the recent discovery of a ten-keyed teponaztli? some will ask. Any precontact teponaztli with ten slabs, each sounding a different pitch, would sensationally confirm Brinton's thesis and make him a prophet crying in the wilderness. The "ten-keyed" teponaztli, however, came from Colima (or Nayarit), belonged in March, 1967, to José Luis Franco (Mexico City, Salamanca 30A), and is a wooden plank (instead of a cylinder) incised with three keys, not ten. The two-keyed teponaztli still remains, therefore, the provable precontact norm.

By striking the same "platform" key, first on one side of the platform and then on the other, two different pitches can be produced, claims one recent writer.[120] In the same breath, however, he states that the differing pitches

---

[118] *Anales*, 4ª ép., VIII, 12–14 (lám. 3, right side, and fot. 8a = Macuilxóchitl), 654–656 (fot. 117).

[119] Daniel G. Brinton, *The Güegüence: A Comedy-Ballet in the Nahuatl-Spanish Dialect Of Nicaragua* (Philadelphia: Privately printed, 1883), p. xxx: "That it [marimba] was not unknown to the ancient Aztecs seems shown from the following drawing from an original Mexican painting in Durán's *Historia*, where the player does not appear to be striking a drum, but the keys of the marimba, or an instrument of that nature" [cut shows teponaztli].

[120] Martí, *Canto*, p. 335: "Como las lengüetas son de differentes longitudes, cada una produce un sonido, o dos, cuando la lengüeta está dividida en dos secciones de diferente grosor." María de Baratta, *Cuzcatlán Típico* (San Salvador: Ministerio de Cultura, 1952), I, 87, gives *CE* as the two notes produced by striking the two tongues of the teponaztli in the Museo Nacional at San Salvador. "But Indian players sometimes hit the two ends of the cylinder, producing the notes FD♭ instead," she adds ("Los indios algunas veces acostumbran dar con los bolillos en las paredes laterales a las

of the two keys are determined by their differing lengths. Castañeda demonstrated in 1933 that this is not so.[121] The same recent writer takes passing note of a stone teponaztli, in the National Museum, already studied at length by Castañeda.[122] Dedicated to Macuilxóchitl (Five Flower), this teponaztli sits on a base resembling a braided straw mat. Both round ends of the cylinder are capped with what appear to be drumskins. Thus decked out, the stone effigy strongly reminded Castañeda of the Dos Coatls teponaztli in the mustem, which is a wooden cylinder open at both round ends, with the standard ⊥-shaped incision above, but without any aperture directly below this incision.

Of what use was a stone teponaztli? It served as a votive offering, if one may believe Castañeda and Leopoldo Batres.[123] The latter, while general inspector of archaeological monuments, published illustrations and descriptions of numerous stone teponaztlis dug up at Mexico City on December 13, 1900. *Canto, danza y música precortesianos* (pp. 218–219) suggests that during ceremonies honoring Our Grandmother, a female impersonator of Toci kicked or stamped on a stone teponaztli. Sahagún's Náhuatl original, however, does not bear out such an interpretation.[124]

Sahagún does underline the versatility of the teponaztli family when he writes that, on the night when captives impersonating the Rain Gods were to be slain, teponaztlis "croaked, growled, and droned," all in the same ceremony.[125] Another proof of their versatility is recorded in *Book 9—The Merchants*, chapter 10. According to the account in this book, a merchant did not reach the apex of his career until he could invite his peers to a banquet at which the choice viands were cooked slave. Not any slave would do, but only the ones who danced best to the sound of the teponaztli. Sahagún tells where and how such Nijinskys were found.

---

lengüetas, en ese caso, este tepunahuaste [teponaztli] del Museo Nacional da en las paredes laterales las siguientes notas: Fa, Re♭").

From observation of the depressions on museum instruments caused by hammer strokes, Franco concludes that precontact players struck their teponaztlis customarily in three spots: at the tips of the two facing keys, and just above the intersection of transverse and lateral cuts.

[121] *Anales*, 4ª ép., VIII, 64–65.

[122] *Ibid.*, p. 23. Plates 2 and 13 (between pp. 80 and 81) show front and rear views.

[123] *Ibid.*, p. 6; Leopoldo Batres, *Archaeological Explorations in Escalerillas Street* (México: J. Águilar Vera & Co., 1902), pp. 47–49. All the various clay instruments—including ayacachtli, áyotl, omichicahuaztli (14.5 cm long), flute (22 cm long), teponaztlis (length 20 cm, diameter 10 cm)—as well as the teponaztlis of tezontle stone, were "painted with a vermilion red," as was also the statue of Macuilxóchitl to whom they were offered. Cf. Seler, *Gesammelte Abhandlungen*, II (1904), 887–890.

[124] Martí quotes only the Spanish (Garibay ed., I, 193.26–.27); Sahagún here uses *atabal* to translate huehuetl (Anderson and Dibble, *Book 2—The Ceremonies*, p. 114).

[125] *Book 2—The Ceremonies*, chap. 25 (Anderson and Dibble, p. 83): "yn teponaztli, mjmjlcatoc, nanalcatoc, iuhqujn qujqujnacatoc."

Slave dealers in the Azcapotzalco market place hired professional musicians to sing and play the teponaztli. These stirred up lively enough music to make even the most reluctant slave dance his best before the assembled crowd. The purchaser carefully considered which one to buy. He sought above all else a slave sensitive enough to keep exact time to the beat of the teponaztli; also someone handsome, with an excellent body. If a handsome slave danced well he sold for a third as much again as a mediocre dancer. Upon getting the slave home, the merchant jailed him in a wooden box all night but the next morning took him out to start dancing in preparation for the banquet.[126] At the banquet the bathed slave was cooked in *olla* and served in tidbits with maize and salt, but without chili.[127]

The customary season of the year for millionaire merchants to indulge themselves in such conspicuous consumption was the fifteenth month, which came around November 19–December 8. During this month, dedicated to the Aztec tutelar deity Huitzilopochtli, Panquetzaliztli ("feast of the flags") was celebrated. In another book, *The Ceremonies* (Anderson and Dibble, pp. 134–135 = *Historia General,* Garibay ed., I, 210.32–211.33), Sahagún describes in some detail the intermezzi preceding the final trumpet blast for the chosen victims. Having had all their hair cut off by the merchants grooming them for the grand finale when their hearts would become "precious-eagle-cactus-fruit," the bathed slaves proceeded to pirouette before Moctezuma. One of their entr'actes consisted of a staged battle. To make it lifelike, some real soldiers "wearing armor jackets of yellow cotton and carrying shields painted with wolf eyes" rushed into the fray. Against their pine swords, the slaves had little chance with no other weapons than stone-tipped bird arrows. Occasionally a slave did manage to fell an armed soldier, however. In such an event, the slave's reward sounded a musical overtone: his downed opponent was slung over a teponaztli. An expert sacrificer then wielded an obsidian knife to extract the heart of the weakling warrior. The blood that gushed into the inner resonance chamber of the teponaztli gave it new "life."

Our other supreme authority on Aztec matters, Diego Durán, emphasizes the versatility of the teponaztli when he recounts its role in the obsequies of the two kings Axayacatl (d. 1481) and Ahuitzotl (d. 1502). At the first exequies,

After the king's corpse was costumed in the manner of four deities, singers began the funeral chants and responses. His hunchbacks, dwarfs, and other slaves who were to die were next brought in and given the jewels, feet rattles, and other articles that they would need in the after life in order to keep on

---

[126] *Book 9—The Merchants,* pp. 45–46 (condensed) = *Historia General* (Garibay ed.), III, 43–44: "El tratante que compraba y vendía los esclavos alquilaba los cantores para que cantasen y tañesen el *teponaztli. . . .* Los que querían comprar los esclavos . . . . al que veía que mejor cantaba y más sentidamente danzaba, conforme al son . . . luego hablaba al mercader en el precio del esclavo."

[127] *Book 9—The Merchants,* p. 67 = *Historia General,* III, 56.27.

pleasing the king as they had heretofore done in this life. After various further rites the royal corpse and mummy bundle were cremated. All the ashes were placed inside a teponaztli, whereupon the slaves were cast down on their backs beside it, their chests slashed open and their hearts torn out. The blood collected in vessels was then poured over the embers of the fire in which the corpse and mummy bundle had burned.[128]

Similar extravagance distinguished the 1502 ceremonies:

Two hundred slaves sumptuously attired were killed so that they might go on serving Ahuitzotl in the next world. After the royal corpse was set aflame, the priests took their sacrificial knives and one by one slew all those slaves offered by the royal and noble guests as funeral presents. The victims were stretched on their backs over the same teponaztli that played the funeral music, and while pinned on top of it their breasts were slashed open and their hearts extracted.[129]

Alvarado Tezozomoc, whose *Crónica Mexicana* Orozco y Berra assigned to approximately 1598, confirms Durán's account of Ahuitzotl's sumptuous funeral ceremonies. At the close of his chapter 81 (p. 570 in the 1878 ed.), Tezozomoc insists that the slaves were slung over the "large teponaztli, because that was the king's instrument." The sacrificers instructed each before death: "Go enjoy the good life in the seventh afterworld." Museum teponaztlis rarely exceed 2 feet in length, and 6 or 7 inches in height. Their small size would alone suggest that none was the "gran *teponaztli, música que era del rey,*" alluded to by Tezozomoc.

If these citations sufficiently establish the versatile and always virile role of the teponaztli in Aztec music, what of its use elsewhere—in Yucatán, for instance? Within only a decade of the pacification of Yucatán, an inspector named Tomás López Medel was sent there by the Audiencia of Guatemala to reform abuses.[130] One paragraph of the statutes drawn up by López in 1552 reads: [131]

---

[128] Condensed from Durán's *Historia de las Indias de Nueva-España,* I, 307–308 (chap. 39). The translators of *The Aztecs,* 1964, p. 178, authorize the royal ashes being placed "*in* a teponaztli," although the Spanish reads "poniendo *junto à* las ceniças un teponaztli."

[129] *Historia,* I, 408 (chap. 51). Footnote 28 above documents the analogous funeral honors paid Tarascan royalty.

[130] Yucatán came temporarily under administrative supervision of the Guatemala Audiencia *ca.* 1550. Data concerning López' visit is conveniently assembled in Alfred M. Tozzer, ed., *Landa's Relación de las Cosas de Yucatán* (Cambridge: Peabody Museum [Papers, Vol. XVIII], 1941), pp. 70–72.

[131] First printed in Diego López Cogolludo, *Historia de Yucathan* (Madrid: Juan García Infanzón, 1688), Bk. V, xvi–xix, Tomás López' *Ordenanzas* have been frequently republished. The quoted passage may be consulted in Diego de Landa, *Relación de las Cosas de Yucatán,* ed. Hector Pérez Martínez (México: Pedro Robredo, 1938), pp. 354–355.

No Indian girl is to bathe with men nor go about dressed as a man, nor shall a man dress as a woman, even under the pretense of making merry. Nor shall the upright drum or *toponobuzles* [corruption for teponaztlis = tunkules] be played at night. If played in the daytime, at least they ought not to interfere with Mass or sermon.

On August 3, 1588, a welcoming festival in the Yucatán village of Katunil [132] rose to its climax with a preconquest Maya dance thus described in a contemporary *Relación breve y verdadera:* [133]

Among the many dances and devices of the Indians, one made a specially fine impression. Six porters, dancing and singing as they went, carried on their shoulders a float. Atop it rose a narrow, six-foot-high, circular turret. This looked somewhat like a pulpit with sides of painted cotton cloth and with two flags waving on the right and left of it. Inside, a finely attired, handsome Indian [134] was visible from the waist up. In one hand he carried a rattle [*zoot* [135]], in the other a feather fan. All the while he kept bowing and whistling the tune being played on the teponaztli by a musician nearby the float. Meanwhile, many others went along singing to the same accompaniment and whistling loudly and shrilly.

[132] For location of this village (near Tabi in central Yucatán), see map at the end of *Landa's Relación,* Tozzer ed.

[133] *Colección de documentos inéditos para la historia de España* (*Relación de las cosas que sucedieron al Padre Fray Alonso Ponce*) LVIII (Madrid: Vda. de Calero, 1872), 411–412. Literal English translation in Tozzer, p. 94; better translated in J. Eric S. Thompson, *The Rise and Fall of Maya Civilization* (Norman: University of Oklahoma Press, 1954), pp. 257–258. Bartolomé de las Casas, *Apologética Historia* (*Biblioteca de Autores Españoles,* CVI [1958], p. 151, chap. 178), writes "cantos y sones y juegos y bailes." Similar uses by Oviedo and other contemporaries seem to authorize occasionally translating *son* as "instrumental piece."

[134] Martí, *Canto,* pp. 54–55, identified the handsome Indian in the turret atop the float as the Mayan equivalent of the Aztec Flower Prince, Xochipilli. As authority for doing so, he pointed to a similar scene in the Mexican picture book alluded to above, on pp. 27–28 and 60.

The anonymous author of the explanatory notes in this picture book identified the figure borne aloft not as Xochipilli but as "Tlaçopilli which means 'honored lord.' " The painting in question comes at plate 23 [35] in the post-1562 manuscript copied from the Codex Tudela of 1553 (Codex Magliabecchi XIII, 11, 3, Biblioteca Nazionale Centrale, Florence). The anonymous annotator also identified the fiesta as Tecuilhuitl. Tlaçopilli carries a feathered baton called *yolo topili* and wears a parrot disguise. Before him marches not a teponaztli player but a conch-shell trumpeter. See Zelia Nuttall, *The Book of the Life of the Ancient Mexicans* (Berkeley: University of California Press, 1903), for color facsimile of the codex; for date of the manuscript, cf. Donald Robertson, *Mexican Manuscript Painting* (New Haven: Yale University Press, 1959), pp. 126, 128.

[135] Ermilo Solís Alcalá, *Diccionario Español–Maya* (Mérida: Editorial Yikal Maya Than, 1950), p. 529 (sonaja). For bibliography of the term *zoot,* see Ralph L. Roys, *The Book of Chilam Balam of Chumayel* (Washington: Carnegie Institution, 1933), pp. 20 (par. 1: "pecnom u pax [= huehuetl], pecnom u zoot"), 25 (last par.), 29 (last line), 55 (line 21: *zot*), 56 (8); also, indexed entries, "rattle."

The porters themselves went through the same dance routine as the crowd, keeping step to the music of the teponaztli. The turret swaying from side to side atop the float was really something to see, being so tall and well painted. An infinity of Indians came from all around to see this dance, which was a great favorite before the Spaniards arrived, and which in their language is called *zonó*.

Later colonial authors continued mentioning the teponaztli as an indispensable Mayan musical instrument—from Pedro Sánchez de Águilar (*Informe contra idolorvm cvltores del obispado de Yvcatan*, (1639) to Bartolomé José Granado y Baeza (*Imforme del cura de Yaxcabá, Yucatán* [1813], 1845).[136] It was this latter *cura* who quoted the prophet Isaiah (18.1: *Vae terrae cymbalo alarum*) to prove teponaztlis were foreseen in Scripture. Isaiah's apostrophe, "Ah, land with the whirring of wings for its music, lying beyond the rivers of Cush," could refer only to the teponaztli (= tunkul), claimed Granado y Baeza. His reasoning ran thus: (1) Isaiah's instrument had two keys, corresponding to two wings; (2) these made a whirring sound; (3) the land referred to in the prophecy lay beyond the limits of the world known to Isaiah's contemporaries. No other exotic instrument but the teponaztli (= tunkul) fitted all three conditions.

The fine staple of Granado y Baeza's argument ought not to obscure the very real value of his detailed description of the instrument.[137] Among his useful precisions was a flat statement that in Yucatán players placed the tunkul directly on the ground—not on any mat, trestle, or other support. Among the Aztecs, it was frequently laid on a braided straw mat. If the player stood, the teponaztli (with or without mat) rested on a trestle support bearing the zigzag name of *teponaztzatzaztli*.[138] If he sat, he availed himself of a low stool (called *icpalli*), or just squatted.[139] War chiefs carried small teponaztlis into battle, just as they sometimes carried huehuetls. The portable kind was pierced with two small holes through which to pass the cord that tied it on.[140]

[136] Sánchez de Águilar (3rd ed.; Mérida: E. G. Triay e hijos, 1937), p. 149; Granado y Baeza, repr. ([first publ. *Registro Yucateco*, I, Mérida, 1845] México: Bibl. Aportación Histórica Vargas Rea, 1946), pp. 25–27 (describing the tunkul = tankul = teponaztli).
[137] Granado y Baeza prefers the spelling *tankul* (p. 26). Formerly the instrument was an idol. Now the sense has been reduced to "idolize."
[138] Sahagún, *Book 8—Kings and Lords* (Anderson and Dibble [1954]), p. 28. Teponaztzatzaztli = "supports" for teponaztlis.
[139] *Anales del Museo Nacional de Arqueología, Historia y Etnografía*, 4ª época, VIII, 6. For the term *icpalli* see Molina, fols. 15 (Spanish–Náhuatl) and 33v (Náhuatl–Spanish). Icpalli usually guarantee the player's social distinction (Rémi Siméon, *Dictionnaire de la langue nahuatl* [Paris: Imprimerie Nationale, 1885], p. 153: "marque de la puissance chez les anciens chefs, qui avaient seuls le droit de s'en servir").
[140] Both the Tlaxcala and Cuauhtli-Ocelotl teponaztlis were so pierced. See *Anales*, 4ª ép., VIII, 6–7.

To Granado y Baeza's ears the bounce of the rubber-tipped sticks stirred up a lively echoing music that, when heard seven miles across the Yucatán countryside on a good night, sounded like nothing less than the *Ve, Ve, Ve* ("way, way, way") with which the Vulgate "prophecy" of the teponaztli begins. Such a confounding of fact and fancy is merely amusing. But he was not alone in trying to find the monosyllable triplets that best suggest the bleating sound of the instrument. Onomatopoeia dictated the very name of the teponaztli in the Tarascan language, if we may believe Lagunas (1574). *Cuir[hu]ingua* is its name in Tarascan, "because when struck or played, it makes the sound of *kween, kween, kween*." Or at least so says Lagunas, the most painstaking Tarascan linguist of his period.[141]

Knowing that it was so staple an instrument among Aztecs, Tarascans, Mayas, and for that matter every civilized tribe of mainland Mesoamerica, we next inquire: where else did it dominate indigenous music? One answer cannot be contested: in its Mexican shape, it never funneled down through the isthmus into Andean America.[142] Neither the Chibcha of Colombia[143] nor the Inca of Peru knew it.

It did win favor in the Antilles. Such cultural drift is the more interesting because in pre-Cortesian times, according to Heinrich Berlin's "Relaciones precolombinas entre Cuba y Yucatán" (*Revista Mexicana de Estudios Antropológicos*, IV/1–2 [Jan.–Aug., 1940], 141–160), no trade passed between Yucatán and even the nearest isle. Nonetheless, Gonzalo Fernández de Oviedo (1478–1557) met a Haitian version of the teponaztli on the island of Hispaniola as early as 1515, and made a drawing of it to accompany the precise description in Book V, chapter 1, of his monumental *Historia general y natural de las Indias* (*Biblioteca de Autores Españoles,* CXVII, 114, 116;

---

[141] Lagunas, *Dictionarito* [1574], p. 138: "Porque quando le tocan, o tañen haze con su sonido *cuincuincuin.*" Lagunas finds so many examples of onomatopoeia in the language that on p. 76 he writes: Kombz "signifies the sound of something hitting the water for, as has been said already, many words derive from the sound of the action or imitate the blow."

[142] Charles Wisdom, *The Chorti Indians of Guatemala* (Chicago: University of Chicago Press, 1940), pp. 175–176, 379–380, discusses the *tun* (small teponaztli) and *teponagua* (large) played by the Chortis living in the Maya area (Guatemala-Honduras) of which Copan was the culture center. See also photograph 35 after page 336 in Rafael Girard, *Los Chortis ante el problema Maya* (México: Antigua Librería Robredo, 1949), I. South of the Maya area, the teponaztli disappears. *Anales,* 4ª ép., VIII, 282, cites a few "ancestral" types found in South America, Polynesia, and Africa. Baratta (n. 120 above), I, 96, copies the d'Harcourts (cf. *Anales,* 4ª ép., VIII, 284) when she mentions the tunkuli of the Jívaros in Ecuador.

[143] R. d'Harcourt, "L'ocarina à cinq sons dans l'Amérique préhispanique," *Journal de la Société des Américanistes,* n.s., XXII, 348–349, makes a strong case for the ocarina as the most characteristic Chibcha instrument. For the best recent account of precontact Chibcha instruments, see Fritz Bose, "Die Musik der Chibcha und ihrer heutigen Nachkommen," *Internationales Archiv für Ethnographie,* XLVIII, pt. 2 (Leiden: E. J. Brill, 1958), 149–198. Idiophones and membranophones, pp. 158–159.

CXXI, 501). In his experience, the Hispaniola islanders followed the peculiarly Mayan custom reported by Granado y Baeza of placing the instrument on the ground. Their reason was that the sound carried farther ("y este atambor ha de estar echado en el suelo, porque teniéndole en el aire no suena" [CXVII, 116]).[144]

Oviedo's precise drawing was first published in Spain at folio 46v, column 2, of his *La historia general de las Indias* (Seville: Juan Cromberger, 1535), and in Italy at folio 112v of the Italian translation published in Giovanni Battista Ramusio's *Terzo Volume delle Navigationi et Viaggi* (Venice: Stamperia de Giunti, 1556). In both the primitive Spanish and Italian publications, Oviedo accompanies the drawing with a description substantially the same as that published from his original manuscript by the Real Academia de la Historia in 1851 (IV, 130), but without the questionable claim that the teponaztli does not sound well except when placed on the ground.

tepuzquiquiztli

Defined by Molina (fol. 104) with no more than the laconic "trompeta," the tepuzquiquiztli, according to Rémi Siméon (*Dictionnaire de la langue nahuatl* [Paris: Imprimerie Nationale, 1855], p. 453), was a "trompette en metal," and the root of the word is *quiquiztli* (discussed at pp. 60–61, above) preceded by *tepuztli*, which he and Molina agree means *cuivre* = *cobre* = "copper." Precontact copper rattles (also called "clapperless bells") cast by the lost wax process can be documented in numerous archaeological finds.[145] Metal trumpets are more difficult to find, but

---

[144] A polite musician brought up in Prince John's company and within constant earshot of Juan de Anchieta's precepts, Oviedo found little to his liking in the instrument. What is more, he thought Antilles music in 1515 poorer than the indigenous music at Darién (Panamá)—that "muy gentil población" of 1500 Indians and 500 Spaniards which preceded all other New World settlements in blending Europeans and indigenes into a cordial mixture (cf. Juan Pérez de Tudela Bueso's introduction, *Biblioteca de Autores Españoles* [1959], CXVII, lii–liii).

Fray Ramón Pane—a Catalonian *ermitaño* who learned the language of Hispaniola in order to convert the natives (see Mendieta, *Historia Eclesiástica Indiana* [1870], p. 35)—was commissioned by Christopher Columbus in 1496 to describe Taino life. Pane mentioned a Hispaniola drum called *mayohavau*. Made of a stout hollowed-out tree trunk something less than 4 feet long and 2 feet in diameter, this slit-drum had two keys that reminded him of blacksmith's tongs. To its accompaniment the Tainos sang their religious chants. Its sound carried "a league and a half." This may well be the same congener of the teponaztli later described in Oviedo's *Historia general y natural*. See Pane's chapter 14 translated by Benjamin Keen in *The Life of the Admiral Christopher Columbus by his son Ferdinand* (New Brunswick: Rutgers University Press, 1959), pp. 158–159.

[145] Batres, *Archaeological Explorations* (1902), p. 14, pictured "thirty copper morris-bells" dug up in only one day during the sewer excavations at Mexico City, September 4, 1900. Before the digging ended, 150 had been collected. For a unique type of

their disappearance may mean no more than that they were melted down.

At best, metallurgy arrived late in Mesoamerica. The Mayas lacked metal at the time the Bonampak murals were painted, nor did they know it except as an import much later.[146] What material did they use, then, for their trumpets that rival the hatzotzerah on the Arch of Titus for extraordinary length? Wood, according to the leading contemporary Maya authority.[147] So far as color is concerned, the four Bonampak trumpets—longer than a man's arm—are painted tan near the mouth. Halfway to the flaring bell the tan changes abruptly to a deep ruddy brown, possibly because two kinds of tropical wood join here. A black ring around the trumpet an inch or so from the lips suggests a mouthpiece. Twin trumpeters stand side by side in the twelve-man orchestra [148] shown in one mural. In another scene, depicting the tumult of battle, the trumpeters mix singly with the fighters. The paintings show the lips of the players always tightly pursed, with the trumpet itself jutting upward. Because of their material, the obsolete *Zink* would be their nearest European equivalent.

Not only were the Bonampak long trumpets evidently made of wood, but also long wood trumpets continued to be the only kind used in Mayan indigenous ceremonies throughout the colonial period. Landa's *Relación* of ca. 1566 mentions "long thin trumpets of hollow wood with long twisted gourds at the ends" as a principal Mayan instrument.[149] An eyewitness account, dated 1624, describes a dance ceremony in the Mayan area during which these "long, twisted trumpets . . . fill the whole town with excite-

---

Tarascan copper cascabel, tortoise-shaped, and made of soldered copper wire, see Krickeberg, *Las antiguas culturas*, p. 364. "No other New World culture produced anything like it," he wrote.

[146] On the metal famine in Maya areas, see Tozzer ed. of Landa, pp. 18.104, 111.506. All pre-Cortesian metal objects in Yucatán were imports from Tabasco, Honduras, and Nicaragua. Copper bells were the only metal musical instruments in the peninsula when Grijalva skirted its shores in 1518. "The money which they used was little bells [of copper]" at the time the Spaniards arrived, so reported the first native of Yucatán to learn both Spanish and Latin, Gaspar Antonio Chi (= Xiu, 1531–ca. 1610; son of a Maya priest, Xiu served as organist of Mérida Cathedral as late as 1596). Xiu's *Relación*, 1582, translated, is in Tozzer's ed. of Landa, p. 231; confirmation of the use of copper bells for money (from Landa and Cogolludo), p. 95.418.

[147] J. Eric S. Thompson, "The Orchestra," in *Bonampak, Chiapas, Mexico* (n. 10, above), p. 60.

[148] Except for players of large huehuetl and teponaztli, all are in a procession moving from left to right. The others are four ayacachtli players, three áyotl, and one other rattler. See inset in Martí, *Instrumentos*, after p. 58.

[149] Héctor Pérez Martínez ed. (1938), p. 109; Tozzer ed. (1941), p. 93. The Mayan word for trumpet is *hom*. For distinction between *chul* (= flute) and hom, see Ralph L. Roys, *The Book of Chilam Balam of Chumayel* (Washington: Carnegie Institution, 1933), p. 127.3.

ment." The witness [150] claimed that in the Quiché language the dance, with which he had been familiar for seventeen years, was called *teleche,* and in Sotohil (= Tzutujil = Zutujil, the language of his village [151]) was called *loj-tum.*[152]

This dance enacts the sacrifice of a prisoner taken in battle. Tied to a stake, he is attacked by four dancers disguised as a jaguar, a puma, an eagle, and another animal—these four supposedly representing his naguals [= familiars].[153] They try to kill him to a terrible din caused by yells and the calls of some long twisted trumpets that look like sackbuts and whose frighteningly dismal sounds are enough to scare the wits out of anyone. In other villages where I have seen this dance the same trumpets are played and the same thing happens: the whole town is thrown into an uproar and everyone down to the smallest child rushes out panting to be present—which does not happen when the usual dance is held.

Another witness to the supernatural powers ascribed to long wooden trumpets is the chronicler Francisco Antonio de Fuentes y Guzmán (1643–*ca.* 1699), who recalls their use in the thirty-day camp meetings that preceded war. While imploring the aid of their god Exbalanquen, the

[150] Thompson, *The Rise and Fall of Maya Civilization,* p. 257, identifies the witness as "the Spanish priest of the town of Mazatenango." However, the witness was Bartolomé Resinos Cabrera, *beneficiado* of the village of San Antonio Suchitepéquez. Cf. the original document (Archivo General de la Nación [Mexico], Ramo de Inquisición, CCCIII, 54, fols. 357–365) transcribed in Ernesto Chinchilla Águilar, "La Danza del Tum-Teleche o Loj-Tum," *Antropología e Historia de Guatemala,* III/2 (June, 1951), esp. pp. 19–20.

[151] *Diccionario Geográfico de Guatemala* (Guatemala: Talleres de la Tipografía Nacional, 1962), II, 132, identifies the language spoken in San Antonio Suchitepéquez today as predominantly Quiché and limits the use of Sotohil (= Tzutujil = Zutujil) to two places in Sololá (pp. 448–450).

[152] Tozzer, *Landa's Relación,* p. 117 n. 536, assembles a comprehensive bibliography of the arrow-death sacrifice. Martí, *Canto,* pp. 56, 59, reproduces two of the plates to which Tozzer refers. One of these comes from the Codex Fernández Leal now belonging to the Bancroft Library at Berkeley. For reproduction in entirety and interpretation, see John Barr Tompkins, "Codex Fernandez Leal," *Pacific Art Review,* II/1–2 (Summer, 1942), 39–59. Plate 4 showing the arrow death is on p. 49. Manuel Carrera Stampa, "Fuentes para el Estudio de la Historia Indígena," *Esplendor del México Antiguo,* II (1959), 1184, classes this codex as *posthispánico.*

Alfredo Barrera Vásquez translated a "Canción de la Danza del Arquero Flechador" from the village of Dzitbalché (between Mérida and Campeche), *Tlalocan,* I/4 (1944), 273–277. The original poem belongs to a group of fifteen Mayan songs, not all complete. Though copied in the eighteenth century, they faithfully reflect precontact Mayan religious concepts.

[153] Daniel G. Brinton, whom James A. H. Murray, *A New English Dictionary,* 1908, credits with having introduced the term into the English language in 1883, published the earliest monograph on the subject, *Nagualism. A Study in Native American Folk-Lore and History* (Philadelphia: MacCalla, 1894). Current dictionaries consider the word to be derived from the Zapotec, whence it passed into Quiché and Náhuatl. Cf. Friederici, *op. cit.,* pp. 443–444.

Guatemala Indians were in the habit of "singing all the reasons that impelled them to do battle to the accompaniment of their teponaztlis, their long trumpets made of black wood, their flutes, and their shell trumpets" (*Recordación Florida*, Vol. I, edited from the two-volume manuscript original, 1690, 1699, in the Archivo de la Municipalidad de Guatemala [Biblioteca "Goathemala," Vol. VI, 1932], p. 18). Better still, they were indispensable instruments for the Oxtum dance. So vital were they considered by the Indians of Alotenango (a town on the road from Antigua Guatemala to Escuintla in Sacatepéquez department), that within Fuentes y Guzmán's time these villagers had offered their governor, Martín Carlos de Mencos, 1,000 pesos for a license to play their "trompetas largas, de maderas negras . . . por una vez sola." They were willing to pay so high a price because in the Oxtum dance "they invoked their deity with that kind of trumpet" (*Recordación Florida*, I, 20–21).

The Bonampak murals are but the first of several precontact evidences pointing to paired use of these lengthy vertical trumpets. Numbers 10:1 documents a similar predilection for paired trumpets in ancient Israel. Of course the parallel cannot be exact, because the yard-long hatzotzerah used in pairs were made of silver, a metal not readily available to the Aztecs.[154] Despite the fame that silver gave Zacatecas and other Mexican states, "white excrement of the gods" (as the Aztecs called silver) was a precious metal that none of the Náhuatl-speaking tribes learned how to extract in quantity. Apart from the exaggerated length of both hatzotzerah in Israel and vertical trumpet in Mexico, still another parallel can be drawn: both forwent finger holes. The two players painted in Sahagún, *Florentine Codex*, chapter 24, illustration 19,[155] must be trumpeters if for no other reason than that their long twin instruments flaring into a bell lack finger holes.

In his *Historia de Tlaxcala* written between 1576 and 1595, Diego Muñoz Camargo (*ca.* 1527–1612[156]) tended to exaggerate the *grandezas* of his own immediate Indian forebears. This is understandable; his mother was a noble Indian maiden from Tlaxcala and at one time he himself governed that

---

[154] The *Jewish Encyclopedia* (1916), XII, 268, neatly summarizes the literature on the twinning of *hatzotzerah*. Concerning silver in pre-Cortesian Mexico, see Krickeberg, *Las antiguas culturas*, pp. 96–98, 404.

[155] Repr. Martí, *Instrumentos*, p. 58; Anderson and Dibble, *Book 2—The Ceremonies*, between pp. 102 and 103.

[156] Manuel Carrera Stampa, "Algunos aspectos de la *Historia de Tlaxcala*," *Estudios de Historiografía de la Nueva España* (México: El Colegio de México, 1945), pp. 94–103. For an earlier dating of the *Historia* and other background information see Alberto Escalona Ramos, "Estudio sobre la *Historia de Tlaxcala*," in the 1947 ed. of Muñoz Camargo's work (Publicaciones del Ateneo Nacional de Ciencias y Artes de México), pp. 315–342.

town. His partiality for Tlaxcala does not, however, make him any great apologist for indigenous music, nor does he wish to sing any auld lang syne to its strains. According to him, the vertical trumpets that in countless temples throughout the Aztec empire joined with large shell trumpets to signal nightfall, midnight, four in the morning, daybreak, eight, midday, and mid-afternoon,[157] were always *trompetas de palo,* or wooden trumpets. Not too flattering when he called the sound of the temple instruments a "hideous din," he demurred from them with the educated ears of a mestizo who has visited Madrid, Valladolid, and Medina del Campo.[158] He recalled that wooden trumpets were war as well as temple instruments and remembered their role in the famous battle of 1384 between Huexotzincas and Chichimecas. It was this battle that inspired the song cycle composed by a chieftain named Tequanitzin Chichimecatl Tecuhtli.[159] The songs in the cycle served Muñoz Camargo as historical source material (or so he claims at the close of Bk. I, chap. 6).

If not still used by Aztec musicians when Cortés arrived, a vertical trumpet surmounted by a "tied-on tongue" serving as resonator was popular in eleventh-century Mixtec ensembles; or, at any rate, so contends Vicente T. Mendoza in "Tres instrumentos musicales prehispánicos" (*Anales del Instituto de Investigaciones Estéticas,* VII [México, 1941], 71–86). Mendoza proposes calling this "bocina con resonador en las orquestas mixtecas" by a name that Náhuatl lexicographers from Molina in 1571 (fol. 7v) to Rémi Siméon in 1885 (p. 31) reserve exclusively for the conch shell trumpet: atecocolli.[160]

The panels in Codex Becker I which inspired Mendoza's argument had already been lengthily discussed by both Saville and Seler (see above, pp. 24–27). As noted on page 28, the foremost warrior-king of the second Tilantongo dynasty, 8 Deer (1011–1063; nicknamed "Tiger Claw"), joined his brother Prince 9 Flower (b. 1012), his half brother Prince 12 Movement, Lord "Belching Mountain," and two other musicians in panels 8 and 9 of this codex to celebrate a victory dated 1048. Mendoza correctly proposes

[157] *Historia de Tlaxcala,* ed. Alfredo Chavero (México: Secretaría de Fomento, 1892), p. 159 (chap. 20). Sahagún, *Book 2—The Ceremonies* (1951 trans.), p. 202 (= *Historia General,* Garibay ed., I, 252–253), agrees that trumpets signaled the "hours" for incensing the gods only four times during daylight. But instead of four times during the night, he says five times, thus making a total of nine calls each twenty-four hours. See below, pp. 157 and 163, for the importance of the "hours" in newly founded Christian churches throughout Mexico.

[158] Chavero ed., p. 262 (Bk. II, chap. 9). His father was a Spanish captain.

[159] *Ibid.,* p. 66: "trompetas de palo y otros instrumentos de guerra sonoros"; p. 68: "Tequanitzin Chichimecatl Tecuhtli, en unos cantares o versos que compuso de sus antepasados."

[160] "Tres instrumentos," p. 83. He picked up the Náhuatl term not from a dictionary but from Campos' vade mecum, *El Folklore,* p. 24.

ollin ("movement" [161]) as the hieroglyph beneath Prince 9 Flower's feet but trips in his attempt to identify the crouching figure as the god of music Macuilxóchitl = 5 Flower.

Prince 9 Flower blows the larger of the two gourd trumpets. Its very size forces him to rest it on a wicker support. King 8 Deer blows the smaller gourd and therefore needs nothing on which to lay his. Both grasp their trumpets with their left hands. Both likewise lift their right hands in the open-palm gesture of a modern conductor asking for quiet.

Apart from shape, it is reasonable to suppose that these trumpets are of gourd, since both are colored yellow in the codex. Fat in the middle, both trumpets narrow at distal and proximal ends. The first trumpeter seems to blow through a mouthpiece colored blue. The distal ends of both trumpets are swagged with painted paper bells through which emerge glyphs for "sound." Tied securely above each gourd runs a tongue jutting upward at its farther end from the mouth. In all likelihood this is a resonator with thin vibrating membrane, like the resonators that give low notes on the present-day marimba so rich and prolonged a quality.[162] The reason that no such trumpet survives today, nor even its name, is explained by the perishable material. However, the several facts thus far listed authorize (1) my contending that it is indeed a gourd trumpet and (2) my looking for a possible name. Perhaps the name applied by Rubén M. Campos to the conch, *atecocolli*, may more properly apply to the gourd trumpet. Our indigenes still today suck the juice out of maguey with long gourds called *acocotes* > Náhuatl *acocotli*. Whatever their name, Saville erred in calling these codex trumpets flageolets [163] with covered finger holes.[164]

---

[161] Séjourné, *Burning Water*, p. 97, shows six forms the *ollin* hieroglyph may take (p. 97, fig. 11), and explains what "movement" means (pp. 93–94). See also Vaillant, *op. cit.*, p. 157.

[162] "Tres instrumentos," p. 85: "como sucede también en las marimbas actualmente en uso, cuyas cajas de resonancia, provistas de una perforación en su base, están cubiertas de una membrana muy delgada de papel." Chenoweth (p. 16) says that the membrane covering the small opening near the bottom of the marimba resonator is "taken from the intestine of a pig." See also the other entries in *The Marimbas of Guatemala* indexed under "vibration membrane."

[163] "The term flageolet is now constantly applied to any fipple flute, especially if it be of small size," warned Christopher Welch in 1911. See his *Lectures on the Recorder* (London: Oxford University Press, 1961), p. 47. Saville evidently meant nothing more than "fipple flute."

[164] Mendoza, pp. 83–84; he refers to Saville's "The Musical Bow in Ancient Mexico," *American Anthropologist*, XI/9 (Sept., 1898), 283. For an indisputable pair of vertical trumpets tied with tongues that Mendoza wished to consider resonators, see the twelfth-century "Toltec trumpeters playing for the ritual sacrifice of a woman," painted by Agustín Villagra after an original "on a hillside in Devil's Glen" near the old mining center of Valle de Bravo (founded 1530), State of Mexico (Martí, *Instrumentos,* p. 58; color reproduction, between pp. 60 and 61). The Toltec trumpets, of wood painted bright red and rose, look like modern megaphones, along the top of which lengthwise poles have been tied.

tetzilácatl

In *Globus* (LXXIV [1898], 86), Seler wrote: "According to Molina's vocabulary [fol. 111: "cierto instrumento de cobre que tañen quando dançan, o baylan"] [this was] an instrument made of copper, which was beaten at the dance; nothing exact is known concerning its form." Nor was he able to improve on this explanation when, the following year, he published another article ("Mittelamerikanische Musikinstrumente," *Globus*, LXXVI [1899], 112) where he confessed that "among the articles which were stored in the *mixcoacalli* [palace warehouse for musical instruments and dance regalia] Sahagún names a metal instrument, tetzilácatl, which was probably beaten."[165]

Sahagún mentioned the tetzilácatl at least twice in *Book 8—Kings and Lords.*[166] Seler knew the second allusion, in chapter 14. In chapter 9 Sahagún listed among the properties for royal dances *tetzilácatl coztic teucujtlatl,* the last two words of which mean that the instrument was in this instance made "of gold."[167] In an article published in 1901 Seler foresaw from archaeological evidence the possibility of identifying tetzilácatl as stone gongs.[168] Evidence for considering them as metal gongs can be found in one early written source, Alva Ixtlilxóchitl's already mentioned *Historia Chichimeca,* in chapter 45 of which the tetzilácatl is described as a concave sheet of metal struck with a metal hammer and sounding very much like a bell.[169]

These explanations conflict with the Luis Reyes etymology, "twisted cane" (communicated by Boilés in March, 1967), the identification with a *silbato bucal* (suggested in the same month by Franco), and the "mention of a metal flute, *tetzilakatl,* for which to my knowledge no surviving example exists archaeologically" (Stanford in *Yearbook II* [1966], p. 112).

tlapitzalli

The central figure in Picasso's cubist *The Three Musicians* of 1921 (Philadelphia Museum of Art, A. E. Gallatin Collection) is Pierrot playing a

---

[165] *Gesammelte Abhandlungen,* II (1904), 677, 702.

[166] Anderson and Dibble (1954), pp. 28, 45.

[167] Molina, *Vocabvlario en lengva mexicana,* fol. 27v: "cuztic teocuitlatl, oro." Cuztic = yellow; teocuitlatl = gold or sliver.

[168] *Gesammelte Abhandlungen,* II, 890 (pl. 93). Seler here discusses the votive instruments dug up December 13, 1900, on the site of the principal temple in Tenochtitlan. These were offerings to the 40-inch-tall vermilion statue of Macuilxóchitl (= Five Flower, god of games, amusements, and music) found in the same diggings (*ibid.,* p. 885). See also *Anales del Museo,* 4ª ép., VIII, 557.

[169] Ixtlilxóchitl, II, 228 (see nn. 31, 32, above): "un artezón de metal que llamaban tetzilacatl que servía de campana, que con un martillo asimismo de metal le tañían, y tenía casi el mismo tañido de una campana."

three-hole vertical flute. Similarly, the central instrument in the pre-Cortesian organology is the vertical flute and its relatives. Or at least this is so judging from the space given vertical flutes in general, and panpipes, ceremonial flutes, double flutes, and multiple flutes in particular, in *Instrumentos musicales precortesianos* (1955, pp. 79–143). Against sixty-four pages for flutes plus another sixteen for huilacapitztli, the whole percussion group of huehuetl, teponaztli, and áyotl together eke out a mere fourteen pages in this handsome book.

The first questions asked by a European-minded musician seeking parallels include these: (1) Were any transverse flutes known? (2) How many finger holes were available? (3) What was the mouthpiece like? Martí answers the first question with a qualified negative. Only one transverse flute has been discovered to date, he says. This solitary example is of Gulf Coast provenience and belongs now to the Museo de Jalapa, Veracruz.[170] In answer to the second question, he points to the six finger holes cut in a 9½-inch-long decorated clay flute found on Jaina Island (east of Dzitbalché off the coast of Campeche State [171]). These give "a white-note diatonic scale of seven sounds, which is the most extensive found in [Mexican] archaeological instruments." [172] Much the more usual number of holes even in Mayan flutes of the best period must have been the four implied for the flute in the Dresden Codex, top of panel 34.[173] Aztec flutes, wherever found, obey the four-finger-hole rule—at least to judge from all the examples in *Instrumentos musicales precortesianos* (pp. 75, 83, 85, 89). When a "ceremonial flute" of human bone incised with five finger holes comes to light it proves to have been Toltec (p. 123, with the two lowest finger holes farther apart than the distance between the other holes), and when one of clay in the shape of a serpent and with five finger holes appears it is identified as Cultura Arcaica (p. 156). Apparently the Aztecs frowned as much on holes that to them were superfluous as the Spartans frowned on Timotheus' superfluous strings.[174]

[170] *Canto*, p. 341. Concerning transverse flutes in Inca territory see Arturo Jiménez Borja, *Instrumentos Musicales del Perú* (Lima: Museo de la Cultura, 1951), p. 45: "The museum of the University of Trujillo owns a Chimú vase showing a man playing a transverse flute." See also below, p. 268 n. 65.

[171] A principal center of Mayan art, Jaina may be found on the map in *Encyclopedia Americana* (1963 or 1965 ed.), XVIII, 819. See text, XVIII, 787, lauding the handmodeled figurines of warriors, priests, ballplayers, and women, dated *ca.* 600 as "small masterpieces of realistic art." The quality of the Jaina art declined between 700 and 1000; during these centuries moldmade conventional animals and women replaced the earlier handmade figurines.

[172] *Instrumentos*, pp. 114 (color reproduction on facing plate), 116. Martí again reproduced this Jaina six-hole flute (Museo Nacional de Antropología) in *Dances of Anáhuac* (1964), p. 176.

[173] Reproduced Seler, *Globus*, LXXVI, 111, and *Gesammelte Abhandlungen*, II, 701; Martí, *Canto*, p. 49, and *Dances of Anáhuac*, p. 178. Also frequently elsewhere.

[174] Even though the Timotheus anecdote is apocryphal (Oliver Strunk, *Source*

Eight steps in the evolution of whistle (fipple) mouthpieces are drawn diagrammatically in Mendoza's "Tres instrumentos musicales prehispánicos" (1941, plate facing p. 76), and Martí reproduces this same diagram in *Instrumentos* (p. 65). Such variety of mouthpieces can be found in pre-Cortesian flutes if the whole gamut of cultures is taken into account. However, the Aztecs made characteristically their own an end-blown flute with a whistle mouthpiece extending through as much as a third of the whole length of the flute. Also, Aztec flutes end in bells that flare, sometimes so abruptly and widely as to look like a flower opening at the end of a stalk.[175]

End-notched flutes to match the *quenaquena* of Peru rarely turn up, and the authenticity of the few in museums is impugned. Mendoza bought an end-notched flute in November, 1934, from an entrepreneur of local antiquities at Oaxaca. Made of human bone, it is pierced with six finger holes that permit emission of the following seven pitches beginning a semitone above middle C: d♭, d♮, e♭, *f*, *g*, b♭, *c*¹.[176] Only the upper five notes of this series utter a pentatonic scale of the type that investigators such as Castañeda decreed to be characteristic of Aztec flutes.[177] Two Tarascan clay flutes in the Museo de Morelia—both pierced with four finger holes and both ornamented at the mouth with gargoyles—produce whole-note scales of five notes.[178] Without ascertaining their exact provenience and without using plus or minus signs to indicate their departures from tempered pitch, Dr. Miguel Galindo in 1933 examined five clay flutes at the Museo Nacional. He hoped to prove that the pre-Cortesian "pentatonic" series occasionally strayed beyond the bounds of the conventional pentatonic scales that can be

---

Readings in Music History [New York: W. W. Norton, 1950], pp. 81–82), the analogy holds. Why four holes, and four only, in Aztec flutes? The four cardinal points and the center comprehended the entire Náhuatl universe, is the answer given by some writers.

[175] *Instrumentos*, pp. 81, 85. The Náhuatl term for bell of a flute or trumpet is *tlapitzaltençouhcayotl*. The two flutes with flowering bells photographed at p. 90 are, on pp. 117–120, identified as those played in the month of Tóxcatl by a priest calling all classes and conditions of men to repentance. Found in 1940 by Hugo Moedano Koer at the Toltec center of Tezatlán (Tlaxcala) in association with other musical instruments dedicated to Macuilxóchitl-Xochipilli, they sound *f*² *g*² *a*² *c*³ *d*³ (last note of this series is the highest *d* on the piano). Martí's "Flautilla de la penitencia: Fiesta grande de Tezcatlipoca," *Cuadernos Americanos*, LXXII/6 (Nov.–Dec., 1953), 147–157, credits Adela Ramón Ligé with having guided him to these piccolo-range "flautillas" in the Museo Nacional de Antropología collections. Because in 1615 Torquemada (*Segunda parte delos veinte i un libros rituales* [Madrid: N. Rodríguez Franco, 1723], p. 256) classed the clay flutes played before 1521 in the fifth Aztec ritual month of Tóxcatl as "very shrill," we are now asked to accept these two Anthropological Museum flutes from a Toltec ceremonial center antedating Torquemada by more than three centuries as the high-pitched flutes to which he refers.

[176] "Tres instrumentos," p. 77. Photographs of this bone flute, front and rear views, are opposite.

[177] *Instrumentos*, p. 108.

[178] *Ibid.*, p. 109.

produced by playing only black keys. The "scales" of his five flutes, as
shown on pages 100–101 of his *Nociones de Historia de Música Mejicana*
(Colima: Tipografía de "El Dragón," 1933), read thus:

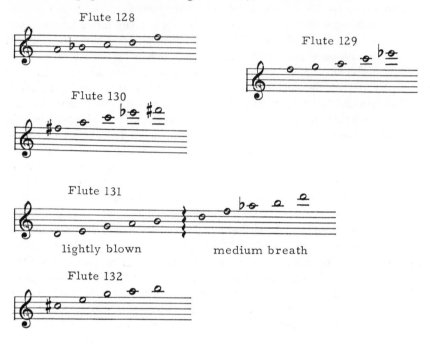

Flute 128

Flute 129

Flute 130

Flute 131

lightly blown   medium breath

Flute 132

The photographs of Flutes 128 and 132 (*Nociones*, pp. 62–63) fortunately
reveal them to be the same flutes, 10½ and 6 inches long, respectively, which
Martí was to choose for an illustration of "pentaphonic flutes of the Aztec
type" in *Instrumentos* (1955, p. 85).

Did precontact flutists overblow and half-stop? Yes, answered H. T. Cresson, whose essay on "Aztec Music" published in *Proceedings of the
Academy of Natural Sciences of Philadelphia,* Part I (1883, pp. 86–94), was
one of the earliest on the subject. Given even a "pentatonic" flute, an
amazing spectrum of pitches becomes available with these added techniques.
As late as 1670 Francisco de Burgoa (1605–1681) continued to complain of
the "out-of-tune flutes" [179] played by the natives to invoke their gods, before
missionaries began instilling in them European pitch ideals. He could not
have made a point of their *destempladas flautas* if they had been blowing,
in simple and straightforward manner, nothing but innocent pentatonic
flutes.

[179] Burgoa, *Palestra Historial* (México: Talleres Gráficos de la Nación, 1934
[Publicaciones del Archivo General, XXIV]), p. 106 (chap. 13). He here discusses
musical conditions in the Oaxaca region before the Dominicans entered upon their
labors.

Viewed from a European stance, the true glories among pre-Cortesian blown instruments were the multiple flutes. As long ago as 1928, Rubén M. Campos' *El folklore y la música mexicana* (p. 22) pictured a four-tube clay whistle.[180] A single mouthpiece served all four tubes. Dr. Galindo in his 1933 *Nociones* (pp. 67–68) pictured and studied the same museum piece. Martí's *Instrumentos* (p. 131) returns with a better photograph of the same specimen (Museo Nacional de Antropología), identifying it as "Cultura Azteca." Much more sensational, however, are the Gulf Coast multiple flutes pictured in *Instrumentos* on pages 132–133 (José Raúl Hellmer collection [181]), 135–136 and 138–139 (Museo Nacional), 141 (Diego Rivera collection); in *Canto, danza y música precortesianos,* on pages 332, 337, 342–343, 345 (this last specimen from Jaina Island represents in effigy a priest playing a triple flute); and in *Dances of Anáhuac,* on pages 173 (= *Canto,* p. 345), 181 (= p. 337), 182, 183 (left = p. 342*b*), 184, 185 (= *Instrumentos,* p. 113, *Canto,* p. 332).

Just as the quality of the photographs grows plangently from the 1928 to the 1964 publication, so also increases the emphasis on these pre-Aztec multiple flutes as the crowning jewels of ancient Mexican music. One of the first triple flutes to receive careful attention was dug up at Tres Zapotes, Veracruz,[182] by C. W. Weiant, in the same excavations that brought to light "the first and only" panpipe to have "turned up anywhere in North America." [183] Could Cortés have heard such exquisite music as this triple flute was capable of making, he would have lauded instead of condemning native music, opines Martí.[184] Even more exciting are the harmonic resources of a quadruple flute in the Diego Rivera collection. "We can assert that Mesoamerican instrument making reached its zenith with these extraordinary

[180] In Leopoldo Batres' *Civilización Prehistórica de las Riberas de Papaloapam* (México: Buznego y León, 1908), lám. 44 (no. 2) pictures a double whistle from San Andrés Tuxtla.

[181] Actually a multiple whistle, since none of the tubes is pierced with finger holes. This exemplar was "acquired on Teotihuacán near the capital, but is revealed by its characteristics as the product of a Gulf Coast culture" (p. 134).

[182] Lower Tres Zapotes (= Tres Zapotes 3) falls at 500 B.C. on the time charts in Peterson, *Ancient Mexico* (1959), p. 299, and Vaillant, *Aztecs of Mexico* (1962), p. 20; Tres Zapotes 2 comes at A.D. 200, Tres Zapotes 1 some 500 years later (Vaillant, *op. cit.,* p. 21).

[183] C. W. Weiant, *An Introduction to the Ceramics of Tres Zapotes* (Washington: Government Printing Office, 1943 [Smithsonian Institution Bureau of American Ethnology, Bulletin 139]), p. 111. His identification of the panpipe and his other musical remarks were corroborated by George Herzog (p. xii). The panpipe is shown at pl. 53, 13.

[184] *Instrumentos,* p. 134. Martí himself constantly strains for just those elements in aboriginal Mexican music which have the best chance of pampering European taste: "seven-tone scale similar to the European diatonic scale . . . whole-tone scale . . . three- and four-part chords" (Kurath and Martí, *Dances,* p. 172); "*organum, gymel y discanto europeos* (*Canto,* p. 343).

quadruple flutes," he writes (p. 140), adding (p. 165) a table of ten chords obtainable from the Diego Rivera exemplar:

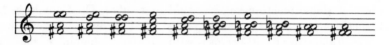

Boilés in his already cited essay published in the spring of 1965, "La Flauta Triple de Tenenexpan," confirms Martí's opinion that classical horizon multiple flutes marked the apogee of Mesoamerican organology. At page 218 of this article he lists the fifteen three-note chords (one two-note) that blowing the Tenenexpan triple flute with various fingerings produces:

At page 217 Boilés emphasizes that the fourths are "well tuned" and at page 218 assures us that the Totonac instrument makers (who, some seven hundred years before the Spaniards arrived, baked this and other multiple flutes) knew the harmonic series. Two tubes of this flute measure 19.5 cm, the other (bourdon) 27 cm. Like cantor, alto, and drone, the three tubes are respectively bored with three finger holes, two, and one; an added hole on the back side of the "cantor" tube serves as "transposition key" (*cambia-registro*, to use Boilés' term).

Why was the secret of making so proleptic an instrument lost? The same baffling question may be asked about many superb facets of the Maya culture, mastery in one epoch giving way to mediocrity in the next.

As it becomes more and more apparent to Mexican diggers that a multiple flute will fetch large prices, the number in private collections both in Mexico and abroad will doubtless continue to grow. The more active specialists in Mexican folklore and indigenous music already tend to dismiss Aztec instruments as only slightly interesting when compared with those from the Teotihuacán II and III periods (200 B.C.–A.D. 250; A.D. 250–650) or from several of the still only partly explored Gulf Coast cultures that flourished simultaneously. "There are numberless clay flutes of the Archaic and Totonac [185] cultures that show diatonic scales; there are also cornet-like clay

---

[185] A goiter-like protuberance at the necks of some clay flutes deflected the air through an "oscillating air chamber" and gave them a reedy timbre. See reference to Franco's articles, p. 7 n. 5 above. Clay pellets to induce a warbling effect are frequent in the Tres Zapotes instruments discovered by Weiant, *op. cit.*, p. 111.

instruments with mouthpieces as perfectly formed as a modern cornet and melodic possibilities limited only by the skill of the player; there exist double, triple, and even quadruple flutes, which not only produce chords but are also capable in skilled hands of producing two or more melodic lines simultaneously," wrote José Raúl Hellmer (*Toluca Gazette,* June 1, 1960).[186]

REACTION OF EUROPEAN-BORN OBSERVERS TO ABORIGINAL MUSIC

Above (pp. 17–18) are listed three lines of investigation that have proved fruitful: scrutiny of archaeological instruments, reevaluation of early Spanish opinion on indigenous music, and the gathering of melodic fragments from remote tribes. The more important conclusions reached by researchists working with museum instruments have now been listed, and we pass therefore to the second principal method of research, which involves a restudy of early Spanish opinion on aboriginal music.

The excerpt chosen by Carlos Chávez as the most valuable comes from Fray Juan de Torquemada's *Veinte i vn libros rituales i Monarchia Indiana,* the original edition of which was published at Seville in 1615. An English translation of this excerpt, "Of the manner in which these Natives had Dances, and of the great dexterity and conformity they all had, in the Dance and in the Song" (Bk. XIV, chap. 11), appears in *Renascent Mexico,* a book published in 1935 under the auspices of the Committee on Cultural Relations with Latin America; the same excerpt can be found in *Mexican Music,* a brochure edited by Herbert Weinstock and published in 1940 by the Museum of Modern Art at the time of the Chávez concerts.

Torquemada's description is of paramount value to the student of Aztec music, in the opinion of Chávez, who wrote: "It will be helpful to transcribe the description . . . since nothing will be likely to give with better authority

---

Franco was preparing in February, 1967, a full-scale monograph on "oscillating air chamber" instruments, to be published by the Institute of Ethnomusicology, University of California, Los Angeles. The absolute novelties that he will announce cannot be anticipated here.

[186] Repr. *Katunob,* II/1 (March, 1961), 70. Illustrating these points during a public lecture in Mexico City, October 9, 1962, Hellmer gave a foretaste of the sensational sounds obtainable from instruments so far apart in their geographic origin as Colima and Veracruz. Not only he but also such other *coleccionistas* as Francisco Villanueva (six-finger-hole Tarascan flute) have made "astounding discoveries." What seems obvious, however, is that none of these pre-Cortesian musical "spectaculars" will enhance Aztec music. Martí proposes only one double flute as Cultura Azteca (*Instrumentos,* p. 128) and does not here consider Hellmer's suggestion that the twin finger holes served to produce a single vibrato tone.

In private conversation in February, 1967, Hellmer placed me more heavily than ever in his debt not only by reading the entire section on Aztec instruments, but also by offering many concrete suggestions for its improvement. In his article reprinted from *Toluca Gazette,* he now wishes "*numberless* clay flutes of the Archaic and *Totonac* cultures" changed to "*a number of*" and "*Occidental West Coast.*"

a clear general idea of the development of these arts [music and dancing] in Mexican antiquity." [187] On page 208 Chávez said: "This narrative of Torquemada's is a very important document, illustrating our understanding of pre-Cortesian music."

Torquemada (1565?–1624), who is not to be confused with his namesake who became a cardinal, wrote his narrative eighty years after the conquest; his description, because of its lateness, would have considerably less value were it not that he, as a Franciscan missionary, relied heavily upon unpublished descriptions of Indian life written by two predecessor Franciscan historians: Toribio de Motolinía (1490?–1565), one of the pioneer missionaries in Mexico, and Gerónimo de Mendieta (1525?–1604), who, if not a missionary of the first generation, nevertheless wrote a uniquely valuable account of Indian life which he spent some twenty-five years in preparing. Since Torquemada relied upon these two, it seems advisable to study not only his second hand account but also the unpublished accounts upon which he drew when compiling his book (see below, pp. 96, 113, and 119).

CONTRIBUTION OF THE MISSIONARIES TO OUR UNDERSTANDING OF INDIAN CULTURE

Despite the fact that "nothing will be more likely to give a clear general idea of the development of music and dancing in Mexican antiquity" than the accounts left us by such missionaries as Motolinía, Mendieta, and Torquemada, as a group they are often accused of having attacked everything Indian. Such missionary bishops of Mexico and Yucatán as Zumárraga and Landa are often charged with having "wantonly destroyed every available record of Indian culture," and of having deliberately set out to "sow with Carthaginian salt" the prostrate Indian mind. This charge cannot be fully substantiated, however.

Present-day understanding of the few Mayan codices that do remain is, after all, founded largely on Landa's own *Relación de las cosas de Yucatán*. Without its rediscovery by Brasseur de Bourbourg and its publication in 1864, the epochal results achieved by so signal a scholar as Ernst Förstemann are scarcely thinkable. "Landa's description of the calendar and his illustrations of day and month signs supplied a firm foundation on which

---

[187] *Renascent Mexico*, p. 203. The excerpt occupies pages 203–208, nearly equaling all the rest of what he has to say on aboriginal music. Torquemala's text (*Segunda parte delos veinte i vn libros* [1723 ed.], pp. 550–552) poses some problems that the translation does not meet successfully. Whoever made it failed to meet the challenge of such musical expressions in Spanish as these: "hace su diapente," "contra bajo," "bemolados," "compasillo," "compás entero," "contra compás," "tiple," "flautillas no mui entonadas," "alçando los tonos."

to reconstruct Maya hieroglyphic writing; it is as close to a Rosetta Stone as we are ever like to get," wrote J. Eric S. Thompson as recently as 1960.[188]

So far as preservation of records is concerned, it must be remembered also that many codices collected in the eighteenth century by Boturini Benaduci perished simply through neglect, and the small number that now remain would be doubled or tripled if those known to have existed 250 years after the conquest were still extant. "It is a sad commentary on our supposed progress that more manuscript-treatises on every aspect of Indian life were destroyed through negligence, bigotry, and ignorance during the second half of the nineteenth century than were lost during the three preceding centuries," [189] is an informed summary that should be remembered by musicologists as well as by Mayanists.

At the same time that we mention the alleged loss of twenty-seven "rolls of signs and hieroglyphics on deerskin" in Landa's famous bonfire of July 12, 1562, in Mani (Yucatán), we shall do well to remember that missionaries such as José de Acosta (who was in Mexico in 1586) argued for the preservation of the Indian records. In his *Historia Natvral y Moral de las Indias,* Acosta, after deploring the loss of Maya writings, continued thus:

The same has happened in other cases where our people, thinking that all is superstition, have lost many memorials of ancient and hidden things which might have been used to no small advantage. This follows from a stupid zeal, when without knowing or without wishing to know the things of the Indies, they say as in the sealed package, that everything is sorcery and that the peoples there are only a drunken lot and what can they know and understand. The ones who have wished earnestly to be informed of these have found many things worthy of consideration.[190]

In like vein wrote Antonio de Cibdad Real, the most erudite Mayanist of the sixteenth century. Among three principal reasons for praising the Mayas he listed first their system of hieroglyphics (which he had himself mastered). Because their codices recorded many antiquities of the area, worthy of being known, he regretted their loss as much as did Acosta.[191]

The missionaries came with the express idea of living and working with the Indians. They made it their business first to learn the Indian tongues. Insofar as they could, they strove to understand the patterns of Indian life, and to accommodate their teachings to the Indian mentality. If they were

---

[188] Thompson, *Maya Hieroglyphic Writing,* p. 28.

[189] *Ibid.* See also Landa's *Relación* (Tozzer ed.), pp. 28–29 n. 156, 77–79 n. 340.

[190] Acosta, Bk. VI, chap. 7: "De modo de letras y escritura que usaron los mejicanos" (*Obras,* ed. Francisco Mateos [Biblioteca de Autores Españoles, LXXIII (Madrid, 1954)], p. 188).

[191] *Colección de Documentos Inéditos para las Historia de España,* LVIII (Madrid: Vda. de Calero, 1872), 392: "así se perdió la noticia de muchas antiguallas de aquella tierra, que por ellos se pudieran saber."

not all so outspoken as Las Casas in denouncing the abuses of the encomienda system, nevertheless they all befriended the Indian in his struggle with the encomendero and sought to alleviate the lot of the oppressed.

The conclusions that can be reached on the basis of missionary evidence concerning indigenous music are, because of the missionaries' friendliness, generally favorable. Clarity will perhaps best be achieved if we list first the general conclusions the evidence enables us to reach, and then quote the passages upon which the conclusions rest. The passages documenting the general conclusions are each prefaced by a short biographical account of the author who wrote the particular passage; with certain of the lengthier passages a précis is affixed defining its contents. By quoting in extenso the passages upon which our conclusions rest, we leave the reader freedom to draw any other conclusions he chooses from the basic data here supplied.

CONCLUSIONS DRAWN FROM SIXTEENTH-CENTURY REPORTS BY EYEWITNESSES

During the late summer of 1520 (August 26 to September 3), Albrecht Dürer—the supreme German painter and engraver of the epoch—visited Brussels. At that moment, the first display of aboriginal Mexican art to reach the other side of the Atlantic had on Charles V's order been sent north from Spain to his headquarters in the Low Countries. Fortunately for art history, Dürer saw this Mexican exhibit and recorded his delight and wonder in a memorandum book, a copy of which is in the Staatlichen Bibliothek at Bamberg. Edited in 1884 and frequently thereafter in the original German (as well as in translations), his remarks still bear repetition.

Dürer's father was a goldsmith and he begins with exclamations over "a sun all of gold a whole fathom broad, and a moon all of silver of the same size." He stands in awe of "wonderful objects of human use, much better than prodigies," which range from armor and raiment to litters. Summarizing his feelings at an art exhibit valued at 100,000 florins, he writes (*Schriften. Tagebücher. Briefe,* ed. Max Steck [Stuttgart: W. Kohlhammer, 1961], p. 48): "Und ich hab aber all mein Lebtag nichts gesehen, das mein Herz also erfreuet hat als diese Dinge. Denn ich hab dabei gesehen wunderbare kunstvolle Dinge und hab mich verwundert der subtilen ingenia der Menschen in fremden Landen." William Martin Conway translates this to read: "All the days of my life I have seen nothing that rejoiced my heart so much as these things, for I saw amongst them wonderful works of art, and I marvelled at the subtle *Ingenia* of men in foreign lands." Dürer concludes: "Indeed I cannot express all that I thought there." What he did express challenges us to find a similar testimony from someone so competent musically as was Cristóbal de Morales, maestro in either nearby Ávila or Plasencia when Charles V spent a whole morning marveling at the dance and music of a company collected by Cortés for the emperor's pleasure at Valladolid.

Rhetorica Christiana (Perusia: Pietro Giacomo Petrucci, 1579) was the first book published in Europe by a native-born Mexican—Diego Valadés (1533–ca. 1582). In a memorable passage (beginning at page 169 thus: "Illa verò tripudia sunt inprimis memorabilia, nam cum tantus esset populi confluxus omnes tamen ad eosdem numeros & sonos pariter cantabant & saltabant nec obstabat varia soni mutatio"), Valadés wrote: "Their dances are very worthy of mention, since despite such a multitude they sing in the most perfect unison and move in perfect synchronism, whatever the shifts of measure and melody. The invincible emperor Charles V could not believe the report of so great a number of dancers and their rhythmic perfection, until he witnessed their performance at Valladolid, where he and a number of his principal courtiers were enthralled by their demonstration an entire morning."

Esteban J. Palomera suggests in *Fray Diego Valadés o.f.m.* (México: Editorial Jus, S.A., 1960), p. 218 n. 4, that this Aztec ballet troupe found so delightful by Charles V and his courtiers in 1527 was the same troupe dispatched to Rome for Clement VII's amazement. Whether this conjecture is accepted or not, the ethnomusicologist cannot but hope for a report from a musician to equal Dürer's report of Mexican art. For his pains, the searcher soon discovers that no musician of Morales' caliber recorded his reactions to Aztec dance and song. Instead of the competent testimony of someone as exalted as Dürer, the music investigator must content himself with the opinions of nonprofessionals writing in nontechnical language. Nonetheless, the testimony from the most alert and observant of these witnesses does sufficiently jibe to justify making several generalizations.

The following conclusions (some of which necessarily duplicate those already arrived at through the study of archaeological instruments) may be drawn from Spanish accounts of Aztec life:

1) Music had no independent life of its own apart from religious and cult observances; music as an art (in our sense of the word) was a concept alien to Aztec mentality.

2) A professionalized caste, similar to the Levitical guild in ancient Israel, controlled public musical life.

3) Training of an extremely rigid kind was prerequisite to a career in music; since music itself was always thought of as a necessary adjunct to ritual, absolutely perfect performances, such as only the most highly trained singers and players could give, were demanded.

4) Imperfectly executed rituals were thought to offend rather than to appease the gods, and therefore errors in the performance of ritual music, such as missed drumbeats, carried the death penalty.

5) Singers and players, because of the important part music played in Aztec life, enjoyed considerable social prestige.

6) Despite this prestige, however, the names of musicians were not recorded, just as the names of poets—unless the poet was a royal personage like King Nezahualcóyotl of Texcoco—were not preserved.

7) Music was regarded as essentially a means of communal rather than of individual expression, and therefore concerted rather than solo music was the norm.

8) Instrumental performance and singing went together, insofar as we can judge from the descriptions of Aztec musical performance bequeathed us by the Spanish chroniclers.

9) Certain instruments were thought to be of divine origin, and the teponaztli and huehuetl, for instance, were even held to be gods temporarily forced to endure earthly exile; the teponaztli and the huehuetl were therefore often treated as idols as well as musical instruments.

10) Not only were certain instruments thought to have mana in them—that is to say, mysterious supernatural powers—but also certain instruments were held to represent symbolically such emotional states as joy, delight, or sensual pleasure.

11) Aztec music communicated states of feeling that even the Spaniards, habituated in alien patterns of musical expression, could grasp and appreciate; whereas much of the Indian music of tribes who lived in the territory now embraced by the United States meant nothing to European ears, Aztec music seems to have communicated in many instances the same emotions to Indian and European listener alike. Thus a sad song, as the Aztecs conceived it, was sad not only in the opinion of the Indians who heard it and understood the words, but also in the opinion of the Spaniards who heard it and did not understand the words.

12) Every piece of music was composed for a certain time, place, and occasion, and therefore the musician needed a wide repertory if he was to satisfy the demands of the different days in the religious calendar. The religious cycle lasted 260 days, and just as the priests consulted the omens for each of the 260 days, so the players had to have appropriate songs ready for each of the days.

13) The Aztecs possessed no system of music notation—or, if they did, none that the Europeans knew anything about; therefore the Aztec musicians needed prodigious memories.

14) Musicians not only learned the old songs, but composed new ones. Creative ability was prized, especially in the households of those powerful caciques who were able to employ singers to compose ballads telling of their military successes.

15) Court music, at least in the Aztec and Tarascan kingdoms, differed as much from the music of the *maceualli*,[192] the lower classes, as court speech

---

[192] For historical uses of *macehual* (= *macegual*), see Francisco J. Santamaría, *Diccionario de Mejicanismos* (México: Ed. Porrúa, 1959), pp. 673–674.

differed from the rude Náhuatl [193] and the rustic [194] Tarascan spoken by the common clay in those kingdoms.

16) Though their music lacked string tone and was predominantly percussive, the Aztecs had acute pitch sense and tuned their instruments with considerable care.

Obviously the chroniclers listened with their ears, not ours, and what they considered "predominantly percussive" might not now be so regarded. Just so with their other observations summarized above.

In addition to the testimony of the chroniclers, lexicographers can be invoked as witnesses to precontact music. In his already cited 59-page article published in the Charles Seeger Festschrift (*Yearbook II* [1966], Inter-American Institute for Musical Research), E. Thomas Stanford draws together lexicographical evidence to sustain three generalizations. Paraphrased from the "conclusions" at pages 115–116 of "A Linguistic Analysis of Music and Dance Terms from Three Sixteenth-Century Dictionaries of Mexican Indian Languages," Stanford's generalizations take the following turn:

1) Dance and music linked everywhere in precontact times as inseparably as Siamese twins.

2) Brazen, assertive qualities such as loudness, clarity, and high pitch were preferred by players and singers alike.

3) This "crying aloud" to their gods served their purpose even when plebeians danced (as is still done in indigenous Mexico) to do penance.

PEDRO DE GANTE (1480?–1572) [195]

Born at Iseghem some miles southwest of Ghent (= Gante in Spanish) "in Audenarde province," Fray Pedro signed himself in a Latin letter "de

[193] Molina, *Arte de la lengua Mexicana* (1571), fols. 34v–35: "enlas cortes delos reyes y principes y entre psonas yllustres, se habla la lengua materna cō mas curiosidad y policia, que entre gente labradora y de baxa suerte. De manera que estos hablā la misma lengua vulgar y materna, tā impfectamente y cō tātas incōgruidades que las mas vezes no se dexan entender dela gente noble."

[194] Lagunas, *Arte dictionario: con otras obras, en lengua Michoacana* (México: Pedro Balli, 1574), pp. 76–77: "En todas las lenguas vulgares, ay pronunciacion pulitica, curiosa y bien pronunciada y tambien ay otra Tosca, plebeya, imperfecta y mal pronunciada. . . . Y de aduertir, que la pulitica cortesana sea universal, e muy perceptible a todos, como la Toledana a los Castellanos. Y la Tezcucana a los Mexicanos." After making norms of the upper-class Spanish spoken at Toledo and the courtly Náhuatl spoken at Texcoco, Lagunas assures us that the language spoken by the upper classes at Pátzcuaro and Tzintzuntzan is the true Tarascan, not the "incongrua, barbara y mal pronunciada, que algunos pueblos vsan: puesto que la lengua Michuacana, es toda vna."

[195] Unless otherwise credited, the biographical facts accord with the footnoted account in García Icazbalceta, *Bibliografía Mexicana* (1954, see n. 20), pp. 90–104.

Mura." [196] Closely but illegitimately related to Charles V, he spent an undetermined period in royal service before his conversion. He thereupon entered the Franciscan house at Ghent as a lay brother. When the first news of Cortés' successes in Mexico reached Charles V in June, 1520, the young emperor (crowned October 23) was at Ghent. Several friars at once applied for leave to go as missionaries, but only three made the journey with Charles to Santander and thence through the port of Seville to Veracruz, where they landed on August 30, 1523. The two older missionaries, Jean van Dak (= de Toit = de Tecto) and Jean d'Aire (= Aora = Ayora), soon succumbed to hardships.

Gante's first three years in Mexico were largely spent at Texcoco mastering the best palace brand of Náhuatl. No other missionary of his generation more thoroughly mastered this tongue, which lacks the six consonants b, d, f, g, r, and s. So much of a stutterer in Spanish that at times his fellow friars could not understand him, he learned to speak a language devoid of these six consonants as fluently as Moctezuma II's own children. His sphere of action in Texcoco, in Tlaxcala, and in Mexico City (1527–1572) revealed him as a teacher of youth. At Cortés' instance, young boys from all the most influential families in the Valley of Mexico were congregated in the schools supervised by Gante and by the Spanish friars who soon began joining him. The curriculum leaned heavily not only on reading and writing, but also on music.[197]

Explaining the unusual emphasis on music, Gante wrote a letter to Philip II, dated June 23, 1557, which is worth quoting. Although it had been simple enough to gather in noble children by mere fiat,[198] it had proved

---

For Gante's birth year Icazbalceta preferred 1479/80; José Toribio Medina opted for 1486.

[196] Émile de Borchgrave, "Pierre de Gand," *Biographie Nationale* (Brussels: Bruylant-Christophe & Cie., 1903), XVII, 443–458, suggests "de Muer" as the best Flemish equivalent. Bartolomé de las Casas, *Historia de las Indias*, Bk. III, chap. 104, 133 (Biblioteca de Autores Españoles, XCVI [Madrid, 1957], pp. 422, 496), highly praised the Christianity of Charles V's Flemish confidant in August, 1518, named "Monsieur de La Mure." Ezequiel A. Chávez, *El ambiente geográfico, histórico y social de Fray Pedro de Gante* (México: Editorial Jus, 1943), pp. 137–138, conjectured that this La Mure and Petrus de Mura were the same person. It was La Mure who in this year so signally aided Las Casas in his campaign for Indian rights. However, Manuel Giménez Fernández, *Bartolomé de las Casas*, II (Seville: Publicaciones de la Escuela de Estudios Hispano-Americanos [CXXI], 1960), 207 n. 666, finds no evidence to sustain the conjectural identification.

[197] Lota M. Spell, "The First Teacher of European Music in America," *Catholic Historical Review*, n.s., II/3 (Oct., 1922), 372–378.

[198] Chávez, "Fray Pedro de Gante: The First of the Great Educators of America," trans. Hermenegildo Corbató, *Modern Language Forum*, XIX/3 (Sept., 1934), 136–137, misrepresents what actually happened. See Gante's own account of what transpired in Francisco González Vera, "De los primeros misioneros en Nueva España, y Carta de Fray Pedro de Gante, deudo del Emperador Carlos V," *Revista de España*, primer año, Tomo III, núm. 11 (Aug. 15, 1868), p. 389.

almost impossible to attract anybody to religious services by mere persuasion.

We were here more than three years, as I told you, without ever being able to attract them. Instead they fled from us, and much more from the Spanish, like savages. But by the grace of Almighty God I began to perceive their mentality and to understand how they should be dealt with. Their whole worship had consisted in dancing and singing before their own gods. When the time came to make sacrifices for victory over their enemies or for the supplying of their daily wants, before killing the victims, they first must needs dance in front of the idol. Upon comprehending this and realizing that all their songs were composed to honor their gods, I composed a very elaborate one myself, but the subject-matter was God's law and our faith that Christ was born of the holy and undefiled Virgin Mary. About two months before Christmas I also gave them some designs to paint on their dancing togs because they always danced and sang in costumes that bespoke happiness, sorrow, or victory.

When Christmas approached, we then invited everyone within ten leagues [35 miles] to come see Our Redeemer's Nativity Feast. So many came that the patio, although very large, could not contain them. Each province had set up its own booths to entertain its chieftains, and even infirm persons came from a distance of seven and eight leagues [25 and 30 miles], carried on hammocks, and others came almost equal distances by water, to hear the singing.[199]

Gante's willingness to accommodate himself to native custom won him such standing amongst the indigenes that Alonso de Montúfar, the Dominican who served as second archbishop of Mexico, 1551–1572, complained: "Not I, but Peter of Ghent, rules as archbishop here." [200] A 56-stanza Náhuatl

[199] *Revista de España*, Aug. 15, 1868, pp. 390–391: "Empero la gente, como estaba como animales sin rason, indomables, que no los podiamos traer al gremio y congregacion de la iglesia, ni a la doctrina, ni a sermon, sino que huian desto como el demonio de la [cruz] y estuvimos mas de tres años en esto que nunca, como tengo dicho, los pudimos atraer, sino que huian como salvajes de los frailes y mucho mas de los españoles, mas por la gracia de Dios empeceles a conocer y entender sus condiciones y quilates y como me debia haber con ellos y es que toda su adoracion dellos a sus dioses era cantar y bailar delante dellos, porque cuando habian de sacrificar a algunos por alguna cosa, ansi como por alcanzar vitoria de sus enemigos, o por temporales necesidades, antes que los matasen habian de danzar delante del idolo, y como yo oi esto y que todos sus cantares eran dedicados a sus dioses, compuse un cantar muy solemne sobre la ley de Dios . . . y tambien diles libreas para pintar en sus mantas, para bailar con ellas, porque ansi se usaba entre ellos conforme a los bailes y a los cantares que ellos cantaban, asi se vestian de alegria o de luto o de vitoria. . . ."

Alberto María Carreño, unacquainted with González Vera's transcription, made his own from the original in the Department of MSS, Biblioteca Nacional, Madrid, publishing it in "Una Desconocida Carta de Fray Pedro de Gante," *Memorias de la Academia Mexicana de la Historia*, XX/1 (Jan.–March, 1961), 14–20. The passage above borrows some improvements from Carreño's transcription, p. 18.

[200] Robert Ricard, "Notes sur la biographie de Fr. Alonso de Montúfar, second archevêque de Mexico," *Bulletin hispanique*, XXV/3 (July–Sept., 1925), 245. This

song composed for his pupils to sing on October 4, 1530 or 1531,[201] pictures Gante so far gone in native custom that he grabs an ayacachtli. At this, the drummers discontinue *tocoto cotiti tocoto cotititi quiti quiti* and start *totocoto tototocototo titiquititi titiqui titiquito*. Their affection for him took such diverse forms as a petition to Charles V in 1552 for more friars from Flanders, and especially from Ghent, "so that when Pedro de Gante dies Mexico will not be left forlorn";[202] or taking his name for their own. One of the best Indian teachers in the Colegio de Tlatelolco was precisely a Pedro de Gante who died in 1605.[203] Sahagún praised this Indian who adopted

---

quotation may be apocryphal. But it is certain that Montúfar complained to Philip II in a letter dated June 20, 1558: "this lay friar has more influence with the Viceroy than I . . . even when this lay friar wishes to contradict the desire of prelates, his wishes are obeyed, to the shame and scorn of prelates" (p. 246). Archbishop Montúfar blamed Gante for never having taken priest's orders, instead remaining always a lay brother. (Illegitimacy perhaps barred Gante's first steps to the priesthood, however.) See Montúfar's letter of April 30, 1562, *Epistolario de Nueva España 1505–1818*, IX, transcribed by Francisco del Paso y Troncoso (México: Antigua Librería Robredo, 1940 [*Biblioteca Histórica Mexicana de Obras Inéditas*, seg. sér.]), p. 161 (no. 515).

[201] Garibay, *Historia de la Literatura Náhuatl*, II, 116. See the complete song in Schultze Jena, *op. cit.*, pp. 257–271 (No. XLIII). German translation faces Náhuatl text. When pioneer Jesuits at Bahia tried dancing and singing in native Brazilian style, Bishop Pedro Fernandes Sardinha rebuked them in a letter dated October 6, 1553. Among others, Salvador Rodrigues, a Jesuit who died on August 15, 1553, at the age of thirty-five, had offended against the bishop's sense of propriety by adopting the "tom gentílico" and playing the same "instrumentos que êstes bárbaros tocam." Various Portuguese youths brought over to help convert the tribal children in the Bahia area joined their Jesuit mentors in singing "pagan tunes" and in playing the "instruments of these barbarians" while "dancing their measures." For documents, see Serafim Leite, "Cantos, músicas e danças nas aldeias do Brasil (século XVI)," *Brotéria*, XXIV (1937), 48. Although Archbishop Montúfar arrived in Mexico too late to stop Gante, the problem of "overadapting" to aboriginal custom and of "going native" worried him no less than Sardinha. The famous "Chinese Rites" controversy swirled around the same problems of "accommodation" and was settled with decisions in 1645, 1704, 1715, and 1742 against accommodation.

[202] *Cartas de Indias* (Madrid: Manuel G. Hernández, 1877), p. 101. Letter XVIII dated February 15, 1552. Las Casas, *Historia de las Indias*, Bk. III, chap. 104 (*Biblioteca de Autores Españoles*, XCVI [1957]), 422, gave a good enough reason for the Indians to prefer Flemings when he wrote: "the Flemish are kinder and more humane than we are" (*cuanto a la gente flamenca, que es más blanda y más humana que nosotros*). A principal downtown street in Mexico City today still bears the name "Gante" in Peter of Ghent's honor (José Fernando Ramírez was responsible for naming it thus; see García Icazbalceta [1954 edition], p. 95 n. 27).

[203] Agustín de Vetancurt, *Menologio franciscano* (México: Vda. de Ribera, 1698) = *Teatro Mexicano*, IV (Madrid: José Porrúa Turanzas, 1961), p. 371. It was extremely common for a "converted Indian to take the name of some Spaniard to whom he was indebted for a favor" in this century. See Francis Borgia Steck, *El primer colegio de América: Santa Cruz de Tlatelolco* (México: Centro de Estudios Franciscanos, 1944), p. 59 n. 95.

Peter of Ghent as his name: "I consulted with him constantly, and his ability and talent made him an ideal aide." [204] When at the age of ninety-two Fray Pedro de Gante died, it is scarcely surprising that the Indian community throughout the entire countryside went into mourning. [205]

Chimalpahin Quauhtlehuanitzin, an Indian annalist born in 1579, found only three events of 1572 sufficiently notable to be recorded: (1) Archbishop Montúfar died; (2) the first Jesuits reached Mexico; (3) Fray Pedro de Gante, "maestro of Mexico's singers," died. [206] Not only are these the events that made the year memorable for Chimalpahin, but also Gante is remembered by this Indian chronicler for a single facet of his multiple services: his having protected native singers. What the Franciscan provincial who wrote Philip II the news of Gante's decease most remembered were the favors that Gante's having been a near kinsman of Charles V enabled him to solicit successfully for the Franciscan mission in Mexico, and also Gante's having stayed with the Indians to the end, instead of abandoning them in mid-course, as did their other great champion, Las Casas. [207]

TORIBIO DE MOTOLINÍA (1490?–1565)

Fray Toribio de Paredes from Benavente (north of Zamora, Spain) arrived in 1524 with the pioneer group of twelve Franciscans headed by Martín de Valencia. The Indians, seeing his miserable habit and noting that he walked

[204] Garibay, *Historia de la Literatura Náhuatl*, II, 225.

[205] Vetancurt, *Teatro Mexicano*, IV (1961), 179: "todos se pusieron luto, convocaron à todos los comarcanos à su entierro, cada qual de las Cofradias, y pueblos le hizo cantar su Missa. . . ." One of Gante's most brilliant strokes was his introduction of the *cofradía* system.

[206] Chimalpahin, *Annales*, trans. Rémi Siméon, p. 284: "No ypan in momiquilli yn Fray Pedro de Gante Cuateçontzin, teopixqui S. Francisco, yn maestro catca yn cantores Mexica. . . ." Chimalpahin continued: "He was buried Sunday, April 20, in the chapel of San José [de Belén] of the Franciscans. Although our dear father always remained a lay brother, the Emperor Charles V wished to name him archbishop. He refused twice, preferring to remain no more than a humble lay brother."

A historian who had every opportunity to know was Vetancurt. He confirmed Charles V's nomination (*Teatro Mexicano*, p. 177) and Montúfar's calling Gante the de facto archbishop. The attitude of Montúfar, as the emperor's second or even third choice, can be the more readily understood.

[207] *Revista de España*, Aug. 15, 1868, p. 386. Also, García Icazbalceta (1954), p. 91. Concerning Fray Alonso de Escalona elected provincial in 1570 see Vetancurt, *Teatro Mexicano*, IV (1961), 72–76. After three years as bishop of Chiapas, Las Casas left for Spain, where he remained the rest of his life (1547–1566). His fellow clergy blamed him for thus deserting his flock.

While Las Casas concentrated on correct doctrine and denounced abuses, "Pedro de Gante taught his Indian charges every useful art known among us," wrote Diego Valadés in *Rhetorica Christiana* (Perusia: Pietro Giacomo Petrucci, 1579), p. 110 (*recte* 210): "Petrus Gandensis . . . omnes artes mechanicas quae apud nos in vsu habentur

barefoot, called him *motolinía*, meaning "poor." Since this was the first word he learned, he adopted it as his name. Although his life-span did not equal that of Las Casas, who lived to be ninety-two, or of Pedro de Gante, who lived to the same age, or of Sahagún, who lived to be ninety, he did live to be the last survivor of the "twelve apostles" of 1524.[208] His two principal works still extant were written in middle life. The *Historia de los Indios* (drafted 1536–1541) and the *Memoriales* (less easily dated [209]) both remained unpublished until 1858 and 1903, respectively; however, both circulated widely in manuscript. Nearly everything said by Torquemada on aboriginal music was transcribed either directly from Motolinía, or from Mendieta (who copied Motolinía's description of preconquest music); Motolinía's early arrival assures authenticity.

Motolinía hated Spanish rapacity no less than did the crusading Las Casas; at one time Motolinía was even accused of petitioning for the recall of all Spaniards from Mexico (except the clergy) because the bad example and conduct of the laity impeded the work of conversion.[210] What in truth he did come to find almost less supportable than the plague of the carpetbagging *calpixques* (majordomos sent into Indian villages to collect tributes) was the roving shepherd of Indian souls unwilling to settle anywhere long enough to learn even one Indian tongue.[211]

In the following extract, which combines several passages from chapter

illos docebat." Valadés spoke with authority. He had studied with Gante, and served as his secretary when affectionate letters arrived from Charles V (*Rhetorica Christiana*, p. 222, quoted in Francisco de la Maza, *Fray Diego Valadés: Escritor y Grabador Franciscano del Siglo XVI* [México: Sobretiro de Número 13 de los Anales del Instituto de Investigaciones Estéticas, 1945], p. 10).

[208] Francis Borgia Steck, translator of *Motolinía's History of the Indians of New Spain* (Washington: Academy of American Franciscan History, 1951), p. 2, places his birth in 1495 "or shortly before"; and, pp. 2, 31, fixes his death in 1565, four years before García Icazbalceta's suggested 1569 (see Steck's footnote 76).

[209] Robert Ricard, "Remarques bibliographiques sur les ouvrages de Fr. Toribio Motolonía," *Journal de la Société des Américanistes*, n.s., XXV/1 (1933), 149–151, extracted dates from the *Memoriales* ranging from 1536 to 1542. Written as a notebook from which the *Historia* and another now lost large work were compiled, the *Memoriales* lacks the polish that Motolinía gave his works intended for public circulation.

[210] On August 23, 1529, a suborned friar named Juan de Paredes (not related to Fray Toribio despite having the same family name) accused Motolinía and three other Franciscans of plotting to kill Nuño de Guzmán, plus several other high civil officials—thereafter packing the rest of the Spanish force home. Having been already severely punished by his Franciscan superiors for corrupting Indian girls, Paredes perhaps hoped to even scores. See Document 53 in García Icazbalceta, *Don Fray Juan de Zumárraga* (México: Andrade y Morales, 1881), p. 244.

[211] See his letter to Charles V, January 2, 1555, translated in Lesley B. Simpson, *The Encomienda in New Spain* (Berkeley and Los Angeles: University of California Press, 1950), p. 239. Spanish text: Motolinía, *Carta al Emperador*, ed. José Bravo Ugarte (México: Editorial Jus, 1949), p. 65: "ni deprendió lengua de indios." Prior Spanish printings listed by Simpson, p. 234 n. 1.

26 in Part II of the *Memoriales*,[212] Motolinía tells how music functioned in
Aztec life, what kinds of instruments were used, how the Aztecs rehearsed
and performed their songs and dance music, how musicians were valued in
Aztec society, and why composers enjoyed special prestige.

One of the main happenings everywhere in this country were the festivals of song
and dance, which were organized not only for the delight of inhabitants themselves, but more especially to honor their gods, whom they thought well pleased
by such service. Because they took their festivals with extreme seriousness and set
great store by them, it was the custom in each town for the nobility to maintain in
their own houses choirs of singers, amongst whom some were composers of new
songs and dances. Composers skilled in fashioning songs and ballads were
everywhere in great demand. Among singers those with good bass voices were
the most sought after for the frequent private ritual observances held inside the
houses of the nobility.

Singing and dancing usually enlivened the principal fiestas occurring every
twenty days, and also less important fiestas. The more important dances took
place usually in the plazas; but also from time to time in the private patios of the
nobility or indoors in the houses of the nobles. When a battle victory was
celebrated, or when a new member of the nobility was created, or when a
chieftain married, or when some other striking event occurred, the singing-
masters composed new songs especially for the occasion. These singing-masters
also sang the old songs appropriate for the various observances in honor of their
gods, or in celebration of historical exploits, or in praise of their deceased
chieftains.

The singers always decided what they were going to use several days beforehand
and practiced. In the large towns (where there was always an abundance of
good singers) those who were to participate got together for rehearsal well in
advance, especially if there were a new song or dance to be performed, so that on
the day of the fiesta all might go off with smoothness and propriety. The day of
the fiesta a large mat was spread in the middle of the plaza, and on this mat they
placed their teponaztlis and huehuetls. The musicians all gathered at the house of
the chieftain and there dressed themselves for the fiesta. They came out of the
lord's house singing and dancing. Sometimes they started their dances in the
early morning and other times at the hour we celebrate high mass. At nightfall
they returned to the chieftain's house where their singing ended either soon after
dark, or occasionally later, sometimes even at midnight.

The two types of drum were: one, the huehuetl, a tall round drum, bigger around
than a man's body, and between three and four feet high. It was made of
excellent wood, and expertly hollowed out inside. The exterior of the huehuetl
was painted; over its mouth was carefully stretched a cured deerskin. Striking at
the edge and then the middle of the drumskin made the interval of a fifth. When
the singers shifted from one tune to another, the huehuetl was retuned to match.
The other drum, the teponaztli, cannot adequately be described in words with-

[212] *Memoriales* (México: Casa del Editor [Luis García Pimemtel], 1903), pp.
339–343.

out a picture at hand to show its appearance. This other drum served as a countertenor; [213] both made a fine sound which carried a great distance.

While the dancers were getting in position the players prepared to strike their drums. Two of the best singers acted as song leaders and set the pitch. The large drum with the animal drumskin was played with the bare hands; but the other (like the drums in Spain) was played with sticks.

.   .   .   .

When they were ready to begin the dance three or four sounded some shrill whistles. Then the drumming began in a low, muffled tone, gradually increasing in volume. Hearing the sound of the drums at the beginning of the dance, the dancers [took the pitch of their song from the sound of the drums, and then] [214] started singing. The first songs were pitched low, sounding as if everything had been flatted, and the tempo was slow. The first song had to do with the particular occasion of the fiesta. Two leaders (as we already said) always began the singing whereupon the entire ring joined in singing and dancing. The crowd often united in a dance routine that would challenge the skill of the best dancers in Spain. More remarkable yet was the fact that not only their feet, but the entire body, head, arms, and hands, heeded an absolutely exact beat. Following their leaders in the singing and drumming, everyone changed position at the same instant, and with such precision that the best Spanish dancers were astonished upon seeing them in action, and greatly admired the dances of these people. . . . The dancers in the outside ring adopted a beat twice as fast as those who danced in the inside ring; [215] this was done so that both outside and inside circles might stay together. Those in the inner circle, perfectly coordinating their movements, shifted their feet and bodies more slowly than those in the outside circle, and it was marvelous to see with what graceful dignity they moved their arms.

[213] John Minsheu, *Vocabvlarivm Hispanicolatinvm et Anglicum copiosissimum* . . . *A Most Copiovs Spanish Dictionarie* (London, 1617), fol. F3, translates *Contrabajo* as "the countertenor."

[214] This phrase joins several other explanatory remarks inserted in Mendieta's "improvement" of Motolinía's account. See Gerónimo de Mendieta, *Historia Eclesiástica Indiana* (México: Antigua Librería [F. Díaz y Santiago White], 1870), pp. 140–143.

[215] For *compás entero* and *compasillo*, the terms used by Motolinía to define the two different beats kept by inner and outer circles of dancers, see Juan Bermudo, *Declaración de instrumentos musicales* (Osuna: Juan de León, 1555), fol. 51v: "El compas mayor es nombrado delos authores entero, y en España compas largo: el qual es medida con movimiento tardio, y quasi reciproco. . . . El compas menor es la mitad del mayor, y es llamado compasete, o medio compas." At fol. 52 he noted that the *pesadumbre de tiempo perfecto, y compas entero* irritated many Spanish singers, who much preferred the allegro of *compasillo* (= *compasete*) to the grave of *compás entero*. Further remarks on *compás llano* (= *compás entero* = *compás largo*) and of the *compás partido* (= *compasete* = *compasillo*) in Stevenson, *Spanish Music in the Age of Columbus* (The Hague: Martinus Nijhoff, 1960), p. 70. Motolinía's correct use of technical terms implies better than casual musical training.

Each verse or couplet was repeated three or four times, the singing, drums, and dancing remaining throughout perfectly coordinated. Upon finishing one song, everyone stopped singing for several measures (although the dancing kept going). This interval gave the huehuetl time to tune for the next song. Then the leaders began anew at a somewhat higher pitch and in a faster tempo, thus ascending the musical scale as if a bass were to change by degrees into a soprano, and a dance into a scramble.[216]

When seven- and eight-year-old sons of chieftains joined their fathers in the dance, singing simultaneously, their high voices notably improved the effect. At times trumpets and also flageolets were played; but the flageolets often seemed not too well tuned. Occasionally also they blew small bone whistles that made a bright sound. . . . From the hour of vespers until nightfall their songs and dances became extremely lively, and the pitch of the songs ascended into ever higher registers so that the sound became extremely brilliant, somewhat like that of our tuneful carols in fast tempo. When the crowds were large, the sound of the singing carried a tremendous distance, especially at night. The spectacle then with their large flares and torches was really something to see.

The Spaniards call these dances *areito*,[217] a word of island origin which whether singular or plural, noun or verb, active or passive, no one can tell me. Perhaps it is an infinitive, like the strings of infinitives used by Negroes [218] just learning

[216] Concerning the *contrapás*, rendered here loosely as "scramble," see Emilio Cotarelo y Mori, *Colección de Entremeses, Loas, Bailes, Jácaras y Mojigangas,* Tomo I, vol. 1 (Madrid: Bailly-Bailliére, 1911), pp. ccxxxix–ccxl; also, Adolfo Salazar, *La Música en Cervantes* (Madrid: Ograma, 1961), pp. 195–196.

[217] Ramón Pane, the "friar" who at Columbus' request wrote, *ca.* 1496, the first description of Indian customs in Hispaniola (see n. 144 above), ignored the term *areito* in his chapter xiv where it should occur (*Colección de libros raros ó curiosos que tratan de América*, V [Madrid: Imprenta de T. Minuesa, 1892], 295–296). Friederici, *op. cit.,* pp. 59–60, gives 1510 as the approximate year in which Peter Martyr introduced the term into European literature. Emiliano Tejera, *Palabras indíjenas de la isla de Santo Domingo* (Santo Domingo: Editorial "La Nación," 1935), pp. 24–28, assembles nine passages from Las Casas, Peter Martyr, Oviedo, López de Gómara, Zorita, and Acosta illustrating early uses of the word.

According to Oviedo, the Hispaniola areito was call-and-response dance song. While everyone kept step to the beat of the dance, the leader improvised short verses which the crowd immediately shouted back (*Sumario de la Natural Historia de las Indias,* in *Historiadores Primitivos de Indias,* ed. Enrique de Vedia [*Biblioteca de Autores Españoles*, XXII], p. 484). Oviedo had seen this kind of leader-follower dance not only among countryfolk in Spain but also in Flanders (*Natural History of the West Indies,* trans. Sterling A. Stoudemire [Chapel Hill: University of North Carolina Press, 1959], p. 39).

Jacob M. Coopersmith, "Music and Musicians of the Dominican Republic: A Survey—Part I," *Musical Quarterly,* XXX/1 (Jan., 1945), 72–75, translates Las Casas and Oviedo's remarks on the West Indian *areito.*

[218] Negroes flooded New Spain with the first wave of Europeans. Some Spanish conquistadores made them supervisors of Indian granaries, tribute gatherers, and overlords of the natives. Motolinía mentioned their prominent role in his *Historia de los*

Spanish, and means "to dance" or "everybody dance in a ring." When I stopped in the West Indies on my way here I encountered some rustic dancing and singing, but nothing to compare with New Spain,[219] where as was said above, they dance in most exquisite and refined fashion.

BERNARDINO DE SAHAGÚN (1500?-1590)

Fray Bernardino Ribeira, a native of Sahagún, studied at Salamanca University, early distinguishing himself as a student of languages. Upon reaching New Spain in 1529, five years after Motolinía, he immediately addressed himself to Náhuatl. In time he became as proficient an Aztecist as any in his order, and indeed the idea of an exhaustive Náhuatl dictionary seeded the magnificent tree now known as his "General History of the Things of New Spain." His first biographer says that the impurities draining into so "marvelously elegant" a language, after the natives began imitating the uncouth attempts of Spaniards to speak Náhuatl, distressed him no end.[220] By record-

---

Indios de Nueva España, trat. 1, cap. 1 (*Colección de Documentos para la Historia de México,* ed. García Icazbalceta, I [México: J. M. Andrade, 1858]), 17: "los calpixques, ó estancieros, y negros."

[219] Alonso de Zurita (= Zorita), a shameless copier of Motolinía, made this comparison his own when he said of the Hispaniola areito: "el bayle que en ellos se usava y el canto era mui tosco" (*Historia de la Nueva España* [*Colección de Libros y Documentos referentes á la Historia de America,* IX], ed. Manuel Serrano y Sanz [Madrid: Lib. Gen. de Victoriano Suárez, 1909], p. 315). Zurita here claimed to be transcribing "ch. 28 of Motolinía's part 4"; however, it is chapter 26 in part 2 of the *Memoriales* that corresponds. Inasmuch as he had access to a final version, now lost, Zurita authorized the opinion that Fray Toribio himself made some changes when preparing his final draft. Cf. *Memoriales,* p. 312, "flautillas no muy entonadas," with Zurita, p. 315, where the last three words are omitted.

[220] Gerónimo de Mendieta, *op. cit.,* p. 663: "At one time I had in my keeping eleven books on good paper. In the best Náhuatl, with accompanying Spanish translation, these told everything concerning the pre-Hispanic usages of the Aztecs, such as their gods, manner of worship, government, polity, laws, traditions, and professions. He wrote these to serve as a sort of Calepino [Ambrogio Calepino, Augustinian, 1435–1510, was the Noah Webster of the sixteenth century]—thereby hoping that all the marvelous finesses of the Aztec language would be revealed, and its original purity guarded from the decline setting in after certain Indians began giving up their own natural and refined way of speaking to imitate our barbarous butchering of their tongue. Misfortune dogged these eleven books, however. At the request of a chronicler in Spain who wanted information concerning the Indies, a viceroy here had them all bundled up and dispatched overseas."

Mendieta's account finds interesting confirmation in Archbishop Montúfar's letter of March 30, 1578, to Philip II (Archivo General de Indias, Audiencia de México, sección quinta, 336 [old no. 66–4–1], 18c [included with "Descripción eclesiástica del Arzobispado," 1572], fol. 1): "La historia vniuersal delos naturales y de sus ritos y ceremonias, compuesta por frai bernardino de Sahagun de la orden de s^t fr^co, que V. M. mando se embie originalmente, sin quedar aca traslado, ni ande impresa ni de mano, por justas consideraciones, me a dicho el autor que la a dado con todos sus papeles originales, al virrey, en lengua castellana y mexicana, y ciertos trasladados q̃ auia sacado."

ing for posterity the purest and most refined Náhuatl he hoped to stave off its decay.[221]

Mexicanists today invariably recognize Sahagún as the unique authority on precontact culture.[222] His *Historia General de las Cosas de Nueva España*, at which he worked for more than a quarter-century (1558–1585), rightfully earns him such fame.[223] At first a mere four "chapters" on gods and men, by 1569 it had already grown to a twelve-book encyclopedia covering every phase of Aztec life. His methodology leaves little to be desired. First at Tepepulco (1558–1560), next at Tlatelolco (1564–1565), he gathered raw material for the "literary" translation made at Mexico City (1565–1569). At Tlatelolco, "eight or ten especially selected nobility, those best informed in their antiquities and most competent in Náhuatl, together with four or five trilingual students" [224] from the college established there for upper-class Indian youth,[225] "shut themselves up together for more than a year [1561–1562] to classify, clarify, and write out anew in careful handwriting" various data gathered at both Tepepulco and Tlatelolco. This extraordinary labor can now be traced through the successive manuscripts that survive at Madrid ("Primeros Memoriales" from Tepepulco and "Códices Matritenses" from Tlatelolco) and at Florence ("Códice Florentino" from Mexico City).[226]

[221] Overleaf (fol. 1*v*) Montúfar adds: "Your Majesty will appreciate his command of the most elegant and correct Aztec known hereabouts; as time passes, his grasp of the ancient forms will be even more highly valued, because decay is already setting in" ("V Mag^d estime la lengua mexicana deste religioso, q̃ es la mas elegante y propria q̃ ay enestas partes, y con el tpo terna mas calidad, por que con el se va perdiendo la propriedad de la antiguedad"). Montúfar was right in foreseeing that the "ancient ways" would be known in their "purity and perfection" only through Sahagún's records.

[222] Typical of the estimate taken by both Mexican musicology and folklore is Dr. Jesús C. Romero's calling "Fray Bernardino de Sahagún nuestro folklorista máximo, honradísimo, acucioso y competente" in "¿Existió la Música Precortesiana?" *Boletín de la Sociedad Mexicana de Geografía y Estadística*, LVI/2 (March–April, 1942), 269. Five years later Dr. Romero lifted Sahagún out of folklore ranks (*Boletín*, LXIII/3 [May–June, 1947], 704).

[223] For an extremely useful résumé of Sahagún's travail in putting together his monumental work, see Wigberto Jiménez Moreno, "Fr. Bernardino de Sahagún y su obra," in Sahagún's *Historia General* (1938 ed.), I, xxxvi–liii. Jiménez Moreno's chart between pages xl and xli codifies his extensive discussion of the way in which Sahagún went about the task.

[224] *Ibid.*, p. xli. Not many of the oldsters who supplied Sahagún with data are now known by name. Fortunately the names and even biographies of the "four or five" Mexican youths versed in Latin, Spanish, and Náhuatl survive. See Garibay, *Historia de la Literatura Náhuatl*, II (1954), 78–79.

[225] Garibay, *Historia de la Literatura Náhuatl*, II (1954), 214–232, summarizes the history of the Colegio de Santa Cruz de Tlatelolco (opened January 6, 1536, with sixty Náhuatl-speaking youths of the most influential families as the first students). See also Steck, *El primer colegio de América*.

[226] The Náhuatl in the Códice Florentino is not as refined as that in the Códices Matritenses because the Indians who helped Sahagún at Mexico City spoke the impure

If the data came from the mouths of Texcocan sachems, the overall plan and classification of material in Sahagún's *Historia General* shows his own meticulously orderly mind at work. So far as organization is concerned, the Náhuatl text as well as the Spanish translation betray the constant influence of the prime medieval encyclopedia produced by a Franciscan— Bartholomaeus Anglicus' *De proprietatibus rerum* (*ca.* 1240), fourteen editions of which had already been printed before 1500. Any sophisticated use of "such assumedly 'native' sources as Sahagún's Náhuatl texts" must therefore take into account an easily overlooked fact: the data was theirs but the agenda and the rules of order were his.[227]

Not only does the organization of his data under conventional encyclopedic headings betray an orderly European mind at work, but certain European value judgments creep in, even when he discusses matters supposedly artistic. According to Vetancurt, Sahagún himself taught music in the Tlatelolco College for Indian youth, opened January 6, 1536.[228] Who is speaking when he lists the qualities of "good" and "bad" Aztec singers in Book X, chapter 8, of his *Historia General de las Cosas de Nueva España*[229]—the ethnologist, or the teacher trained at Salamanca? According to Sahagún, the bad singer "has a hollow, harsh, or raucous voice" (*tiene voz hueca, o áspera, o ronca*). But these are exactly Bartholomaeus Anglicus' adjectives describing a bad voice—*ceca, aspa,* and *rauca!*[230] The bad singer, says Sahagún, tries to hide what he knows from others, and is extremely stingy and proud. But the good singer, on the contrary, "spends his time composing and teaching music" (*ocúpase en componer y en enseñar la música*). When performing, he avoids falsetto (*canta en tenor*), shrinks from monotone (*levanta y baja la voz*), and "sweetens and tunes" his voice. Were these indeed the criteria accepted by precontact Aztec

dialect of Tenochtitlan rather than the more "elegant" Náhuatl of Texcoco—or so reported Paso y Troncoso. Cf. Jiménez Moreno, *op. cit.*, pp. xlvi, lxxv–lxxvi n. 85. The ethnomusicologist who assumes uniform levels of musical accomplishment among Náhuatl-speaking tribes joins company with the linguist who presumes upon a similar uniformity of speech habits.

[227] See Donald Robertson's review of León Portilla's *Los Antiguos Mexicanos a Través de Sus Crónicas y Cantares* in *American Anthropologist*, 63/6 (Dec., 1961), 1376. At pages 1374–1375 Charles E. Dibble reviews Robertson's *Mexican Manuscript Painting of the Early Colonial Period: The Metropolitan Schools* (New Haven: Yale University Press, 1959).

[228] Vetancurt, *Menologio* (*Teatro Mexicano*, IV), p. 298: "enseñarles à leer, y escribir, gramatica, música, y otras cosas del servició de Dios, y la Republica, hasta que el año de 590."

[229] Garibay ed. (1956), III, 116: "De los cantores."

[230] *De proprietatibus rerum* (Nuremberg: Anton Koburger, 1483), Lib. XIX, chap. cxxxij (fourth-from-last page). Dutch, English, French, and Spanish translations of this encyclopedia were published before 1500. Heinrich Mayer printed Vicente de Burgos' Spanish version at Toulouse in 1494.

singers? Or were Sahagún's Indian informants already so acculturated that they supposed their own forefathers capable of agreeing with Bartholomaeus?

In his immediately preceding paragraph, Sahagún had listed the qualities appropriate to an excellent Aztec painter. But according to Donald Robertson, author of *Mexican Manuscript Painting of the Early Colonial Period: The Metropolitan Schools* (New Haven: Yale University Press, 1959): "The contrast of the 'good' artist with the 'bad' artist is in ethical, not artistic terms and comes, as I have shown elsewhere, not from Náhuatl traditions but the encyclopedia of Bartholomaeus Anglicus which served Sahagún as a pattern."

Or, to question another passage from Sahagún frequently quoted in books treating of Aztec music: When the Adonis impersonating Tezcatlipoca ascends the steps of a mean and obscure temple, breaking flutes one by one as he rises to meet his doom, is it the precontact Aztec mind that makes of each flute the symbol of a shattered happiness, or is this "beautiful" symbology European? The passage, despite its having been already quoted to satiety in every popular book on Aztec culture, deserves another repetition here.

The fifth month was called Tóxcatl. In this month was held a feast honoring the principal deity called Tezcatlipoca (whose other names were Titlacáuan, Yáotl, Telpochtli, and Tlamatzíncatl). At this feast they killed a faultless youth whom they had maintained a whole year amidst perfect delights, while he impersonated Tezcatlipoca. As soon as he was killed, another of the same quality was chosen for the ensuing year and always the chosen youth was carefully tended by the majordomos called *calpixques*. Thus, when the day came, a victim was never lacking.

Only the handsomest of captives could be chosen for this sacrifice, the most agile, the best speaker, someone without bodily spot or blemish. Moreover, the youth selected for the sacrifice was taught with greatest care how to play the flute well and how to walk about with a smoking pipe and carrying flowers, after the manner of the highest nobility. Greatly venerated throughout the entire year, he was adored by all who met him. Day after day, he strolled the streets playing his flute, carrying his flowers and pipe, going whither fancy led him. Eight pages always attended him wherever he went. His garments were of the finest and his entire body was painted. . . . Twenty days before the sacrifice, he was allotted new clothing and four lovely maidens to live with him as wives entertaining him and disporting with him until he was taken out to die. Five days before his death, they began treating him as a god. All the court came out to visit him and solemn banquets and magnificent dances were held in his honor. . . .

At the last they took him out to a small mean temple three miles or so from the city on a deserted road. Arriving at the steps of the temple, he began mounting them of his own free will. At the first, then the second, then the third step, he broke in pieces one of the flutes on which he had played during his year of perfect felicity. Thus he continued until reaching the summit where the priests deputed to kill him waited. There they seized him, stretching him on the stone block, face upwards. Then with the swift surgery of the sacrificial knife the chief sacrificer cut open his chest, tore out the heart, and lifted it still beating as an offering to the sun. Thus indeed were all victims sacrificed, but the body of the handsome youth was not tumbled down the steps. Instead, the four who had held him during the tearing out of his heart carried his body reverently down the patio, cut off his head, and skewered it on a stick called *tzonpantli*. Thus ended the life of him whom they had regaled and honored an entire year. Some said that his ending symbolized the end awaiting all those who flaunt riches and enjoy delights in this life: for all shall at the last come down to dust.

(Bk. II, chap. 24.[231])

From the next short excerpt we learn that the young nobles in training for the priesthood at the Calmécac were required to learn vast numbers of hymns honoring the gods in the Aztec pantheon. The Calmécac was "a house of penance and tears, where nobles were reared to become priests of the idols. . . . The fourteenth rule [of instruction] was to teach the boys all the verses of the songs to sing, which they called divine songs; these verses were written in their books by signs" (Bk. III, Appendix, chap. 8 [232]).

In the next excerpt Sahagún's description has been abridged, since it differs in only a few details from Motolinía's. One observation not made by Motolinía has to do with the capital punishment of musicians who made mistakes in performance. The meticulous preparation of the music cannot be wondered at if it was always true that a musician who erred was immediately withdrawn from the ensemble and executed.

One thing that the chiefs took great pains with were the *areitos*, the dances which were festivals for the entire people. The leader of the singing first gave his instructions to the singers in his charge, and told them how to pitch their voices and how to tune them; the leader also told them what kind of rubber sticks they were to use in playing the teponaztli. He also gave orders for the steps and postures that were to be used in dancing. . . . Then they proceeded to the dance. If one of the singers made a mistake in singing, or if one of the teponaztli players erred in the execution of his part, or if one of the leaders who indicated the dance routine made a mistake, immediately the chieftain ordered him seized, and the next day had him summarily executed.

(Bk. VIII, chap. 17, par. 3.[233])

[231] *Historia General*, Jiménez Moreno ed., I, 134–137; Garibay ed., I, 152–155. The Náhuatl text expatiates at much greater length on the youth's physical perfections (Anderson and Dibble, *Book 2*, pp. 64–65). Tezcatlipoca alone claimed the right to turn fortune's wheel, showering blessings or raining ruin (*Historia General*, Bk. I, chap. 3).

[232] Jiménez Moreno ed., I, 298; Garibay, I, 307.16. The verses to sing were written "en sus libros por caracteres," but not necessarily (or even probably) the music.

[233] Jiménez Moreno and Garibay eds., II, 318–319; Anderson and Dibble, *Book 8*, pp. 55–56.

FRANCISCO LÓPEZ DE GÓMARA (1511–1566?)

Gómara has suffered from the reputation of having lied. Bernal Díaz, in writing his "True History," constantly berated him. Only in recent years has it been shown by competent judges that Díaz was himself eaten up by the profound resentment of an ignored underling.[234] Among other detractors of Gómara's history, Las Casas was as outspoken as any in complaining that "he put down only what Cortés testified about himself, so that Cortés and Gómara bedazzled the world." [235]

Of course it is true that Gómara, who became Cortés' personal chaplain in 1541 and remained so until the conqueror's death in 1547, never visited America and instead gleaned much of his data from Cortés.[236] To censure him for failing to visit the scene of action is fair, however, only if such armchair historians as Prescott are also put in the stocks. Besides getting material from Cortés, Gómara also made good use of Motolinía's *Memoriales*, as comparison of such a chapter as 70 in *La istoria de las Indias y conquista de Mexico* (Saragossa, 1552) with chapter 26 in the *Memoriales*, Part II, quickly reveals. All of Gómara's chapter 70, "The Dances of Mexico," would make redundant reading after Motolinía, but at least a few samples may be given.[237]

These two drums [teponaztli and huehuetl] playing in unison with the voices stood out quite strikingly, and sounded not at all badly. The performers sang merry, joyful, and amusing tunes, or else some ballad in praise of past kings, recounting wars and such things. This was all in rhymed couplets and sounded well and was pleasing.

When it was at last time to begin, eight or ten men would blow their whistles lustily. The drums were then beaten very lightly. The dancers were not long in appearing in rich white, red, green, and yellow mantles interwoven with very many different colors. In their hands they carried bouquets of roses, or fans of feathers and gold, while many of them appeared with garlands of exquisitely scented flowers. Many wore fitted featherwork hoods covering the head and shoulders, or else masks made to represent eagle, tiger, alligator, and wild animal heads. Many times a thousand dancers would assemble for this dance and at the

---

[234] Ramón Iglesia, *Cronistas e Historiadores de la Conquista de México* (México: El Colegio de México, 1942), pp. 140–151; Joaquín Ramírez Cabañas' introduction to Gómara's *Historia de la Conquista de México* (México: Pedro Robredo, 1943), I, 10–11.

[235] Lesley B. Simpson, trans., *Cortés: The Life of the Conqueror* (Berkeley and Los Angeles: University of California Press, 1964), p. xvi.

[236] On Gómara's sources, see Ramírez Cabañas, *op. cit.*, I, 18, 246; Simpson, *op. cit.*, pp. xviii, xx–xxi.

[237] Francisco López de Gómara, *Historia de Mexico, con el descvbrimiento dela Nueva España* (Antwerp: Juan Steelsio, 1554), pp. 106–107; Ramírez Cabañas, *op. cit.*, I, 219–220; Simpson, *op. cit.*, pp. 147–148.

least four hundred. They were all leading men, nobles, and even lords. The higher the man's quality the closer was his position with respect to the drums. . . .

At first they sang ballads and move[d] slowly. They played, sang, and danced quietly and everything seemed serious, but when they became more excited, they sang carols and jolly tunes. The dance became more and more animated and the dancers would dance harder and quicken their pace. . . . All those who have seen this dance say it is a most interesting thing to see and superior to the *zambra* [238] of the Moors, which is the best dance of which we have any knowledge in Spain.

ALONSO DE MOLINA (1514?–1585)

Molina was brought to New Spain as a boy of eight or ten, shortly after the Aztec capital fell. His mother, soon left a widow, let him play with Indian children, and he grew up speaking Náhuatl as a second tongue. His was the first dictionary of the language (Spanish–Náhuatl, 1555; Spanish–Náhuatl [enlarged by 4,000 words], Náhuatl–Spanish, 1571).[239]

Molina's definitions of musical instruments have already been canvassed above. Only a lexicographer with considerable musical expertise could have fashioned a dictionary that is so continuously fascinating a document, especially for those interested in acculturation.[240] Like Sahagún, Molina busied himself with providing Náhuatl texts for the newly converted to sing. The translation of the Epistles and Gospels sung throughout the year in parishes for Náhuatl speakers was his.[241]

His dictionary of 1571 suggests several fruitful trains of thought: (1) The Aztecs lacked any generic term for music, coming closest to it with two words meaning "knowledge of singing" (*cuica tlamatiliztli*).[242] (2) Neither did they have a verb meaning *to play*, in our sense of *playing* on an

---

[238] See Joan Corominas, *Diccionario crítico etimológico* (Madrid: Editorial Gredos, 1954), IV, 818–819; Leopoldo de Eguilaz y Yanguas, *Glosario etimológico* (Granada: La Lealtad, 1886), pp. 523–524. Zambra (from Arabic *zámr*) = band of instrumentalists, or the noisy dance for which they played. Soon after Granada was captured, zambras started substituting for organs in mosques converted into churches.

[239] Ramón Zulaica Garate, *Los Franciscanos y la imprenta en México en el siglo XVI* (México: Pedro Robredo, 1939), p. 115. Biography, pp. 83–91. His parents probably came from Extremadura.

[240] Canto de órgano = nauhte*cuicatl* = "four-[part] song" (fol. 24); órgano = euat*lapitzal*ueuetl = "that-flute-drum" (91); vihuela = meca*ueuetl* = "string-drum" (118). Such examples can be greatly multiplied. See Stanford, *op. cit.*, pp. 131–150, for an exhaustive analysis of Molina's music and dance vocabulary.

[241] *Códice Franciscano: Siglo XVI*, ed. J. García Icazbalceta [*Nueva Colección de Documentos para la Historia de México*, II] (México: Francisco Díaz de León, 1889), p. 68: "Epistolas y Evangelios que se cantan en la Iglesia por todo el año."

[242] *Vocabvlario en lengva castellana*, fol. 88; *en lengva mexicana*, fol. 26v.

instrument. (3) On the other hand, their language was immensely rich in specific nouns, such as, for instance:

song sung by a soprano	*tlapitzaualiztli*
song sung to compliment someone	*tecuiqueualiztli*
song sung to insult someone	*tecuicuiqueualiztli*
song sung to someone else	*tecuicatiliztli*

and, although they had no generic nouns meaning "musician," or "player," their language was extremely prolific in specific nouns meaning "player on the huehuetl," "player on the teponaztli," "flute player," "fife player," "trumpet player," and so on. (4) Their language was similarly endowed with verbs of such varied specific meaning as "to sing in praise of someone," "to sing derisive songs," "to sing tenderly," or "to sing in a high voice."

As long ago as Pythagoras and Aristotle, Western civilization began relating music to numbers and assigning simple ratios to consonances. Highly sensitive as were the Mesoamericans to numbers and auguries, no evidence has thus far been adduced from Molina or any other early dictionary to suggest that Aztecs, Zapotecs, Mixtecs, Mayas, or any other tribe conceived of music as an abstraction, thought of numbers as consonance indicators, or related any of their calendrical lore to music in our theoretical sense.[243]

Had any of them done so, E. Thomas Stanford in his Charles Seeger Festschrift article would have listed terms from Mixteco, Náhuatl, or Tarasco tongues for the musical intervals of an octave, fifth, fourth, third, and so on. Charles L. Boilés, however, does permit our believing that as early as the classical epoch Totonac instrument makers knew the harmonic series empirically, and also differential ("Tartini") tones (*La Palabra y el Hombre*, II Época/34 [April–June, 1965], 215, 217).

DIEGO DE LANDA (1524–1579)

The Spanish penetration of Yucatán began in 1526, five years after Cortés' conquest of Mexico, but the complete domination of the peninsula was delayed until twenty years later. Landa's *Relación de las cosas de Yucatán* was written about 1566 while Landa was in Spain to exonerate himself from charges brought by the first resident bishop Francisco Toral (1562–1571). For informants Landa relied principally on (Juan) Nachi Cocom, the territorial ruler of Sotuta who died in 1562 after having had four boys sacrificed in a vain effort to recover his health,[244] and Gaspar Antonio Chi [= Xiu] de

---

[243] Ángel M. Garibay, "Huehuetlatolli, Documento A," *Tlalocan: A Journal of Source Materials* [Sacramento, California: The House of Tlaloc], I/2 (1943), 102, uses the word *música* to translate *huehuetl*. His document: mPM 4068.J83 in the Bancroft Library, Berkeley.

[244] Tozzer ed. (1941), pp. 43–44 nn. 216, 217. He also ordered the crucifixion of two girls. After they were taken down alive, their hearts were extracted (p. 116 n. 533).

Herrera (1531–1610?).[245] The latter, probably born at Mani, "was the son of a pagan priest; he learned to speak Spanish perfectly and knew Latin moderately." [246] In Sánchez de Águilar's *Informe,* published at Madrid in 1639, Chi enjoys the distinction of being the first Indian organist and choirmaster to win voluble praise in a European book: [247] "He sang plain-song and figural music excellently. After being choirmaster at Tecemin [= Tizimin [248]], he became organist of Mérida Cathedral, and later the governor's official interpreter."

Landa's enumeration of Mayan musical instruments included: [249]

Drums which they play with the hand, and another drum made of hollow wood with a heavy and sad sound. They beat it with a rather long stick with a certain gum from a tree at the end of it, and they have long thin trumpets of hollow wood with long twisted gourds at the ends. And they have another instrument made of a whole tortoise with its shell, and having taken out the flesh, they strike it with the palm of the hand.[250] The sound is doleful and sad. They have whistles made of leg bones of deer; great conch shells and flutes made of reeds, and with these instruments they make music for the dancers.

DIEGO DURÁN (1537–1588)

Durán, a Dominican missionary who immersed himself in Indian lore, was formerly thought to have been born in Mexico, but Francisco Fernández

[245] Chi's biography is summarized in Ralph L. Roys, *The Indian Background of Colonial Yucatan* (Washington: Carnegie Institution, 1943), pp. 123–124. Chi's *Relación* (1582) is translated in Tozzer, *Landa's Relación* (1941), pp. 230–232. Both these Mayanists neglect Chi's musical acquirements, however.

[246] Pedro Sánchez de Águilar, *Informe Contra Idolorum Cultores* (3d ed.; Mérida: E. G. Triay, 1937), pp. 144–145.

[247] *Ibid.* He thus describes Chi's musical ability: "Cantaua canto llano y canto de organo diestramente, y tocaua tecla. Yo le conoci Organista en esta Santa Iglesia."

[248] Concerning the Chilam Balam of Tizimin, see Alfredo Barrera Vásquez and Silvia Rendón, *El Libro de los Libros de Chilam Balam* (México: Fondo de Cultura Económica, 1948), pp. 29–32; Barrera Vásquez and Sylvanus G. Morley, *The Maya Chronicles* (Washington: Carnegie Institution, 1949 [Publication 585]), pp. 18–19.

Sánchez de Águilar (1937 ed.), p. 149, defines the functions of the *Holpop:* "He is the principal singer, he sets the pitch, he teaches the song, and is greatly venerated and respected. To him belongs the principal seat at gatherings and weddings. In his charge are the musical instruments, such as flutes, small trumpets, tortoise shells, teponaztli. . . ." Cogolludo confirms the holpop's important role (see Tozzer, *op. cit.,* p. 93 n. 403). Throughout the Mayan area, the colonial maestro de capilla fell heir to the holpop's authority, even the preservation of the books of Chilam Balam coming within his jurisdiction (see *Códice Pérez* [Mérida: Imprenta Oriente, 1949], p. 270).

[249] Tozzer ed., p. 93; Pérez Martínez ed. (1938), p. 109. Further information on Mayan song and dance may be found in Juan Francisco Molina Solís, *Historia del decubrimiento y conquista de Yucatán* (Mérida: R. Caballero, 1896), I, 272–273, 302–303.

[250] In the Maya area the *kayab,* which Landa says was struck with the palm, was also struck with animal horn, according to Castañeda and Mendoza, *Anales,* 4ª época, VIII, 549, 553; also pl. 46 (between pp. 310 and 311).

del Castillo discovered an Inquisition document dated June 14, 1587, proving him to have been born at Seville.[251] His magnificent *Historia de las Indias de Nueva-España,* like Landa's invaluable *Relación,* awaited the nineteenth century for its publication. In it (*Historia,* I, 12) he says that, when a young lad, he was living on the shores of Lake Texcoco (Mexico) with relatives who owned Indian slaves (II, 67). His experiences with the Indians in this area remained vivid in his memory, and he could never praise them and their delightful region sufficiently (I, 12, 16). On May 8, 1556, when he was nineteen, he professed in Santo Domingo monastery at Mexico City. Three years later (September, 1559), he was already so distinguished as to be named deacon of the monastery; in 1561 he was assigned to Oaxaca. A perfect speaker of Náhuatl, he was rotated among various pueblos during the next twenty years (II, 193, 216, 218, 236). In 1581 he was vicar of Santo Domingo de Hueyapan, and in Hueyapan he probably wrote his history. He was extremely sick a month before his deposition to the Holy Office in 1587, and died in 1588.

He expressly states that he wrote his *Historia* for the missionaries working in New Spain. Not until the missionaries really understand the idolatries of the indigenes can they successfully convert them (II, 68, 71). He continually warns his fellow friars working in Mexico not to change the dates of Christian festivals, even when requested to do so by the Indians (II, 246, 266, 267). He describes the dances, songs, and festivals of the indigenes to warn missionaries in New Spain against allowing idolatrous intrusions into Christian festivals, songs, and dances (II, 102, 227, 233, 284). Further invaluable data on Durán's *Historia* is assembled by Fernando B. Sandoval in *Estudios de historiografía de la Nueva España* (México: El Colegio de México, 1845), pages 51–90.

Durán dated his manuscript; the part here quoted was finished in 1579. The *Atlas* appended to the history is a collection of pictures showing preconquest customs; the pictures postdate the Conquest but are probably as authentic records as the paintings in Sahagún's Florentine Codex. In the first extract Durán compares Indian and Spanish musical praxis;[252] the second excerpt contains an early mention of the sarabande.[253]

Kings and nobility all maintained professional singers who composed songs celebrating their important deeds and those of their ancestors. . . . I have heard these many times in public dances and although they celebrate past glories I was delighted to hear such praises sung. There were also singers who composed sacred songs in honor of their idols; these temple singers likewise received regular stipends and they were called *cuycapicque*[254] meaning "composers of

[251] "Fray Diego Durán. Aclaraciones históricas," *Anales del Museo Nacional de Arqueología, Historia y Etnografía,* 4ª ép., III (1925), 228. On the day he signed, he was fifty years old (lám. xi).

[252] Durán, *Historia de las Indias,* II (México: Ignacio Escalante, 1880), 233.

[253] *Ibid.,* p. 230.

[254] Cuicapicqui = "componedor de canto" (Molina, fol. 26v).

songs." Those who criticize Indian customs might well reflect that this custom of maintaining professional singers in no wise differs from the present-day practice of maintaining paid singers in the royal chapel, or a band of musicians in the chapel of the Archbishop of Toledo or of any other noble person. In New Spain there are yet today in certain towns members of the native nobility who still follow their ancient custom of maintaining singers. I myself do not think this old custom undesirable, but think rather that it conduces to good ends; for the prestige of these descendants of kings and chieftains should not be allowed to decay. The metaphors are often so obscure that the songs can scarcely be understood if they are not studied and explained. I have listened to their songs very attentively at times and have found that what at first seemed nonsense made excellent sense after the metaphors were elucidated.

Since the young men were intensely eager to learn how to dance and sing well, and always wished to be leaders in the dancing and singing, they spent much time and effort mastering the particular types of body movement required. It was the custom of the dancers to dance and sing at the same time. Their dance movements were regulated not only by the beat of the music, but also by the pitch of their singing. . . . Their poets gave each song and dance a different tune, just as we employ a different tune when we are singing different types of poetry such as the sonnet or the *octava rima* or the *terceto*. Typical of the pronounced differences encountered in their dance music was the contrast between the solemn and majestic songs and dances performed by the nobility, and the lighter love songs danced by the youths. And still more different in type was another dance they performed which might have been derived from that lascivious sarabande which our own people dance with such indecent contortions of the body and such lewd grimaces.

Although Durán's scattered references to music in the first seventy-eight chapters of his history have never been systematically studied, there are at least twenty-five allusions that should interest ethnologists.[255] He tells us that *ca.* 1450 the neighboring cities around Mexico began instituting municipal "colleges and schools of singing and dancing" in direct imitation of the Aztecs (chap. 23).[256] At the last great celebration of Axayacatl's reign (1469–1481) a new sacrificial stone was dedicated with new songs especially composed to honor the stone (chap. 36).[257] The teponaztli having been placed in the center of the courtyard, the bewigged "Singers of the Round Stone" trooped in, each wearing on his back an ornament resembling a millstone. The importance invariably given "new songs" at such dedications helps explain why composers enjoyed such prestige among the Aztecs.

[255] *The Aztecs,* pp. 58, 111, 113, 122, 158, 159, 162, 163, 167, 177, 178, 180, 187, 190, 204, 212, 219, 235, 242, 250–253, 281, 293, 297, 298, 313.

[256] *Historia,* I, 198: "así empeçaron . . . á ordenar . . . colegios y escuelas de cantar y dançar . . ."; *The Aztecs,* p. 122.

[257] *Historia,* I, 283; *The Aztecs,* p. 163.

Inasmuch as even kings and nobility cannot "sing or dance or enjoy the odor of flowers" in the next world, these supreme pleasures should be all the more savored in this present life (chap. 40).[258] Or at least so decided Tizoc, who reigned only four or five years (1481–1486). Because song and dance epitomize delight, silence is the only fitting response after a defeat, or after a battle in which only a few prisoners are taken (chaps. 57,[259] 61 [260]). A proper welcome for an alien leader, even if it is Cortés spreading terror as he goes, cannot be extended without the clamor of priests' *vocinas y caracoles* (chap. 74 [261]).

GERÓNIMO DE MENDIETA (1525–1604)

Mendieta came to Mexico in 1554 and immediately began the study of Náhuatl, which he learned to speak with signal "elegance." While revisiting Spain (1570–1573) he was commissioned by the Franciscan superior general to prepare a history of the Indians and started the *Historia Eclesiástica Indiana* in 1571; the pressure of missionary duties and the involvement in unforeseen administrative responsibilities delayed its completion, however, until 1596.

Mendieta tells us (in the extract offered below) that the Aztecs ascribed a divine origin to their two most assertive instruments, the teponaztli and the huehuetl. The legendary account runs like this: Teponaztli and Huehuetl dwelt at the court of the Sun. A priestly messenger from earth invaded the heavenly precincts and poured forth in song the story of man's grief. The Sun, however, forbade his servitors to listen to the earthly messenger. Teponaztli and Huehuetl disobeyed the Sun, and for their disobedience were expelled from the heavens. They fell to earth and assumed the form of musical instruments. Ever since their expulsion from the skies they have assuaged man's grief with the sound of their music.

This legendary account is interesting if for no other reason than that it affirms the magic power (having nothing to do with music) that inhered in these instruments. Since the teponaztli and the huehuetl were actually divine beings temporarily condemned to earthly exile, they deserved to be worshiped. Even today certain Indians in out-of-the-way places have the

---

[258] *Historia*, I, 321; *The Aztecs*, p. 180.

[259] *Historia*, I, 453: "no se tocaron caracoles, ni bocinas, ni flautas, como solian, ni atambores, sino todo sordo y sin alegría, y así entraron en la ciudad los que venian desta guerra"; *The Aztecs*, p. 235.

[260] *Historia*, I, 481: "ni se tocase caracol ni otro ningun instrumento"; *The Aztecs*, p. 242. Moctezuma thus displayed his anger at his troops' returning from battle with no more than eighty prisoners for the sacrificial stone.

[261] *Historia*, II, 36; *The Aztecs*, p. 293. Durán reports that at Cortés' first entry Moctezuma's feet were already clapped in irons—although this supreme indignity was hidden from his people by a mantle.

reputation of hoarding their teponaztlis, and of venerating them as if they were sacred objects. Despite long-continued efforts to extirpate such vestiges of idolatry, Indians have been found in our own time who still ascribed mana to their teponaztlis and huehuetls, and the Church's campaign against idolatry has therefore not fully succeeded.[262]

As late as 1939 Rodney Gallop reported several instances, all of which he had seen at first hand, involving the superstitious veneration of teponaztlis.[263] According to Gallop, "There is a suspicion of idolatry in the reverence paid to the drums of San Juan Acingo, Tepoztlan, and Xico, which comes out even more strongly in other parts of the Sierras of Puebla and Hidalgo." Gallop continued by citing an Aztec village, named Xolotla, where the chief sorcerer guarded a teponaztli kept wrapped in a garment, as if it were something human needing protection. The sorcerer, furthermore, called his teponaztli by a human name. "When the priest's back is turned this drum is sometimes smuggled into the village church and hidden behind the altar." [264]

In the legendary account given by Mendieta, priests pictured themselves as the bringers of every good gift man possessed. With music as with maize. the gift of the gods awaited priestly intercession in sorrowing man's behalf. For certain details of the legend, Mendieta cited the authority of the pioneer Náhuatl grammarian, Fray Andrés de Olmos. [65]

Seeing that they were utterly unable to prevail in their struggle with the newly created Sun, the old gods of Teotihuacán in desperation decided to sacrifice themselves. Xolotl, the appointed sacrificer, opened each of their breasts with a large knife and drew out the heart; he then killed himself. By their deaths, the Sun's anger was appeased.

[262] Seler's "Götzendienerei unter den heutigen Indianern Mexikos," Globus, LXIX/23 (June, 1896), 367–370, gives moving accounts of idolatries in the Zapotec area. See p. 369 for two views of a wooden idol representing the wind god, who holds a sacrificial knife in his right hand. In July, 1889, this idol was found sitting on the main altar in the parish church at Santa María Mixistlan.

[263] Among the instruments that Rodney Gallop classed as idols was a teponaztli kept "jealously hidden away" except for "three occasions of the year" ("The Music of Indian Mexico," Musical Quarterly, XXV/2 [April, 1939], 217). The figure carved on it was identified for him by an archaeologist as "Xochipilli, god of song, dance, and festivity" (p. 218). At Xico (Villa Juárez) he found "an Aztec Indian whom I more than half suspect of being a brujo (sorcerer)." This old man guarded a teponaztli "carved in the shape of a monkey with ear-plugs and eyes which, once of gold, have now been replaced by earthenware." On St. John's Day, an Aztec hymn in honor of Xochipilli was chanted to its thud. Gallop was able to transcribe six lines. He calls the sound of a teponaztli a "sinister throb."

[264] Ibid., p. 219.

[265] Vetancurt, Menologio (Teatro Mexicano, IV), pp. 218–222, summarizes the glowing account of Olmos' life in Mendieta, op. cit., pp. 644–651. The legendary origin of teponaztli and huehuetl is in Mendieta's Bk. II, chaps. 2–3 (pp. 79–80).

ℰach god bequeathed his sacred clothing to a priest who had worshiped him. Realizing the great weight of their responsibility for such sacred relics, the priests guarded the vestments most zealously. Their grief, however, on account of the deaths of their gods was not assuaged even though they now had in their possession the sacred vestments. Their grief instead of abating, in time grew insupportable, and they therefore decided to undertake a pilgrimage, hoping that somewhere they might find solace for their anguish.

After wandering about together for a time, they separated and one priest traveled toward the seacoast. When he arrived at the ocean he met there Tezcatlipoca, lord of being, who instructed him to proceed onward to the Court of the Sun, and there to beg the Sun for musical instruments. With songs and musical instruments man would be able fittingly to praise his new gods.

In order to assist him in this long journey to the Court of the Sun, various animals in the sea, among them the tortoise, the whale, and the sea-cow, were asked to form themselves into a bridge so that the grief-stricken priest might pass over them. When the priest arrived at the Court of the Sun he explained the motive of his visit. The Sun, however, not wishing to diminish his own retinue of followers, forbade any of his servitors to listen to the priest's sung entreaties.

But so eloquently and earnestly did the earthly messenger sing his plea that two servants of the Sun, the one named Huehuetl and the other Teponaztli, disobeyed and listened. For their presumption in disobeying him, the Sun cast them forth from his presence in disgrace. They then accompanied the priest in his return to earth.

The huehuetl and teponaztli forever remember the sorrow they felt when first they heard the story of man's extremity, as the priest told it in heaven. If man's anguish because the gods of Teotihuacán are dead has now abated and if instead he has learned how to dance and make merry in song and dance, the sounds of the huehuetl and teponaztli still continue to remind him of the sighs Huehuetl and Teponaztli long ago breathed in heaven when first they heard the sad entreaties of the earthly messenger.[266]

Mendieta's Book II, chapters 2 and 3, later found their way into Torquemada, where they reappear word for word as chapters 42 and 43 in Book VI of the *Monarquia Indiana*.[267] Such Handelian laxity in lifting the property of predecessors explains chapter 31 of Mendieta's Book II (native dances), copied from Motolinía. Because so much sharing of material was the rule, it is not surprising to find even a foe of Franciscan "laxity" like Las Casas repeating the same observations on aboriginal music in his *Apologé-*

---

[266] The paraphrase here given follows Saldívar, *Historia de la Música en México,* pp. 4–5; the last paragraph is his, not Mendieta's.

[267] In the 1723 ed., *segunda parte,* pp. 77–78. See García Icazbalceta's introduction to Mendieta, p. xxxviii.

tica Historia which had already been made or were to be made by Olmos, Motolinía, and Torquemada.[268]

The legend transmitted by Mendieta and repeated by Torquemada fails to give the divine teponaztli and huehuetl who dwelt at the Sun's court any personal names. However, the Indians of Chiapas, Las Casas' polyglot see, gave the Lord of the Tepanahuaste (= teponaztli) the name of Votan. After several decades of exposure to Dominican mission activity, these Chiapas Indians began mixing up Votan with Old Testament history to such an extent that he emerged as a grandson of Noah who watched the Tower of Babel go up. Bishop Francisco Núñez de la Vega's *Constituciones Dioecesanas del Obispado de Chiappa* (Rome: C. Zenobi, 1702) contains a paragraph on Votan "whom all the Indians venerate and whom some provinces call the 'people's heart.' "[269]

In 1691, while touring the Chiapas diocese, Núñez de la Vega came upon a house "built by Votan" in the village of Huehuetan. According to the natives, Votan had built it with his mere breath after fleeing the Tower of Babel on heavenly orders and beginning the establishment of Indian vil-

---

[268] Compare Mendieta, *op. cit.*, Bk. II, chap. 40 (p. 162): "At funerals of chieftains, some marched along singing; but not playing drums—although their custom always forbade singing unless drums were played simultaneously" with the identical statement in Las Casas, *Apologética Historia*, chap. 227 (*Biblioteca de Autores Españoles*, CVI [1958]), p. 317. Mendieta's text: "Algunos otros iban cantando; mas en este acto no tañian atabales, aunque tienen siempre de costumbre no cantar sin tañer juntamente atabales"; Las Casas': "algunos otros cantando; pero en este acto no tañian instrumento alguno, puesto que siempre tenían y tienen de costumbre no cantar sin tañer atabales."

Las Casas' willingness to draw on the common stock of Franciscan writers is not so disappointing as is the discovery that he so rarely mentions music at all. Even the few borrowed allusions tend to repeat themselves and none gives a flattering picture (*Biblioteca de Autores Españoles*, CVI, 144 ["chanzonetas y cantares y saltos de placer que no se podría explicar"], 146 ["unos atambores muy roncos y tristes"], 151 ["en procesión por el patio del templo con grandes cantos y sones y juegos y bailes y personajes"], 189 ["este tormento sufrían cantando"], 192 ["callaban los atabales y cantaban los cantores ayes tristes"], 193 ["los señores y caballeros cantaban coplas y cantares de alegría en alabanzas de sus dioses"], 317, 320 ["poníanle cascabeles de oro en las gargantas de los pies"], 321 ["todos los cantares suyos son muy escuros y entricados," referring to Tarascan funeral songs], 337 ["los mexicanos no usaban tañer instrumento alguno," at royal exequies], 370 ["todos al son de sus instrumentos musicales cantaban unos y respondían otros, como los nuestros suelen hacer en España," discussing festival dances in Nicaragua and Honduras]).

Las Casas' penchant for comparisons with classical antiquity causes us to wonder why he neglected contrasting Boethius with the musical precepts taught in the Calmécac.

[269] Lorenzo Boturini Benaduc[c]i, *Idea de una nueva historia general de la América Septentrional* (Madrid: Juan de Zúñiga, 1746), p. 115, gave this reference wide notoriety. Flavio Antonio Paniagua, *Documentos y datos para un Diccionario Etimológico, Histórico y Geográfico de Chiapas*, I (San Cristóbal–Las Casas [Chiapas]: Manuel Bermúdez R., 1908), p. 56, reprints the appropriate constitution (núm. 34, xxx).

lages in the Chiapas territory. His house in Huehuetan, guarded by a priestess, contained some clay jars and the stone effigies of numerous other deities worshiped before Christianity reached the region. Lord of the Teponaztli, Votan spoke to all in the language of the two-toned drum, according to the villagers. But in their confusion of the Old Testament with native mythology, the Indians claimed also that the "Señor del Palo hueco" was the divine being who had taught each village in the Chiapas polyglot area its distinctive tongue.

ANTONIO DE CIBDAD REAL (= CIUDAD REAL) (1551–1617)

Tozzer, who should have known, rated Cibdad Real as the prince of Mayanists in colonial times.[270] Arriving in Yucatán in 1573, Cibdad Real spent the next forty years preparing a Maya "calepine." The copy now in Providence (John Carter Brown Library) has 701 leaves and lists some 11,180 words in the Spanish–Maya section alone.[271] After suffering from quartan fever for three years, Cibdad Real was ordered to Texcoco ("seven leagues from Mexico City"). Upon recovering, he was named secretary[272] to the Franciscan commissary Fray Alonso Ponce, who toured Mesoamerica (1584–1588) inspecting missions. During this lengthy trip Cibdad Real gathered the data for his *Relación breve y verdadera de algunas cosas de las muchas que sucedieron al Padre Fray Alonso Ponce en las provincias de la Nueva España* (published 1872–1873, 2 vols.).

Few accounts ever written contain so many vivid descriptions of music in the rural districts of colonial Mexico.[273] What Cibdad Real reports of city music can also be very enlightening—if only to prove how utterly the aborigines in more exposed areas had succumbed to European musical influences. Even where Indian governors ruled, European music was fast ousting their own—because they wished it so. One Indian-ruled town where Cibdad Real met nothing but European music was Tlaxcala. From October 26 to 31, 1585, the inspecting party visited Tlaxcala, there meeting Gerónimo de Mendieta. This was also the week when the new viceroy Álvaro Manrique de Zúñiga passed through.[274] Tlaxcala had, of course, been Cortés' headquarters for the assault on Mexico. So far had music acculturation proceeded here that on Corpus Christi, 1538, Tlaxcala had already boasted

---

[270] Landa ed. (1941), p. 45: ". . . to me the great Maya scholar of the century."

[271] Alfred M. Tozzer, *A Maya Grammar* (Cambridge: Peabody Museum [Papers, Vol. IX], 1921), pp. 170–171, 251 [*Diccionario de Motul*].

[272] *Colección de Documentos Inéditos para la Historia de España*, LVII (1872), 24.

[273] See the ninety-two entries for "Música" in Raúl Guerrero's *Indice clasificado* (México: Biblioteca Aportación Histórica [Editor Vargas Rea], 1949), p. 48.

[274] *Colección de Documentos Inéditos para la Historia de España*, LVII, 168. Cf. Mendieta, *op. cit.*, p. xx.

a choir singing the best Spanish polyphonic motets,[275] and the next year had counted two choirs, each of more than twenty singers abetted by rebecks and axabebas.[276] A Tlaxcala Indian had been the first to compose an entire polyphonic Mass in New Spain, and its quality had reaped praise from the best Castilian singers.[277] When all this had already happened in the 1530's, it was small wonder that a half century later Cibdad Real found this proud Indian town competing with the best European musical entertainment that the capital could offer the new viceroy.

Not in Cibdad Real's account of such a stopover as that at Tlaxcala, but in his diary of visits to much remoter parts of the viceroyalty, must one therefore look for his record of the old *ritos y supersticiones* still flourishing in full vigor. After having left San Salvador (capital of present-day El Salvador), the inspecting party traveled east during mid-May, 1586. In the vicinity of the 6,985-foot San Miguel volcano, they encountered a deep crystal-clear spring named Uluapan.[278] From it issued a short river running

[275] *Colección de Documentos para la Historia de México*, ed. J. García Icazbalceta, I (México: J. M. Andrade, 1858), 81 ("capilla de canto de órgano"), 82 ("motete en canto de órgano"). Both Steck (*Motolinía's History of the Indians of New Spain*, pp. 154 ["choir with the organ playing"], 155 ["motet with organ accompaniment"]) and Elizabeth Andros Foster (*Documents and Narratives*, IV [Berkeley: Cortés Society, 1950], 104 n. 7 [*canto de órgano* = "organum"]) stumble over Spanish Renaissance musical terminology.

[276] The shrill axabeba joined trumpets and drums at tourneys and other martial exercises in fifteenth-century Spain. In 1434, at the most famous joust in the Castilian John II's reign, "tocaron al arma las trompetas, chirumbelas, e atabales, e xabebas Moriscas" (Juan de Pineda, *Libro del Passo Honroso, defendido por el excelente caballero Suero de Quiñones* [2d ed.; Madrid: Antonio de Sancha, 1783], p. 61 [chap. 72]). For Motolinía's letter of 1539 to his provincial mentioning the Moorish "jabebas" popular already in Tlaxcala, see CDHM (1858; cf. n. 275 above), I, 84. Eguílaz y Yanguas, *Glosario etimológico* (1886), p. 426, authorizes our equating jabeba with axabeba, and, on p. 311, quotes from quatrain 1233 of Juan Ruiz's *El libro de buen amor*, written *ca.* 1350: "Dulçema, e axabeba, el finchado albogon, / Çinfonia e baldosa en esta fiesta son." *Al-shabbāba*, from which ajabeba derives, signifies transverse flute in Arabic. See Stevenson, *Spanish Music in the Age of Columbus* (1960), p. 22; also pp. 23, 45, and 46.148.

J. Delgado Campos, editor of *El libro de buen amor* (Paris: Ch. Bouret, n.d.), defined *axabeba* as "reed flute." Muñoz Camargo, *Historia de Tlaxcala*, chap. 16 (1892 ed., p. 135; 1947 ed., p. 147) mentioned *fabebas* (= jabebas = axabebas); "instruments of similar type" enjoyed a vogue in Tlaxcala long before the Spaniards, he wrote.

[277] CDHM, I, 210: "Un Indio de estos cantores, vecino de esta ciudad de Tlaxcallan, ha compuesto una misa entera, apuntada por puro ingenio, aprobada por buenos cantores de Castilla que la han visto." Decades later, after a drastic drop in population, music at Tlaxcala still continued outstanding (see Boturini Benaduci [*ca.* 1698–1749], *Idea de una nueva historia*, p. 95).

[278] The Ulúa language was one of five spoken in 1576 by tribes inhabiting what is now El Salvador. References in María de Baratta, *Cuzcatlán Típico* (n. 120, above), p. 18. Those speaking Ulúa lived in San Miguel province, which was exactly the area

into the Pacific. Though iguanas abounded and though the spring was filled with *mojarras* and other delectable fish, none of the Indians in the region dared touch any of them; nor would they even make a fire nearby, "because they said that the fish and the iguanas were formerly humans and to prove it they told this fable": [279]

At the edge of the spring four hundred boys were dancing one day to the sound of a teponaztli [280] that an old man was playing. Finally they all became so tired and so satiated with dancing that they one and all decided to cast themselves into the spring and drown. So that their fate would be a common one, they tied themselves together with a long stout rope. First the leader jumped in. Then all followed one by one until but a single boy remained of the entire lot. However, by the time all the others had drowned themselves, he had changed his mind, and had decided to untie himself. Freed, he ran to the village with the news that all of his erstwhile companions had changed to iguanas and fish. This is the reason no one disturbs the spring; and even now they say that at night one can hear music-making and dancing at the edge of the spring.

The folklore of El Salvador is so little known outside the country [281] that this tale is repeated from Cibdad Real in preference to some of the legends that he collected in other parts of Mesoamerica. Contrasting with this legend is the "true" story that he collected among the primitive Lacandones [282] (inhabiting the area where the Bonampak musical murals were found).

That year, 1586, some of these Indians set out for the mainland with their arms (which are bow and arrows). After passing the night on the farm of a Spaniard from Chiapas, they killed a Negro who defended himself; and then carried off nine or ten young and old captives to their island fortress in the middle of the

---

through which Cibdad Real was traveling when he came upon the "ojo de agua llamado Uluapan."

[279] *CDIHE*, LVII, 333–334.

[280] Cibdad Real's text reads *tamborilejo*. Sahagún translates huehuetl with "atambor," teponaztli with "atamboril." See his *Book 8—Kings and Lords*, trans. Anderson and Dibble (1954), p. 28, for the Náhuatl; his *Historia General*, Garibay ed. (1956), II, 298.17 for the Spanish: "Usaban de atambor y de atamboril, el atambor era alto, como hasta la cinta, de la manera de los de España en la cobertura; era el tamboril de madera, hueco, tan grueso como un cuerpo de un hombre, y tan largo como tres palmos, unos poco más y otros poco menos, y muy pintados; este atambor, y este atamboril ahora lo usan de la misma manera."

[281] Baratta, *Cuzcatlán Típico* (see n. 120 above), I, 16: "Los estudios y trabajos sobre la etnografía cuzcatleca, desgraciadamente no están tan avanzados como era de desearse." For her discussion of the *tepunahuaste* (= teponaztli), see I, 84–97. "Ten tepunahuastes still survive here in El Salvador," she says (I, 86). On the next page are photographs of the Museo Nacional exemplar (sounding *CE*) and of her personally owned specimen (sounding B_2b-D_1, according to her).

[282] Tozzer, *Landa's Relación*, p. 104 n. 474, translated this "true" tale. Thompson found it in Cibdad Real's *Relación*, I (= *CDIHE*, LVII), 473–475.

lake. There they fattened them like pigs for sacrifice to their gods. At night the prisoners were herded together into a jail made of thick wooden stakes driven into the ground. Above them guards kept watch in a hut. But by day they were taken out, fed well, and paraded up and down the village streets with jingles on their feet. Finally came the awaited day of sacrifice, and one by one they were brought out to be killed. However, it so happened that the drummer playing the teponaztli [283] made a mistake with his mallets and the music lost a beat. At once the Indian priest ordered the ceremony stopped. Taking the lost measure in the music for a bad omen, he forthwith ordered the teponaztli player guilty of the mistake to be killed [284]—so enormous was the crime. But the rest of the Indians interceded for him, and he was spared. Nevertheless, the captive remaining to be sacrificed was ordered back to the wooden jail, there to await death another day.[285]

On Wednesday, February 18, 1587, the inspecting party stopped at a village named Matzatlan (located in southeastern Jalisco on the road from Ciudad Guzmán to Colima). The several festivities in their honor included an exhibition by a juggler lying flat on his back. With his feet high in the air he made a thick log 6 feet long dance on the soles of his bare feet.[286]

This sport is a commonplace everywhere among the Indians of New Spain but few are masters of it—and of the few, no one that we saw surpassed the marvelous skill of this exhibitor. Were he in Spain, he would in no time make a mint with this entertainment because it makes such a brilliant show and requires such agility and virtuosity. The heavy log, a hand's breadth thick and some six feet long, is usually inscribed with carvings and painted. The acrobat lies on his back with a small pillow beneath his loins. With legs high in the air and the heavy log balanced on his bare soles he throws it up and catches it on his soles, all in strictest time to music provided by an Indian playing a small teponaztli. Some others, shaking rattles and singing, join the teponaztli player in a ring dance around the log juggler. The rattles, with their perforated heads, and granules or pebbles inside, make a brave sound. Sometimes the juggler spins the log around on the sole of one foot, very fast, wriggling the other foot simultaneously. Other times with only one foot he flings the log into the air and catches it as it descends on his bare sole, always as I have said keeping time with the beat of the music.

At great length Cibdad Real continues telling how the log is sometimes placed on the thigh, or calf, or on the back of the thigh, whence it is cast aloft, then caught on bare soles and spun around, the juggler never using anything but his feet. Or two boys mount the ends of the log, to be hoisted aloft on the juggler's soles. The boys dance and mime, all to the teponaztli

[283] "El que estaba tañendo el teponastle, que es un instrumento de madera que se oye media legua y más, erró el golpear y el compás de la musica" (p. 474).

[284] Cf. Sahagún, Bk. VIII, chap. 17, par. 3 (n. 233 above).

[285] The last captive, a converted Indian, managed miraculously to escape; it was from him that a Dominican friar heard what had happened on the island (p. 475).

[286] *CDIHE*, LVIII, 104–106.

beat. After describing other feats, Cibdad Real stops with the observation: "It would make a very prolix tale if all were told, but this sport is mentioned here because it is unique and most admirable."

As he recounts it, the spectacle becomes the analogue of a ballet. Sahagún's Náhuatl informants told him that Aztec kings and lords maintained just such acrobats: "Their deeds are marvelous; for with the soles of his feet one man lying on his back made a thick, round log dance up and down" (Bk. VIII, chap. 10).[287] The painting illustrating Sahagún's description specifies two musicians. Both sing and dance while at the same time one plays a portable teponaztli, the other a portable huehuetl.

SEVENTEENTH- AND EIGHTEENTH-CENTURY REDACTORS

As was intimated above at page 86, the well-known seventeenth-century author Juan de Torquemada said little that had not already been said by his predecessors.[288] It is therefore not necessary to quote long passages from him or from such other later historians as Boturini Benaduci and Clavijero, both of whom, like Torquemada, summarized rather than added fresh information. Torquemada did, however, add a few glosses which must here be repeated: (1) He affirmed positively that part-singing of the kind practiced in Spain was unknown in Mexico before the Conquest.[289] (2) He said that during their dances the Indians always sang in unison with the teponaztli tune. (3) He stated that the teponaztli and huehuetl players, during all the cult dances but one, were placed where the dancers could see them, and thus better follow their beat, the one exception being a dance honoring Huitzilopochtli.[290] (4) He listed the instruments Moctezuma particularly delighted in hearing at mealtime—clay flutes, reed flutes, conch shells, bones, and huehuetls—but said none of Cortés' men much cared for the Emperor's favorite music, heard invariably at all the Emperor's meals.

Boturini Benaduci's 1746 *Idea de una nueva historia general* repeats some of Torquemada's better anecdotes, in the process "improving" them. For instance, Torquemada told of Nezahualcóyotl's falsely accused son-in-law.

---

[287] Anderson and Dibble (1954), p. 30. The illustration for the log dance comes between pages 36 and 37 (pl. 64).

[288] In his introduction to Mendieta, *op. cit.*, pp. xxv–xxxii, García Icazbalceta drafted a chapter-by-chapter comparison to prove that Torquemada ruthlessly plagiarized. John Leddy Phelan, *The Millennial Kingdom of the Franciscans in the New World* (Berkeley and Los Angeles: University of California Press, 1956 [Publications in History, 52]), p. 143 n. 4, defends Torquemada. One virtue that will continue to endear Torquemada to all users of the 1723 edition is its exceptionally full index.

[289] *Primera parte de los veinte i vn libros rituales* (1723), p. 229.

[290] *Segunda parte*, p. 265. The corresponding chapter in Sahagún (*Book 2—The Ceremonies* [1951], p. 72) fails to mention teponaztli but does specify tlalpanhuehuetl, áyotl, and ayacachtli. Sahagún's informants limited themselves to saying that during this dance the musicians remained inside the tribal temples.

After keeping this son-in-law imprisoned for four years, Nezahualcóyotl learned that the charges were baseless and at once ordered the youth's release from jail. Along the way to Nezahualcóyotl's palace, the much maligned son-in-law composed a song, which he sang with great effect when ushered into the King's presence. So taken with the song was the King that he not only reinstated his son-in-law as ruler of the town of Otumba but also bestowed upon him many new honors.[291]

As if so suspenseful a story were not enough, Boturini Benaduci must heighten dramatic interest by making the accused a culprit. Because guilty, the prisoner can confute no charges. Only a miracle, a mellifluous siren's song, can buy his release. If we are to believe the *Idea de una nueva historia* (p. 97), friendly palace singers arrange the rescue. Having heard his sad farewell song composed in prison, they inveigle the King into hearing the Aloha Oe. It is this song that softens the sovereign's stony heart.

Obviously, Torquemada's tale has undergone considerable European influence when Boturini Benaduci can so alter it that a New World Orpheus emerges and Nezahualcóyotl becomes some sort of Texcocan Pluto. Enough of a Mexicanist to prefer the Náhuatl language to Latin, Boturini Benaduci still betrays his own upbringing when he insists on decking everything Mexican in lace and ruffles for the benefit of Europeans. His constant urge to prettify everything Indian ultimately recoils on itself. The pretense that the Aztecs, Texcocans, or any other tribe subscribed to a European *esthétique* not only traduces them but also shows that the writer cannot escape his own preconceived value judgments.

Much of what Boturini Benaduci wrote about cantares would be more interesting to the musicologist if he had discussed the music instead of the texts. What he said on pages 90–91 provides an example. "After gaining a battle on Ce Xóchitl [1 Flower] the Culhuas [= Colhuas] decided to institute a feast in which only new songs would be permitted: with nothing of old songs mixed in," he wrote. "Professional singers who intruded any old bits would forfeit their posts." These observations would be even more interesting if one could be sure that music rather than texts were at stake.

ABSENCE OF MUSICAL QUOTATIONS IN SIXTEENTH-CENTURY CHRONICLES OF PRECONQUEST LIFE

Doubtless the missionaries and their Indian pupils wrote down various samples of indigenous melody. Shortly after the advent of the friars, Chris-

---

[291] *Primera parte*, pp. 165–166 (Bk. II, chap. 51). Martí, *Canto*, p. 123, professed to follow Torquemada's version of this incident. Nonetheless he echoed Boturini Benaduci's misstatement. Explaining Nezahualcóyotl's reason for pardoning the *yerno*, Martí wrote: "Impresionó tanto el canto a *Netzahualcóyotl* que le perdonó la vida." This is not so. The *yerno*'s life was spared because Nezahualcóyotl learned that the charges were false—not because the yerno swayed him with song (see *Hispanic American Historical Review*, XLII/3 [Aug., 1962], 450).

tian texts began to be sung in such native languages as Náhuatl, but with indigenous tunes. Sahagún's *Psalmodia Christiana* comprises just such a collection of hymn texts in Náhuatl, intended to be sung with indigenous tunes.[292] This hymnbook, published in 1583, was (as Sahagún said in its preface) a collection of hymn texts composed several decades before actual publication; furthermore, according to Sahagún, many other missionaries had tried the same expedient of composing Christian texts in native languages, in order to give the Indians acceptable words to sing to their old tunes.

Acosta, writing on this same subject, said one of the popes had encouraged the missionaries to retain everything Indian that did not conflict with Christianity (Edward Grimstone translation):

> Our men that have conversed among them, have laboured to reduce matters of our holy faith to *their tunes*, the which hath profited well: for that they imploy whole daies to rehearse and sing them, for the great pleasure and content they take in their tunes. . . . We must therefore conclude, following the counsel of pope *Gregory*, that it was very convenient to leave vnto the Indians that which they had vsually of custom, so as they be not mingled nor corrupt with their ancient errors. [293]

Regrettably, however, these indigenous tunes, like some of the original music composed by the Indians after the Spanish arrival, seem to have been lost irretrievably. The sole surviving sixteenth-century music with Náhuatl texts is the polyphonic music composed by an Indian who followed common custom of the time in taking for his own the name of a benefactor—Hernando Franco, chapelmaster of the Mexico City Cathedral between 1575 and 1585.[294]

If no transcriptions of Aztec melodies notated during the first half century have come to light, it need not be concluded that none will ever be

[292] Sahagún's sole work published in his lifetime survives in such few copies that García Icazbalceta (*Obras* [México: V. Agüeros, 1896], III, 175) thought he owned a unique copy. Garibay, *Historia de la Literatura Náhuatl* (1954), II, 100, mentions six extant copies.

Although published in 1583, the hymns in *Psalmodia Christiana* date from a quarter-century earlier. According to Garibay, *op. cit.* (II, 99–100) the work (which comprises not Davidic psalms but hymns to Christ and the saints) appeared too late to do its intended good. This may well be so; but the Huntington Library copy (San Marino, Calif.) contains dated jottings revealing its use so late as 1640. A copy in the Rare Books Division, New York Public Library (*KE, 1583), showing signs of long and hard use, bears a Náhuatl-speaking maestro de capilla's signature at folio 169v (Antres [*sic*] Damiya *maestro*, followed by a flourish).

[293] Acosta, *Historia natural y moral*, 1954 ed. (*BAE*, LXXIII), pp. 207–208 (Bk. VI, chap. 28); translated as *The Natvrale and Morall Historie* (London: Edward Blount, 1604), pp. 492, 494.

[294] Garibay, *Historia de la Literatura Náhuatl*, II, 225; Steck, *El primer colegio de América* (1944), p. 59 nn. 95–96. For names of other outstanding Indian musicians flourishing before 1600, consult "*Indios* músicos" in Garibay's index (II, 425).

found. When it is remembered that such prose accounts as Sahagún's, Motolinía's, Durán's, and Mendieta's were not published until three centuries after they were written, that even the mangled texts of the Náhuatl songs, *Cantares en idioma mexicano,* were not published until 1899, that as yet no one has made a complete and trustworthy translation of these preconquest songs into any modern language, that publication of other important Náhuatl texts has been delayed, and that numerous sources in Indian tongues resting in Spanish and Mexican archives still await the eye of competent linguists, then it need hardly be wondered at that no authentic Aztec music—a much more fragile kind of cultural remains than writing—has thus far been published.

In the peninsula, Francisco de Salinas (1513–1590) published *De musica libri septem* (1577), containing what has been called "the first Arab tune to be noted in western musical notation." [295] Salinas also included Portuguese, Spanish, and Italian folk songs in his *De musica.* In Mexico there were certainly musicians as adequate as Salinas for the task of noting down "melodies." What may easily have happened is simply neglect; at the Archive of the Indies in Seville, just as in Mexico or Guatemala, there probably exist certain unexploited bits of indigenous melody awaiting study and publication. [296] Why have they not been found? Competent musicians do not

[295] *De musica libri septem* (Salamanca: Mathias Gastius, 1577 [*Documenta Musicologica,* 1.XIII, Kassel, Bärenreiter, 1958]), p. 339. Felipe Pedrell, "Folk-lore musical castillan du XVI° siècle," *Sammelbände der Internationalen Musik-Gesellschaft,* I (1899–1900), 372–400, rifled Salinas for sixty "folk songs." *Calui ui calui Calui araui,* p. 392 of Pedrell's article (see also *Qalbi qalb a'rabi* in J. B. Trend, *The Music of Spanish History* [London: Oxford University Press, 1926], p. 201), turns out to be something so coy as this:

Who can foresee that an authentic Mexican melody of the conquest century would look any more distinctively "Mexican" than the above looks "Moorish"? In his *Intabulatura de Lauto Libro Quarto,* 1508, Joan Ambrosio Dalza not only published the first pavanes (*pauane = padoane*) and pioneered in grouping dances into three-movement suites, but also began with a variation set entitled *Caldibi castigliano* which is "one of the most interesting of the whole book" (Robert J. Snow, "Petrucci: Intabulatura de Lauto Libro Quarto" [M.A. thesis, Indiana University, 1955], p. 14). Dalza borrows *Calui ui calui* for the "theme" of his *Caldibi.* But who now descries anything "Moorish" in Dalza's recension? Similarly, colonial composers incorporating indigenous materials have been passed by contemptuously by investigators with preconceived notions of what must be "Mexican."

[296] See "Un códice cultural del siglo XVIII," *Historia* [Buenos Aires], IV/14 (Oct.–Dec., 1958), 65–107, for facsimiles of a cantata, the music of which was composed in 1790 by three Mojos Indians at Trinidad, Bolivia, to a libretto in their own

usually have time or inclination to go foraging in archives devoted to regional history on the bare chance that, after looking through a hundred manuscripts in obsolete handwriting, an exceptional one with music will turn up.[297] Worse still, when one is found, it often gets "lost" soon after discovery. For instance, in 1922 a manuscript containing large quantities of music composed by Indians from what is now Trinidad, Bolivia, was found at the Archivo de Indias by José Vázquez-Machicado. Thirty-six years later his brother Humberto published a facsimile of the manuscript (dated 1790) but in March, 1966, no one on the staff of the Archivo de Indias could find the Indian music manuscript discovered in 1922, despite the evidence of the published facsimile!

But to return to a more hopeful note: Colonial composers in Mexico, such as Juan Gutiérrez de Padilla and Francisco López Capillas, wrote parody Masses; transcriptions are just beginning to be made or still await publication. At the moment of publishing the present book, the magnificent corpus of Mexican colonial Masses and motets cataloged in 1966–67 by the distinguished team, Lincoln Bunce Spiess (professor of musicology, Washington University, St. Louis) and E. Thomas Stanford (ethnomusicologist, Museo Nacional de Antropología e Historia, Mexico City), still awaited publication by the Music Division, Pan American Union, Washington. Already available, however, were the microfilms of this monumental material made under their personal supervision (orders to be placed with the librarian of

---

language. Don Lázaro de Ribera, governor of the Mojos, forwarded the cantata to the Spanish court with a covering note dated September 18, 1790. The three who composed the music were Francisco Semo, Marcelino Ycho, and Juan José Nosa (p. 77). Ribera's *informe*—now at the Bolivian National Archive in Sucre (Archivo de Mojos y Chiquitos, 10, Mojos V: Gobierno de Ribera 1788–1793, núm. 111)—first gained notoriety when Gabriel René-Moreno mentioned the "composiciones músicas hechas por los indios . . . que se despacharon á Su Magestad" in his *Biblioteca Boliviana* (Santiago de Chile: Imprenta Gutenberg, 1888), p. 180. How tardily this entry was followed up can be judged by the thirty-four years that elapsed before these "music compositions by Indians composed in Her Majesty's honor" were found at Seville and the lapse of another thirty-six before notice of their discovery reached print.

[297] Elnathan Chauncy, *ca.* 1639–1684, Harvard A.B. 1661, copied several bars of 3/2 music into a commonplace book that he kept while at college. The facsimile opposite p. 116 in Samuel E. Morison, *Harvard College in the Seventeenth Century* (Cambridge: Harvard University Press, 1936), shows this scrap of melody:

Before an English-speaking investigator casts stones at his Mexican colleagues for failing to identify more examples of sixteenth-century indigenous melody in the colonial manuscripts that survive at Puebla, Mexico City, or at points farther south, he might pause to consider how hard it is to identify the exact composer of even so innocent-looking a New England snippet as the above.

the Escuela Nacional de Antropología e Historia, Don Antonio Pompa y Pompa). Only when this corpus begins to be investigated with the care lavished on European products of the same periods will it be safe to rule on the lurking here or there—like nopal cactus on a 1556 title page—of an Indian *L'homme armé*. All written evidence goes to prove that the missionaries favored preserving the Indian tunes wherever possible. The surviving written evidence reveals also that the Indians who studied under Pedro de Gante, Juan Caro, and other teachers, soon learned the craft of music well enough to compose, themselves; in certain instances they composed polyphonic music that excited the admiration of their own Spanish mentors. A fortiori, there must have been Indians who could themselves notate their own tunes used for such hymns as those included in *Psalmodia Christiana*.

Another possible approach to the Aztec melodic system should here be briefly mentioned. Certain classical Náhuatl scholars, such as Antonio del Rincón, stressed the fact that Náhuatl was recited with a pronounced up-and-down inflection in the pitch of successive syllables. Appropriate accent marks, according to Rincón in Book V of his *Arte Mexicana* (published in 1595),[298] showed the rise and fall of pitch in successive syllables. If such rules of pitch as Rincón gave were applied to a collection of Náhuatl songs, *Cantares en idioma mexicano*, for instance, a graph of the melodic rise and fall might be traced. The drum notations heading the *teponazcuícatl* indicate the teponaztli rhythm;[299] might not a graph showing the rise and fall of the voice be superimposed on a graph of the teponaztli rhythmic patterns? It is not too much to expect that the prevailing shape of Aztec melody might emerge from such a composite study.[300] Preliminary results now already

---

[298] Antonio del Rincón, *Arte Mexicana* (México [1595], new ed. by Antonio Peñafiel, Secretaría de Fomento, 1885), Bk. V, chaps. 1–2 (Peñafiel, pp. 60–66). Sample observations: "Accento agudo es el que fuera de alagar la syllaba le añade vn tono que leuanta la pronunciacion con sonido agudo, v.g. milli. tlilli, accento graue es el que fuera de alagar la syllaba, añade vn sonido graue con que la abaja el tono, v.g. teotl. ciuatl" (p. 61).

[299] The fourteen songs occupying fols. 26v–31v of *Cantares en idioma mexicano* (nos. 21–34) belong to a section in the MS headed *Teponazcuícatl* ("teponaztli songs"). Schultze Jena translates these into German: *Alt-Aztekische Gesänge*, pp. 139–169.

Garibay, *Historia de la Literatura Náhuatl*, I, 157, divides the contents of this manuscript into twelve sections. Section 6 is headed *teponazcuícatl*. As Garibay lengthily demonstrates (I, 350–369), *teponazcuícatl* means more than simply "songs accompanied by teponaztli." The term, when used as title, means "theatrical songs." In the midst of each song so headed, the beat changes once or oftener to keep step with new situations as they develop in the unfolding drama. Miming and acting are the distinguishing features of *teponazcuícatl*, so-called.

[300] Vicente T. Mendoza, "Música precolombina de América," *Boletín Latino-Americano de Música* (Bogotá, 1938), iv, 244–247, claimed that the prevailing direction of indigenous melody is down, that primitive tribal melody uses fewer scale notes than melodies of civilized tribes, that an approach to formal unity can be seen in beginning each successive strophe of a long *cantar* with identical melodic incises, that

show that Aztec melody often covered so wide a range as to call for falsetto singing.[301]

THE MELODIC SYSTEM OF THE EARLY ABORIGINES

Should the methods just mentioned seem unduly roundabout, we can only reply that the Achilles heel hobbling all discussions of the Aztec musical system continues to be the lack of melodies transcribed in the conquest period. Because no tunes of clearly provable antiquity have come to light, scholars have had to guess at the Aztec melodic system. What else could they do with no better evidence in hand than melodies recorded since the 1890's (in remote sections of Mexico where it has been hoped that European influences never effectively penetrated)? A good example of an ethnologist working with the aid of phonograph recordings is Carl Lumholtz, whose two-volume *Unknown Mexico* appeared at the beginning of this century (1902). Lumholtz' transcriptions of Huichol and Tarahumara Indian melodies were all made from field recordings, and can therefore withstand the most rigorous assay.[302]

Lumholtz journeyed southward from Bisbee, Arizona. He first visited tribes in Sonora, thence passing into Chihuahua where he investigated the habits of the isolated Tarahumaras. Wending his way down the western cordilleras through Durango and Zacatecas, he next stopped in Jalisco where he spent considerable time with the Huicholes. Obviously none of the tribes he visited were descendants of the Aztecs.[303] Even had they been, it is too much to suppose that from 1519 until 1902 the musical culture of any

---

men are the singers, not women. His last generalization is perhaps not infallible. Sahagún, Bk. II, chap. 30 (Anderson and Dibble, p. 113), writes: "And the medicine [women] and those who sold lime went ranged on both sides singing."

[301] See Martí, *Canto*, pp. 186, 193. Sahagún's informants, Bk. II, chap. 26 (English trans., p. 87), mention men who dress up as women, sing in a high falsetto, and dance after "the manner of women." Transvestitism was so common at certain festivals that both Durán and Sahagún slip into the personal pronoun "she" for female impersonators.

[302] Henrietta Yurchenco, "La Recopilación de Música Indígena," *América Indígena*, VI/4 (Oct., 1946), p. 322. Herself the leading collector in Mexico and Guatemala during World War II, she laments the hundreds of field recordings in the Peabody Museum, Harvard, made by Lumholtz' contemporaries of just such tribal music as he collected, but which still await transcription and analysis. The excitement of fieldwork contrasts disadvantageously with the ennui of transcription.

[303] According to the *Encyclopaedia Britannica* (1964 ed.), XIV, 484, the Tarahumaras with whom Lumholtz succeeded in "communicating" were "descendants of the Aztecs." No ethnologist will agree. Filiberto Gómez González, "Los Tarahumaras, el grupo étnico mexicano más numeroso que aun conserva su primitiva cultura," *América Indígena*, XIII/2 (April, 1953), 114, mentions their *tutuguri* (= *rutuburi*) and *yumare* dances to the sound of "rustic violins." Campbell W. Pennington, *The Tarahumar of Mexico* (Salt Lake City: University of Utah Press, 1963), abundantly demonstrates the role of Jesuit colonial missions in acculturating this tribe.

people, however primitive, would have remained completely static. But since Lumholtz' transcriptions have been so frequently quoted to illustrate the aboriginal musical habits of the Mexicans, we must here quote several of his examples—always bearing in mind, however, the date of his transcriptions, their source, and the unlikelihood that these melodies recapture in any significant way the essential flavor of preconquest music in the proud heart of ancient Mexico, Tenochtitlan.

The first three short melodies given below were taken in Chihuahua during Lumholtz' stay with the Tarahumaras; prefacing the first song, he says: "Although the Tarahumare, as a rule, has a harsh and not very powerful singing voice, still there are some noteworthy exceptions, and the airs of the rutuburi songs are quite pleasing to the ear. These, as all their dancing-songs, are of great antiquity." [304] He translates the first song: "In flowers is jaltomate, in flowers stands up getting ripe." The second: "Ridge yonder, ridge fog."

Two Rutuburi Dances

No. 1 (Vol. I, p. 338)

Vá- sa- ma   du- lú   (-hu - ru) - si

Sae-va-gá wi-li   Sae-va- gá   wi - li   wū-ka wū-ka.

No. 2 (Vol. I, p. 338)

Rā- ya-bó   va- mí   va - mí-(ra)   Rā - ya - bó

be- mó-ko   rā - ya - bó   be - mó-ko.

---

[304] Lumholtz, *Unknown Mexico* (New York: Charles Scribner's Sons, 1902), I, 338. Throughout his long life (1851–1922) Lumholtz specialized in cannibals of Australia, headhunters of Borneo, and other exciting primitive men—always returning with a best-seller.

Another type of dance popular with the Tarahumaras at the time Lumholtz visited them was the *yumari*.

The yumari songs tell that the Cricket wants to dance; the Frog wants to dance and jump; and the Blue Heron wants to fish; the Goatsucker is dancing, so is the Turtle, and the Grey Fox is whistling. But it is characteristic of the yumari songs that they generally consist only of an unintelligible jargon, or, rather, of a mere succession of vocables, which the dancers murmur.

Unlike the rutuburi, the yumari soon becomes tiresome, in spite of its greater animation. . . . According to tradition it [the yumari] is the oldest dance.[305]

Before setting down a yumari dance with two variants, Lumholtz explained that the accent sign (>) in each of the following snatches meant a grunt rather than musical tone.

Yumari Dance and Variants

(Vol. I, p. 339-340)

The next two musical quotations were taken by Lumholtz during a short stay with the Tepehuane Indians (extreme southwest corner of the state of Chihuahua).

[305] *Unknown Mexico*, I, 339–340. Both rutuburi and yumari dances are linked to the peyote cult that dominated Huichol ceremonial life.

Tepehuane Tribal Song

(Vol. I, p. 425)

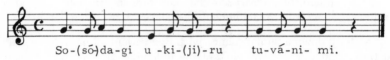

Feast Song Sung at the Appearance of the Morning Star

So-(sŏ)da-gi u -ki-(ji)-ru   tu-vá-ni- mi.

The next several examples were collected during Lumholtz' excursion into the extreme northwesterly portion of Jalisco. To judge from his printed examples, the Huichol Indians strongly favored rhythmically free melodies founded on simple triad arpeggios. Nearly all have religious texts. As might be expected, the rain songs invoke the aid of gods—the deer god in the first song, and the mother-eagle goddess in the second.

Huichol Rain Songs

No. 1 (Vol. II, p. 10)

O - to Tá - wi me - ma - nó - ti

Wa-wat-sá - li me - ma - nó - ti

Sa - kai-mó - ka me-ma - nó - ti

Ko - yo - (yo) - ni me-ma - nó - ti

To - la - hŭ - li - pa me - ma - nó - ti

Sa - kai - mo-ka me-ma-nó - ti   a - a.

No. 2 (Vol. II, p. 18)

Vae - li-ka u-i-má-li   Vae - li-ka u-i-má-li

(Va - vae -)   me - má - na   kaui   (Va -

vae-) me-má-na kaui (Va -vae-) me-má-na Kaui (Va-)

ta - hae-má-me   (me-)má-na kaui (Va-) ta-hae-má-me

(me-)má-na   kaui (Va - vae-) me-má-na kaui (Va -

vae-) me-má-na kaui (Va - vae-) me- má- na   kaui.

Lumholtz tells of having mightily pleased his Huichol hosts by learning several such rain songs as the two just given.[306]

Anticipating 1913, when Stravinsky caught "the primitive mood" by constantly changing time signatures, Lumholtz bars the next two Hikuli songs in constantly shifting meters. The first is a dance in honor of the mescal button from which is fermented the highly intoxicating liquor that induces visions and ecstasies; the other precedes a deer hunt.[307] Because of their frenetic character, Lumholtz again insists that he has transcribed none of

[306] Yurchenco found it equally expedient to learn the songs of the secretive Seris when visiting the coasts of Sonora in the summer of 1941. See "La Recopilación," p. 324.

[307] To collect peyote, the Huichol tribesmen every September or October trekked east to the plateaus where it grows. "As soon as the peyote-seekers reach the ground where the peyote grows, the leader of the band cries out 'there is a deer'—and they advance with drawn bows and arrows ready to shoot. According to Huichol belief, the peyote springs up from footprints left by a magic deer or god in the form of a deer." To go on a Deer Hunt in September or October meant therefore to make a pilgrimage for peyote, not to seek an actual deer. See Seler, "Die Huichol-Indianer des Staates Jalisco in México," *Gesammelte Abhandlungen*, III, 361.

the songs and dances at actual ceremonial performances, where he would have had only a flickering fire for light; instead, they were all recorded at the moment of actual performance and then later committed to paper. Even so, our conventional notation can give no idea of the methods used in performance.

Huichol Hikuli Dance Song

(Vol. II, p. 278)

Huichol Deer-Hunting Song

(Vol. II, p. 154)

accompanied by rubbing two notched deer bones

Commenting on these last two songs, Lumholtz again reminds us that infinite repetition of the same fragments of melody was the rule. From a narrowly Europeanized point of view such repetition soon becomes tedious, but from the tribal viewpoint the repetition of a ritual enhances its efficacy.

The Huichol instruments included their version of the huehuetl (three-legged hollow cylindrical drum with a covering of deerskin upon which the player rapped with his fingers), the four-hole flute, and the notched bone rasp. Since the typical Huichol and Aztec *instruments* obviously resemble each other, many observers have chosen to draw parallels between existent Huichol and nonexistent Aztec *melodies;* this inference is drawn easily enough: as the instruments are demonstrably similar, why should not the melodies sung in conjunction with the instruments have been similar? [308]

A sampling of melody from every tribe visited by Lumholtz would leave no room for later examples recorded by Preuss and Yurchenco. We therefore pause briefly to summarize the general principles that he deduced from the Tarahumara and Huichol melodies: (1) the melodies are preeminently pentatonic; (2) they are nonexpressive in the Western sense; (3) however, they usually end on a note that Europeans recognize as a "satisfactory" tonic; (4) their range is an octave or a tenth; (5) melodic climax is not their goal; (6) a strong, rhythmic, propulsive force informs all the songs; (7) nearly all are cult or ritual songs; (8) dance and song are twins in the native culture areas.

Lumholtz, a Norwegian, was soon followed by K. T. Preuss, whose *Die Nayarit-Expedition* (Leipzig, 1912) records his work among the Cora Indians. Frances Densmore, well-known American student of Indian music, contributed two articles, one on Pápago and another on Yaqui music, in 1929 and 1932 respectively.[309] Rodney Gallop collected two Otomí songs at the village of San Pedro Tlachichilco in 1938; these he considered authentic enough to call "the first truly Indian music which I discovered among the Otomis." His article, "Otomí Indian Music from Mexico" (*Musical Quarterly*, XXVI/1 [Jan., 1940], 87–100), accordingly begins with these choice

---

[308] Seler endorsed the drawing of musical parallels between precontact Aztecs and latter-day Huicholes (*GA*, III, 362–363). But Auguste Génin, "Notes on the Dances, Music, and Songs of the Ancient and Modern Mexicans," *Annual Report of The Smithsonian Institution . . . 1920* (Washington: Government Printing Office, 1922), pp. 657–658, strongly opposed the tendency to lump all tribes of Mexico together in one pot, and especially opposed the assumption that the civilized usages of the Mayas and Aztecs can be safely inferred from modern practices of primitive tribes. To Génin's caveats still another must be added—at least for "Aztec" dances, music, and songs. All such Aztec diversion would have to be reduced to a very low common denominator indeed if what passed for polite usage at Moctezuma II's court differed in no significant way from *macehual* entertainment.

[309] In *Yuman and Yaqui Music* (Smithsonian Institution, Bureau of American Ethnology, Bulletin 110 [Washington: Government Printing Office, 1932), pp. 154–165, she transcribes thirteen Yaqui songs (discussion on pp. 22–24). See also "Music of the American Indians at Public Gatherings," *Musical Quarterly*, XVII/4 (October, 1931), 464–475; exx. 1–2: Pápago; ex. 4: Yaqui.

bits. But he announced the thesis of his article in its opening sentence: "Nothing is rarer in Mexico than authentic indigenous melody."

During the 1940's the most ambitious recording project to date was consummated, at least so far as the tribal music of Mexico and Guatemala is concerned. Between 1942 and 1946 the New Yorker Henrietta Yurchenco showed superlative skill in inducing even the most reticent tribal singers to record for her. Her methods included (1) the obtaining of strong official backing, national and local, before visiting a remote area; (2) always paying her informants; (3) the discreet use of alcohol to wet dry throats; (4) concentration on recording itself, to the exclusion of transcription. She explains her methods at length in her already cited essay, "La Recopilación de Música Indígena" (*América Indígena*, VI/4 [Oct., 1946], 321–331). To the question that has puzzled so many collectors, not only of Mexican folk music but also of South American, "How can one tell whether the piece being recorded is indigenous or imported?" she replies (p. 328): "The hard truth is that one cannot really be sure; the best informed musical scholars themselves agree that at times the native and the foreign styles cannot be distinguished; some primitive melodies look all too suspiciously European."

Another pitfall against which Yurchenco warns is best uncovered by her own experience in Chiapas. After her first trip she would have guaranteed that the natives delighted in playing instruments, but only rarely sang. Unaware that to them the request to make "music" meant to play, not to sing, she came away with only such "music" as the piece for reed flute and drum recorded during Holy Week at Ixtepa and transcribed by Roberto Téllez Girón for her article "La Música Indígena en Chiapas" (*América Indígena*, III/4 [Oct., 1943], 310). On going back to the same Tzotzil villages in Chiapas three years later she discovered her mistake, and this time departed with a true treasure trove of song.[310]

Her archive of Cora and Huichol song and instrumental music recorded in 1944 under the auspices of the Instituto Indigenista Interamericano, the Departamento de Bellas Artes of the Secretaría de Educación Pública at Mexico City, and the Library of Congress, has served Jorge González Ávila [311] for a most useful set of transcriptions. These accompany the impor-

[310] "La Recopilación," p. 325: "Acabo ahora de regresar de un segundo viaje a la misma región e hice grabaciones en las mismas aldeas que tres años antes; esta vez hice el descubrimiento de que la mayoría de los discos contienen canciones. El por qué . . . se explica porque el canto no se considera como música ni por los ladinos ni por los indios: la música en el concepto popular es sólo la instrumental."

Raul G. Guerrero, "Música de Chiapas," *Revista de Estudios Musicales*, I/2 (Dec., 1949), 140, found his informants equally reluctant to sing. Each of the four *sones* for reed flute and drum, p. 142, is a lively 6/8 melody, strongly implying tonic-dominant harmony. Instrumental or vocal, his ten examples (pp. 138, 142, 145) fall outside our present topic, all betraying mestizo origins.

[311] *Cuadernos de Bellas Artes*, 1V/6 (June, 1963), 29. He makes no attempt to transcribe words, because "el texto cantado es ininteligible." The disks were recorded

tant monograph, "Investigación Folklórico-Musical de la Señora Henrietta Yurchenco en Nayarit y Jalisco" (serialized in *Boletín de la Sección de Investigaciones Musicales del Departamento de Música*, nos. 13–22 [June, 1963–March, 1964]; the bulletins appeared as monthly inserts in *Cuadernos de Bellas Artes*, IV/6–V/3).

The value of González Ávila's transcriptions is much enhanced by his willingness to continue lengthily with a repetitive pattern. A typical example of his procedure can be seen in the *Son del elote* ("Green Corn Piece"). In the two pages of this *son*, for instance, he puts down on paper eight repetitions of the basic formula. The changes from one repetition to the next are always minute; nonetheless, the student who sees several repetitions written out does profit thereby. Analysis cannot but reveal how aleatory are the changes from strophe to strophe. One may even question: Are the changes ever intentional?

González Ávila designates the speed metronomically. Accompanied by a sixteenth-note persistent tapping of the musical bow—this being an autochthonous instrument according to Yurchenco [312]—the following eight-bar formula constitutes the "Green Corn Piece." [313] Either the first, second, or third of the repetitions can equally well be considered the formula, so minor are the changes.

For study purposes, Yurchenco (1947) herself fortunately edited Album XIX in a series issued by the Library of Congress, Music Division Recording

---

at San Pedro Ixcatán, San Juan Corapan, Jesús María (name now changed to El Nayar), and the nearby hamlet of San Francisco, all in the Sierra of Nayarit (due north of Tepic). This duplicates the area covered by Preuss (*Die Nayarit-Expedition*, 1912).

[312] *Cuadernos de Bellas Artes*, IV/10 (Oct., 1963), 22. Since the songs accompanied by musical bow are the most primitive, since the festivals at which they are sung betray a pagan origin, and since the Coras attach such importance to the musical bow, it must surely be pre-Hispanic, argues Yurchenco. Lumholtz held the same opinion.

Seler disagrees (*GA*, III, 363): "In the same ways that the Huicholes [and Coras] obtained possession of sheep, cattle, mules, and the use of a distilling apparatus, they probably learned of the musical bow which is surely of African origin." Seler refuses to accept the music bow as a native New World instrument despite the fact that its use was already traditional among the Coras as early as 1754. In that year José Ortega, *Historia del Nayarit* (Barcelona: Pablo Nadal, 1754; repr. México: E. Abadiano, 1887), chap. 3 (p. 22 of 1887 ed.), described the musical bow used at Cora dances. Ortega's description exactly tallied with Yurchenco's published in 1947, almost two centuries later: "This is a percussion instrument consisting of a long wooden bow with gourd resonator [beneath]. An ordinary string is stretched taut and wound around the two notched ends of the bow. The bow is stretched on the gourd, which rests on the ground. The performer holds the two together with his foot, striking the string with two thin wooden sticks." See p. 3 of her explanatory pamphlet for Album XIX, Library of Congress, Music Division, Recording Laboratory ("The Folk Music of Mexico").

[313] *Cuadernos*, IV/7 (July, 1963), 39–40; González Ávila transcribes the *Son del Elote* with five sharps and changes meter frequently. New bars begin at mm 1.3, 2.1, 2.3, 3.2, 3.4, 4.2, 4.4, 5.2, 6.1, 6.3, 7.3, 8.2, and 8.4 (of our numbering).

Laboratory. This 78-rpm album is called "Folk Music of Mexico." The *Son del elote* [314] begins the second band of 91A (LC 1460). According to the record label, it was taken from a Cora Indian informant at Jesús María, Nayarit. Lacking contact with Yurchenco's informant, González Ávila failed to decipher the text. Despite his conscientious transcription of the pitches, no one who knows the recording will believe that such a piece can be penned up in the trammels of European notation.

Son del elote

[314] Labeled *Son del venado* on LC 1460 (91A). Either the record label errs, or González Ávila's transcription is mislabeled.

(5 more repetitions follow.   See Cuadernos de Bellas Artes,
IV/7, 39-40)

Commenting on the music transcribed for an exceptional article, "La lírica popular de la costa michoacana," *Anales del Instituto Nacional de Antropología e Historia,* XVI–1963 (1964), 275, E. Thomas Stanford bespoke the impotence of conventional notation when confronted with the challenge of his examples also, and the inevitable recourse to recordings for any comprehension of them. Stanford's examples require *el disco fonograbado para su difusión;* whatever other differences separate them, so do Yurchenco's.

In the next excerpt, *Son para la siembra,* two repetitions of the melodic formula sung when "seed is sown" should suffice to show again how the scheme of "slight variation" works. (As in the preceding example, the accompaniment consists of only sixteenth-note tappings on the musical bow.)

Son para la siembra

(<u>Cuadernos</u>, IV/10', 23)

In González Ávila's transcription of "The Cricket's [315] Song," the perky insect dances the same six-bar routine to the point of exhaustion. What is more, the insect's formula is so internally repetitious that almost every bar begins with an inverted mordent. Only bar 3 (second and third repetitions) breaks this rule.

Son de la chicharra

[315] *Chicharra* = cicada; *grillo* = cricket. Yurchenco explanatory booklet, p. 3, translates *chicharra* as "cricket."

(Cuadernos, IV/8, 36)

As transcribed by González Ávila, the four shaman's chants sung at the Huichol fiesta "to cure illness" [316] are freer rhythmically, but no less repetitious melodically than the preceding Cora *sones*. Antiphony now relieves the soloist from the burden of continuous singing. The tireless repetitions constantly travel back and forth between the shaman (= *maracami*) and his assistants. In all four transcribed songs of this class, swooping down from high notes is the rule. For that matter no interval is "clean" in a Western sense. Band 2 of LC 1466 (94B in "The Folk Music of Mexico") begins with the following song, recorded at Huilotita, Jalisco, 1944, according to Yurchenco's label.

Canto para curar enfermos

[316] *Cuadernos*, IV/11, p. 44; IV/12, p. 52; V/1, p. 44; V/2, p. 44.

Since González Avila limits himself to transcription and eschews analysis, it is to Yurchenco herself that one turns for comments on her recorded collections. The *American Record Guide*, 25/4 (Dec., 1958), 25/8 (April, 1959), and 33/1 (Sept., 1966), included her articles, "Taping History in Guatemala," "Singing Mexico," and "Taping History in Mexico." Her review of a record edited by E. Richard Sorenson and Philip R. Lenna, "Cora Indian Festive Music" (Folkways FE-4327), appeared in the same monthly (32/11 [July, 1966], 1090–1091). The *Journal of the International Folk Music Council*, XV (1963), contains her "Survivals of Pre-Hispanic Music in New Mexico" and her "Primitive Music in Indian Mexico: A Journey of Musical Discovery" entered *HiFi Stereo Review*, IX/4 (Oct., 1962).

A younger investigator than Yurchenco, Charles L. Boilés published his first extended analysis of field-recorded autochthonous excerpts as recently as 1966 in *Yearbook II* of the Inter-American Institute for Musical Research at Tulane University, pages 43–74 and 188–198 of which are devoted to his brilliant article with musical supplement, "The Pipe and Tabor in Mesoamerica." Limiting himself to flute tunes, he concluded (pp. 71–73) that in the indigenous examples selected for comparison, intervals as large as a fourth or fifth tend to ascend whereas smaller intervals descend, "the periods are usually formed of short phrases," "the ranges extend well over an octave," ornamentation rarely disturbs the "essential simplicity" of the melody, there are fewer notes per minute than in analogous European melody, and the final note is "in the highest register if not the highest note itself."

XTOLES

The scraps of indigenous melody quoted thus far from Lumholtz and from Yurchenco's anthologies still remain the respected property of ethnomusicology. Not so the next "native" melody. Printed as an annex to Gerónimo Baqueiro Fóster's "El Secreto Armónico y Modal de un Antiguo Aire Maya" in *Los Mayas Antiguos* (México: El Colegio de México, 1941, p. 265), a miscellany edited by César Lizardi Ramos to mark the centenary of John L. Stephens' explorations in Yucatán, *Xtoles* reached a still wider audience when the same article was republished intact in the first issue of *Revista Musical Mexicana* (Jan. 7, 1942, p. 16). Seven or eight years earlier, Gabriel Saldívar had published substantially the same air (same title) when treating "Mayas" in his definitive *Historia de la música en México* (1934, p. 72). Vicente T. Mendoza was to print it again in 1950 ("Música indígena de México," *México en el arte*, IX, 62).[317] With better knowledge than those outside Mexico possess, Mendoza (p. 61) credited not Saldívar, but Baqueiro Fóster, with having discovered the air—"which he heard as a child during carnivals in the city of Mérida as accompaniment for the Ribbon Dance or Dance of the Xtoles [= buffoons]."

On the other hand, Pablo Castellanos credits, not Baqueiro Fóster, but rather José Jacinto Cuevas (1821–1878), born in Mérida of Cuban parents (*Enciclopedia Yucatense*, IV [1944], 675), with having been the first to collect and publish *Xtoles*. As evidence, Castellanos points to a medley called *Mosaico Yucateco* composed as long ago as 1869 and republished at Mérida by Luis H. Espinosa in 1951. Cuevas unified his medley by repeating *Xtoles* three times (pp. 1, 2, 14 of 1951 ed.), but each time introduced it without

---

[317] Mendoza again introduces it as example 4, *Panorama de la Música Tradicional de México*, between pages 110 and 111. Baqueiro Fóster "reconstructed it in 1932," says Mendoza (p. 111).

baptizing it *Xtoles;* also the key and meter differ from Baqueiro Fóster's version, thus further impeding easy identification of Cuevas' version as having been the anterior. Whoever deserves credit for its discovery, *Xtoles* really came into its own when the Ballet Folklórico de México, directed by Amalia Hernández, took it up. This group, prize winner at a 1961 international festival in Paris and internationally hailed thereafter, made it for several years the crown of their opening act ("The Gods").

Widely popular as it has now become, can the melody of *Xtoles* be called an authentic hand-me-down from the Maya precontact past? Baqueiro Fóster, unwilling to pronounce on its exact age, limits himself to guessing: "By its rhythm, one could believe that it was a religious song." [318] Perhaps an analogous bit of "aboriginal" melody from the West Indies will help fix the age of *Xtoles.* The best-known "Indian" relic from the West Indies is the *Areito Antillano* which purports to be the Song of Anacaona, beauteous but betrayed queen of Haiti who was killed in 1503. The Maya *Xtoles* had to wait until 1869, but her song made its debut in an American imprint several years earlier, in Henry R. Schoolcraft's *Information Respecting the History, Condition and Prospects of the Indian Tribes of the United States* (Philadelphia: Lippincott, Grambo, 1852), II, 312. Hamilton W. Pierson [319] collected it *ca.* 1849 and published it in 1852 in the following form (metathesis changes the queen's name from Anacaona to Anacoana and the French spelling *bombai* replaces the Spanish *bombé*):

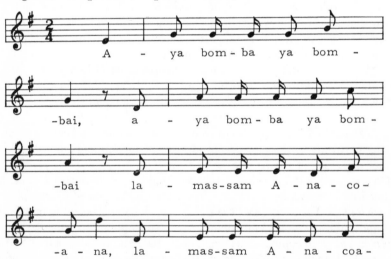

---

[318] *Los Mayas Antiguos,* p. 270: "por el carácter austero de su melodía y por su ritmo podría creerse que fué un canto religioso." But it could also have been a war song, he continues.

[319] Colporteur for the American Bible Society in Haiti *ca.* 1849, Pierson (1817–1888) was a Presbyterian minister. See *Dictionary of American Biography* (New York: Charles Scribner's Sons, 1934), VII, 591.

na   Van   van ta - va - na   do —

gai, van   van ta - va - na   do - gai.

Pierson clarifies the circumstances under which he obtained this da capo song:

The accompanying song was presented to me by William S. Simonise, Esq., of Port au Prince, a native of Charleston, South Carolina, but for many years a resident of Hayti, and one of her first lawyers. In my travels upon the island I have met with nothing else that professed to be a relic of the language or music of its aboriginal inhabitants. As to the autenticity of this song, I have neither the knowledge of music, nor other means of investigation, that would enable me to give an intelligent opinion upon the subject. I therefore submit it as it came to me.[320]

The above melody gained a new lease on life when Antonio Bachiller y Morales published it, slightly modified, at page 45 in the second edition of *Cuba Primitiva* (Havana: Miguel de Villa, 1883), with the title "Areito Antillano." But a better friend yet proved to be the president of the Academia Nacional de Artes y Letras in Cuba, Eduardo Sánchez de Fuentes (1874–1944). Composer of *Anacaona*, a four-movement symphonic poem premiered in 1928 which exploits this very melody, he reprinted the melody twice in a book issued that same year—*Folklorismo* (Havana: Imp. Molina y Cía., 1928, pp. 11, 83)—each time with the changes introduced by Bachiller y Morales.[321] In the same book he indulged in a long polemic "Sobre nuestro folklore" (pp. 79–108) defending it as an authentic melody of the Hispaniola aborigines. It remained for another much more acute Cuban, Fernando Ortiz, to point out[322] that the text of the "Anacaona Song" collected by Pierson at Port-au-Prince *ca.* 1849 had already been published in Paris in 1814 (Drouin de Bercy, *De Saint-Domingue, de ses guerres, de ses révolutions*, p. 178). In 1814 guise, the text read: "Aia bombaia, bombé /

---

[320] *Information*, II, 309.

[321] Facsimile of the Bachiller y Morales version in Fernando Ortiz, *La africanía de la música folklórica de Cuba* (Havana: Ministerio de Educación, 1950), p. 62. Bachiller y Morales changed the first note to *f♯*, the fifth to *a*.

[322] Ortiz, op. cit., pp. 76–77. Unfortunately, he mistook the order in which Drouin de Bercy and Moreau de Saint-Méry published the works cited in footnotes 163, 164. He copied the page numbers uncritically from Pierre de Vaissière, *Saint-Domingue* (Paris: Perrin et Cie., 1909), p. 179. Cf. also Ortiz' citation, p. 472, fourth line from bottom. His footnotes are notoriously unreliable, however prescient his insights.

Lamma samana quana, / E van vanta, vana docki / Aia, bombaia, bombé, / Lama samana quana!" The translation into French [323] at once reveals Pierson's fatuousness in ascribing the song to Anacaona. Instead, its origin is proved to have been purely Negro; the song belonged to their "Vaudoux" rites.

Having now allowed the footprints of this one famous Caribbean "Indian" areito to lead us to its lair, we may profitably make a comparison of "Anacaona's Song" with the equally "Indian" *Xtoles* from Mérida. Three versions are shown below: Baqueiro Fóster's (1941, 1942), Salvídar's (1934), and Mendoza's (1950, 1956 [*Panorama*, Ex. 4]).

Xtoles

[323] Translation reprinted, Vaissière, *op. cit.*, p. 179 n. 2.

Vicente T. Mendoza

Co - nex

co - nex pa - le - xen xi - cu - bin

xi - cu - bin yo - kol - kin.   Co - nex

co - nex pa - le - xen xi - cu - bin

xi - cu - bin yo - kol - kin.

These may profitably be compared with the version divulged in 1869 by the
Cuban-descended José Jacinto Cuevas, and reprinted in Mérida in 1951.

SINFONÍA INDIA

What can be made of the melodies thus far cited from Lumholtz, Yurchenco, and others? Can they be properly used to reconstruct the melodic system and the rhythmic system of the ancient indigenes? Such fragments of ancient Greek melody as the Delphic Hymns to Apollo (written about 130 B.C.) and the so-called Seikilos Song (written still later) are nowadays invoked by writers who are attempting to reconstruct the musical system in vogue among the Greeks of the Periclean age. Should not scholars who permit themselves the liberty of bringing late Alexandrian examples into discussions of music in the age of Aeschylus or Sophocles admit the equal propriety of using such indigenous fragments as Lumholtz collected in discussions of the melodic system in vogue among the Mexican aborigines of an earlier epoch?

These are, of course, merely academic questions. If, however, we ask what can be made of these melodies, this time asking not as musical antiquarians but as practical musicians, we can speak somewhat more enthusiastically in their behalf. In a country such as Mexico, which contains so many more Indians than it does persons of pure European blood, the indigenous expressions in art and music assume almost the value of national palladiums. As symbols of Indian cultural achievement in a nation so largely made up even yet of pure-blooded Indians, any fragment or shard of Indian music gathers to itself a transcendental significance. Only those who have troubled to acquaint themselves with the divided character of the Mexican national soul can realize how important it is to the formerly oppressed Indian now to assert himself spiritually and artistically, even if in so doing he lights on "aboriginal" specimens that, objectively considered, boast a very dubious pedigree.

In the United States where a competent musician such as Edward Mac-Dowell in his *Second Orchestral Suite* (1895), or Charles T. Griffes in his *Two Sketches for String Quartet* (1922), has used Indian themes, the musical result has had to stand on its own merits and not on its appeal to lineal descendants of Powhatan and Squanto.[324] In Mexico, however, even an Indian name, such as Candelario Huízar affixed to his symphony entitled *Oxpaniztli*—whether or not genuine Indian themes are used—guarantees a certain type of success that those unfamiliar with the spirit of Cárdenas' Mexico have no way of properly anticipating. If a return to the speaking of Náhuatl as a national language has not yet been suggested in Mexico, it is certain that many leading artists and musicians would bear the effacement of all cultural intrusions between 1519 and 1821 with perfect equanimity. In such a climate of opinion it is not to be wondered at that even pseudoaboriginal music stimulates more enthusiasm than a genuine colonial masterpiece.

The most widely known and universally admired composition founded on

---

[324] MacDowell, who borrowed his Indian melodies from Theodore Baker's doctoral dissertation, *Über die Musik der nordamerikanischen Wilden* (Leipzig: Breitkopf und Härtel, 1882), found in them "an occasional similarity to Northern European themes." These likenesses he deemed "a direct testimony in corroboration of Thorfinnkarlsefni's Saga" (cf. p. 1, orchestral score). For data on Griffes' posthumously published *Two Sketches*, see Edward M. Maisel, *Charles T. Griffes* (New York: Alfred A. Knopf, 1943), p. 328.

"aboriginal" melody is undoubtedly Chávez' twelve-minute *Sinfonía India*. Yet, in this unique achievement, can any surer precontact authenticity be claimed for the melodies than can be claimed for the melody Pierson collected? The Cora melody from Jesús Nayarit, which dominates the exposition of this one-movement symphony is shown at pages 146–147.

Konrad Theodor Preuss (1869–1938) obtained this melody not from Huichol Indians, but from Cora. The middle-aged informant who, in 1905, sang it into the wax cylinders that were later dispatched to Berlin for Erich M. von Hornbostel to transcribe, bore so Spanish-sounding a name as Ascensión Díaz (*Die Nayarit-Expedition* [Leipzig: B. G. Teubner, 1912], p. 377). Preuss made his headquarters during early 1905 at Jesús María,[325] and it was from this village of less than a thousand that he sent back his report "Der Mitotentanz der Coraindianer" (*Globus*, XC/5 [Aug. 2 ,1906], 69–72). The third photograph accompanying this report shows Ascensión Díaz playing the music bow (p. 71). To make him sing, Preuss had to ply him with "much whiskey." But the first session with him alone yielded a lode of ten songs, filling twenty cylinders.

Preuss's principal goal during his seven months with the Coras was linguistic. Not since José Ortega's *Vocabulario en Lengua Castellana y Cora* (1732) had anyone studied their language.[326] Also, he correlated their calendar of religious feasts. Incompetent musically, he had the good fortune to enlist as transcriber of the melody—eventually printed in *Die Nayarit-Expedition* (p. 373)—the most authoritative and best-known ethnomusicologist of the era, Hornbostel (1877–1935). The text of the song reproduced above deals with the setting of Our Father, the sun, the onset of twilight, the

---

[325] Now Nayar, Jesús María supplied not only Preuss but several subsequent investigators with a wealth of ethnic documentation. Roberto Téllez Girón's posthumously published "Informe sobre la investigación folklórico-musical realizada en la región de los Coras, Estado de Nayarit, Enero a Marzo 1939," relies more heavily on Jesús María than any other locale. See the handsome tome issued by the Secretaría de Educación Pública, Instituto Nacional de Bellas Artes, Departamento de Música, Sección de Investigaciones Musicales, in 1964 with the title *Investigación Folklórica en México: Materiales*, Volume II. The music for the popular Cora Danza del Arco was communicated by the Cora Indian informant at Jesús María, Lorenzo Sóstenes, in late March, 1939 (pp. 337–356), and the pipe-and-tabor music of the Danza de los Maromeros by another Jesús María informant (picture at p. 139), Carlos Altamirano (music at pp. 297–334). Having shown where the best veins for ethnic research lay, Preuss inspired others like Téllez Girón to follow in his footsteps. But Preuss, the earlier researcher, recorded his airs, while Téllez Girón transcribed his in the field. Téllez Girón nowhere correlates his data with "Materiales" obtained in the same specific area by his predecessors, nor does his bibliography pay credit to them.

[326] Preuss, "Reise zu den Stämmen der westlichen Sierra Madre in Mexiko," *Zeitschrift der Gesellschaft für Erdkunde zu Berlin*, 1908, p. 149. His interpreter among the Coras was Francisco Molina, the only sufficiently convinced Christian to burn his fellow tribesmen's offerings to their gods (pp. 157–158). Preuss met Ascensión Díaz at the pueblo of San Francisco near Jesús María his second month in the area (p. 158). See also "Un viaje a la Sierra Madre Occidental de México," *Boletín de la Sociedad de Geografía y Estadística*, 5ª época, Tomo III (México, 1908), p. 201.

sun's descent to the netherworld.[327] Since the concepts in the text are basically pagan, Hornbostel was surprised to find massive European influences in the melody. He could only postulate that the Coras had as eagerly accepted Spanish folk music as they had adopted Spanish violins and oboes.[328]

The Coras were reduced to Spanish rule in 1722 [329] and Jesús María at once became the center of Jesuit missions in the area. The signal success of these missions inspired the *Apostolicos Afanes de la Compañia de Jesus en la America Septentrional* (Barcelona: Pablo Nadal, 1754) by José Ortega (1700–1768). Ortega—a native of Tlaxcala who entered the Jesuit novitiate at Tepotzotlán in 1717; who, upon completing his studies, was assigned to Nayarit; and whose *Doctrina cristiana, oraciones, confesonario, arte y vocabulario de la lengua Cora* was published at the expense of the bishop of Guadalajara in 1729—in 1754 classed the Coras, when not drunk, as nearly model Christians.[330]

To say that overwhelming European influences had not intruded upon the Jesús María area before Preuss visited it in 1905 would therefore require abdicating a historian's responsibility. With acculturation already so far advanced in 1754, who can be surprised at Ascensión Díaz' waxing a melody at Jesús María in 1905 which to Hornbostel's expert ears in Berlin sounded far from purely indigenous? Only truth is served when the melody quoted *ipsissima verba* in 1935–36 as principal subject of Chávez' *Sinfonia India* (New York: G. Schirmer, 1950 [exposition, pp. 9–15; recapitulation, pp. 43–48]) is recognized as in fact betraying very strong European influences—in its intervals and in its metrical and formal organization. To go further: only its essentially European character explains how Chávez could so successfully have integrated it into a symphony written in New York City for an essentially European-minded music public.

No matter that the program notes for the Boston premiere on April 10, 1936 (55th season [1935–36], *Concert Bulletin*, p. 985), called the theme a "Huichol" melody, and that its pure indigenous sound was harped upon. The program notes erred. So do the numerous notes written since, when

---

[327] *Die Nayarit-Expedition*, pp. 220, 377–378. Spanish translation from the German in Vicente T. Mendoza, *Panorama* (1956), pp. 133–134. The music (ex. 7 between pp. 110 and 111) suffers from careless copying.

[328] *Die Nayarit-Expedition*, p. 367: "Die Melodien zeigen, in Gegensatz zu den Texten, durchweg mehr oder minder starke europäische Beeinflussung."

[329] Ortega, *Historia del Nayarit*, p. 231, mentions the founding of both Jesús María and San Francisco de Paula. Ascensión Díaz (Preuss's informant) came from the latter hamlet.

[330] *Historia del Nayarit* (1887 ed.), pp. 274–275. Eduard Seler, *Encyclopedia of Religion and Ethics*, ed. James Hastings (Edinburgh: T. and T. Clark, 1913), VI, 828 (col. 2), wrote that the Coras (at the time of his article) still retained a priest and called themselves Christian, even though after Jesuit expulsion their religious instruction had lapsed.

they call it "Huichol" instead of Cora.[331] A factual error that can creep into the notes for the concert premiere at Boston, that can be repeated in the explanatory booklet for the RCA Musical Masterpiece Series recording (M503 [12337–12340]),[332] that can rear its head in the program notes of even the Orquesta Sinfónica Nacional in Mexico City,[333] and that, very bluntly, can be accepted by the composer himself when he lauds "pure indigenous art," has long since become the property of too many vested interests to be eradicated easily.

What cannot be contested is the excellence of the symphony. When it was first played over the air on January 23, 1936, it joined two other Indian evocations (Daniel Ayala's *U Kayil Chaac* and Luis Sandi's *El Venado*). Colin McPhee reviewed the radio premiere, decreeing that all three were built on Indian motifs, but that only Chávez' symphony was a prizewinner in the group: "the Sinfonia India . . . is admirable music sharp and clear in outline." [334] Charles Seeger, whose word is law, declared in his review of the full score published in 1950 by G. Schirmer: "Without question the *Sinfonia India* is one of Chávez's best works, and one of the best produced recently in the hemisphere." [335] Richard Franko Goldman rated it thus in his review of Everest LPBR-6029:

The *Sinfonia India* represents perhaps the best kind of sophisticated primitivism we have in contemporary music, and can still [1960] serve as a lesson to all others who have tried it. Given native material of considerable interest to begin with, Chávez puts a strong and vigorous imagination to work on it.[336]

To Goldman's estimate need now be added only the proper credit line— for the "native material of considerable interest."

No one can deny that *Sinfonía India* contrasts markedly with the bow to Indian melody by that other paladin of Latin-American music, Heitor Villa-

[331] Preuss found that "Curiously enough, Huichol songs lack the recurrent beat necessary for the dance—peyote and corn toasting songs excepted. If the Huicholes wish to dance, then two musicians standing next to the shaman play homemade violin and guitar." See his article, "Reise zu den Stämmen" (n. 326 above), p. 160: "Die Gesänge der Huichol haben merkwürdigerweise keinen Tanzrhythmus, mit Ausnahme des Gesanges vom Feste des Peyote und des Maisröstens." The words for the melody under discussion (*Sinfonía India*) laud our father, the Sun, in his daily course. The religious subject would alone interdict a strong dance pulse, were it really a Huichol song. But as Hornbostel transcribed it, and as Chávez quotes it, its very veins course with the stamping rhythms of a dance (*mitote*).

[332] Information supplied by Herbert Weinstock and Herbert Brodsky was used to compose the booklet.

[333] *Inter-American Music Bulletin*, 11 (May, 1959), p. 2, quoting Francisco Agea's OSN program notes of August 1 and 3, 1958. Edward Downes, annotating "Latin American Fiesta" (Columbia Monaural ML 5914 [R63–1346]), alludes to the "melodies, which may be pre-Columbian in origin" used in Chávez's *Sinfonía India*.

[334] *Modern Music*, XIII/3 (March–April, 1936), 42.

[335] *Notes of the Music Library Association*, 2d ser., VII/4 (Sept., 1950), 628.

[336] *Musical Quarterly*, XLVI/3 (July, 1960), 396.

Lobos, whose fifty-page score entitled *Trois Poêmes Indiens* (*chant et orchestre*) is dated Rio de Janeiro, 1926. Villa-Lobos begins with a *Mouv' de Marche Lente* exploiting two Tupinambá songs collected around 1557 by Jean de Léry in the Rio de Janeiro region and first published in 1585 at pages 159 and 285 of Léry's *Histoire d'vn Voyage faict en la terre dv Bresil, avtrement dite Amerique.* . . . *Avec les figvres, reveve, corrigee & bien augmentee de discours notables, en ceste troisieme Edition* ([Geneva], Antoine Chuppin). As reprinted the next year in the Latin translation, *Historia Navigationis in Brasiliam, qvae et America dicitvr* (Geneva: Eustache Vignon, 1586), pages 128 and 219, the melodies quoted by Villa-Lobos take the following form:

Since the several Tupinambá bits rank as the sole specimens of native New World song to have reached print in the Conquest century, Luiz Heitor Corrêa de Azevedo learnedly discusses Léry's pioneer collecting activity, and traces the fate of the Tupinambá melodies in a thesis for the Folklore Chair, Escola Nacional de Música da Universidade do Brasil, published with the title, *Escala, ritmo e melodia na música dos índios brasileiros* (Rio de Janeiro: "Jornal do Commercio," Rodrigues & Cia., 1938). Villa-Lobos picked the melodies up from Guilherme Pereira de Melo, the first edition of whose history of music in Brazil appeared in 1908.

Another composer hardly less famous than Chávez and Villa-Lobos whose genuflections to "indigenous" melody can be compared with theirs is Ottorino Respighi. In 1950, fourteen years after his death, Ricordi published Respighi's *Impressioni Brasiliane*, the three movements of which are called *Notte tropicale, Butantan,* and *Canzone e Danza.* According to Mário de Andrade (introduction to Luciano Gallet's *Estudos de Folclore* [Rio: Carlos Wehrs & Cia., 1934], p. 19), Gallet's *Dois Cadernos de Melodias Populares Brasileiras* (1924) served Respighi as source. The weakness of Respighi's score cannot be explained solely by such lapses as his having quoted "A Perdiz piou no Campo" with four sharps in the signature, rather than three.

Still other comparisons with renowned composers might be drawn, but perhaps Villa-Lobos' and Respighi's attempts at garbing indigenous melodies in symphonic robes offer sufficient examples. In contrast with the authentic hand-me-downs from the Indian past which served Villa-Lobos, Chávez availed himself of material already so imbued with "massive European influences" that it can hold its own in a symphonic environment. The "native material of considerable interest" used by Chávez needed neither disguise nor heavy makeup.

FUTURE OF AZTEC RESEARCH

Mexican composers since *Sinfonía India* have faced sober reality: the more nearly authentic the tribal music, the less comfortably does it don European concert dress. Any attempt to "elevate" such tribal music by incorporating it in a symphony forces Cinderella's sisters into tight shoes and leaves a bloody trail in the Popocatépetl snow. Even were it possible to find "pure" Indian survivals today, another question arises: Who would pretend that rural music of the 1900's significantly resembles court music of the 1400's?

At best, the connecting of Mexico's present-day rural Indian music with the music of Moctezuma's court involves us in a historical fallacy. True, other historical errors have fathered gracious offspring in music history. The birth of opera *ca.* 1597 can, for instance, be attributed to a fond notion of Greek drama indulged in by certain Florentine gentlemen clustered around Count Giovanni Bardi. They were certainly as mistaken in their notions of the Greek past as was Columbus in thinking that he had landed on the coast of Asia. However far off base the musicologists of the 1930's who descried the proud Aztec past in contemporary indigenous music may have been, still a useful purpose may have been served by their fancies.

In those decades, Mexican composers were stimulated by an ideal of a Homeric age, as it were, and in their mouths was placed a rallying cry. So far as practical results are concerned it hardly matters whether such ideas on Aztec music as Chávez propagated were really accurate or not; they were accepted and believed, thereby fulfilling their purpose. Because they were indeed believed, Mexican musicians for the first time since 1821 succeeded in convincing *norteamericanos* that they deserved to be taken seriously. Scenes from the Aztec past are the culminating glory of Mexico's history, as Diego Rivera conceived them in his highly idealized versions of preconquest life painted for the National Palace. Mexican music profited for a few years from the same kind of idealizations.

But where does the "back to the Aztecs" battle cry lead in the more sophisticated 1960's? Joaquín Gutiérrez Heras discusses the problem in "Mexico's Music in Transition" (*Mexican Life,* XL/9 [Sept., 1964], 25–26, 48–51). His prognosis of the nativist's future cannot be called encouraging.

For him, the nationalist period ended abruptly in 1940, and all the worthwhile Mexican efforts at reconstruction preceded that cutoff date.[337] What came after was nothing more than a "warming over," or a "withdrawal" in search of a more personal style. In the future, he foresees that "the reconstruction of pre-Columbian music, usually based on traditional tunes, on historical documents, and on musical instruments found in excavations," will be no more than a musical game guided by the musical empathy of the composer. He reaches much the same conclusions in his important article, "Music in Transition," *Atlantic Monthly*, 213/3 (March, 1964), 112–117.

For him, there is nothing authentically Mexican, anyway, in a game played principally to attract the United States buyer. Never again can the breath of life be blown into museum instruments. The best "preconquest" tunes woven into present-day Indian symphonies have a strange way of turning out to be as purely "Aztec" as Jesús María. Any vision of a "vast treasury of aboriginal melody which can still be heard in out-of-the-way places in Mexico and Guatemala" and any belief that "centuries after the Conquest and after the initial contact between Spaniard and Indian, numerous Indian groups still preserve intact their ancient musical culture" [338] must be dismissed as a mere mirage shining with the bright glow of the Seven Cities of Cibola.

Or at least so claim the new critics. Are they right? If the works at the June–July, 1966, Festival of Contemporary Music in the Mexico City Palace of Fine Arts programmed by Manuel Enríquez, González Avila, and other younger *valores* sufficiently attest the trend twenty years after *Nuestra Música* was founded, one fact does rise clear. No young composer looks to his "Aztec" past for musical salvation. When José Antonio Alcaraz, music critic for the Mexico City newspaper *El Heraldo* and a promising composer in his own right, conducts a symposium of five young creators, Mario Lavista (aged twenty-three), Héctor Quintanar (thirty), Mario Kuri, Joaquín Gutiérrez Heras (thirty-nine; author of the articles mentioned in the preceding paragraph), and Manuel Enríquez (forty), on the topic "¿Como puede librarse México del subdesarrollo musical que padece?" (*El Heraldo de México Cultural*, no. 67 [Feb. 19, 1967], pp. 6–7), they each offer solutions for the present plight of Mexican music. But "back to the Aztecs," or back to any indigenes' music, is never the solution suggested by any of the emerging composers of our decade.

---

[337] Carlos Chávez "back to the aborigines" enthusiasm of the 1930's caused him to boast of "the knowledge of music possessed by the contemporary Indians, who still, in many regions of the country, preserve the manner of execution and the forms of the most ancient traditions" (*American Composers on American Music*, ed. Henry Cowell [Stanford University Press, 1933], p. 170). In the 1960's he had evolved into one of the professors that he criticized (p. 168), according to certain ex-pupils.

[338] *Nuestra Música*, I/2 (May, 1946), 78.

3 ACCULTURATION: THE COLONIAL PHASE

APTITUDE OF THE INDIANS

European music was taken up and mastered by the Indians immediately after the arrival of the conquerors. Such chroniclers as were quoted in the preceding chapter unite in extolling the quick talent of their Indian charges. The Indians could hardly have so soon mastered the Gregorian chant and so readily embraced polyphonic singing had they not already built up a strong musical tradition among themselves. Because the Indians showed such inordinate fondness for the music brought them by missionaries, the first bishop of Mexico instructed the missionaries within his diocese to teach music wherever they went as "an indispensable aid in the process of conversion."

A number of Cortés' own men, as is shown later, were competent singers and instrumentalists. Wherever Cortés traveled he carried professional Spanish minstrels along with his army to entertain himself and his soldiers. The Indians everywhere were fascinated with the music of these sixteenth-century "USO" entertainers and began to imitate them as soon as possible. Certain ones among Cortés' followers who were gifted musically began to teach after their warring days had ended, and a number of amusing stories are recounted by the chroniclers of the conquest period telling how speedily the Indians wheedled out of their masters all their best professional secrets.

MUSIC AS AN AID IN CONVERSION

From the moment of initial contact with the Indians, the Spaniards emphasized the primacy of music in worship. What band of three hundred would-be conquistadores would today stop negotiations with emissaries of Moctezuma in order to build an altar where their chaplain could not say, but *sing*, Mass? Bernal Díaz writes that the first Sunday after they set foot on the spot later rechristened Veracruz two Indian governors arrived on an embassage from Moctezuma; before any business could be transacted Cortés ordered an altar built, after the hasty erection of which Fray Barto-lomé de Olmedo, "who was a fine singer, chanted Mass." [1] Symbolically this chanting of Mass was an excellent prelude to the later efforts of the mission-aries who, everywhere they went, sang their services. What the Indians failed to grasp in words was at least partly conveyed in music.

Cortés' own chaplains, because of their duties with his troops, were unable to give more than incidental attention to the Indians; missionaries specifically assigned to Indian work soon arrived, however. In the summer of 1523, two years after the fall of Tenochtitlan, the first three missionaries specially picked for the task of converting the Indians arrived. One had spent fourteen years as professor of theology at the University of Paris; another—the Fleming who had been employed in state business by his relative, Charles V, before his conversion and joining of the Franciscan order—was to become known as Pedro de Gante in Mexico (see above, pp. 91–95 [2]); the third claimed Scottish antecedents. All three had spent sev-eral years in a Franciscan house at Ghent before applying to Charles V for permission to go as pioneers to Mexico, and had therefore lived in the atmosphere that produced masters such as Josquin des Prez, Pierre de la Rue, Jean Mouton, and Nicolas Gombert. At the time the three asked permission to go, Jean van Dak (= Juan de Tecto), the senior friar of the trio, was guardian of the Ghent house and Charles V had invited him to become his confessor. Their journey from Ghent to Seville before embarking was taken in Charles V's company. Charles, wherever he traveled, always carried with him his own private chapel choir,[3] which included several of the most illustrious musicians of the age. When Pedro later wrote his near relative, Charles V, claiming the Indians under his charge had already gained sufficient skill to rival the chapel singers in Charles's own private chapel, he was therefore pitting them against a choir known to be superla-tive.

The first year after their arrival in Mexico the missionaries devoted them-selves almost exclusively to Náhuatl. "This is the theology that St. Augustine ignored," was their reply to missionaries in the second wave who questioned

---

[1] Bernal Díaz del Castillo, *Historia Verdadera*, ed. Genaro García (México: Secre-taría de Fomento, 1904), I, 107: "dixo misa Cantada fray bartolome de olmedo que Era gran Cantor."

[2] For further biographical details see Joaquín García Icazbalceta, *Obras* (México: Imp. de V. Agüeros, 1896), III, 5–39.

[3] Higinio Anglés, *La música en la Corte de Carlos V* (Barcelona: Instituto Español de Musicología, 1944), p. 20.

their methods.[4] The lay friar in the 1523 group, Fray Pedro, soon founded a school at Texcoco which has been called the first school for the teaching of European subjects in America. He also instigated the founding of the first church for the Indians, the Church of San José de Belén.[5] This Indian chapel was later chosen as the scene for the most impressive pageantry in sixteenth-century Mexico. Because it was the finest and largest church in the city (larger than the primitive cathedral) it was chosen for such great ceremonial occasions as the commemorative services after Charles V's death, in which the entire civil and ecclesiastical hierarchy participated. Adjacent to the chapel was the school for Indians founded by Fray Pedro upon his removal from Texcoco to Mexico City.

Even though music was only one of several arts taught in the San Francisco school founded by Fray Pedro, his surviving portraits carry a notice to the effect that his music teaching was the subject in which he gained his most phenomenal results.[6] His own early years in Flanders doubtless prepared him for his role as music mentor, for his was of course the epoch when Church musicians everywhere throughout Europe looked for inspiration to Flemish masters. Fray Pedro was assisted in his music instruction by others who were not Flemings, such as Fray Arnaldo de Bassacio, listed as a Frenchman, and the venerable Spanish priest, Fray Juan Caro.[7] But they were all united in their belief that music provided an indispensable adjunct to worship. The music they approved for instructional purposes included the finest European art music of their period.

Pedro de Gante's remarkable success with the Indians may be ascribed to certain factors other than mere goodwill: he first learned the Náhuatl language; the schools he then proceeded to found were modeled on those maintained by the celebrated Brethren of the Common Life in Flanders; he taught the Indians and not the children of the Spanish invaders, thus eliminating any possible racial friction. His importance as an educator has been stressed by recent historians of education in Mexico.[8] The best tribute paid him, however, was the widespread adoption of his educational plan by other missionaries.

His letter dated October 31, 1532, just nine years after the advent of the band of three missionaries in Mexico, tells what Pedro de Gante felt had been accomplished in music since his arrival:

---

[4] Gerónimo de Mendieta, *Historia Eclesiástica Indiana* (1870 ed.), p. 606: "Aprendemos la teología que de todo punto ignoró S. Augustín."

[5] For a brilliant history of San José "de los Naturales" see John McAndrew, *The Open-Air Churches of Sixteenth-Century Mexico* (Cambridge, Mass.: Harvard University Press, 1965), pp. 368–399.

[6] Jesús Romero Flores, *Iconografía Colonial* (México: Museo Nacional, 1940), p. 90. Cf. *Annales de Chimalpahin* (1889 ed.), p. 284.

[7] Mendieta, *op. cit.*, pp. 412, 414.

[8] Ezequiel A. Chávez, *El primero de los grandes educadores de la América* (México: Editorial Jus, 1943), pp. 49–60.

I can tell Your Majesty [Charles V] without exaggeration that there are already Indians here who are fully capable of preaching, teaching, and writing. And with the utmost sincerity I can affirm that there are now trained singers among them who if they were to sing in Your Majesty's Chapel would at this moment do so well that perhaps you would have to see them actually singing in order to believe it possible.[9]

Had he been alone in his enthusiasm for music his labors would soon have ended abortively. But others, perceiving his results, wholeheartedly seized upon his educational plan. Numerous other missionaries wrote letters describing their successes in music education. Fray Martín de Valencia, leader of the band of twelve who came out the year after Fray Pedro's arrival in Mexico, wrote a letter to the Emperor on November 17, 1532, endorsing music as a prime aid in the task of conversion. A short excerpt will show why he valued music instruction. The training given the natives in music helped to wean them from their former beliefs; music was the sweetening added to make their new instruction more palatable.

Likewise we take all the children of the caciques (insofar as we are able to get these nobles to send us their children), and also children from other of the more influential Indian families, hoping to separate them from heathen influences by rearing and educating them in our monasteries. We devote much time to them, teaching them not only how to read and write, but also how to sing both plainchant and polyphonic music. We teach them how to sing the canonical hours and how to assist at Mass; and we strive to inculcate the highest standards of living and conduct.[10]

Motolinía, one of the same band of twelve arriving in 1524 with Fray Martín de Valencia as leader, gives in his *Historia de los Indios* several remarkable instances showing how avidly the Indians took to the music of the friars.

At the time when the Indians began to learn the Ave Maria and the Pater Noster the friars in order to make the learning easier and more pleasurable gave them these and other prayers, along with the Commandments, in their own tongue and set to a pleasing plainchant melody. They were so eager to learn, and there were so many of them, that they fairly piled up in the courtyards of the churches and shrines and in their own sections of the town, singing and learning prayers for three or four hours on end; and their haste was so great that wherever they went, by day or by night, one could hear them on all sides singing and reciting the whole catechism. The Spaniards were amazed.[11]

[9] *Cartas de Indias* (Madrid: Manuel G. Hernández, 1877), p. 52.

[10] *Ibid.*, p. 56.

[11] Joaquín García Icazbalceta, *Colección de Documentos* (México: J. M. Andrade, 1858), I, 30. E. A. Foster, *Motolinía's History of the Indians of New Spain* (Berkeley: The Cortés Society, 1950), p. 52.

Elsewhere in his *Historia de los Indios* Motolinía comments at length on the astounding facility with which the Indians mastered even the most complicated elements in the European music system.

Their understanding is keen, modest, and quiet, not proud or showy as in other nations. They learned to read quickly, both in Spanish and in Latin, in print and in manuscript. . . . They learned to write in a short time. . . . The third year we started to teach them singing and some people laughed and made fun of it, both because the Indians seemed to be singing off pitch, and because they seemed to have weak voices. It is true that they do not have voices as strong or as sweet as the Spaniards. Probably this comes about because they go barefooted, with unprotected chests, and eat food that is poor fare. But since there are so many of them to choose from, the Indian choirs are all reasonably good.

It was quite a sight to see the first man who began to teach them [part-] [12] singing. He happened to be an old friar who knew scarcely anything of the Indian language, only Castilian, and he talked with the boys as correctly and sensibly as if he were talking with intelligent Spaniards. Those of us who heard him were beside ourselves with laughter as we watched the boys standing openmouthed to see what he meant. It was marvelous that, although at first they did not understand a thing and the old man had no interpreter, in a short time they understood him and learned to sing so that now there are many of them so skilful that they direct choirs. As they are quick-witted and have an excellent memory, most of what they sing they know by heart, so that if the pages get mixed up or the book falls while they are singing this does not prevent them from singing on without the slightest error. Also, if they lay the book on a table, the ones who see it upside down or from the side sing just as well as those who are in front of it. One of these Indian singers, an inhabitant of this city of Tlaxcala, has composed unaided a whole Mass which has been approved by good Castilian singers who have seen it.

Instead of organs they use flutes playing in harmony, and the sound resembles that of a pipe organ because of the large number of flutes playing together. Instrumentalists who came from Spain taught them how to play; so many instrumentalists arrived together that we asked them to divide themselves up among the Indian towns where they might receive pay for their lessons, instead of becoming a burden on one community. The Indians have learned to make chirimías [double-reed instruments] though it cannot be said that as yet they know how to produce from them a satisfactorily tuned scale. . . .

Notably to be valued in these Indian students is their exceptionally good deportment. The teacher has to expend very little effort, for they are so eager to learn that they are soon ready to teach themselves. Indian instructors are used along with the friars in such schools as those at Mexico City and at Santiago de Tlatelolco.[13]

---

[12] *Colección de Documentos*, I, 109: "Fray Juan Caro, un honrado viejo, el cual introdujo y enseñó primero en esta tierra el castellano y el *canto de órgano*. . . ."

[13] *Ibid.*, I, 209–211; Foster, *op. cit.*, pp. 238–240.

Motolinía dated the dedication of his history February 24, 1541. For a considerable period of time before its completion he had centralized his missionary activities in Tlaxcala,[14] capital of the province where Cortés had found his staunchest Indian allies. He selected the 1538 festival of Corpus Christi at Tlaxcala to illustrate how successfully the Indians of this province had woven certain Spanish strands into the fabric of their own indigenous culture—within less than two decades.

On the holy day of Corpus Christi in the year 1538, the Tlaxcaltecas held a very solemn festival which deserves to be recorded, because I believe that if the Pope and Emperor had been there with their courts they would have been delighted. . . . This was the first day that the Tlaxcaltecas used the coat of arms granted them by the Emperor when the town was made a city. This favor has not yet been accorded any other Indian town but this one, which well deserves it, for its people greatly assisted Don Hernando Cortés, acting for His Majesty. . . . In the procession there marched a large choir trained to sing polyphonic music; their singing was accompanied by music of flutes harmonizing with the vocal parts, and also by trumpets and drums, sounding together with bells, large and small. Since all these instruments sounded together at their entering and at their leaving the church, it seemed that the very heavens were falling just then. . . .

On the following Monday they presented four one-act plays . . . written in prose. . . . One scene ended with the singing of *Benedictus Dominus Deus Israel.*

Motolinía then tells of the Easter celebration in Tlaxcala the next year (1539).

These Tlaxcaltecas have greatly enlivened the divine service with polyphonic music written for voices and for groups of instruments. They have two choirs which alternate with each other in singing the divine office. Each choir has more than twenty singers; they have also two groups of flutists who accompany these choirs, and they also use in their performances the rebec and Moorish flutes [*ajabebas*] which aptly imitate the sound of the organ. Besides these they have skilful drummers who when they sound their drums tuned with the small bells they carry, create a delightful effect. . . .

The Wednesday of the Easter octave . . . they had a play ready to be performed. It represented the fall of our first parents. . . . When the angels brought two garments, very clever imitations of the skins of animals, to dress Adam and Eve, the most striking thing was to see them go out in exile weeping, Adam escorted by three angels and Eve by another three. As they went out they sang together a polyphonic setting of the psalm *Circumdederunt me.*[15] This was so well per-

[14] Foster, *op. cit.,* p. 8. Francis B. Steck, *Motolinía's History of the Indians of New Spain* (Washington: Academy of American Franciscan History, 1951), pp. 18–19, 21–25.

[15] Psalm 114:3 (Vulgate) = 116:3 (A.V.): "The sorrows of death compassed me, and the pains of hell gat hold on me. . . ." This same psalm in a polyphonic setting by Morales was sung by the Mexico City Cathedral choir at the funeral commemoration for Charles V in 1559.

formed that no one who saw it could keep from weeping bitterly. . . . Consoling the disconsolate pair, the angels went off singing, in parts, by way of farewell, a *villancico* [16] whose words were:

Oh, why did she eat
—that first married woman—
Oh, why did she eat
The forbidden fruit?

That first married woman
—she and her husband—
Have brought Our Lord down
To a humble abode
Because they both ate
The forbidden fruit.

This play was performed by the Indians in their own tongue.[17]

Among the other plays mentioned by Motolinía some two or three seem to have shown considerable imagination and constructive skill; music was a necessary incidental in all. Most of them were of a type popular in New Spain and Spain alike during the sixteenth century—the *auto sacramental*. The blending of the various arts—scenic, literary, dramatic, and musical—seems to have been remarkably well contrived. Motolinía was understandably proud of the Christian Indian cultural achievements. Although the period between 1519 and 1538 saw the decline of many artistic customs that must have been ideal expressions of the aboriginal spirit, the assimilation of Spanish customs compensated at least partly for the loss of certain older modes of cultural expression.

The first bishop of Mexico, Fray Juan de Zumárraga (appointed in 1528), though by no means as exclusively concerned with the problems of Indian welfare as was Motolinía, nevertheless applied himself earnestly to the problems invovled in converting them.[18] Because he learned soon after his arrival in the New World that no inducement had proved so alluring to the Indians as the music of the friars, he wholeheartedly endorsed the program of music instruction which Fray Pedro had already set up in the school attached to the San Francisco monastery, and also encouraged the founding of several other schools where reading, writing, and especially music could

[16] For data on the villancico during this epoch see Stevenson, *Spanish Music in the Age of Columbus*, pp. 18, 208, 252, and examples at pp. 267–271.

[17] *Colección de Documentos* (1858), I, 79, 81–82, 84–87. Foster, *op. cit.*, pp. 101–104, 106–109.

[18] Pedro de Gante's letter to Charles V dated July 20, 1548, laments Zumárraga's death above all else because of his untiring devotion to the Indians. See Joaquín García Icazbalceta, *Nueva Colección de Documentos para la Historia de México* (México: Imp. de Francisco Díaz de León, 1889), II (*Códice Franciscano*), p. 197.

be taught the Indians. The steps taken toward instituting a full musical program in the primitive cathedral fell short of his desires; but he did appoint Canon Juan Xuárez (who arrived in 1530) chapelmaster,[19] and for a quarter of a century Xuárez labored with the Indian youths preparing and rehearsing them for musical service in the cathedral.

Despite his own Franciscan vow of poverty, Zumárraga understood the necessity of paying a trained resident choir and hiring instrumentalists if the cathedral was to be served properly. To furnish his cathedral, which started as a dependency of Seville, he spent on accessories the whole revenue of his bishopric during four years.[20] His ideal for a physical plant was a cathedral that in every detail would equal that of the parent church at Seville.[21] In musical matters he was equally ambitious. His letter to Charles V, dated April 17, 1540, illustrates not only his understanding of the unusual value of music as a tool for plowing and furrowing the Indian mind, but also his conviction that paid choirs were necessary.

He began his plea for paid choirs with no little astuteness. He pointed out to the Emperor that the Masses appointed for the members of the royal house and particularly for Charles himself were celebrated with insufficient solemnity. Zumárraga's line of reasoning ran thus:

I believe the deed of erection for these Masses obliges us to sing them, not merely recite them. Some of our cabildo, however, disagree with me. But it seems to me that it is preferable to err on the side of more rather than less in such important matters. However, since there are insufficient funds to pay the singers, and since those now singing under Canon Xuárez' direction can devote only a small part of their time (for they must do outside work), I beg you to increase the stipends of the singers.

Zumárraga also pointed out to Charles in this letter other values that would accrue from a costlier music program.

At present, numbers of the cathedral clergy are absent on business elsewhere during the week, and some that remain do not know how to sing plainchant properly. . . . Experience has shown how greatly edified the Indians are by polyphony, and how fond they are of music in general; indeed the fathers who work directly with them and who hear their confessions tell us that more than by preaching the Indians are converted by the music. They come from great distances in order to hear it, and they work hard to learn it and to become really proficient in it. Since there is no endowment to pay them, it would be well for

[19] Jesús Estrada, "Clásicos de Nueva España," *Schola Cantorum* [Morelia], VII/7 (July, 1945), 91. The date of appointment to the chapelmastership was February 1, 1539, but Xuárez had filled various musical posts after his arrival almost a decade earlier.

[20] *Colección de Documentos*, (1858), I, 24–25.

[21] See Lota M. Spell, "Music in the Cathedral of Mexico in the Sixteenth Century," *Hispanic American Historical Review*, XXVI/3 (Aug., 1946), 296.

those who sing in the choir to be freed from other business so that the Masses of Your Majesty may be celebrated with befitting solemnity.[22]

Zumárraga did not simply content himself with pleas to the Emperor, however; while detained in Spain on a lengthy visit he himself engaged various professional Church musicians and purchased manuscript choir books for Mexico City.

Music having proved itself so effective a tool in missionary work around Mexico City, it was but natural that elsewhere in New Spain the same emphasis should have manifested itself. On November 8, 1569, Fray Alonso de Peraleja wrote from Guadalajara:

We support in every religious house an Indian master whose duties consist in teaching reading, writing, arithmetic, and music. Music is taught all the boys who wish to learn it, and many have become skilful singers and players. Unfortunately, however, we can keep none of them because we have nothing to give or pay them. Were Your Majesty to order that these singers who compose the choirs of our churches and monasteries be paid, it would be accounted a deed glorious in the sight of God, and would enhance our work with those who still remain heathen. A suggested stipend would be, let us say, ten pesos annually.

We are extremely careful to see that in our churches and monasteries the Office of Our Lady is sung daily, and on saints' days to see that polyphonic music is sung, accompanied by chirimías and flutes, for the Indians find all this extremely attractive. We are also careful to see that the Indians know how to sing in their own houses at night suitable Christian doctrine and hymns.[23]

Another account may be here abridged from the Spanish. The Council of the Indies, supreme governing body in Spain, sent over to Mexico in 1568 an inspector whose duties included the gathering of reports from the various religious orders on the progress of their missionary labors. The longest account of Indian musicians who played and sang in the mission churches probably occurs in the report prepared by the Franciscans for this visiting inspector, Licenciado Juan de Ovando. The section reproduced below carries the heading, "Singers and Instrumentalists."

The Indian singers and instrumentalists who play in church gather together every day in order to rehearse their singing and playing, using our schools for a place to

[22] Mariano Cuevas, *Documentos Inéditos del Siglo XVI* (México: Talleres Gráficos del Museo Nacional de Arqueología, Historia y Etnología, 1914), p. 99: "Y porque el canto de órgano suple las faltas de los absentes, y la experiencia muestra cuánto se edifican de ello los naturales, que son muy dados a la música, y los religiosos que oyen sus confesiones nos lo dicen, que más que por las predicaciones se convierten por la música, y los vemos venir de partes remotas para la oír y trabajan por la aprender y salen con ello, y pues la sustentamos no de las bolsas, es razon que las misas de V.M. se digan con toda la solemnidad, pues se puede hacer buenamente y los que en el coro residen no se ocupen en otras cosas."

[23] *Nueva Colección de Documentos para la Historia de México*, II (*Códice Francis-cano*), p. 169.

practice. We recommend the continuation of this custom: for one thing, because without daily practice they do not progress in their singing, and for another, because they soon forget what they have learned already if they stop practicing. They can hardly practice elsewhere than at our schools.

It is customary in the towns large enough to warrant the stationing of clergy for the singers and players to divide into two groups; these alternate weekly so those who are married and have families may see them regularly. Also they need every other week free so they can earn enough to pay taxes. It would be cruel for us to allow them to serve continuously in church, doing nothing but singing. They are all so long-suffering that we feel conscience-stricken not to give then any financial aid. In each of the two choirs there are ordinarily fifteen or sixteen Indians. While a lesser number might suffice, still the thinness of their voices prevents them from sounding well unless there are at least that many. Also, that many are needed because each member of the choir both sings and plays, and therefore must have moments when he can rest. Conformable to the instructions given by the fathers, they sing Mass and the Divine Office in all the churches attached to monasteries, performing both plainchant and polyphony with agreeable skill. In some of the more favored towns where time and circumstance propitiously unite, they perform the Offices of the Church with as great solemnity and with as impressive music as can be encountered in many of the cathedral churches of Spain itself.

Polyphonic music is the vogue everywhere, and accompaniment of flutes and chirimías is common. In a number of places dolcians [*dulzainas*] and reeds [*orlos*] along with viols [*vihuelas de arco*] and other types of instruments are used. Organs are also found in a number of places.

The Indians themselves play all these instruments, and their harmonious sounding together is truly a wonderful allurement toward Christianity as far as the generality of the natives is concerned. The music is most necessary. The adornment of the church itself and all the beauty of the music lifts their spirits to God and centers their minds on spiritual things. They are naturally inclined to be careless and forgetful unless they are reminded of the unseen by the seen and the unheard by the heard. Because of their very tendency to forget and to neglect, their own governors during the times of their infidelity made a point of occupying them incessantly in the building of huge and sumptuous temples, and also in the adornment of them with numberless beautiful flowers, requiring them, moreover, to offer gifts of gold and silver, and to participate in endless sacrifices and ceremonies, more severe and arduous than those imposed by the law of Moses.[24]

After serving as procurator for the entire Franciscan order in Rome, Diego Valadés published his *Rhetorica Christiana* (1579), containing a large full-sheet copper engraving of an Aztec ceremony. Between pages 168 and 169, this engraving shows eight pairs of dancers circling about a public square in front of a temple, with two musicians at the "gospel" side playing

[24] *Ibid.*, pp. 65–66.

teponaztli and huehuetl and another accompanist between the viewer and the altar playing a teponaztli set on a trestle. Born at Tlaxcala a dozen years after Cortés subdued the capital, Valadés cannot have been an eyewitness to a precontact ceremony. But what he reports of the magnificence with which the indigenes celebrated Christian ceremonies (chap. 25, pt. 4 [pp. 226–227]) can on no account be impugned. His extensive traveling convinces him that nowhere in Spain does the splendor of the cult exceed the mode of celebrating festivals among the Indians of New Spain. Written in Latin, his report not only bolsters the best boasts of accounts in Spanish, but also adds piquant details. He alludes to the Indian waits who ascended into high church towers to mix their native teponaztlis and other drums with Spanish instruments and with the tintinnabulation of the bells, bells, bells (sometimes antiphonally, sometimes together). Their dawn and dusk concerts threw the whole community into joyous expectation and delirious excitement, reports Valadés. He also knows that critics complain of these "Christian" fiestas as being the old pagan rites with nothing changed but the name of the patron. As a native-born Mexican (Spanish father, Indian mother) he refuses to agree.

The Franciscans were, of course, the first order to undertake the conversion of the Indians. The Dominicans arrived in 1526, and the Augustinians followed in 1532. Juan de Grijalva's *Cronica dela Orden de N. P. S. Augustin en las prouincias dela nueua españa En quatro edades desde el año de .1533 hasta el de .1592* (México: Juan Ruyz, 1624) testifies no less frequently to the native appetite for European music than do the Franciscan chronicles of the same sixty years.[25] After the three orders already named, a fourth, the Society of Jesus, entered Mexico in 1572. Andrés Pérez de Ribas (1576–1655), a Jesuit, testified a century after the conquest that in his experience music instruction and performance were still one of the best means of attracting and holding the Indians. Jesuit Indian work was concentrated in northwestern Mexico; but the Jesuits also maintained a *seminario* for Indian youths at Mexico City enrolling ordinarily some fifty *colegiales* at the time Pérez de Ribas wrote his *Historia de los trivnfos de nvestra santa fee entre gentes las mas barbaras* (Madrid: Alonso de Paredes, 1645). Wherever they worked in Sinaloa and Sonora, they founded schools for apt

---

[25] In 1556 Augustinians sponsored the first New World music publication. See pp. 175–178. Their Indian work proved especially successful in what is now the State of Hidalgo, north of the State of Mexico. Vicente T. Mendoza, "Música Indígena Otomí: investigación musical en el Valle del Mezquital (1936)," *Revista de Estudios Musicales* (Mendoza, Argentina), II/5–6 (Dec., 1950–April, 1951), 370–371, 383, 399, 401, 414–415, 417, 452–453, 458, 460–463, 465–466, quotes Grijalva, sometimes at great length. See especially pp. 452, 458, 463. No Augustinian church lacked an organ. To train organists, a talented youth from each village was sent at community expense to Mexico City, where his keep and instruction were paid for. Players of other instruments were trained in each village.

Indian children; "reading, writing, and music" were always the three R's.[26] But music in the villages was rustic compared with that in the capital. Each year at Mexico City the privileged Indian youths enrolled in San Gregorio staged several big entertainments of the kind that would today be called "folklore festivals." Pérez de Ribas devotes an entire chapter (Bk. XII, chap. 11) to "Moctezuma's mitote," the dance-and-music extravaganza offered the public every Mardi Gras by the San Gregorio *colegiales*.

The first remarkable attraction of this mitote is the costuming of the dancers, who come out decked in all the finery of Mexico's former rulers. . . . In his right hand the dancer grasps an ayacachtli—a small pumpkin on a handle with rattling pellets inside. He shakes this, keeping time with the dance beat, and the sound is fascinating. . . . The platform for the festival is strewn with fragrant flowers. The seat of honor is Moctezum's icpalli, which looks like a low gilded stool. A teponaztli on a stand is placed at one side of the stage. This instrument guides both dance and song. Made of fine wood, painted or carved, the teponaztli is played with rubber-tipped sticks. The two facing keys are cut above a hollowed-out interior. No European instrument resembles the teponaztli. However, under Spanish influence three other instruments are now often added to the native ensemble: harp, cornett, and bassoon.[27] Around the huehuetl huddle the older Indian nobility. They sing—singing always being a necessary part of the Mexican dance—but avoid any agitated steps. As a rule there are fourteen dancers, not counting the Emperor Moctezuma who enters toward the close. . . . At the moment when the dancers emerge from the palace, their song has these words: "Go forth, Mexicans! Dance the Tocontín, for the King of Glory has entered our ranks." [28] The three syllables of the word *Tocontín* imitate the sound that the teponaztli makes and from these sounds the dance takes its name.[29] The dancers come out in double file, as in the Spanish *hacha*.[30] The majestic movements of feet, hands, and arms keep pace with the *largo* of the dance beat. . . . After Moctezuma enters and all have paid him due reverence, the tempo picks up. Then he rises to dance alone, and with three children attending him. Upon his passing between the two files of dancers, each prostrate dancer shakes his

[26] Pérez de Ribas, *Historia* (México: Luis Álvarez y Álvarez de la Cadena, 1944), I, 231; II, 122, 252. Pérez de Ribas reprehends trying to teach music merely "by ear"; the child must begin by learning to read and write (II, 122: "porque era menester enseñar primero a escribir, leer y luego el punto de canto a los músicos y escoger voces."

[27] According to Mendoza, "Música Indígena Otomí," p. 443, a sixteenth-century mural in a small Indian church of the Valley of Mezquital pictures a band of angelic musicians playing harp, trumpet, shawm, and teponaztli—in concert.

[28] Mendoza, *Panorama de la Música Tradicional* (México: Imprenta Universitaria, 1956), pp. 159–161, prints six *toco[n]tines* dated 1620, 1625, 1640, and 1651.

[29] See above, pp. 50n–51n.

[30] Juan de Esquivel Navarro, *Discvrsos sobre el Arte del Dançado* (Seville: Juan Gómez de Blas, 1642), fol. 38, classed the *hacha* (torch dance) with the españoleta, English branle, and tourdion as a traditional court dance. In ternary meter, the hacha moved in *grave*.

ayacachtli around Moctezuma's passing feet. The Emperor next retires to his seat and the dancers rise to renew their various routines, all of which are intriguing and never grow monotonous. What is sung (and the singing never stops) always corresponds with what the teponaztli plays. Two choirs answer back and forth: one, the group around the huehuetl; the other, an antiphonal choir placed behind a curtain or a lattice. Finally, be it said that this dance with its splendid costuming, apparatus, movements, and song, has been praised by the very highest Spanish authorities and has been imitated by the flower of Spanish youth. With such endorsement, it certainly belongs among the school exercises of the Indian youth enrolled at San Gregorio. The mitotes in vogue among the macehuales and vassals are another matter. Commonplace and lacking in any distinction, the ordinary mitote cannot be compared with the dance traditional among Indian ruling families.[31]

It is quite probable that the level of musical ability declined among the missionaries sent out during the later colonial period. Only a few of the later missionaries in what is now the southwestern part of the United States can have come into the field with so extensive a background of training as Pedro de Gante.[32] But where one did appear in California, Felipe Arroyo de la Cuesta for example, musical emphasis was still found an invaluable aid in the conversion process. Elsewhere also, music training given by competent instructors still proved invaluable. Anthony Sepp (who had received his own thorough musical training at Augsburg) found that "one secret of [his] popularity among the Indians was his decided talent and love for music."[33] Sepp's "brilliant success in the musical training of the Indians" won him a large "harvest" of converts, and "being the first to have introduced harps, cornet[t]s, clari[o]nets, and organs into these parts, [he] has earned for him[self] undying praise."[34]

Many other notable examples of missionary success traceable, on the human level at least, to emotional conditioning through music have been culled from Jesuit missionary documents and published in Guillermo Furlong, *Músicos Argentinos durante la dominación hispánica* (Buenos Aires: Talleres Gráficos de San Pablo, 1945), Pedro J. Grenón, "Nuestra primera música instrumental," *Revista de Estudios Musicales*, II/5–6 (Dec., 1950–

---

[31] Pérez de Ribas, *op. cit.*, III, 326–327. All comments not relating to the music of the tocontín have been abbreviated or paraphrased. Neither Martí, *Canto, danza y música precortesianos*, 1961, nor Martí-Kurath, *Dances of Anáhuac*, 1964, indexes the tocontín, despite its preconquest origins.

[32] Rafael Montejano y Aguíñaga, "La Conversión de los indios por medio de la música," *Schola Cantorum: Revista de Cultura Sacro-Musical* (Morelia), Año IX, Núm. 9 (Sept., 1947), pp. 134–136.

Montejano y Aguíñaga continued his monograph in *Schola Cantorum*, IX/11 (Nov., 1947) and 12 (Dec., 1947).

[33] Angela Blankenburg, "German Missionary Writers in Paraguay," *Mid-America* (Chicago), XXIX [n.s., XVIII] (Jan., 1947), 43.

[34] *Ibid.*, p. 44. (Quoted from a letter written June 15, 1729, by Matthias Strobel.)

April, 1951), Serafim Leite, *Artes e ofícios dos Jesuítas no Brasil* (*1549–1760*) (Lisbon: Edições Brotéria, 1953), and other books. The medal for being the first to apply a successful missionary technique should be struck in Pedro de Gante's honor, however, for it was he who first showed the way.

THE RESULTING SUPERFLUITY OF INDIAN SINGERS AND INSTRUMENTALISTS

The gathering of further statements attesting the Mexican Indian's extraordinary fondness for music would be an easy task, simply because so many of the friars mentioned the role music played in winning tribes to Christianity. But if we can appreciate why the early friars so gladly inaugurated music instruction, we still perhaps cannot quite understand why such large numbers of Indians gladly undertook careers as professional Church musicians, especially when the friars were not usually able to pay them living wages. The problem of oversupply in the number who presented themselves for service as musicians was studied by the president of the second audiencia, Bishop Sebastián Ramírez de Fuenleal. Fuenleal ascribed the plethora of Church musicians (1) to the prestige they enjoyed among their fellow Indians by virtue of their profession, and (2) to the exemption from taxation they often enjoyed. Both these advantages descended to them from their preconquest antecessors. As Fuenleal remarked, "Among the Indians [before the conquest] instrumentalists and singers were highly esteemed, because by means of songs their musicians preserved the memory of the past; and not only was respect given those who devoted themselves to music but also the privilege of exemption from taxation." [35]

The first official notice of the excessive number of singers and instrumentalists was taken at the initial Church council called by Archbishop Alonso de Montúfar. The printed provisions of this council, which were published in 1556, the year after the meeting of the council, explain what had taken place.

The great excess in our archdiocese of musical instruments, of chirimías, flutes, viols, trumpets, and the large number of Indians who spend their time in playing and singing obliges us to apply a remedy and to place a limit on all this superabundance. We therefore require and order that from henceforth trumpets shall not be played in churches during divine service, and require that no more be bought; those that are already in possession of the churches shall be used only in outdoor processions, and not as accompaniment for the liturgy. As for the chirimías and flutes, we require that they be stored in the principal towns and distributed for use in the villages only on festival days of their patron saints; and as for viols and other instruments, we request that these too be no longer used; we urge all the clergy to install organs everywhere so that indecorous and improper instruments may be banished from the Church. The organ is the correct

[35] Quoted from Henri Ternaux-Compans, *Voyages, Relations et Mémoires* (Paris: Arthus Bertrand, 1840), XVI, 218–219, in Montejano y Aguíñaga, *op. cit.*, p. 134.

instrument for use in the Church, and we wish its use to become universal in Mexico.

We charge all clergy in our archdiocese, and all other clergy in Mexico residing outside our archdiocese but under our spiritual jurisdiction, carefully to limit the number of singers throughout our jurisdiction so that no more than are necessary shall continue to spend their time simply in singing. Those who are permitted to continue must be able to sing plainchant intelligently. They shall sing polyphonic music only when their singing conforms to standards which we consider acceptable.[36]

. . . .

Because of the vast number of churches that have sprung up everywhere in our archdiocese, proper regulation has proved difficult. . . . We therefore decree that only those which in the judgment of the Ordinary seem really necessary shall be permitted to continue; the others shall be taken down. Those that remain shall be decently equipped with all the proper furnishings and ornaments. No more Indians than are absolutely necessary shall be permitted to become choristers and custodians. They should be few in number, and should live lives that are without blemish or spot. They moreover should know the doctrines of our holy faith and the traditional customs of the Church. They should be married and not bachelors, and they should be persons who know how to give sound instruction in doctrine to those who are still ignorant.[37] . . . Indian catechists who work in villages where there are no priests must be able to sing the various prayers, so they can teach the people.[38] . . . The Indian singers shall be examined by the clergy who know the native languages, and shall not be permitted to sing songs that remind the people of their old idolatrous customs; they shall sing nothing that savors of heathenism or that offends against sound doctrine.[39]

. . . .

The Indians of this nation continue to delight in the kind of dancing, of festivity, and of mirthmaking that they delighted in during the days of their heathenism; but in order to avoid contamination from customs that may contain seeds of evil, we ask (as said the Apostle Paul) that the appearance of evil be avoided. . . .[40] Furthermore they shall not begin dancing before the hour of High Mass; they may dance, however, during the afternoon and in the evening.

No more convincing proof need be given than these extracts from the printed proceedings of the council to show with what extravagance the Indians had taken to the music of the friars. One chronicler caustically remarked that the Indians liked Mass best when it was an instrumental concert as well. But churches in Mexico during this period were by no means unique in allowing a wide assortment of wind and string instruments.

[36] *Constituciones del arçobispado* . . . *de Tenuxtitlan Mexico* (México: Juan Pablos, 1556), fol. xxxiii recto (cap. 66).

[37] *Ibid.*, fol. xix recto (cap. 35).

[38] *Ibid.*, fol. xxxiii verso (cap. 66).

[39] *Ibid.*, fol. xxxv recto (cap. 72).

[40] *Ibid.*, fol. xxxiv verso (cap. 72).

They were commonplace even in the chapel music at Charles V's court. His chapel payroll included salaries for eight trumpeters and four drummers [41] in addition to salaries for woodwinds and strings. More austere than Charles, Philip preferred plainchant woven in a polyphonic web, rather than Masses parodying *Mille regretz;* and the instruments accompanying his "Spanish Chapel" rarely went beyond organ and bassoon.[42] Even so, a cappella polyphony never prospered anywhere in Renaissance Spain; and Victoria himself began publishing his Masses with organ accompaniment as soon as he relocated in Castile (1592, 1600).

It is only to be expected, then, that in Mexico as in the Peninsula instrumental accompaniment should have been the invariable rule. What the First Mexican Council denounced was not instrumental accompaniment as such, but the unmanageable superfluity of Indian instrumentalists. Philip II was not slow in adding the force of his authority to the decisions of the bishops. In February of 1561 he issued to the president and oidores of the royal audiencia a cedula that read in part:

> Because of the cost of maintaining the present excessive number of instrumentalists who consume their time playing trumpets, clarions, chirimías, sackbuts, flutes, cornetts, dulzainas, fifes, viols, rebecs, and other kinds of instruments, an inordinate variety of which are now in use in the monasteries, . . . and because the number of musicians and singers is reported to be increasing constantly in both large and small towns, . . . and because very many of those reared simply to sing and play on instruments soon become lazy scoundrels whose morals are reported to be extremely bad, . . . and because in many places they do not pay tribute and resist lawful authority, we require a reduction in the number of Indians who shall be permitted to occupy themselves as musicians.[43]

Even Philip's strongly worded cedula, enforcing as it did the decisions of the First Mexican Council, failed to procure the desired results; the Second Mexican Provincial Council meeting in 1565, a decade after the First Council, was again forced to occupy itself with the same problem. In addressing itself October 11, 1565, to Philip, the Second Council petitioned: "Item, that Your Higness order a further abatement in the excessive number of Indian singers; . . . the small payment they now receive almost always is insufficient for them even to eat, much less pay tribute." [44]

[41] Anglés, *op cit.*, p. 23.

[42] Isabel Pope, "The 'Spanish Chapel' of Philip II," *Renaissance News*, V/2 (Summer, 1952), 36. For Philip II's personal tastes, see R. Stevenson, *Spanish Cathedral Music in the Golden Age* (Berkeley and Los Angeles: University of California Press, 1961), pp. 331–332, 341 n. 151.

[43] Genaro García, *Documentos inéditos ó muy raros para la historia de México* (1907), XV, 141–142.

[44] *Colección de Documentos Inéditos . . . del Archivo de Indias* (Madrid: J. M. Pérez, 1870), 1ª sér., XIII, 287.

In general, throughout the sixteenth century prelates and the secular clergy favored a drastic curtailment in the numbers of Indians whom the regulars, that is to say the friars, were willing to place in such semiofficial church positions as janitors, building custodians, decorators, music instrument makers, and players and singers. Since Montúfar was himself a Dominican, the members of his own order perhaps took his injunctions seriously, but the Franciscans and even the Augustinians seem at times blandly to have disregarded him. Admirable men often disagreed on vital points of missionary procedure during the sixteenth century, as the clash between the Dominican Las Casas and the Franciscan Motolinía on mass baptism of Indians illustrates. Because of this possibility of disagreement, Indian musical life could continue to flourish, at least in Franciscan environments, long after Church councils had ordered an abatement, and after Philip II had himself intervened to halt the excess.

High secular and ecclesiastical authorities had to keep reminding Indian singers, even as late as the end of the century, that they could no longer expect the tax exemptions and high social status that their preconquest forebears had enjoyed. And, similarly, Indian musicians had to be reminded that, whatever kindnesses had been done them by the friars, in the minds of bureaucratic bishops their place in God's economy was as Gibeonite hewers of wood and drawers of water rather than as children of the covenant.[45]

Saldívar, during his epoch-making investigation of Mexican colonial music, found a petition presented by a group of Indian singers who prayed Viceroy Martín Enríquez in 1576 for relief from the tribute. Enríquez roughly reminded them that they must pay it like every other Indian, no matter how poor they were or how little they received for their services as Church musicians. Saldívar also unearthed evidence to show that the cash salaries paid a sampling of 1,376 Indian singers averaged during Enríquez' administration only a little more than two pesos annually. Even this munificent cash salary was begrudged by Spanish self-styled grandees. It is of course well known that many prelates came to regard the Mexican Church simply as a choice haven for impecunious immigrants. In the 123 towns whose records

---

[45] For a striking illustration of the changed attitude toward the Indian, see Alonso de Montúfar, "Carta del Arzobispo de Mexico al Consejo de Indias Sobre la Necesidad de que los Indios Pagasen Diezmos" [May 15, 1556], *Anales del Museo Nacional de Arqueología, Historia y Etnografía*, 5ª época, I/3 (July–Dec., 1934), 355. True, Montúfar voiced his complaint against the "ornamentos mui ricos e ynstrumentos de música, mejores y más que los ay en la capilla de Su Magestad" and against the "cantores" and those who played "cheremias y sacabuches y trompetas y orlos y dulçainas y cornetas y en muchos monesterios ay bigüelas de arco" under cloak of protecting the Indians from too much free service to the friars. The letter itself, credited to the Archive of the Indies (Papeles de Simancas, Est. 60, Caj. 4, Leg. 1 [Libro de Cartas]), eloquently testifies to the artistic zeal of the Augustinians, who in that very year of 1556 were sponsoring publication of the first New World music imprint.

Saldívar studied, the average number of Indian Church musicians was 11.2, a figure that in some instances represented instrumentalists as well as singers. Since the towns included in this count were often mere hamlets or villages numbering a total population of hundreds rather than thousands, a figure of eleven musicians for each is quite sufficient proof that Mendieta and Torquemada knew their arithmetic when they boasted of the tremendous interest the Indians took in music. But the average cash salary paid the 1,376 Indian singers whose records Saldívar studied reached only about 4 percent of the average cash salary paid Spanish and Creole singers who functioned at the same time in the important metropolitan churches of New Spain.[46]

THE MUSICAL ACHIEVEMENT OF INDIAN CHOIRS

As Torquemada summed up the achievement of sixteenth-century Indian choirs when he wrote his *Monarquía Indiana* (published in 1615), their record seems notable.

1) Without receiving any lavish gifts of choirbooks, the Indians nevertheless were able to create splendid libraries of Church music by painstakingly copying books brought over by Zumárraga and his deputies.

After they had learned to write, they then learned how to draw lines on paper and write music notes; they then made excellent copies both of plainsong and of polyphonic music in large letters suitable for use in choirs. Their copies were used by the friars as well as by themselves, and were beautifully done with illuminated letters throughout.[47]

2) By sharing among themselves the teaching that certain privileged ones were able to get from Spanish masters, musical culture of the European type became sufficiently diffused for them to develop polyphonic choirs, even in their smaller villages.

Nowadays every town of one hundred population or more contains singers who have learned how to sing the Offices, the Mass, Vespers, and are proficient in polyphonic music; competent instrumentalists are also found everywhere. The small towns all have their supply of instruments, and even the smallest hamlets, no matter how insignificant, have three or four Indians who sing every day in church. Especially is this true in the provinces of Michoacán and Jalisco.[48]

---

[46] Gabrial Saldívar, *Historia de la Música en México* (1934), pp. 90–94. For an index of the volume from which he extracted his data, see Luis Chávez Orozco, *Índice del Ramo de Indios del Archivo General de la Nación* (México: Instituto Indigenista Interamericano, 1951), pp. 4–30 (Vol. I, Expediente 46 [fol. 18v], 93 [35v], 95 [36], 96 [36], 115 [42v], 116 [43], 138 [51v], 165 [61], 167 [61v], 168 [61v], 176 [64v], 321 [144v], 329 [147], 338 [150]).

[47] Juan de Torquemada, *Tercera parte de los veinte i vn libros rituales* (1723), p. 213, col. 2 [Bk. XVII, chap. 3].

[48] *Ibid.*, p. 214, col. 1.

3) Because the Indians, in addition to making their own instruments, soon developed among themselves the art of fabricating clever imitations of European instruments brought over by the invaders, they were able to develop instrumental accompanying ensembles with unique and unforeseen tone color possibilities.

The first instruments of music manufactured here were flutes, then oboes, and afterwards viols and bassoons and cornetts. After a while there was no single instrument used in churches which Indians in the larger towns had not learned to make and play. It became unnecessary to import any of these from Spain. One thing can be asserted without fear of contradiction; in all Christendom there is nowhere a greater abundance of flutes, sackbuts, trumpets, and drums, than here in New Spain. Organs have also been installed here in nearly all the churches which are administered by the orders. However, with these, not the Indians but rather Spanish builders have taken charge of construction, since the Indians do not have capital for such larger enterprises. The Indians make the organs under supervision, and they play the organs in our monasteries and convents. The other instruments which serve for solace or delight on secular occasions are all made here by the Indians, who also play them: rebecs, guitars, trebles, viols, harps, spinets.

So far as centers of instrument-making were concerned, Pátzcuaro in Michoacán took the lead as early as 1586 in making "bells, trumpets, flutes, and shawms for all New Spain." Nearby Tzintzuntzan, capital of the Tarascans, specialized in *trompetas y chirimías.*[49]

4) Indian musical accomplishment was by no means limited to clever imitation of European performance, but included also a certain amount of original creative activity in the European idiom.

With this I conclude (and this is an important observation): only a few years after the Indians began to learn the chant, they also began to compose. Their villancicos, their polyphonic music in four parts, certain masses and other liturgical works, all composed with adroitness, have been adjudged superior works of art when shown Spanish masters of composition. Indeed the Spanish masters often thought they could not have been written by Indians.[50]

MUSIC PRINTING DURING THE SIXTEENTH CENTURY

At least 220 books were published in Mexico during the sixteenth century. A

[49] [Antonio de Cibdad Real], *Relación breve y verdadera* (*Colección de Documentos Inéditos para la Historia de España,* LVII [Madrid: Vda. de Calero, 1872]), 532 (Pátzcuaro), 538 (Tzintzuntzan). Pátzcuaro today remains the "holy city" of the Tarascans. See Nicolás León, "Los Indios Tarascos del Lago de Pátzcuaro," *Anales del Museo Nacional de Arqueología, Historia y Etnografía,* 5ª ép., I/1 (1934), 152. In certain out-of-the-way Indian villages of Jalisco and Nayarit the fabrication of long-obsolete Spanish string instruments still remained a specialty when Léon Diguet wrote his "Le Chimalhuacan et ses populations avant la Conquête espagnole," *Journal de la Société des Américanistes,* n.s., I/1 (1903), 13–14.

[50] Torquemada, *op. cit.,* III, 214. Most of what Torquemada says on this page copies Mendieta, *op. cit.,* pp. 412–413.

large proportion of these were printed in Indian tongues. Grammars, dictionaries, and religious tracts were published in at least ten Indian languages, including Náhuatl, Otomí, Tarasco, Maya, Zapotec, Huastec, Mixtec, Utlatec (= Quiché), Tzotzil, and Chuchon. Those who controlled the press obviously had no intention of neglecting the Indian. The books published in Spanish included treatises on navigation, medicinal herbs, and surgery; leaflets on how to teach reading and elementary arithmetic; records of notable current events such as earthquakes; stories of voyages and explorations; and a large number of devotional texts.

Of the 220-odd Mexican imprints, thirteen contained music. The first such book appeared in 1556, thirty-five years after Cortés crushed the Aztec nation. The remainder was published between 1560 and 1589. No other colony except Mexico rang up such a record of liturgical imprints containing music. Even at Lima, in Peru, where another viceroyalty whose importance equaled that of Mexico had its seat, no missals, antiphoners, or graduals, were printed; true printing started in Lima forty-five years later than in Mexico. But in most respects, except for the printing of liturgical books, both Lima and Mexico presses followed a similar course.

In both capitals the first book was a manual of Christian doctrine in an Indian tongue. The 1539 *Breve y mas compendiosa doctrina* published at Mexico City in the language of the Aztec was the counterpart of the 1584 *Doctrina christiana* published at Lima in the language of the Incas.[51] The first printers in both capitals were Italians, and from the beginning printing was rigidly circumscribed by government regulations. From both presses flowed a stream of titles betraying similar cultural interests. The literary life in both capitals followed a parallel course; a long heroic poem such as Pedro de Oña's *Arauco domado* (1596), published in Lima, was soon joined by another similarly ambitious poem on a New World theme, Bernardo de Balbuena's *Grandeza Mexicana* (1604), published in Mexico.[52] These comparisons between the cultural life of Mexico and of the other Hispanic colony nearest it in political importance, Peru, reinforce the capital importance of the music books now to be discussed. If it is not further recognized

[51] *Cartas de Indias* (Madrid: Manuel G. Hernández, 1877), p. 787, col. 1, lists the 1539 Mexican *doctrina*, but Zumárraga's letter of May 6, 1538 (p. 786, col. 2), vouches for earlier printing. The first Mexican imprint, a copy of which can now be located, is a *Manual de Adultos* published in 1540. See facsimiles of two leaves, Agustín Millares Carlo and Julián Calvo, *Juan Pablos: Primer impresor que a esta tierra vino* (México: Manuel Porrua, 1953), pp. 129–131. The polemic loosed by Francisco Vindel's *El Primer Libro Impreso en América* (1953), *Apéndice* (1954), and *En papel de fabricación azteca fue impreso el primer libro en América* (1956) has yielded no generally accepted results. *Doctrina Christiana* (Lima: Antonio Ricardo, 1584) initiated printing in both the Quechua of the Incas and the Aymara of their subjects living in the altiplano.

[52] José Rojas Garcidueñas, *Bernardo de Balbuena* (México: Instituto de Investigaciones Estéticas, 1958), pp. 115–138, summarizes *Grandeza Mexicana* ("Músicas, bailes,

that in no other Hispanic colony of the colonial period were such publication ventures involving music attempted, and if it is not realized that during this same short thirty-three-year period even Madrid, the Spanish capital (after 1561), saw publication of only one liturgical book, the significance of the thirteen Mexican music books will not be properly appreciated. Ironically enough, the first and only liturgical music book printed at Madrid (1571) during the period 1556–1589 turns out to be merely a pallid reprint of the first Mexican music publication (1556).[53]

DESCRIPTION OF SIXTEENTH-CENTURY MEXICAN IMPRINTS CONTAINING MUSIC

Four of the thirteen music books printed in Mexico between 1556 and 1589 contain the plainchant portions of the Mass sung by the choir; these bear the collective title *Graduale Dominicale*.

Lota M. Spell explained the word "Dominicale" in this title as meaning "Dominican." The Order of Preachers, second of the mendicants in Mexico, subsidized publication of numerous handsome liturgical music imprints at Seville, beginning wih a *Liber processionum secundum ordinem fratum predicatorum* (Meynard Ungut and Stanislaus Polonus, 1494); and elsewhere also, of course. Their choirbook titles included either the Latin equivalent of "Order of Preachers" or, more rarely, *secundum consuetudinem sancti Dominici*. Only in Spanish and in colloquial parlance does such a title as "Misal Dominico. Fo. becerro" crop up—as in the manifest of forty boxes of books sent to Mexico City in 1584 (boxes 17, 21, and 25 contained Dominican Missals and Psalters[54] printed at Venice and elsewhere). Such books were needed because the Dominicans used a liturgy of their own, differing somewhat from standard Roman use. But their own individual liturgical needs were more usually met by importing books into Mexico, rather than by undergoing the expense of printing small runs in the colony. "Dominicale" in the title, *Graduale Dominicale*, means simply that the choirbook in question contains the plainchant sung in all Sunday and feast-day Masses.

The second largest group among the dozen with music printed in Mexico comprises three antiphonaries. These contain the plainchant sung during canonical hours. The other six liturgical books with music include two manuals, or directories, for the proper administration of the sacraments; a

---

danzas," p. 124). Soon after accepting the miter of Puerto Rico (and after arriving in San Juan in Lent, 1623 [p. 40]), Balbuena fell victim to pirates, whose raids so hampered any musical advance in the islands. Not only was his own splendid library burned by Dutch buccaneers in September, 1625, but in their month-long sacking of San Juan they even carried off the cathedral bells and organ (p. 47).

[53] Cristóbal Pérez Pastor, *Bibliografía Madrileña* (Madrid: Tip. de los Huérfanos, 1891), I, 23–24 (item 48).

[54] Francisco Fernández del Castillo, *Libros y Libreros en el Siglo XVI* [Publicaciones del Archivo General de la Nación, VI] (México: Tip. Guerrero Hnos., 1914), pp. 272–274.

missal (which contains the music sung by the celebrant at Mass, rather than the music sung by the choir); a passioner; a psalter; and a directory for Augustinian novices (containing a tabloid version of music sung by the priest at Mass).

I. The earliest book is musically the most elementary. Printed in 1556 by Juan Pablos (Giovanni Paoli), a native of Brescia who emigrated to Mexico in 1539, this directory of worship "purified of errors" was designed by Diego de Vertauillo, Augustinian provincial (1554–1557). Trained at Burgos, he arrived in Mexico the same year as Pablos. For a specialty he chose the training of novices. Not addicted to any personal luxuries, he insisted that everything endorsed and used by Augustinians in Mexico—including even the stones to build churches and the ornaments on the altars—be of absolutely first-rate quality (Juan de Grijalva, *Crónica*, 1962 ed., pp. 272–273, 443–445). Similarly, with the music, he insisted that the chants taught novices be "correct" to the last note. The title page of the music book printed under his supervision reads: *ORDINARIVM / sacri ordinis hęremitarū / sancti Augustini episco / pi & regularis obser / uātię, nūc denuò / correctū sic q3 / nõ secūdum / morē an / tiquū / ce- / remonię fiant, sed se- / cūdū choros altos.// Mexici. anno. / dñi. 1556 / idibus / Iulij.*[55]

Although reaching only eighty pages, the first twelve already cover: (1) how and when to ring bells, (2) when to face the altar, (3) when to stand and when to sit, (4) when to sing, (5) the proper tone for benedictions and absolutions, (6) when to kneel while in choir, (7) when to genuflect, (8) when to bow, and (9) versicles and invitatories. The music scattered through the *Ordinarium* includes the priest's intonations at various classes of Church feasts throughout the year: "minora simplicia," "maiora simplicia," "minora semiduplicia," "maiora semiduplicia," "minora duplicia," "maiora duplicia."

After studying the *Ordinarium* the young Augustinian seminarian would know the intonations for the Kyries, Glorias, Sanctuses, and Agnuses suitable at various classes of feasts; how to form processions; what colors of ecclesiastical vestments to wear throughout the Church year; how to swing incense; the proper melodic formulas for the intoning of gospels; how to be a subdeacon or a deacon at Mass; how to give the *pax;* and what to do when the bishop visited his church. As an instruction manual its virtues are manifest: rules are clearly set down in simple language, the easiest rules are given first with an orderly progression toward the more difficult, only the bare essentials are stressed with all superfluous verbiage stripped away.

Alonso de la Vera Cruz (*ca.* 1504–1584) attested the success of the triptych to which the *Ordinarium* belongs when he published an open letter some years later (November, 1559) claiming that all three parts— *Constitutiones, Ordinarium, Regula*—had been applauded not only in New

[55] Facsimile of title page in Vindel, *Apéndice* (Madrid: Talleres tipográficos de Góngora, 1954), p. 24. See his comments, p. 20.

Spain but in the Peninsula and in Peru.[56] Even better proof of the popularity of these publications can be found in the Madrid reprint of 1571, issued by the pioneer printer in the Spanish capital, Pierres Cosín. In the Madrid republication, the *Ordinarium* takes up folios 192–234 of a continuously numbered series, thus clinching the proof that it formed the middle panel between constitutions and rule.

All the melodies in the *Ordinarium* were already several centuries old at the time the book was compiled; if Solesmes datings are accepted, none of the chants printed in this 1556 book can have originated later than the twelfth century. Creed melodies are omitted; however, the 1556 book does supply melodies for the *Ite missa est* sung by the priest at the end of Mass. In consonance with the instructional purpose of the book, most of the melodies included are of an easy syllabic rather than a melismatic type.

To show how nearly the 1556 melodies approximate those printed in such an easily accessible book as the 1934 edition of the *Liber Usualis*, the opening phrases of four different Kyries are shown below, the first Kyrie in each pair being the 1556 version and the second being the Solesmes version. The Solesmes monks, of course, made no claims to infallibility, but they did attempt to determine the exact shape of a melody at the time it was originally divulged. If a melody as printed in 1556 closely adheres to the Solesmes version, then at least it was not badly corrupted by the time it reached Mexico.

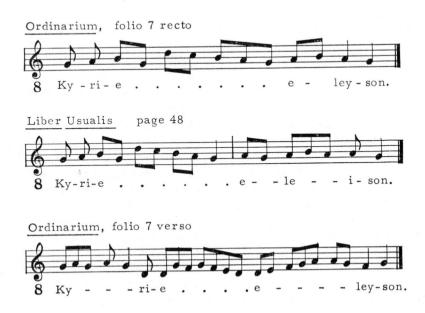

Ordinarium, folio 7 recto

Ky - ri- e . . . . e - ley - son.

Liber Usualis   page 48

Ky-ri-e . . . . . . e - - le - - i- son.

Ordinarium, folio 7 verso

Ky - - - ri- e . . . .e - - - - ley-son.

[56] Millares Carlo and Calvo, *op. cit.*, p. 58.

Apart from being the first New World music imprint, the 1556 *Ordinarium* enjoys another priority. It is the first New World publication to show a completely nude man and woman facing each other on the title page (Adam and Eve before the Fall). Interestingly enough, Aztec pictorial art always played more the Puritan, so far as nudes are concerned, and carefully eschewed the pudenda. Following the *Ordinarium*, Maturino Gilberti's *Vocabulario en lengua de Mechuacan* (1559) and Alonso de Molina's *Confessionario Mayor* (México: Pedro Balli, 1578) repeat the same nude Adam and Eve compartment.

Only three copies of the *Ordinarium* have come to light: the first formerly owned by a resident of Titusville, Pennsylvania, and now in the New York Public Library; the second owned by the British Museum; and the third belonging to Salvador Ugarte in 1953 [57] (now in the William H. Scheide Collection, Princeton, New Jersey).

II. The second book with music published in the New World was the *Manuale Sacramentorum secundum vsum ecclesię Mexicanę . . .* , printed by Juan Pablos in 1560 as his swan song. This manual was by no means the manual for beginners that the 1556 *Ordinarium* had been; it has 354 pages, and its use was made mandatory throughout the archbishopric of Mexico by Montúfar. Not knowing what kind of liturgical usage would finally be prescribed by the Council of Trent, then in adjourned session, the bishops under Montúfar's presidency committed themselves in 1560 to an eclectic use derived from the usages of Rome, Toledo, Salamanca, Seville, Granada, Plasencia, "y otros." A certain liturgical independence, a Neo-Hispanic "Gallicanism," if one may call it that, distinguishes not only this sacramentary "according to the use of the Mexican Church," but several later liturgical books issued before Pius V's bull *Quod a nobis* "swept away all the numerous variations and exuberances then common in the Roman Rite, and established one uniform Mass, and one uniform method of saying Mass." [58]

III. In 1561 Antonio de Espinosa [59] published a *Missale Romanum Ordinarium* which has long been recognized as the handsomest New World book of the sixteenth century.

The most splendid product of the Mexican press, a volume whose pre-eminence has been challenged only two or three times during the centuries which have elapsed since its publication, is the *Missale Romanum Ordinarium*, printed in the city of Mexico in 1561. It is a magnificent folio volume of 330 leaves, printed in red and black, with historiated initials and occasional woodcut borders.[60]

Music printing appears on fifty-two pages. As was the European printing custom, the notes themselves are black; the five-line staff is red. The music,

[57] *Ibid.*, p. 151; New York Public Library, *Library Treasures: An Exhibition, 1966* (New York: New York Public Library, 1966), p. 13.

[58] William R. Bonniwell, *A History of the Dominican Liturgy, 1215–1945* (New York: Joseph F. Wagner, 1945), p. 295.

[59] Espinosa was an Andalusian typefounder recruited in September, 1550, by Juan Pablos' scout Juan López. The latter was a Mexico City luthier who had recently returned to Seville on business. Espinosa's keeping company with a maker of viols and guitars shows the trend of his interests long before he became the great Mexico City music printer. See José Gestoso y Pérez, *Noticias Inéditas de Impresores Sevillanos* (Seville: Gómez Hnos., 1924), p. 115; Alexandre A. M. Stols, *Antonio de Espinosa* (México: Biblioteca Nacional, 1962), pp. 6–7.

[60] Samuel A. Green, *A Second Supplementary List of Early American Imprints* (Cambridge, Mass.: University Press, 1899), p. 20. (Quotation from George P. Winship.)

like that of the 1556 *Ordinarium,* was chosen from the repertory of simpler chants, both books having been printed for the use of celebrants rather than of choirs. Most of the melodies are syllabic. Two-note neumes appear frequently (podatus and clivis), three-note neumes rarely (torculus and climacus). Liquescent neumes or the quilisma appear nowhere in the missal, but neither are they found in European chant books of the epoch. Even so, the music could never have been sung by a tyro in plainsong. The competence expected of clergy in New Spain may be gauged not only from the character of the melodies in this book, but also from rules already promulgated by Archbishop Montúfar five years before the printing of this *Missale.* In the 1556 *Constituciones del arçobispado,* Montúfar required that candidates for minor orders "know the fundamentals of plainchant, and at the very least be able to sightsing creditably." Candidates for the diaconate and the priesthood were required to demonstrate a still higher degree of accomplishment as plainchanters. If his rules were at all implemented, Montúfar had a right to expect that the music notes printed in the 1561 *Missale* would serve more than a merely decorative purpose.

The viceroyal printing privilege issued August 20, 1560, to Juan Pablos' widow, Gerónima Gutiérrez, reveals that San Francisco and San Agustín monasteries in the capital had together commissioned the printing of the missal (Archivo General de la Nación, Ramo de Mercedes, Vol. V, fol. 87).[61] This fact alone assures us that the copies were destined for Indian parishes served by regulars, rather than Spanish parishes served by diocesan clergy. A Dominican, Bartolomé de Ledesma, took the responsibility of censoring the *Missale.* With three orders participating, a somewhat eclectic choice of chants and prayers would be expected, and such eclecticism is exactly what García Icazbalceta [62] found to be the rule, so far as texts are concerned. Comparing the 1561 *Missale* with others available to him, he discovered that the editors had selected their texts from no single European source, but had instead pieced together material from many different sources. Once having chosen a preface or a postcommunion or other matter, however, the editors adhered faithfully to the source from which they were at the moment copying. The music in the 1561 *Missale* obeys the same rule. Some such antiphon as the one given below shows how faithfully a model was copied, once it had been selected. The underlined notes in the 1497 *Missale* differ from those in the 1561 *Missale;* otherwise the two examples are identical.

---

[61] Alberto M. Carreño, "El Primer Misal Romano Impreso en México," *Boletín de la Biblioteca Nacional,* XIII/1–2 (Jan.–June, 1962), 55–56.

[62] García Icazbalceta, *Bibliographía Mexicana del Siglo XVI* (México: Librería de Andrade . . . , 1886), p. 124. Variants from modern usage were found in the prefaces of St. John Baptist, St. Francis, St. Augustine, and in the use of benediction at requiem; this latter was a custom continued by the Dominicans into the next century.

Missale (Mexico: Antonio de Espinosa, 1561),folio 121 verso

Ves - pe - re au - tem Sab - - ba - ti:

quae lu - - - ces-cit in . . pri -ma Sab-ba - ti:

ve - nit Ma - ri - a Mag - da - le - - - ne

et al - te - ra Ma - ri - - a, vi - de -

re . . se - pul - crum, al - - le - lu - ia.

Missale (Venice: Joannes Herzog, 1497), folio 219 recto

Ves - pe - re au - tem- Sab - -- ba - ti . .

et al - te - ra Ma - ri - a . . . . .

IV. Two years after Espinosa's much lauded *Missale,* a new printer from Rouen published his first liturgical book. Conforming with the general practice of his century, Pedro de Ocharte [63] (he Hispanicized himself thus in Mexico) invaded the publishing business by marrying the daughter of his

[63] For a résumé of Ocharte's career, see García Icazbalceta, *Bibliographía Mexicana* (1954 ed.), p. 36 n. 65; supporting documents at pp. 51–53 (nos. 46–52, 54–57, 60–61, 63, 66, 68–69).

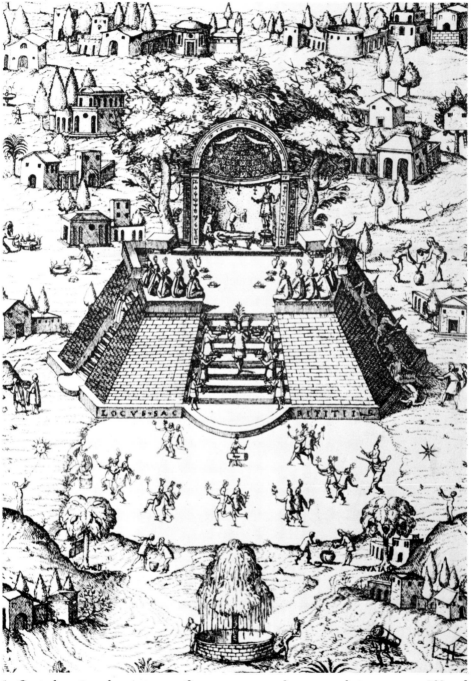

1. Central portion of an Aztec sacrifice scene engraved on copper between pages 168 and 169 in Diego Valadés's *Rhetorica Christiana* (Perusia: Pietro Giacomo Petrucci, 1579). In addition to the players of teponaztlis and huehuetl mentioned in our text at pages 163–164, the two dancing figures at the viewer's extreme right may be playing a long trumpet or flute and a bone rasp=omichicahuaztli.

2. Three wooden teponaztlis, the top exemplar in the British Museum, 36.8 cm in length, the other two in the Museo Nacional de Antropología e Historia, Mexico City, 47 cm and 60 cm. The top two teponaztlis are of Mixtec provenience, Oaxaca area, 1300–1500. The bottom teponaztli, made of nogal wood and presented to the Tlaxcala Indians by Cortés, was probably also carved by Mixtecs. The crouching feathered human figure recalls the deity Quetzalcóatl. The two keys sound a minor third interval. Concerning teponaztlis, see pages 21–22, 49–52, 63–73, 111–113, 118–119 and 163–164.

3. Aztec teponaztli, Museo Regional de Toluca, 50 cm long. Matlazinca culture. The two tongues sound the fifth a–e¹ when struck on the platforms adjacent to the center cut. When struck on the outer troughs, the tongues sound an octave. Concerning such "platform" keyed teponaztlis, see pages 65–67 of the text.

4. Tlalpanhuehuetl, Museo Regional de Toluca, 97 cm high, 42 cm diameter. This is the so-called Malinalco drum, Matlazinca culture. See text, pages 20–22, 42–44, for extensive description and interpretation.

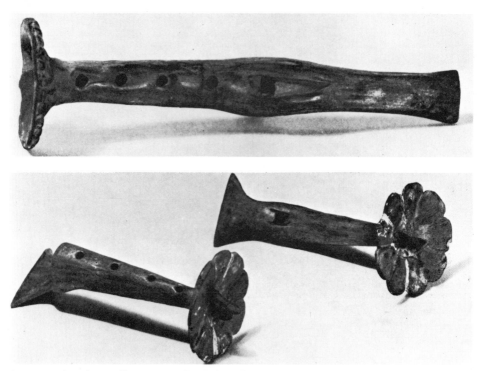

5. Aztec clay tlapitzalli, 16.3 cm long; 8 and 8.5 cm long. The two smaller flower petal flutes are at the Museo Nacional de Antropología e Historia, Mexico City, the larger in the Martí private collection. See pages 79–82 and 103–104.

7. Clay ocarina in the shape of priest blowing a three-tube multiple flute, 13 cm high. Martí private collection. Maya culture, *ca.* 500 A.D. Emitting the notes a^1 and b^1, this ocarina came from a gravesite on Jaina island. One of the tubes of a multiple flute such as is shown in the effigy was characteristically longer than the other two. All three notes sounded simultaneously.

6. Two Mayan six-fingerhole clay flutes, Museo Nacional de Antropología e Historia, Mexico City, and Museo Regional de Villahermosa, Tabasco, 23.5 and 19.8 cm long. The first comes from Jaina island, Campeche. Both are dated *ca.* 500 A.D. Both were plugged at the top to begin with, but the top of the Tabasco flute is broken. The fingerholes of the National Museum flute are exactly spaced 1.5 cm from each other and below the mouth hole is an exquisite decoration 2.5 cm in width. The Tabasco flute is ornamented with a priest's head above the proximal fingerhole. At the distal end is a clay ornamental ring.

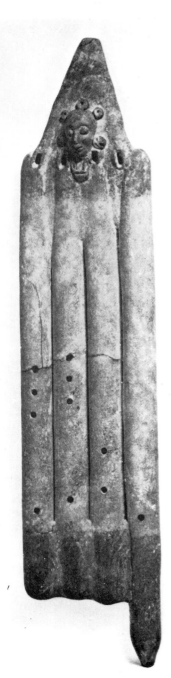

8. Clay multiple flute, Museum of the American Indian, Heye Foundation, New York City, Gulf Coast culture, *ca.* 500 A.D. See pages 83–85 of accompanying text.

9. Goiter-type clay flute producing oboe sound, Museo Nacional de Antropología e Historia, Mexico City, 16 cm long. Maya culture, *ca.* 500, Jaina island. See page 7 of text.

10. Three Peruvian panpipes, the top a casting in the American Museum of Natural History, New York City, of a now lost eight-tube stone panpipe 16 cm wide, 13.5 cm high; the bottom left a six-tube Inca stone panpipe in the Museum der Völkerkunde, Berlin (VA 8589), 9 cm wide, 8 cm high; the bottom right an eleven-tube Nazca clay panpipe in the Museo Nacional de Antropologia, Lima. Both the first and second exemplars have auxiliary side holes in the tubes that permitted the player to sound more notes than there were tubes. When stopped, the three side holes in the Inca stone panpipe at Berlin dated 1300–1500 A.D. (2nd, 4th, and 5th tubes) raised the vibration frequencies by about 10 percent. To carry this panpipe, string was passed through the two holes in the knob at the viewer's right. The Nazca panpipe dated about 500 A.D. was broken after having been examined by Andrés Sas in 1939. According to him, the eleven pipes sounded a series beginning with a semitone above Middle C and ending with d^2 above high c^2 thus: c# e g# a# b; e^1 f + ^{1} g^1 b^1 c^2 d^2. Sas remarked on the symmetry of c# e g# b and e^1 g^1 b^1 d^2 (*Revista del Museo Nacional*, VIII/1 [1939], 129). Further data on panpipes=antaras in the text at pages 245–255.

11. Coiled clay trumpet, from Chimbote, Peru, in the Nathan Cummings collection, The Art Institute of Chicago, 28 cm long. Mochica III culture *ca.* 400 A.D. Painted in reddish brown and white, this trumpet flares into a bell depicting an open jaguar's mouth. When blown, it emits the first four partials in the overtone series. Further data on Peruvian trumpets, pages 256–258.

predecessor—Juan Pablos. His 1563 liturgical imprint, *Psalterium Chorale*, pays further tribute to his predecessor (d. early August, 1560) by listing as copublisher Juan Pablos' widow, Gerónima Gutiérrez. To prove how elusive can be this class of Mexican incunabulum, the 1563 *Psalterium* first showed up as recently as 1963 and was found in a small, difficult-of-access Guatemalan upland village. Previously, no one had even suspected its existence. On the other hand, the Vasco de Puga Cedulario published by Ocharte in 1563 had been known to all bibliographers, ever since interest first awakened in Mexican incunabula.

Even were the copy discovered in 1963 not a unicum, the *Psalterium* would still excite interest because of the valuable new light thrown on Mexican liturgical printing by the *licencia* (dorse of the title page). Both the title and the vignette of St. Dominic at the bottom of the title page identify it as a Dominican psalter. Its retrieval and present preservation in an area that was so distinctively Dominican mission territory during the sixteenth and seventeenth centuries as San Miguel Acatán [64] (in the present department of Huehuetenango, Guatemala) therefore seem quite logical. The title reads:

Psalterium Chorale secundū cō- / suetudinem sancti Dominici: cū versiculis responsorijs ho- / rarū & psalmorum intonationibus: ac omnibus antiphonis / notatis nec non & hymnis antiquis & nouis ordinari/is & extrauagantibus cum propijs cantibus: ac / vesperis & vigilijs & defunctorum similiter / ex integro notatis: & omnibus alijs / que ad Psalterium perti = / nent additis.

The verso of the title page begins with a letter from the Dominican prior [65] at Mexico City to Montúfar (also a Dominican, archbishop 1551–1572), stating that arrangements to print the *Psalterium* had been made with Juan Pablos shortly before the latter's death in 1560. The prior's letter contains other information worth having in his words:

Muy illustre y Reuerendissimo Señor. Fray Pedro de feria prior del cōuento de scto Domingo de Mexico dela ordē delos predicadores enesta nueva España: por quanto en los conuentos de la dicha orden, ay necesidad de Salterios de choro pa

---

[64] The Maryknoll father Daniel Jensen, while serving with Father Edward Moore at San Miguel Acatán, gathered a fine library of early liturgical books used at Santa Eulalia, San Juan Ixcoi, and San Mateo Ixtatán. Typical are a Dominican *Processionarium* (Venice: Antonio Junta, 1545) purchased for San Juan Ixcoi in 1561, a Cistercian missal (Paris: Ambrose Girault, 1545) inscribed at Santa Eulalia, and a Dominican missal (Salamanca: Antonio Álvarez, 1550).

[65] Concerning Pedro de Feria, the last fourteen years of whose life were spent as bishop of Chiapas, see Antonio de Remesal, *Historia General . . . de Chiapa y Guatemala* (Guatemala City: Tip. Nacional [Biblioteca "Goathemala," IV–V], 1932), II, 472–473. Remesal defined Dominican mission territory as reaching "from Tehuantepec to San Salvador" (I, 429).

celebrar los oficios diuinos: y en la officina de Juan pablos difunto impressor que fue de libros en esta dicha ciudad, ay todo buen recaudo y aparejo para los imprimir: y a ello le ha ofrecido la parte del dicho Juan pablos. A vuestra señoria reuerendissima supplico, sea seruido de lo auer por bueno y dar licencia para ello.

Next comes the archbishop's *licencia*,[66] transferring to Pedro de Ocharte and Pablos' widow permission to print, and requiring two Dominicans to certify the exact agreement of the final text with that of a Dominican *Psalterium* published at Venice in 1523 by Petrus Liechtenstein.[67]

V. In 1568 Pedro de Ocharte published a *Manuale Sacramētorū, secundū vsum almę Ecclesię Mexicanę, nouissime impressum cū decretis sancti cōcilij Tridē.* Like the 1560 *Manuale,* this was published under a ceiling-price regulation. Diego de Sansores (= Sansoric), at whose cost the book was printed, was enjoined not to sell it in a paperback covering for more than 4 pesos de oro común. The 1568 *Manuale* duplicates the 1560 except for revisions of the sacramentary approved by the Council of Trent. Although printed from worn type, the 1568 sold for a peso more than the 1560 *Manuale.*

Of the 183 numbered leaves, 47 show music. The largest block of chants belongs to the section headed *Officium mortuorum* (fols. 88–95v, 96v–97v, 100–123). Words are bar-lined, lozenges mix with squares to denote short and long syllables (see, for instance, *Requiem aeternam,* fol. 93). Accidentals, however, fall within the singer's discretion. An 11-page *Index co-*

[66] Assi presentada y por su Señoria reuerendissima vista: dixo que daua & dio la dicha licencia para que Pedro ocharte y Geronima gutierrez su suegra impressores de libros, puedan imprimir en su imprenta el dicho Salterio: con tanto que todo lo que se fuere imprimiendo, vaya firmado de dos padres de la dicha orden de señor sancto Domingo abiles y suficientes para el examen de lo que se fuere imprimiendo. Y en virtud de sancta obediencia so pena de excomunion mayor, cuya absolucion a si reseruo, dixo que mandauan & mando, que despues de impresso el dicho Salterio no se publique ni de a ninguna persona hasta presentallo ante su Señoria reuerendissima para mandallo corregir concertar con el original, que fue impresso en Venencia, [*sic*] por Petrilietestyn el año de mill y quinientos y veynte y tres: que assi se cumpla y guarde, y firmo lo su señoria reuerendissima: a veynte y vn dias del dicho mes de setiembre, de mill y quiniētos y sesenta y tres años.

Fr. A. Archiepiscopus
Mexicanus
Ante mi Diego Maldonado Secretario

[67] The Biblioteca Nacional at Lisbon owns the Venetian original (*Reservado 1328*) which served as model for the Mexican imprint of 1563. Differing from the 1563 title only in the abbreviations, the 1523 title begins thus: *Psalteriū chorale sm consue- / tudinē sci dñici: cū versiculis respō- / sorijs horarū & psalmo4 intonatio- / nibus: ac oībus antiphonis no- / tatis.* The *Tabula hymno4* at folio 202 lists 139 hymns, and the colophon overleaf reads: *Finis. Laus deo optimo maximoq3, Anno 1523 Venetijs Petrus Liechtenstein.* Antiphons for each psalm, Athanasian and Apostles' creeds, the Litany, and the *Te Deum laudamus* enrich both imprints.

piosus separates usages peculiar to the Indies from those allowed in Europe.

VI. The exact dating of a mutilated *Graduale Dominicale* has proved difficult because the one extant copy lacks both title page and colophon. Formerly the damaged copy, now shelved at the Biblioteca Nacional in Mexico City, was thought to have been printed in 1576; now, however, it is conceded to have been printed before 1572, and possibly as early as 1568.[68]

To summarize Emilio Valtón's description of this pre-1572 Gradual: Antonio de Espinosa printed this 35 by 21 cm folio in red and black throughout, the red lines sometimes smearing because he was reduced to using the oil of Mexican *chía* in preparing the red ink, much against his will. The Mexican National Library exemplar, cataloged as 0-I-7-1 in 1935 and as 264.15 GRA. in 1967, begins with *Dnica. ij. Aduentus* (Second Sunday in Advent) and breaks off in the midst of a Mass honoring St. Dominic after folio 280. At folio 268, after *Dominica xxii. Post trinitatem,* start Votive Masses. The Mass *In feria iii. quādo celebratur de beato Dnico* (beginning at fol. 278) suggests that Dominicans commissioned this Gradual.

As if this were not enough, at folio 149v in the Holy Saturday Litany a rubric inserted before the invocation "Sancte pater Dominice" reads: "Hic vox exaltetur, & bis nomen quod sequitur, dicatur." Only Dominicans could have required St. Dominic's name to be sung twice, forte. In the 1576 Graduals issued by Espinosa and Ocharte all such telltale Dominican signs have been expunged and numerous other significant changes are made. Some Masses are dropped, others added; introits, offertories, and other chants for the same Mass can be quite different in the pre-1572 and 1576 Graduals.

According to Valtón (pp. 124, 145), the pre-1572 Gradual suffers from superfluous notes in the plainchant which, in the 1576, have been cut away. For proof he inserts facsimiles of the Mode VII Introit, *Puer natus est nobis* (Christmas High Mass), which comes at folio 22 in the pre-1572 Gradual (Valtón, lám. 30, p. 129) and at folio 20 in the 1576 (lám. 35, p. 141). Unfortunately, his case is not proved by this introit, which runs ninety-eight notes in the pre-1572 Gradual and ninety-seven in the 1576. However, some significance can perhaps be attached to the contour of the phrase at "magni consilii Angelus." The pre-1572 version here more closely resembles the Solesmes editors' approved version than does the 1576. The latter version, which avoids the downward leap of a fifth after "magni," is perhaps easier to sing.

[68] Emilio Valtón discovered this gradual and dated it 1571; see Henry R. Wagner, *Nueva Bibliografía Mexicana del Siglo XVI* (México: Editorial Polis, 1940), p. 25. Valtón, *Impresos Mexicanos del Siglo XVI* (México: Imprenta Universitaria, 1935), pp. 122–146. Valtón seems not to have taken into account the exemption from liturgical reform allowed the Dominicans and other old orders by Pius V. A Gradual printed in 1576 or even later could have gone "unreformed," if it were for their use.

pre-1572 Graduale, folio 22

ma - gni con - si - li - i   An - - -

-ge - - lus.

1576 Graduale, folio 20

ma - gni con - si - li - i   An - - -

-ge - - lus.

Graduale Romanum
    (Tournai: Desclée, 1952),   page 33

ma - gni con - si - li - - - i   An - -

- ge - - lus.

The pre-1572 Gradual also differs by virtue of the five pre-Tridentine sequences in it which invade no later Mexican imprint: *Laetabandus exultet
fidelis chorus* (Christmas *prosa* at fols. 23–24), *Omnes gentes plaudite* (Ascension *sequentia* at 186–187v), *Sancti Spiritus adsit nobis gratia* (Pentecost
sequentia, 195v–197v), *Profitentes unitatem veneremur Trinitatem* (Trinity
sequentia, 212–214), and *Laudes ergo Dominico* (*sequentia* lauding Dominic at 279v–280). To these, the pre-1572 adds the Easter *prosa*, *Victimae
paschali laudes*, and the Corpus Christi *sequentia*, *Lauda Sion Salvatorem*.
Even these last two fail to appear in Antonio de Espinosa's 1576 Gradual
(149v, 183), although the Tridentine fathers endorsed their continued use.

VII. The next two books were also printed by Pedro de Ocharte, who by
1572 had become so heartily envied and disliked by certain Spaniards at

Mexico City as to have been denounced to the Inquisition. At the moment he was in the process of completing one hundred passion books ordered by Antonio Ruiz de Morales y Molina, bishop of Michoacán. Because the bishop's order was pressing, Ocharte while still in prison begged Antonio de Espinosa to finish printing the books. In a letter to his wife, Ocharte described the contents, which included music for Maundy Thursday, Good Friday, and Holy Saturday.

The depositions taken by the Inquisition authorities during their investigation include several that bear on Ocharte's passion books. In all he printed 310 of them, and for each one he asked the handsome sum of 20 pesos, five times the price placed on his 1568 *Manuale*. The Inquisition file reveals, moreover, who read proof, who took charge of delivering the books while Ocharte was in prison, and even the name of the person who pulled sheets while he was awaiting trial.[69] We know when Ocharte was apprehended, and that the printing of the *Pasioneros* was completed shortly before March 1, 1572. Pedro Balli, who bound them, claimed on April 18 that a fourth of the lot was owned by a thirty-four-year-old French employee of Ocharte who had changed his name to the less suspicious Juan Ortiz. Yet despite all this specific information, not one copy is extant today. Where did 310 books selling for such an extraordinary price disappear to? The documents of the Inquisition trial were published shortly before the First World War, but no copy of the *Pasionero* itself had ever been seen.

Finally, in the late 1930's, battered sheets of a Passion According to St. John were found in an Indian village near Tlaxcala. Here at last was a possible fragment. Along with the eight pages of passion music was found a fragment of a *Graduale Dominicale* later identified as one of the issues of 1576. Interest rose in the passion fragment. Ruiz de Morales, the music-loving bishop for whom the passioners were printed, was translated to the see of Tlaxcala (= Puebla) only a year after they were ready. What more natural than his taking books already purchased into his new diocese? Federico Gómez de Orozco and a collector named Conway shared possession of the battered sheets that had been found.[70] Mexican bibliographers examining the questioned sheets finally pronounced them authentic fragments of a sixteenth-century passion book that could be none other than Ocharte's; specimens of type from the known Ocharte books confirmed their having been printed at his press.

The finding of these several sheets demonstrated once more the hazards that have beset Mexican sixteenth-century imprints. It is no wonder that only two copies of the 1556 book, one copy of the 1560 book, two copies of the 1561 book, and one or two copies of certain other books here mentioned have come into the possession of libraries in the United States, despite the

---

[69] *Libros y Libreros en el Siglo XVI*, pp. 99, 139, 242.
[70] Wagner, *op. cit.*, p. 273.

high prices paid for them. The British Museum and the Biblioteca Nacional in Chile have acquired occasional copies offered for sale by private Mexican collectors, but even the National Library in Mexico still lacks some of the most important music imprints. In view of the scattered places in which the books now rest—some at the Biblioteca Nacional in Mexico City, others at the University of Texas in the García Icazbalceta collection, at the New York Public Library, at the Newberry Library in Chicago, at the Huntington Library in San Marino, and at the Library of Congress in Washington—it is not surprising that so little is actually known concerning these Mexican music imprints. Henry R. Wagner, whose studies in Mexican bibliography are classic, has more than once called attention to the inadequate canvassing of Mexican music imprints, due simply to the wide dispersal of the books and the difficulty of making comparisons.

VIII. The next book with music has disappeared also. The same Inquisition documents that revealed the existence of an Ocharte *Pasionero* speak of an *Antiphonario Dominical* being printed for him by Espinosa while he was imprisoned. In March, Ocharte ordered his brother-in-law and factotum, Diego de Sansores, to give Espinosa all the paper "de marca mayor" (of superior quality) which he had still at his shop so that Espinosa might finish the *Antiphonario* without delay.[71] This may be the antiphonary mentioned in the Mexico City cathedral capitular act, dated February 12, 1577, which ordered 40 pesos de tepuzque paid to Pedro de Ocharte (freed from prison in 1574) for an antiphonary that had already been delivered to the cathedral authorities at an earlier unspecified date.[72]

IX, X, XI. In 1576 at least three (and possibly four) [73] editions of a new *Graduale Dominicale* were issued. One of these was printed by Espinosa "at the expenses of Ocharte"; Ocharte himself published two other editions of the same book. Three different editions of so large a book—comprising more than four hundred large folio pages—needs explanation. Such a book printed throughout in two impressions, black over red, with music of the more elaborate plainsong variety printed on nearly every page, must have been expensive to produce. The pressure of a real emergency is needed if the simultaneous issue of three editions is to be explained. No decision independently made by the Mexican hierarchy was responsible for the sudden and urgent demand for new choir books. Rather it was Pope Pius V's decree issued in 1571 concerning the reform of both missal and gradual which made necessary the immediate acquisition of new missals and graduals everywhere. Pius V's decree implemented liturgical decisions already made by the Council of Trent, and in issuing it he stipulated that henceforth

[71] *Libros y Libreros . . .* , p. 139.

[72] José T. Medina, *La Imprenta en México* (Santiago: Casa del Autor, 1909 [1912]), I, 357–359.

[73] Spell, *op. cit.*, p. 315. When Archbishop Francisco Plancarte in 1916 presented the Newberry Library in Chicago with a copy he stated that he himself had seen copies of each of the *four* editions of the 1576 gradual.

all liturgical books should be printed under the direct supervision of the Holy See. Although the purpose of this ruling was to halt all liturgical printing undertaken elsewhere, Philip II soon overrode the stipulation that all books should be printed at Rome. But the requirement for new missals and graduals exactly conforming to papal requirements stood, and in Mexico as elsewhere new books had immediately to be procured.

The capacity of any one press to produce new books within a given time was severely limited during the sixteenth century. When a sudden need arose for quantity production, the work had to be divided between two printers. In England, for instance, when a new prayer book was adopted by Parliament in 1548, and its use throughout the whole realm became mandatory on Whitsunday in 1549, a sufficient number of books could be produced only by dividing the work between two printers, Whitchurch [74] and Grafton. In Mexico the responsibility for the new graduals was shared by Ocharte and Espinosa. Ocharte alone may have produced three editions, but in any event he undertook two.

How does this extraneous information concerning printers and publication dates add to our knowledge concerning music in sixteenth-century Mexico? In this fashion: from the different bits of information now assembled one can estimate the number of choirs ready in 1576 for an elaborate plainsong version of the entire liturgy. Mendieta and Torquemada boasted of an astounding development of Indian choirs. The evidence pieced together here bolsters the truth of their claims.

In 1572 Ocharte stated that he had just finished printing 310 passioners, of which 100 had been ordered by the bishop of Michoacán. If, in 1572, with no pressure upon him to produce more than 100 books, he could print an extra 210, certainly he was able to turn out no less than twice 310 when he produced two editions of the *Graduale*. Espinosa's contribution of a third batch of graduals in 1576 means we should multiply 310, our test figure, by three. The result, 930, can be accepted as a minimal figure; probably the actual number was in excess of 1,000. Because these graduals were "libros de facistol," only one copy for each choir was required. That a thousand choirs with singers all trained to sing the full service in the elaborate plainsong version of the 1576 *Graduale Dominicale* should have existed in New Spain at that time seems indeed remarkable. In all New Spain in 1580 there were 14,711 Spaniards.[75] If every Spaniard in the realm had been singing plainchant there would still have been scarcely enough to

[74] Whitchurch's border design ("compartment") on the title page of *The booke of the common prayer* (London, 1549) reached Mexico, where it was copied on the title page of Alonso de la Vera Cruz's Aristotle, published by Juan Pablos, 1554, and again at various times between 1559 and 1639. For a fascinating tale of two cities—London and Mexico—see Lucy E. Osborne, "The Whitchurch Compartment in London and Mexico," *The Library*, 4th ser., VIII (1928), 303–311.

[75] Gonzalo Aguirre Beltrán in his article, "The Slave Trade in Mexico," *Hispanic American Historical Review*, XXIV/3 (Aug., 1944), quotes this population figure (p. 414).

188

fill the choirs for whose specific use the 1576 *Graduales* were printed. But the records of the Metropolitan Church at Mexico City show that Spanish singers were notoriously difficult to come by; only a few of the cathedrals, such as those at Mexico City, Puebla, and Guadalajara, can have used any Spanish singers whatsoever. Nearly all the 10,000 or more choir singers who began singing the service out of the 1576 graduals must therefore have been Indians. Perhaps never at any time in any colony has a veneer of European musical culture been so quickly and thoroughly applied as in sixteenth-century Mexico.

The best preserved of the 1576 graduals published by Ocharte and printed by Espinosa is the copy at the Newberry Library (VM 2149 G73) obtained in 1916 from the exiled archbishop of Linares (= Monterrey), Francisco Plancarte. On the title page, beneath a worn woodcut of Christ presenting Peter with the keys of the kingdom, appears a seven-line legend [76] stating that the contents conform with Tridentine decrees and that the old chants have been thoroughly emended and purified throughout by the reverend *bachiller* Juan Hernández. According to the legend, he had also composed certain graduals, alleluias, tracts, offertories, and communions heretofore lacking. If Juan Fernández really wrote "new" music, he qualifies as the first "composer" to have had anything of his own printed in the New World. Born in 1545 at Tarazona, Spain, he emigrated to Mexico City in 1567 or 1568, where on May 25, 1574, he obtained a bachelor's degree in canon law from the recently founded university.[77] His voice and musicianship won him a singer's appointment in the cathedral, and after 1585 promotion to the music directorship.

Despite the explicit assurances on both title and colophon pages that "superfluous" notes have been removed, many melodies still trailed long garlands of melismas. In opposition to the Medicean 1614 pruners of the Roman gradual, Hernández also permitted many ligatures on unaccented syllables. To show what difficulties the soloist singing Hernández' Palm Sunday tract must surmount, the following excerpts can be studied (fols. 116*v*–117; 118*v*):

---

[76] Secūdum normam Missalis noui: ex decreto / Sancti Concilij Triden. nunc denuo, ex industria, studio & labore admodum Reue / rendi Bachalaurei Joannis Hernandez, excussum, & in numeris mendis et su / perfluitatibus (quibus scaturiebat) notularum cantus repurgatum. Su / peradditis et de nouo compositis per eundem Bachalaureum, cum In / troitibus officij, cum Gradualibus, Alleluia, & Tractibus tum demum / Offertorijs, & Communionibus, quorum antea non fuerat vsus.

The inked title page of the Library of Congress exemplar (M2149. M5 1576 Case) offers certain minor variations from the above.

[77] *Cartas de Indias*, p. 208 (information in Archbishop Pedro de Moya y Contreras' letter to Philip II, March 24, 1575). Valtón, *op. cit.*, p. 145, citing Archivo General de la Nación, Sección de la Universidad: Grados de Bachilleres en Cánones 1566–1699, Letra J, Tomo IV. Hernández may also have corrected Ocharte's 1572 passioners (*Libros y Libreros*, p. 99).

No less melismatic were the alleluias for Ascension, Pentecost, and Trinity. The alleluias at folios 170, 172v, and 175v provided the melodic scaffolding for versicles that follow. The alleluia for the Sunday in the Ascension octave will illustrate (fol. 170):

Even though accidentals are frequently indispensable (as above for "gau-de-bit"), Hernández nowhere specified them. For another departure from

Sevillian music printing rules, he refused to bar-line every individual word.

XII, XIII. Pedro de Ocharte's 300-leaf *Psalterivm, Aniphonarium* [*sic*] *Sanctorale, cū Psalmis, & Hymnis* published in 1584, and 329-leaf Antiphonary *de tempore* issued five years later, make a crowning pair of sixteenth-century Mexican imprints with music. The antiphons, hymns, and responsories for saints' offices in the 1584 book, and the liturgical season offices in the 1589, conform with the texts of the revised breviary promulgated by Pius two years before the announcement of the revised missal. To meet criticism of the delay until 1584 and 1589 in issuing office chants to complement the Mass chants of 1576, Ocharte bespoke the difficulty of notating correctly so much music. "Extreme care" and lengthy revision had proved necessary, according to the colophon of the 1589 book (*notatis summa cura, longissimisq3 vigilijs perfectum, correctum: nuperrime reuisum & emendatū*). To expedite in some degree the 1589 imprint, he was forced to sacrifice consistency by entrusting edition of the Holy Week chants to an editor who followed the Dominican custom of bar-lining words, but the Advent to Palm Sunday and Easter to Advent chants to an editor who acted as if only Franciscan houses were to be buyers of the book. (Obviously, the special appendix of chants for St. Francis' octave does not fit the overall plan of the 1589 book [third gathering, fols. 60–62].)

The 1584 book (foliated consecutively throughout) has the virtue of being the best cross-referenced of the Mexican musical imprints. The notation of such hymns as the SS. Peter and Paul *Aurea luce* and the Transfiguration *Quicumque Christum queritis* (fols. 215 and 239*v*) mixes squares and lozenges to indicate an unequivocal measured rhythm:

Qui-cum-que Chri- stum   que - - ri - tis:

O - cu -los in al - tum   tol - - li - te il -

-lic li - ce - bit   vi - - se - re: sig -

-num pe - ren - - nis   glo - ri - e.

Toward the close of the 1584 book, the same mixing of squares and dia-
monds to indicate measure can be found not only with the poetry of hymns
but even with the prose of the Office for the Dead, as for instance in
Quoniam ipsius est mare at folio 293*v*. Melismatic chants occur much less
frequently than do syllabic in this book, although the Compline antiphons
Alma redemptoris and *Ave Regina coelorum* by way of exception begin thus
(fols. 80 and 81):

The 1589 imprint goes beyond the 1584 in showing both printed sharps
and flats. For instance, the fifth note in the antiphon on folios 87*v* and 88
(second foliation) is preceded by a printed sharp:

Almost as interesting as these unusual printed sharps are the contemporary
handwritten comments that can be found here and there in copies of the
1584 and 1589 books purchased by the University of Texas from García
Icazbalceta's heirs. For instance, the modes of all the Annunciation chants at
folios 190*v*–191*v* of the 1584 imprint are inked into the ornate initials. At
folio 46*v* in the 1589, the *Christus natus est* invitatory bears a marginal note
telling the organist to transpose the chant accompaniment (*organo da tono
de solfaut para la mediasion en fefaut*).

PRESENT-DAY SIGNIFICANCE OF SIXTEENTH-CENTURY MUSIC IMPRINTS

The present-day significance of these music imprints may be summarized
under seven statement headings: (1) These were the first books containing
music printed in the New World. (2) They were the only liturgical books
with music published in any of the Spanish colonies and in their own way
were as distinctive as *The Open-Air Churches of Sixteenth-Century Mexico,*
the subject of John McAndrew's 1965 book (Harvard University Press). (3)
They provide imposing examples of the printer's art in sixteenth-century

America. (4) The plainchant printed in them is less "corrupted" than had previously been thought universal in sixteenth-century liturgical books. (5) From them can be ascertained the general level of musical culture in churches of New Spain during the epoch. (6) They introduce us to some of the commanding musical personalities of the time at Mexico City, where all the books were printed. (7) From circumstances connected with their publication we can adduce corroborating evidence concerning the number, geographic spread, and performance ability of Indian choirs.[78]

A POSTHUMOUS IMPRINT (1604)

In 1605 Tomás Luis de Victoria published at Madrid his "swan song"—the *Officium Defunctorum* written to commemorate the Dowager Empress María, who had died two years earlier. None familiar with it would class it as anything but a work in purest sixteenth-century a cappella style. In 1604 Juan Navarro, a Franciscan born at Cádiz but stationed in the Michoacán province, published at Mexico City what may with equal propriety be called the swan song of Mexican sixteenth-century music printing. Because of the slight discrepancy in dates, it does fall outside the enchanted circle of Mexican incunabula. To pass it by in complete silence, however, would be to overlook its raison d'être. As surely as any of the imprints heretofore discussed, Navarro's *Quatuor Passiones* was designed for use in Indian missionary parishes under mendicant supervision.

To link it still further with the preceding century, this is the last Mexican publication to have been printed in Gothic type. José Toribio Medina—who gave his personally owned copy to the National Library in Chile—calls it "a typographical masterpiece, admirable alike for the splendid paper on which it is printed, the registration of the black notes on the red staves." [79] With such praise from the prince of Latin-American bibliographers, we next ask: who could have been the printer? Navarro's *Liber in qvo qvatvor passiones Christi Domini continentur* [80] was printed by Diego López Dávalos, husband of María de Espinosa. Since it was her father, Antonio de Espinosa, native of Jaén, who had published the Mexican typographical masterpiece of the sixteenth century, the *Missale Romanum Ordinarium* of 1561, it was all the more fitting that her husband continue in her father's footsteps with a

---

[78] If Indian choirs used the books, those who pulled sheets for Ocharte, publisher of music books dated 1563, 1572, 1576, 1584, and 1589, were, as often as not, Negroes. See *Libros y Libreros,* p. 99. The Cromberger parent firm in Seville relied heavily on Negro laborors. Juan Cromberger had six working for him at his death in 1540 (Gestoso y Pérez, *op. cit.,* p. 74).

[79] *Historia de la Imprenta en los antiguos dominios españoles* (Santiago de Chile: Fondo Histórico y Bibliográfico José Toribio Medina, 1958), I, 140.

[80] José T. Medina, *La Imprenta en México,* II (Santiago: Casa del Autor, 1907), 19–22, gives a useful bibliographic description.

music imprint the luxury and length of which were not to be duplicated anywhere in the Americas until the nineteenth century (and not in Mexico until 1952).

López Dávalos began his recorded printing career in Mexico with Juan de Torquemada's *Vida y Milagros*.[81] The colophon reads: "Enel Collegio Real de Sanctiago Tlatilulco. a 15. de Iulio. Año 1602." Tlatelolco college, as has been noted above (p. 101), functioned from its foundation on January 6, 1536, as a school for noble Indian youths; but by 1602 it had suspended liberal arts courses.[82] Instead, trades were emphasized, with printing serving as an example (1597–1602 [83]). López Dávalos' last book came out in 1613. The next year he was dead.

For reasons stated above (p. 185), the actual music in Navarro's passioner of 1604 cannot well be compared with that in the 100 passioners printed by Pedro Ocharte in 1572 to satisfy the bishop of Michoacán. But in any event Navarro's melos is cobbled on the last of conventional plainsong. Navarro, himself a vicar choral in Michoacán, may well have been stimulated to add passions according to the Synoptic Gospels—Matthew, Mark, and Luke—precisely because these were omitted from the 1572 book. To eke out the further music needed for Holy Week, Navarro granted the first eighty-nine folios to the four passions, but the rest of his book to lamentations and the Prayer of Jeremy.

Obviously, *Quatuor Passiones* was meant for mission churches under mendicant supervision. Navarro's insistence on securing recommendations from Dominican and Augustinian vicars choral in the capital shows the scope intended for his work.[84] Not the endorsement of cathedral musicians in Mexico, Puebla, or elsewhere, but precisely the blessing of mendicant-order musicians was sought, because their Indian parishes were to be buyers of the book.

In his dedication to the Franciscan provincial, Navarro claimed to have purloined no time from his major duties, but rather to have composed his chants as a "nocturnal exercise." Following the dedication comes a letter to

[81] *Ibid.*, II, 9–12 (Torquemada's life, pp. 10–12 [b. Spain *ca.* 1563; professed San Francisco in Mexico, 1579; official Franciscan chronicler, 1609; d. Tlatelolco college, January, 1624]).

[82] Francisco B. Steck, *El primer colegio de América* (México: Centro de Estudios Franciscanos, 1954), pp. 82–83, describes the character of the Colegio de Santa Cruz at Tlatelolco *ca.* 1600. The copy of *Quatuor Passiones* cataloged in the first bibliography to mention it, *Bibliotheca Mexicana* (1755) by Juan José Eguiara y Eguren (1691–1763), p. 1121, "extat in Bibliotheca Franciscanorum ad Tlatelolco."

[83] Stols, *op. cit.* (see n. 59 above), pp. 21–23.

[84] Dominican endorsement is dated November 24, 1601; Augustinian, November 28, 1601. These appear at the front of the book with such other preliminary matter as the viceroyal twelve-year printing privilege (Dec. 13, 1601), and other necessary licenses. The viceroyal privilege declared a fine of 1,000 Castile ducats against anyone who presumed to break Navarro's copyright.

the reader emphasizing the role of music in the Western Church. His frequent and, on the whole, apt quotation from Scripture and from patristic authorities [85] indicates either his own extensive reading or the easy availability of a catena of well-selected passages. To justify his time spent composing music, he reminded his fellow friars that according to Revelation their chief occupation in heaven would be musical exercise. He then continued with an apologia pro vita sua which can be paraphrased thus:

I have as a man endeavored to devote all my time to a heavenly work. . . . Whether I have excelled in that work or not, let others judge. . . . Those who always disparage the labors of others which they cannot duplicate, and those who clamor against the unceasing nightly toil of others, are but asked to recall the story of Michal, daughter of King Saul, and wife of David. She despised David for his playing and dancing before the Ark of the Covenant, and for her gesture of contempt she was punished with sterility. Those who deride the conscientious endeavor of those who devote themselves to music, and who rail at the nightly labor of others while giving themselves to rest, relaxation, and leisurely living, lack sweetness of disposition. But just as David was not at all impaired in his joyful praise despite Michal's derision (for he said: "I shall go on playing before the Lord, and I shall yet be more shameless than I was hitherto, and will be base in mine own sight," 2 Reg. 6 [21b–22]) so in like manner I shall also delight in the Lord and praise Him for His kindness. In His praise I shall spend my time with carefree mind, overlooking the assembly of those who unfeelingly mock and carp at my endeavor.

Juan Navarro, the author of *Quatuor Passiones*, was formerly confused with another Juan Navarro, the Spanish polyphonist who died at Palencia in 1580.[86] Eitner's *Quellen-Lexicon* and *Grove's Dictionary* are but two of the more available authorities that confused the two men. Gilbert Chase in an article entitled "Juan Navarro *Hispalensis* and Juan Navarro *Gaditanus*" (*Musical Quarterly*, XXXI/2 [April, 1945]) disentangled the two. The mistake had been a natural one: Juan Navarro Hispalensis ("of Seville") reached international fame with a posthumous volume published at Rome in 1590—*Psalmi, Hymni ac Magnificat*.[87] A copy of this book was preserved in the Puebla cathedral archive. Why, therefore, should not Navarro Hispalensis have emigrated to Mexico? Rafael Mitjana, who first confused the two, did not know that Juan Navarro Hispalensis was old enough in 1553 to compete for the Málaga chapelmastership left vacant in that year by Morales' death.[88]

The temptation to carry over famous figures from the Old to the New

---

[85] His patristic authorities include Ambrose, Augustine, Gregory, Isidore, and Hrabanus Maurus.

[86] Juan B. de Elústiza and G. Castrillo Hernández, *Antología Musical* (Barcelona: Rafael Casulleras, 1933), p. lxxv.

[87] Stevenson, *Spanish Cathedral Music in the Golden Age*, pp. 254–258.

[88] *Journal of the American Musicological Society*, VI/1 (Spring, 1953), 37 n. 168,

World still persists, even if the Navarros have been forcibly separated into two distinct personalities. Was the Juan de Padilla who served successively as chapelmaster of Zamora Cathedral (May 7, 1661—January 27, 1663) and Toledo Cathedral (September 7, 1663—December 16, 1673) the same person as the Juan Gutiérrez de Padilla who became maestro of Puebla Cathedral in 1629 and made a great name for himself at the dedication ceremonies in April, 1649? [89] The answer must be "No." Was Domenico Zipoli, the organist of the Jesuit church at Rome whose *Sonate d'intavolatvra* were published in 1716, the same Zipoli who crossed seas to serve as a Jesuit in Argentina—arriving in 1717 and dying of tuberculosis at Córdoba on January 2, 1726? Adolfo Salazar, warned by the Navarro fiasco, considered it unlikely that such a European musical celebrity as Zipoli could have buried himself in Argentine obscurity saving Indian souls.[90] More recently, however, Lauro Ayestarán decisively tipped the scales against Salazar and made "Yes" now the confident answer to this question.[91]

Whatever the Zipoli outcome, the Navarro of 1604 fame was no polyphonist. His book finds its nearest European congeners in the *Passionarivm ivxta capellae Regis Lvsitaniae consvetvdinem,* by the Portuguese precentor Manuel Cardoso (Leiria: Antonio à Mariz, 1575), or the *Liber Passionum et eorum quae Dominica in Palmis, vsque ad Vesperas Sabbathi sancti inclusiué, cantari solent,* compiled by Frei Estevão of Thomar (Lisbon: Simão Lopez, 1595) and approved by Duarte Lobo.[92] The Manuel Cardoso makes an especially apt comparison because there was another roughly contemporary Portuguese composer named Manuel Cardoso, the polyphonic genius who was a Calced Carmelite. The two Manuel Cardosos just as easily trap the unwary as do the two Juan Navarros and the two Juan de Padillas.

All three passioners—Cardoso's of 1575, Frei Estevão's of 1595, and Juan Navarro's of 1604—observe similar conventions. They open with the Matthew narrative, run through the other three, then proceed to lamentations, lessons, and the Prayer of Jeremy. All three differentiate the turba, the Evangelist, and the Saviour's parts by making Jesus' a bass role and the others baritone and tenor. Only at moments of utmost desolation on the Cross does Jesus' bass climb so high as Bb in the Cardoso, and only at like moments of final agony does Navarro require the same ascents. Of the three settings Cardoso's is the plainest, and Navarro's the most uniformly Dorian. Frei Estevão claims to have improved on Cardoso by distinguishing ac-

---

[89] "The 'Distinguished Maestro' of New Spain: Juan Gutiérrez de Padilla," *Hispanic American Historical Review,* XXXV/3 (Aug., 1955), 363–373.

[90] "El caso de Domenico Zipoli," *Nuestra Música,* I/2 (May, 1946).

[91] *Domenico Zipoli: Vida y obra* (Buenos Aires: Pontificia Universidad Católica Argentina, 1962).

[92] Already chapelmaster of Lisbon Cathedral in 1595, Duarte Lobo (*ca.* 1563–1646) ranks as one of the paramount composers of the age. Navarro found no such recommender in Mexico.

cented from unaccented syllables (squares and lozenges); he also joins
Navarro in preferring Mode I against the *Alamire* chosen by Cardoso for
Tenebrae.

All three settings are rigorously syllabic, with only an occasional eruption
into melisma. Navarro reserves melismas for words or expressions of such
dramatic intensity as "My God, My God, why hast Thou forsaken Me?" and
uses the punctum for unaccented syllables in the text, the virga for accented
syllables. His neumes of two or more notes are the podatus, clivis, scandicus,
climacus, and porrectus. The F clef on the middle line is the most common
in Navarro. *B*-flats and *b*-naturals are the only accidentals used. The following example illustrates Navarro's style in one of his more expansive moments
(notes with dashes over them are virgas in the original): [93]

[93] *Quatuor Passiones,* fol. 8v.

("What, could ye not watch with me one hour? Watch and pray, that ye enter not into temptation: the spirit indeed is willing, but the flesh is weak." Matt. 26:40b–41)

Duarte Lobo recommends the 1595 Portuguese passioner as having been "composed" (= *composto*) by Frei Estevão. If that is allowed, then Navarro has equal right to present his book as an "original" creation, despite all the affinities with Roman chant. For the English-speaking reader, a more familiar instance of "composed" plainchant may be *The Booke of Common Praier noted* (1550), by John Marbeck (= Merbecke); or Luther's *Deudsche Messe* can serve as a convenient analogy.

In Spain, Hernando de Issasi (= Yssasi) "composed" a Holy Week Office (*Spanish Cathedral Music in the Golden Age*, p. 468) which he at last succeeded in having published with the title *Qvatvor Passiones Domini, cvm Benedictione Cerei* (Salamanca: Mathias Gastius' heirs, 1582). This 130-leaf volume of monody could certainly have served as Navarro's model in Mexico, if no other—one of the rare extant copies now belonging to the Museo de Arte "José Luis Bello y González" in Puebla to prove that the *officio dela semana santa que a compuesto en canto el maestro de capilla hernando de ysasi* was known in Mexico before 1600. (Another copy of this rare Salamanca *Qvatvor Passiones*, lacking a title page, belongs to the Newberry Library, Chicago; call number: Case VM2184.92C36 1582.) In his pompous preface, Issasi, chapelmaster at Ávila, vaunts the "immense labor and lengthy vigils" his compilation of chants has cost him. Toledan plainchant has been his source, but everything has been "corrected and emended to conform" with Pius V's new liturgical decrees.

What light does all this information throw on the musical situation in Mexico *ca.* 1604? Navarro's book, distressingly European though it may appear to those searching for the exotic, does add one more document proving how congenial the soil was into which the whole Gregorian system was thrown in Indian Mexico. Just as (1) the division of the day into canonical hours, (2) the hiring of temple singers, and (3) the complicated musical ritual not breachable in an iota were all part of precontact Aztec and Tarascan religious practice, so also were (4) the parallelistic setting of psalm verses, (5) the recitation on a central pitch (departed from only at beginning, middle, and end of a strophe), and (6) the constant answering back and forth between soloists and crowd in plainsong passions.

Torquemada (1615) noted the flourishing state of Church music in Michoacán, and it therefore appears likely that enough sales of Navarro's book were made in his own territory to return him the costs of printing it. Throughout the seventeenth century sporadic notices of indigenous musical life keep cropping up in Michoacán. It is obvious that Indian musical talent was for a longer time officially encouraged in such outlying centers as Valladolid (now Morelia) than in Mexico City. Diego Basalenque, whose early studies at Puebla equipped him to speak more authoritatively on music than any other Augustinian chronicler, wrote a chronicle of Michoacán in which he told of two exceptionally talented Indians, father and son; the father took Francisco for his Christian name, the son took Mateo.

So eminent and knowledgeable an organist was the father that he asked to compete with the great Spanish maestro Manuel Rodríguez [in January, 1567 [94]] when the latter was trying out for organist of Mexico City Cathedral. No one would believe that an Indian could best Rodríguez but he asked to prove what an Indian could do musically; and was therefore allowed to try his skill, first improvising [*tañó de fantasía*] and next playing a set piece [*un paso*]. So outstanding did he show himself to be that all the musicians were left gasping with admiration.

Although the imported Rodríguez did triumph in 1567 at Mexico City, this Indian virtuoso's son Mateo captured the organist's bench at Valladolid (= Morelia) Cathedral, and when Basalenque knew him was playing there "as well as any skilled Spaniard that you please." [95]

GEBRAUCHSMUSIK IN NEW SPAIN

In the fullest sense of the term all early Mexican polyphony was *Gebrauchsmusik* ("music for use"). This rule applied to pieces by Christian Indians no less than by Spaniards. Inasmuch as the forum in which this music for use was heard seems usually to have been some Church occasion, we may predispose ourselves to a more favorable view of the surviving canvases if we first measure the frames they were intended to fill. Formal public worship provided many of the available opportunities for the performance of part music. There were also, however, numerous nonliturgical occasions sponsored by the Church, such as processions, public acts of mourning, welcome ceremonies for new viceroys, or congratulatory acts staged for important public officials, when polyphonic music was required. The nonli-

[94] Mexico City Cathedral, *Actas Capitulares, Libro 2°* (1559–1576), fol. 209v (Jan. 28, 1567). Rodríguez continued for almost thirty years, dying in 1594 or 1595 (*A.C., Libro 4°* [1588–1605], fol. 119v).

[95] Diego Basalenque, *Historia de la Provincia de San Nicolás de Tolentino de Michoacán* [1st ed., 1673] (México: Editorial Jus, 1963), p. 62. Among other subjects, Basalenque taught music. For samples of his acute musical observations, see pp. 85 (between 1540 and 1545 Tacámbaro developed a finished band of instrumentalists and singers able to do polyphony), 151 (at Charo, the only town in Michoacán speaking Matlaltzinga, there flourished after 1550 fine choirs singing the Te Deum in their own language, to the Gregorian tune, the *Miserere mei* and Responses from the Office of the Dead in polyphony, and many hymns in their own tongue and in Latin), 153 (abundance of shawmers [= chirimías]), 216 (Pátzcuaro became a center for the making of instruments [*chirimías, flautas, trompetas, sacabuches, organos*] and of bells as early as the time of Vasco de Quiroga, first bishop of Michoacán). Map of the places mentioned by Basalenque in the 1963 ed., p. xv.

turgical occasions most relished by the humbler classes and best stimulating the Indian composer were without doubt the processions and outdoor fiestas where popularized part music, such as hymns to the Virgin, or villancicos in honor of the saints, or chanzonetas of thanksgiving were sung.

On the other hand, the nonliturgical occasions during which more pretentious types of part music were attempted were the welcoming ceremonies for new viceroys, or the acts of mourning for deceased sovereigns such as Charles V (d. 1558) and Philip II (d. 1598). It was at such welcoming or memorial occasions that the mass demonstrations of huge Indian throngs were always considered an indispensable prerequisite to success.

MUSIC IN COMMEMORATIVE ACTS

A detailed account of the commemorative pageant honoring the memory of Charles V may be found in the fifty-two-page pamphlet published by Antonio de Espinosa at Mexico City in 1560, *Tvmvlo Imperial dela gran ciudad de Mexico*. Its author, Francisco Cervantes de Salazar, though not a musician but a professor of rhetoric in the newly founded (1553) University of Mexico, was nevertheless well qualified to discuss the musical aspects of the pageant. Born in Toledo and a professor in the University of Osuna before emigrating to Mexico, he had while in Osuna enjoyed the friendship of so eminent an authority as the music theorist, Juan Bermudo, who held him in high enough personal esteem to ask that he write the introduction to his 1550 music manual, *El Arte tripharia*. Correspondence between the two evidently continued after Cervantes came to the New World, for it was at the latter's suggestion that Bermudo added a section of his original organ pieces in the second (1555) edition of his well-known treatise, the *Declaración de instrumentos*. In this second edition, Bermudo (fol. 113v) gratefully acknowledged the request from the New World for the addition of his own original compositions.

Cervantes de Salazar's description of the commemorative ceremony in Mexico City shows it to have been an occasion when the colonials set out to surpass the pomp and circumstance of the acts already staged at Brussels and in the Peninsula. Because Charles V had died at Yuste in the odor of sanctity, Church authorities in Mexico as elsewhere were eager to do his memory every possible homage. *Tvmvlo Imperial*, because of its contemporaneity, because of the vividness with which it describes individual details, because of its specific mention of performance methods, and especially because of its references to the music of Cristóbal de Morales and Lázaro del Álamo, deserves close scrutiny by every student who would understand sixteenth-century music in New Spain. The abridged and paraphrased extracts below by no means exhaust the passages that might interest a music student.

Having discussed the matter with the Royal Audiencia, with the archbishop, and with other officials, the viceroy [Luis de Velasco] decided to stage the ceremonies in San José [the first church erected for the Indians] and in the adjoining patio between it and San Francisco, the monastery to which it belongs. The Church of San José was chosen rather than the cathedral because the latter is entirely too small to accommodate any great throng and its ceiling is too low to permit the erection of a suitably imposing funeral monument. Also, the viceregal palace is so close to the cathedral that a procession could hardly have started moving before it would have reached the cathedral door.

The Order of the Procession on the Afternoon of St. Andrew's Day (November 30, 1559)

The procession from the viceregal palace was divided into four sections; in the first were the Indians, many of whom when they neared the monastery broke into sobs so heartfelt as to augment our own tears. Before the Indians was carried aloft a cross covered with black cloth; this was flanked on both sides with candlesticks carried on poles. The governors of Mexico, Tacuba, Texcoco, and Tlaxcala, all wore formal mourning attire. Each governor carried the banner of his provincial capital, with the coat of arms bestowed by His Majesty woven into the banner in gilt and silver threads running over a black background. More than two hundred village chieftains marched in solemn procession with their governors, all observing ceremonious silence. Approximately two thousand prominent persons in mourning followed them. The spectators who awaited the procession in the patio and in the streets adjacent to the monastery numbered at least forty thousand. This tremendous crowd was kept under control by interpreters who knew the Indian languages and by peace officers from the local constabulary. Upon arriving at the monastery patio the four governors—those of Mexico, Tacuba, Texcoco, and Tlaxcala—laid their banners at the four corners of the memorial monument.

The procession of the clergy included the archbishop, the bishop of Michoacán, the bishop of Nueva Galicia; provincials, priors, and guardians of the orders of St. Augustine, St. Dominic, and St. Francis; and some four hundred priests.

.   .   .   .

The dignitaries having finally entered the Church of San José and having seated themselves [the procession itself lasted two and a half hours] the vigil began. Outside and inside the church stood a huge crowd of onlookers. The cathedral chapelmaster [Lázaro del Álamo] began by directing one of his two antiphonal choirs in the singing of the invitatory, *Circumdederunt me,* by Cristóbal de Morales; and then the other in the singing of the psalm, *Exultemus,* also by Morales. Since both settings are polyphonic throughout and the choirs sang them with the utmost sweetness, the vigil began with a devotional fervor that elevated the minds of everyone present.

After the invitatory eight cope-bearers intoned the first antiphon in plainchant; the succentor then started the first psalm, *Verba mea auribus percipe, Domine,* and the same eight cope-bearers then sang the verses antiphonally with a chorus made up of friars and clergy, carrying it through with utmost solemnity. After the psalm, *Verba mea,* there followed an antiphon sung by the choirs in a polyphonic setting, and then another antiphon sung by the cope-bearers in plainchant.

Next the succentor started the psalm [*Domine ne in furore*]; when he reached the mediation, a group of six boys with the chapelmaster responded in a four-part setting of the remainder of the psalm-verse. The rest of this psalm was sung antiphonally: verses in plainchant sung by succentor and cope-bearers succeeded polyphonic verses sung by the boy choir. The chapelmaster [Álamo] had himself composed the music sung by the boys. After the psalm, *Domine ne in furore,* came another antiphon and psalm, sung again in the same way with polyphony and plainchant alternating. In the middle of the last psalm the cope-bearers advanced to the main altar.

There the archbishop [Montúfar] started the *Pater noster.* After it, Morales's polyphonic setting of *Parce mihi, Domine* was sung, the beauty of which enthralled everyone. The response was sung in plainsong, the cope-bearers remaining at the main altar during the singing of the verses of the response. The second lesson was confided to the bishop of Michoacán [Vasco de Quiroga]. After this, *Qui Lazarum resuscitasti* (in polyphonic setting) was sung: whereupon the archbishop began the last lesson. At its conclusion the cope-bearers began the psalm, *De profundis,* during which the clergy and the friars prepared to form their recessional. At the conclusion of *De profundis,* the singing of the response, *Libera me,* aroused the deepest devotion. The response completed, archbishop and all the choristers joined in the final prayer.

Early Mass the next day [December 1] was sung by thirty friars with such fervor and pathos that tears involuntarily started in the eyes of those present. . . . High Mass later during the day was sung in a five-voice setting.[96]

A generation later the exequies of Philip II provided New Spain with another opportunity for an ostentatious display of public grief. Dr. Dionysio de Ribera Flórez, canon of the metropolitan cathedral, wrote the official account in his *Relacion historiada de las Exequias Funerales . . . del Rey D. Philippo II,* which was printed by Pedro Balli at Mexico City in 1600. Though not as informed a person, musically speaking, as Cervantes de Salazar, Ribera Flórez nevertheless emphasized the role of music in the pageantry. After the death of every subsequent Spanish sovereign a similar public act was staged in Mexico, and then the account printed for distribution in Spain as well as the colony. Among its rare books the Biblioteca Nacional in Madrid now houses a series of these accounts; the musical extracts from them enable the reader to gain insight into some of the shifting currents of musical taste in the colony.

[96] Cervantes de Salazar, *Tvmvlo Imperial dela grand ciudad de Mexico* (México: Antonio de Espinosa, 1560), fols. 1r, 1v, 23v, 24r, 25r, 25v, 26r. The Huntington Library, San Marino, and the New York Public Library, Rare Books Division, own copies, but seven leaves before signature C in the latter's copy have been supplied in facsimile.

In all the Spanish colonies, for that matter, commemorative acts marking royal deaths, births, weddings, and accessions stimulated a constant stream of *relaciones* sent back to Spain in manuscript, or printed—the purpose usually being to invoke royal favor on the colonial officials who staged the events. For the ethnomusicologist these relaciones can be particularly useful. They are mines from which to extract descriptions not only of the European-type music but also of the indigenous dance and song heard at these commemorations.

INDIAN PARTICIPATION IN PUBLIC GALAS

As if commemorative acts for royalty were not enough, the young colony also reveled in receptions for viceroys, oidores, archbishops, and other high officials. Beginning November 1, 1578, a week-long gala marked the arrival of various religious relics sent from Rome. "By order of the Viceroy, Indian musicians were summoned from everywhere" to add the greatest possible sparkle.[97] All the decorations and ornaments saved from Charles V's commemoration two decades earlier came out of storage, all the same types of poetical tourney were again staged, all the customary triumphal arches were again erected.

According to Pedro de Morales' account, printed in 1579,[98] when the procession reached the Roman arch erected at the corner of Tacuba and Santo Domingo streets (= present-day Tacuba and República del Brasil streets), a band of Indian youths, bravely decked in native costume and featherwork, started dancing to the sound of a four-part song. Flutes and teponaztli accompanied the song, which, in Náhuatl, lauded Hippolytus (d. 236), patron of Mexico City. Morales printed the song in full. The pattern is exactly that of the sixteenth-century villancico: an opening *estribillo* (four lines), followed by two strophes (of eight lines each). The last line of the estribillo reads: "matiquinto tlapaluiti" (= "to do them [Hippolytus and other saints] homage"). This serves as refrain line at the close of each strophe (= *coplas*). In the five-act *Tragedia* written for the Mexico City festival and printed at folios 110–185 of Morales' *Carta*, villancicos close both Act II (ll. 674–693) and Act V (ll. 698–725). Again, the pattern repeats itself: four-line estribillo, two (or three) eight-line strophes. The last line of estribillo recurs at the close of each strophe.[99]

---

[97] José Rojas Garcidueñas, "Fiestas en México en 1578," *Anales del Instituto de Investigaciones Estéticas*, IX (1942), 40.

[98] *Carta del Padre Pedro de Morales* (México: Antonio Ricardo, 1579); copy at The Hispanic Society of New York. The best-known portion of this *carta* is the *Tragedia intitulada Trivmpho de los Sanctos*, a play dealing with Diocletian's persecutions of Christians and Constantine's eventual espousal of the faith.

[99] Harvey L. Johnson, *An Edition of Triunfo de los Santos* (Philadelphia: University of Pennsylvania [Publications. Series in Romance Languages and Literature, XXXI], 1941), pp. 100–101, 151. Act III ends with the chorus' singing of the *Circumdederunt*

Typical of Indian participation in a gala for a new viceroy was the welcome given Diego López Pacheco, Marqués of Villena (seventeenth viceroy) on November 18, 1640, when "youths dressed as Aztecs, adorned with feathers and precious stones, performed in his honor the indigenous majestic and solemn dance known as the *tocotín*. Ayacachtlis and teponaztlis accompanied the song, which began: 'Go forth, Mexicans, dance the tocotín.' " [100]

Celebrations away from Mexico City and Puebla sometimes inspired descriptive comment published at the capital itself. In 1675 the well-known mathematics professor and savant Don Carlos de Sigüenza y Góngora remarked that they played the tlalpanhuehuetl (= huehuetl sitting on the ground), the teponaztli, the omichicahuaztli (bone rasp), the ayacachtli, the cuauhtlapitzalli, "and other instruments suitable to the Mexican nation." With these "they praised the Virgin in holy songs conceived in a most elegant style." The Spaniards, on the other hand, had their own band of "suavissimos instrumentos" (p. 60), played indoors during respites between readings in a poetical tourney. At church, Sigüenza y Góngora assisted at a Mass sung by Padre Juan de Robles, whose singing he paid the very dubious compliment of comparing to that of a swan (p. 56).

TWO AZTECAN CHANZONETAS (*ca.* 1599)

Manuscript copies of the Tlaxcala Indian's *Missa a 4* praised before 1541 by Motolinía, and of the various sixteenth-century villancicos by Indians lauded in 1615 by Torquemada (Bk. XVII, chap. 3 [1723 ed., III, 214]) may still survive. Luis Reyes of the Universidad Veracruzana, Xalapa, announced discovery in early 1967 of what may prove just some such work, or a portion of it, copied on the *amatl*-leaf used in the binding of a book in Teopantlan, a village 20 miles northeast of Izúcar de Matamoros, state of Puebla. However, no really comprehensive search for sixteenth-century Indian-composed pieces has yet been attempted outside the capital city itself, and it is therefore not surprising that the earliest pieces by a Mexican Indian composer thus far available intrude at folios 121v–123 of a 139-folio codex now, or formerly, owned by Canon Octaviano Valdés of Mexico City. [101] Only the second of the Valdés Codex pieces is ascribed.

---

me invitatory. See above, p. 201, for Cervantes de Salazar's mention of Cristóbal de Morales' setting of the *Circumdederunt me* sung during the Charles V ceremony of 1559.

[100] Cristóbal Gutiérrez de Medina, *Viaje del Virrey Marqués de Villena*, ed. Manuel Romero de Terreros (México: Imp. Universitaria, 1947), p. 88. See above, pp. 51n, 165, for other references to the toco[n]tín.

[101] Contents listed, "Sixteenth- and Seventeenth-Century Resources in Mexico," *Fontes artis musicae*, 1955/1, pp. 12–13. The Mass at folios 101v–109 ascribed to Palestrina is by Pierre Colin.

This codex—31 x 22 cm—was, in July, 1954, bound on a crinkled, worn parchment cover that was once the leaf of a psalter (Psalm LXI, 7–9, Vulgate). The date "1599

That the composer was an Indian of noble descent (as were most Indians given a first-class education in sixteenth-century Mexico) can immediately be learned from his having been "Don" Hernando Franco. Nowadays, the use of "Don" as an honorific has become so widespread in Spain and in Latin America that not many stop to consider how few had a right to use it in the sixteenth century.

At that time the use of *don* was restricted to people of the very highest classes in Spain. Not a single member of Cortés's expedition was a *don,* not even Cortés himself. The first document referring to him as a *don* is dated Toledo, May 5, 1525. Alonso de Santa Cruz, who seems to have been very careful about the use of honorific titles, in his *Crónica* first refers to Cortés as a *don* in 1526. Previously he called him *capitán.*

A curious use of the title is found in its application to the leading *caciques* of Mexico. When the crown in Spain began granting coats of arms to them they were invariably referred to as *dons.* Numerous Spaniards, who performed far greater services, in receiving coats of arms, did not attain the use of the title *don.*[102]

With the choice of Christian names that was his at baptism, many a cacique opted for the name of his Spanish godfather, with the result that the Ixtlilxóchitl who ruled Texcoco, and who joined Cortés against Moctezuma, became "Don Fernando Cortés Ixtlilxóchitl" once he was baptized by Fray Juan de Ayora.[103] The *Annales de Chimalpahin* preserve the name of a Don Hernando Cortés, lord of Itztlacoçauhcan.[104] Quite often the Indian part of the name disappeared entirely. Thus, a cacique of Coatlán, Oaxaca, turns up in the *Relación de Coatlán* as "Don Fernando Cortés," no more.[105] Another styled himself "Don Pedro de Alvarado," after Cortés' hotheaded captain of the same name.[106] Earlier, on page 94, attention was called to Pedro de Gante who died in 1605 after a lifetime spent teaching in Tlatelolco College.

Años" at folio 87r (upper right-hand corner of the page) should probably be taken as the date of copying. The watermark at folios 101v–109 agrees with that cataloged in C. M. Briquet, *Les Filigranes: Dictionnaire historique des marques du papier* (2d ed.; Leipzig: Karl W. Hiersemann, 1923), II, 335 (no. 5693). On its evidence the paper is of Madrid provenience (1561–1571). The watermark consists of a Latin cross tipped with a small ornament and enclosed within a lozenge, beneath which appear the letters *I* and *A* with a vertical line between them.

[102] Henry R. Wagner, *The Rise of Fernando Cortés* (Berkeley: The Cortés Society [Documents and Narratives concerning the Discovery and Conquest of Latin America, n.s., III], 1944), pp. 382–383 (abridged).

[103] Agustín de Vetancurt, *Teatro Mexicano,* IV (Madrid: José Porrúa Turanzas, 1961), p. 197.

[104] Rafael García Granados, *Diccionario Biográfico de Historia Antigua de Méjico* (México: Instituto de Historia, 1953), III, 44 (no. 4170).

[105] *Ibid.,* p. 43 (no. 4162).

[106] *Ibid.,* p. 18 (no. 3993).

For those who wish to multiply the list of famous names adopted by Indian converts, *Indios Cristianos de los Siglos XVI y XVII* provides a happy hunting ground. To this group belongs the composer of the two chanzonetas transcribed below from the Valdés Codex.

Only lack of full information concerning the Mexico City Cathedral chapelmaster Hernando Franco (1532–1585),[107] from whom Don Hernando Franco copied his name, previously permitted confusion of the two. Now that his antecedents have been canvassed, it becomes obvious that the cathedral chapelmaster can never have merited the "don" honorific. For that matter, the peninsula itself boasted few composers of that social category. "Don" Fernando de las Infantas (1534–*ca.* 1610) came of sufficiently important stock to be thus styled.[108] Any other reputable composer who was a don will be found with great difficulty.

The text of Don Hernando Franco's two apostrophes to the Virgin—the first *a* 5 (fols. 121*v*–122), the second *a 4* (122*v*–123)—read thus:

1. Sancta maria yn ilhuicac cihuapille tinatzin dios yn titotenpantlatocantzin.
   ‖: Ma huel tehuatzin topan ximotlatolti yn titlatlaconhuanimen. :‖
2. ‖: Dios itlaçonantzine cemicac ichpochtle cenca timitztotlatlauhtiliya ma topan ximotlatolti yn ilhuicac ixpantzinco in motlaçoconetzin Jesu Christo. : ‖ Ca onpa timoyeztica yn inahuactzinco yn motlaço conetzin Jesu Christo.

The eminent Aztecist Charles E. Dibble, professor of anthropology at the University of Utah, translates the texts:

1. Holy Mary, Queen of Heaven, Mother of God, thou art our mediator. Intercede ["speak thou well"] for us who are sinners.
2. Oh precious Mother of God, oh eternal Virgin, we earnestly implore of thee: intercede for us. In heaven thou art in the presence of thy dearest Son, Jesus Christ. For thou art there beside Him. In heaven thou art in the presence of thy dearest Son, Jesus Christ.

Facsimiles of the appropriate openings from the Valdés Codex were published as long ago as 1934 (by Saldívar, *Historia de la Música en México*, pp. 102–105) and, as a result, Don Hernando Franco's notational expertise was never for a moment left in doubt among those acquainted with Spanish mensural practice in the period. Like the Náhuatl-speaking maestro de capilla of San Juan Ixcoi (Huehuetenango department, Guatemala) who was his contemporary—Tomás Pascual, active 1595–1635 [109]—our composer liked ternary meter. But, as taught by Spaniards, the mensurations for triple movement still involved all the medieval intricacies of imperfection, alteration, coloration, punctus additionis, and punctus divisionis, long after musicians in other parts of Europe had taken off their hair shirts and found

---

[107] Biography in "European Music in 16th-Century Guatemala," *Musical Quarterly*, L/3 (July, 1964), 342–343.

[108] Stevenson, *Spanish Cathedral Music in the Golden Age*, pp. 316–318.

[109] Transcriptions of three villancicos by Tomás Pascual in *Musical Quarterly*, L/3, pp. 347–348, 350.

easier solutions. Don Hernando showed his complete mastery of the prickly system still being taught in the peninsula. As applied in Spain, the rules meant that in C3 ♩ ♪ ♩ and ♩·♪ ♩ could both demand the same rhythmic figure when transcribed into modern ⅜, namely: ♫♩ In C3 ♩ ♩ ♩ ♩ and ♩ ♩ ♩ ♩ could both mean, in modern ⅜, ♫♩ ♪ . For the record, these and other pieces of barbed wire scratch any neophyte's foot who today tries scaling the fence erected around Don Hernando's piece in C3. The first transcriber to try left a bleeding trail, for lack of the necessary preliminary training in Spanish notational practice of the period.[110]

But at the same moment that his notation was building fences that not all doctoral candidates can today climb over, Don Hernando was showing a certain clumsiness in his part-writing that a harmony student can detect. Within the Spanish Renaissance context, his management of suspensions, of consecutive fifths and octaves—to mention no other niceties—is frequently distressing. When his teacher from whom he took his name (the cathedral chapelmaster) wrote a triple-meter piece, the part-writing is everywhere elegant—witness the Gloria in the chapelmaster's *Magnificat Septimi toni*.[111] The paradox glaring at us from the Indian pupil's chanzonetas therefore needs explaining. How can such command of the mensural notation system combine in the same composer with so amateurish a part-writing concept? Perhaps the native tradition that idolized rhythmic instruments and made a fetish of beat helps explain Don Hernando's mastery in one area and his naïveté in another.

In this same connection, we also do well to remember that in 1527 when Aztec dance and music made their debut in Europe it was the rhythmic ingenuity of it all which kept Charles V and his court at Valladolid enthralled an entire morning. According to Valadés (*Rhetorica Christiana*, p. 169), the precision with which the troupe executed the most complicated changes in exact unison surpassed anything heretofore seen at court. Throughout the lapse from 1527 to 1599, the presumed date of Don Hernando's chanzonetas, the native traditions obviously suffered some losses. For instance, Valadés himself states that after becoming Christianized men and women no longer danced promiscuously together. But in such chanzonetas as Don Hernando's, not to mention those of the Indian maestro Tomás Pascual transcribed in the *Musical Quarterly*, L/3 (July, 1964), 347–350, they show that the mastery of notation gave each his opportunity to vaunt himself in dance measures as vigorous as any that their ancestors may have known.

Their "religious" texts certainly do not prevent either of Don Hernando's chanzonetas from being dance music. Fortunately for the native tradition in Mexico, Spanish custom throughout the sixteenth century permitted even

---

[110] Saldívar, *op. cit.*, p. 106.
[111] Steven Barwick, *The Franco Codex* (Carbondale: Southern Illinois University Press, 1964), pp. 134–136.

so prominent a composer as Francisco Guerrero of Seville to use the same
music with secular and sacred texts, as his *Canciones y villanescas espirituales* published at Venice in 1589 amply testifies. Only those unacquainted with the habit of making the same music do for profane and
for *a lo divino* texts will imagine that Don Hernando let his musical wings
be clipped by any presently surviving "religious" texts.

Judged by European canons, his melodies are attractive enough to continue to be appealing after several hearings. At the Tlatelolco college for
noble Indian youths, preliminary music training was given by Bernardino
de Sahagún himself. Many of his pupils emerged so competent musically
"that the [Mexico City] Cathedral itself took them into choir service" ("de
mucho de ellos se ha valido la Catedral para su capilla").[112] But this Tlatelolco training took them only through canto llano and those rules of
mensuration that would enable them to bear their own part in *canto de
órgano.* Soigné part-writing, no less than the rules of mensural notation,
must be learned. The explanation for Don Hernando's weaknesses probably
lies in the system that gave Indian musicians sufficient rhythmic and melodic background to enter even the Cathedral capilla but that forswore the
counterpoint needed to make them highly sophisticated composers of part
music.

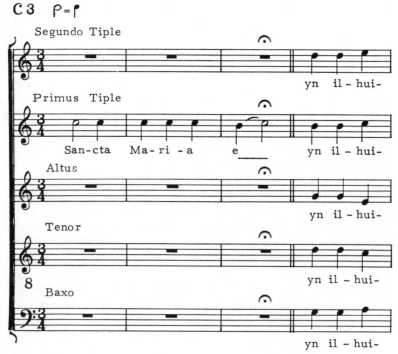

[112] García Icazbalceta, *Bibliografía Mexicana del Siglo XVI* (1954), p. 340 (quoting
from Agustín de Vetancurt, *Menologio,* October 23, *Theatro,* pte. IV, trat. 2, cap. 2, no.
159).

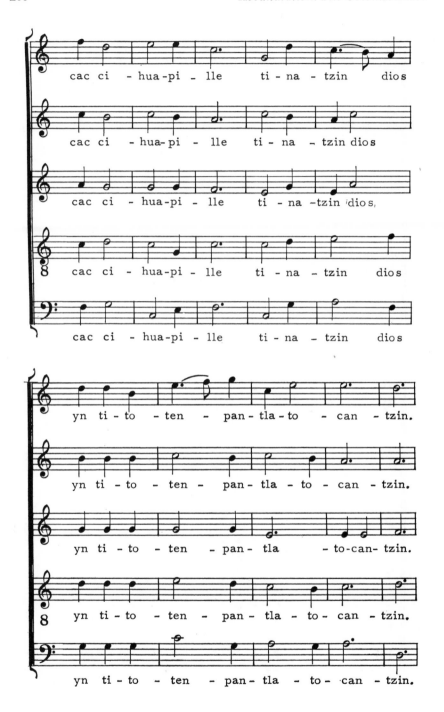

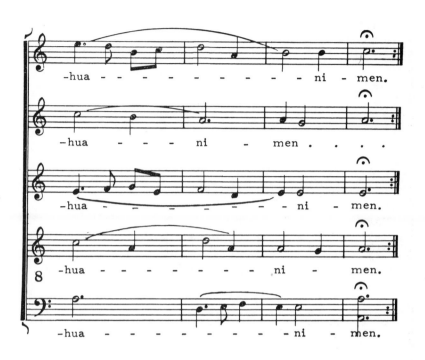

-hua - - - - - - - - ni - men.

-hua - - - ni - men . . . .

-hua - - - - - - ni - men.

-hua - - - - - - - ni - men.

-hua - - - - - - - ni - men.

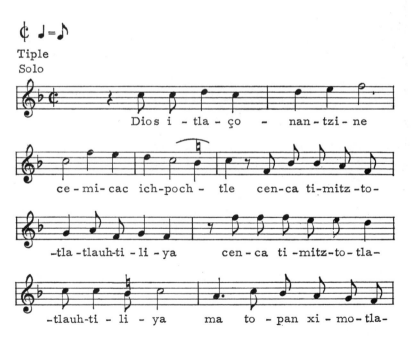

Tiple
Solo

Dios i - tla - ço - nan - tzi - ne

ce - mi - cac ich - poch - tle   cen - ca ti - mitz - to-

-tla - tlauh - ti - li - ya   cen - ca ti - mitz - to - tla-

-tlauh - ti - li - ya   ma   to - pan xi - mo - tla-

Codex Philipp J. Becker I (*Le Manuscrit du Cacique*), panels 8–9, upper strip. Vertical shading in the above reproduction represents red in the original codex, horizontal equals blue, no shading means yellow. Consisting of three fragments, this codex depicts an eleventh-century Mixtec dynastic struggle. The royal musicians in panels 8–9 play instruments still in vogue not only in 1521 but also much later. See above, pages 24, 26–28, 34, and 77–78 for references to this codex. Since such chanzonetas as those just shown at pages 208–219 resounded to the accompaniment of teponaztlis, huehuetls, and other indigenous instruments, they thereby acquired a local flavor denied them when nowadays they are performed *a cappella* with Spanish-translated texts.

SECULAR MUSIC AND MUSICIANS IN THE YOUNG COLONY

In the *Historia Eclesiástica Indiana* (Bk. III, chap. xix [p. 225]), Mendieta claimed that Indians by the hundreds started humming the simple and catchy tunes with which religious instruction was baited by the pioneer Franciscan Francisco Ximénez. When joined to doctrine in their own tongue, the tunes so fascinated them that the boys in the friars' school would crowd into the patio to sing them. Later, they would spend "three and four hours at a time repeating the tunes at home and at their various meeting places." This craze began in 1525, four years after Mexico City was gained.

Motolinía, Mendieta, and Torquemada agree that during the next year, 1526, the Franciscan Juan Caro began the first formal teaching of figural music in Mexico.[113] Motolinía, however, goes on to confirm a fact that must be immediately apparent to anyone who reads conquest histories written by laymen. The bulk of the early teaching—especially of the common classes —fell to Spanish secular musicians, not friars. So many instrumentalists eager to reap riches flooded into Mexico before 1530 that they had to be partitioned out among the villages.

Since so many instrumentalists could never be boarded and lodged all in one place, they were asked to separate and go through the Indian towns, teaching the natives how to play shawms and their other instruments. How fast the Indians learned can be gauged from the following: a Spanish rebeck-player in Tlaxcala gave an Indian owning a homemade rebeck three lessons. In ten days the Indian had made such headway with it that he was able to join an ensemble of recorders and take the leading part. Just now there is a teacher of viols at Mexico City, and he has all four sizes [soprano, alto, tenor, bass]. I will be much surprised if the Indians studying with him do not master every secret of his art before the year is out.[114]

To avoid bogging the reader down with detail, Motolinía does not name the Mexico City teacher of the *vihuela de arco* with all four sizes of the instrument, but this teacher may well have been the same viol player named Ortiz who joined Cortés' expedition at Trinidad, Cuba. A man of substance, he and Bartolomé García "sold or gave" Cortés the best steed in the expedition. After Mexico City was gained, Ortiz was among the first to set up as a dancing master and viol teacher.[115] He was soon forced, however, to change

---

[113] *Colección de Documentos*, I, 109: "Fray Juan Caro, un honrado viejo, el cual introdujo y enseñó primero en esta tierra el castellano y el canto de órgano"; *Historia Eclesiástica Indiana* (1870), p. 412; *Monarquía Indiana* (1723), III, 213, col. 2.

[114] *Col. de Doc.* (1858), I, 210–211 (paraphrased and abridged).

[115] Bernal Díaz del Castillo, *op. cit.*, I, 58, 66 ("ortiz el musico"), 138 ("En aquella sazon se le murio el cavallo a cortes y compro o le dieron otro, q̃ se dezia el harriero, q̃ era castaño oscuro que fue de ortiz El musico"); II, 465 ("ortiz gran tañedor de byola e amostraba a dançar").

his studio location after three bordellos opened nearby. His clientele included numerous Indians. Had it not, his gaining such mastery of Náhuatl as to be called a *Nahuatlato* [116] ("interpreter") would be more difficult to explain. The buildings used for his dancing and music academy were converted after his death into a part of the first Jeronymite nuns' convent in Mexico [117] (inaugural ceremony, September 29, 1585), and in them lived Sor Juana Inés de la Cruz, the famous Mexican poetess.

Another pioneer music teacher in the capital was a Valencian (and therefore compatriot of Luys Milán) whose name in both Bernal Díaz del Castillo's *Historia verdadera* and in the first book of the Mexico City cabildo acts is reduced to Maese Pedro "de la harpa." [118] On October 30, 1526, he and another musical conquistador—the drum-and-fife player for Cortés' invading forces, Benito de Bejel [119]—petitioned the cabildo for rights to a choice plaza location where they proposed "setting up a dancing school to give luster to the City." [120] The cabildo acceded with a permit to build on a plot 50 feet wide and 30 deep. How great were the rewards Mexico offered Benito de Bejel (who had started life as a mere drum-and-fife player for Spanish forces in Italy) is shown by his rising, before 1543, to the status of an encomendero, gathering tributes and personal services every eighty days from Indians at Axacuba. [121] Some idea of the demand for the instruments that were being taught by these and by other musical conquistadores in the reviving city can be gathered from the cabildo deliberations of February 8, 1527, which mention the shops where music accessories were being sold. [122]

On Cortés' journey to Honduras (October, 1524—April 25, 1526) [123] he

---

Another musician whose first name Bernal Díaz ignored settled at Colima: "vn hulano moron gran musico vezino de colimar" (II, 453). Saldívar (p. 161) baptized him Alfonso Morón and made him a vihuela player.

[116] Julio Jiménez Rueda, *Historia de la Cultura en México: El Virreinato* (México: Editorial Cultura, 1950), p. 254.

[117] Josefina Muriel, *Conventos de Monjas en la Nueva España* (México: Editorial Santiago, 1946), p. 252, quoting Francisco Fernández del Castillo, *Doña Catalina Xuárez Marcayda, primera esposa de Hernán Cortés* (México: Imprenta Victória, 1920), p. 72. In his *Índice alfabético,* p. vii, Fernández del Castillo gives "Alonso" as Ortiz' Christian name.

[118] Bernal Díaz, *op. cit.,* II, 464–465; *Actas del Cabildo de la Ciudad de México* (México: Ignacio Bejarano, 1889), I, 109 (Oct. 30, 1526).

[119] Bernal Díaz, *op. cit.,* I, 386: "benito de beger, nro pifano"; II, 460: "benyto de bejel fue atanbor y tanborino de exerçitos de ytalia e tambien lo fue en esta nueva españa."

[120] *Actas,* I, 109–110: "pedieron que les hiciesen merced de les dar un sytio para en que hagan donde agora esta la plaza una escuela de danzar por ser ennoblecimiento de la Cibdad."

[121] *El Libro de las Tasaciones de Pueblos de Nueva España, Siglo XVI,* prologue by Francisco González de Cossío (México: Archivo General de la Nación, 1952), p. 97.

[122] *Ibid.,* I, 121: "donde agora estan las tendezuelas de los tañedores."

[123] Fernando Ramírez, *Expedición de Hernán Cortés a Las Hibueras* (México: Vargas Rea, 1947), pp. 7, 27 (dates from Gómara).

took along "five players of shawms, sackbuts, and dolcians; also a tumbler and a puppeteer who did sleight of hand tricks." [124] The trip lasted much longer than planned, many died from hunger, and Cuauhtémoc—the last Aztec king—was hanged in Lent, 1525, with two other chieftains, on conspiracy charges.[125]

The players of the shawms, sackbuts, and dolcians whom I mentioned before were accustomed to dainties in Castile and could not endure the hardships. Having fallen ill from hunger, they made no music—except one of them, and all the soldiers cursed the sound of it and complained that it was no better than foxes or the howling of jackals. We said that it would be better to have maize to eat than music.[126]

Some of the Indians in the expedition resorted to the time-honored expedient of cannibalism, and Cortés was later accused of abetting their deed.[127] Worse still, four of the musicians ended in the stomachs of the starving soldiers. Only one of the original five instrumentalists lived to tell the tale, the shawmer Bartolomé de Medrano. In 1544 when Cristóbal de Pedraza, bishop of Honduras, wrote his *Relacion de la Prouincia de Honduras y Higueras,* he recorded that the expeditioners were reduced first to eating their horses, and next to eating each other.

Medrano who at present [1544] is shawmer at Toledo Cathedral [128] told me, and many others as well, that he had eaten the brains of the sackbut player Montesinos, native of Seville, and the intestines and brains of Bernardo Caldera, brother of the licenciado Caldera who was a long time in Peru. Also he said he helped eat Bernardo Caldera's cousin. These four instrumentalists were all natives of Seville, specially contracted for Cortés' service, and all four perished of hunger in the expedition.[129]

This makes of course the kind of piquant anecdote that a Ricardo Palma could embellish with rare effect. But as sober history it needs to be recalled if only to counterbalance the impression that all emigrating musicians and dancers struck it rich in sixteenth-century America. The acculturative process operated on a two-way street. What habits were picked up by the Indians from Europeans must in fairness be weighed against those learned by the Spaniards from the Indians.

[124] Bernal Díaz, *op. cit.,* II, 278: "çinco chirimías y çacabuches y dulçaynas."

[125] López de Gómara, chap. 179 (Simpson trans., p. 356).

[126] Bernal Díaz, *op. cit.,* II, 287.

[127] *Documentos para la Historia de México,* I: *Sumaria de la Residencia tomada, á D. Fernando Cortés,* transcribed by Ignacio López Rayon (México: Vicente García Torres, 1852), p. 231 (XXXV).

[128] Stevenson, *Spanish Cathedral Music in the Golden Age,* pp. 121 n. 170, 228 n. 74.

[129] *Colección de Documentos Inéditos relativos al descubrimiento, conquista y organización de las antiguas posesiones españolas,* 2d ser., XI: *Relaciones de Yucatán,* I (Madrid: Sucs. de Rivadeneyra, 1898), 413.

At the same time that Cortés was urging conversion on his captives, he was accused of restraining friars from destroying their temples and of allowing the common folk to continue unhindered in their former beliefs.

In the villages for which he was personally responsible more idols and sacrifices continued than elsewhere. Whereas it is a known fact that Franciscans went about burning many heathen temples in the Mexico City area, Cortés said it would have been better to let them stand, and he showed himself greatly annoyed that their temples had not been allowed to remain as memorials ["mostro tener grand enojo por que queria que estuviesen aquellas casas de ydolos por memoria"].[130]

Ever addicted to display, Cortés insisted on surrounding himself with all the apparatus of a great Spanish lord. His personal panoply always included some such band of musicians as the group too delicate for the harsh Honduras march or as the still larger band that entertained guests at a sumptuous banquet held at Mexico City to commemorate the peace pact agreed to (June, 1538) by Francis I and Charles V at Nice.[131] Bernal Díaz attended the Mexico City banquet. More than twenty years later he could still savor the brilliance of the "tronpeteria y generos de instrumentos harpas biguelas [vihuelas] flavtas dulçainas chirimias" announcing the change of courses during the banquet [132] (jointly given by Viceroy Antonio de Mendoza and Cortés).

But when he revisited Spain, arriving in May, 1527,[133] not Spanish instrumentalists but native Mexican entertainers—Indian jugglers and dancers especially—made up Cortés' train. A sensation was caused by those who could juggle a tree trunk with bare feet while lying on their backs (see above, p. 118 for description of the musical accompaniment). Rather than

---

[130] *Documentos para la Historia de México*, I: *Sumaria de la Residencia* (1852), pp. 231–232. Testimony taken from Rodrigo de Castañeda, January 3, 1529. One of the first conquistadores, Castañeda was named *alférez real* in 1528.

[131] Morales wrote a famous festal motet for the occasion; see Stevenson, *Spanish Cathedral Music*, pp. 18–19.

[132] *Historia verdadera*, II, 423.

[133] Bernal Díaz, *op. cit.*, II, 383, and Gómara, *op. cit.*, chap. 192 (Simpson trans., p. 390), quarrel on the date of Cortés' arrival in Spain. "Toward the end of the year 1528," wrote Gómara; Bernal Díaz placed their arrival a year earlier. Herrera y Tordesillas, followed by Lucas Alamán, *Disertaciones sobre la historia de la república mexicana* (México: José Mariano Lara, 1844), II, 22, opts for 1528. The conflict of dates puts us on guard against the many other discrepancies in published accounts of this trip. Diego Valadés refers to the impression made by the Indian dancers and singers in Cortes' tow (*Rhetorica Christiana*, 1579, p. 169): "dum in Valle Soletana specimen eius rei coram eo ederetur. . . ." According to Manuel de Foronda y Aguilera, "Estancias y Viajes de Carlos V," *Boletín de la Sociedad Geográfica de Madrid*, XXXVII/7 (July, 1895), 26, Charles V spent nearly all his time at Valladolid from January 24 to August 23, 1527. But in 1528 he did not reside there so much as a day. Valadés strengthens Bernal Diaz' date.

hoarding such spectacle, which proved vastly entertaining to the highborn of Spain and opened for Cortés several doors to powerful officialdom,[134] Charles V agreed that the same Indian entertainers should be sent to amuse Popè Clement VII.[135] As marks of favor, the thirty-nine Indians in Cortés' entourage were all given travel money back to Mexico out of the royal coffers, outfits of gaudy European clothing, and various other bounties.[136]

Not only did the Indians dance before the Spanish court, but so did Cortés himself. Clad in full armor, he allegedly danced a pavane.[137] Before dance historians discovered that the lutanist Joan Ambrosio Dalza began publishing pavanes in 1508, Charles Compan's *Dictionnaire de danse* (Paris: Cailleau, 1787, pp. 294–295) and other dance lexicons habitually classed the pavane as a Spanish dance imitating a turkey's movements (*pavo* = turkey), and seized on Cortés' return to Spain in 1527 as the year the pavane reached the Peninsula. This unfortunate surmise falls even flatter before the obstacle posed by Luys Millán. The first to publish *pavanas* in Spain (*Libro de mvsica de vihuela de mano. Intitulado El maestro*, Valencia, 1535), Milán prefaced his pavanes with the explicit statement that his "imitated the sound of those composed in Italy." [138]

This attempt to foist a Mexican origin on a European dance [139] having

[134] *Historia verdadera*, II, 385.

[135] *Ibid.*, p. 391; Alamán, *op. cit.*, II, 28; Niceto de Zamacois, *Historia de Méjico* (Barcelona: J. F. Parres, 1877), IV, 462.

[136] Alamán, *op. cit.*, II, 29.

[137] *Enciclopedia dello Spettacolo* (1960), VII, col. 1789. Describing the ceremonious character of the Spanish pavane, Gino Tani writes: "Nobile, magnifica, processionale divenne soprattutto alla corte spagnolo: Hernán Cortés in armatura completa la danzò a Madrid coi suoi ufficiali al ritorno della conquista del Messico."

Despite long wear, this anecdote smacks of fable. Like Voltaire's anecdote of Cortés' vainly seeking an audience with Charles V and being rebuffed, it makes a good story. Voltaire ends his "Conquête du Mexique" (*Essai sur les moeurs et l'esprit des nations*, III [Œuvres complètes, 1785 ed., XVIII], 329) thus: "A peine put-il obtenir audience de *Charles-Quint:* un jour il fendit la presse qui entourait la coche de l'empereur, & monta sur l'étrier de la portière. *Charles* demanda quel était cet homme: 'C'est, répondit *Cortez*, celui qui vous a donné plus d'Etats que vos pères ne vous ont laissé de villes.' "

Fabricated out of whole cloth by Voltaire, this anecdote still finds a place in encyclopedias—because so *bien trouvé*. Voltaire also pioneered in claiming that the human sacrifices of the Aztecs were an exaggeration spread abroad by the conquistadores to justify their own cruelties ("C'est une très-grande exagération; on sent qu'on a voulu colorer par-là les injustices du vainqueur de *Montezuma*" [p. 323]). According to him they were never cannibals ("ils n'étaient point anthropophages" [p. 324]).

[138] *Publikationen älterer Musik*. Zweiter Jahrgang (Leipzig: Breitkopf & Härtel, 1927), p. 65. Authoritative descriptions of the Italian *pavana* and *padoana* in Lawrence H. Moe, "Dance Music in Printed Italian Lute Tablatures" (Harvard University Ph.D. dissertation, 1956), I, 37–41, 43–46.

[139] Both Gabriel Saldívar (*Historia de la Música* [1934], p. 159) and Carlos Chávez (Herbert Weinstock, *Mexican Music* [1940], p. 9) fell into the trap. For claiming a

ended in fiasco, attempts to find American antecedents for any other European dance immediately raise dust clouds of suspicion. The sarabande offers a good illustration. Several years after the death of Bartolomé José Gallardo (1776–1852), his bibliographic jottings were compiled in *Ensayo de una biblioteca española de libros raros y curiosos,* Volume IV (Madrid: Manuel Tello, 1889). Item 4542 in the *suplemento* (p. 1527) records a manuscript miscellany copied in various hands. "En la ciudad de Panamá" and "Año 1539" identify the place and date of the manuscript, according to Gallardo's editors, who give the manuscript the factitious title of *Varios.* If they may be believed, a long poem by Fernando Guzmán Mexía on the "Vida y tiempo de Maricastaña" takes up folios 207–281*v.* After invoking the *burlescas musas* the poet recalls the sound of *zambapalo y zarabanda* (1. 18). Does this allusion mean that the poet, risiding in Panama in 1539, already knew the zarabanda = sarabande?

Hernán Mejía de Guzmán (= Fernando Guzmán Mexía) does figure in the history of Panama during this very epoch. Son of Pedro de Mejía (1496–*ca.* 1552), Charles V's chronicler, Hernán Mejía de Guzmán was born at Seville and came out to Tierra Firme with his father-in-law Luis de Cabrera. Thence he passed to Peru where he gained fame as an infantry captain in the civil wars. Upon Gonzalo Pizarro's defeat he was posted back to Spain with news of Pedro de la Gasca's successful pacifying of the country.[140] Arriving in Seville on December 8, 1548, he immediately continued north to present the good news at court. Unfortunately for Mejía de Guzmán's reputation as the first to mention the sarabande, the manuscript from which the allusion came has yet to be studied and dated scientifically.

Better can be said of the earliest known Mexican document for the prehistory of the sarabande. The text of a six-strophe *çarauanda* (= *zarabanda*) by Pedro de Trejo has survived from the year 1556. Born at Plasencia, Extremadura, in 1536,[141] Trejo left home for Seville in 1556, proceeding thence to Mexico the next year, after a brief visit home to pick up his belongings. During the first four years in Mexico he resided in what are now the states of Jalisco and Michoacán, with one or two side trips to Zacatecas (the great silver mining center). In 1561 he married the wealthy Doña Isabel Corona, by whom he had two children, Francisco, born in 1564, and Esteban, born in 1566. However, their married life ran so unevenly that she

---

Mexican origin for the pavane, they could appeal to so standard an encyclopedia as the *Grand Dictionnaire Universel du XIXe Siècle* (Paris: P. Larousse, 1874), XII, 444, col. 3.

[140] *Enciclopedia Universal Ilustrada* (Espasa-Calpe), XXXIV, 257. Gonzalo Fernández de Oviedo, *Historia General y Natural de las Indias* (Madrid: Gráficas Orbe, 1959 [Biblioteca de Autores Españoles, CXXI]), pp. 288, 290, 299–300.

[141] Archivo General de la Nación [Mexico City], Ramo de Inquisición, CXIII, fol. 310.

later accused him (to the Santo Oficio) of brutal conduct, extending even to beatings.

His favorite diversion in the 1560's seems to have been versifying. Within this decade he not only composed but also copied in a writing master's hand the *Cancionero general de obras del poeta Pedro de Trejo,* dedicating it to Philip II. It is this cancionero and an enlarged version of his poems dated 1569 that contained the text of the çarauanda.[142] Although certain of Trejo's poems boasted such distinguished literary models as Jorge Manrique and Juan Rodríguez del Padrón (a musical version of whose *Viue leda* is in the Colombina Cancionero, MS 7-I-28), they frequently mixed the sacred and secular in ways that offended the delicate sensibilities of Holy Office authorities at Mexico City, with the result that after 1572 Trejo was denied the happy pastime of penning coplas on either sacred or secular topics.

His poems do enjoy enough lasting literary merit for Alfonso Méndez Plancarte to have included several in *Poetas Novohispanos: Primer Siglo* (Mexico City: Universidad Nacional Autónoma, 1942, pp. 5–9) and to have praised them (p. xx) for their "grave o graciosa inspiración." Méndez Plancarte seems also to have been the first who descried the historical importance of Trejo's sarabande when he wrote (p. 9) that it antedated the first peninsular mention of the sarabande by fourteen years and therefore goes far to confirm the origins in the New World of this universally known European dance.

The line in Trejo's sarabande which caused Inquisition censors at Mexico City the greatest disquiet read: "el Criador es ya criatura." In defense of this line (written to rhyme with the refrain line, "Çarauanda ven y dura"), Trejo alleged that the bishop of Michoacán, after submitting the text of the whole zarabanda to three friars for approval, had himself ordered it sung at Pátzcuaro (holy city of the Tarascans) on Corpus Christi. Trejo's testimony, preserved at the Archivo General de la Nación in Ramo de Inquisición, Volume CXIII, folio 334, proved irrefragably the 1569 date of the zarabanda. The refrain line, "Çarauanda ven y dura," finds an echo as late as Quevedo's *El Entremetido y la dueña y el soplón,*[143] when a demon accuses "el poeta de los pícaros" of having invented such filthy things as the 'tengue tengue, don golondrón, pisaré yo el polvillo, zarabanda y dura, vámonos á chacona."

Quevedo's coupling of zarabanda and chacona in the same list takes on

---

[142] For facsimile of the çarauanda copied in the *cancionero,* see *Revista de Literatura Mexicana,* Año 1, no. 1 (July–Sept., 1940), pp. 92–94. At pp. 230–231 of the *Boletín del Archivo General de la Nación,* XV/2 (April–June 1944), a printed transcription appeared of the çarauanda copied by Trejo into the 1569 enlarged version of his poems. The 1569 manuscript poems are bound in Ramo de Inquisición, CXIII, after folio 46.

[143] Francisco de Quevedo Villegas, *Obras satíricas y festivas* (Madrid: Sucs. de Hernando, 1904), p. 308.

added interest in the light of Curt Sachs's contention that both sarabande and chaconne originated in the New World.[144] In Spain the earliest reference to the sarabande that he could cite was a prohibition dated 1583. Diego Durán the Dominican historian of preconquest Mexico, mentioned it as a familiar dance in New Spain before 1579. For him it was the epitome of lewdness and only such an Indian provocation to vice as their "tickle dance" (*cuecuecheuycatl*[145]) could compete with "this sarabande which our creoles dance" (*esta zarabanda que nuestros naturales*[146] *usan*).

Less than two decades later, some of the more brazen belles of Lima, Peru, took up both the sarabande and the chaconne. Lines 1219 and 1221 of a 1598 poetical satire against Peruvian loose living (copied first in the 210-folio MS 19387 at the Biblioteca Nacional in Madrid with the title "Sátira hecha por Mateo Rosas de Oquendo a las cosas que pasan en el Pirú. Año de 1598") attest the currency of both dances in the South American viceroyalty. Rosas de Oquendo had been in Mexico before Peru, and nowhere hints that Peruvians had invented the *Puertorrico* ("too bad for the person who takes it up," he exclaims). Nor had they invented "La zarabanda y balona, / el churunba y el taparque, / la chacona y el totarque / y otros sones semexantes." Instead, it was the devil who invented them to seduce even a stone statue to acts of vice, contends the poet. The context of these earliest South American allusions to the sarabande and the chaconne can best be studied in A. Paz y Melia's pioneer edition of the poem (*Bulletin*

[144] *World History of the Dance* (New York: W. W. Norton, 1937), p. 367.

[145] *Historia de las Indias de Nueva España*, II (México: Ignacio Escalante, 1880), p. 231. See also Biblioteca Nacional, Madrid, MS 1982, fol. 147. The 1579 date comes at folio 168v and *sarabande* begins with ç (not z) in this manuscript (*çarabanda*). Indian men dressed as women to dance the *cuecuecheuycatl*, thus increasing its stench.

[146] Durán uses "los naturales" to mean the indigenes of Mexico. For examples, see his *Historia*, II, 68 (l. 10), 69 (24), 192 (1), 203 (3), 220 (32), 252 (4), 295 (10). He uses "los Españoles" to mean Spaniards born in Spain, including those who emigrated to the New World. Examples: *Historia*, II, 60 (ll. 1, 17, 18, 23–24, 25–26, 34), 63 (6, 8), 255 (19). When he wishes to refer to Spain, he writes "en España" (69 [19]). When referring to persons reared in Spain he writes "los que se criaron en España" (169 [36]). He uses "nuestros naturales" to mean Creoles.

According to the *Diccionario de la Lengua Española* issued by the Real Academia Española (Madrid: Espasa-Calpe, 1956), p. 913, "natural" signifies "nativo, originario de un pueblo o nación." Martín Alonso, *Enciclopedia del Idioma* (Madrid: Águilar, 1958), III, 2944, agrees. Sebastián de Covarrubias in his 1611 *Tesoro de la Lengua Castellana o Española* (Barcelona: S. A. Horta, I.E., 1943), p. 824, concurs thus: "Natural de Toledo, el que nació y tiene su parentela en Toledo." Expanding on this last distinction ("parentela"), Elías Zerolo, *Diccionario Enciclopédico de la Lengua Castellana, H-Z*, II (Paris; Garnier Hnos., n.d.), 368, writes: "*Natural* supone el domicilio fijo de los padres, mientras que *nacido* no supone más que simplemente el nacimiento" ("*natural* implies parents' residence [at the place of one's birth] whereas *nacido* implies no more than simply birth [at such-and-such a place]").

hispanique, VIII/2 [April–June, 1906] and 3 [July–Sept., 1906]) or in Rubén Vargas Ugarte's *Rosas de Oquendo y otros* (Lima: Tipografía Peruana, s.a., 1955), p. 29 [Clásicos Peruanos, V]).

What kind of figure did the youthful sarabande flaunt in Europe? The references collected by Sachs can serve as a summary. Mariano [147] excoriated it, Cervantes [148] denounced it, Marino [149] was disgusted with it. In Giambattista Marino's long poem *L'Adone* (published 1623) he identified and described as twins the sarabande and the chaconne. He complained that in both dances obscene motions and lewd gestures were the rule. He called down the wrath of heaven on the lascivious inventors of these vulgar dances. Both came from New Spain and the dancers pantomimed the ultimate intimacies of the conjugal act, according to him. Wanton maidens clacked castanets and snapped their fingers to enliven the beat, while the men banged tambourines. Far from the staid dance of the late Baroque, Marino knew it as a frenetic orgy accompanied by noisemakers.[150]

In France also it was known as the "mad sarabande" at least as early as 1605. Malherbe (1555–1628) mentions one such sarabande, inspired by the dancing of American savages, in a letter dated August 20, 1613 (*Œuvres,* ed. L. Lalanne [Paris: L. Hachette, 1862], III, 327). Six Tupinambá Indians captured on the island of Maranhão had arrived naked at Rouen earlier that year, but by the time they reached Paris they were being paraded fully clothed. Caught in the craze caused by their presence in the capital, the famous court lutanist Ennemond Gaultier (*ca.* 1580–1651) based a lute sarabande on one of their dances, and Malherbe sent a copy of this "Tupinambá" sarabande to his son, Marc-Antoine; he was confident that upon having learned it, his son would be delighted, because "it is considered one

[147] Juan de Mariana, *Tratado contra los juegos públicos,* chap. 12, "Del baile y cantar llamado zarabanda," in *Obras,* II (Madrid: M. Rivadeneyra, 1854 [Biblioteca de Autores Españoles, XXXI]), 432–434. The severity of Mariana's morals inspired him to inveigh with no less vigor against bullfighting.

[148] Cervantes mentioned the sarabande at least seven times. Sample reference: "el endemoniado son de la çarabanda" (*El celoso extremeño,* IV, 146). For the others, see Carlos Fernández Gómez, *Vocabulario de Cervantes* (Madrid: Imprenta Silverio Aguirre Torre, 1962), pp. 1097 and 1096 (under "zambapalo"). He mentions the chaconne four times, twice in conjunction with the sarabande (p. 287).

[149] G. B. Marino, *L'Adone* (Turin: G. B. Paravia, n.d.), p. 376. The stanzas in question are in Canto Ventecismo, 83–85.

[150] Although long disused anywhere in Mexico, the term *zarabanda* survived as late as 1936 for a drunken dance staged by a confraternity in highland Guatemala. See Ruth Bunzel, *Chichicastenango: A Guatemalan Village* (Locust Valley: J. J. Augustin, 1952 [Publications of the American Ethnological Society, XXII]), pp. 82, 85, 432. "When they have *zarabandas* they hire a marimba and they sell drinks, *chicha* and *aguardiente* for the expenses of the *cofradía.* They start on Sunday after the market starts to break up and it goes on all Sunday night and Monday until evening. The people dance and drink" (p. 85).

of the most excellent pieces that one can hear." If the sarabande "du vieux G." at page 40 of the *Livre de Tablature des Pièces de Luth. de M: Gaultier S: de Nèiie* (Paris: Chez la veufue de M: Gaultier, 1664?) comes close to the style of Gaultier's "Tupinambá" sarabande it should be transcribed into modern notation. The bizarre costumes forced on the six Tupinambá Indians when they danced in Paris, maracas in hand, inspired a contemporary print which, as plate 1 in the *Journal de la Société des Américanistes* (n.s., V/1 [1908]) serves as frontispiece for E.-T. Hamy's article, "Les Indiens de Rasilly: Étude iconographique et ethnographique" (pp. 21–52).

In England, Ben Jonson mentions the sarabande in plays produced in 1616 and 1625, calling it the "bawdy Saraband" in his *Staple of News* (1625), Act IV, scene 2. Even better evidence for the lascivious character of the youthful sarabande, however, crops up in so faraway a place from Mexico as Goa, India. In 1606 the Fifth Ecclesiastical Council banned the dance (Decreto 12: of Acção Quarta, printed in *Archivo Portuguez-Oriental*, fasc. 4: [Nova-Goa: Imprensa Nacional, 1862], p. 266):

Since nothing more conduces to sensuality than lascivious and unseemly songs and dances, this holy Synod requires that henceforth no one under pain of excommunion dare to dance or sing the sarabande . . .	Como não ha cousa, que mais incite a sensualidade, que cantos, e bailes lascivos, e deshonestos, manda esta sagrada Synodo sob pena de excommunhão que nenhuma pessoa daquy por diante seja ousada a bailar ou cantar a sarabanda . . .

But to return from the Far East to the New World: Taking his cue from Emilio Cotarelo y Mori,[151] Sachs adduced numerous passages from Cervantes, Lope de Vega, and Quevedo Villegas to show that the chaconne as well as the sarabande took root in the New World. In 1599 Simón Aguado "wrote an entremés *El Platillo* for Philip III's wedding festivities; during its course four players dance the chaconne, which Aguado tabs as of American provenience." [152] Tampico, Mexico, is suggested as its home base. While dancing it, Pobreto, Novato, and their girl friends work a confidence game on a rich Indian. Lope de Vega introduces a band of musicians in *La prueba de los amigos*. They are importuned to play. "Play what?" they ask. "Play that chaconne with the words beginning: 'Go to Tampico,'" [153] comes the reply. In another Lope de Vega comedy, *El amante agradecido* (1618), a troop of musicians start singing: "A jolly life, a jolly life we lead, dancing

---

[151] *Colección de Entremeses, Loas, Bailes, Jácaras y Mojigangas*, I, 1 (Madrid: Bailly-Bailliére, 1911), pp. cclxix–cclxxi.

[152] *Ibid.*, p. ccxl. See also p. 227 ("bailaban la chacona por extremo") and p. 229 ("vamanos, vida, á Tampico"). Aguado's manuscript (National Library, Madrid) is dated July 16, 1602, at Granada (p. 230n).

[153] Ricardo del Arco y Garay, *La Sociedad Española en las Obras Dramáticas de Lope de Vega* (Madrid: Escelicer, S.L., 1942), p. 916.

the chaconne. It came over from the Indies by mail, and now it dwells here in this house as its home; here it will live and die." [154]

From his several references, Sachs inferred not only that both the sarabande and the chaconne originated in New Spain but also that they showed Negroid influences. Negroes came with the conquistadores; one of Cortés' gunners was a Negro. Another named Juan Garrido was the first to sow wheat in Mexico.[155] After Las Casas suggested substituting Negro for Indian labor (to save the less hardy Indians from extermination) they arrived in ever-increasing numbers. On May 4, 1553, Viceroy Luis de Velasco importuned Charles V to allow the introduction of no more, because already there were in Mexico more than 20,000 and there were not nearly that many Spaniards in the land.[156] In 1580 New Spain still counted slightly fewer than 15,000 Spaniards, whereas the Negro population stood at more than 18,500, with another 1,500 registered as mulattoes.[157]

Small wonder that Negroes so mightily impressed the Indians, especially when they were named calpixques (= overseers of Indian pueblos [see above, p. 96]). At Mexico City their favorite diversion was to gather around the famous Aztec calendar stone (carved before 1481 for King Axayacatl) and play, sometimes so roughly that they ended by killing each other. Archbishop Montúfar (d. 1572) put a stop to this by ordering the stone buried.[158] By the end of the century (1598) Negro drums were so much better known in Mexico than the preconquest tlalpanhuehuetl that even an Indian historian, Alvarado Tezozomoc, felt obliged to explain the dread death drum of his ancestors by comparing it with *un atambor de los negros que hoy bailan en las plazas* ("a drum of the Negroes who nowadays dance in the plazas").[159] So much concrete data has in recent years come to light on the mutual interaction of Negro, Indian, and Spanish musics in colonial Mexico that Saldívar could devote a whole chapter to "La Influencia Africana" (*Historia de la Música en México*, pp. 219–229). From the sixteenth century he quoted Viceroy Luis de Velasco's decree dated January 2, 1569, confining the hours of dancing in the main Mexico City plaza to

---

[154] *Ibid.*, p. 915.

[155] Gonzalo Aguirre Beltrán, *La población negra de México 1519–1810* (México: Ediciones Fuente Cultural, 1946), p. 8 (quoting Francisco A. de Icaza, *Conquistadores y pobladores* [1923], I, 169).

[156] *Cartas de Indias*, pp. 264–265.

[157] Aguirre Beltrán, "The Slave Trade in Mexico," p. 414, quoting Germán Latorre, *Relaciones geográficas de Indias* [Biblioteca colonial americana, IV, Seville, 1920], pp. 97–99.

[158] Durán, *Historia*, II, 151–152: "Las dos piedras . . . la vna de las quales bimos mucho tiempo en la plaça grande . . . frontero de las cassas reales donde perpetuamente se recoxian cantidad de negros a jugar. . . . Alᵒ de Montúfar . . . la mando enterrar biendo lo que alli pasaua de males y omicidios."

[159] Hernando Alvarado Tezozomoc, *Crónica Mexicana* (México: Editorial Leyenda, 1944), p. 87 (chap. 24).

Sunday and feast-day afternoons, from noon until six o'clock. Mexico City was the capital, and regulations were better obeyed there than elsewhere. Following the example of the capital, nearby Puebla ruled in 1612 against the excessive Negro mixing and mingling in public dancing (*Libro de Cabildos de la Niña Ciudad de Puebla Año de 1606. 1612*, fol. 219*v* [April 7, 1612])—but only after Mexico City had renewed her decree against the Negro *cofradías* that sponsored the excessive diversion. The context of the 1612 decrees at Mexico City and Puebla clearly establishes that what was most feared from the Negro *cofradías*, *cantillos*, and *bayles* was the rioting, bloodshed, and killings that so frequently followed. Not manners, nor even public morals, were so much in issue as public peace. Where this was not jeopardized, free mixing meant the eventual submission of all native Indian dances to overriding Negro (and Spanish) influences. The rumba, the bomba, and even the huapango—all bear the Negro stamp.

An eyewitness report sent to Mexico City from the coastal province of Pánuco (north of Veracruz) will illustrate what kind of Negro-Indian mixing prevailed in 1624.[160]

The Huastec Indians throughout the whole province of Pánuco worshiped as their major deity a jug made of different-colored feathers from the mouth of which protruded artificial flowers made of the same featherwork. Balancing it, the Indians lightest on their feet whirled about, rattles in hand, dancing to the sounds of the wooden instrument called teponaztli by the Mexicans and of an indigenous drum. An elaborate headdress completed their costumes.

To summarize the rest of the report: This preconquest dance, called the *payà*, was formerly diffused throughout the whole province. Once purely Indian, it had by then (1624) been taken up by Negroes, mulattoes, and mestizos, with Lucas Olola, the Negro slave of Hernán Pérez, leading it. He wore Indian costume, put on an act of being enraptured, fell on the ground as dead, rose frothing at the mouth, and pretended to be seven gods, able to pass through walls. The terrified Indian men curried his favor by leaving their women alone with him. He convinced the Indians that a mulatto named Quintero had cast an evil eye on them, causing sickness, but claimed that he alone could cure them. (No missionaries worked in the area, but the Negroes and mulattoes spoke the Indian tongue.)

While accepting Negro leadership, the Huastecs continued to resist Spanish influences. What kind of acculturation Pánuco underwent during the next several decades can be learned from a report dispatched in 1783 to Mexico City by Francisco Xavier Rodríguez Barquero, parish priest assigned to the area.

---

[160] Archivo General de la Nación, Ramo de Inquisición, 303, fols. 255 (bis)–256*v*. Sample text: "Los indios mas ligeros baylan al son de vn instrumento q̃ llaman en mexicano teponastle, y de vn atambor a su usansa, llevando sonajas de madera en las manos."

In the missions subject to Tampico the Indians still perform their old prohibited dances such as the *volador,* danced on the tip of an enormously high pole. The music of teponaztli and of a clarion that they give the same name as their old dance, payà, serves as accompaniment for this dance performed nightly at their festivals. Beforehand, they prepare with fasting and abstinence from their wives. These are the same superstitions that Carlos de Tapia Centeno censured in a book in the Huastec tongue printed at Mexico City, 1767.[161] Worse still, missionaries who have seen their dances pretend that they contain nothing bad—because they do not wish to alienate their flocks.[162]

Negro or mulatto directors of the pole dance can still be documented at the close of the colonial period. On August 23, 1809, a mulatto maestro from Quezaltenango (Guatemala) arrived with a company of pole dancers in the town of San Antonio de Ciudad Real in Chiapas. They were promptly driven out when they added to the music of drum and fife a pantomime of a robber paying a confessor 1 peso for forgiveness of crime.[163]

Negroes in cities taught music and dancing, directed "oratorios," and ran what would now be called musical comedy theaters. For example: Joseph Chamorro, a free man of color, taught dancing and guitar playing at Oaxaca in 1682. His name is preserved because he was convicted in that year of bigamy.[164]

In 1669 at Puebla and again in 1684 in the Cuernavaca area, Negroes and mulattoes were cited for directing oratorios, although these had been forbidden by a printed edict issued at Mexico City on December 5, 1643. This edict identified an oratorio as a nighttime musical party (held in an interior patio as a rule), with dancing and refreshments (especially chocolate), all ostensibly in honor of the Holy Cross, Our Lady, or some saint. An altar

[161] Tapia Centeno's *Noticia de la lengua huasteca* (México: Imp. de la Bibliotheca Mexicana), written *ca.* 1725, was not licensed until 1746. According to the *Noticia,* p. 106, "the paya is an amphora decked with dyed featherwork flowers. Dressed as women with long false hair they balance it on their shoulders. They dance in a circle around a teponaztli played by the dancing master who with a clay thurible first incenses the musical instruments and next those around him. He warns them that unless thus incensed they will encounter ill fortune or die shortly." Tapia Centeno claimed that this dance honored *Teem,* "whom the Mexicans call Xochiquetzatl" (i.e., goddess of love).

[162] Ramo de Inquisición, 1283, fifth gathering, fols. 99*v*–100*v*. Like many other purists, Rodríguez Barquero got nowhere. When he demanded, on August 15, 1783, that the Tampico *alcalde mayor* prevent such a heathen dance from desecrating Assumption, Don Manuel Vasquez refused (fol. 101), saying that it had been permitted for a long time. At the mission of Osuluama the *palo volador* was approved as long ago as 1581, the zealous *cura* was informed. Digging around the pole set up in Tampico plaza, he found "many tamales, roast chickens, and other eatables." No one buries all that food around a high pole merely to enliven a *bayle* danced to the sound of teponaztli, he indignantly countered.

[163] Ramo de Inquisición, 1449 (1810), fol. 198.

[164] Ramo de Inquisición, 671, fols. 18–26.

would usually be set up in the patio, lit with many candles, and above the altar would be hung pictures of deceased friends or family. The oratorio would recur nightly for nine days with different guest lists each night and with the variety entertainment including a monologue by a dramatic reader accompanied by harp or guitar.

Two such oratorios were running at Puebla in early May, 1669. Both were being managed by Negroes belonging to Nicolás Alvares, prominent local citizen. Chorillo (= Melchor), a mulatto nicknamed "el cantor de la Virgen," led a combination of "muchos instrumentos de harpa y guitarras." Cervantes gave readings to the "musica de arpa y guitarra." [165] Everyone, "españoles, negros y mulatos," came and went freely during the nightly performances.

In time, entertainments given by Negro troupes gained such popularity among the richest classes that complaints of irreverence and misuse of sacred symbols were conveniently overlooked. In 1746, a complainant from Guadalajara denounced "Los combentticulos, y Prozesiones, Que los Mulattos, i Negros de la Ciudad de Guadalaxara han introduzido." At three in the afternoon, small bands of Negroes playing trumpet and drum would start making the rounds of the local wine shops to advertise the nighttime "Musicas, bailes, &." in their small homemade musical-comedy houses where (says the complainant) "grandissimo disorden" always prevailed. To this bill of particulars the Mexico City authorities replied that if prominent townspeople looked on it all as mere theater, then who were the capital inquisitors to start interfering with local entertainment given by Negroes? [166]

Two tablatures in the private collection of Gabriel Saldívar—one from Puebla, the other from León, Guanajuato—await publication. The first, a *Método de Cítara* (four courses), was assembled by Sebastián de Aguirre *ca.* 1650,[167] and contains in four-line cipher two *tocotines,* an *El Guasteco*

---

[165] Ramo de Inquisición, 612, fols. 509 (May 14, 1669), 511v–512 (Sept. 12, 1669). See also, "Denunciaciones . . . zerca de oratorios y Bailes," Ramo de Inquisición, 661 (1684). Ramo de Inquisición, 677, fol. 532, contains a letter from Oaxaca dated June 1, 1689, complaining that oratorios have flared up there, despite the effort to stamp them out.

[166] Ramo de Inquisición, 897, fols. 375 (complaint from Guadalajara, Sept. 19, 1746) and 378 (reply from Mexico City). Negro influences even today still make themselves felt in much of the entertainment music preferred in Mexico. See Carmen Sordo Sodi, "África en los Orígenes del 'a Go-Go,'" *El Sol de México,* Sección C, January 21, 1967, p. 8. The African influence was mediated in colonial times through the Caribbean Isles. It continues to be transmitted through those same islands now, writes Miss Sordo.

[167] Provisional date suggested by Dr. Saldívar who kindly permitted the taking of quick notes on the two tablatures kept at his house in Colonia Roma Sur (Anáhuac 86) in October, 1962. Without unhurried and unimpeded scrutiny of his tablatures I cannot guarantee the accuracy of the notes taken then, however. Although folios 31–37 are intabulated for a *vihuela de cinco órdenes,* the tablature is mostly for a *cítara* of four

(Huastec dance), a *panamá,* and a *portorrico de los Negros* (fol. 20). These tributes to the native environment joined such other dances in the Puebla tablature as the following: [168] a bacas (= vacas), six balonas (= valonas), three bran[le]s,[169] five canarios, one chanberga (= chamberga), two folías, three gallardas, twenty-one hachas, two jácaras, three marionas, one marizápalos, one morisca, eight pasacalles, four pavanas, three torbellinos,[170] four villanos, and one zarabanda. The titles of several dances include local qualifiers. For instance, the tablature includes a *Chiqueador de la Puebla* and a *Puerto Rico de la Puebla* (in addition to seven dances entitled simply *portorrico*). *El prado de San Gerónimo* precedes a *pasacalle de este prado* and another two pieces called simply *El prado.* Apart from pavanas and gallardas, the manuscript includes also a *pavana francés* and a *gallarda portugués.* The fact that the compiler calls one piece a *Balona de Bailar* but another six pieces simply *balonas* may mean nothing,[171] but it is significant that *La Oleada* is called a canción. Of the two villancicos in the tablature, the first inspires a pair of *diferencias* (variations), which follow immediately after. If the entire tablature antedates 1700, the two corridos precede all other notated examples of this popular Mexican song type.[172]

The compiler of Saldívar's handsome eighteenth-century tablature from Guanajuato—ninety-four folios of five-course guitar music—designates strummed chords with the capital letters well known to everyone who has looked at the third or eighth editions of Gaspar Sanz's *Instrvccion de mvsica*

---

courses. Until Dr. Saldívar publishes several musical documents in his possession, no comprehensive history of secular music in New Spain can be undertaken. The many personal courtesies extended by Dr. Saldívar, by his son Gabriel Saldívar Osorio, and by other members of his family are here gratefully remembered. New address in 1967: Calle Diez 27, San Pedro de los Pinos, México 18, D.F.

[168] All the entries in our alphabetical list turn up in Cotarelo y Mori's useful dictionary of Baroque Spanish dances, with the exception of *balona* (= valona, probably not a dance) and *torbellino.* See *Colección de Entremeses* . . . , I, i, pp. ccxxxv–cclxxi.

[169] The third with diferencias (= variations).

[170] Martín Alonso, *Enciclopedia del Idioma* (Madrid: Águilar, 1958), III (N-Z), 3985, defines torbellino *inter alia* as a Negro couples' dance. Such French "whirlwinds" as *Les Tourbillons* in Rameau's *Pièces de clavecin,* 1724, come too late to bear any relation to our torbellinos.

[171] Alonso, *op. cit.,* III, 4115, defines *valona* (Walloon) as a type of song (on the authority of Richard Perceval's *A dictionarie in Spanish and English* [1599], and César Oudin's *Tesoro de las dos lenguas* [1607]).

[172] See Vicente T. Mendoza, *El romance español y el corrido mexicano* (México: Universidad Nacional Autónoma, 1939), pp. 125–132, for a not very decisive study of the "Antigüedad del Corrido en México." The Real Academia Español dictionary defines *corrido de la costa* as a "romance ó jácara que se suele acompañar con la guitarra al son del fandango"—without documenting the earliest usage of corrido in this sense. Mendoza mentions some *Coplas del Tapado* dated August 19, 1684. But this is a secondhand reference not buttressed by J. T. Medina or F. González de Cossío's bibliographies (1907, 1947, 1952).

sobre la guitarra española (Saragossa, 1674, 1697). In order, the contents run thus (time signatures in parentheses): jácaras (3), marionas (3), gallardas (C), españoletas (3), villanos (C), El Caballero (C), canarios ($\frac{6}{4}$), Baylad Caracoles (3), Los Impossibiles ($\frac{3}{4}$), jota ($\frac{3}{4}$), fandango ($\frac{3}{4}$), tarantelas ($\frac{6}{8}$), folías españolas (3), las bacas (3), El Amor (3), jácaras francesas (3), marizápalos (3 [with 7 diferencias]), Las Sombras (C), jácaras de la costa (3), gaitas (3), cumbees (3), zarambeque o muecas (3), El Paloteado (C), folías gallegas (3), zangarilleja ($\frac{6}{4}$), chamberga (3), passacalles para comenzar las seguidillas manchegas (3), Gran Duque (C), marssellas (3 [with 6 diferencias]), folías italianas (3), Al Verde Retamar (3), las penas ($\frac{6}{8}$), sarao o bailete de El Retiro ($\frac{3}{4}$), La Amable (3), Fustamberg ($\math4{C}\!\!\!\!/$), payssanos ($\frac{6}{4}$), allemanda ($\math4{C}\!\!\!\!/$), paspied viejo ($\frac{3}{8}$), La Cadena (3), El Cotillo ($\math4{C}\!\!\!\!/$), La Christian ($\math4{C}\!\!\!\!/$), La Bacante ($\math4{C}\!\!\!\!/$), cotillon nuevo ($\math4{C}\!\!\!\!/$), rigodon ($\math4{C}\!\!\!\!/$). Seventeen minuets conclude the intriguing series of dances: three menuetas "de trompas," three "del soldado," two without qualifier, one menuet "amoroso," one "afectuoso," another "de el Zisne," and another six not qualified.

So far as bows to Africa go, the Negro cumbees do the Guinea Coast homage with a subtitle reading "cantos en idioma guineo." Saldívar's transcription is still eagerly awaited. Another African-influenced piece follows the cumbees, the zarambeque (defined and illustrated in Cotarelo y Mori as a "frenetic Negro dance" [173]).

A third colonial tablature is more accessible, since it is kept in the manuscripts division of the Mexican National Library: MS 1560 (olim 1686). This "Tablatura Musical" of 99 + vii folios contains enough ambitious music by unknown composers to tax the ingenuity of any American doctoral candidate. True, Corelli tops the list. But certainly Samuel Trent and Bartolomé Gerardo are composers who have thus far eluded lexicographers. The repertory belongs to the first half of the eighteenth century and the copying was done piecemeal. Forty-two leaves were ciphered for guitar. Then another copyist turned the oblong book upside down and started anew in staff notation, reverting at least twice, however, to Corelli pieces already ciphered. Gross errors spoil the spelling of titles in both the guitar and violin portions of the book. But for the piquant local color that these titles can give they are left uncorrected in the following list:

fol. 1, Pasacalle; 1*v*, Valona de Voca Negra; 2, Rondaut de Coruet; 2*v*, Alemanda; 3, Coranta; 4, Burro; 5, [something in] $\frac{6}{8}$; 5*v*, Rigaudon; 7, Adagio (in $\frac{3}{8}$); 7*v*, Sarab' despacio; 8, Giga alegre; 9*v*, Rondaus; 10, Minuete; 10*v*, Minuete otro; 11, La dansa de la Cadena; 11*v*, Minuete la E; 12, Minuet el exselente; 12*v*, Matilde Vaile de la opera de Mercurio; 13, enamorado; 13*v*, La Cadena; 14*v*, Alemanda; 15, Minuet, Jiga; 15*v*, Gabot p° la C., g°, Ariua, Higue, Canarie; 16, Bridi turoli, Rond. de la Babet; 17, Paspiet; 17*v*, Excuseme Monsiur; 18, Minuet; 18*v*,

---

[173] *Col. de Entremeses*, I, 1, pp. cclxxi–cclxxiii.

Sapateros El Corte; 19, La faborita Sarabanda largo; 20, music scribbles, El Consuelo; 20v, Minuet de las fugas; 21, La Gashe; 21v, Minuet que se toca despues del Bure del fustamber; 22, Las 4 Caras; 22v, Minuet, pª los Aficionados; 23, Guastala, Minuet; 24, Reverencia Yngleza por el H, Su Minuet; 24v–25, cadences in the 8 tones (IV–V–I), some transposed; 25v, La Maria Burè; 26v, Sonata IX de la Opera V de Coreli [*XII Suonate a violino e violone o cembalo*, Rome, 1700], Preludio largo; 27, Giga Alegro; 28, Adagio; 28v, Tempo de Gavota; 29v, Sonata de Samuel Trent [Preludio, Largo, Giga, Alegro]; 30v, Giga de la Sonata 3ª de la Opera V de Coreli; 32, De la Sonata X Sarabanda Largo, Gavota Alegro; 32v, Giga Alegro; 33v, Follia Sonata 12 de Coreli [Adagio, Andante, Alegro continued through fol. 36]; 37 and 38 [untitled]; 39v, Giga pʳ la M. de Ricardo; 41, Deidades, Su Voz; 42, untitled.

Turning the tablature upside down and leaving the ciphered part for the section in staff notation, we plunge at once into the violinist's studio with exercises on folios 1–4. Pieces follow in this order:

fol. 4v, El Florecido Nicolⁿⁱ 1° [starts with bass downbeat, G minor, $\frac{3}{4}$]; 5, 2 Minuets; 5v, Minuet de Ansou, Baylete de la Bretaña; 6, Minuet; 6v, Paspiet viejo, Su Minuet; 7, Minuet de Pichiforte; 7v, El Agraviado; 8, more minuets [for violin solo]; 8v, Area Si eres Pheniz; 9, Min. Nicol.; 9v, Borgoña [siciliano rhythm]; 10, Minuet de Ant°; 10v, Min. Nic.; 11, Minuet de Ger° [Bartolomé Gerardo]; 11v, M. Ruizeñor Ric° Marcha del Principe Eug°; 12, Minuet de Nicolini; 12v, Sonata Gerardo [G major]:𝄞 |♪ ♪ ♫ | ♩ ♪ ♪ ♪ | Bajo [bass part for Gerardo's 1st and 2d movements]; 13v, Minuet de Gerardo, Con Bajo [E major, 4-sharp signature]; 14, Minuet figurado; 14v, 2 more minuets [the second by Nicolini]; the next four leaves contain more minuets; 19v–20, Chiga de Coreli Opera 5ª [last movement of Sonata 5]; 20v–24v, Adagio and Allegro unattributed [not from Corelli's Op. 5]; 25v–26, Lesion del maestro Bartholomê Gerardo [two violins]; 26v–27, Lezion [*sic*] del Maestro Corelio [not from Corelli's Op. 5, and probably not by Corelli]; 27v, Lezion a solo del M. Jerardo; 28v–29v, exercises; 30, Oracion funebre; 30v, La amable [violin with bass]; 31v, Sonata by Gerardo [not complete]; 32, Paspie nuevo; 32v–33, Folias Coreli [Op. 5]; 34–35, minuets; 37, El Dengue, Otro Minuet; 38; untitled ciphered minuet.

Nineteen blank leaves in the middle of the book separate the guitar repertory from the violin. Both repertories document Corelli's Mexican reputation. Corelli's impact in Mexico matches his proven popularity with guitarists in eighteenth-century Spain. For example, Santiago de Murzia's *Passacalles y Obras de Guitarra por Todos los Tonos Naturales y Acidentales*, a 128-folio manuscript now in the British Museum (Add. 31640, dated 1732), includes a Toccata and Giga "de Coreli" at folios 86 and 95v.

The neglected name of Samuel Trent, guitarist and sonata composer, may perhaps startle the reader so unacquainted with Latin-American currents as to imagine that Mexico successfully resisted all British cultural inroads until independence. Martín Cortés, the conqueror's son, visited England in

1554.[174] Enough English merchants visited Mexico City in the same century for García Icazbalceta to publish a 95-page translation of their travel accounts in his *Obras* (VII [México, V. Agüeros, 1898], 55–150), and in the same volume to devote another 145 pages to the raiders with Sir John Hawkins who fell into Mexican hands in 1568. Miles Phillips, who returned to England in 1582, learned Náhuatl to perfection while foreman of an Indian construction gang (VII, 199). Among the other Englishmen in sixteenth-century Mexico who left their mark on history were David Alexander (Cornwall), William Brown (London), William Collins (Oxford), John Farrington (Windsor), William Griffin (Bristol), John Moon (Cornwall), Robert Plimpton (Plymouth), John Williams (Cornwall).[175]

What Samuel Trent's musical presence in Mexico can at the very least do for us is put us on guard against any easy assumption that acculturation in New Spain involved only Spanish and Indian heritages. Welcome or resisted, Negro, Jewish,[176] English, Dutch, French—all reached Mexico and left their impress. Even the vocabulary of so traditionally Spanish a type as the *pasacalle* (first item in MS 1560) may well surprise the layman of today who fancies that colonial Mexico remained a closed and static culture throughout its three centuries.

---

[174] Lucas Alamán, *Disertaciones sobre la historia de la República Mexicana* (México: José M. Lara, 1844), II, 109.

[175] *Corsarios franceses e ingleses en la Inquisición de la Nueva España. Siglo XVI* (Mexico: Imprenta Universitaria, 1945), pp. 507–510, gathers a list of Englishmen (taken from G. R. G. Conway).

[176] Having left Mexico City for the mines of Pachuca, Luis de Carvajal (b. 1566) was in the habit of recreating himself at night by singing "a song to the harp accompaniment of Manuel de Lucena on the departure of the Jews from Egypt, their pursuit by Pharaoh, and their wanderings in the desert." Their stay in Pachuca antedated 1594. On October 27, 1594, Domingo Gómez, of Portuguese Jewish descent, testified that Carvajal and Lucena (both Jewish) assembled at the house of Manuel Álvarez to sing Psalm 137 ("esta çierto que el cantar que el dho Luis de Caruajal canto y Manuel de Luçena tañio en vna Arpa fue vn cantar que comiença Sobre los Rios de Babilonia"). So early a date for Jewish musical beginnings in the New World gives Mexico another musical priority. Documentation in Archivo General de la Nación, Ramo de Inquisición, 236 (1592–1594), fols. 166, 172. See also *Publicaciones del Archivo General de la Nación*, XXVIII (México: Talleres Gráficos de la Nación, 1935), 304–306, for early data on Jewish music in Mexico.

The first Jewish congregation in South America flourished at Recife, Brazil, 1648–1653. In 1646 the rabbi, Isaac Aboab da Fonseca, wrote at Recife a still extant poem. In 1653 the hazzan = cantor was *Ieosua velosino*, according to the book of acts of the congregation. See Dr. Arnold Wiznitzer's transcription and notes in "O livro de Atas das Congregações Judaicas 'Zur Israel' em Recife e 'Magen Abraham' em Maurícia, Brasil, 1648–1653," *Anais da Biblioteca Nacional de Rio de Janeiro*, LXXIV (1953), 213–240, and especially 215 (poetry-writing rabbi) and 235 (hazzan in 5413 = 1653).

Pasacalle p.^r la C. Selecto

The distinguished Mexican guitarist, Miguel Alcázar, who recorded this pasacalle as the opening selection in his disc entitled *Tablatura Mexicana para Guitarra Barroca*[177] (Discos de Capitol de México, S.A. de C.V., Angel recording SAM–35029) repeats every four bars (ornamenting the repeats), adds after measure 36 a cadencing chord of D Major, and uses the re-entrant guitar tuning first recommended by Luis de Briceño in his *Metodo mui facilissimo para aprender a tañer la guitarra a lo Español* (Paris: 1626). Briceño's tuning of doubled unison courses 5 through 2 calls for a fourth up, fifth down, third up. Course 1, which is single, sounds a fourth above course 2.

The details of the various possible tunings of the baroque Spanish guitar were first assembled from Briceño, Doizi de Velasco, Gaspar Sanz, and others, in Sylvia Murphy's "The Tuning of the Five Course Guitar," *Galpin Society Journal*, XXIII (August, 1970), 49–63. The transcription shown above conforms with the transcription principles taught in the 303–page Mexican guitar treatise dated 1776 at The Newberry Iibrary, Chicago, with the call-number Case MS VMT 582 V29e, "Explicacion para tocar la guitar[r]a . . . por D[n] Juan Antonio Vargas y Guzmán, Profesor de este ynstrumento en la Ciudad de Veracruz Año de 1776." According to him, courses 4 and 5 are each tuned in octaves, courses 1, 2, 3 each at the unison. As a result every note below g on the second line in our transcription is doubled at the octave. These doublings are not however written into our transcription, on the authority of Vargas y Guzmán's own transcribed example at page 121 of his treatise.

---

[177] The other selections (all transcribed from MS 1560), are Guastala, Matilde, Excuseme Monsiur, Valona de Voca Negra, and Corelli's Folia on Side One; La Dansa de la Cadena, Reverencia Yngleza-Su Minuet, Las 4 Casas, Minuet el exselante, Minuet de las fugas, Minuet p[a] los Aficionados, and a Sonata including three sections ascribed to Samuel Trent plus the anonymous Sarab[a] despacio.

PART II

THE
INCA
AREA

INSTRUMENTS USED BY THE INCAS
                    AND THEIR PREDECESSORS

If variety of instrumental types and skilful fabrication sufficiently index
their musical culture, then such early Peruvian peoples as the Nazca, Mochica, and Chimú compete advantageously with any contemporary group in
Mexico or Central America. The Aztecs characteristically chose the *huehuetl* and the *teponaztli* for their favorite instruments. The throb of these
virile *percutores* provided the indispensable background for any larger
ensemble—even for the *musique de table* with which Moctezuma regaled
himself when he ate.[1] With Spartan reserve, the Aztecs contented themselves with flutes numbering fewer finger holes than were cut in Mayan-
area flutes half a millennium before Tenochtitlan was founded.[2] But as early
as the Paracas horizon in Peru (beginning of the Christian era), bone flutes
with unequally spaced holes and *antaras* of six pipes in three pairs enter the
bottle-shaped tombs of a people whose otherworld sounded with melody
involving intervals alien to the overtone series.

From Paracas Necropolis graves (*ca.* A.D. 400), located on one of the
world's bleakest desert peninsulas, Jorge C. Muelle, director of the Peruvian

[1] Juan de Torquemada, *Veinte i vn libros rituales i monarchia indiana* (Madrid:
Nicolás de Rodríguez Franco, 1723), I, 229. The *Caracoles, Huesos, Atabales, y otros
Instrumentos, de poco deleite a los oidos de los Españoles* played at his banquets were
distasteful to the soldiers assigned to him. Friedrich Blume, *Renaissance and Baroque
Music* (New York: Norton, 1967), p. 16, emphasizes the European taste of the epoch
for "sweetness" (*suavitas*). Whatever else can be said of Aztec music, it was not
"sweet."

[2] Curt Sachs, *The History of Musical Instruments* (New York: W. W. Norton, 1940),
p. 194.

Museo Nacional de Antropología y Arqueología, even took a mummy bundled with some twenty-two pelican ulnae and llama tibiae.[3] In three llamas and two pelicans, finger holes had been drilled. Places in the others had been marked for drilling. The mummy itself may therefore well be the remains of an American *musicarius* who expected to continue piercing finger holes in the next world.[4]

In Bolivia, as well as in Peru, proofs can be adduced of a significant musical development long antedating the Inca conquest. Around 500 A.D. the Tiahuanaco culture flourishing near the southern tip of Lake Titicaca already knew panpipes, as a stone statue of a player holding a syrinx to his lips demonstrates. A photograph of this statue (now in La Paz) appears in Dick Edgar Ibarra Grasso's *Prehistoria de Bolivia* (La Paz: Editorial "Los Amigos del Libro," 1965), p. 121, and it was also at Ibarra Grasso's instance that the Museo Arqueológico of the Universidad Mayor de San Simón in Cochabamba obtained, not effigies of players, but, better still, several instruments themselves which antedate the Tiahuanaco culture.

Two llama-bone rasps cataloged as Cliza 2171 and 2172 recall the Mexican omichicahuaztli but belong to the Cultura Megalítica, according to the museum's datings. A clay ocarina (three holes, Cliza 658) from the same horizon and a whistle (5028) were found some 30 miles south of Cochabamba. The whistle trills e^2–$f^2\sharp$; another clay whistle sounding a resonant $c^1\sharp$ (Mojocoya 3271) in the same Cochabamba museum takes the shape of a fish with coffee-bean eyes, and dates from the Yampará culture (*Prehistoria de Bolivia*, pp. 221–225).

The Bolivian museums, however, still lack any single centralized collection to compare with the splendid array of instruments from Inca-controlled territory which the National Museum in Lima houses. The following alpha-

[3] These bones, now on file at the National Museum in Lima, bear serial numbers under 33.148 and 33.149. For a photograph, see pl. 3 after p. 28 in *Cultura*, II (Lima: Ministerio de Educación Pública, 1956). Josafat Roel Pineda, who in 1967 served as staff ethnomusicologist at the Casa de la Cultura in Lima, published "Un Instrumento Musical de Parakas y Q'ero" in the *Boletín* of the Conservatorio Nacional de Música, 2ª época, Año II, no. 30 (Jan.–Sept., 1961), pp. 18–29. The continuation of Roel Pineda's article (foreseen in 1961) promises to extend very substantially the horizon of Peruvian organological studies.

[4] Molds used to mass-produce pottery were buried with a Mochica skeleton now on deposit at the National Museum. Quite evidently, the deceased "specialized" in making pottery. The prepared, half-prepared, and unprepared bones buried with Muelle's Paracas find similarly uphold the idea that these remains belong to a "specialist" in making instruments.

Frans Blom, *The Conquest of Yucatan* (p. 136), mentions molds to mass-produce pottery found in northern Honduras excavations of imprecisely dated, but remote, age (Ulúa River valley). See his Plate VI. The pottery included ocarinas sounding six notes. Any comparative study of instrument making and its history, so far as the Americas are concerned, remains still in its nonage.

betical synopsis therefore concentrates on those instruments favored within the confines of present-day Peru, with only incidental side-glances at organology in Bolivian, Chilean, and Ecuadorean reaches of the Inca empire. Also, names of instruments are those in the imperial language, Quechua, with only occasional mention of Aymara equivalents.

The variety of archaeological instruments found in the area comprising modern Ecuador can be surmised from the twenty indexed references to "drums," "flute," "Pan-pipes," "trumpet," "whistles," and "whistling jars" in Betty J. Meggers' *Ecuador* (London: Thames and Hudson, 1966; vol. 49 in the "Ancient Peoples and Places" series). Despite the seventy-six photographs and forty-two line drawings, however, this useful introduction to the archaeology of Ecuador lacks any visual documentation of the various instruments mentioned and fails even to hint at their present-day museum locations. According to Meggers, transpacific contacts during the Bahía phase (the millennium before A.D. 500) account for panpipes "graduated from both sides toward the center" (p. 117) "rather than from one side to the other in typical New World fashion" (p. 93).

antaras

When the hole of a bone flute has been corrected by being partly refilled, or filled and another drilled in its place,[5] as in specimens both at the National Museum and in the private collection of Arturo Jiménez Borja at Lima, it is obvious that the maker sought a predetermined sound. But far more decisive in proving pitch intention are the numerous syrinxes surviving from the Peruvian archaeological past. Today in Lima, both the San Marcos University Museum at Samudio 660[6] and the National Museum facing the Plaza Bolívar house collections of Nazca clay antaras fashioned well before Alfred ruled England. Because the pitch sounded by each tube differs in no wise from that sounded when Nazca lips first touched it more than a millennium ago, the gamuts of these clay antaras can be taken with no more trouble than it costs to blow them.

[5] For an incontrovertible example see bone flute 33.148/56.2/3.24 at the National Museum. The museum official who amiably consented to act as mentor and cicerone during my instrument studies in Lima was Julio Espejo Núñez, whose help is here gratefully remembered. He published the extremely useful "Bibliografía Básica de Arqueología Andina. V. Música Precolombina" in the *Boletín Bibliográfico*, XXIX/1–4 (Lima: Dec., 1956), pp. 70–81, issued by the Biblioteca Central of the Universidad Nacional Mayor de San Marcos. This bibliography lists 152 titles and concludes with an author index.

[6] Félix Caycho Quispe, Curator of the San Marcos collection, kindly demonstrated antaras 1/1108, 1/376, and 767/5. From lowest to highest the eleven pipes in the latter measure 39.5, 30.9, 25.5, 22.3, 19.7, 15.5, 12.4, 10.5, 9.9, 9.0, and 8.6 cm. On the other hand, the longest of the seven tubes in 1/376 reaches only 20 cm. Like the Pisco antaras in the National Museum, 1/376 carries certain distinguishing "trademarks." Two trophy heads and a feline deity have been painted on its sides.

Raoul and Marguerite d'Harcourt in their classic text, *La musique des Incas et ses survivances,* Volume II, showed at plates 16, 17, and 19 several such Nazca syrinxes. They specified the pitch systems of a representative four *en argile* (pl. 16, 1; pl. 17, 1, 2, 3) as: *x* A *d g a b d¹ e¹ g¹ a¹ a¹♯ b¹ c²♯ d²*; F A♭ B *d e f♯ a b d¹ f¹*; *f a♭ b d¹ e¹ f¹♯ a¹ b¹ d² f²*; and C♯ F♯ A *c d f g c¹♯ d¹♯* respectively. They conceded that the pitches of the latter strayed quarter tones away, except for the note *c.* Because Andean players today often blow five-note melodies, the d'Harcourts had, however, some years earlier committed themselves to a pentatonic thesis. The evidence of the only surviving pre-Hispanic instruments whose pitch cannot have changed—these very clay antaras—uncomfortably conflicts with any such neat hypothesis.[7] Even if the original players blew only selected notes from any given series, the rest of the tubes cannot be dismissed as mere makers' errors. According to Jorge C. Muelle (*Revista del Museo Nacional,* VIII/1 [1939], 137), the tubes in Nazca antaras were individually rolled around molds. After the tubes were individually fashioned, their makers assembled them in a finished instrument of from three to fifteen pipes. Laid out in a graded row, the tubes were cemented with clay fillings. Faulty tubes, or pipes sounding undesired pitches, need never have entered any assembled antara. If any archaeological instrument sounding fixed pitches should reflect a maker's intention, then it is a Nazca syrinx. What is more, the d'Harcourts' third Nazca antara exactly duplicates the pitch series of the second, but an octave higher. No two instruments sounding the same series of ten letter-name pitches, but at an octave's distance, can have been fashioned haphazardly.

The d'Harcourts chose therefore to say as little as possible concerning the

---

[7] As Carlos Vega, now a third of a century ago, showed in his *Escalas con semitonos en la música de los antiguos peruanos* (Buenos Aires: Imp. y Casa Edit. "Cori," 1934), the bulk of the d'Harcourts' own evidence from modern as well as ancient sources fails to bear out their thesis. Frédéric Lacroix originated the pentatonic thesis when he decreed in 1843: "Ajoutons que les Péruviens ne connaissaient pas les demitons" (*L'Univers. Histoire et Description de tous les peuples: Mexique, Guatemala et Pérou* [Paris: Firmin Didot Frères, 1843], p. 386, col. 1).

In 1843, evidence had already reached Europe countering this very thesis. James Paroissien (1784–1827), an English-born soldier of fortune who rose to brigadier general during the war in Peru, 1820–1821, returned home as the first Peruvian diplomatic representative in London, 1822–1823. With him he carried an eight-tube stone panpipe which he presented to the surgeon, Thomas Stewart Traill (1781–1862). Before sending a plaster cast of it to Berlin for Alexander von Humboldt's inspection, Traill showed the stone panpipe to Mendelssohn, who made some prescient comments. Starting a major third above middle *c* the eight tubes emitted *e, f♯, g, a, d¹, c¹♯, f¹, a¹.* For a somewhat garbled account of this archaeological panpipe, see Mariano Eduardo de Rivero and Juan Diego de Tschudi [*sic*], *Antigüedades Peruanas* (Vienna: Imprenta Imperial, 1851), pp. 139–140.

pitch systems of the Nazca clay antaras.[8] A decade later a Peruvian, Mariano Béjar Pacheco, returned to them with an article in *El Comercio* (Lima) for July 28, 1935, "Deducciones del sistema musical de la cultura nazca." After examining a representative half-dozen Nazca antaras at the National Museum, he showed that semitones entered the pitch series of each (instruments numbered 3/6763, 3/6774, 3/6775, 3/6790, 3/6791, 3/6792). He also discovered that enharmonic intervals cropped up between adjacent tubes. Leaving the d'Harcourts with their pentatonic article of faith if they still wished to believe it, he contended that Inca music, if ever really pentatonic, had become decadent, just as had postclassical Greek, by loss of the enharmonic genus. Following in Béjar Pacheco's wake, the distinguished Belgian-born Andrés Sas studied twenty-eight antaras culled from the same collection in a conscientious *Ensayo sobra la música nazca*. His article—published twice, first in the *Boletín Latino-Americano de Música*, IV/4 (Oct., 1938), and later in the *Revista del Museo Nacional*, VIII/1 (1939)—should have dissipated all remaining doubt concerning the vaunted pentatonic series. Far from being usual in these archaeological instruments, he showed it to be quite rare—at least in pure form. Then again, only ten of the twenty-eight antaras submitted for his examination blew a series capable of being expressed in Western notation without plus or minus signs to show appreciable divergences from written pitches.

More recently, still other antaras from both Pisco and Nazca valleys have been added to the National Museum collection. As in those examined by Sas, tubes are sometimes broken or fissured. The larger instruments are those that have been more often cracked; and even in the smaller antaras the tubes that should utter the deepest notes are the ones most frequently broken off. To facilitate comparison by presenting our findings in the same way that Sas gave his, we show in conventional notation the pitches of the two dozen antaras submitted for our inspection during October and November of 1958 (see accompanying musical examples).

[8] Karl Gustav Izikowitz, *Musical and Other Sound Instruments of the South American Indians* (Gothenburg: Elanders Boktryckeri Aktiebolag, 1935), follows suit when he devotes only one paragraph to "The Musical and Acoustic Properties of the Pan-pipe" (p. 400). Peruvian scholars are themselves fully aware of the deficiencies in the d'Harcourt study. See Museo del Arte (Lima), *Instrumentos musicales del antiguo Perú* (1961), p. 7 (unnumbered).

Nazca Antaras

None of the National Museum antaras submitted for Sas's now twenty-nine-year-old study or for my more recent examination runs to nine tubes. Only one in his survey, and none in mine, consists of eight. The eight-tubed exemplar (35/1684) in his survey differs from the others in being the only antara whose pipes make a stairway of equal-sized steps. In still other respects it reveals its primitive workmanship. The individual tubes were not rolled separately in advance. They bend slightly, but not after any set plan. No glaze has been applied to the exterior. This eight-tubed antara can therefore be dismissed as a primitive piece or as the work of an isolated craftsman.

Of the two dozen in my· survey, nineteen run between ten and thirteen tubes. Sas's set included in addition a pair of fourteen-tube antaras (32/415 and 32/417), the second of which carried "etchings" of four striped tunny fish beneath the tubes. The lowest tube, sounding E below middle C, reaches 46 cm. For the rest of the ten- to fourteen-tubers in his survey, the only decoration is an occasional geometric pattern glazed on the clay surface. The same holds true of my ten- to thirteen-tubers. These larger antaras were meant to be played, not looked at or used as amulets.

Those with three to seven tubes tell a different story. Of the five three- to seven-tubers entering my survey, antara 3/6783 came from Pisco. Since the other four make a family with it, all these lesser antaras are hereafter called Pisco. They differ from Nazca ten- to fourteen-tubers in such crucial respects as the following: (1) design of the tube proper; (2) shape of the blowholes; (3) distance between adjacent tubes; (4) type of glaze applied to the exterior; (5) insertion of string holes. The one Pisco antara with the fewest tubes happens to be also the only National Museum instrument with human features shaped and painted on the clay. The lowest of the three tubes has been painted with a tan face, a red mouth, and black eyes looking away from the higher tubes.

All Pisco tubes in my survey flare from a thinner cylinder in the bottom half of the pipe to a fatter cylinder in the top half. What is more, the blowholes are round, or nearly so. They are equally spaced, and the same size. Nazca ten- to fourteen-tubers, on the other hand, show egg-shaped blowholes that are by no means equally spaced.[9] The lowest pipes not only have larger diameters, but also more space has been left between them than between higher pipes. Nazca tubes continue the same bore from top to bottom, except for the narrowing in the last 5 mm to the ellipsoidal blowhole. Nazca antaras characteristically show a rich, firebrick-red glaze, Pisco a more lustrous but also a blacker glaze. None of the Nazca ten- to fourteen-tubers has been bored for a string hole. All the Pisco syrinxes show small holes between pipes, through which twine to carry them was doubtless passed. The tone quality of Pisco tubes tends to be shriller, perhaps because they were primarily signaling instruments. They also seem to speak more easily. To play the Nazca antaras calls for a steady stream of air directed more precisely, but for his reward the player produced a more delicate and retreating sound.

The doublets that keep intruding both in Sas's survey and in mine (his *Ensayo* listed three pairs, my survey includes five twins) appear all the more remarkable if the scattering of excavations which yielded these an-

----

[9] In such a typical eleven-tuber as 3/6785, the distance from the left side of the bottom pipe to the right side of pipe 4 is 5.6 cm, but from the left side of pipe 5 to the right of 8 is only 5.1 cm. In 767/5, an eleven-tuber at the San Marcos University Museum, the bottom four holes measure 6.5 cm, the next four 5.5; blowholes 8 through 11 measure only 5.3 cm. This tale repeats itself everywhere among Nazca ten- to fourteen-tubers.

taras is remembered. When native Quechua-speaking players have been handed the Museum clay instruments to play, not only have they at once made pipes speak which European lips blew in vain, but also their first instinct has always been (in my observation) to pick out the antaras that make pairs and hold them together while blowing. It is of course a recognized fact that all over the highlands of modern Peru and Bolivia the double-rowed syrinx is the indigenes' instrument, not the single-rowed. The d'Harcourts, after various conjectures, could think of no better reason for the universal insistence on double-rowed panpipes than the greater strength and solidity gained from tying a double rather than a single row.[10] If such be the true reason, it operated as long ago as the Huari-Tiahuanaco horizon (*ca.* 1200). Just outside Lima at the Huallamarca grave site in San Isidro, a geminated set of closed-tube cane panpipes recently came to light. The dozen pipes divide into complementary sets of six tied with cotton multi-wound string. Arturo Jiménez Borja, who now guards them in his private collection, blew first one side and then the other to produce out-of-tune hexachords.[11]

The clay antaras, if the d'Harcourts reasoned rightly, needed none of the strength imparted by tying a double row of canes. Why then do so many still surviving clay antaras reveal themselves as twins? Was it because of the Andean aborigines' well-known belief that mana resided in twins as such? Such pairs as 1/1118 and 1/1119, 1/1130 and 1/1133, 1/1134 and 1/1135, 3/6791, and 3/6808, even show duplicate exterior marks. With one pair it is a characteristic red band surrounding the antara at the tip of the third lowest pipe, dividing the lower tan glaze from the upper blackish-brown (1/1130 and 1/1133).[12] With another, it is alternate bands of dainty red and black crow's-feet over a light background (3/6791 and 3/6808).

Whatever else their gemination indicates, at least these twins prove that their designers know how to reenact predetermined pitches. Haphazard as may seem any given series to us, the makers never allowed a wider interval than a perfect fourth to intervene between adjacent pipes.[13] If a fourth does enter a series, it comes, as a rule, near the bottom. It never appears between pipes in the upper half. This is the more remarkable because a much wider difference in pipe lengths must be allowed for between low pipes than between high to produce so large an interval as a fourth.

[10] R. and M. d'Harcourt, *La musique des Incas et ses survivances* (Paris: Lib. Orientaliste Paul Geuthner, 1925), I, 37: The double series makes the Peruvian syrinx *plus épais, plus solide, et les ligatures plus efficaces,* but serves no other purpose.

[11] Izikowitz found that in most double-seried syrinxes "the pipes of one row are open" (p. 392). But both rows are closed in Jiménez Borja's Huallamarca syrinx. On one side the pipes are a trifle longer.

[12] To this same thirteen-tube family belong 1/1134 and 1/1135.

[13] This rule seems to be transgressed in 3/6712 only because pipes 8 and 9 (counting from the bottom) have been clumsily repaired. Obviously these clay antaras must be clean and unbroken if musical data taken from them is to be trusted.

Somewhere between adjacent pipes in antaras 1/1130, 1/1133, 1/1134, 1/1135, 3/6809, 1/6777, 3/6806, and 3/6785 of the twenty-four submitted for my inspection, intervals distinctly smaller than a minor second creep into the series. Where such microtones do insinuate themselves, they always come in the upper half. These fine pitch distinctions near the top of a series must obviously have cost the maker some pains. Just as it is easier to fret microtones near the pegbox than near the bridge, so such fine distinctions would have taxed the antara maker less at the bottom of his series than at the top. And not only do such microtones crop up in a third of the instruments in my survey, but they also entered some fourth of the syrinxes studied by Sas in the 1930's.[14] All the instruments yielding such microtones between adjacent pipes in his survey as well as in mine are Nazca-type antaras, and all are of eleven or more tubes. But to show that the makers worked according to a preconceived plan, only once in each antara does a microtone between neighboring tubes intrude.

Until tonometric analyses in cents can be calculated, further generalizations concerning Nazca pitch series must be forgone.[15] But since nearly every major museum began to acquire Nazca artifacts after Max Uhle first opened their tombs in 1901, enough antaras are now spread around the world to challenge a united effort at breaking their musical code.[16] Curt Sachs has of course warned against confusing pitch series with scale (*The History of Musical Instruments*, p. 167). Even so, there must somehow be meaning in such a series as 3/6785 blows, pipes 3 and 8 (counted from the bottom) sounding a perfect octave, but pipes 3 and 7 ever so slightly flat an octave.

If we can never again hear the music the Nazca dead hoped to continue playing on these antaras in the afterlife, at least we can predispose ourselves to a more sympathetic understanding of the pitch differences by studying

---

[14] Antaras numbered 3/6785, 3/6809, 3/6792, 35/7769, 32/416, 32/417, 32/418.

[15] Izikowitz (*op. cit.*, p. 400) suggested the need for just such measurements with a tonometer. An M. Hohner No. P3 chromatic pitch pipe (A-440) served as a standard during my tests.

[16] The University of California, Berkeley, can pride itself on having been one of the institutions to have profited earliest from Uhle's excavations, especially those at Ocucaje in the lower Ica Valley. In their seminal study, *The Uhle Pottery Collections from Ica* (University of California Publications in American Archaeology and Ethnology, vol. 21, no. 3, pp. 95–133), Alfred L. Kroeber and William Duncan Strong published as long ago as 1924 a plate of a twelve-tubed antara taken out of Ocucaje gravesite B (pl. 29). Ornamented with what look like painted bowls—five or six stalks growing out of each— this syrinx belongs to what Kroeber in 1924 called the Proto-Nazca phase (A.D. 50–650, p. 120). Whatever the revisions of nomenclature and dating Kroeber willingly accepted in such a later monograph as *Toward Definition of the Nazca Style*, none will deny him the credit of having pioneered in publishing data on a Nazca syrinx in an American university museum. On the other side of the globe, the British Museum owns Nazca antaras, one of which is pictured in Plate VII, *Galpin Society Journal*, XII (1959).

the sound distinctions in the aboriginal spoken languages at the moment the Spaniards arrived. Bertonio, when making his classic dictionary of the Aymara tongue (1612), was thrown back on such factitious letters as *cc, chh, cch, cqu, qhu, pp,* and *tt* for sounds that were not counterparted in Romance languages. On the other hand, while distinguishing between *t* and *tt, c* and *cc,* the Aymara Indian pronounced *e* and *i* so indifferently, as well as *o* and *u,* that the same lexicographer struggled to decide whether so common an instrument as the flute (generic sense) should be spelled *pincollo* or *pincullu,* the cane variety as *quenaquena* or *quinaquina.* In despair, he allowed both spellings to invade the same dictionary,[17] so ambivalent a sound did the Titicaca-region Indians give these vowels. Quechua, the official empire tongue, knew important distinctions between *q* and *qq* while lacking *b, d, f,* and some other consonantal sounds. By analogy, the clay antara makers may have infinitely busied themselves with microtonic pitch distinctions that elude us while remaining quite oblivious to other differences that European ears both at the conquest and now consider fundamental.

In addition to the evidence of museum instruments, iconographic testimony can be taken to establish the wide popularity of the antara, the diverse shapes it took at various horizons, and the characteristic methods of playing it. Mochica ceramics from the north coast abound in lifelike painted tableaux. The d'Harcourts reproduced a Mochica pottery scene. Two antara players face each other, apparently dancing.[18] A piece of string connects their six-tubed antaras. Here at least evidence survives which tends to prove that twins were played simultaneously by facing players. Jiménez Borja in his masterful *Instrumentos Musicales del Perú* (1951, p. 115) offered a photograph of a Mochica stirrup vase. The squatting player blows a six-tubed antara. He grasps the ends of the two lower tubes with his right hand, and drapes the fingers of his left over the top four. Jiménez Borja's private collection includes a Mochica whistle whose vent has been ornamented with the molded figurine of an erect antara blower. A feline motif centers his diadem. His syrinx, like nearly all in representational art, contains six pipes of graded size. But in this instance the clay artist makes the geminated pipes appear to be lying horizontally, rather than in facing couplets. This particular whistle effigy served as model for the huge cast flanking the left entrance to the Nazca Hall in the National Museum.

Antaras of less than six tubes were sometimes played drum-and-fife fashion, at least in the twilight of southern coastal culture before the Inca conquest (Ica period). The player in an Ica pottery piece at the National Museum holds the four-tubed syrinx in his left hand while beating the

---

[17] *Segunda Parte del Vocabulario* (Juli [Lima]: Francisco del Canto, 1612), pp. 266, 288, 289.
[18] D'Harcourt, *op. cit.,* I, 37.

cylindrical drum with the other.[19] In a companion Nazca piece, a player who must have been a juggler presses the five-tubed antara to his mouth with his right hand.[20] His left grasps a trumpet and a rattle. Beside his left knee lies a small barrel drum ready to beat with the rattle, the trumpet, or his free hand if ever he puts these other two instruments down.

Whatever the cultural horizon, only men played the antara (or for that matter the sexually symbolical vertical flute). As a rule, antaras seem to have been laid beside the dead in good condition, ready to play. But at Huallamarca some broken clay antaras recently dug up show every sign of having been shattered before being cast over the dead. These shards form part of the Jiménez Borja collection which has in recent years taken second place only to the National Museum insofar as instruments are concerned. They proceed from a late Tiahuanaco site.

Occasionally syrinxes made, not of clay, but of stone have been dug up, even in South American areas peripheral to the Inca empire. A five-tubed antara of *talcito* stone came to light on the wooded shores of the Toltén River in Araucanian Chile more than a half century ago, and Jerónimo de Amberga described it in "Una flauta de Pan, araucana," *Revista Chilena de Historia y Geografía*, XXXVII (1921), 98–100. Amberga convincingly explained the duplication of the lowest note by the two longest tubes, each 9 cm long and each sounding $a\flat$ (second space, treble clef). The other three tubes sound the C minor triad just above. According to Amberga, some old Araucanians remembered having heard of syrinxes made of cane. Juan Orrego-Salas, however, vetoes our accepting syrinxes as instruments native to an area so far south of the confines of the Inca empire (Maule River), when he writes in "Araucanian Indian Instruments," *Ethnomusicology*, X/1 (Jan., 1966), 56: "Panpipes, which were so extensively developed by all groups of the Central and Northern Andean regions, never reached the Araucanians. Araucanian scales and melodic patterns also appear to be clearly divorced from the prevailing pentatonic features of Andean music."

Apart from clay and stone (and, of course, cane), silver syrinxes can be documented from Orsúa y Vela's *Historia de la Villa Imperial de Potosí*. A century before his history, the Indians were still playing silver ayarichis = antaras = syrinxes. In December, 1622, according to Orsúa y Vela (1965 ed., I, 349), a band of native Indian musicians played various ethnic instruments, including "sweet-sounding silver ayarichis" ("Traían también unos cañoncitos de plata alternativamente puestos a manera de órgano (que lla-

---

[19] Jiménez Borja, *Instrumentos Musicales* (Lima: Imp. del Politécnico Nacional "José Pardo," 1951), p. 91. See Charles L. Boilés' "The Pipe and Tabor in Mesoamerica," *Yearbook II* (1966) of the Inter-American Institute for Musical Research (Tulane University), pp. 43–74, for rebuttal of Mendoza's argument for Hispanic transplant. Boilés limits his area but his thesis can be extended to Peru.

[20] Jiménez Borja, *op. cit.*, p. 20.

man los indios *ayarichis*), que hacen una suave armonia"). Their delicious music was one of the more notable events of a prolonged festival.

pincollos (= *pincullus*) and *quenaquenas*

Bone flutes, unlike antaras, cannot be summoned as witnesses to ancient Peruvian musical systems. But they do nonetheless testify to a consuming interest in pitched instruments as early as the Chavín horizon. The Chavín period retreats, of course, at least beyond 400 B.C., and probably begins as early as 850.[21] The National Museum's Gotush llama-bone flute taken during 1941 excavations at a Chavín site measures 13.2 cm. Already an end-notched flute, the first finger hole has been pierced at 6 cm from the playing end, the second at 7.9, the third at 9.8. Equal distances therefore intervene between the three finger holes. But a Paracas pelican-ulna flute at the same museum already shows unequal spacing of the five finger holes. So also does a puma-bone flute (no. [39] 14) of 13.5 cm. From the notched playing end of the puma flute, hole distances read respectively 3.2, 5.0, 6.9, 8.9, and 11.7 cm. An experienced Quechua player employed at the National Museum— Filomeno Límaco Lloclla (born in Cangallo province, Ayacucho department)—was able to extract the following approximate sounds from llama and puma flutes: d^2 e^2 $f^2\sharp$ a^2+; $e^2\sharp$ $f^2\sharp$ $g^2\sharp$ — $a^2\sharp$ b^2 $c^3\sharp$ —. Because the pelican flute lacks an end notch, he could not make it speak. By "whistling" into the llama bone he could shift the four-note series to begin on approximately b^1 or c^2. He was also able to introduce some of the characteristic glissandos between notes in both llama and puma series which native quena players today so highly favor.

The National Museum's deer-bone flute from Paracas boasts a proximal cup that reaches the exaggerated length of 3.2 cm in an instrument only 17 cm from blowing to sounding end. A pair of horizontally placed eyes 1 cm apart have been drilled 1 cm below the "notch." The Chavín and Paracas flutes end with semicircular notches. Nazca bone flutes, on the other hand, already begin to employ rectangular notches, the shape that was to become universal after 1532.[22] As a rule, the archaeological notches have been delicately incised. The deer flute alone among the Paracas horizon instruments has been heavily wound with cordage at the distal end. Even today, indigenous players often wind their quenas with coils of thread, especially at the sounding end. They do so to prevent air from leaking through cracks. With the slightest fissure, a bone, clay, or cane tube can scarcely be made to speak.

During the Chimú period, last before the Incas subjugated the north

---

[21] Although earliest of the cultural horizons, the "Chavín is generally regarded as the greatest art style evolved in Peru" (J. Alden Mason, *The Ancient Civilizations of Peru* [Harmondsworth: Penguin Books, 1957], p. 46).

[22] D'Harcourt, *op. cit.*, I, 65, corrected by Jiménez Borja, *op. cit.*, pp. 34, 109.

coast, cross flutes came into vogue. Decisive evidence can be taken not only from the recovered flutes but also from the clay effigies astride Chimú stirrup jars. Such a jar in the Trujillo University museum collection as that numbered U 3509 (see p. 138 of Jiménez Borja's *Instrumentos Musicales del Perú*) is mounted by a sitting player who blows a cross flute. He fingers it with his right hand while holding it to his mouth with the left. In Jiménez Borja's private collection, a pair stands atop another such jar: one blows a transverse flute, the other beats a drum.[23]

The emphasis on museum clay and bone specimens of course belies the past; doubtless cane flutes like cane antaras vastly outnumbered the others in any given period. But at least the museum flutes can be marshaled to prove that ancient Peruvian instrument makers moved forward from Chavín with three equidistant holes to Paracas Necropolis and Nazca with five unequally spaced finger holes, from Paracas round notches to Nazca rectangular, from Chavín vertical to Chimú transverse flutes.

qquepas

Though ample evidence for metal trumpets can be taken from the chronicles of the conquest, those that enter museum collections most often are of clay or conch. Conch trumpets with their penetrating and awe-inspiring blasts came into use at least as early as the Chavín. While the field for an air base was being cleared some forty years ago at Chiclayo (south of the Lambayeque River), a conch trumpet incised with a Chavín deity himself blowing a conch came to light. Now in the private collection of Dr. Abraham Pickman,[24] this shell trumpet measures 23 cm in length. The top is pierced with a blowhole, the bottom spiral with a small aperture through which to pass a carrying string. Still a favorite with the Incas in 1532, the large conch trumpet had therefore enjoyed a privileged position in aboriginal cults for some two millennia before the Spanish conquest. Every culture thus far unearthed testifies to its dominant role.

Perhaps because the *strombus galeatus* does not flourish in Peruvian coastal waters and has to be imported from so great a distance as the Isthmus of Panama, the Mochica instrument makers fell back on clay imitations of the large conch. The National Museum at Lima owns some half dozen of these clay contrafacta. Their usual length runs between 16 and 17 cm. Sometimes the clay even imitates the shell edge (35/86). The mouthpiece always comes at the apex, and in 35/86—an instrument sounding an awesome d (space below the treble staff)—has been painted red while the rest is glazed a light tan. Clay conch 1/2623—molded with a carrying hole

---

[23] Another distinctive late development was the black sausage flute that became popular in the Chincha region (southern coast) shortly before the Inca conquest. Five finger holes appear to be the normal number.

[24] Jiménez Borja, *op. cit.*, p. 120.

at the base and originally covered with tan paint—blows a sonorous d♯+. Clay 1/2626, a small undecorated trumpet, blows a piercing g♯.

Powerful and sinister demons capable of wreaking havoc on one's enemies took up their abode inside conch trumpets. Mochica ceramics at the National Museum attest the ever more horrific shapes Mochica pottery painters were willing to believe lurked inside such trumpets. The earliest demon has merely a shell for his back, six teeth, and two tusks. But a more developed type sports a vicious tail, a razorback, two pairs of tusks and fangs, and many more teeth besides.[25]

Clay trumpets, apart from conch imitations, came also in vertical and coiled forms. The Museo Nacional owns a pair of verticals from Pucará, the earliest known culture site between Cuzco and Lake Titicaca. Though perhaps even earlier than the Mochica clay conches, the Pucará tubulars are the more elaborately decorated. From each, a feline juts out at one side of the bell in bas-relief, while a loop matches the head at the opposite side. Six stylized human heads rim the bell, their faces so turned that the three in each semicircle look toward the feline deity. Meanwhile his bulbous eyes peer above a mouthful of exposed teeth. The tube of 39/30 extends to 26.7 cm, the ornamentation beginning 17 cm from the blowing end. The proximal diameter, because so large as 1.5 cm, suggests that some sort of mouthpiece was fitted in;[26] the blowing end in any event has been painted maroon to distinguish it from the glossy black, red, and white used in ornamenting the bell end (diameter, 7.4 cm).

Clay verticals break much more readily than coiled, and the Mochica trumpet bells 1/2738 and 1/2743 at the National Museum may belong to fractured specimens. Each flares into a gaping feline head, 1/2743 with thirteen vicious lower and fifteen upper teeth. Mochica coiled trumpets flare into bells that sometimes protrude horizontally from the player (1/2740), sometimes straight up (1/2741), sometimes at an oblique angle (1/2735), and sometimes down (1/2739). One diademed figure decorating a bell (1/2739) beats a drum, while the diademed deity ornamenting another bell (1/2740) holds rattles or cymbals. The tubes in the first three of these coiled trumpets measure approximately 59, 36, and 58 cm, but the coils bring their horizontal extension down to only 29, 14, and 30 cm. The cupped mouthpieces issue into 0.4 or 0.5 air columns, but the bells flare to diameters of from 6 to 8 cm. Though, like the clay conches, the coiled trumpets blow notes just above middle *C*, their tone more resembles that of the modern cornet—in contrast with the noble trombone sound of the conch trumpets.

Both mouthpiece and bell of the one Recuay clay trumpet (*ca.* A.D. 500)

---

[25] *Ibid.*, pp. 118–119.

[26] Even conches were sometimes fitted with metal mouthpieces. See d'Harcourt, *op. cit.*, I, 26; and Charles W. Mead, "The Musical Instruments of the Incas" (Supplement to American Museum Journal, III/4 [New York, 1903]), p. 15, Pl. III, fig. 1.

in the national collection (1/852) have unfortunately broken off. But even
so the tube length of what is left (sounds d) extends to no less than 97 cm,
starting with a 0.5 cm. bore. Its WWW geometrical black bands over a bright
tan glaze at once suggest alien provenance. The tube has been carried out
horizontally, then bent back in the curvature of a bow, then again brought
forward horizontally. Still another distinctive type of coil characterizes
Mochica trumpet 1/2744 (sounds $d\sharp$). The tube winds three times around
the top of a chicha bowl in coils that suggest a serpent.

A Mochica whistle in Jiménez Borja's collection very graphically winds
about in three coils dabbed with red. The snake grasps a rodent in his
mouth, ready to swallow him. Numerous other graphic shapes, animal and
human, ornament the dozen or so Mochica whistles in the same collection.
Many of the figurines were doubtless cast from molds. No ancient Peruvian
culture has bequeathed us a richer repertory of bizarrely and excitingly
decorated instruments.

Julio Castro Franco suggests that Mochica zoomorphic whistles formed
consorts, each whistle player timing his pitch to succeed another's so that
melodies could be performed.[27] The antara players around Puno even today
use the same group discipline to produce music beyond the power of any
one player.

DICTIONARY NAMES FOR INSTRUMENTS

The Spaniards entering Peru discovered certain instrumental types, such as
trumpets of deers' and dogs' skulls, for which no peninsular cognates were
known. They also found the Indians themselves speaking numerous local
languages, often with different names for the same instruments. The Inca
official tongue, imposed with the same authority as was Latin throughout
the Roman Empire, was of course Quechua. But Aymara occupied a place
analogous to Greek. Poma de Ayala names two other tongues that were still
widely spoken as late as 1615: Mochica and Puquina.[28]

Spanish lexicographers active about that date ignored all but Quechua
and Aymara. Even so, modern organologists have frequently been trapped
into confusing names of instruments in the two languages and even into
supposing that different names always meant different instruments. True,
some names did carry over from language to language. The best dictionaries
of these two tongues were published in 1608 at Lima for Quechua (Diego
González Holguín) and in 1612 at Juli on the shores of Lake Titicaca for

[27] Museo de Arte, *Instrumentos musicales del antiguo Perú* (program booklet for
recital and exposition), p. 15. Chancay excavations provided the bizarre zoomorphic
whistles illustrated in the last plate of this booklet. On antara consorts, see below, pp.
264, 276–277.

[28] Felipe Huamán Poma de Ayala, *Nueva Corónica y Buen Gobierno* (París: Institut
d'Ethnologie, 1936), p. 113.

Aymara (Ludovico Bertonio). In both tongues, *huancar* (Q.) = *huancara* (A.) meant drum, *qquepa* (Q.) = *qhuepa* (A.) meant trumpet, and *pincullu* = *pincollo* meant flute. But for *antara* in Quechua, the Aymara knew two terms: *sico* for small size and *ayarichi* [29] for large. The Aymara also distinguished between bone flute (*cchaca pincollo*) and cane. The cane variety they called *quenaquena* or *quinaquina*, meaning "full of holes." They also knew it as *tupa pincollo*. Bertonio himself interdicted our supposing that *quenaquena* could mean a double flute when, on pages 284 and 288 of his *Segunda Parte del Vocabulario*, he twice declared that *quena quena*, *ppia ppia*, and *lutu lutu* meant anything made of stone or of other material and which was full of holes (*piedra o qualquiera otra cosa muy agugereada*). On page 243 of his *Primera Parte* and page 289 of his *Segunda* he repeats *Flauta de caña: Quenaquena; Qenaquena* (!) *pincollo: Flauta de caña*. The Quechua dictionaries not only of González Holguín but also of Juan Martínez de Ormachea (1604), Diego de Torres Rubio (1619), Juan Roxo Mexia y Ocón (1648), and Esteban Sancho de Melgar (1691) unite in ignoring *quena* or *quenaquena*.[30] Poma de Ayala, who in his *Nueva Corónica y Buen Gobierno* drew pictures of numerous native instruments and listed some ten still commonly used *ca.* 1615, and Cobo in his *Historia del Nuevo Mundo* (1653), are in fact the first chroniclers to mention the quenaquena by its Aymara name. Modern Peruvianists who give the end-notch flute this name [31] avail themselves of an Aymara term not found in classical Quechua

---

[29] Bartolomé Arzáns de Orsúa y Vela, in his *Historia de la Villa Imperial de Potosí*, ed. Lewis Hanke and Gunnar Mendoza (Providence: Brown University Press, 1965), I, 96, describes a festival in April, 1555, during which a band of forty richly dressed Indians played "diversos instrumentos a su usanza." He defines the ayarichi as "unos cañutillos aunados duplicadamente, que siendo mayor el primero van disminuyéndose hasta el último que es pequeñito, y soplando de cabo a otro hace la harmonía conforme el tamaño de la caña, y llaman a este instrumento ayarichi" ("some double-rowed tubes graded in size from largest to smallest, which when blown emit sounds ranging from low to high depending on the size of the tube, and they call this instrument ayarichi"). Mendoza footnotes this passage and another mentioning the ayarichi (III, 69): "un instrumento fúnebre."

[30] It also fails to appear in the great nineteenth-century dictionary, J. J. von Tschudi's *Die Kechua-Sprache* (Vienna: Kaiserlich-Koeniglichen Hof- und Staatsdruckerei, 1853), III. Abtheilung.

[31] Philip Ainsworth Means erred in his *Ancient Civilizations of the Andes* (New York: Charles Scribner's Sons, 1942), p. 444, when he alluded to "the panpipe or syrinx, called *quena* in Quechua." Even composers who have used the term know better than an Andean specialist such as Means what the word *quena* means. Witness Alberto Williams (1862–1952) who called his press "La Quena"; and his compatriot Alberto Ginastera who entitled the first movement of his *Impresiones de la Puna* "Quena" (premiered at Buenos Aires November 30, 1934). The reviewer in *La Prensa*, December 3, 1934, praised Ginastera for penetrating the "misterios de la música aymaro-queschua pentatónica" and for catching the true "carácter melódico del Altiplano boliviano." Again in *La Prensa* Ginastera reaped praise for his devotion to "el arte

dictionaries or, for that matter, in sixteenth-century Spanish literature dealing with the Incas.

Anyone who has made use of the dictionaries soon comes to know them as the organologist's best friends. They not only enable us to distinguish Cobo's *zacapa* ($=$ *saccapa*) as Aymara for leg rattles of *maichil,* his *churu* as Quechua for snail as well as conch shell, and his *chanrara* as Quechua for copper and silver jingles, but also point to Poma de Ayala's *pomatinya* (*poma* $+$ *ttinya*) as a drum stretched with puma skin, his *pipo* as made of large canes, his *catauri* as a rattle simulating the rattlesnake, and his *chiuca* as fashioned of a piebald animal's skull. The dictionaries go further. They reveal that for the Aymara a "musician" in the general sense was a *pincollori,* "player of the pincollo," "because ordinarily a musician plays it." But for the Quechua he was the one who knew how to make a *taqui,* or "dance song," or had memorized large numbers of them. "Music" in the European sense became "all kinds of sweetened made-up taquis" in Quechua; "plainsong" became "any kind of taught song," and *canto de órgano,* "sweetened orderly song." These and other translations into Quechua suggest that the native vocal as well as instrumental music sounded harsh and astringent to Spanish ears.[32] Since for such a European sound as that of a *campana,* "bell," the Quechua had no native word, to translate it the lexicographers had to fall back on *huaccan,* which meant "the sound of all kinds of animal," or else use their own word.[33]

If the flute fascinated the Aymara, the drum galvanized the Quechua. All kinds of compounds were made of *huancar,* Quechua for "drum." A potbelly was a *huancarmanani.* A giddy, foolish woman was a *huancar huayñu.* A braggart or person with coarse voice was a *huancar hina cuncca.* To curse a person ("may you swell up and die") was *huancarmanay.* To force food on the satiated was *huancaraypascam.* So large did the drum idea loom that when the Spaniards introduced their *guitarra* and *vihuela* the Quechua called them *ttinya,* the same word they applied to any hand drum.

The Quechua and Aymara dictionaries have only to be compared with

---

autóctono" when two years later *Impresiones de la Puna* gained a rehearing in Buenos Aires (issue of Sept. 1, 1936).

[32] Diego González Holguín *Vocabvlario dela lengva general de todo el Perv llamada lengva Qquichua, o del Inca* (Lima: Francisco del Canto, 1608), II, 310, even offers a whole pat Quechua sentence for missionaries to use when trying to improve voice quality. The idea runs: "Sound your voice more gently and sweetly so that you will delight and astonish **everyone.**"

[33] Small bells of the jingling kind were common enough before the Spaniards arrived, but evidently not large church-type bells. According to Joan de Santacruz Pachacuti Yamqui, "Relación de Antigüedades deste Reyno del Pirú," *Tres Relaciones de Antigüedades Peruanas* (Madrid: M. Tello, 1879), p. 275, the Inca Pachacuti, *ca.* 1450, found a stone bell at Cajamarca. The small-size ones were made of copper and silver.

a classic Náhuatl lexicon like Alonso de Molina's *Vocabvlario en Lengva Mexicana* (Mexico City: Antonio de Espinosa, 1571) to convince one that musical instruments of all kinds enjoyed at least as prominent a role in Inca as in Aztec life, that they came in no less subtly varied shapes and sizes, and that as many metaphors suggested by instruments entered Quechua and Aymara speech as Náhuatl.

LITERARY ALLUSIONS

Just as the dictionaries tell their tale, so even more convincingly do the fables handed down from the preconquest past, the memories of religious rites before the Spaniards stopped them, and the pictures drawn in such an illustrated chronicle of aboriginal life as Poma de Ayala's. A catena of literary allusions could begin with Oviedo's account of the first ship that ventured across the equator into Peruvian waters.[34] Bartolomé Ruiz, who captained it, met a balsa with sails—the first Indian craft seen by the Spaniards anywhere in the New World which could travel oceanic distances. This raft was on its way to trade for the large conches that the Incas preferred above all others for their war trumpets. To obtain them, says Oviedo, they were glad to trade "all the gold, silver, and raiment that they carried" (*todo el oro é plata é ropas que traen*). But since space cannot be given any exhaustive list of allusions we must forgo a chronological catalog and here confine ourselves to only a few of the more suggestive. They are grouped under instruments in the same order chosen for our discussion of archaeological specimens.

A fable having to do with the antara that persisted in mid-coastal folklore until at least the beginning of the seventeenth century, at which time Francisco de Ávila collected it for his "Idolatrias de los Indios de Huarochirí," [35] runs as follows. In the remote past, Pariacaca lived in one of five big egg-shaped mounds on the coast. He instructed his hero son Huathiacuri how to cure a local chieftain by killing a pair of serpents in his roof and a two-headed toad under his grinding stone. In payment, the chieftain had to give Huathiacuri—who traveled in poor and shabby disguise—his beautiful daughter. Family connection with such an upstart medicine man so annoyed the brother-in-law of the daughter that he challenged Huathiacuri to a musical contest. To make sure that his son would win, Pariacaca told Huathiacuri how to find a magic antara and drum. When he met a fox and a

---

[34] Gonzalo Fernández de Oviedo y Valdés, *Historia General y Natural de las Indias*, IV (Madrid: Imp. de la Real Academia de la Historia, 1855), p. 122, col. 1.

[35] See *Informaciones acerca de la Religión y Gobierno de los Incas*, ed. H. H. Urteaga (Lima: Sanmarti, 1918), pp. 120–121.

skunk who had stopped to feast on a dead guanaco, they would run away, the fox leaving his antara, the skunk her drum. With these he would be sure to conquer. The brother-in-law assembled two hundred women to shake their small drums and numerous men to help him play the antara, but Huathiacuri defeated them all. Moreover, he drank as much chicha beer as two hundred guests.

Huathiacuri was later joined in his exploits by five falcons who flew out of the egg-shaped mounds and then turned into men. This fable, like others of its class, emphasized that men—not women—played antaras and pincollos. Both sexes beat drums. Skilful playing of the antara was considered the ultimate test and the measure of a hero.

Both Cristóbal de Molina of Cuzco (1575) and Bernabé Cobo (1653) describe the August [36] festival of *citua* in which the Incas gave thanks for not having succumbed to sickness during the past year, and purified Cuzco for the year to come. At the height of the fiesta they devoted a whole day to banqueting and singing an *haravi* [37] in honor of the sun. For this occasion they donned long red smocks reaching to their feet, wore special diadems called *pilco casa,* and played cane syrinxes, "making with them music of the type called *tica tica.*" On this day the mummies of the ancestors were brought out into the Great Square to be venerated and to enjoy the open-air festivity.

Poma de Ayala (*ca.* 1615) shows on page 322 of his illustrated chronicle a darce scene in which four Antisuyos (indigenes living north and east of Cuzco) perform the [h]*uarmi auca.*[38] In this dance "all the men dress up as women," thus paying tribute to the Amazons of the selva.[39] His picture shows both sexes nude to the waist and barefooted. Even so, only the men string maichil rattles around their ankles and a man plays the six-tubed antara. The participants cross hands as they dance.[40] Among other instruments accompanying this taqui, Poma de Ayala mentions a pipo, which he classes as a flute, and a drum played by a man who sings above its beat in praise of the Amazons of Chihuanay. The men dancers meantime chant

---

[36] *Las Crónicas de los Molinas,* ed. Francisco A. Loayza (Lima: Ed. Domingo Miranda, 1943 [*Los pequeños grandes libros de historia americana, ser. 1, t. 4*], pp. 29–36); Bernabé Cobo, *Historia del Nuevo Mundo* (Seville: Imp. de E. Rasco, 1893), IV, 113–118. Cobo placed this festival in the tenth month of the Inca year. Miguel Cabello Balboa, *Miscelánea Antártica* (Lima: Universidad Nacional Mayor de San Marcos [Instituto de Etnología], 1951), p. 351, gives it to September.

[37] Diego González Holguín, *op. cit.,* I, 145, thus defined *haraui:* "Cantares de hechos de otros o memoria de los amados ausentes y de amor y aficion y agora se ha recibido por cantares deuotos y espirituales."

[38] Poma de Ayala, *op. cit.,* (facs. ed.), p. 323.

[39] Francisco de Orellana during his 1542 voyage of discovery down the Amazon heard of these female warriors. See Oviedo, IV, 388–389.

[40] Cobo, *op. cit.,* IV, 231, describes another cross-hands dance of only three persons (Inca between two *pallas* = princesses) as the best in the indigenous repertory.

"caya, cayaya" in a rhythm involving four beats, with triplets on the third and duplets on the rest, to which the women reply in alternating triplets and duplets using the same syllables.

Wherever native festivals occur, Poma de Ayala always mentions the end-notched flute, whether pincollo or quenaquena (pp. 315, 319, 323, 325, 327), as the indispensable "melody" instrument.[41] Invariably it is played by a man, never by a woman. He can see only innocent delight in the native dances and songs. But Arriaga, who published his well-informed *Extirpacion de la Idolatria del Pirv* in 1621, held a less sanguine view. Poma de Ayala pleads even for those such as the *Uauco,* which they sang to the accompaniment of deer-skull whistles or trumpets. He sees all these with the eyes of a Christianized hankerer after the glories of his own people's past. But Arriaga contended that the very instruments themselves breathed the errors of aboriginal religion. His viewpoint so prevailed at Lima that already the *Constitvciones Synodales del Arçobispado de los Reyes,* enacted in 1613, advised curates serving native parishes not to allow any dances, songs, or *taquies antiguos* which were accompanied by such infected instruments as the antara, deer skull, or *tamborillo.*[42]

Arriaga, who had traveled the length and breadth of Peru ferreting out superstitions, complained that the antaras (*antari* in his spelling), pincollos (flutes of bone and cane in his definition), *pututu* (gourd trumpet), trumpets made of deer and taruga skulls, and even those of copper and silver which survived from the pagan past, served but to summon people to fiestas at which they worshiped idols.[43] What is more, he mentioned many supposedly Christian celebrations at which idols were hidden around a Virgin or saint. After fasting and confessing themselves to wizards, they all danced and sang and drank themselves into a stupor at their three principal yearly feasts. The women at these festivals banged on their tamborines, "which they all own," meantime singing antiphonally. The men used such instruments as "*succhas*—skulls of the guanaco, and animal horns of which they always have a superfluity."[44] At intervals they sang the fables of their past, invoked the local deity by raising their hands or turning around after a verse in his praise. "Their usual custom is not to pronounce his name out loud, but to mouth it silently between syllables. They always dress up in their gaudiest finery for these events, clothe themselves in vicuña wool, wear silver diadems and brightly colored feather plumes, and put on wide-sleeved short shirts adorned with silver bangles."

[41] See his lively drawing of two players serenading two nude maidens from a cliff (p. 316).

[42] Reprinted in *Constituciones Synodales* (Lima: Ignacio de Luna, 1722), fol. 7 (chap. 6, par. 8).

[43] Pablo Joseph de Arriaga, *Extirpacion de la Idolatria del Pirv* (Lima: Geronymo de Contreras, 1621), pp. 44–45.

[44] *Ibid.,* p. 30.

Many Spaniards thought all this very attractive, Arriaga was willing to admit, allowing themselves the delusion that the Indians were honoring Christian saints in their native way. But such customs smacked as much of superstition, he claimed, as did their practice of "beating dogs and drums and crying up a din to revive the 'dead' moon during a lunar eclipse"; or of burying rich viands, vessels, and conches with the dead to make their next life a happier one.[45]

Archbishop Pedro de Villagómez so thoroughly agreed that he copied Arriaga verbatim when he came to publish his *Carta Pastoral de Exortacion e Instrvccion contra las Idolatrias de los Indios del Arçobispado de Lima* (Lima: Iorge López de Herrera, 1649). The archbishop's chapter 44, "De las fiestas que hacen los Indios a las huacas," equals Arriaga's chapter 5, his chapter 45 matches Arriaga's chapter 4, and his chapter 46, "De los abusos y supersticiones que tienen los Indios," omits only the few sentences in Arriaga's like-named chapter 6 which were written in the first person. To combat all idolatry, Archbishop Villagómez counsels his *visitadores* to enter Indian villages carrying with them stacks of printed devotional songs, leaving them for the Indians to learn and sing (fol. 48v: "A de llenar copias impressas de cantares deuotos a proposito de lo que an menester saber los Indios, y dexarselas para que los aprendan, y canten"). Repeating a ruling of the 1612 Lima Synod, he again urges that under no circumstances shall the missionaries allow their charges to "play tamborillos, dance, or sing in the old-fashioned way, or revive the heathenish dances and songs in their native language" (fol. 71v).

Garcilaso de la Vega, as usual, painted a prettier picture. For him the antara invoked no diabolical rites but was a delicate instrument on which virtuosi performed before the Inca. Like a chest of viols, antaras—as he remembered them from his noble youth at Cuzco in the 1550's—came in several voice registers. They did not sound polyphony, he admitted, but they did answer one another antiphonally at consonant intervals. Four players made a playing group. To play the antara well the entertainer had to practice assiduously.[46] The bone or cane flute also needed practice. A knowledgeable performer could extract a tune so individual that he could call his beloved from a great distance.[47] Each Quechua song had its own "proper" tune, and a pincollo player spoke the individual sentiment just as power-

---

[45] *Ibid.*, pp. 38, 14.

[46] *Primera parte de los Commentarios Reales* (Lisbon: Pedro Crasbeeck, 1609), fol. 52v, col. 2: "la musica no era commun, sino que la aprendian y alçauan con su trabajo."

[47] *Ibid.*, fol. 53, col. 1. Pedro Gutiérrez de Santa Clara affirmed as much in his *Historia de las Guerras Civiles del Perú* (Madrid: Lib. de V. Suárez, 1905), III, 549–550, when he wrote: "These Indians have some small flutes with two holes on one side and another beneath, called pingollos. They sing their *romances* with them as clearly as if they were speaking. With these they call their loves, and the young ladies at night shut up in their houses or with their guardians when they hear who is playing the pingollo secretly steal out to him."

fully with his flute as with his voice. The fact that Garcilaso could transcribe
a Quechua song into European notation, and also that during his noble
youth a Cuzco chapelmaster had already delighted the Indians and satisfied
the Spaniards at a Corpus Christi celebration by adding parts to an Inca
paean proved that Inca music, if not an Isaac, was at least an Ishmael.[48] Any
tune that can be notated and still remain recognizable when woven into a
polyphonic web must obviously consist of melodic intervals that the European system recognizes. Inca antara as well as vocal music proceeded in
consonancias.

In contrast with the relatively small numbers gathered to make an antara
consort before the Inca, pincollo bands included as many as a hundred
players. According to Poma de Ayala, the eleventh *coya*—wife of Huayna
Capac (d. 1525)—assembled a band of more than a hundred *pincollori* to
accompany her private dancers. Drums beat out the rhythms. She was the
first to insist that proper "acoustical" surroundings be found for each group
of instruments. Pincollos, for instance, had to be played on a recessed stone
platform against a wall called a *pincollonapata,* or in one or two other
special places—always different from those in which she listened to her
female singers chant haravis.[49]

If the antara, pincollo, and cognates served to entertain the Incas in
peaceful hours, the qquepa found its principal use in battle or warrior
ceremonies. Molina of Cuzco described the initiation rites for future empire
soldiers at the festival of Capac Raymi.[50] Their ears were pierced, their
weapons were given them, and they were scourged several times. After
sleeping some cold distance from Cuzco, they arose to meet the shepherd of
the sacred llama flock, who came out to them "playing on bored conches of
the kind called *hayllayquepa.*" They were whipped before sitting down
some half league outside the city to sing the *huarita* to the accompaniment
of conch trumpets. This lasted one hour, after which they were again heavily
scourged. Manco Capac, the first Inca, arose from Tambo hole teaching his
subjects to sing this very taqui in honor of the Creator—and on one occasion
of the year only—at this very ceremony.

The sound of the large conch carried tremendous distances, especially in
the mountains. After one of Huascar's battles with Atahuallpa, the usurper's
two generals, Challcuchima and Quisquis, rallied their decimated forces
"ten leagues from the place of battle, with blasts of *guayllaquipas.*" [51] The
Spaniards themselves had recourse to the same large conches more than
once to find one another in difficult terrain. Hernando de Soto, later to

---

[48] Garcilaso de la Vega, *Commentarios,* fol. 101v, col. 2.

[49] Poma de Ayala, *op. cit.* (facs. ed.), p. 141. See also his drawing of a *pingollona-
pata* on p. 316.

[50] *Las Crónicas de los Molinas,* pp. 51–57.

[51] Joan de Santacruz Pachacuti Yamqui, "Relacion de Antigüedades deste Reyno del
Piru," in *Tres Relaciones de Antigüedades Peruanas* (Madrid: M. Tello, 1879), p. 321.

discover the Mississippi River and to govern Florida, would never have survived the ambuscade set for him on his way to Cuzco had not Almagro discovered him with repeated blasts at midnight on these same awesome war conches.[52] When the indigenes heard these blown, realized that succor had arrived, and that Soto was joining with Almagro, they dispersed before dawn.

In Poma de Ayala's two drawings of trumpeters—one an imperial *chasqui* (runner) and the other a guard set by Atahuallpa over the defeated Huascar [53]—both players adopt the same posture seen in Mochica clay figurines. They throw their heads back so that they look upward while pressing the trumpet to their mouths. Poma de Ayala's chasqui holds a gourd trumpet (called *putoto* [54]) to his mouth with his right hand and carries a *quipu* (the knotted cord that served the Incas in place of writing) and a small basket in his left hand. Huascar's forward guard blows a conch, which he presses to his mouth with his left hand. His right remains free to hold both a spear and the rope that goes around Huascar's neck.

Therefore, though both trumpeters throw their heads back, they play different materials and use different arms.

Not only because of the difficulty in obtaining them, but also because of their nobler sound, conches remained the "aristocratic" instruments. They alone were deemed suitable sacrifices to such *huacas* as fountains and springs.[55] Only conches were buried with chieftains. To obtain the largest specimens, both Xérez (Pizarro's secretary) and Oviedo agree that a brisk coastal commerce had been developed. Because Xérez' account (as redacted by Juan de Sámano) tells exactly what prizes the Incas were willing to exchange for conches, it dramatizes the role of the conch trumpet in Inca times as does perhaps no other.[56]

[52] Pedro Pizarro, *Relación del descubrimiento y conquista de los reinos del Perú* (Buenos Aires: Editorial Futuro, 1944), p. 73.

[53] Poma de Ayala, *op. cit.*, pp. 350 (chasqui) and 115 (Huascar guarded).

[54] *Ibid.*, p. 351. On p. 334 he spelled it *pototo*. Bernardo de Vargas Machuca in his *Milicia y descripción de las Indias* dated 1599 (Madrid: Lib. de V. Suárez, 1892), I, 40, gave it as *fotuto*. *Putoto* was made to serve in a 1781 document as a synonym for the conch trumpet. See the famous sentence of death passed May 15, 1781, by the Spanish officer José Antonio Areche, on the rebel Tupac Amaru (who had usurped royal powers on the strength of his Inca descent). This sentence was reprinted in Manuel de Odriozola, *Documentos históricos del Perú* (Lima: Aurelio Alfaro, 1863), I, 159: "Del proprio modo se prohiben y quitan las trompetas ó clarines que usan los indios en sus funciones, á las que llaman *pututos,* y son unos caracoles marinos de un sonido estraño y lugubre, con que anuncian el duelo y lamentable memoria que hacen de su antigüedad."

[55] Polo de Ondegardo, *Informaciones acerca de la Religión y Gobierno de los Incas* (Lima: Sanmarti, 1916), p. 39.

[56] *Las Relaciones Primitivas de la Conquista del Perú*, ed. Raúl Porras Barrenechea (Paris: Imp. les Presses modernes, 1937), p. 66.

The first European ship entered Peruvian waters in September, 1526. The oceanic raft captured by the Spanish pilot Ruiz hoisted "as fine cotton sails as ours." [57] The merchandise, all of which was being offered to barter for *caracoles,* included

. . . many pieces of silver and gold for personal adornment . . . crowns, diadems, girdles, bracelets, leg- and breast-armour, tweezers, little bells, bead necklaces . . . mirrors edged with silver, drinking vessels, many woollen and cotton shawls, and shirts . . . beautifully and richly woven in scarlet, crimson, blue, yellow, and all other colours, with figures of birds, animals, fish, and shrubs . . . some small scales like the Roman kind to weigh gold . . . and some emeralds and chalcedonies and other jewels and pieces of crystal; and all of this they carried aboard to trade for conches.

Because the Inca imperial color was vermilion, the conches they preferred above all others had to be not only outsize, but also had to show coral or other reddish tints on the interior.

The esteem in which the instrument itself was held carried over to its players. Ñaimlap, the earliest ruler of the northern province of Lambayeque whom the Indians at the time of the conquest could still recall by name, entered his realm from afar with forty officials. Pita Çofi, the officer who headed his list, *era su trompetero ó Tañedor de unos grandes caracoles, que entre los Yndios estiman en mucho* ("was the trumpeter, or player of large conches, which are among the Indians held in great esteem").[58]

In addition to the folkloric antlers and guanaco skulls execrated by Arriaga [59] (but gratefully remembered in a naïve drawing by Poma de Ayala [60]), the skulls of dogs were turned into trumpets by at least one nation conquered during the reign of Pachacuti (d. 1471)—the Huanca. According to Garcilaso, Huancas adored their god in a dog's form, feasted on dog flesh, and

---

[57] Of the twenty aboard, eleven escaped. Only three of the nine captured were retained. The trio later served as interpreters when the Spaniards conversed with Atahuallpa at Cajamarca.

[58] Cabello Balboa, *op. cit.,* p. 327.

[59] Arriaga is by no means the only witness to the superstitious use of *cuernos de venado.* The first Augustinians found antlers being adored in fertility rites. They were warned not to approach the antlers on pain of swelling up and dying. See "Relación de idolatrías en Huamachuco por los primeros Agustinos," in *Informaciones acerca de la Religión y Gobierno de los Incas,* ed. H. H. Urteaga (Lima: Sanmarti, 1918), p. 37.

[60] Poma de Ayala, *op. cit.,* p. 320. Overleaf he described the festival. Girls of sixteen lifted their small drums aloft and, while beating them with mallets, sang in Quechua: "Dear brother, I do not see the taruga in your hands which you seem to be holding; I do not see the deer . . . ," to which the men players responded by blowing two notes on one deer skull and then another. In his drawing the skulls are held in two hands. Each has a mouthpiece. One player bends low, the other stands erect. Both wear elaborate feather headdress.

. . . to show their more ardent devotion made of dog skulls a kind of trumpet [*vna manera de bozinas*] which they played at their festivals and dances. They themselves considered the music very soothing to the ears [*muy suaue a sus oydos*]. But in their wars they played it to terrorize their enemies. They said that their dog-god endowed it with the ability to produce contrary effects at one and the same time. Because of their worship, it sounded well to them, while simultaneously it shocked their enemies and made them flee.[61]

In 1633 Cobo described as still current a dance called *guayayturilla,* which was accompanied by dried antlers made into an instrument.[62] Both men and women painted their faces crimson with a gold or silver band stretching from ear to ear above the nose. The leader started very slowly, setting the tempo for the others. The popularity of this dance so late as the middle of the seventeenth century proves clearly enough that none of the bans urged by such Christianizers as Arriaga[63] had effectually torn the Indians from their beloved antlers and skulls.[64]

Silver, bronze, and copper trumpets sounded at all the principal shrines when the Spaniards arrived. Catequil, an idol who dared "contest" Atahuallpa's right to supplant Huascar and for such temerity was later broken to pieces, enjoyed in palmier days the praise of *trompetas de plata baxa y metal.*[65] Tantazoro, another favorite idol, commanded fourteen *trompetas de plata y cobre* which sounded bravely against the din of *muy hermosos atambores* ("very beautiful drums") for the celebration of his rites.[66] He "drank" out of forty-one silver vases, and from his nose and ears dangled five silver crowns "like horseshoes." When he was taken from his shrine for processions about the countryside, his devotees protected him from the weather with seven richly worked canopies and fanned him with a splen-

---

[61] Garcilaso de la Vega, *op. cit.,* fol. 138*v,* col. 1.

[62] Cobo, *op. cit.,* IV, 230.

[63] See "Relación de idolatrías en Huamachuco por los primeros Agustinos," p. 28, for description of the ruses by which the Indians retained their old "errors." Avila, for his pains in trying to root out superstition, had to suffer from false charges brought against him by the very Indians whose ways he was trying to change.

[64] Leather trumpets (*bozinas de cuero*) provided still another type in addition to conch, clay, and animal skull. Martín de Morúa, *Historia del origen y genealogía real de los Reyes Inças* (Madrid: C. Bermejo, 1946), p. 197, cites the leather *bozinas* as hunting horns. The chase in preconquest Peru (as in Europe) was a royal sport denied all but the Inca and highest nobility.

[65] "Relación . . . por los primeros Agustinos," p. 24. The only metal trumpet that has come to my attention in a Peruvian museum is an unnumbered silver specimen 27 cm long, with a bore beginning at 3.5 cm and emerging into an 8.5 cm bell. Owned by the Trujillo University Museum, this metal trumpet is joined by a four-tube metal antara (the longest tube measuring 9 cm with a 3 cm diameter) and metal transverse flute (three holes, closed at both ends, 25 cm long, 6 cm in diameter) in the same collection.

[66] *Ibid.,* p. 33.

didly wrought featherpiece of *diversos colores*. Ozorpillao, still another idol in Huamachuco (northern highlands), "owned" two houses stocked with vases, trumpets, drums, and clothing.[67] In the same vicinity another nine huacas already famous in the time of Huayna Capac (ruled 1493–1525) "owned" clothing, trumpets, and llamas donated by the Inca and his predecessor, Topa Inca Yupanqui (ruled 1471–1493). In general, metal trumpets seem to have been preferred for shrines, conch for martial events, gourd for the imperial post, and skull for "folk" festivals.

Size so mattered in syrinxes and flutes that quite different names were given large and small (*ayarichi* and *sico* [A.]; *pincollo* and *pirutu* or *piruru* [Q.]).[68] It meant so much in conches that coastal merchandise was carried afar in exchange for the largest specimens.[69] It also mattered insofar as drums were concerned. The timber frames of the largest varied from nine to eleven feet. The heads were of leather, tied with V-shaped thongs. The drummers beat these large drums with their hands, and the sound carried "two or three leagues." When Negroes began to be imported soon after the conquest, they were surprised to find the Indians using the same monster sizes they had known in Africa, but even "their own drums were not as large as those of the Indians." The indigenes used these big sizes, especially in the region of Quito, to signal—say both Rocha [70] and Vargas Machuca [71]—because "their sound like that of *fotutos* [= *putoto* = *potutu*] carries great distances in the mountains."

At a dance so solemn that in preconquest times it could be danced only by members of the blood royal, the *guayyaya*, a huge drum mounted on the back of a poor male porter was beaten by a woman. As many as three or four hundred dancers took part. To each beat they would take three steps, one back and two forward, thus slowly approaching the Inca or highest official present.[72] While dancing they sang responsorially a *cantar* peculiar to this *bayle*. Men and women threaded their way, sometimes with locked arms, at others in single file. This was one of the few dances in which they abstained from jumping.

Triumphs were celebrated with big drums, but deaths and losses were mourned with small. When Pachacuti (1438–1471) rose to the defense of

[67] *Ibid.*, p. 34.

[68] González Holguín, *op. cit.*, I, 285, says that the small-size ones were made of bone or cane.

[69] According to González Holguín, *huayllaqquepa* had to mean *la bozina de caracol grande*, and no ordinary size (I, 187, col. 2).

[70] Diego Andrés Rocha, *Tratado vnico, y singvlar del origen de los Indios Occidentales del Piru* (Lima: Imp. de Manuel de los Olivos, 1681), fol. 39.

[71] *Milicia y descripción de las Indias* (1892 ed.), I, 40.

[72] Cobo, *op. cit.*, IV, 231.

Cuzco he brought forth from the armory the biggest drums, conches, and antaras.[73] But when his father died, the principal widows mourned with *tamborçillos pequeñuelos* (tiny drums) and *campanillas* (small bells). They scourged themselves, cropped their hair, came out in procession bare to their waists with ashes on their heads, and their faces painted black. Meantime, to show his satisfaction in at last being sole ruler, Pachacuti proudly armed his warriors with oval shields, large spears, and clubs, and had them march in slow procession to the sound of large drums. The other blood survivors blamed him for insulting the dead.

All the chroniclers from Cieza de León [74] to Cobo [75] agree that drums were played to mourn the dead. The bereaved went from one favorite haunt of the deceased to another, playing drums and flutes and wailing sad songs in which they rehearsed his whole life history. Women seem to have been the principal mourners. Since they all owned small, portable drums which they held aloft by attached thongs and beat with bulbous mallets,[76] they were always ready to raise a mourner's din at any required moment. Pedro Pizarro, even in old age at Arequipa, still remembered how the mourners at Cajamarca for Atahuallpa's death had all been women beating small drums, and how they had all gone about from his one favorite haunt to another singing his life story.[77]

The numbers 4 and 8 fascinated the Inca. The highest yearly feast, that of Capac Raymi, closed with llama sacrifices by four old men to the accompaniment of four drums of the Sun so large that each could be played by four chieftains. Dressed in vermilion smocks, which trailed to their feet, the four beaters at each of the four drums went masked in puma skins fitted with vicious false teeth and golden claws.[78]

To frighten their enemies, the rebels after Pachacuti's death hung up eight drums on four wooden poles.[79] Inca Roca, to insure his infant son a victorious life, ordained at his birth a great feast sung to the accompaniment of eight large drums.[80]

---

[73] Santacruz Pachacuti Yamqui, *op. cit.*, p. 270.

[74] *Parte Primera de la Chronica del Peru* (Antwerp: Juan Steelsio, 1554), fol. 170*v*.

[75] Cobo, *op. cit.*, IV, 237.

[76] Arriaga, *op. cit.*, p. 45.

[77] Pedro Pizarro, *op. cit.*, p. 66.

[78] Cobo, *op. cit.*, IV, 102.

[79] Santacruz Pachacuti Yamqui, *op. cit.*, p. 288.

[80] *Ibid.*, p. 265. How closely the Indians clung to their old numerological fancies as late as 1725 becomes very apparent in Gerónimo Fernández de Castro y Bocángel's *Elisio Peruano. Solemnidades Heroicas, y Festivas Demonstraciones de jvbilos, que se han logrado en la muy Noble, y muy Leal Ciudad de los Reyes Lima* . . . (Lima: Francisco Sobrino, 1725), fol. L2 of which carries a description of "D. Juan de Abendaño *Saba Capac* noble natural del Pueblo de Miraflores, y Pachacamac." Dressed up to represent Huayna Capac, he was attended by a troupe of eight dancers playing native instru-

Vermilion, the Inca color,[81] reappeared frequently on their cult drums. The first Augustinian missionaries (arrived in 1551) found the native priests and diviners "beating drums covered with blood."[82] They came out shaking bags full of jingles, beating copper *cencerros* (bells, or possibly gongs), and banging their bloody drums to summon the *demonio* whose advice they required on sickness and other problems. According to the Augustinian report, all this infernal racket confused even the shamans themselves into believing that they had established contact with the demon.

Though generally drums were made of hollow logs covered with cured llama hide at both ends,[83] drum cases of clay and metal were also quite common. Cieza de León vouches for the playing of "golden drums, some set with precious stones," at Cuzco during the annual feast of Hatun Raimi.[84] They were beaten by women who responded at intervals to the "high" voices of the men praising their gods. According to Cieza, the great conqueror Pachacuti rounded up the needed metallurgists during his conquest of the Chimú kingdom, transporting them to Cuzco. Previously, skilled metalworking such as would be necessary for the more intricate shapes, the *cire perdue*, and the techniques of sintering, alloying, and annealing, belonged to the coastal kingdoms.[85]

Because one of the Incas' most sensational practices was their habit—

---

ments. The eighth Inca marching in the same procession was also attended by *ocho gentiles hombres de la Corte* who danced to the strains of conch trumpets and quena-quenas ("traìa delante vna tropa de instrumentos musicos de su tiempo, marinos Caracoles, ciertas Flautas, a quien llaman *quenaquenas*, cuya musica tiene mas de lugubre, que de apacible" [fol. L3*v*]). Manco Capac exceeded all the other Incas in glory, with eight *meninos* dancing about him.

Eight still cuts a wide swath in Francisco de Arrese y Layseca's *Descripcion de las Reales Fiestas* that celebrated Charles IV's ascent to the throne (Lima: Imp. Real de los Niños Expósitos, 1790), pp. 94–96. Eight *chimbos* and eight *pallas* danced in the procession. For a culminating pair of dances *ocho personas cada una baylaban gallardamente al son de instrumentos.* The accompaniment consisted mostly of *cascaueles y tixeras* (jingles and scissors).

[81] The walls and all the wooden trimmings in Atahuallpa's private apartments at Cajamarca were "daubed with a bright red bitumen which was extremely lustrous and fierier than ochre." See Francisco de Xérez's graphic eyewitness account, *Conquista del Peru,* repr. in *Historiadores Primitivos de las Indias Occidentales,* III (Madrid, 1749 [ed. Andrés González Barcia]), p. 201, col. 1 (ll. 41–45).

[82] "Relación . . . de los primeros Agustinos," p. 46.

[83] Cobo, *op. cit.,* IV, 229.

[84] Pedro de Cieza de León, *Del Señorío de los Incas* (Buenos Aires: Ediciones Argentinas "Solar," 1943), pp. 167–168.

[85] Pedro Pizarro, *op. cit.,* p. 98, mentions the *muchos plateros y muy delicados oficiales* (many silversmiths and other cunning workmen) assembled by the Incas in Cuzco. For a list of the exquisite metal objets d'art brought home to Spain by the Pizarros in the Santa María del Campo (January, 1534) as part of the royal fifth, see Xérez, p. 236, col. 1 (1749 ed.; see n. 81 above). Two small gold or silver drums entered the royal fifth.

popularized by Pachacuti—of flaying their defeated foes and stuffing their skins to make drums, nearly all the chroniclers dwell on it.[86] To this day, their cured human-skin drums (the dead man's arm being stuffed to beat his own puffed stomach) remain the best-known "Inca instruments." All popular books on organology mention them. Poma de Ayala even tells how Rumiñaui, a traitor to Huascar but an extremely able captain, killed the heir apparent Illescas, made of his skin a drum, of his bones an antara, and of his teeth a necklace.[87] Poma's drawing shows the fiendish captain in the act of disemboweling the prince.[88] His naked quivering body hangs upside down from a tree, the skin over chest and abdomen already incised and folded back. With left hand the captain braces himself against the expiring prince's tied foot, and with right prepares to dig out the entrails with a sharp anchor-shaped lancet.

Of the several methods that can be used to study preconquest Andean music, investigation of museum instruments tempered by a reading of the literary allusions will surely continue to be the most fruitful. The d'Harcourts, who in the transcriptions that bulk so large in their first volume rendered the same kind of service to Andean music that Liszt's "Hungarian" Rhapsodies rendered to "Hungarian," controlled their results neither culturally nor geographically.[89]

From the instruments themselves, some such conclusions as the following can be drawn. (1) Musically speaking, the Andean peoples have nothing to fear from comparison with the Aztecs or Mayas. (2) If their instruments provide sufficient clues, their musical culture did not remain static but advanced from the equidistant finger-hole stage to the unequal; from the three-hole to the five- and six-hole; from the single-row antara to the double-row; from the six-tube antara to the fourteen- and fifteen-tube; from the stairway antara to the unequal pipe-growth; from the vertical to the cross flute. (3) Materials, except the conch, were native to the Andean region. (4) Number, color, size, and sex mattered intensely to the indigenous player. (5) Nazca and Mochica instruments, to name no others, were not fashioned haphazardly, but according to exact, preconceived plans. (6) Individual "schools" of instrument making flourished, even at the same cultural horizon. (7) If different names within the same language prove anything, both Aymara- and Quechua-speaking indigenes sharply distinguished between different sizes of the "same" instrument, and different substances used in making it. (8) The peoples with the largest thoracic

---

[86] Although all the Spaniards from Oviedo to Montesinos mentioned the custom, this was no mere conqueror's libel. Santacruz Pachacuti and Poma de Ayala, both full-blooded indigenes, give the goriest descriptions.

[87] Poma de Ayala, *op. cit.*, p. 164.

[88] *Ibid.*, p. 163.

[89] John H. Rowe, "Inca Culture at the Time of the Spanish Conquest" (Bulletin 143 [*Handbook of South American Indians*], Vol. II [Washington: Smithsonian Institution, 1946], p. 289), drew attention to these weaknesses.

capacity of any around the world [90] justly made so breath-consuming an instrument as the antara their specialty. (9) Communal playing, as befits a society built on the *ayllu* pattern, was well enough advanced to bring together bands of a hundred pincollo players and smaller groups of antara blowers. (10) The wide and broadly differing gamuts of surviving antaras may justify Garcilaso's claim that for each *tonada* there existed a quite different tune. (11) The indigenes certainly did not allow themselves to be confined by pentatonic, nor for that matter by diatonic, restrictions. (12) Some attention was already being given to "acoustical" surroundings by so famous a musical patroness as the eleventh coya. (13) None of the archaeological instruments thus far inventoried blows notes lower than a violist's open *C*—a fact that may help to explain why the Spaniards found their vocal ideal so high and strident. (14) For that matter, their only groups of professional singers at Cuzco before the conquest reflected a similar trend, since they were always composed exclusively of young girls not out of their teens. (15) Though instrument making had probably become a recognized craft before A.D. 500, the more intricate metal instruments seem to have awaited the Chimú period. (16) Museum instruments stress clay and bone because precious metals attracted the Spanish eye for profit and cane is fragile.[91] (17) Coastal cultures are the best represented in collections, but, like the Romans, the Incas seem to have availed themselves of the most advanced knowledge of the subjugated. (18) Just as trumpeters enjoyed superior social status in Renaissance Europe, so also did trumpeters in the Inca empire—especially those who blew the large conch. (19) Buried instruments, such as qquepas and antaras, reflect the sharply varying social status of their owners. (20) The first contact between Peruvians and Europeans symbolized their musical interests—the Peruvians navigating an ocean-going balsa to trade "all that they had" for the large conches that alone they considered suitable for their war trumpets.

[90] Mason, *op. cit.*, p. 7.

[91] As long ago as the 1870's metal instruments were so scarce that E. George Squier in *Peru: Incidents of Travel and Exploration in the Land of the Incas* (London: Macmillan, 1877), pp. 181–182, had to depend entirely on stone and clay musical specimens for his assessment of ancient Peruvian music, even in the coastal areas where metallurgy had reached its highest development. His cuts, made from photographs, were the earliest illustrations of the antara and coiled qquepa to appear in an English book. At pages 305–307 he describes and illustrates the Aymara pototo dance at Tiahuanaco, identified as a preconquest survival. Nothing heard by Cortés' band could have been "more fascinating, more weird or savage" than the music of syrinxes, shallow drums, and cow's horns during his Tiahuanaco visit.

In 1954 the Metropolitan Museum of Art in New York City exhibited eighty gold pieces from Colombia (Museo del Oro, Banco de la República), including a scepter-like pin with a jingle in its head and the golden effigy of a ceremonial conch trumpet (both objects from the Cauca Valley, Calima Style). For detailed descriptions see items 39 and 43 in the guide to the exhibit, *80 masterpieces from the Gold Museum* (Bogotá: Banco de la República, 1954). The Cauca Valley fell outside Inca territory.

2 MUSIC TEACHING IN THE INCA AREA: BEFORE AND AFTER THE CONQUEST

ANTIQUITY OF FORMAL INSTRUCTION

Not only did the Andean peoples ruled by the Incas perfect so advanced a musical instrument as the antara, but also the Incas were apparently the earliest Americans to institute any formal schemes of musical training. The Inca Roca (*ca.* 1350)

. . . was the first to establish schools in the royal city of Cuzco in which *amautas* [masters] taught those sciences which the royal family and the nobles of the empire needed to know. They did not teach from writings, because they had none. But by rote and by actual participation they inculcated the rites, precepts, and ceremonies of their false religion. They taught the grounds and reasons for their system of laws, and how to apply them in governing subject peoples; . . . also how to speak elegantly and correctly, how to bring up their children, and how to regulate their households. In addition, the amautas taught poetry and music.[1]

The songs taught by these highly venerated[2] amautas served the same mnemonic purpose as did their varicolored, knotted quipus.[3] The four-year

[1] Garcilaso de la Vega, *Primera Parte de los Commentarios Reales* (Lisbon: Pedro Crasbeeck, 1609), fol. 95, col. 2.

[2] *Ibid.* (*eran tenidos en suma veneracion*), and fol. 137, col. 2.

[3] For an English summary of references to the knotted strands used by the ancient Peruvians to record statistics—culled from Garcilaso de la Vega (fol. 134, col. 2; fol. 136, col. 1) and other chroniclers—see John R. Swanton, "The Quipu and Peruvian Civilization," *Bureau of American Ethnology Bulletin No. 133* (Washington: Smithsonian Institution, 1943), pp. 587–596.

course of study in the *yachahuasi*—as they called the school for noble youths in their 11,440-foot capital—indeed culminated in oral examinations testing their memory of the wars, conquests, and sacrifices celebrated in these very songs.[4]

If the future warriors and governors of the empire were assembled from its outer reaches to be drilled in a palace school under the ruling Inca's watchful eye, so also were elect virgins gathered from the four quarters of the Inca's world to inhabit nunneries at Cuzco. Their persons were regarded as so sacred that the eyes of those known even to lust after them were plucked out.[5] Virgins of the Sun occupied the first of the six houses set aside for these *acllas* ("chosen ones"). The fourth house contained a younger group of girls than the other five, and was called a *taquiaclla*[6] because it was set aside for the musically talented. In this house resided

. . . the singers and drummers elected to entertain the Inca, his captains and the principal nobility when they banqueted. . . . All the girls in it were chosen for their beauty as well as their voices. Their ages ranged from 9 to 15. At the end of the sixth year they were let go to make way for newcomers. As in the other houses, they had their *pongocamayos* or superintendents and their tutors who watched them and made sure that they lacked for nothing. By day the girls of this fourth house guarded the Inca's flock of sacrificial animals. . . . Above all, they were excellent singers of the *arabices* and other songs that they used.[7]

Huamán Poma de Ayala (*ca.* 1590) confirmed Morúa's account (1591) of the regimented life these girl singers endured. He added that they were also trained in flute playing, that they sang before the ruling Inca and Coya (emperor and empress) at mixed banquets rather than at all-male affairs, and that they enlivened imperial marriages and calendar festivals.[8]

As for their repertory, it was the ninth Inca, Pachacuti (1438–1471), builder of the stupendous Sun Temple at Cuzco, who first ordered the *yanaconas* and *mamaconas* of their sun-worshiping religion to gather standard collections of songs. In these song cycles, the deeds of the various emperors, beginning with the first Inca, Manco Capac, were to be rehearsed

[4] Martín de Morúa, *Historia del origen y genealogía real de los Reyes Inças del Perú*, ed. C. Bayle (Madrid: C. Bermejo, 1946), p. 169.

[5] Francisco López de Gómara, *Historia de las Indias*, ed. Andrés González Barcia (Madrid: [*Historiadores Primitivos*, II], 1749), p. 113, col. 1. Eunuchs whose very lips and noses had been cut off guarded them.

[6] In Quechua, *taqui*—joined with other vocables—signified "music" (in a general sense), and *aclla*, "chosen." See Diego González Holguín, *Vocabvlario dela lengva general de todo el Perv llamada lengva Qquichua* (Lima: Francisco del Canto, 1608), I, 339, col. 1; 7, col. 2.

[7] Morúa, *op. cit.*, pp. 252–253. *Arabice = Haraui =* chansons de geste, as well as love songs. See González Holguín, *op. cit.*, I, 145, col. 2, ll. 6–11.

[8] Felipe Huamán Poma de Ayala, *Nueva Corónica y Buen Gobierno* (Paris: Institut d'Ethnologie, 1936), p. 300.

"so that they would be remembered." [9] The songs in these extended cycles were to be distributed among the various festivals of the year and sung in appointed order. The priests and priestesses were to spread out in every "valley and village; and they and their descendants serve forever the holy places where the mummies of their chieftains were kept."

Even away from Cuzco, then, song still served the same formal purposes. In the high Andean villages where they

. . . knew neither letters nor statutes nor ordinances but only the kind of dance song which they called (and still call) an *arabice* they brought to mind and recounted old happenings in this way: Both men and women joined hands, or locked arms. The leader of the group started singing. All the rest then sang in reply. This responsorial singing lasted three or four hours until the leader had finished with his account. Sometimes a drumbeat accompanied the singers. Their tales had to do with the manner of the various Incas' deaths, who each was, what each did, and whatever else old and young were not supposed to forget. While all this singing went on, stand-bys brought up mugs of chicha for them to drink without their stopping the dance. After several hours they one by one dropped drunk on the ground. General intoxication served as the finale for every such dance.[10]

Garcilaso de la Vega—born at Cuzco of a Spanish captain and an Inca princess—best explains the character of preconquest Peruvian music. According to his *Commentarios Reales,* the chorus needed no instrumental accompaniment when chanting war and hero songs in solemn public ceremonies. Love songs were a different matter. The tunes of these were as often played on *flautas* as sung. Each song was mated with its own particular tune. "No two lyrics could be sung to the same tune." So hypnotic a spell was one love tune able to weave, even when played on a flute without the ditty, that a Cuzco Indian woman rushed to her husband's arms from a far distance when she heard but the sound of his *flauta.*[11]

Their instrumental repertory included pieces other than just the tunes of songs. Those players who were permitted to perform on the antara before the Inca or his principal chieftains had to have studied a long time, "because even if their music was so ethnic, it was by no means vulgar. On the contrary, it had to be laboriously learned and continuously practiced." The range of an antara roughly corresponded to either baritone, tenor, alto, or soprano. The players of the four sizes formed a quartet; but they did not play polyphonic pieces, since they knew nothing of part music. Rather, they formed a quartet so that their instrumental melodies could range at will

[9] Juan de Betanzos, *Suma y narración de los Incas,* ed. M. Jiménez de la Espada (Madrid: M. G. Hernández, 1880), p. 128: *para que de aquella manera hubiese memoria dellos y sus antigüedades.*

[10] Morúa, *op. cit.,* p. 176.

[11] Garcilaso de la Vega, *op. cit.,* fol. 53 [*recte* 52], col. 1.

from the lowest note of the bass to the highest of the treble. Each antara consisted of

. . . four or five double pipes of cane. These were bound together so that the pitch of each pipe would successively rise a degree above its neighbor, after the manner of organs. . . . Their way of playing was this. One member of the quartet would start by blowing a note. Then another player would blow a pipe sounding at the distance of a fifth or any other desired consonance above or below the first note. Next, still another player would blow his note, again at any desired consonantal distance. Finally, the fourth played his note. By keeping up this sort of thing they ranged from lowest to highest notes at will, but always in strict time. They did not know how to vary their melodies with small-value notes but always stuck with whole notes.[12]

Garcilaso does not necessarily mean to say that they never played fast music, but rather that their idea of rhythm was aggregative instead of partitive. The way in which several antaras played together recalls, of course, the Russian horn bands that wealthy nobles assembled during the reign of Catherine the Great. Each hornist blew only a note, but by careful drilling the players could simulate any legato melody that they chose.[13]

MISSIONARY METHODS AND REPERTORY

In Peru, as in Mexico, the Indians took immediately to the music of their conquerors. European polyphony indeed so quickly seized the fancy of the Quechua-speaking Indians that when Garcilaso left Peru in 1560 "there was already in Cuzco a band of Indian flautists in the employ of Juan Rodríguez de Villa Lobos, a resident of that city, so extremely proficient that they could play perfectly any piece of polyphony put before them." [14] By 1602, Garcilaso added, excellent players were to be found not only in the ancient Inca capital, but everywhere.

Because European music so swayed their charges, the Franciscans, Dominicans, and Augustinians always made music a principal subject in the schools set up wherever they were sent to evangelize the Indian— from Quito, the northernmost city of the ancient Inca empire, to Copacabana, on the shores of Lake Titicaca. At Quito, for instance, where, from 1550–1581, the Franciscans ran a school for sons of chieftains (the Colegio de San Andrés), they were even able to teach their pupils such advanced

---

[12] *Ibid.*, fols. 52v–53 [*recte* 51v–52].

[13] On J. A. Maresch (*ca.* 1719–1794), organizer of the first Russian horn band, see M. J. Pénable, "Le Cor," *Encyclopédie de la Musique et Dictionnaire du Conservatoire,* 2ᵐᵉ partie, III (Paris: Lib. Delagrave, 1925), p. 1647.

[14] Garcilaso de la Vega, *op. cit.*, fol. 53, col. 2. Concerning Rodríguez de Villalobos, native of Cáceres (Extremadura), see *Primera Parte*, fol. 178v, col. 1; fol. 244; and *Historia General del Peru* (Cordova: Vda. de Andrés Barrera, 1617), fol. 254, col. 1; fol. 271v, col. 2.

European polyphony as Francisco Guerrero's motets (Venice: Antonio Gardano's Sons, 1570), printed copies of which reached the colegio within a decade of publication.[15] One of their prize alumni was Cristóbal de Caranqui, "who had a most beautiful voice, and also played the organ masterfully." [16] Those who did not sing received instruction in shawm playing. Such hard use did the school *chirimías* (shawms) endure that already in 1581 when inventory was taken they were set down as "old."

Another alumnus who excited the admiration even of the Spanish governor at Quito bore the hybrid name of Francisco Tomalá (first name Christian, last Indian). Sole son of the chieftain who ruled the island of Puná (guarding Guayaquil harbor), he graduated from the three R's to a course in both branches of European music, plainsong and polyphony. The governor, who praised him in a geography of Peru written about 1571 for Philip II to see,[17] was surprised at the versatility of an Indian who could have become so fine a horseman—when there were no horses before Pizarro —who could have accumulated 100,000 pesos, and who could at the same time have developed into so good a musician.[18]

At Cajamarca—where the Inca Atahuallpa filled a famous room full of gold to placate Pizarro and was for his pains strangled on August 29, 1533—the music of the conqueror proved similarly useful to those friars who preferred converting Indians by gentler means than the choice between burning and strangling. By 1615 the Indian singers at Cajamarca had become so outstanding that a traveler from Mexico to Peru chose only them among the many such groups of singers in Peru for special praise.

They have a chapelmaster who teaches them music. They sing in church every day as regularly as if they were canons. . . . They play shawms and other instruments to celebrate the Office Hours, a custom which had become general throughout the Indies. Those who perform are sons of chieftains and other principal Indians. They value this privilege highly and vie for it as a great honor.[19]

At Jauja, due east over the mountains from Lima, the Franciscan friar Gerónimo de Oré (1554–1629) labored twenty-odd years before issuing a

---

[15] Federico González Suárez, *Historia General de la República del Ecuador* (Quito: Imprenta del Clero, 1892), III, 339n.

[16] *Ibid.*, III, 336.

[17] Salazar de Villasante, "Relación General de las poblaciones españolas del Perú," in *Relaciones Geográficas de Indias*, ed. M. Jiménez de la Espada (Madrid: Tip. Manuel G. Hernández, 1881), I, 9.

[18] Marcos Jiménez de la Espada, ed., *Una Antigualla Peruana* (Madrid: Imp. de Fortanet, 1892), p. 42: Carlos Inquill Topa Inga, grandson of the eleventh Inca, "was a very good writer and a good horseman, skilled in arms, *a fine musician,* and very manly." Francisco Tomalá was therefore not a unique Indian prince.

[19] Antonio Vázquez de Espinosa, *Compendio y descripción de las indias occidentales* (Washington: Smithsonian Institution, 1948), p. 375.

manual of religious lyrics in Quechua to be sung with native as well as European tunes. In his *Symbolo Catholico Indiano* (Lima: Antonio Ricardo, 1598), he insisted that the Peruvian Indians should everywhere be taught not only plainsong but also polyphony by competent masters. They should study recorders, shawms, and trumpets,[20] "because all this music study leads to their conversion."[21] To enforce his point, he quoted a decision of the 1583 Council of Lima which encouraged the setting up of formal music curricula, both vocal and instrumental (woodwinds), at every Indian mission.[22] The vocal program had so prospered at Jauja that his own charges "had been singing Our Lady's Office from memory for forty years."[23]

Every evening his flock gathered to sing the Apostles' Creed to the tune of *Sacris Solemniis:* [24]

[20] Gerónimo de Oré, *Symbolo Catholico Indiano,* fol. 51v.

[21] *Pues todo esto autoriza y ayuda, para el fin principal de la conuersion delos indios. . . .*

[22] Rubén Vargas Ugarte, *Concilios Limenses* (Lima: Tip. Peruana, 1951), I, 311.

[23] Oré, *op. cit.,* fol. 53.

[24] *Ibid.,* fol. 53v. *Symbolo Menor* at fol. 160.

Capac eterno Dios

1) Almighty and eternal God, I kiss you with all
     my strength, to you I cry, hear me. Open my lips so that I may praise
     you.
2) You Holy Trinity, God the Father, God the Son,
     God the Holy Ghost
   You are the only one, Three Persons.

After singing the sixteen versified articles of the Creed, they then began practicing whatever they were to sing the next morning. On Sundays, Wednesdays, and Fridays, old and young in his Indian valley gathered at the church door under a streaming pennant. The two best boy soloists in the mission school—"those with the finest voices, and who have been taught the most"—commenced singing. The rest of the schoolboys responded. Meanwhile the older Indians filed into the church in parallel columns of men and women. On other days of the week, only the schoolchildren assembled. To keep the juniors quiet and orderly, Oré counseled that on these days of the week they should "proceed into the church singing their lesson slowly and devoutly in the fourth tone." [25] His choice of the fourth tone proves that he recognized the distinctions between the eight tones taught by the leading Spanish theorists of his century. Juan Bermudo had, for instance, claimed that the fourth tone "instils authority without being offensive; and uncouth voices singing in it sound agreeable." [26]

If the Franciscans emphasized music in their Colegio de San Andrés at Quito, and if Oré found music sufficiently potent a means of attracting the thirty thousand Indians in the middle valley of Jauja [27] to justify the expense of printing a book of Quechua lyrics on the first press in South America, so also at Cuzco itself a Franciscan tertiary, Juan Pérez Bocanegra, found music so keen an inducement that he could bring his *Ritual* of 1631 to a close with the first piece of vocal polyphony printed in any New World book. [28] The words are again in Quechua, the imperial language of the Incas. [29] Prior to publication of this 720-page Ritual, the complier had spent

[25] *Ibid.,* fol. 55.

[26] *Declaración de instrumentos* (Osuna: Juan de León, 1555), fol. 121v, col. 2.

[27] Diego de Córdova Salinas, *Coronica dela Religiosissima Provincia delos doze apostoles del Peru* (Lima: Jorge López Herrera, 1651), p. 551, col. 1. Huayna Capac had erected a large temple in this valley, *ca.* 1500.

[28] Despite the spate of Mexican musical imprints between 1556 and 1604, no polyphonic printing seems to have been undertaken by Pablos, Espinosa, Ocharte, or López Dávalos.

[29] Quechua, the dialect of Cuzco, marched with the Inca wherever he conquered, and was imposed by force. The number of completely distinct native idioms within the empire was legion.

forty years in and around Cuzco ministering to Indians, first as *cura* at Our Lady of Bethlehem Church in the ancient imperial capital and later as *párroco* at Andahuaylillas. His knowledge of both Quechua and Aymara had won him appointment as diocesan examiner in both tongues while still cura.[30]

He printed the following *oración* in sapphic verse on pages 708–709 of his *Ritual* (treble and tenor on p. 708, alto and bass on p. 709). The music, though he does not name the composer, may well have been written by an Indian. He does say that it "has been composed to be sung in processions as they [Indian parishioners] enter their churches on Lady-Days." [31] In the transcription below, the words of only two stanzas are shown, but several others follow on page 710 of the 1631 imprint. The music divides neatly into 3 + 3 + 4 + 3 + 3 + 4 bars. The lilt of the syncopated episodes at bars 7, 11, and 14 is especially fetching.

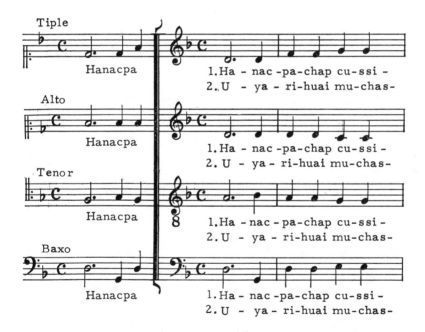

[30] Diego de Mendoza, *Chronica de la Provincia de S. Antonio de los Charcas* (Madrid, 1665), p. 551, col. 2. Bocanegra's musical competence is vouched for in his record of a dozen years or so as Cuzco Cathedral singer (*ca.* 1599–1611). During La Raya's episcopacy (1598–1604) he even served as a choir-book corrector.

[31] Juan Pérez Bocanegra, *Ritual Formulario, e institucion de curas* (Lima: Gerónimo de Contreras, 1631), p. 707: *va compuesta en musica a quatro vozes, para que la canten los cantores, en las processiones, al entrar en la Iglesia.*

No one religious order monopolized the musical education of the Peruvian Indians. Pedro de la Gasca (1492–1565)—who, as Charles V's personal delegate in Peru from June 13, 1547, until January 25, 1550, became the viceroyalty's first lawgiver—summoned representatives of all three mendicant orders to Lima as early as 1549 to tell them that they must learn Quechua, erect churches, teach the Indians how to pray, and everywhere set up schools. In these *escuelas* they were to teach reading, writing, hygiene, and such other "good things" as how to sing according to the rules of art and how to solfa (*dezir el sol, fa, mi, re*).[32] Gasca's very precise instructions were of course later strengthened by the ruling of the Third Lima Council (1583) in favor of music instruction at every Indian mission.[33]

In conformity with his mandate and with Act V, chapter 5, of the council's rulings, the Dominicans placed so excellent a musician at Cochangara as Fray Pedro de Vega, "a fine singer who taught his parishioners how to sing . . . and it is inspiring to observe the musical skill which the Indians have acquired throughout this whole valley, because there are bands of instrumentalists and choruses of singers in these parts who yield to none of the best anywhere in the world."[34] His missionary neighbor, the Franciscan Gerónimo de Oré (1554–1629), though of Spanish parentage, was born in Peru and studied only at Lima, never in Spain. The Dominican Vega, on the other hand, was trained at a motherhouse in Seville which had become famous for its music as early as 1494.[35]

The Jesuit fathers entered Peru in 1568, a generation after the three mendicant orders. In Europe, of course, they tended from the beginning to emphasize classics rather than fine arts in schools under their auspices. But in Lima, where they were called by the great viceroy Francisco de Toledo to take charge of the exclusively Indian parish of Santiago del Cercado in the early 1570's, they found that their Indian charges responded to European music so enthusiastically that it prepared the way for their conversion. In the school they at once founded for *cercado* children they therefore made it a principal subject. So vigorously did they teach both vocal and instrumental music that already in 1598 Anello Oliva, in his *Historia del Reino y Provincias del Perú*, could boast that Indian musicians trained in the cercado school competed with the best professionals in Lima. In 1622 Bernabé Cobo in his *Historia de la Fundación de Lima* could rate the music

---

[32] Pedro Gutiérrez de Santa Clara, *Historia de las Guerras Civiles del Perú* (1544–1548) (Madrid: Lib. de Victoriano Suárez, 1904–1929), VI (1929), 232.

[33] *Lima Limata Conciliis*, ed. Francis Harold (Rome: Giuseppe Corvi, 1673), p. 43 (cap. v).

[34] Juan Meléndez, *Tesoros Verdaderos de la Yndias* (Rome: Nicholas Angel Tinassio, 1681), p. 617, col. 2.

[35] The Dominicans of Seville underwrote the *Processionarium ordinis praedicatorum* published by Meynard Ungut and Stanislaus Polonus two years after Columbus' discovery. More copies of this book survive than of any other Spanish musical incunabulum.

at Santiago del Cercado as equal to the best in any cathedral he could name. Though only eight hundred adult Indians resided in the parish, "many had become finished vocalists and instrumentalists." [36] The church in that year owned two organs, four sets of shawms, two trumpets, viols of various sizes, and other instruments for feast-day use.

At Arequipa, Nicolás de Tolentino, chapelmaster of the church later to become the Arequipa Cathedral, contracted on September 17, 1611, with the maestro of the Jesuit-sponsored Indian choir to borrow the band of Jesuit-trained Indians for all important musical events in the cathedral-to-be, so superior had the Indian musicians become to all others in the area.[37] At Juli on the shores of Lake Titicaca the Indian musicians trained at the Jesuit mission were still the best in the region when the Bavarian Wolfgang Bayer was stationed in Peru (1752–1766).[38]

The fact that such a missionary as Oré could, by studying only at Lima, have become proficient in plainsong and polyphony, as well as at the keyboard, shows that already in his youth the capital entertained good music teachers. Pizarro traced the lines of the new city on Epiphany, 1535. Thirteen years later a Dominican from Pizarro's home town of Trujillo—Gerónimo de Loayza—received the pallium, and thus became Lima's first archbishop. Almost at once the *clérigo* Domingo Álvarez became *maestro de*

---

[36] Oliva, *Historia del Reino* (Lima: Imp. y Lib. de S. Pedro, 1895), p. 204; Cobo, *Historia de la Fundación de Lima*, ed. M. González de la Rosa (Lima: Imprenta Liberal, 1882), p. 138. Oliva, an Italian, extols (pp. 205–206) the painter Bernardo Billi brought in 1575 from Italy to decorate the cercado church and other Jesuit churches.

[37] Vargas Ugarte, "Notas sobre la Música en el Perú," *Cuaderno de Estudio* (Pontificia Universidad Católica del Perú, Instituto de Investigaciones Históricas), III/7 (1949), 29. For his documentation, Vargas Ugarte appealed to Victor M. Barriga, "Los Músicos y Cantores de la Iglesia Mayor y la Compañía en 1611: Los Maestros de Capilla Nicolás de Tolentino y Juan Castelo—Acuerdos para tocar y cantar en diversos templos," a fundamental article published in *El Deber* (Arequipa), Aug. 29, 1945, p. 3, cols. 5–7. Nicolás de Tolentino, himself an Indian, signed "en nombre de Juan Caquia y Juan Taipe indios cantores sus discipulos." Juan de Castelo, "maestro de capilla de los indios cantores del dicho colegio de la Compañía de Jesús," headed a group of nine musicians banded together in a *cofradía*—Diego Ignacio, Juan Casa, Baltazar de Vargas, Vicente Gualpa (these four were present for the signing of the contract), Francisco Chani, Diego Chani, Juan Baustista, Juan de Jesús, and Sebastián Tito (these five were absent from the signing ceremony). The "cantores de la Compañía de Jesús con su maestro de capilla instrumentos altos y bajos cada cosa en su tiempo" obligated themselves to perform at all the principal feasts and during Holy Week in the *Iglesia mayor* (parent church of the present cathedral). One of the Jesuit Indian musicians enjoys the honorific "Don" in the contract (Don Francisco Chani), as does also Nicolás de Tolentino. These were the only two *curacas* (caciques) in the two bands.

[38] J. T. Medina, *Jesuitas Expulsos de América en 1767* (Santiago de Chile: Imp. Elzeviriana, 1915), pp. 49–50.

capilla. On February 20, 1552, he signed the cathedral constitutions adopted at the first Lima Council. His duties included, of course, the teaching of both plainsong and polyphony to cathedral staff members.[39]

Although our concern here does not fly so high as the learned reaches of cathedral music but sticks to the more commonplace European music taught by missionaries, still we do well to remind ourselves that the Lima Provincial Council of 1567 passed a rule requiring the *chantre*, or a paid substitute, in every cathedral of the archdiocese to teach singing.[40] Indians as well as Creoles were eligible for this free instruction. The Lima Council of 1583 repeated the same rule,[41] and to put teeth into it ordained that no one could aspire to a benefice who had not learned to sing *cantum ecclesiasticum.*[42] In Spanish parishes throughout the archdiocese the 1583 council ruled that Mass must always be sung, not said. If a full choral celebration could not be held, then at least it should be recited *in tono.* In parishes without a regularly appointed maestro de capilla, the sacristan should teach the boys to sing, read, and write.[43] In both Spanish and Indian parishes the *Salve Regina* should always be sung at Saturday vespers, ruled this same council.[44] In exclusively Indian parishes, suitable candidates should be trained to sing the Epistle at Mass and to provide whatever musical assistance was needed.[45]

Each successive council passed more exacting ordinances, insofar as the music in Lima Cathedral itself was concerned. The maestro de capilla should teach a dozen boy choristers, ruled the 1593 council, six at cathedral chapter expense, the other six at *fábrica* expense.[46] Like other New World cathedrals, Lima had started as a suffragan of Seville, and throughout the sixteenth century took every step possible to imitate the grandeur of Sevillian music during Francisco Guerrero's mastership. Just as at Quito, so at Lima, his polyphonic publications were the first to be purchased.[47] The

---

[39] *Concilios Limenses,* I, 92, 355.

[40] *Sumario del Concilio Provincial* (Seville: Matias Clavijo, 1614), p. 21 (par. 75).

[41] *Concilium Limense Celebratum anno 1583* (Madrid: Pedro Madrigal, 1591), fol. 64v (chap. 29).

[42] *Sumario* (Seville, 1614), p. 170 (chap. 29).

[43] *Lima Limata Conciliis,* p. 200 (chap. 16).

[44] See p. 29 (chap. 27); also p. 223 (chap. 3) for 1585 diocesan ruling.

[45] *Sumario,* p. 55 (par. 74).

[46] *Lima Limata Conciliis,* p. 159 (chap. 26).

[47] A battered copy of Guerrero's *Liber vesperarum* of 1584 can still be seen among the forty-six choral books preserved in Lima Cathedral. Over Psalm 111 (*Beatus vir que timet*) some hard-pressed chapelmaster has scribbled: *si toca Vergara por falsa ut negro y si toca valentin por los bajones.* . . . At folio 68 (*Exultet orbis*) the printed leaf is gone. A handwritten substitute makes good the loss.

Doubtless this came with the shipment of seventeen copies (Boxes 40–55) approved for shipment from Seville to Portobelo (Panama) on January 10, 1601. The manifest lists Guerrero's 1584 *Liber vesperarum* thus: "Vn libro de canto de Guerrero con las

repertory, as well as the system of training, therefore approached Sevillian standards.

At Cuzco, even during the civil wars that racked the infant colony from 1544 to 1548, *monaçillos* and *moços de coro* (acolytes and choirboys) were already being trained to sing Spanish polyphony.[48] Garcilaso de la Vega assures us that as early as 1551 or 1552, when he was still a lad of twelve, Cuzco Cathedral already boasted a chapelmaster who was sufficiently a composer to make an effective polyphonic arrangement of the Inca haylli monody sung to the sun at summer solstice. After dressing up eight of his mestizo choirboys in Indian costume and giving each a plow to carry in his hand, he had them sing the verses. "At each refrain, the whole choir joined in: to the great content of the Spaniards and the supreme delight of the Indians at seeing their own songs and dances used by the Spaniards to celebrate Our Lord's festival [Corpus Christi]." [49]

Garcilaso implies that the choirboys were being used as much to entertain the crowd that gathered in the Cuzco Cathedral at important church feasts as to uplift them. For that matter, so does Gutiérrez de Santa Clara when he tells of an Epiphany service during which they sang Spanish coplas which ran, "Where dwells the butterfly?" [50] But at least the choirboys were on these occasions enlivening the Church's traditional festivals. The chapelmaster Pedro Serrano who was hired in April, 1580, went too far, however, when he began renting the choirboys out for secular evening entertainments. After warning him, the cathedral chapter dismissed him in August, 1582, "because he did it every night, and they had asked him to stop." [51] Gonzalo de Mora, who succeeded him as both organist and chapelmaster in April, 1583, had to bind himself to a strict regimen of teaching and of ceremonial observances. Even though only sixteen of the assigned twenty-four boys actually attended his classes, his hands were full. Besides teaching them to read and write church Latin, he was required to give them hour-and-a-half daily lessons in counterpoint.[52]

Visperas de todo el año." See Irving A. Leonard, *Romances of Chivalry in the Spanish Indies* (Berkeley: University of California Press [Publications in Modern Philology, XVI/3], 1933), pp. 310–312; Leonard cites Archivo General de Indias, Contratación 1137, for his supporting document.

[48] Gutiérrez de Santa Clara, *op. cit.*, VI, 186.

[49] Concerning Juan de Fuentes, the Cuzco chapelmaster responsible for the arrangement, see Stevenson, *The Music of Peru: Aboriginal and Viceroyal Epochs* (Washington: Pan American Union, 1960), p. 66. On the *haylli*, see Bernabé Cobo, *Historia del Nuevo Mundo* (Seville: E. Rasco, 1893), IV, 230; also n. 4 on p. 294 below.

[50] *Guerras Civiles*, VI, 186: "¿adónde posa la mariposa?"

[51] Vargas Ugarte, "Notas," p. 26. Supporting documents in the *Libro de auctos capitulares 1549–1556* (actually 1546–1590) at Cuzco Cathedral, fol. 54 (Aug. 10, 1582).

[52] Counterpoint, as taught by sixteenth-century Spanish theorists, meant more than written work. Improvising a melody above a given plainsong at sight was the goal.

SECULAR MUSICIANS OF THE CONQUEST EPOCH

At Lima, Trujillo, Quito, Cuzco, Arequipa, and elsewhere throughout the colony, European musical culture was spread, usually, by some church arm. But secular musicians also entered the colony in considerable numbers from its earliest days. During the quadrennium in which he sought to make himself an independent ruler, Gonzalo Pizarro—half brother of the conqueror, Francisco—hired a band of six instrumentalists to travel with him wherever he went. When he entered Cuzco, Lima, or Quito, they sounded a flourish of "drums, trumpets, and shawms" to herald his approach.[53] After Gasca had mustered sufficient military strength to defeat him on April 10, 1548, on the plains of Sacsahuamán he, too, entered Cuzco, "marching to the sound of drums and fifes, many trumpets and shawms . . . after which he made a triumphal entry into the cathedral, where the canticle *Te Deum Laudamus* was sung with great jubilance."[54]

The names of twenty-one secular musicians active in Peru before 1553 have been recovered. If this many entered the colony during the first two decades, probably two hundred professionals reached Peru before the first centenary of Atahuallpa's death. Not all remained, of course. Gasca, after quelling Gonzalo Pizarro's forces, condemned his six personal *ministriles* to the galleys.[55] He banished two other Pizarro partisans—one, a psaltery and viol player, to Chile; the other, a trumpeter, to Mexico. But even those who were exiled had already planted musical seed that was to be harvested during the next several decades. Garcilaso, for instance, still remembered those condemned to the galleys when, as an old man, he came to publish his *Commentarios Reales* at Lisbon in 1609. Agustín Ramírez, whose name he remembered in particular,[56] may very well have taught him how to notate music in parts.[57]

Of the twenty-one arrivals before 1553 whose cases have been studied, five played shawms for their principal instrument—Antón Alonso, Rodrigo de Azer,[58] Juan de Contreras,[59] Alonso de Palma, Guillermo de Villa; three

[53] Gutiérrez de Santa Clara, *op. cit.*, II (1904), 392, 468; IV (1910), 552. See also I (1904), 121, for the band music that greeted the four *oidores* at their entry into Lima. Diego Fernández in his *La Segunda Parte de la Historia del Peru* (Seville: Hernando Díaz, 1571), fol. 121v, col. 1, confirmed the use of *mucha musica de trompetas, cherimías, y atabales* to ornament state occasions in Lima (1557).

[54] Gutiérrez de Santa Clara, *op. cit.*, VI, 153–154.

[55] Garcilaso, *Historia* (1617), fol. 218v, col. 2.

[56] Both he and Ramírez were mestizos.

[57] *Primera Parte*, fol. 53v [recte 52v], col. 2: *Holgara poner tambien la tonada en puntos de canto de organo.*

[58] *Colección de documentos inéditos relativos al descubrimiento, conquista y organización . . . de América . . . sacados de los archivos del reino y muy especialmente del de Indias*, ed. L. Torres de Mendoza (Madrid: Imp. del Hospicio, 1873), XX, 511.

[59] *Ibid.*, XX, 510.

played trumpet—Diego García de Villalón,[60] Baltazar de Monzón,[61] Tomás Obres; three played the plucked vihuela—Gerónimo Carrillo, Francisco Marcián Diañez,[62] Juan de la Peña Madrid;[63] one played flageolet—Hernando de Escobar;[64] one played sackbut—Juan Ramírez. Juan de Acuña and Juan de Soria majored in drums.[65] Pedro Bejarano made verses that he put to music.[66] Alonso Muñoz de Benavente sang.[67] Juan Vázquez, a man of many parts, played not only psaltery and viol but also taught dancing.[68]

Francisco Lobato y López came from the same town in Portugal which gave birth to the greatest of Portuguese theorists, Vicente Lusitano.[69] If they did not know each other in Olivença before they went their separate ways, at least they were contemporaries. The shawmer Azer was a Fleming. The rest of the twenty-one were of Spanish blood. The shawmer Contreras came from Almoroxo, the troubadour Diañez from Valencia province, Juan Díaz from the province of Cádiz, Juan de Estrada from Seville,[70] the trumpeter García de Villalón from Villalobos, the trumpeter Monzón from Granada by way of Mexico, the balladeer and jester Peña Madrid from Jaén,[71] Agustín Ramírez from Mexico City (where his father was a Spaniard, his mother an Indian), Juan Ramírez from Guadalajara, and Vázquez from Zalamea de la Serena. If Andalusia and Extremadura are the best represented Spanish provinces, so also were they the best represented among early Peruvian settlers who were not musicians.

In Peru as in Mexico, it was this horde of free-lance Peninsular instrumentalists who fanned out through the colony and from whom the Indians learned not only how to play but also how to make new guitars,

[60] Rafael Loredo, "Sentencias contra los que participaron en el alzamiento de Gonzalo Pizarro," *Mercurio Peruano,* año XV, no. 159 (May, 1940), p. 267.

[61] *Colección,* ed. Torres de Mendoza, XX, 487; also Cristóbal Bermúdez Plata, *Catálogo de Pasajeros a Indias* (Seville: Imp. Ed. de la Gavidia, 1942), II, 78, no. 1291. Monzón sailed for Mexico on June 26, 1535.

[62] Gutiérrez de Santa Clara, *op. cit.,* V, 280–289.

[63] *Colección de documentos inéditos para la historia de España,* XCIV (Madrid: M. Ginesta, 1889), 153–154.

[64] Loredo, *op. cit.,* p. 274.

[65] *Colección,* ed. Torres de Mondoza, XX, 536, 539.

[66] Gutiérrez de Santa Clara, *op. cit.,* IV, 465. Bejarano settled at Andahuaylas.

[67] *Colección de documentos inéditos para la historia de España,* XCIV, 143. At fifty he still remained a bachelor. By inference, the other musicians in this list were married.

[68] Loredo, *op. cit.,* p. 267; also *Colección,* ed. Torres de Mendoza, XX, 507.

[69] *Col. de doc. inéd. para la hist. de Esp.,* XCIV, 145.

[70] Gutiérrez de Santa Clara, *op. cit.,* IV, 526.

[71] Arrived at Lima before 1553; resided at Cuzco 1566–1567; moved to La Plata (= present-day Sucre) in 1568. He was so illiterate that he had a hard time signing his own name. At La Plata where he opened a dancing school he did, however, insist on adding to his quality with a "de" between Peña and Madrid (his signatures).

vihuelas, sackbuts, shawms. In the process of adapting these to their own local materials, some became so indigenized that unaware folklorists today will swear on their purely American, even entirely local, origin. The *charango*, an armadillo-backed adaptation of the Spanish bandurría, provides a good example. Only recently José Díaz Gainza in his *Historia Musical de Bolivia* (*Época Precolonial*) (Potosí: Universidad Tomás Frías, 1962, pp. 55, 172–174) reverted again to the problem. The charango is not an autochthonous instrument, and allusion to it anywhere awaits the year 1813 when, at Tupiza, the Indians' pleasure in playing this "small guitar called charango around here" is first mentioned in a document now at the Archivo de Indias. Carlos Vega announced this date in *Los Instrumentos Musicales aborígines y criollos de la Argentina* (Buenos Aires: Ediciones Centurión, 1946), page 151.

Although the Peninsular secular musicians in the new viceroyalty can be more easily documented, Negroes from Africa began playing a vital role no later than 1551. Within a decade after Francisco Pizarro's death, the Lima cabildo hired Negro drummers to welcome Viceroy Antonio de Mendoza, paying to have their *atabales* draped in the Inca color (*Libros de Cabildos de Lima*, transcribed by Bertram T. Lee, *Libro Cuarto* (*Años 1548–1553*), act of Aug. 31, 1551, p. 434). A dozen years later, the vast popularity of Negro dancing and drumming in the public streets made many of them impassable at times. The Lima cabildo responded by confining such dancing, and the Negro music accompanying it, to either the public plaza or the plaza of Nicolás de Ribera *el mozo*. The act of August 13, 1563 (*Libros de Cabildos: Libro Sexto* (*Años 1562–1568*), *Segunda Parte*, p. 144), limits the locales, because Negro dancing and music stopped even beasts of burden in their tracks.[72]

To welcome Lope García de Castro, the Lima cabildo again called on Negro drummers, dressing each in bright new taffeta outfits (*Libro Sexto*, p. 274, act of Oct. 27, 1564[73]). The trumpeters for the reception ceremonies were Indians. None of the names of the Negro drummers survives. Names of

[72] As transcribed by Lee for publication in 1935, this act begins: "eneste cabildo se trato sobre que los negros hazen bayles con atambores en las calles publicas desta çibdad donde Resulta que no se puede pasar por ellas e las cavalgaduras se espantan e suçeden otros daños e ynconvenientes e conviene se Recojan en partes publicas. . . ." Except in the said two plazas, they may not henceforth dance, drum, or play other instruments: "ni toquen atambores ni otros ynstrumentos para baylar sino fuere en la plaça publica. . . ." Rodolfo Barbacci kindly called this act to my attention.

[73] "Eneste cabildo se mando que atento este çibdad haze fiesta e Regozijo como es Razon por la venida del señor presidente e an de sacar al Regozijo tronpetas y atabales y para semejante Regozijo an de salir vestidos los que an de tañer las tronpetas y atabales se proveyo y mando que el mayordomo desta çibdad de a los negros que tañeren los atabales a cada uno una chimiRa y cuperuça de tafetan y a los yndios que an de tañer las tronpetas a cada uno una manta ansi mismo."

the trumpeters who hailed Viceroy Antonio Hurtado de Mendoza's arrival
do enter the Lima cabildo records.[74] Those mentioned in the act of July 10,
1556, were all Mexican Indians. Luis Herrera de la Fuente, the internationally renowned Mexican conductor brought to Peru to conduct the Lima
orchestra in 1966, is no Náhuatl-speaking Aztec. But for a precedent, the
governing powers of the Lima orchestra can look back more than four centuries to Pedro de Tapia, and a pair of Aztec trumpeters with the Christian
names of Francisco and Antón, brought south from Mexico City no later
than the year in which Philip II began his reign.

Only by taking account of the diverse strains sounding in Peruvian ears
from the start of the viceroyalty can the cosmopolitan musical life in Peru
today be set in proper historical context, or the happy blending of contribu-
tions from the European-born like Andrés Sas, Rodolfo Holzmann, and Rodolfo Barbacci, the Mexican-born like Herrera de la Fuente, and the native-
born like the father and son Carlos and Armando Sánchez Málaga, Roberto
Carpio Valdés, Enrique Iturriaga, Enrique Pinilla, César Arróspide de la
Flor, Celso Garrido-Lecca, Josafat Roel Pineda, and others of the younger
generation, be properly appreciated.

[74] "Eneste cabildo el señor francisco de anpuero Regidor dixo e hizo Relaçion que con-
çertaron el y el fator [Bernaldino de] Romany a quien fue cometido que se les diesen
a los tres yndios tronpetas de salario por ser tronpetas desta çibdad e otros çinquenta
pesos por lo que sirvieron en la entrada y Resçebimiento de su eçelencia del señor
visoRey y en sus fiestas e que açebtandolo se les libren / llamanse los yndios / pedro de
tapia y francisco y anton naturales de mexico" / [signatures of six cabildo members
conclude the act].

PERUVIAN "FOLK MUSIC," 1500-1790: LITERARY AND MUSICAL SOURCES FOR A FRESH STUDY

HUAMÁN POMA DE AYALA (1534?–1615?)

Our best informant on sixteenth-century indigenous folklore, Huamán Poma de Ayala, enjoyed the double advantage of being himself an egoistic Andean of pure blood and of being an adept illustrator of his own text. His 1179-page *Nueva Corónica y Buen Gobierno* (finished *ca.* 1613) reeks with the pride of a native who considered his own Lucanas lineage worthier than even that of the Incas, for after all the Incas were but parvenus unjustly seizing power in a land with a pre-Inca history that stretched back to 6000 B.C.[1]

Only so fanatical an Indian purist as he would perhaps have considered the folk music nurtured in his native soil sufficiently important to merit a full dozen pages of connected text and illustration (pp. 316–327), not to count numerous other pages on which he makes passing allusions. He frames

---

[1] Felipe Huamán Poma de Ayala, *Nueva Corónica* (Paris: Institut d'Ethnologie, 1936), p. 87. The son of Huamán Mallqui who saved Luis Ávalos de Ayala's life in a battle against the insurrectionary Gonzalo Pizarro, Felipe Huamán Poma de Ayala adopted the Ayala name after his father did the same. Luis Ávalos de Ayala subsequently became the protector of the family and fathered Felipe's half brother Martín de Ayala, a *clérigo de misa* in Huamanga (= present-day Ayacucho) after 1582. See Raúl Porras Barrenechea, "El Rastro Autobiográfico de Huamán Poma (De un estudio inédito que comprende su vida y su obra)," *La Prensa*, July 28, 1945, pp. 17, 22–23. In Peru, as in Mexico, Indian nobility frequently adopted the names of Spanish captains with whom they became especially friendly. Despite the mixed parentage of his half brother (whom he respected highly), Felipe Huamán Poma decried the *mezcla de razas* on principle.

his chapters on canciones and música by loudly proclaiming that the dances and song of his aboriginal brethren hide no idolatries or wizardry.[2] On the contrary, he declares that they serve only the innocent purposes of diverting and refreshing the common folk. True, they often end in drunkenness, but except for this unfortunate aftermath they serve as the most precious surviving testimonies of his people's greatness.

Because he stood so close to preconquest times, and because he so sympathetically entered into the spirit of aboriginal music, his description merits a synopsis in English.

The most frequent song type met with is the *haravi*. But such other types as the *cachiua*[3] and the *haylli*[4]—not to mention numerous special types belonging to the shepherds of llamas, sowers of seed, and tillers of the soil—must be distinguished. Every *ayllu* [clan] has its particular dances and songs.

As a general rule, end-notched flutes (whether of bone or cane) support the melody when an haravi is sung. The pangs of love form their most frequent theme. The singer in a typical haravi[5] complains that unlucky chance separates

---

[2] *Ibid.*, pp. 315, 328.

[3] Diego González Holguín, *Vocabvlario dela lengva general de todo el Perv* (Lima: Francisco del Canto, 1608), II, 59, defined *cachua* as a "choral dance with joined hands." Bernabé Cobo in his *Historia del Nuevo Mundo*, IV (Seville: E. Rasco 1893), 231, called the cachua a "very important *baile* which in former times [i.e., before the conquest] they did not dance except at principal festivals, and then as a choral dance with men and women joining hands to form a circle while around them wove the dancers."

[4] González Holguín, *op. cit.*, defined the *haylli* (I, 151) as a "joyful victory-song after battle or after the sowing of seed." Ludovico Bertonio, *Vocabvlario dela lengva aymara* (Juli: Francisco del Canto, 1612), *Segunda Parte*, p. 126, without defining the noun lists the meanings of the corresponding verbs, *hayllita* and *hayllitha*. Quite evidently haylli was fraught with identical connotations in both Quechua and Aymara. Diego de Torres Rubio, *Arte de la Lengua Aymara* (Lima: Francisco del Canto, 1616), defined *hayllitha* "to sing in victory," and haylli as *aquel canto*.

[5] So far as the Aymara tongue was concerned, any song, whether decorous or risqué in text, could be called a haravi—or at least so Bertonio affirmed when, in his *primera parte*, p. 114, he gave it as translation for *cancion honesta, o torpe que sea*. In his *segunda parte*, p. 122, he defined it concisely as any *cantar o cancion*. Huayñu, another Aymara term that survives in Peruvian folk music today as huayno, he defined as any *dança, bayle* or *sarao* (or also it could serve, he claimed, to mean simply a friend or companion of either sex). Josafat Roel Pineda, "El Wayno del Cuzco," *Folklore Americano*, VI–VII, no. 6–7 (Lima, 1959), pp. 129–246, prints 151 huaynos, text and music, collected from the presently surviving repertory.

As early as 1586, when Antonio Ricardo issued the first *Arte, y vocabvlario en la Lengva general del Perv llamada Quichua* at Lima, the term "haravi" was defined in the Inca tongue as *cancion, endechas* ("lament"). González Holguín followed suit in his Lib. 1 at p. 145 when he defined it as a song of "absent loved ones." Already, however, in 1608 it was changing its meaning to include *cantares deuotos y espirituales*. Cobo, *op. cit.*, spelled the word arabi[s] (IV, 232); Hipólito Unánue writing under the pseudonym of Aristeo in *Mercurio Peruano*, March 17, 1791 (p. 207), spelled it without the *h*, and derived *yaravi* from it.

him from his beloved, who is as beautiful as the yellow mountain flower of the Andes, the chinchircoma. But though apart, he always thinks of her and pursues her like a precious but elusive reflection in the waters. Her deceitful mother seeks to separate them. Her evil father also tries to keep them apart. Even now when he but thinks of her smiling eyes he loses his senses. He has been searching everywhere for her, traversing mountain, river, and villages. Now he can only sit and weep.

The Aymara call their songs of love's sorrows *uanca*. A typical text reads somewhat as follows. Two by two we can travel through the coldest regions. For you have completely enfolded me and I am surrounded with your tenderness. How sweet is the taste of it! Your mother would keep us apart, as would also your perverse father. But come alone. I will take you in my lucky arms. Then we will mount and ride away by day and by night like wandering orphans, fed by only the roots and herbs that sustain the llamas you are accustomed to tend. He who seeks to snatch you away from me will die at my hands, cut off forever like a severed thread. Hear me in this freezing night. Come to my breast and I will tend you forever. But if you refuse, my sad heart will weep.

A typical *cachiua* on the other hand tells a happier tale, like the following: Sweetheart, wherever you are, come, for I am waiting. Wear your most beautiful and costliest dress so that we can assist at the Holy Sacrifice.[6] Then put on your oldest and commonest dress and we will travel afar. Sweetheart, I am waiting. We shall be happy together. Wear your kerchief, your sash, and come when you hear the linnet sing.

In preconquest times, however, the haravi did not necessarily weep a lover's woes. At the Inca festival in honor of the Creator called the *uaricza*, a red llama was tied and to his soft ee-ee-ee, the chief responded with the burden of an haravi that was not sad. He kept repeating een-een-een in slow rhythm at the llama's pitch level. The noblewomen standing by interspersed stanzas that began very high but gradually, during the half hour that the women continued singing, dropped by small steps to the pitch of the llama's bleat. Their stanzas (inserted between the Inca's refrains) said such things as this: Your field is sown with capsicum. I shall come gather pimiento. Your field is sown in flowers. I shall come to cut blossoms. The men standing by meanwhile interjected, yes, lady, I have so sown it, yes, princess, yes, dear lovely girl, yes, sweet flower.

Or still another way in which an haravi could be sung in preconquest times was by noble young maidens to the accompaniment of pincollos played by young men. Even then, however, the texts seem always to have voiced the young men's

---

[6] The mention of Mass makes this, of course, a postconquest cach[i]ua. (For still a third spelling, see Domingo de S. Thomas' *Lexicon, o Vocabulario de la lengua general del Perv* [Valladolid: Francisco Fernández de Córdova, 1560], fol. 112v, who gave it as *cachuay*, and defined it as *corro de bayle, o dança*.) Other allusions prove how many postcontact novelties Poma de Ayala takes for granted. When he speaks of mounting and riding away by day and by night, he presupposes horses, for instance. Only *curaca*-class Indians rode them.

sorrows, not the girls'. The lyrics might run as follows, while being sung by noble maidens. My dear love, my sweet little one, does not your heart sigh and are not you ready to weep, you who are my precious blossom, my sovereign queen, my princess? See how I have been seized and carried away like the water borne away by the stream when it rains. When I behold your dress, everything else goes black. At night as I lie wakeful I think that dawn will never come because you, my queen, do not remember me. I am in a prison, devoured by the jaguar and the fox, forgotten, overwhelmed, and lost, my princess.

In that quarter of the world stretching northwest of Cuzco the uauco sung by sixteen-year-old girls to the beat of the drum is likely to tell such a tale as this: I do not see the taruga that you seem to be holding in your hands. I do not see the deer skull, dear brother, dear brother.[7] The men blow their antlers to reply in a kind of seesaw response that sounds like "wowkoh, wowkoh, wowkoh, wowkoh; cheechoh, cheechoh, cheechoh, cheechoh." In the [g]uacones[8] dance, the girls sing a rhythmical refrain that sounds like "pahnohnigh, pahnoh, pahnonigh, pahnoh," against youths singing "yahahaha, yahaha, I saw you among the happy Chosen Ones,[9] my lady, I saw you in the place of the llama, yahahaha." The Yauyos use a refrain that sounds like "yahpuhpuh, yahpoh." Those among them who till the soil—women as well as men—sing a refrain that sounds like "ahrah-wahyoh" repeated many times. The shepherds sing a ditty that goes like this: my llama, my dear llama, you are mine, my llama.

Among the other songs popular with the Chinchaysuyos[10] are the *saucataqui* [= the making-fun-of-someone type]; and the *cochotaqui* [= the full-of-happiness type]. These two types have their own characteristic refrains. The dance song that belongs to the highest chieftain in a locality is called the *hatuntaqui*. Every ayllu from Cuzco to Quito cultivates its specialties.[11]

---

[7] This refrain, "dear brother, dear brother" (*uayayay turilla, uayayay turilla*) gave Cobo, *op. cit.*, the right to name this particular dance the Guayayturilla (IV, 230). He described it thus: "Men and women paint their faces with red lead and fasten a silver or gold band from ear to ear above the nostrils. They play the dance music on dried deer skulls, the antlers serving as flutes. The leader starts, and the others follow with great precision."

[8] Martín de Morúa, *Historia del origen y genealogía real de los Reyes Inças del Peru,* ed. C. Bayle (Madrid: C. Bermejo, 1946), p. 342, mentions *guacones* as a dance-and-song type that by 1590 had become especially popular at Corpus Christi celebrations. Cobo (IV, 230) claimed that in his day (1653) guacones were danced by men only; they masked and jumped about with the skin of some wild animal in their hands.

[9] For the *acllacuna* selected by government officials during periodic visits of inspection, see J. Alden Mason, *The Ancient Civilizations of Peru* (Harmondsworth: Penguin Books, 1957), p. 181.

[10] Inhabitants of the northwestern quarter of the Inca world, i.e., Ecuador and the part of modern Peru northwest of Cuzco.

[11] Morúa, *op. cit.*, p. 343, insists on the same idea. So does Joan de Santacruz Pachacuti Yamqui in his "Relacion de Antigüedades deste Reyno del Piru," *Tres Relaciones de Antigüedades Peruanas,* ed. M. Jiménez de la Espada (Madrid: M. Tello, 1879), p. 318, when he speaks of the *tantos cantos* which *cada nacion o prouincia tenian*—enough to overflow the earth.

Southeast of Cuzco as far as Tucumán and Paraguay the same individuality of dances and lyrics still prevails in every ayllu. They call the songs sung by the girls *uanca*. The youths play the quena quena. Everyone from highest to lowest dances and sings in all the festivals, even in the bleak areas around Potosí.

Southwest of Cuzco in the region inhabited by the Yanauaras, the Pomatambos, the Qullauaconde, and toward Arequipa, they mask for the dances that they call *saynatas*. The women sing *ayamilla, saynata, saynata* [= "scabrous Death, you shameless, shameless Destroyer"], to which the men sing in reply, ah ah oh, ah ah oh.

Then the women continue: *cauquiro pimanata saynata conarupi manata saynata, a a o, a a o; minarotipi manata saynata tocllo; cocharotipi manata saynata* ["your mask does not frighten me; when you take it off I shall soon enough recognize you"]. The men then reply to the women: *acaropi manha acaropi manha halla halla ana ana* ["take our masks off if you can, but you will not be able"]. Here the song comes to an end, and the men all burst out laughing.

In fine, all four quarters of the Inca world specialize in their own varied songs and dances. Nowadays the Collas [southwest of Cuzco] praise their Spanish overlords with new songs incorporating words borrowed from Castilian, and inviting them to dance with Indian maidens.[12]

BERNABÉ COBO (1572–1659)

Poma de Ayala's insistence on the "infinite" variety of indigenous dance songs cannot be written off as mere chauvinism. Bernabé Cobo, the Andalusian-born Jesuit who finished his carefully researched *Historia del Nuevo Mundo* a generation later, echoed the same idea when he wrote:

Each province over the whole Inca empire had its own inviolable dance songs. Nowadays, however, each tribal group imitates the dances of others as well, especially at church festivals. The infinite variety which can be seen at a procession of the Blessed Sacrament and at other special times is really amazing. Once I happened to be in a small town near Puno at Corpus Christi. I counted forty different dances, each imitating the costumes, the music, and the steps of the various tribes to which the dances originally belonged.[13]

Cobo and Cieza de León unite in claiming that different levels of society cultivated their own particular songs and dances. When Cobo described the guayyaya [14] as a dance into which only members of the blood royal might enter, he left behind the domain of "folk" music. According to him, "They

[12] Poma de Ayala decries, however, the irregular unions that resulted, and laments the mixing of the races as the worst catastrophe that has befallen Peru.

[13] IV, 230. One of the most frequent dances was the *gaucones,* for masked men only.

[14] IV, 231.

danced it to the sound of a huge drum mounted on the back of a servant. A woman played it. The music was solemn and dignified." Cieza de León told of Inca festivals at which hired rhetoricians and composers furnished songs "resembling our romances and villancicos." [15] These cantares recounted the exploits of former brave Incas, and they

. . . sang them in order to fortify the present generation with memories of ancient glories. Those who by royal command learned these romances and taught them to the princes [in Cuzco] and leaders in the provinces received high honors and rich rewards. Thus they preserved five hundred years of history as fresh in the memory as ten. . . . These *cantares* were by no means sung or told abroad at every session or to the vulgar; but only at some great concourse of nobility assembled from the four quarters of the empire. At some such solemn meeting, and in the royal presence, those who knew these romances telling of past kings' glories sang them while gazing on the Inca. . . . Only the brave and valiant were remembered in song; the others were buried in oblivion.

After the conquest, naturally enough, it was this sort of courtly romance and villancico which proved most fragile. Just as the type of concerted antara playing Garcilaso described as peculiarly apt for the entertainment of the Inca [16] soonest suffered for want of patronage, so also the *musica reservada* of the royal bards who celebrated past Incas' prowess must soonest have died out for want of a continuing dynasty.

CUZCO FESTIVAL (1610)

The proud descendant claiming royal blood, if he wished to celebrate his ancestors as late as 1610, had only one recourse—to change any still extant songs and dances praising the Inca *a lo divino*. This indeed is exactly what he did when in that year at Cuzco the Jesuits celebrated the beatification of Ignatius Loyola. The *Relacion de las fiestas qve en la Civdad del Cvzco se hicieron* [17] (Lima: Francisco del Canto, 1610) tells how thirty thousand adult males claiming Inca blood assembled at Cuzco to begin a festival on May 2 lasting some twenty-five days. On Tuesday, May 3, they sang in Ignatius' honor a song likening him to the black Andean eagle, the *Curiquenque* [Aymara]. On Wednesday, May 4, they revived the pomp of authentic dance and song still remembered from Huayna Capac's era, but "Christianized it all" by bringing forth the infant Jesus clad in Inca garments, incredibly rich, to do Him obeisance. On Saturday the 7th the

[15] Pedro de Cieza de León, *Del Señorio de los Incas* (Buenos Aires: Edic. "Solar," 1943), pp. 75–77.

[16] Garcilaso de la Vega, *Commentarios Reales* (Lisbon: Pedro Crasbeeck, 1609), fol. 52 (*recte* 51) v, col. 2.

[17] Repr. in Carlos A. Romero, *Los Orígines del Periodismo en el Perú* (Lima: Imp. Gil, 1940), pp. 14–21.

parishioners of San Blas did Ignatius the homage of singing to the accompaniment of big drums, trumpets, and other warlike instruments, all the
many acclamations once composed in praise of a victorious captain who had
led their ancestors to victory in battle. On Sunday, five thousand Indians
staged a sham battle in Cuzco plaza to the sound of drums. On Monday
those of Inca blood residing a half league outside Cuzco in San Sebastián
parish, and on Tuesday those in San Gerónimo a league and a half away,
contributed their still remembered *danças y cantares*. On Thursday (Ascension), ten thousand Spaniards and Indians watched a review of several
hundred *yanaconas* (Inca official class) to the sound of chirimías. On
Sunday the 15th the descendants of the Inca's élite guards, the *cañares*,
staged a second mock battle (again to the sound of their ancient warlike
instruments) during which they "routed' the Inca's traditional enemies, the
Canas of Ancocava.

But all this revival of Huayna Capac's panoply ("the like of which had
never been seen" [18]) could ill conceal the plight of the vanquished. More
and more during the later colonial period the typical indigenous song was to
be the haravi (= *yaraví*) [19] defined by González Holguín in 1608 as a
memoria de los amados ausentes y de amor y aficion. The haylli, once
publishing the number of the Inca's slain enemies, became at best a victory
song after successful sowing of seed or lifting of a heavy burden. Even at
Cuzco itself, the indigenous types had to give way to European music when
anything like public rejoicing was ordered toward the close of the eighteenth century. Or at least this had become true in 1788 when news reached
Cuzco of its elevation to become the seat of a royal *audiencia*.[20]

THE YARAVÍ

At the end of the colonial epoch the yaraví had not only supplanted all other
indigenous musical types as the Andeans' favorite, but it had also come to

---

[18] *por no auerse hecho otras semejantes en el Cuzco.* . . .

[19] *Mercurio Peruano*, no. 22 (March 17, 1791), p. 207 n. 9: "the elegaic songs known
as *yaravies* take their name from the [h]aravi. . . ."

[20] See Ignacio de Castro, *Relación de la fundación de la Real Audiencia del Cuzco
en 1788* (Madrid: Vda. de Ibarra, 1795), pp. 115, 172 (*sinfonía*), 128 (*serenata*),
198–199 (*piezas Francesas, Inglesas, y Alemanas*). Indigenous music was dealt its
heaviest blow at Cuzco when at one and the same time José Antonio Areche forbade
all further native finery reminiscent of the Inca past, all mention of genealogical trees
rooted in Inca rulers, all "plays and other public functions used by the Indians to
memorialize their ancient past," and even the use of any distinctively native musical
instruments. Areche's edict, dated May 15, 1781, came after the quelling of the most
dangerous native revolt (that of Tupac Amaru) in late colonial times. See Odriozola,
Documentos, I (1863), 160, for the text (copied from Pedro de Angelis). The year
1788 was much too early for any relaxation of so drastic a decree as Areche's.

be known among European observers as always a sad song. Writing on Andean music for *Mercurio Peruano* (no. 101 [Dec. 22, 1791], pp. 285–286, 290–291) under the pseudonym of Sicramio, one alert connoisseur thus described the yaraví:

The tonality is regularly minor with only transitory modulations into major. Accidentals often color harmony—which is also as a rule enriched with appoggiaturas, suspensions, and those other ornaments that give breath and soul to music.[21] The meter varies between 3/8, 3/4, and 6/8; but the tempo never exceeds *moderato*, scaling on down through *andante* and *andantino* to *largo*. Invariably the sentiment is serious. As for performance, yaravíes require no set number of voices, a soloist or duet sufficing, but a trio or even more often taking part. . . . The poetry [22] has much to do with their melancholy effect. The verse may refer to some cruelty, or to some dreary memory of a loved one, or to the unjust forgetfulness of such a dear one, or to the despair arising from jealousy, or to love's tyrannies. But whatever the immediate occasion, the subject still retains its pangs. Some yaravíes run in five-syllable lines, others in six- or seven-syllable lines. Seven-syllable quatrains with alternate rhyming, five-line stanzas, and even ten-line stanzas now and then enter the poetic scheme. Similes and other figures of speech adorn the verse, as well as numerous references to indigenous myths, and allusions to birds, forests, rivers, mountains, and other natural phenomena.

[21] This description cannot be verified because the yaravíes to which he refers do not survive. Mariano Eduardo de Rivero printed three "haravis" in *Antigüedades Peruanas* (Vienna: Imprenta Imperial, 1851), pp. 135–138. Mateo Paz Soldán copied all three in his *Geografía del Perú* (Paris: Lib. de Firmin Didot, 1862). Oscar Comettant included five yaravíes in his pioneer article, "La Musique en Amérique avant la découverte de Christophe Colomb," *Compte-Rendu du Congrès International des Américanistes, 1ʳᵉ Session* (Nancy, 1875), II, 295–299. The two unaccompanied yaravíes at pages 295–296 came from a collection made by a Swede who spent five years in Peru, Carl Erik Södling (1819–1884). Södling's seven-page *Indianska dans-melodier upptecknade i Södra Amerika* and *Indianska sånger*, both published at Stockholm by Abr. Hirsch in 1874, are bound together in the copies at Yale University.

Of the yaravíes printed at pages 297–299 of Comettant's 1875 report to the International Congress of Americanists, two have been arranged for saxophone trio by the renowned composer Ambroise Thomas. The melodies thus arranged were collected by a long-term resident in Peru, Bernier de Valois (Comettant, *op. cit.*, p. 292).

Commenting on the three yaravíes borrowed from *Antigüedades Peruanas* for his *Geografía del Perú*, Paz Soldán categorically claims that his three (G minor, p. 37; A minor, p. 38; D minor, p. 40) are all ancient: *Existen aun varias tonadas antiguas muy melodiosas que pueden servir para averiguar los conocimientos músicos de los antiguos Peruanos*. His three are all slow pieces cast in irregular phrase lengths (5 + [8 + 6] + [10 + 6]; 7 + 8 + 8; 7 + 6 + 19). The mawkish Italian sentiment and frequent parallel thirds in the first, the Alberti bass in the second, and the "thirdsiness" of the third make it hard to believe any of them a purely indigenous composition.

[22] On yaraví poetry see *Literatura Inca*, ed. Jorge Basadre (*Biblioteca de Cultura Peruana*) (Paris: Desclée, De Brouwer, 1938), p. 403. The yaravíes in *Ollantay* (pp. 209, 215) are the best-known Quechua examples. For a popular reprint of Poma de Ayala's three, see Luis M. Baudizzone, *Poesía, Música y Danza Inca* (Buenos Aires: Editorial Nova, 1943).

Thus it comes about that music and poetry unite to evoke painful nostalgia. . . . Every nation has evolved its own characteristic musical types, in which it strikes its favorite pose. The French leans toward pomp, the German to profundity, the Spaniard recreates himself with jaunty abandon, the Portuguese delights in elevated martial strains. . . . Among us, only the Indian betrays no foreign influence—and his yaravies reveal his innate affinity for all that is tetric and gloomy. His natural condition conduces to the same melancholy, his dark rooms, low ceilings, the poor building materials, his insufficient fare, hard couch on the floor, his poor and dark clothing. . . . Even the birds whose song he prefers are those that, like the *cuculí,* emit a funereal note. . . .

What a contrast with all this sad music does the Spanish fandango make, or such derivatives of Spanish dances as we favor here in Peru! Take, for instance, the *Don Mateo,* the *Punto,* and other joyful dance tunes that abound among us. If not all are as exciting as the fandango, they at least show how closely we can approach the gaiety of the Spaniard, and at what an opposite pole our Creole music lives from the melancholy world that gives birth to yaravies.[23]

Another contributor to *Mercurio Peruano,* signing himself T. J. C. y P.,[24] answered this essay on the yaraví with a "Carta sobre la música" in the issue of February 16, 1792 (no. 117). While not denying the generally sad character of the yaraví, he accused Sicramio (the pseudonymous essayist in the December 22, 1791, issue) of negligence when he omitted any mention of the still-sung *cachuas.* T. J. C. y P. also dissented from Sicramio's musical analyses. He found more yaravies cast in duple than in ternary meter, and none in ⁶⁄₈. He also called attention to the molds of four-bar phrases, eight-bar periods, and sixteen-bar sections into which the composers of yaravies customarily poured their inspirations. He claimed to possess a collection of twelve yaravies which included the very one analyzed by Sicramio.

[23] "Sicramio" was Dr. J. M. Tirado's pseudonym. For an easily accessible reprint of his comments see Consuelo Pagaza Galdo, "El Yaraví del Cuzco," *Folklore Americano,* VIII–IX, nos. 8–9 (Lima, 1960–1961), pp. 77–82. Her article contains fifty examples, text and music. As late as May 14, 1829, the *Don Mateo* retained its popularity in the theater as the epitome of gaiety. See *Mercurio Peruano,* no. 519 (of that date), calling it *el delicioso y agradable intermedio nacional.*

[24] Toribio José del Campo y Pando enjoyed various appointments in Lima Cathedral between 1788 and 1818, in which latter year he died. See Enrique Iturriaga, "Las investigaciones de Andrés Sas sobre la música de la Colonia," *El Comercio,* Sunday Supplement, Sept. 5, 1954, p. 10, col. 5 (second section). Also Lima Cathedral, *Acuerdos Capitulares,* XV (1793–1808), fol. 44v (Nov. 6, 1798); XVI (1809–1816), fol. 69v (Jan. 7, 1814), fol. 70 (Jan. 14, 21), fol. 72 (Feb. 14); XVII (1817–1828), fol. 22v (July 14, 1818). At first an organ repairer and builder, he was promoted from second to first flautist on January 21, 1814, at an annual salary of 150 pesos. At p. 109 of his *Mercurio Peruano* article he claims (in the third person) to have deduced the scale by geometrical means, and to have arrived at more certain rules for tempering the scale than Rameau's.

But he found that it fell into eight-bar periods, that B minor was the key, and $\frac{2}{4}$ (not any ternary meter) the time signature. Already at bar 3 the composer [25] modulated to A, awkwardly allowing $f\sharp$ -e in the voice part to make consecutive fifths with B-A in the instrumental bass. This fault was in a manner "masked by the contrast of minor and major," that is, B minor–A major. The composer then circumambulated from A major back to his home key at bar 8.

I find in this yaraví, just as in the others (and for that matter in nearly all indigenous music, whatever the type), that the first and second 8-bar periods both end on the tonic, whereas in our European music, with the exception of seguidillas, the first period ends with the dominant; or if the home key is minor then with the relative major (unless, of course, some great genius of a composer following the bent of his inspiration chooses to half-cadence, or passes to a parallel minor dominant, or cadences deceptively).

T. J. C. y P., because he wishes to compare indigenous music to its disadvantage with European, at once reveals himself as a culturano who will ultimately be pleased with nothing less than Pergolesi, or at least Terradellas. "My analysis reveals the small merit of this class of music," he claims in the Mercurio Peruano of February 19 [1792]. "The captious transitions do not permit the laws of harmony to govern, nor does any musical logic control the argument. The chords ramble without rhyme or reason while the melody soon collapses into tedious and boring commonplaces." Sicramio revealed himself a mere sentimentalist, adds T. J. C. y P., when he allowed himself to confound the pathos, the misery, and the destitution of the Andean with any vaunted unique powers in the music of these unfortunate people. Just because Christian charity moves us to salve the sores of Lazarus is no reason to magnify his moans into "uniquely great" art. It would have been better for Sicramio to have studied the Quechua language—which loses more than most in translation—if he had wished to expound the "glories" of indigenous art. The best expression of the truly indigenous spirit which T. J. C. y P. has seen is un perfecto drama musico, que yo mismo he oido y visto representar. "This tragedy showed that a nation esteemed as barbarous had already before the conquest produced models of art worthy of comparison with Racine and Voltaire." [26] Quechua

[25] Though he does not identify the composer he makes it hard to believe that this yaraví was indeed an anonymous piece of "folk music."

[26] Ollantay may even have been the drama to which he alludes. His comparing it with works by Racine and Voltaire shows how thoroughly he had succumbed to French taste. Although not published until 1853 (in J. J. von Tschudi's Die Kechua-Sprache), Ollantay antedates the execution of Tupac Amaru (1781), according to Clement Markham (Ollanta [London: Trübner, 1871], p. 10). The incidental music for Ricardo Rojas' "restoration" of Ollantay (Buenos Aires: Editorial Losada, 1939, pp. 169–191) includes a huaino, yaraví, serpent dance, prayer, and cortège by Gilardo Gilardi,

is, moreover, better suited to musical setting than is French, with its nasals and elisions, he adds.

Not indigenous art as such, but the exalting of the yaraví above every other musical and poetic achievement, makes him question Sicramio's taste. Why do you call the yaraví 'inimitable"? he asks Sicramio. Every street corner boasts as much. That little Negro tune called the *zango* that the Negro Galindo plays in every alley has just as much right to be called inimitable, roundly concludes T. J. C. y P. Both zango and yaraví, after all, use the same melodic intervals and accompanying chords. With the same modulations and chord patterns the yaraví induces melancholy, the zango wayward delight. The two go at different speeds, and one is heavily accented. But neither deserves to be called "unique" or "inimitable."

NEGRO FOLK MUSIC

T. J. C. y P. merely touches on the Negro folk music of colonial Peru. But another *Mercurio Peruano* contributor with none of his or Sicramio's musical pretension—José Rossi y Rubí, vice-president of the Sociedad de Amantes del País—had previously treated it at length.[27] The Negroes imported from the coasts of Guinea and Senegal and from the Congo were already very numerous in Lima as early as 1628.[28] By 1748 they numbered some ten thousand.[29] Describing the music of those who still spoke only their native tongues in 1791, Rossi y Rubí wrote:

Their principal instrument is the drum, the skin of which they stretch over a hollow cylindrical log or over a clay frame. They play it not with mallets but with their hands. They also favor small nose flutes. They make dried horses' or asses' jawbones into a clattering instrument, with the teeth knocking against each other. They also make a sort of music with striated wooden blocks rubbed against each other. Their most melodious instrument is the marimba, fashioned of wooden slabs which serve as keys of different sizes. Beneath the slabs they adjust dried hollow gourds, also of different sizes, to serve as resonators. Slabs and resonators

---

composed in a style probably as close to the Inca as *Ollantay* comes to precontact Quechua drama. Cf. Leopoldo Vidal Martínez, *Poesía de los Incas* (Lima: Ed. Amauta, 1947), pp. 203–208. Alberto Ginastera's *Ollantay: Tres Movimientos Sinfónicos* (Buenos Aires: Barry, 1964) greatly improves on Gilardi. Lasting fifteen minutes, this work sets a high-water mark for symphonic reconstructions of "Inca" music. The three movements picture (1) The Landscape of Ollantaytambo, (2) Warriors [rushing to the fray], and (3) Ollantay's death.

[27] *Mercurio Peruano*, no. 49 (June 19, 1791), p. 122.

[28] *Instruccion para remediar, y assegurar, quanto con la diuina gracia fuere possible, que ninguno de los Negros, que vienen de Guinea, Angola, y otras Prouincias de aquella costa de Africa, carezca del sagrado Baptismo* (Lima: Gerónimo de Contreras, 1628), fol. 1.

[29] *A true and Particular Relation of the Dreadful Earthquake Which happen'd at Lima* (London: T. Osborne, 1748), p. 48.

are together mounted on an arched wooden frame. They play the marimba with two small sticks, like Bohemian psalteries. The diameter of the gourds is graduated with the ascending scale; and the sound that is emitted at times pleases the most fastidious ear. On the whole, however, we must confess that Negro song and dance, like many other manifestations of their talent and taste, lag as far behind the Indian as does the Indian behind the European.

As the citations from the sixteenth-century *Libros de Cabildos de Lima* given at the close of the preceding chapter reveal, Negro musicians and dancers took a prominent role in Peruvian music life as early as 1551. The important part played by those of Negro blood not only in the economy but more particularly in the musical life of what was throughout colonial times called Alto Perú (= modern-day Bolivia) is attested as early as June 12, 1568, the date on which Juan de la Peña Madrid contracted with a married mulatto, Hernán García, to open a school in the capital of the Audiencia de Charcas, each teaching his own specialty: Peña Madrid, how to sing and dance, and García, how to play and dance (documents in Sucre, Bolivia, National Archive, Escrituras Públicas, Águila 1568, fol. 226*v*, Bravo 1569, fols. 29*v*, 148*v*, 156). With such a head start, Negroes continued throughout the seventeenth and eighteenth centuries as leading entertainers in all districts of the viceroyalty. No welcome ceremony, no birthday or accession celebration, failed to include Negroes, or actors made up as Negroes. Even in a clime so inhospitable for them as 13,600-foot Potosí, they topped off such an *Aclamacion festiva de la mvy noble imperial Villa de Potosí* as Juan de la Torre reported (Lima: Francisco Sobrino, 1716), folio 26. A *mogiganga de treinta figurones* after the loa on Sunday, April 26 (1716), listed as protagonists a *Rey, y Reyna de Angola* of dark enough hue for "all Ethiopia to have given them their shade."

What is probably the earliest picture of Negroes playing a marimba and dancing (the painting at fol. E142 is listed in the index of the manuscript as "Negros tocando Marimba y bailando") can be found in a miscellany of curiosities collected in northern Peru and now preserved in the Biblioteca de Palacio at Madrid with the call number 90/344 ("Trujillo del Peru, II"). This bound manuscript miscellany, 10 by 6½ inches, has 1794 stamped on the back of the thick spine, and as will be shown below when discussed at greater length, gathers ethnographic materials forwarded by Baltasar Jaime Martínez Compañón during the preceding decade. The picture to which we refer shows two Negroes playing a diatonic marimba while a quartet of Negroes dance to its strains. Among other paintings of Negroes in this same miscellany, folio E140 shows a Negro pair doing a handkerchief dance to the tune supplied by a Negro drum-and-fife player.

The articles in *Mercurio Peruano* of June 19, 1791, by Rossi y Rubí and in the issue of February 19, 1792, by T. J. C. y P. pass value judgments but do not obscure the popularity of the very music they condemn. Far from fading, the memory of the street-corner entertainer Galindo, whom T. J. C.

y P. affected to disdain, continued so much alive a half century later that the *Correo Peruano* of November 6, 1845 (p. 3, col. 3), still called him to mind with an "Anécdota histórica." This pleasant reminiscence starts thus: "At the close of the preceding century there roamed through the streets of Lima a Negro named Galindo who, although able neither to read nor to write, made up verses to sing with the accompaniment of his bandurria." His ready wit enabled him to best even a reverend *cura* in a public test of improvising ability.

ANTONIO PEREYRA Y RUIZ' AREQUIPA "NOTICE"

The reactions of T. J. C. y P. and of Rossi y Rubí crystallized capital opinion at the close of the colonial period. But was their big-city distrust of indigenous rural music any more patronizing than that current in the second largest city, Arequipa? To judge from the manuscript "Noticia de la Muy Noble, y Muy Leal Ciudad de Arequipa" of 1816 (deposited with the *cabildo insular* of Tenerife for safekeeping by its author, Antonio Pereyra y Ruiz), provincial prejudice against Quechua music at Arequipa could match the bias at the capital. At folio 34 in a copy of his trenchant "Noticia," now at the National Library in Lima, Pereyra y Ruiz labeled the Indian of the Arequipa region "el animal mas indomito" and "el menos agradecido" anywhere to be encountered. His chapter on music in the Arequipa region begins at folio 32 thus:

The Peruvian indigenes never learned to use the beautiful science of music as a means of expressing joy, "which is the first and most natural sensation expressed by song," as Tomás de Yriarte well said in his poem *La Música* [*Colección de obras en verso y prosa* (Madrid: Benito Cano, 1787), I, 193: "la alegría, primera y más natural sensación que se expresa con el canto"]. In conformity with their apathetic nature, they instead composed nothing but sad songs venting their sorrows and complaints to their idols. At funerals they sang similarly doleful songs rehearsing the deeds, good and bad, of the deceased.

Some of these passed into the drawing room with the progress of civilization—in the transit undergoing some improvements but not enough to lose their lethargic character. Their grief-laden strains now became vehicles for a lover's sorrows and, circulating throughout Peru under the name of *yaraví*, so vitiated public taste that the public will not be satisfied at a concert nowadays without something of the yaraví type mixed in. The center where the style of the yaraví is set is Chuquisaca [= La Plata = modern Sucre]. The many students there have taken this sad type so much to heart that they are continually composing them, usually in as lugubrious a vein as possible.

As opposed to literary descriptions of early Peruvian folk music, actual music is less easily come by. Even so, the eighteenth century did bequeath three collections of anonymous music, and the just-mentioned Arequipa

"Noticia" of 1816 a fourth collection. Some of these pieces of anonymous music exhale perhaps too much "art" to be classifiable as "folk" expression. Still, the music in all four collections shows what was being played and sung by the nonprofessional in the area now called Peru.

For the area known in colonial times as High Peru (present-day Bolivia), the earliest extensive secular collection cannot be called folk music, even though Indians composed it all. The High Peru secular collection in question was a 1790 festival cantata. It was composed at Trinidad (Bolivia) by three Mojos Indians, Francisco Semo, Marcelino Ycho, and Juan José Nosa, to compliment the Spanish queen, María Luisa de Borbón. The score, discovered at the Archivo de Indias in Seville (see above, p. 123), was published in facsimile by Humberto Vázquez-Machicado ("Un códice cultural del siglo XVIII," *Historia*, IV/14 [Oct.–Dec., 1958], 65–107), with a study of the music by Hugo Patiño Torres. This ambitious cantata for chorus and soloists accompanied by violins, cello, and continuo, can at least warn us against expecting the remote areas of High Peru to have resisted European influences any more successfully than did the more exposed Lima, Arequipa, Trujillo, and Cuzco. What does survive as a witness to High Peruvian folk music are the few scraps to be discussed at the end of this chapter, among them a Potosí dance called "El Cielito" (reduced to writing in the Arequipa "Noticia" of 1816, this is another typical colonial testimony to Spanish folk influences), several indigenous songs taken by a French traveler during a visit to the Chiquitos and Morotocas tribes (published at Paris in 1844), and the musical museum found in "Ilustraciones del Potosí Colonial" (section dated 1859).

The best method for studying this material from coastal and inland areas is to divide it geographically and chronologically, with the older material from Cuzco, Lima, Trujillo, and Arequipa coming first, and the music representative of the High Peruvian tribes and the silver paradise of Potosí coming last.

GREGORIO DE ZUOLA (1645?–1709)

The earliest collection was brought together by Fray Gregorio de Zuola, a Franciscan who, after serving some dozen years at Cochabamba in what is now Bolivia (1666–1678), was transferred to the *doctrina* (Indian mission) of Urquillos near Cuzco and thence, in the 1690's, to the Cuzco motherhouse, where he died on November 28, 1709.[30] He left his 500-page commonplace book to his cousin-in-law, Matías Ramos Delgado of Cuzco, who rose from being a captain to a general (d. 1725).[31] For that matter, all

[30] Carlos Vega, *La música de un códice colonial del siglo XVII* (Buenos Aires: Imprenta de la Universidad, 1931), p. 11.

[31] *Ibid.*, pp. 13–14.

Zuola's Cuzco relations were gentry (in his commonplace book he noted the deaths of two ladies of quality at Cuzco, one of whom was his niece, the other his cousin [32]).

Throughout all seventeen items copied on pages 136, 160–161, 354–364, 368–369, 372, 389, and 391 he set Spanish texts, except on 160–161 (a version of the *Credo Romano*). In all but two pieces he chose secular lyrics. Lope de Vega's *Las fortunas de Diana* served as the source of his monodic *Entre los álamos verdes.*[33] The other texts, though in every instance anonymous, so frequently copy or echo known Peninsular originals (e.g., lyrics on pp. 356, 361, 363, 389 [34]) that all may quite well be derivative. He credited the music of the three-voiced *Hijos de Eva tributarios* [35] to Tomás de Herrera, of the four-voiced *Dime Pedro por tu vida* and *Por qué tan firme os adoro* to Correa. For the rest he omitted any composers' names. Since he was acknowledged to be not only a *gran Plumario* ("great penman") but also *Gran diestro en la música* ("very skilled in music"),[36] he may himself have been the composer of at least the *Credo Romano* on pages 160–161 of his commonplace book.[37] In any event, the lowest voice in this setting has been

[32] *Ibid.*, pp. 9–10. His connections in Cuzco suggest that he himself was a *natural*. His own commonplace book is not the only witness to Zuola's life. See the *Anales del Cuzco, 1600 á 1750*, compiled before the middle of the eighteenth century (Lima: Imprenta de "El Estado," 1901), pp. 168–169 (events of 1685). According to Carlos A. Romero (*Revista Histórica: Órgano del Instituto Histórico del Perú*, V/2 [1916], 224), the compiler of these *anales* was Diego de Esquivel y Navía, dean of Cuzco Cathedral in 1740.

Quite evidently, the dean had access to Zuola's book. The incident in Urquillos to which Zuola referred was a Siamese birth on April 5: the dean quotes from page 140 of Zuola's MS (which shows a picture of the twins). The dean (printed edition, p. 154) refers also to Buenaventura de Hotón, the same provincial who visited Cochabamba at the beginning of 1666 (p. 458 of Zuola's MS).

When republishing his 1931 monograph with a new title, "Un códice peruano colonial del siglo XVII," *Revista Musical Chilena*, XVI/81–82 (July–Dec., 1962), 54–93, Vega still did not notice the concordances of the Zuola MS with the *Anales del Cuzco*. Despite the lapse of thirty-one years, the 1962 article fails to improve significantly upon the 1931 monograph in other respects.

[33] For a polyphonic version, see J. Bal y Gay, *Treinta Canciones de Lope de Vega* (Madrid: Residencia de Estudiantes, 1935), pp. 1–6 (*Romance a 4* by Juan Blas de Castro).

[34] *Marizápalos baja una tarde, Don Pedro a quien los crueles, Malograda fuentecilla, Por qué tan firme os adoro.*

[35] A religious item developing the idea of "to thee do we cry, poor banished children of Eve," *Hijos de Eva* takes precedence as the earliest piece of vernacular polyphony extant by a colonial Peruvian composer. The composer, Tomás de Herrera, flourished at Cuzco *ca.* 1611; see *Musical Quarterly*, LIII/2 (April, 1967), 296–297.

[36] Vega, *op. cit.*, p. 11.

[37] Vega, *op. cit.*, p. 86, remarks: "the deterioration of page 160 [Zuola's MS] sensibly prejudices the third staff of the second voice; under such circumstances our transcription would be defective or guesswork."

completely written out,[38] whereas the two others betray the amateur composer who still struggled for exactly the right notes. On page 389 he copied the four-part *Por qué tan firme os adoro*. This last, like *Dime Pedro* (a 4), attests the mastery of one of the most sophisticated composers at work in seventeenth-century Spain.[39]

None of the seventeen items can be unreservedly classed as modal. True, the monodic *Don Pedro* on page 361, *Malograda fuentecilla* on page 363, and the polyphonic *Por qué tan firme* do eschew the extra flat that belongs to minor signatures. But $b\flat$ in the first and $e\flat$ in the other two songs intrude so often that any pure dorian feeling soon evaporates. The keys of the remaining items are always C major (*Pardos ojos, Poco a poco pensamiento, Yo sé que no ha de ganar*), A minor (*A cierto galán, Marizápalos baja una tarde, Qué importa que yo lo calle, Don Pedro a quien los crueles, Paxarillo fugitivo*, all monodic; *Hijos de Eva*, polyphonic), or F major (*No sé a que sombras funestas* [a 2] and *Dime Pedro* [a 4]). Only four of the seventeen songs go in triple meter—in each example indicated simply by the numeral 3—the rest all choosing common for their meter. The rhythms, especially in the common-meter monodies, often disport themselves in such supple and lithe ways as to suggest declamation rather than metronomic measure.

The two items that, because they are most vigorously rhythmical, do exude a distinctively popular aroma are *Marizápalos* and *Yo sé que no ha de ganar*. Just as *Barbara Allen* sung in the Carolina mountains harked back to a distant English past, so *Marizápalos* had been popular in Spain for at least two centuries before Zuola copied the melody into his book.[40] The lyrics recount how Marizápalos, the niece of a curate and the belle of Madrid, went walking in a thicket. She there hallooed Pedro Martín. They thence returned to disport themselves in lovemaking. But they heard footsteps at a compromising moment, whereupon he fled as fast as Adonis before the boar's tusks. The curate, entering hard after, would have used some very bad Latin had he only seen what they were doing. This pic-

---

[38] It can hardly be a plainchant; between *Dominum* and *Jesum Christum* it jumps a seventh. Moreover, it favors the leaps of a fourth and fifth which characterize basses in part music.

[39] Manuel Correa (d. 1653) was born at Lisbon, became a Calced Carmelite, served as maestro de capilla at Sigüenza and Saragossa. MS M1262 at the Biblioteca Nacional in Madrid contains a rich store of his secular part songs. Vega's opinion that the Correa of the Zuola commonplace book "is surely Francisco Correa de Araujo" betrays singular inattentiveness (*Revista Musical Chilena*, XVI/81–82, p. 55). His transcription of *Por qué* foists parallel octaves and other errors on Correa that do not enter the manuscript of the "amateurish" Zuola (cf. *ibid.*, XVI, 87, 88).

[40] Emilio Cotarelo y Mori, *Colección de Entremeses, Loas, Bailes, Jácaras y Mojigangas*, Tomo 1, vol. 1 (Madrid: Bailly-Bailliére, 1911), p. ccliii. For earlier versions of the coplas, see p. ccxiii.

turesque subject matches perfectly with the jaunty music [41] copied on Zuola's page 356.

In *Yo sé que no ha de ganar* the swain boasts that, because he is Portuguese, he can love more in one hour than others can in twenty-three. Whatever he has to lose in the game of love will be hers to gain. He proposes in the *estribillo* (refrain) that they try the game for at least a month. The first stanza poses a typical double entendre: "I know that she is not going to gain nor I to lose, because she does not love me nor I her." *Querer* is of course fraught here with more than one meaning. The estribillo with its invitation

[41] For a polyphonic *Marizápalos*, see Francisco Guerau's published at pp. 72–73 in Felipe Pedrell's *Cancionero Musical Popular Español* (Valls: Eduardo Castells, 1922), IV. Both Zuola's monody and Guerau's polyphonic setting (1694) hew to the same key (A minor) and gallop at the same gait; but the tunes are not identical.

to try the game for "only a month" comes after the strophe—a most unusual order in the baroque villancico [42] (and virtually unknown in the Renaissance villancico).

Zuola himself placed *Don Pedro* [43] first among the *Romances varios* [44]

[42] See *Romances y Letras a tres voces,* ed. Miguel Querol Gavaldá (Barcelona: Instituto Español de Musicología, 1956), pp. *16–17.*

[43] Printed with sixteen additional lines in Agustín Durán's *Romancero general* (*Biblioteca de Autores Españoles,* XVI), II, 218 (no. 1238).

[44] The texts of three romances entering the Zuola collection—*Don Pedro* at p. 361, *Malograda fuentecilla* at p. 363, and *Por qué tan firme os adoro* at p. 389—derive from the same printed source, *Romances varios de differentes authores, nuevamente impresos por un curioso* (Amsterdam: Ishaq Coen Faro, 1688); two of the three are not to be found in any other printed source.

copied in his commonplace book. He also designated the melody as Tenor (but without adding any other voice parts). He perhaps gave it priority because the subject here harked back to so bygone an event as the crowning of Inés de Castro's corpse after her assassination in 1355. Pedro, one of the

Don Pe - dro a quien los cru - el -

-es   Sin ra - zon lla - man cru -

el   des- de Coim-bra(a)Al- co - ba - ça cien mil

ha-chas hi-zo ar-der cien mil   ha - chas hi-zo ar-

der   cien mil   ha - chas hi - zo ar - der.

Don Pedro

Don Pedro, whom cruel men call cruel without reason, had a hundred thousand torches burnt from Coimbra to Alcobaça.

three Peters who were to rule contemporaneously in Castile, Aragon, and Portugal, had loved her passionately but adulterously. To prevent her from becoming queen, his father gave orders for her to be killed. When soon afterward Pedro himself ascended to the Portuguese throne he brought her dead body back from Coimbra to Alcobaça to have her crowned and obeisance done her.[45]

[45] Luis Vélez de Guevara (d. 1645) made this the culminating episode in his dramatic masterpiece, *Reinar después de morir*.

Zuola's melody adheres to traditional Renaissance form insofar as its repetition with every successive four lines and lack of a refrain are concerned. Because he sticks to the old romance form which does not allow for a musical refrain, it might also be expected that the melody line would betray certain archaic features. Actually, however, the modulation to G major implied at bars 4–5, the rhythmical expansion of bar 7_{1-3} at bars 8–9, the drop of a fifth to the final note, and the avoidance of fermatas at phrase ends, suggest that the melody, though poured into a vintage bottle, is new wine of the seventeenth century.

AMÉDÉE FRANÇOIS FRÉZIER (1682–1773)

In contrast with Zuola's commonplace book, the music of which had to lie for two centuries in manuscript, the next source to preserve music of a popular type was printed in Paris as early as two years after Amédée François Frézier had completed the Pacific Coast voyage during which he collected his melodies. On page 60 of his *Relation du voyage de la Mer du Sud* (Paris: J. G. Nyon [etc.], 1716) he printed the earliest surviving example of a melody sung by the aborigines of Chile, and on a plate opposite page 59 he offered the first pictures of their *thouthouca* (a trumpet of an arm's length, cut in sections, and flaring into a snoutlike bell), of their *pivellca* (a cup-shaped whistle), and of their *coulthun* (a barrel-shaped drum circled with grooves).[46] In his section on Peru he printed two bits of Creole popular music, one a *zapateo* (danced in both Peru and Chile) and the other a hymn to the Virgin. He claimed that the zapateo enjoyed as much popularity as did the minuet in France.[47] "In dancing, they alternately strike with the heel and the toes, taking some steps, and coupeeing without moving far from one place." He listed the harp, guitar, and *bandola* (mandolin) as the usual accompanying instruments. "The bandola has a much sharper and louder sound" than the usual guitar, according to him.

For an example of popular music set to a devotional text he offered, on page 217, a vernacular hymn in five stanzas. He testified to the enormous vogue of this class of music, especially at Lima, but he deplored what he considered the unsound theology. The structure, as befitted a hymn for the masses to sing, is extremely simple—four three-bar phrases. The second stanza antedates 1617, and was written by Miguel Cid, a Sevillian poet.[48] Bernardo de Toro (1570–1643) of Seville gave Cid's poem a popular musical

[46] On aboriginal Chilean instruments, see Eugenio Pereira Salas, *Los Orígenes del Arte Musical en Chile* (Santiago: Imp. Universitaria, 1941), chap. 1, and Juan Orrego-Salas, "Araucanian Indian Instruments," *Ethnomusicology*, X/1 (Jan., 1966).

[47] The zapateo had been popular in the peninsula a century earlier. See Cervantes, *Segunda parte del ingenioso cavallero Don Quixote* (Madrid: Juan dela Cuesta, 1615), fol. 239v.

[48] Rafael Mitjana, *Estudios sobre algunos músicos españoles del siglo XVI* (Madrid: Sucs. de Hernando, 1918), p. 156.

Zapateo

setting that was sung every night at Rosary. His triple-meter music differs from that sung after 1700 (Lima version reprinted in *The Music of Peru* [1960], p. 157).

BALTASAR JAIME MARTÍNEZ COMPAÑÓN (1737-1797)

If the atmosphere throughout the Zuola collection remains always as rarefied as the mountain air over 2-mile-high Cuzco, and if Frézier's zapateo and Lady hymn smack too much of *música culta*, the next important collection—gathered in the northern Peruvian diocese of Trujillo by the great humanist bishop Baltasar Jaime Martínez [de] Compañón y Bujanda (1737–1797) during his episcopal visits of 1782–1785 (forwarded to Charles IV of Spain in 1788–1790)—leaves no doubt of its origins among the baser commonfolk. The very commonness and "vulgarity" of the music have kept the collection from receiving the recognition it deserves. When Marcos Jiménez de la Espada first called attention to this source (in 1881 at the Fourth International Congress of Americanists), he readily enough admitted that the airs were Peruvian, whether Creole or indigenous. But when he delivered three songs and an instrumental dance to the press two years later,[49] he allowed the music to be characterized as "worthless" (*su música no tiene valor alguno*). To compound the mischief, he permitted the music

---

[49] Congreso Internacional de Americanistas, *Actas de la Cuarta Reunión* (Madrid: Imp. de Fortanet, 1883), pp. lxi–lxxx. These were the first pieces to be printed from movable type in Spain (*por primera vez en España, con caracteres tipográficos*), p. lxxxiii.

to appear incorrectly titled (e.g., *Láuchas* for *Lanchas*) and with numerous wrong notes. As a result, those few musical scholars who had seen even so much as the four pieces printed in 1883 carried away unfortunate impressions.[50] In the interim since 1883 the texts of the seventeen songs have been twice reprinted,[51] but no further attempt has been made to transcribe the music, which is, after all, the more distinctive part. What is therefore now needed is a publication that will include all twenty items (seventeen songs and three instrumental dances), will follow the order of the manuscript, and will faithfully adhere to both the original notes and texts.[52]

Martínez Compañón's nine tomes, averaging two hundred leaves each, form no less than a vast encyclopedia of Trujillo provincial life. Maps, drawings, paintings, chronologies, indices, fill its pages. To preserve some system, he devotes Volumes III, IV, and V to flora, VI to fauna, VII to birds, VIII to sea dwellers, IX to archaeological remains. Music occupies doubled folios 176–194 of Volume II. Because he is rumored to have later (1792) opposed construction of a theater across the street from the cathedral in Bogotá,[53] it might be guessed that he also expurgated the material collected during his Trujillo diocesan visits. Actually, however, his truly scientific spirit did not quail before texts that at times border on the coarse. The music, probably written out by some such professional aide as Pedro José Solís (chapelmaster of Trujillo Cathedral from March, 1781, to September, 1823[54]), also breathes throughout a crudeness that confirms its commonplace origin.

Martínez Compañón himself tells the exact locales at which he took the songs copied on folios 184 and 185 (Lambayeque), 187 and 189 (Chachapoyas), 188 and 191*b* (Cajamarca), 190 and 191*a* (Huamachuco), and 192 (Otusco). He had personally visited each of these towns, letters written by him from Lambayeque reaching Trujillo on January 7 and February 22, 1784;[55] from Cajamarca (Atahuallpa's death place) on November 5, 1784;[56] from Chachapoyas on November 24, 1782.[57] Himself an informed musician

---

[50] Neither Manuel Ballesteros Gaibrois in "Un manuscrito colonial del siglo XVIII," *Journal de la Société des Américanistes,* nouv. sér., XXVII, 145–173, nor Jesús Domínguez Bordona in *Trujillo del Perú a fines del siglo XVIII* (Madrid: C. Bermejo, 1936), pays the music any mind. They do take note of the texts.

[51] Rubén Vargas Ugarte, *Folklore Musical del Siglo XVIII* (Lima: Empresa Gráfica Scheuch, 1946 [Universidad Católica del Perú: Instituto de Investigaciones Artísticas]); José Manuel Pérez Ayala, *Baltasar Jaime Martínez Compañón y Bujanda (1737–1797)* (Bogotá: Imprenta Nacional, 1955), pp. 247–251.

[52] There are two songs on folio E. 191: Pérez Ayala prints them as one. Vargas Ugarte rearranges the order, but does at least give facsimiles of the music.

[53] Pérez Ayala, *op. cit.,* pp. 86–93.

[54] Trujillo Cathedral, *Actas Capitulares,* VII (1777–1786), fol. 67; XI (1814–1839), fol. 163*v*.

[55] Trujillo Cathedral, *Actas Capitulares,* VII, fols. 125*v*, 127.

[56] *Ibid.,* fol. 137.

[57] *Ibid.,* fol. 100.

(he was chantre, or precentor, of Lima Cathedral from 1768–1778), he taught plainchant at various times during his diocesan visits, from 1782 to 1785.[58] He was probably himself equal to the task of taking down the melodies in his collection; but even if he confided the task to a professional aide, he must have made such decisions as the following: (1) the logical order in which the songs were disposed, those from Trujillo city coming first (Christmas carols followed by secular songs), then secular songs taken at progressively greater distances from Trujillo; (2) the writing out of all the many repeats, and also the writing out in full of an accompanying instrumental part even when it traveled in unison with the voice.

The Christmas songs with which the collection begins are carols in the old sense: "round dances." Both are indeed subtitled *cachuas*, which in the Quechua tongue means exactly a round dance. The text of the second reads: "Give us leave, sirs, since it is Christmas Eve, to dance and sing after the manner of our own land." In both, phrases of text are many times repeated, the music complying with corresponding reiterations. So homely is the "harmonization" that in the first the bass does nothing but drone out *A-E, A-E, A-E,* in broken quaver octaves. The bass in the second breaks away from the charmed circle of *A-E,* but only for the most transitory of excursions to the key of C. The unmistakable key of each is A minor. The fact that the fiddle intervenes in the accompaniment of both but confirms the violin's folk status in eighteenth-century Peru. The voice parts in the first make a rudimentary four-part harmony, but with the lowest never descending below *E.* For that matter, in no song of the entire collection does any lower note appear. High tessitura for all the voices is the rule: in one solo song ("The Jealous Woman," collected at Lambayeque) no lower note than *b* (middle line of treble clef) appears anywhere.

The other pieces that he collected in and around Trujillo include one Negro song, *El Congo* (Negro slave labor began to account for the prosperity of Trujillo as early as 1600), two Chimú dances (Chimú curacas ruled the region around Trujillo before the Inca conquest, *ca.* 1475, Chanchán just outside present-day Trujillo serving as their capital), a song in the now extinct Mochica tongue (Mochicas ruled the area before the Chimú, i.e., before 1300), and finally three bold and lusty mestizo dance songs.

The Negro song, after a four-bar introduction, sticks with a persistent bass throughout. The tonic-dominant harmony justifies T. J. C. y P.'s complaint that such corner musicians as the Negro Galindo took up only the most ordinary harmonic progressions of the European music to which they were exposed. The text has it that "They carried me off to the coast without just cause, ‖: making me leave my mother whom I loved;:‖ What says the

---

[58] *Actas Capitulares*, VIII (1786–1796), fol. 160v. He had resided at Piura, Lambayeque, and Cajamarca (three months in each) *explicando diariamente las lecciones . . . de Canto llano a sus seminaristas hasta que dexo establecida su disciplina.*

Congo; cusucu, go see, cusucu, go; There's ||: nothing new, nothing new :||
but the stick of the white man; get, get to your place!" [59]

The two Chimú (= Chimo) instrumental dances should not be understood as music in any way affiliated with the archaeological past, but rather
as the kind of fare Chimú descendants provided their Spanish masters to
win favor, *ca.* 1782. The intervals and rhythms border on the trite; but in
defense it should be said that the native music among even such tribes of
eastern Peru as today retain an untouched culture does not appear very
distinctive when reduced to Western notation. The tone color and rhythmic
twists too subtle for conventional notation give such music as that of the
remote jungle Caxinahuas its distinctive flavor.

After these two Chimú dances Martínez Compañón next offered the only
surviving song with Mochica text. Fernando de la Carrera had already, of
course, on pages 258–264 of his classic text of the Mochica language—*Arte
dela Lengva Yvnga de los Valles del Obispado de Truxillo* (Lima: Joseph de
Contreras, 1644)—printed *Seys Hymnos, traducidos en la lengua, los quales
se cantan por los puntos de los latinos de a donde se traduxeron* ("Six
hymns, translated into the [Mochica] language, which are to be sung to the
notes of the Latin hymns from which they have been translated"). But
Martínez Compañón gave us an original song with independent music. The
Mochica tongue, spoken by only forty thousand in 1644, was in Carrera's
day (as in Martínez Compañón's) a coastal language filled with difficult
sounds for which Spanish orthography yielded no counterpart.[60] By the
1780's its users had been still further diminished and its purity sullied by the
intrusion of many Castilian words. Obviously Martínez Compañón's text is
corrupted Mochica when it contains such Spanish words as *jesuchristo* and
perdonar. But after the onomatopoetic *ja ya llunch, ja ya lloch* repeated by
way of introduction, the first two words, *iñ poc* do mean "I am called."
Fama (= *fam.az*) means "you are crying." *Lens* (= *len*) after the Spanish
word *cuerpo* means "with." Even if Carrera's *Arte* does not enable us to
translate the whole of Martínez Compañón's text, we shall probably not be
going far astray if we suppose it to be a prayer for pardon, antiphonally
sung. The fact that it is to be danced with drum and bass drone in andantino tempo in no way detracts from its penitential character. In B minor, the
vocal melody makes use of only five notes, but not after the pentatonic
fashion that the d'Harcourts wished to believe universal in Inca music.

The three mestizo songs at folios 181, 182, and 183 share several musical

[59] Negro dialect songs, or songs depicting Negroes, were nothing new in Peru: at
Cuzco a *Villancico de Negro, para Navidad a 4 voces* survives in the San Antonio Abad
Seminary Library (along with notice of a pascualillo for Christmas *a 5, El Negro*). See
R. Vargas Ugarte, "Un archivo de música colonial en la ciudad del Cuzco," *Mar del
Sur,* Año V, no. 26 (March–April, 1953), pp. 3, 6.

[60] See Carrera's preface *Al lector* for an explanation of the difficulties. He turned
letters upside down and combined vowels to obtain new written characters.

characteristics. Each is in brisk triple meter; each falls into clear four-bar phrases; in each the vocal melody drives forward at least part of the time over a "boogie"-type bass; in each the frequent textual repetitions inspire corresponding musical repeats. The vocal melody in the two major songs ever and anon favors the flatted "blue" seventh degree of the scale. The jazzy sound of bars 33–40 in the one minor song, *La lata* ("The Can"), comes from the nervous syncopations in every other bar.

The texts must not be translated here. In *La lata* (fol. 181), *oficiales de marina* sally forth at night to roast the fat in the can of a mulatta. "Take it, take it, take it," they roisteringly cry, "you who give my love its glory moment." She knows how to conjure all their anxieties. The third song (fol. 183) starts innocently enough with Don Felis de Soto issuing orders against the selling of tobacco, but soon gets down to such loose talk as "pretty thing, my rabbit, let me come in your nest; pretty thing, my heart's delight, you slay me; pretty thing, what a beautiful conjunction, you lovely tramp; pretty thing, love calls me when in bed." The second of this group of three (fol. 182) develops a more courtly vein: "You, adorable, are the only one whom I love; for you alone I would die." At the close, he bids her a sad farewell.

After these three bold mestizo songs collected in Trujillo itself, Martínez Compañón began his hegira through the province with two wholly decorous items, from the coastal town of Lambayeque (120 miles north of Trujillo city). In the first the singer asks whether it is prudent to await a later moment for a disclosure of feelings. In the second he acclaims his ungrateful *samba* (mixture of Indian and Negro) as queen of the flowers, birds, fish, and animal realm; she merits the adoration of all. The music of both Lambayeque songs goes in an andantino 3/8. Both show one trait not shared with any other songs in this collection: the interruption of the voice part with frequent rests on fourth bars (or even second and fourth) of a phrase. Meanwhile the bass plays what might be called the Lambayeque motto, consisting of an arpeggio triad on beat 1 (triplet) returning to root on beat 2 (quarter note). In both songs four-bar phrases are the rule. These always begin with an obsessive rhythm in the voice part (two sixteenth notes followed by a pair of eighths). Both share one further mannerism: seesawing between tonic and dominant from four-bar to four-bar phrase. The dominant usually takes off with an ascending scale. One song is in major (D), the other in minor (A).

The next song pairs with a later lover's lament in this same Martínez Compañón collection, even though the words are quite different and one was taken at Chachapoyas (*El Diamante*, fol. 187), the other at Cajamarca (*El Tuppa maro*, fol. 191*b*), more than 100 miles distant in the central highlands. The first six bars of the Chachapoyas vocal part may be compared with the first nine of the Cajamarca.

The introductory and concluding instrumental portions are also substantially the same music. The musical likenesses are the more interesting

In - fe - li - zes o- jos mi- os   de - jad

ya de a-tor-men - tar me con el▪   llan - to.

Infelizes ojos mios

Unfortunate eyes of mine, stop tormenting me
with your tears.

De los ba-ños don-de estu - be   lue- go

vi- ne a tu lla- ma - da Sin-tien-do yo tu be-ni-

-da con-fu - so de tu   lle - ga - da

De los baños

From the baths where I was, I promptly came to
your call, hearing of your coming,
confused at your arrival.

because here for the first time we meet pentatonic melodies of the type that
modern investigators, beginning with Leandro Alviña's *La música Incaica*
(Cuzco, 1919),[61] have chosen as typical of Peruvian highland music. On
circumstantial evidence, this melody in both its Chachapoyas and Cajamarca versions may well be an authentic survival. As for the texts, in the
first the singer complains of woes that turn his unhappy eyes into rivers of
tears; in the second, he comes from the baths (*De los baños donde estuve*)

[61] See especially "Los Diversos Tonos Pentafónicos," pp. 20–21.

at his loved one's call, but is confused at her arrival. The Inca baths outside Cajamarca remain even today, of course, and are the most renowned historical site near this town in which Atahuallpa met his death.

Another song taken at Cajamarca follows at folio 188, but this one is clearly mestizo. The tempo shifts from an opening allegro (with frequent "Scotch snaps") to grave when the voice enters. The rhythm in every sung bar repeats itself—a crotchet followed by triplet quavers, with d^1 serving as the lowest note (except at the octave repetition in the penultimate bar). Shifting back to Chachapoyas for its locale, the next song mixes indigenous and Spanish words ("I know you" and "feel sorry for me" are in Castilian). With its numerous grace notes, the vocal melody makes a habit of pitch slides. In this respect it is unique in the collection:

The bishop veers to Huamachuco, a highland town made famous as the scene of the first Augustinian labors in Peru, for his next two songs. In both, the singer begins with a characteristic syncopated rhythmic figure and stays with it throughout: ♪♪♪ . One song, *La brujita* ("The Little Enchantress"), is in D minor; the other, *De bronse' devo de ser* ("I have to be of bronze"), is in D major. Throughout the latter the singer rises only the first six notes of the major scale (with the third touched on only as sixteenth note in passing). Martínez Compañón types it as a cachua for a *despedida* (leave-taking).

At folio 192 he comes to his longest text, that for a cachua to be sung and danced by eight noble Indian maidens (*pallas*) of Otusco in honor of Our Lady of Carmen (Otusco is in the mountains 50 miles east of Trujillo). Typed as a *huicho nuevo* to distinguish it from the old-style *huicho* at folio 189, this is a responsorial song. The leader gives out each strophe, and is at once answered by the whole group singing the same melody as a refrain with only the syllable "na" for each note. The modulations from the prevailing key of A minor to C major and back, along with the frequent sharped leading tones, forbid our supposing that either text or music harks back much beyond Martínez Compañón's own day.

His last item is a *cachuyta* (little cachua) from the *montaña* (which in Peru usually means the lowland east of the mountains). It is unique in the collection, but not because of its "indigenous" character. Indeed, it is his only song that makes much of the vocal arabesque at ends of phrases which visitors to Andalusia always expect in *cante jondo*. These melodic curls together with such unusual features as the drop from sharped leading tone to fifth degree (à la Grieg) and the constant accompaniment of the voice at the distance of a third or sixth (the fiddle usually plays in unison with the voice throughout this collection) force us to believe that the most characteristically Spanish song is the one taken at the greatest distance from Trujillo. As for the text, the metaphor *rueda de la fortuna* ("wheel of fortune") brings in an idea as remote as possible from indigenous thinking among a people who never had so much as heard of the wheel before the Spanish conquest.

In addition to the vocal pieces thus far mentioned, the collection includes the *Bayle del Chimo* followed by drum-and-fife dance at folio 179, and the long *Lanchas* (dance for fiddle and continuo) at folio 186. Extending to more than 150 bars of quick 3/4 music, this last piece veers mainly between A minor and C major, gravitating toward F only after bar 105. Such violent clashes between the chords of B♭ Major and E major as distinguish bars 90–91, 94–95, 98–99 compensate for the lack of harmonic movement. Not only was this one of the pieces chosen for printing in 1883, but also Holzmann and Arróspide de la Flor gave it their cachet of approval in 1946 when they listed it as *seguramente la de mayor valor musical entre todas* [62] ("certainly the piece of the whole collection with the greatest musical

[62] *Folklore Musical del Siglo XVIII*, p. 5.

value"). Since it comes immediately after the two Lambayeque songs, Martínez Compañón probably wished it to be understood as a northern coastal dance taken in the one town of Trujillo province which, along with the capital, had undergone the heaviest Spanish influence.[63]

Six songs from his collection reached print in *The Music of Peru* (Washington: Pan American Union, 1960)—pages 304–320 of which contain transcriptions of two Christmas cachuas, the tonada *El Congo*, the Mochica song for antiphonal trebles, and the tonadas for accompanied soprano, *La lata* ("The Can") and *La Donosa* ("The Pretty Girl"). Taken from Martínez Compañón's Tomo II, folios E. 176–178 and E. 180–182, all these except *La lata* were on April 30, 1961, recorded in Schoenberg Hall, UCLA. Roger Wagner conducted the instrumental ensemble accompanying the soloists, Barbara Wilson, Claire Gordon, Doris Preissler, and Richard Levitt. Pages 9–10 of the program booklet printed under auspices of the UCLA Music Department, *1961 Spring Festival of Latin American Music,* described the songs.

Although no final assessment of Martínez Compañón's folk music can be undertaken until the whole collection is published in a correct edition, at least these generalizations can now be made: (1) his was the earliest American attempt at gathering so extensive a collection; (2) he controlled his takings by presenting them in geographical order; (3) he selected "characteristic" items—those from Lambayeque being typed with much use of a rhythmic figure (a pair of sixteenth notes followed by a pair of eighths) and a fourth-bar vocal rest; those from Huamachuco by a characteristic syncopated figure; those from Trujillo city by a vigorous 3/8 "boogie" bass (with much covert obscenity in the texts); those from Cajamarca and Chachapoyas, the mountain songs, by pentatonicism in the vocal melody; (4) he pioneered also in showing two alternate versions of the same folk song (from mountain points more than 100 miles apart); (5) he began his collection with a pair of Christmas carols (cachuas), but did not allow his miter to prevent some racy songs from entering the group; (6) he served science by incorporating a song in the now extinct Mochica tongue.

LATE COLONIAL "SOCIETY" DANCE MUSIC

Two borderline sources of late colonial folk music remain for brief mention, both of which are manuscript collections of guitar music preserved at Lima (one in the Museo Nacional de Historia, Magdalena Vieja, the other in the

[63] In his *Al Lector* Carrera alludes to his great-grandfather Pedro Gonçalez, the conquistador who began the Hispanicizing process. After the famous earthquake at Trujillo on February 14, 1619, the cathedral chapter for a time even moved to Lambayeque, the most "civilized" place in the province outside Trujillo. See *Actas Capitulares,* I (1616–1628), fol. 33.

National Library). The first, reaching twenty-five leaves with five staves to a page, belonged to Francisco García, *teniente coronel* in the Royal Engineers at Lima in 1805 (signature dated December 18 at folio 25*v;* an earlier owner seems to have been a Don Jorge Tambino). On the yellowed parchment binding, *Libro de Zifra para—* can still be made out, but the tablature breaks off after folio 11, the rest of the book being copied in staff notation. That tablature toward the end of the colonial epoch was a dying system can be surmised from the fact that such intabulated items as those at folios 1*v* (*Marcha de Napoles*) and 2 (*Chiga*) have been recopied in staff notation at folios 23 (*Marche de Naples*) and 12 (*Giga*). Minuets take up by far the largest space in the whole book. Among the fifteen included are a *Minuet de Conde de las Torres* (fol. 3*v*), a *Minuet Portugués* (fol. 4), and a *Minuet de Landabere* (fol. 4*v*) in the tabulated portion; and a *Menuet anglais*[64] in A Major followed by *diferencia* in the staff-notated part (fol. 18*v*). Among the three marches is a *Marcha de Parma* (fol. 9*v*); the rest of the anonymous items include a *Tiro Nuevo* (fol. 3), a *Toc[c]ata* (fol. 16*v*), and a Sonata in A (fol. 21*v*–22*v*). This last may well be by the same Missón who composed the A minor Sonata copied twice in this book,[65] the first time in tablature (fols. 5*v*–6*v*), the second in staff notation (fols. 12*v*–13). Since he is the only named composer in the manuscript, the catalog number was changed in 1966 to 927. *Mis.*

The Biblioteca Nacional MS (D 9950) bears *Cuaderno de Musica / para Viguela* for its title. The paper binding for the nine leaves consists of a broadside printed at La Paz, Bolivia, in 1829, with Andrés Santa Cruz, *ministro de hacienda*, as the signatory. Each of the oblong pages runs to seven staves of staff-notated music. As in the previous guitar book, minuets bulk largest (fols. 1, 2, 3, 7, 9), but a Rondo in E takes up folio 4 and a Sonata in D takes up folios 5 to 8. None of the anonymous music in this or the previous MS savors of the common folk in the way that Martínez Compañón's songs and dances do. Still, the ubiquitous minuets tell the same tale as do the polonaises and *contradanzas* in the late colonial repertory of Mexico. They show how infused was every level of colonial life with stylish music brought over from Europe.

[64] This spelling, along with others in the staff-notated part, suggests that the second half was copied anew by some French émigré. Certainly tablature had long been known and practiced in Peru. At page 365 (not 369) of his commonplace book Zuola lists, for instance, the various guitar positions that Gaspar Sanz had given as the *Abecedario Italiano* in each, writing out the musical notes that the letter position implied. To Sanz's *Abecedario Italiano*, Zuola added still another eight letter positions— Q, R, S, T, V, X, Y, Z.

[65] Luis Missón (d. Madrid, 1766) reputedly originated the genre musical picture known as the *tonadilla*. For biographical data and stylistic appreciation, see José Subirá, *La Tonadilla escénica* (Barcelona: Editorial Labor, 1933), pp. 106, 111–114. Subirá discovered various Missón trio sonatas (flute, viols, continuo) in the Duke of Alva's library.

For late viceroyal music of a more common-clay cast than the cultured minuets in Mexican National Library MS 1560 or in Peruvian Biblioteca Nacional MS D 9950, Pereyra y Ruiz' 1816 "Noticia" of Arequipa serves as a useful source (the copy of this "Noticia" in the Lima National Library was sent by the Tenerife *cabildo insular*).[66] The dances at Arequipa which Pereyra y Ruiz can endorse as a counterthreat to the popularity of the sick, sad yaraví bustle with as much life as any Spanish *tirana* of the epoch.

Fol. 53: El Gallinasito, baile de Arequipa

Fol. 54: El Moro, bayle de Arequipa

BOLIVIAN INDIAN MUSIC

To turn from the area comprising what is now independent Peru to what was called in colonial times High Peru (Alto Perú), Pereyra y Ruiz transcribed at folio 55 of his 1816 "Noticia de . . . Arequipa" (Lima copy) the following brisk dance song from Potosí.

El Cielito,   bayle de Potosi

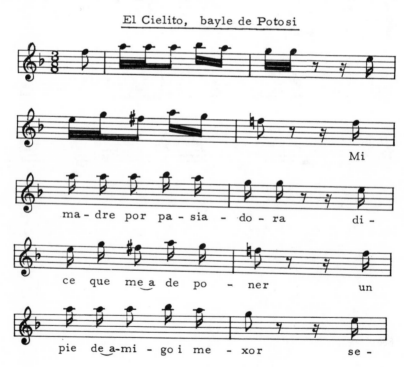

Mi

ma - dre por pa - sia - do - ra   di -

ce que me a de po   -   ner   un

pie de a-mi - go i me - xor   se -

ra un a - mi - go de pie a - na -

na na - na - na na - na

na - na - na na - na - na Ay

cie - lo cie - lo que si, cie -

li - to de Po - to - si.

(D. C.)

Obviously this is music no nearer the indigenous than the Zipoli Mass copied at Potosí in 1784 and now surviving at Sucre Cathedral in testimony of the Italian organist's Argentine sojourn. For indigenous melody we must look elsewhere. What the Frenchman Frézier had done for coastal music when, in 1716, he published at Paris the first excerpts, was repeated for the music of the area now comprising Bolivia when the French Alcide d'Orbigny published at Paris in 1844 the third volume (Pt. I) of his monumental *Voyage dans l'Amérique Méridionale*.[67] Between pages 60 and 61 of the text he inserted seven pieces of music collected among Bolivian tribes. The first nine examples came from Chiquitos Indians, the next eleven from Morotocas. For the Chiquitos items he was able to supply translations into French, but not for the Morotocas.

The Chiquitos melodies show such European influences as sequences (nos. 1 and 4), modulation (from F major to D minor in no. 2), da capo (no. 4). The most unaffected seem to be numbers 3 ("here goes the young stag seeking a hind, a young hind"), 8 ("the feet of the young partridge are as red as pimiento; I recognize you, I recognize you"), 9 ("they got drunk on the honey of the small bee; they thought it was of the large, but they were mistaken").

[67] Tome 3, 1ʳᵉ Partie (Paris-Strasbourg: P. Bertrand-Vᵉ Levrault, 1844). In the Spanish translation, *Viaje a la América Meridional*, Tomo IV (Buenos Aires: Ed. Futuro, 1945), the musical examples are printed at pp. 1273–1279.

ya - e   na   su   ta   pa   re   se

The Morotocas' songs range a tenth or wider (nos. 1–4, 10–11); all except number 7 are essentially pentatonic. They divide evenly between examples in duple and in triple meter; one starts slowly in common meter and changes in mid-course to very fast triple (3/8). Numbers 2 and 3 are distinguished by short breathy phrases punctuated by rests.

Not many native South Americans contemporary with d'Orbigny shared his zest for recording local curiosities. However, the Bolivian Melchor María Mercado did gather between 1841 and 1869 a 148-leaf miscellany of water colors, poetry, music, and travel diary that around 1900 reached the National Library of Bolivia (Colección Rück, nos. 486–488). Appropriately enough, since the Bolivian National Library is at Sucre, the manuscript begins with a fulsome dedication to the memory of Bolivia's first president, Sucre. The title on the opening leaf of the oblong book as presently bound reads "Ilustraciones gráficas del Potosí Colonial." But such a title belies the contents. All the water colors, music, and travel diary after plate 33 (= 30, new numbering) deal with other parts of Bolivia and Peru (La Paz, Cochabamba, Trinidad, and the eastern part of Bolivia; Peru from plate 119 [= 94] through 145 [= 120].

The pages devoted to Beni and to the Mojos Indians (region of Trinidad) make an especially attractive addition to the Bolivian folkloric literature. Among the forty-six leaves added to his manuscript by Mercado in 1859 may be found not only several bits of popular religious music (European-influenced) but also such a lively indigenous item as *El gran baile de los naturales llamado jeruze* (fol. 75, old numbering). *Flautines* are the instruments prescribed for the opening dance in *El gran baile*, but a *flautón bajón* for the second.

In the first description of the Mercado manuscript to reach print, it was called "muy curioso y de mucho interés etnográfico" (*Biblioteca de Ernesto O. Rück: Catálogo* [Lima: Imp. y Encuadernación de Guillermo Stolte, 1898], p. 61), and the sixteen pieces of music were listed (p. 63) with the titles that Mercado gave them. Not only in such a frankly Christian item as the *Verso a la Santísima Trinidad por los naturales de Trinidad* (*Beni*) but also in *Baile de toritos, Trinidad* and even in the *jeruze* from which excerpts have just been given, the problem of authenticity constantly arises. In Mercado's century, as in ours, testimony to the *echt* indigenous spirit can all too frequently be challenged. But in our own generation Bolivian folklorists still continue their efforts to gather melodies that capture the spirit of the preconquest past.

The third volume of *monografías* published at the expense of the La Paz municipality on her fourth centenary contains a generous collection of Aymara melodies gathered in the La Paz vicinity.[68] These are printed attractively, and are accompanied by watercolor reproductions of the native dances at which the music is used. Even more recently the municipality has shown its disposition to continue patronizing folkloric studies with the

---

[68] *La Paz en su IV Centenario* (Buenos Aires: Imp. López, 1948), pp. 427–461.

publication in 1955 of a *Catálogo General de la Exposición de Artesanía Popular Indo-Mestiza* which contains valuable information on both Indian and mestizo musical instruments (pp. 16, 22, 27; also plate at p. 24), and in 1956 of Yolanda Bedregal de Conitzer and Antonio González Bravo's *Calendario Folklórico del Departamento de La Paz, con un pequeño glosario de música y danzas indígenas*. The Bolivian Ministry of Education has caught stride not only with the publication of so valuable a work as Karl Gustav Izikowitz' *Instrumentos Musicales de los Indios Chipaya* but also of Julia Elena Fortún de Ponce's 100-page *Manual para la recolección de material folklórico* (1957). Her *Antología de Navidad* (La Paz: Biblioteca Paceña [Alcadía Municipal], 1956) and "La Navidad en el ámbito chuquisaceño," *Cuaderno de la Sociedad Folklórica de Bolivia*, 1 (Sucre: Imprenta "Bolívar," 1952) reveal two facets of her imposing doctoral labors at the Universidad Central de Madrid.

As Directora Nacional de Antropología, she wrote the prologue to Enrique Oblitas Poblete's *Cultura Callawaya* (La Paz: Talleres Gráficos Bolivianos, 1963), a 509-page treatise awarded first prize in a competition promoted in 1960 by the Bolivian Ministerio de Educación y Bellas Artes. This fundamental study contains not only a chapter on the dances of the Callawayas— qantu, tuaillo, qena-qena, chatri, ulun simppana, chiriguanos, kkarachupa, cullawa, para wajaj, khariciri, machu tusuj, pulipuli, and others—but also plates and a musical supplement. Láminas 9, 38–39, 41–43, 47, 71–72 following page 509 show players of various instruments. The 39-page appendix contains 136 "melodías musicales de sicu o flauta de pan, pincollo, flauta traversa, quena," transcribed by Antonio González Bravo. These 136 melodies (all collected in the Bautista Saavedra province of the department of La Paz) comprise 86 tunes for the qantu, tuaillo, chiriguanos, chatri, qena-qena, chchili, and other regional dances; 14 songs with native text; and an instrumental section beginning at number 101 with "música de flauta traversa." Less than half the melodies from 101 through 136 obey the pentatonic principle (102–103, 108, 112–115, 117, 126, 130–132, 134), but they all do conform with the Andean threnody stereotype.

In the future even more refined studies are promised which will for the first time make it possible for us to separate the qualities that give each major Bolivian tribal music a distinctive individuality. For the department of La Paz, and among the Aymara in the neighboring department of Oruro, a recording project carried on in 1953–1957 by Louis Girault happily eventuated in approximately 250 takes of the ceremonial and festival music still being performed on the altiplano in the mid-1950's. A handsome monograph, *La musique des aymara sur les hauts plateaux boliviens* by Marguerite and Raoul d'Harcourt (Paris: Société des Américanistes [Musée de l'Homme], 1959, 133 pp.), contains transcriptions of 104 melodies from the Girault collection (now deposited at the Phonothèque Nationale in Paris). Although usually transcribed textless, and always reduced to music notation that refuses to hint at any departures from tempered tuning,[69] still this beautiful study boasts eight cachuas (= *kashuas*, pp. 64–70, all recorded September 8, 1955, at Peñas, hard by the shores of Lake Titicaca), ten *huaynos* (= *waynos*, pp. 84–91, the first four taken at La Paz, February 21, 1954), and five *charcas* (pp. 59–64), not to mention other types with Spanish names.

As the authors state, division of the material does not reflect musical differences but rather the varying occasions for its performance. In conformity with their previously enunciated theory that pure Incaic music should hew to pentaphonic modes, they see European influences in all seven-note melodies. Only two examples with chromaticisms are permitted to enter their book (nos. 80–81, pp. 109–110—solo dances taken at Peñas on September 8, 1955).

Foreseeing the eventual demise of all indigenous Andean music, they pen this threnody: [70]

Since our trips to Peru, European influences have steadily gained and indigenous music has suffered severe loss of its distinctive style. The Bolivian airs here presented lack some of that richness which once caused Olivier Messiaen to hail Andean survivals as a treasury comparable with only Japanese and Mongolian folk musics. The examples here shown are less typical of what the pure native music should contain. Perhaps the frustration affecting the Aymara as a people debilitates their music. Nonetheless, the pastorales here transcribed do breathe a moving lyricism and their dances do at times burst with considerable vigor.

[69] Paul Collaer in "Cariban and Mayan Music," *Studia Memoriae Belae Bartók Sacra* (London: Boosey and Hawkes, 1959), pp. 123–139, transcribes four Guatemalan melodies (D, F, G, H, at pp. 130–131), in each instance carefully introducing plus or minus signs above the notes to show departures from tempered pitches. He used copies of *Musica indígena de Guatemala* (1943–1944) deposited at the Brussels Institut National de Radiodiffusion (INR/Volk 73/Audiodisc, 1–12). The originals were taken under Library of Congress subsidy by Henrietta Yurchenco. The only pentatonic piece among the Guatemala transcriptions is the reed flute *Baile del Venado* (credited to Quichés from Nahuala, Sololá, p. 129).

[70] *La musique des Aymara*, pp. 43–44, abridged.

BIBLIOGRAPHY

More than a quarter century ago Latin-American musical bibliography had the rare fortune of enlisting the services of so gifted an investigator of hemispheric literature as Gilbert Chase. A master of all European tongues spoken in the Americas, he at once established himself as the bibliographic authority of both continents when he published *A Guide to Latin American Music* (Washington: Library of Congress, Music Division, 1945). Expanded and updated, thanks to the Martha Baird Rockefeller Aid to Music Program, this manual returned to print in 1962 with a slightly altered title: *A Guide to the Music of Latin America* (411 + xi pp.). Over the long expanse of decades—from Volumes VI through VIII of the *Handbook of Latin American Studies* issued in 1940–1942 to Volume XXVI in 1964—he has consistently remained a foremost figure in Latin-American musicological and bibliographical disciplines. So authoritative and so extensive indeed is the aid available in Chase's many publications that little more need be offered here than a convenient list of the titles cited in the present volume. It goes without saying that any investigator bent on further research in our fields should make Chase's bibliographies his daily companions.

To avoid the obvious, the following bibliography omits compendia on every public library reference shelf, such as Otto Mayer-Serra's handsomely produced *Música y Músicos de Latinoamérica* (2 vols.; Mexico City: Editorial Atlante, 1947) or Nicolas Slonimsky's popular *Music of Latin America* (New York: Thos. Y. Crowell, 1945). Standard encyclopedias in Spanish and English are excluded, as are also unpublished manuscripts.

Anonymous works and liturgical books not edited by a named compiler are alphabetized under the first letter of the title. As a rule, only the first editions of standard histories are here cited, or diplomatic reprints.

Acosta, Jorge R., and others. *Esplendor del México Antiguo*. México: Centro de Investigaciones Antropológicas, 1959. 2 vols.

Acosta, José de. *Historia Natvral y Moral de las Indias*. Seville: Juan de León, 1590.

———. *Obras*. Ed. Francisco Mateos. Madrid: Ediciones Atlas, 1954. (*Biblioteca de Autores Españoles*, LXXIII.)

Actas del Cabildo de la Ciudad de México, I. México: Ignacio Bejarano, 1889.

Aguirre Beltrán, Gonzalo. *La población negra de México, 1519–1810*. México: Ediciones Fuente Cultural, 1946.

———. "The Slave Trade in Mexico," *Hispanic American Historical Review*, XXIV/3 (Aug., 1944).

Alamán, Lucas. *Disertaciones sobre la historia de la república megicana*, II. México: José Mariano Lara, 1844.

Alcina Franch, José. "Sonajas rituales en la cerámica mejicana," *Revista de Indias*, XIII/54 (Oct.–Dec., 1953).

Alva Ixtlilxóchitl, Fernando de. *Obras históricas*. México: Editora Nacional, 1952. 2 vols.

Alvarado, Francisco de. *Vocabvlario en lengva misteca*. México: Pedro Balli, 1593. Facs. ed. supervised by Wigberto Jiménez Moreno, with additions from Antonio de los Reyes' *Arte en lengva mixteca* (1593). México: Instituto Nacional Indigenista, 1962.

Alvarado Tezozomoc, Hernando. *Crónica Mexicana* [*ca.* 1598]. México: Editorial Leyenda, 1944.

Alviña, Leandro. "La Música Incaica," *Revista Universitaria* [Cuzco], XIII/2 (Dec. 31, 1929).

Alvitez, Alexo de. *Puntual descripcion, funebre lamento . . . con que . . . mando solemnizar las Reales Exequias de . . . Mariana Josepha de Austria*. Lima: n.p., 1757.

Amberga, Jerónimo de. "Una flauta de Pan, araucana," *Revista Chilena de Historia y Geografía*, XXXVII (1921).

Amézquita Borja, Francisco. *Música y danza; algunos aspectos de la música y danza de la sierra norte del estado de Puebla*. Puebla: n.p., 1943.

Anales del Cuzco, 1600 á 1750. See Esquivel y Navía.

Ancona H., Ignacio, and R. Martín del Campo. "Malacología precortesiana." In *Memoria del Congreso Científico Mexicano* [1951], VII. México: Universidad Nacional Autónoma, 1953.

Anderson, Arthur J. O. "Aztec Music," *Western Humanities Review*, VIII/2 (Spring, 1954).

Andrade, Vicente de P. *Ensayo bibliográfico mexicano del siglo XVII*. México: Imp. del Museo Nacional, 1899.

"Anécdota histórica," *Correo Peruano* (Lima), I/181 (Nov. 6, 1845).

Anglés, Higinio. *La música en la corte de Carlos V*. Barcelona: Instituto Español de Musicología, 1944.

[*Antiphonarium*]. México: Pedro de Ocharte, 1589.

Aranzáes, Nicanor. *Diccionario Histórico del Departamento de La Paz*. La Paz: J. L. Calderón, 1915.

Arco y Garay, Ricardo del. *La sociedad española en las obras dramáticas de Lope de Vega*. Madrid: Escelicer, 1942.

Arguedas, José María. "Los Himnos Quechuas Católicos Cuzqueños," *Folklore Americano*, III/3 (1935).

Arrese y Layseca, Francisco de. *Descripcion de las Reales Fiestas*. Lima: Imp. de los Niños Expósitos, 1790.

Arriaga, Pablo Joseph de. *Extirpacion de la idolatria del Pirv*. Lima: Geronymo de Contreras, 1621.

Arte, y vocabvlario en la Lengva general del Perv llamada Quichua. Lima: Antonio Ricardo, 1586.

Arzáns de Orsúa y Vela, Bartolomé. *Historia de la Villa Imperial de Potosí.* Ed. Lewis Hanke and Gunnar Mendoza. Providence: Brown University Press, 1965. 3 vols.

Asenjo Barbieri, Francisco. *Las castañuelas.* Madrid: M. Ducazcal, 1878.

Ávila, Francisco de. *Dämonen und Zauber im Inkareich. Aus dem Khetschua übersetzt und eingeleitet von Dr. Hermann Trimborn.* Leipzig: K. F. Koehler, 1939.

Ayestarán, Lauro. *Domenico Zipoli. El gran compositor y organista romano del 1700 en el Rio de la Plata.* Montevideo: Imp. Uruguaya, 1941.

————. *Domenico Zipoli: Vida y obra.* Buenos Aires: Pontificia Universidad Católica Argentina, 1962.

Azevedo, Luiz Heitor Corrêa de. *Escala, ritmo e melodia na música dos índios brasileiros.* Rio de Janeiro: "Jornal do Commercio," Rodrigues & Cia., 1938.

————. "Tupynambá Melodies in Jean de Léry's 'Histoire d'un Voyage Faict en la Terre du Brésil.'" In *Papers of the American Musicological Society: Annual Meeting, 1941.* Richmond: William Byrd Press, 1946.

"Aztec Music, Reconstructed," *Time,* XXXV/22 (May 27, 1940).

Bachiller y Morales, Antonio. *Cuba Primitiva.* Havana: Miguel de Villa, 1883.

Baker, Theodore. *Über die Musik der nordamerikanischen Wilden.* Leipzig: Breitkopf und Härtel, 1882.

Ballesteros Gaibrois, Manuel. "Un manuscrito colonial del siglo XVIII," *Journal de la Société des Américanistes,* nouv. sér, XXVII/1 (1935).

Bal y Gay, Jesús, ed. *Tesoro de la música polifónica en México, I. El Códice del Convento del Carmen.* México: Instituto Nacional de Bellas Artes, Departamento de Música, 1952 [1953].

————. *Treinta Canciones de Lope de Vega.* Madrid: Residencia de Estudiantes, 1935.

Baqueiro Fóster, Gerónimo. "El Huapango," *Revista Musical Mexicana,* no. 8 (April 21, 1942).

————. "El Secreto Armónico y Modal de un Antiguo Aire Maya." In *Los Mayas Antiguos.* México: El Colegio de México, 1941. Also in *Revista Musical Mexicana,* no. 1 (Jan. 7, 1942).

Baratta, María de. *Cuzcatlán Típico.* San Salvador: Ministerio de Cultura, 1952.

Barbacci, Rodolfo. "Apuntes para un Diccionario Biográfico Musical Peruano," *Fénix,* VI (1949).

Barlow, Robert. "El Códice Azcatítlan," *Journal de la Société des Américanistes,* n.s., XXXVIII and suppl. (1949).

Barrera Vásquez, Alfredo. "Canción de la Danza del Arquero Flechador," *Tlalocan,* I/4 (1944).

Barrera Vásquez, Alfredo, and Silvia Rendón. *El Libro de los Libros de Chilam Balam.* México: Fondo de Cultura Económica, 1948.

Barrera Vásquez, Alfredo, and Sylvanus G. Morley. *The Maya Chronicles.* Washington: Carnegie Institution, 1949. (Publication 585.)

Barriga, Victor M. "Los Músicos y Cantores de la Iglesia Mayor y la Compañía en 1611: Los Maestros de Capilla Nicolás de Tolentino y Juan Castelo—Acuerdos para tocar y cantar en diversos templos," *El Deber* (Arequipa), Aug. 29, 1945.

Bartholomaeus Anglicus. *De proprietatibus rerum.* Nuremberg: Anton Koberger, 1483.

Barwick, Steven. *The Franco Codex.* Carbondale: Southern Illinois University Press, 1964.

Basadre, Jorge, ed. *Literatura Inca.* Paris: Desclée, De Brouwer, 1938.

Basalenque, Diego. *Historia de la Provincia de San Nicolás de Tolentino de Michoacán.* [1673.] México: Ed. Jus, 1963.

Bascom, William. "The Main Problems of Stability and Change in Tradition," *Journal of the International Folk Music Council,* XI (1959).

Batres, Leopoldo. *Archaeological Explorations in Escalerillas Street.* México: J. Águilar Vera & Co., 1902.

————. *Civilización Prehistórica de las Riberas del Papaloapam.* México: Buznego y León, 1908.

Baudizzone, Luis M. *Poesía, Música y Danza Inca.* Buenos Aires: Editorial Nova, 1943.

Bedregal de Conitzer, Yolanda, and Antonio González Bravo. *Calendario Folklórico del Departamento de La Paz.* La Paz: Concejo Municipal de Cultura, 1956.

Bejar Pacheco, Mariano. "Deducciones del sistema musical de la cultura nazca," *El Comercio,* July 28, 1935.

Beristaín de Souza, José Mariano. *Biblioteca Hispano-Americana Septentrional.* México: A. Valdés, 1816–1821. 3 vols.

Berlin, Heinrich. "Relaciones precolombinas entre Cubã y Yucatán," *Revista Mexicana de Estudios Antropológicos,* IV/1–2 (Jan.–Aug., 1940).

Bermúdez de la Torre, Pedro Joseph. *El Sol en el Zodiaco* (including *Parte Segunda: Panegirico y poesias*). Lima: Francisco Sobrino, 1717.

Bermúdez Plata, Cristobal. *Catálogo de Pasajeros a Indias,* II. Seville: Imp. Ed. de la Gavidia, 1942.

Bermudo, Juan. *Comiença el libro llamado declaraciõ de instrumẽtos musicales.* Osuna: Juan de León, 1555.

————. *El arte Tripharia.* Osuna: Juan de León, 1550.

Bernal, Ignacio. *Mexico before Cortez.* New York: Doubleday, 1963.

Bertonio, Ludovico. *Arte y Grammatica mvy copiosa dela Lengva Aymara.* Rome: Luis Zannetti, 1603.

————. *Vocabvlario dela lengva aymara.* Juli [Lima]: Francisco del Canto, 1612.

Betanzos, Juan de. *Suma y narración de los Incas.* Ed. M. Jiménez de la Espada. Madrid: M. G. Hernández, 1880.

Beyer, Hermann. "Una representación auténtica del uso del Omichicahuaztli," *Memorias y Revista de la Sociedad Científica "Antonio Alzate,"* XXXIV/4–9 (June, 1916).

Blankenburg, Angela. "German Missionary Writers in Paraguay," *Mid-America,* XXIX [n.s., XVIII] (Jan., 1947).

Blom, Frans. *The Conquest of Yucatan.* Boston: Houghton Mifflin, 1936.

Boilés, Charles Lafayette. "El Arco Musical, ¿Una pervivencia?," *La Palabra y el Hombre: Revista de la Universidad Veracruzana,* II Época/39 (July–Sept., 1966).

————. "La Flauta Triple de Tenenexpan," *La Palabra y el Hombre,* II Época/34 (April–June, 1965).

————. "The Pipe and Tabor in Mesoamerica," *Yearbook II* of the Inter-American Institute for Musical Research (New Orleans: Tulane University, 1966).

Bonniwell, William R. *A History of the Dominican Liturgy, 1215–1945.* New York: Joseph F. Wagner, 1945.

Boone, Olga. "Les Xylophones du Congo Belge," *Annales du Musée du Congo Belge. Ethnographie-Série III. Notes analytiques sur les Collections,* III/2 (Oct., 1936).

Borchgave, Émile de. "Pierre de Gand," *Biographie Nationale,* XVII. Brussels: Bruylant-Christophe, 1903.

Bose, Fritz. "Die Musik der Chibcha und ihrer heutigen Nachkommen," *Internationales Archiv für Ethnographie*, XLVIII, pt. 2. Leiden: E. J. Brill, 1958.

Boturini Benaduc[c]i, Lorenzo. *Idea de una nueva historia general de la America Septentrional*. Madrid: Imp. de J. de Zúñiga, 1746.

Bouronclé Carrión, Alfonso. "Contribución al Estudio de los Aymaras (Segunda Parte)," *América Indígena*, XXIV/3 (July, 1964).

Braden, Charles S. *Religious Aspects of the Conquest of Mexico*. Durham: Duke University Press, 1930.

Brasseur de Bourbourg, Charles Étienne. *Histoire des nations civilisées du Mexique et de l'Amérique-centrale*. Paris: Arthus Bertrand, 1857–1859. 4 vols.

Bretón Fontecilla, Cecilia. "Una obra musical de Fray Juan Navarro," *Schola Cantorum*, IV/8 (Aug., 1942).

Brinton, Daniel G. *Ancient Nahuatl Poetry*. Philadelphia: [Library of Aboriginal American Literature], 1887.

———. *The Güegüence: A Comedy-Ballet*. Philadelphia: Privately printed, 1883.

———. *Nagualism. A Study in native American folk-lore and history*. Philadelphia: MacCalla, 1894.

Briquet, C. M. *Les Filigranes: Dictionnaire historique*. 2d ed. Vol. II. Leipzig: Karl W. Hiersemann, 1923.

Bueno, Miguel. "Instrumentos Musicales Mexicanos," *El Universal* (Mexico City), pictorial supplement, Sept. 18, 1966.

———. "Interesante Exposición de Instrumentos," *El Universal*, Aug. 28, 1966 (signed with pseudonym, Hans Sachs).

Bunzel, Ruth. *Chichicastenango: A Guatemalan Village*. Locust Valley: J. Augustin, 1952. (*Publications of the American Ethnological Society*, XXII.)

Burgoa, Francisco de. *Geografica Descripcion de la Parte Septentrional, del Polo Artico de la America*. México: Juan Ruys, 1674. Repr. 1934. (*Publicaciones del Archivo General*, XXV–XXVI.)

———. *Palestra Historial*. México: Juan Ruyz, 1670. Repr. 1934. (*Publicaciones del Archivo General*, XXIV.)

Bustamante, Manuel E. *Apuntes para el Folklore Peruano*. Ayacucho: Imp. "La Miniatura," 1943.

Caballero, César Augusto A. *Bibliografía del Folklore Peruano (Primera Contribución)*. Lima: n.p., 1952.

Caballero Farfán, Policarpo. *Influencia de la Música Incaica en el Cancionero del Norte Argentino*. Buenos Aires: Comisión Nacional de Cultura, 1946.

Cabello Balboa, Miguel. *Miscelánea Antártica*. Lima: Universidad Nacional Mayor de San Marcos, 1951.

Calancha, Antonio de la. *Coronica Moralizada*. Barcelona: P. Lacavalleria, 1638.

———. *Coronica Moralizada . . . Tomo Segvndo*. Lima: Jorge López de Herrera, 1653.

Campo [y Pando], Toribio José del. "Carta escrita . . . sobre no ser impropria la Música en las Representaciones Dramáticas," *Mercurio Peruano*, no. 83 (Oct. 20, 1791).

———. "Carta sobre la música: en la que se hace ver el estado de sus conocimientos en Lima," *Mercurio Peruano*, nos. 117, 118 (Feb. 16, 19, 1792).

Campos, Rubén M. *El folklore musical de las ciudades*. México: Secretaría de Educación Pública, 1930.

————. *El folklore y la música mexicana*. México: Secretaría de Educación Pública, 1928.

Cano Gutiérrez, Diego. *Relacion de las Fiestas Trivmphales qve la Insigne Vniuersidad de Lima hizo*. Lima: Francisco Lasso, 1619.

Capitan, Joseph Louis. "L'Omichicahuatzli [*sic*] mexicain et son ancêtre de l'époque du renne en Gaule." In *Verhandlungen des XVI. Internationalen Amerikanisten-Kongresses Wien . . . 1908*. Vienna: A. Hartleben's Verlag, 1910.

Cardoso, Manuel. *Passionarivm ivxta capellae Regis Lvsitaniae consvetvdinem*. Leiria: Antonio à Mariz, 1575.

Carpentier, Alejo. *La música en Cuba*. Mexico: Fondo de Cultura Económica, 1946.

Carreño, Alberto M. "El Primer Misal Romano Impreso en México," *Boletín de la Biblioteca Nacional*, XIII/1–2 (Jan.–June, 1962).

————. "Una Desconocida Carta de Fray Pedro de Gante," *Memorias de la Academia Mexicana de la Historia*, XX/1 (Jan.–March, 1961).

Carrera [Daza], Fernando de la. *Arte de la lengva yvnga de los Valles del Obispado de Truxillo del Peru*. Lima: Joseph de Contreras, 1644.

Carrera Stampa, Manuel. "Algunos aspectos de la *Historia de Tlaxcala*." In *Estudios de Historiografía de la Nueva España*. México: El Colegio de México, 1945.

Carvajal y Robles, Rodrigo de. *Fiestas qve celebro la Civdad de los Reyes*. Lima: Geronymo de Contreras, 1632.

Casa de la Cultura Ecuatoriana. *Catálogo General del Museo de Instrumentos Musicales*. Quito, 1961.

Casas, Bertolomé de las. *Apologética Historia*. Madrid: Sucs. J. Sánchez de Ocaña, 1958. (*Biblioteca de Autores Españoles*, CVI.)

————. *Historia de las Indias*, II. Madrid: Estades, 1957. (*Bibl. de Aut. Esp.*, XCVI.)

Caso, Alfonso. "Ensayo de interpretación del disco estelar que aparece en los tres fragmentos del huehuetl del Ozomatli," *Anales del Museo Nacional de Arqueología, Historia y Etnografía*, 4ª época, VIII (1933).

————. *Las Exploraciones en Monte Albán*. México: Imprenta Mundial, 1932. Tacubaya: n.p., 1935. (Instituto Panamericano de Geografía e Historia, Publications 7, 18.)

————. *Interpretation of the Codex Bodley 2858*. Mexico City: Sociedad Mexicana de Antropología, 1960.

————. "Vida y aventuras de 4 Viento 'Serpiente de Fuego.'" In *Miscelánea de estudios dedicados a Fernando Ortiz*, I. Havana: Sociedad Económica de Amigos del País, 1955.

Castañeda, Daniel. "Una flauta de la cultura tarasca," *Revista Musical Mexicana*, 1/5 (March 7, 1942).

Castañeda, Daniel, and Vicente T. Mendoza. "Los Teponaztlis," "Los Percutores Precortesianos," and "Los Huehuetls," *Anales del Museo Nacional de Arqueología, Historia y Etnografía*, 4ª época, VIII (1933).

Castro, Ignacio de. *Relacion de la fundacion de la Real Audiencia del Cuzco en 1788*. Madrid: Vda. de Ibarra, 1795.

Cervantes de Salazar, Francisco. *Crónica de la Nueva España*, Tomo I. Madrid: Hauser y Menet, 1914. (*Papeles de Nueva España, tercera série, Historia*, ed. Francisco del Paso y Troncoso.)

————. *México en 1554*. México: Universidad Nacional Autónoma, 1939.

————. *Tvmvlo Imperial dela gran ciudad*. México: Antonio de Espinosa, 1560.

Chase, Gilbert. *A Guide to Latin American Music.* Washington: Library of Congress, Music Division, 1945.

———. *A Guide to the Music of Latin America.* Washington: Library of Congress and Pan American Union, 1962.

———. "Juan Navarro *Hispalensis* and Juan Navarro *Gaditanus,*" *Musical Quarterly,* XXXI/2 (April, 1945).

Chávez, Carlos. "La Música." In *México y la Cultura.* México: Secretaría de Educación Pública, 1946.

———. "The Music of Mexico." In *American Composers on American Music.* Ed. Henry Cowell. Stanford: Stanford University Press, 1933.

Chávez, Ezequiel A. *El ambiente geográfico, histórico y social de Pedro de Gante.* México: Editorial Jus, 1943.

———. "Fray Pedro de Gante," trans. Hermenegildo Corbató, *Modern Language Forum,* XIX/3 (Sept., 1934).

———. *El primero de los grandes educadores de la América.* México: Editorial Jus, 1943.

Chávez Orozco, Luis. *Índice del Ramo de Indios del Archivo General de la Nación.* México: Instituto Indigenista, 1951.

Chenoweth, Vida. *The Marimbas of Guatemala.* Lexington: University of Kentucky Press, 1964.

Chimalpahin. *See* Siméon, Rémi.

Chinchilla Águilar, Ernesto. "La Danza del Tum-Teleche o Loj-Tum," *Antropología e Historia de Guatemala,* III/2 (June, 1951).

Cibdad Real, Antonio de. *Relación breve y verdadera de algunas cosas de las muchas que sucedieron al Padre Fray Alonso Ponce en las provincias de la Nueva España.* Madrid: Vda. de Calero, 1872–1873. (*Colección de Doc. Inéd. para la Hist. de España,* LVII–LVIII.)

Cieza de León, Pedro de. *Del Señorío de los Incas.* Buenos Aires: Ed. Argentinas "Solar," 1943.

———. *Parte Primera de la Chronica del Perv.* Antwerp: Juan Steelsio, 1554.

———. *The Incas.* Trans. Harriet de Onis. Norman: University of Oklahoma Press, 1959.

Clark, James Cooper. *The Story of "Eight Deer" in Codex Colombino.* London: Taylor and Francis, 1912.

Clavijero, Francisco. *Historia antigua de México.* Ed. Mariano Cuevas from Clavijero's original Spanish. Vol. II. México: Editorial Porrúa, 1945.

———. *Storia antica del Messico,* II. Cesena: Gregorio Biasini, 1780. Trans. Charles Cullen, *The History of Mexico.* 2d ed. London: J. Johnson, 1807.

Cobo, Bernabé. *Historia de la Fundación de Lima.* Ed. M. González de la Rosa. Lima: Imprenta Liberal, 1882.

———. *Historia del Nuevo Mundo,* IV. Seville: Imp. de E. Rasco, 1893.

Códice Pérez. Trans. from Maya into Spanish by Ermilio Solís Alcalá. Mérida: Imprenta Oriente, 1949.

Cogolludo. *See* López Cogolludo, Diego.

Collaer, Paul. "Cariban and Mayan Music." In *Studia Memoriae Belae Bartók Sacra.* London: Boosey and Hawkes, 1959.

Columbus, Ferdinand. *The Life of the Admiral Christopher Columbus.* Trans. Benjamin Keen. New Brunswick: Rutgers University Press, 1959.

Comettant, Oscar. "La Musique en Amérique avant la découverte de Christophe Colomb," *Compte-Rendu du Congrès International des Américanistes, 1ʳᵉ Session,* II (Nancy: G. Crépin-Leblond, 1875).

Compan, Charles. *Dictionnaire de danse.* Paris: Cailleau, 1787.

Congreso Internacional de Americanistas. *Actas de la Cuarta Reunión.* Madrid: Imp. de Fortanet, 1883.

Coopersmith, Jacob M. "Music and Musicians of the Dominican Republic: A Survey—Part I," *Musical Quarterly,* XX/1 (Jan., 1945).

Córdova, Juan de. *Arte en lengva Zapoteca.* México: Pedro Balli, 1578.

———. *Vocabvlario en lengva çapoteca.* Mexico: Pedro Ocharte and Antonio Ricardo, 1578.

Córdova Salinas, Diego de. *Coronica dela Religiosissima Provinçia delos doze Apostoles del Perv.* Lima: Jorge López de Herrera, 1651.

———. *Teatro de la Santa Iglesia Metropolitana de los Reyes. Anales de la Catedral de Lima.* Lima: n.p., 1958. (Biblioteca Histórica Peruana, Vol. VII.)

Cornyn, John H. *The Song of Quetzalcoatl.* Yellow Springs [Ohio]: Antioch Press, 1931.

Corominas, Joan. *Diccionario crítico etimológico.* Madrid: Editorial Gredos, 1954. 4 vols.

Corsarios franceses e ingleses en la Inquisición de la Nueva España. Siglo XVI. México: Imp. Universitaria, 1945.

Cotarelo y Mori, Emilio. *Colección de Entremeses, Loas, Bailes, Jácaras y Mojigangas.* Tomo I, vol. 1. Madrid: Bailly-Bailliére, 1911.

Covarrubias, Sebastián de. *Tesoro de la Lengua Castellana o Española* [1611]. Barcelona: S. A. Horta, I. E., 1943.

Cresson, H. T. "Aztec Music," *Proceedings of the Academy of Natural Sciences of Philadelphia, 1883,* 3d ser., XIII (1884).

Cuevas, José Jacinto. *Mosaico Yucateco.* Mérida: Luis H. Espinosa, 1951.

Cuevas, Mariano. *Documentos Inéditos del Siglo XVI.* México: Talleres Gráficos del Museo Nacional de Arqueología, Historia y Etnología, 1914.

———. *Historia de la Iglesia en México.* El Paso [Texas]: Editorial "Revista Católica," 1928. 5 vols.

Cuzco Cathedral. *Libro de auctos capitulares 1549–1556* (actually 1546–1590). Unpublished.

Densmore, Frances. "Music of the American Indians at Public Gatherings," *Musical Quarterly,* XVII/4 (Oct., 1931).

———. *Papago Music.* Washington: Govt. Printing Office, 1929.

———. *Yuman and Yaqui Music.* Washington: Govt. Printing Office, 1932.

Díaz del Castillo, Bernal. *Historia verdadera de la conqvista de la Nueva-España.* Madrid: Imp. del Reyno, 1632.

———. *Historia verdadera. . . .* Ed. from original manuscript by Genaro García. México: Secretaría de Fomento, 1904. 2 vols.

Diccionario Geográfico de Guatemala. Guatemala: Tipografía Nacional, 1962. 2 vols.

Diguet, Léon. "Le Chimalhuacan et ses populations avant la Conquête espagnole," *Journal de la Société des Américanistes,* n.s., I/1 (1903).

Domínguez Bordona, Jesús. *Trujillo del Perú a fines del siglo XVIII.* Madrid: C. Bermejo, 1936.

Dorantes de Carranza, Baltasar. *Sumaria relación de las cosas de la Nueva España.* México: Imp. del Museo Nacional, 1902.

Drouin de Bercy. *De Saint-Domingue, de ses guerres, de ses révolutions.* Paris: Hocquet, 1814.

Dürer, Albrecht. *Schriften. Tagebücher. Briefe.* Ed. Max Steck. Stuttgart: W. Kohlhammer, 1961.

Durán, Agustín. *Romancero general.* Madrid: M. Rivadeneyra, 1849–1851. (*Biblioteca de Autores Españoles*, X, XVI.)

Durán, Diego. *Historia de las Indias de Nueva-España.* México: Imp. de J. M. Andrade y F. Escalante, 1867–1880. 2 vols. Partially translated by Doris Heyden and Fernando Horcasitas in *The Aztecs.* New York: Orion Press, 1964.

Eguiara y Eguren, Juan José. *Bibliotheca Mexicana sive Eruditorum Historia Virorum. . . . Tomus Primus.* México: In Aedibus Authoris, 1755. Manuscript continuation at University of Texas Library.

Eguilaz y Yanguas, Leopoldo de. *Glosario etimológico.* Granada: La Lealtad, 1886.

Eguiluz, Diego de. *Historia de la Misión de los Mojos . . . escrita en 1696.* Ed. Enrique Torres Saldamando. Lima: Imp. del Universo, 1884.

Elústiza, Juan B. de, and G. Castrillo Hernández. *Antología Musical.* Barcelona: R. Casulleras, 1933.

Escalona Ramos, Alberto. "Estudio sobre la *Historia de Tlaxcala.*" In Muñoz Camargo, 1947 ed.

Espejo Núñez, Julio. "Bibliografía Básica de Arqueología Andina. V. Música Precolombina," *Boletín Bibliográfico* of the Biblioteca Central, Universidad Nacional Mayor de San Marcos, XXIX/1–4 (Dec., 1956).

Esquivel Navarro, Juan de. *Discvrsos sobre el Arte del Dançado.* Seville: Juan Gómez de Blas, 1642.

Esquivel y Navía, Diego de. *Anales del Cuzco, 1600 á 1750.* Lima: Imprenta de "El Estado," 1901.

Estevão, *Frei* of Thomar. *Liber Passionum.* Lisbon: Simão Lopez, 1595. [British Museum. K.7.f.14.]

Estrada, Jesús. "Clásicos de la Nueva España: Ensayo histórico sobre los Maestros de Capilla de la Catedral de México," *Schola Cantorum*, VII/7 (July, 1945).

Farabee, William C. *Indian Tribes of Eastern Peru.* Cambridge [Mass.]: The Museum, 1922.

Fernández, Diego. *Primera, y segvnda parte, de la historia del Perv.* Seville: Hernando Díaz, 1571.

Fernández, Justino. "Una aproximación a Xochipilli." In *Estudios de Cultura Náhuatl*, I.

Fernández de Castro y Bocángel, Gerónimo. *Elisio Pervano. Solemnidades Heroicas y Festivas Demonstraciones de jvbilos.* Lima: Francisco Sobrino, 1725.

Fernández del Castillo, Francisco. *Doña Catalina Xuárez Marcayda, primera esposa de Hernán Cortés.* México: Imprenta Victoria, 1920.

———. "Fray Diego Durán. Aclaraciones históricas," *Anales del Museo Nacional de Arqueología, Historia y Etnografía*, 4ª época, III (1925).

———. *Libros y Libreros en el Siglo XVI.* México: Tip. Guerrero Hnos., 1914. (*Publicaciones del Archivo General de la Nación*, VI.)

Fernández de Oviedo y Valdés, Gonzalo. *Historia general y natural de las Indias.* Madrid: Imp. de la Real Academia de la Historia, 1851–1855. Reprinted in *Biblioteca de Autores Españoles*, CXVII–CXXI (1959).

————. *Sumario de la Natural Historia.* In Enrique de Vedia, *Historiadores Primitivos.*

Fernández Gómez, Carlos. *Vocabulario de Cervantes.* Madrid: Imp. Silverio Aguirre Torre, 1962.

Fernández Naranjo, Nicolás. "La vida musical en La Paz." In *La Paz en su IV centenario.* Buenos Aires: Imp. López, 1948.

Flury, Lázaro. "Danzas, costumbres y creencias de los indios del Gran Chaco," *América Indígena,* XVI/2 (April, 1956).

Foronda y Aguilera, Manuel de. "Estancias y Viajes de Carlos V," *Boletín de la Sociedad Geográfica de Madrid,* XXXVII/7 (July, 1895).

Fortún [de Ponce], Julia Elena. *Antología de Navidad.* La Paz: Biblioteca Paceña, 1956.

————. "La Navidad en el ámbito chuquisaceño," *Cuaderno de la Sociedad Folklórica de Bolivia,* I. Sucre: Imprenta "Bolívar," 1952.

————. *Manual para la recolección de material folklórico.* La Paz: Ministerio de Educación, Departamento de Folklore, 1957.

Foster, E. A., trans. *Motolinía's History of the Indians of New Spain.* Berkeley: The Cortés Society, 1950. (*Documents and Narratives,* IV.)

Franco Carrasco, José Luis. "Sobre un Grupo de Instrumentos Prehispánicos con Sistema Acústico no Conocido," *Actas y Memorias* of the XXXV Congreso Internacional de Americanistas [1962], Vol. III (México: Editorial Libros de México, S.A., 1964).

Frézier, Amédée François. *Relation du voyage de la mer du Sud aux côtes du Chily et du Perou, fait pendant les années 1712, 1713, & 1714.* Paris: Chez Nyon, 1732.

Friederici, Georg. *Amerikanistisches Wörterbuch.* Hamburg: Cram, De Gruyter, 1947.

Fuentes y Guzmán, Francisco Antonio de. *Recordación Florida,* I. Guatemala City: [Biblioteca "Goathemala," VI], 1932.

Furlong Cárdiff, Guillermo. *Los Jesuitas y la cultura rioplatense.* Montevideo: Urta y Curbelo, 1933.

————. *Músicos Argentinos durante la dominación hispánica.* Buenos Aires: Editorial "Huarpes," 1945.

Galindo, Miguel. *Nociones de Historia de Música Mejicana.* Colima: Tip. de "El Dragón," 1933.

Gallardo, Bartolomé José. *Ensayo de una biblioteca española de libros raros y curiosos,* IV. Madrid: Manuel Tello, 1889.

Gallop, Rodney. "Music and Magic in Southern Mexico," *Monthly Musical Record,* LXIX/806 (May, 1939).

————. "Otomí Indian Music from Mexico," *Musical Quarterly,* XXVI/1 (Jan., 1940).

————. "The Music of Indian Mexico," *Musical Quarterly,* XXV/2 (April, 1939).

Galpin, F. W. "Aztec Influence on American Indian Instruments," *Sammelbände der internationalen Musikgesellschaft,* IV (1903).

Gann, Thomas. "Mounds in Northern Honduras." In *Nineteenth Annual Report of the Bureau of American Ethnology 1897–98.* Pt. 2. Washington: Govt. Printing Office, 1900.

García, Genaro. *El Clero de México durante la dominación española.* México: Vda. de C. Bouret, 1907. (*Doc. inéd. ó muy raros para la hist. de México,* XV.)

García, Gregorio. *Origen de los Indios de el Nvevo Mvndo.* Valencia: P. P. Mey, 1607.

García Granados, Rafael. *Diccionario Biográfico de Historia Antigua de Mejico.* México: Instituto de Historia, 1953. 3 vols.

García Icazbalceta, Joaquín. *Bibliografía Mexicana del Siglo XVI*. México: Librería de Andrade, 1886. Rev. and aug. by Agustín Millares Carlo. México: Fondo de Cultura Económica, 1954.

———. *Colección de Documentos para la Historia de México*, I. México: Lib. de J. M. Andrade, 1858.

———. *Don Fray Juan de Zumárraga*. México: Andrade y Morales, 1881.

———. *Nueva Colección de Documentos para la Historia de México*, II. México: Imp. de Francisco Díaz de León, 1889.

———. *Obras*, III and VII. México: Imp. de V. Agüeros, 1896 and 1898.

Garcilaso de la Vega. *See* Vega, Garcilaso de la.

Garibay Kintana, Ángel. *Historia de la Literatura Náhuatl*. México: Editorial Porrúa, 1953–1954. 2 vols.

———. "Huehuetlatolli, Documento A," *Tlalocan: A Journal of Source Materials*, I/2 (1943).

———. *Poesía indígena de la altiplanicie*. 2d ed. México: Universidad Nacional Autónoma, 1952.

Gates, William, trans. *The de la Cruz-Badiano Aztec Herbal of 1552*. Baltimore: Maya Society, 1939.

Génin, Auguste. "Notes on the Dances, Music, and Songs of the Ancient and Modern Mexicans." In *Annual Report of the Smithsonian Institution . . . 1920*. Washington: Govt. Printing Office, 1922.

———. "The Ancient and Modern Dances of Mexico," *Mexican Magazine*, III/1 (July, 1927).

———. "The Musical Instruments of the Ancient Mexicans," *Mexican Magazine*, III/7 (July, 1927).

Gestoso y Pérez, José. *Noticias Inéditas de Impresores Sevillanos*. Seville: Gómez Hnos., 1924.

Gilberti, Maturino. *Vocabulario en lengua de Mechuacan*. México: Juan Pablos, 1559.

Gillmor, Frances. *Flute of the Smoking Mirror*. Albuquerque: University of New Mexico Press, 1949.

Giménez Fernández, Manuel. *Bartolomé de las Casas*, II. Seville: Escuela de Estudios Hispano-Americanos, 1960. (*Publicaciones*, CXXI.)

Ginastera, Alberto. *Impresiones de la Puna para flauta y cuarteto de cuerdas*. Montevideo: Editorial Cooperativa Interamericana de Compositores, 1942. Consisting of "Quena," "Canción" (including Yaraví), and "Danza."

———. *Ollantay*. Buenos Aires: Barry, 1964 (composed, 1947). Three symphonic movements: "Landscape of Ollantaytambo," "The Warriors," and "The Death of Ollantay."

Girard, Rafael. *Los Chortis ante el problema Maya*. México: Antigua Librería Robredo, 1949.

Goldman, Richard Franko. "Chavez: *Sinfonia India* . . ." (record review), *Musical Quarterly*, XLVI/3 (July, 1960).

Gómara. *See* López de Gómara, Francisco.

Gómez González, Filiberto. "Los Tarahumaras, el grupo étnico mexicano más numeroso que aun conserva su primitiva cultura," *América Indígena*, XIII/2 (April, 1953).

González Bravo, Antonio. "Clasificación de los sicus aimaras," *Revista de Estudios Musicales*, I/1 (Aug., 1949).

——. "Música, instrumentos y danzas indígenas." In *La Paz en su IV centenario*. Buenos Aires: Imp. López, 1948.

González Holguín, Diego. *Vocabvlario dela lengva general de todo el Perv llamada lengua Qquichua, o del Inca*. Lima: Francisco del Canto, 1608.

González Obregón, Luis. *Croniquillas de la Nueva España*. México: Ed. Botas, 1936.

——. *México Viejo y Anecdótica*. México: Vda. de C. Bouret, 1909.

González Suárez, Federico. *Historia General de la República del Ecuador*, III. Quito: Imp. del Clero, 1892.

González Vera, Francisco. "De los primeros misioneros en Nueva España y carta de Fray Pedro de Gante," *Revista de España*, I, iii/11 (Aug. 15, 1868).

Graduale Dominicale. México: Antonio de Espinosa, *ca*. 1570 and 1576; Pedro de Ocharte, 1576.

Granado y Baeza, José. *Imforme del cura de Yaxcabá, Yucatán, 1813*. México: Vargas Rea, 1946.

Green, Samuel A. *A Second Supplementary List of Early American Imprints*. Cambridge [Mass.]: University Press, 1899.

Grenon, Pedro J. "Nuestra primera música instrumental," *Revista de Estudios Musicales*, II/5–6 (Dec., 1950–April, 1951).

Grijalva, Juan de. *Cronica dela Orden de N. P. S. Augustin en las prouincias dela nueua españa. En quatro edades desde el año de .1533 haste el de .1592*. México: Juan Ruyz, 1624.

Guerrero, Francisco. *Liber Vesperarum*. Rome: Ex officina Dominici Bassae apud Alexandrum Gardanum, 1584.

Guerrero, Raúl. *Índice clasificado de la Relación breve*. México: Biblioteca Aportación Histórica (Vargas Rea), 1949.

Guerrero, Raúl G. "Música en Chiapas," *Revista de Estudios Musicales*, I/2 (Dec., 1949).

Gumilla, Joseph. *El Orinoco Ilustrado, Historia Natural, Civil, y Geographica, de este gran rio*. Madrid: Manuel Fernández, 1741. Modern edition: Bogotá: Editorial ABC, 1955.

Gutiérrez de Medina, Cristóbal. *Viaje del Virrey Marqués de Villena*. Ed. Manuel Romero de Terreros. México: Imp. Universitaria, 1947.

Gutiérrez de Santa Clara, Pedro. *Historia de las Guerras Civiles del Perú*, I–IV, VI. Madrid: Lib. de V. Suárez, 1904–1910, 1929.

Gutiérrez Heras, Joaquín. "Mexico's Music in Transition," *Mexican Life*, XL/9 (Sept., 1964).

——. "Music in Transition," *Atlantic Monthly*, 213/3 (March, 1964).

Haekel, Joseph. "Zur Problematik des Obersten Goettlichen Paares im Alten Mexiko," *El México Antiguo*, IX (1959).

Harcourt, R. d'. "L'ocarina à cinq sons dans l'Amérique préhispanique," *Journal de la Société des Américanistes*, n.s. XXII/2 (1930).

——. "Sifflets et ocarinas du Nicaragua et du Mexique," *Journal de la Société des Américanistes*, n.s., XXXIII (1941).

Harcourt, R. and M. d'. *La musique des Aymara sur les hauts plateaux boliviens*. Paris: Société des Américanistes, 1959.

——. *La musique des Incas et ses survivances*. Paris: Lib. Orientaliste Paul Geuthner, 1925. 2 vols.

Harold, Francis, ed. *Lima Limata Conciliis*. Rome: Giuseppe Corvi, 1673.

Hellmer, José Raúl. "Los Antiguos Mexicanos y su Música," *Boletín Bibliográfico de la Secretaría de Hacienda y Crédito Público,* X/286, Época Segunda (Jan. 1, 1964).

————. "Mexican Indian Music Today," republished from *Toluca Gazette,* June 1, 1960, in *Katunob,* II/1 (March, 1961).

Hernández, Francisco. *Antigüedades de la Nueva España.* Trans. Joaquín García Pimentel. México: Pedro Robredo, 1945.

Herrera y Ogazón, Alba. *El Arte Musical en México.* México: Dirección General de las Bellas Artes, 1917.

Herrera y Tordesillas, Antonio de. *Historia general de los hechos de los castellanos en las islas i tierra firme del mar oceano.* Madrid: Imp. Real, 1726–1727.

Herring, Hubert, and Herbert Weinstock, eds. *Renascent Mexico.* New York: Covici-Friede, 1935.

Holzmann, Rodolfo. *Panorama de la Música Tradicional del Perú. 53 Piezas transcritas de grabaciones tomadas directamente en el lugar, con su letra y glosas.* Lima: Ministerio de Educación Pública, Escuela Nacional de Música y Danzas Folklóricas, Servicio Musicológico [Casa Mozart, Jirón Arequipa 184], 1966. With *Suplemento ilustrativo,* preface by E. Mildred Merino de Zela, and *presentación* by José María Arguedas.

Huamán Poma de Ayala, Felipe. *Nueva Corónica y Buen Gobierno.* Paris: Institut d'Ethnologie, 1936.

Humphreys, Robert A. *Liberation in South America 1806–1827. The Career of James Paroissien.* London: University of London [The Athlone Press], 1952.

Ibarra Grasso, Dick Edgar. *Prehistoria de Bolivia.* La Paz: Editorial "Los Amigos del Libro," 1965.

Iglesia, Ramón. *Cronistas e Historiadores de la Conquista de México.* México: El Colegio de México, 1942.

Instrvccion para remediar, y assegvrar, qvanto con la diuina gracia fuere possible, que ninguno de los Negros, que vienen de Guinea, Angola, y otras Prouincias de aquella costa de Africa, carezca del sagrado Baptismo. Lima: Geronymo de Contreras, 1628.

"Instrumentos musicales," *Política,* VII/153 (Sept. 1, 1966).

"Investigación Folklórico-Musical de la Señora Henrietta Yurchenco en Nayarit y Jalisco," *Boletín de la Sección de Investigaciones Musicales del Departamento de Música,* nos. 13–22 (June, 1963–March, 1964), inserted in *Cuadernos de Bellas Artes,* IV/6–V/3.

Issasi, Hernando de. *Qvatvor Passiones Domini, cvm Benedictione Cerei.* Salamanca: Typis Haered. Mathiae Gastii, 1582.

Iturriaga, Enrique. "Las investigaciones de Andrés Sas sobre la música de la Colonia," *El Comercio* (Sunday Supplement), Sept. 5, 1954.

Ixtlilxóchitl. *See* Alva Ixtlilxóchitl.

Izikowitz, Karl Gustav. "Les instruments de musique des Indiens Uro-Chipaya," *Revista del Instituto de Etnología de la Universidad de Tucumán,* II (1931–1932).

————. *Musical and Other Sound Instruments of the South American Indians.* Gothenburg: Eleanders Boktryckeri Aktiebolag, 1935.

Jiménez Borja, Arturo. *Instrumentos Musicales del Perú.* Lima: Museo de la Cultura, 1951.

————. *La Danza en el Antiguo Perú (Época Pre-Inca).* Lima: Museo Nacional (offprint from *Revista del Museo Nacional,* XXXIV), 1955.

————. "Peruanische Tänze und Tanzmasken," *Zeitschrift für Ethnologie*, LXXXIV/2 (1959).

Jiménez de la Espada, Marcos, ed. *Relaciones Geográficas de Indias*. Madrid: Manuel G. Hernández, 1881.

————. *Tres Relaciones de Antigüedades Peruanas*. Madrid: M. Tello, 1879.

————. *Una Antigualla Peruana*. Madrid: Imp. de Fortanet, 1892.

Jiménez Moreno, Wigberto. "Fr. Bernardino de Sahagún y su obra." In Sahagún, *Historia General*, I (1938).

Jiménez Rueda, Julio. *Historia de la Cultura en México: El Virreinato*. México: Ed. Cultura, 1950.

Johnson, Harvey L. *An Edition of Triunfo de los Santos*. Philadelphia: University of Pennsylvania, 1941. (*Publications, Series in Romance Languages and Literature*, 31.)

Jones, A. M. "Report on Lecture on 'African Music,'" *African Music Society Newsletter*, I/3 (July, 1950).

Juarros, Domingo. *Compendio de la Historia de la Ciudad de Guatemala*. 3d ed. Guatemala City: Tipografía Nacional, 1936.

Klineberg, Otto. "Notes on the Huichol," *American Anthropologist*, n.s., XXXVI/3 (July–Sept., 1934).

Klüpfel, Karl, ed. *N. Federmanns und H. Stades Reisen in Südamerica 1529 bis 1555*. Stuttgart: Litterarischer Verein, 1859.

Kollmann, J. "Flöten und Pfeifen aus Alt-Mexiko." In *Festschrift für Adolf Bastian*. Berlin: D. Reimer, 1896.

Krickeberg, Walter. *Altmexikanische Kulturen*. Berlin: Safari-Verlag, 1956. Trans. as *Las antiguas culturas mexicanas*. México: Fondo de Cultura Económica, 1961.

Kroeber, Alfred L., and William Duncan Strong. *The Uhle Pottery Collections from Ica* (*University of California Publications in American Archaeology and Ethnology*, XXI/3). Berkeley: University of California Press, 1924.

Kurath, Gertrude, and Samuel Martí. *Dances of Anáhuac*. Chicago: Aldine Publishing Co., 1964. (*Viking Fund Publications in Anthropology*, 38.)

Kutscher, Gerdt. "The Translation of the 'Cantares Mexicanos' by Leonhard Schultze Jena." In *Proceedings of the Thirty-Second International Congress of Americanists* [1956]. Copenhagen: Munksgaard, 1958.

Lach, Robert. "Die musikalischen Konstruktionsprinzipien der altmexikanischen Tempelgesänge." In *Festschrift für Johannes Wolf*. Berlin: Martin Breslauer, 1929.

Lacroix, Frédéric. "Pérou et Bolivie." In *L'Univers. Histoire et Description de tous les peuples: Mexique, Guatémala et Pérou*. Paris: Firmin Didot frères, 1843.

Lagunas, Juan Baptista de. *Arte y dictionario: con otras Obras, en lengua Michuacana*. México: Pedro Balli, 1574.

————. *Dictionarito breve y compendioso en la lēgua de Michuacan*. México: Pedro Balli, 1574.

Landa, Diego de. *Relación de las cosas de Yucatán*. Ed. Hector Pérez Martínez. Mexico: Pedro Robredo, 1938. *See also* Tozzer, A. M.

Las Casas. *See* Casas, Bartolomé de las.

Lehmann, Walter. "Les peintures mixtéco-zapotèques et quelques documents apparentés," *Journal de la Société des Américanistes*, n.s., II/2 (Oct. 15, 1905).

Leite, Serafim. *Artes e ofícios dos Jesuítas no Brasil (1549–1760)*. Lisbon: Edições Brotéria, 1953.

————. "Cantos, músicas e danças nas aldeias do Brasil (século XVI)," *Brotéria,* XXIV (1937).

León, Antonio de. *Constitvciones Synodales, del Obispado de Arequipa.* Lima: Joseph de Contreras, 1688.

León, Nicolás. *Bibliografía Mexicana del Siglo XVIII.* México: Imp. de F. Díaz de León, 1902–1908.

————. "Los Indios Tarascos del Lago de Pátzcuaro," *Anales del Museo Nacional de Arqueología, Historia y Etnografía,* 5ª ép., I/1 (1934).

————. *Los Tarascos: Notas históricas, étnicas y antropológicas.* México: Imp. del Museo Nacional, 1904.

Leonard, Irving A. "Best Sellers of the Lima Book Trade, 1583," *Hispanic American Historical Review,* XXII/1 (Feb., 1942).

————. *Don Carlos de Sigüenza y Góngora: A Mexican Savant of the Seventeenth Century.* Berkeley: University of California Press, 1929.

————. "On the Cuzco Book Trade, 1606," *Hispanic Review,* IX/3 (July, 1941).

————. "On the Mexican Book Trade, 1683," *Hispanic American Historical Review,* XXVII/3 (Aug., 1947).

————. *Romances of Chivalry in the Spanish Indies.* Berkeley: University of California Press, 1933. (*Publications in Modern Philology,* XVI/3.)

León Portilla, Miguel. *Los antiguos mexicanos a través de sus crónicas y cantares.* México: Fondo de Cultura Económica, 1961.

————. *La filosofía náhuatl estudiada en sus fuentes.* México: Instituto Indigenista Interamericano, 1956.

Léry, Jean de. *Histoire d'vn Voyage faict en la terre dv Bresil, avtrement dite Amerique.* 3d ed. [Geneva]: Antoine Chuppin, 1585.

————. *Historia Navigationis in Brasiliam, qvae et America dicitvr.* Geneva: Eustache Vignon, 1586. Latin translation of preceding title.

Liber processionum secundum ordinem fratrum predicatorum. Seville: M. Ungut and S. Polonus, 1494.

Libros de Cabildos de Lima: Libro Cuarto (Años 1548–1555) and *Libro Quinto (Años 1553–1557).* Lima: Torres Aguirre-Sanmartí y Cía., 1935. Transcribed by Bertram T. Lee.

Loayza, Francisco A., ed. *Las Crónicas de los Molinas.* Lima: Domingo Miranda, 1943. (Los Pequeños Grandes Libros de Historia Americana, Ser. 1, Vol. IV.)

Lohmann Villena, Guillermo. *El Corregidor de Indios en el Perú.* Madrid: Ediciones Cultura Hispánica, 1957.

López Cogolludo, Diego. *Historia de Yucathan.* Madrid: Juan García Infanzón, 1688.

López de Gómara, Francisco. *Historia de Mexico, con el descvbrimiento dela Nueva España.* Antwerp: Juan Steelsio, 1554. Trans. Lesley B. Simpson as *Cortés: The Life of the Conqueror.* Berkeley and Los Angeles: University of California Press, 1964.

————. *La Historia general de las Indias y Nuevo Mundo.* Saragossa: Pedro Bernuz, 1554.

López Medel, Tomás. See López Cogolludo.

López Rayon, Ignacio, transcriber. *Documentos para la Historia de México,* I: *Sumaria de la Residencia tomada á D. Fernando Cortés.* México: Vicente García Torres, 1852.

Loredo, Rafael. "Sentencias contra los que participaron en el alzamiento de Gonzalo Pizarro," *Mercurio Peruano,* año XV, no. 159 (May, 1940).

Lorenzana, Francisco Antonio. *Concilium Mexicanum Provinciale*. México: Typ. Josephi Antonii de Hogal, 1770.

Lothrop, S. K. "La Metalúrgia aborígen de América," in *Letras: Organo de la Facultad de Letras* (San Marcos University), I (1953).

Lumholtz, Carl. *New Trails in Mexico*. New York: Charles Scribner's Sons, 1912.

——. "The Huichol Indians of Mexico," *Bulletin of the American Geographic Society*, XXXV/1 (Feb., 1903).

——. *Unknown Mexico*. New York: Charles Scribner's Sons, 1902. 2 vols.

McAndrew, John. *The Open-Air Churches of Sixteenth-Century Mexico*. Cambridge [Mass.]: Harvard University Press, 1965.

McPhee, Colin. "New York—January–February 1936," *Modern Music*, XIII/3 (March–April, 1936).

Maisel, Edward M. *Charles T. Griffes*. New York: Alfred A. Knopf, 1943.

Manuale Sacramētorū, secundū vsum almę Ecclesię Mexicanę. México: Pedro de Ocharte, 1568.

Manuale Sacramentorum secundum vsum Ecclesię Mexicanę. Mexico: Juan Pablos, 1560.

Marban, Pedro. *Arte de la Lengua Moxa, con su Vocabulario*. Lima, 1702.

Mariana, Juan de. *Tratado contra los juegos públicos*, in *Obras*, II. Madrid: M. Rivadeneyra, 1854. (*Biblioteca de Autores Españoles*, XXXI.)

Marino, Giambattista. *L'Adone*. Turin: G. B. Paravia, 1922.

Markham, Clement, trans. *Ollanta*. London: Trübner, 1871.

Martens, Frederick H. "Music in the Life of the Aztecs," *Musical Quarterly*, XIV/3 (July, 1928).

Martí, Samuel. *Canto, danza y música precortesianos*. México: Fondo de Cultura Económica, 1961.

——. "Flautilla de la penitencia: Fiesta grande de Tezcatlipoca," *Cuadernos Americanos*, LXXII/6 (Nov.–Dec., 1953).

——. *Instrumentos musicales precortesianos*. México: Instituto Nacional de Antropología, 1955.

Martínez, Juan. *Vocabulario enla lengua general del Peru llamada Quichua*. Lima, 1604.

Mason, J. Alden. *The Ancient Civilizations of Peru*. Harmondsworth: Penguin Books, 1957.

Mayer-Serra, Otto. "Silvestre Revueltas and Musical Nationalism in Mexico," *Musical Quarterly*, XXVII/2 (April, 1941).

Maza, Francisco de la. *Fray Diego Valadés: Escritor y Grabador Franciscano del Siglo XVI*. México: Sobretiro del Número 13 de los Anales del Instituto de Investigaciones Estéticas, 1945.

Mead, Charles W. "The Musical Instruments of the Incas," *Supplement to American Museum Journal*, III/4 (1903).

Means, Philip Ainsworth. *Ancient Civilizations of the Andes*. New York: Charles Scribner's Sons, 1942.

Medina, José Toribio. *Bartolomé Ruiz de Andrade, primer piloto del Mar del Sur*. Santiago de Chile: Imp. Elzeviriana, 1919.

——. *Biblioteca hispano-americana*. Santiago de Chile: Casa del autor, 1898–1907. 7 vols.

————. *Colección de Documentos Inéditos para la Historia de Chile* . . . *1518–1818*, V and XXIX. Santiago: Imp. Elzeviriana, 1889 and 1901.

————. *Historia de la Imprenta en los antiguos dominios españoles.* Santiago: Fondo Histórico y Bibliográfico, 1958. 2 vols.

————. *La Imprenta en Lima* (*1584–1824*). Santiago: Casa del Autor, 1904–1907. 4 vols.

————. *La Imprenta en México, 1539–1821,* I and II. Santiago: Casa del Autor, 1909 [1912] and 1907.

————. *Noticias biobibliográficas de los Jesuitas Expulsos de América en 1767.* Santiago: Imp. Elzeviriana, 1915.

Meggers, Betty J. *Ecuador.* London: Thames and Hudson, 1966.

Mejía, Estanislao. "El Folklore de Tlaxcala," *Orientación Musical,* VIII/89 (May, 1949).

Meléndez, Juan. *Tesoros Verdaderos de las Yndias.* Rome: Nicholas Angel Tinassio, 1681.

Méndez Plancarte, Gabriel. *Poetas Novohispanos: Primer Siglo.* México: Universidad Nacional Autónoma, 1942.

Mendieta, Gerónimo de. *Historia Eclesiástica Indiana.* México: Antigua Librería, 1870.

Mendoza, Vicente T. *El romance español y el corrido mexicano.* México: Universidad Nacional Autónoma, 1939.

————. "La Música y la Danza." In Jorge R. Acosta and others, *Esplendor del México Antiguo,* I (1959).

————. "Musica indígena de México," *México en el Arte,* IX (1950).

————. "Música Indígena Otomí," *Revista de Estudios Musicales,* II/5–6 (Dec., 1950–April, 1951).

————. "Música precolombina de América," *Boletín Latino-Americano de Música,* IV (1938).

————. *Panorama de la Música Tradicional de México.* México: Imp. Universitaria, 1956.

————. "Tres instrumentos musicales prehispánicos," *Anales del Instituto de Investigaciones Estéticas,* VII (1941).

Mexico City. Archdiocese. *Constituciones del arçobispado . . . de Tenuxtitlā Mexico.* México: Juan Pablos, 1556.

Middendorf, Ernst W. *Das Muchik oder die Chimu-Sprache.* Leipzig: F. A. Brockhaus, 1892.

Milán, Luys. *Libro de mvsica de vihuela de mano.* Valencia: Francisco Díaz Romano, 1536.

Millares Carlo, Agustín, and Julián Calvo. *Juan Pablos: Primer impresor que a esta tierra vino.* México: Manuel Porrua, 1953.

Minsheu, John. *Vocabvlarivm Hispanicolatinvm et Anglicum copiosissimum.* London, 1617.

Missale Romanum Ordinarium. México: Antonio de Espinosa, 1561.

Mitjana, Rafael. *Estudios sobre algunos músicos españoles del siglo XVI.* Madrid: Sucs. de Hernando, 1918.

Molina, Alonso de. *Arte de la lengua Mexicana.* México: Pedro Ocharte, 1571.

————. *Confessionario Mayor.* México: Pedro Balli, 1578.

————. *Vocabvlario en lengva castellana y mexicana.* 1571. México: Antonio de Espinosa, 1571.

Molina, Cristóbal de. *See* Loayza, Francisco A.

Molina Solís, Juan F. *Historia del descubrimiento y conquista de Yucatán,* I. Mérida: Imp. R. Caballero, 1896.

Montejano y Aguíñaga, Rafael. "La conversión de los indios por medio de la música," *Schola Cantorum,* IX/9 (Sept. 1947).

Montesinos, Fernando. *Memorias antiguas historiales y políticas del Perú.* Madrid: Imp. de M. Ginesta, 1882.

Montúfar, Alonso de. "Carta del Arzobispo de México al Consejo de Indias," *Anales del Museo Nacional de Arqueología, Historia y Etnografía,* 5ª época, I/3 (July–Dec., 1934).

Morales, Pedro de. *Carta.* México: Antonio Ricardo, 1579.

Morelet, Arthur. *Voyage dans l'Amérique Centrale.* Paris: Gide et J. Baudry, 1857.

Moreno, Segundo Luis. "La Música en el Ecuador." In J. Gonzalo Orellana, *El Ecuador en cien años de independencia.* Tomo II. Quito: Imp. de la Escuela de Artes y Oficios, 1930.

Morley, Sylvanus G. *The Ancient Maya.* Stanford: Stanford University Press, 1946.

Morúa, Martín de. *Historia del origen y genealogía real de los Reyes Inças.* Madrid: C. Bermejo, 1946.

Motolinía, Toribio de. *Carta al Emperador.* Ed. José Bravo Ugarte. México: Editorial Jus, 1949.

————. *Historia de los Indios de Nueva España.* In *Colección de Documentos para la Historia de México,* I. Ed. J. García Icazbalceta (1858). Translations: *see* Foster, E. A.; Steck, F. B.

————. *Memoriales.* México: Casa del Editor [L. García Pimentel], 1903.

Muelle, Jorge C. "Arqueología y Folklore," *Folklore Americano,* II/2 (1954).

Muñoz Camargo, Diego. *Historia de Tlaxcala.* México: Secretaría de Fomento, 1892.

Muriel, Josefina. *Conventos de Monjas en la Nueva España.* Mexico: Editorial Santiago, 1946.

Museo de Oro. *80 masterpieces from the Gold Museum.* Bogotá: Banco de la República, 1954.

Navarro, Juan. *Liber in quo quatuor passiones Christi Domini continentur.* México: Diego López Dávalos, 1604.

Nicholson, H. B. "The Chapultepec Cliff Sculpture of Motecuhzoma Xocoyotzin," *El México Antiguo,* IX (1959).

Nowotny, Karl A. "Americana," *Archiv für Völkerkunde,* XVI (1961).

————. "Die Notation des *Tono* in den Aztekischen Cantares," *Baessler-Archiv,* Neue Folge, IV/2 [XXIX. Band] (Dec., 1956).

————. "Erläuterungen zum Codex Vindobonensis (Vorderseite)," *Archiv für Völkerkunde,* III (1948).

Nowotny, Karl A., ed. *Codices Becker I/II.* Graz: Akademische Druck- u. Verlagsanstalt, 1961.

Núñez de la Vega, Francisco. *Constituciones Dioecesanas del Obispado de Chiappa.* Rome: C. Zenobi, 1702.

Nuttall, Zelia. *The Book of the Life of the Ancient Mexicans.* Berkeley: University of California Press, 1903.

Oblitas Poblete, Enrique. *Cultura Callawaya.* La Paz: Talleres Gráficos Bolivianos, 1963.

Odriozola, Manuel de. *Documentos históricos del Perú,* I. Lima: Aurelio Alfaro, 1863.

Oliva, Anello, *Historia del Reino y Provincias del Perú de sus Incas Reyes. Descubrimiento y Conquista por los españoles* (1598). Lima: Imp. y Lib. de S. Pedro, 1895.

Orbigny, Alcide d'. *Voyage dans l'Amérique Méridionale.* Tome troisième, 1ʳᵉ Partie. Paris-Strasbourg: P. Bertrand-Vᵉ Levrault, 1844.

Ordinarivm sacri ordinis hȩremitarū sancti Augustini. México: Juan Pablos, 1556.

Oré, Gerónimo de. *Symbolo Catholico Indiano.* Lima: Antonio Ricardo, 1598.

Orrego-Salas, Juan. "Araucanian Indian Instruments," *Ethnomusicology,* X/1 (Jan., 1966).

Ortega, José. *Apostolicos Afanes de la Compañia de Jesus.* Barcelona: Pablo Nadal, 1754.

——. *Historia del Nayarit* (= *Apostólicos Afanes*). México: E. Abadiano, 1887.

——. *Vocabulario en Lengua Castellana y Cora.* Hdos. de la Vda. de F. Rodríguez Lupercio, 1732. Repr. in *Boletín de la Sociedad Mexicana de Geografía y Estadística,* primera época, VIII (1860).

Ortiz, Fernando. *La africania de la música folklórica de Cuba.* Havana: Ministerio de Educación, 1950.

——. "Instrumentos musicales indoamericanos," *Inter-American Review of Bibliography,* VII/4 (Oct.–Dec., 1957).

Osborne, Lucy E. "The Whitchurch Compartment in London and Mexico," *The Library,* 4th ser., VIII (1928).

Pagaza Galdo, Consuelo. "El Yaraví del Cuzco," *Folklore Americano,* VIII-IX/8-9 (1960–1961).

Palomera, Esteban J. *Fray Diego Valadés, o.f.m.* México: Editorial Jus, S.A., 1960.

Pane, Ramón. *See* Ramón Pane.

Paniagua, Flavio Antonio. *Documentos y datos para un Diccionario Etimológico, Histórico y Geográfico de Chiapas,* I. San Cristóbal–Las Casas: Manuel Bermúdez R., 1908.

Paredes, Manuel Rigoberto. "Instrumentos musicales de los Kollas," *Boletín Latino-Americano de Música,* II (Lima: Editorial Lumen, 1936).

Paso y Troncoso, Francisco del. *Epistolario de Nueva España 1505–1818,* IX. México: Antigua Librería Robredo, 1940.

Paz Soldán, Mateo. *Geografía del Perú,* I. Paris: Lib. de Fermin Didot, 1862.

Paz y Melia, A. "Cartapacio de diferentes versos á diversos asuntos compuestos ó recogidos por Mateo Rosas de Oquendo," *Bulletin hispanique,* VIII/2 (April–June, 1906) and 3 (July–Sept., 1906).

Pedraza, Cristóbal de. "Relacion de la Prouincia de Honduras y Higueras." In *Col. de Doc. Inéd. rel. al descubrimiento, conquista y organización de las antiguas posesiones españolas,* sec. ser., XI. Madrid: Sucs. de Rivadeneyra, 1898. (*Relaciones de Yucatán,* I.)

Pedrell, Felipe. *Cancionero Musical Popular Español,* IV. Valls: Eduardo Castells, 1922.

——. "Folk-lore musical castillan du XVIᵉ siècle," *Sammelbände der Internationalen Musik-Gesellschaft,* I (1899–1900).

Pénable, M. J. "Le Cor," *Encyclopédie de la Musique et Dictionnaire du Conservatoire,* 2ᵐᵉ partie, III. Paris: Lib. Delagrave, 1925.

Peñafiel, Antonio. *Monumentos del Arte Mexicano Antiguo.* Berlin: A. Asher & Co., 1890.

Peñafiel, Antonio, ed. *Cantares en idioma mexicano.* México: Secretaría de Fomento, 1899. Reproducción facsimiliaria, same publisher, 1904 [1906].

Pennington, Campbell W. *The Tarahumar of Mexico.* Salt Lake City: University of Utah Press, 1963.

Peralta Barnuevo, Pedro de. *Lima fundada . . . Parte Primera.* Lima: Francisco Sobrino y Bados, 1732.

———. *Lima trivmphante.* Lima: Joseph de Contreras y Alvarado, 1708.

Perdomo Escobar, José Ignacio. *Historia de la música en Colombia.* Bogotá: Imp. Nacional, 1945. Augmented and revised (3d ed.). Bogotá: Editorial ABC, 1963. (*Biblioteca de Historia Nacional,* CIII.)

Pereira Salas, Eugenio. *Los Orígenes del Arte Musical en Chile.* Santiago: Imp. Universitaria, 1941.

Pérez Ayala, José Manuel. *Baltasar Jaime Martínez Compañón y Bujanda.* Bogotá: Imprenta Nacional, 1955.

Pérez Bocanegra, Juan. *Ritval Formvlario, e Institvcion de Cvras.* Lima: Geronymo de Contreras, 1631.

Pérez de Ribas, Andrés. *Historia de los trivnfos de nvestra santa fee entre gentes las mas barbaras.* Madrid: Alonso de Paredes, 1645.

Pérez Pastor, Cristóbal. *Bibliografía Madrileña,* I. Madrid: Tip. de los Huérfanos, 1891.

Peterson, Frederick A. *Ancient Mexico.* New York: G. P. Putnam's Sons, 1959.

Phelan, John Leddy. *The Millennial Kingdom of the Franciscans in the New World.* Berkeley and Los Angeles: University of California Press, 1956. (*Publications in History,* 52.)

Pierson, Hamilton W., "Anacoana [*sic*], Queen of the Caribs." In Henry R. Schoolcraft, *Information respecting the History, Condition and Prospects of the Indian Tribes of the United States,* II. Philadelphia: Lippincott, Grambo, 1852.

Pineda, Juan de, ed. *Libro del Passo Honroso, defendido por el excelente caballero Suero de Quiñones.* Madrid: Antonio de Sancha, 1783.

Pizarro, Pedro. *Relación del descubrimiento y conquista de los reinos del Perú.* Buenos Aires: Editorial Futuro, 1944.

Polo de Ondegardo, Juan. *Informaciones acerca de la Religión y Gobierno de los Incas.* Lima: Sanmartí y Cia., 1916–1917. 2 vols.

Pope, Isabel. "Documentos Relacionados con la Historia de la Música en México," *Nuestra Música,* VI/21 (1er Trimestre, 1951); VI/24 (4° Trimestre, 1951).

———. "The 'Spanish Chapel' of Philip II," *Renaissance News,* V/2 (Summer, 1952).

Popol Vuh: The Sacred Book of the Ancient Quiché Maya. English version by Delia Goetz and Sylvanus G. Morley. London: William Hodge & Co., 1951.

Porras Barrenechea, Raúl. *Cartas del Perú, 1524–1543.* Lima: Sociedad de Bibliófilos Peruanos, 1959.

———. *El cronista indio, Felipe Huamán Poma de Ayala.* Lima: Editorial Lumen, 1948.

———. "El Rastro Autobiográfico de Huamán Poma (De un estudio inédito que comprende su vida y su obra)," *La Prensa* (Lima), July 28, 1945.

———. *Fuentes históricas peruanas.* Lima: J. Mejía Baca and P. L. Villanueva, 1951.

———. *El Inca Garcilaso en Montilla (1561–1614).* Lima: Editorial San Marcos, 1955.

———. *Las Relaciones Primitivas de la Conquista del Perú.* Paris: Imp. les Presses modernes, 1937.

————. "El Sochantre Cristóbal de Molina." In *Las Crónicas de los Molinas*. Ed. F. A. Loayza.

Prescott, William H. *History of the Conquest of Mexico*. New York: Harper and Brothers, 1843. 3 vols.

Preuss, Konrad T. *Die Nayarit-Expedition*. Leipzig: B. G. Teubner, 1912.

————. "Der Mitotentanz der Coraindianer," *Globus*, XC/5 (Aug. 2, 1906).

————. "Reise zu den Stämmen der westlichen Sierra Madre in Mexiko." In *Zeitschrift der Gesellschaft für Erdkunde zu Berlin*, 1908.

————. "Un viage a la Sierra Madre Occidental de México," *Boletín de la Sociedad de Geografía y Estadística*, 5ª época, III (1908).

Psalterivm, Aniphonarium. Mexico: Pedro de Ocharte, 1584.

Psalterium Chorale. México: Pedro de Ocharte and Gerónima Gutiérrez, 1563.

Querol Gavaldá, Miguel, ed. *Romances y Letras a tres voces*. Barcelona: Instituto Español de Musicología, 1956.

Ramírez, Fernando. *Expedición de Hernán Cortés a Las Hibueras*. México: Vargas Rea, 1947.

Ramírez de Fuenleal, Sebastián. *L'évêque de Saint-Domingue à l'impératrice*. In H. Ternaux-Compans, *Voyages, relations et mémoires originaux*, XVI. Paris: Arthus Bertrand, 1840.

Ramón (= Román) Pane. "Escritura. De la antiguedad de los indios." In Fernando Colón, *Historia del Almirante Don Cristóbal Colón*. Madrid: Imp. de T. Minuesa, 1892. (*Colección de libros raros ó curiosos que tratan de América*, V.)

Ranking, John. *Historical Researches on the Conquest of Peru, Mexico*. London: Longman, Rees [etc.], 1827.

Rea, Alonso de la. *Chronica de la Orden de N. Seraphico P. S. Francisco, Prouincia de S. Pedro y S. Pablo de Mechoacan en la Nueua España*. México: Bernardo Calderón, 1643.

Redfield, Robert. *Tepoztlán, a Mexican Village: A Study in Folklife*. Chicago: University of Chicago Press, 1930.

————. *The Folk Culture of Yucatan*. Chicago: University of Chicago Press, 1941.

Relación de la grandiosa fiesta que el señor gobernador D. Luis de Andrade y Sotomayor alcalde ordinario de la Villa Imperial de Potosí hizo á 4 de Marzo de 1663. Seville, 1889.

Relación de las ceremonias y ritos y población y gobierno de los indios de la provincia de Michoacán [1541]. Ed. José Tudela and others. Madrid: Águilar, 1956.

Relación sucinta de las fiestas celebradas en la ciudad de Nuestra Señora de La Paz, en el Perú, a costa del regidor de ella Don Tadeo Diez de Medina con motivo de la exaltación al trono del Señor Rey Don Carlos IV. Madrid, 1791.

Remesal, Antonio de. *Historia de la Prouincia de S. Vicente de Chyapa y Guatemala*. Madrid: Francisco de Angulo, 1619. Repr. *Biblioteca "Goathemala,"* IV–V. Guatemala: Tip. Nacional, 1932.

René-Moreno, Gabriel. *Biblioteca Boliviana: Catálogo del Archivo de Mojos y Chiquitos*. Santiago: Imprenta Gutenberg, 1888.

————. *Les derniers jours de la colonie dans le Haut-Pérou*. Paris: Ed. Nagel, 1954.

Ribera, Juan Antonio. *Pompa funeral en las exequias del . . . Rey . . . Fernando VI*. Lima: Pedro Nolasco Alvarado, 1760.

Ribera Flórez, Dionysio de. *Relacion historiada de las Exeqvias*. México: Pedro Balli, 1600.

Ricard, Robert. *La conquête spirituelle du Mexique*. Paris: Institut d'Ethnologie, 1933.

———. "Notes sur la biographie de Fr. Alonso de Montúfar," *Bulletin hispanique*, XXV/3 (July–Sept., 1925).

———. "Remarques bibliographiques sur les ouvrages de Fr. Toribio Motolinía," *Journal de la Société des Américanistes*, n.s., XXV/1 (1933).

Rincón, Antonio del. *Arte Mexicana*. México: Pedro Balli, 1595. New ed. by Antonio Peñafiel. México: Secretaría de Fomento, 1885.

Río, Marcela del. "Instrumentos musicales prehispánicos," *Excelsior*, Oct. 14, 1962. Interview with José Luis Franco Carrasco.

Rivero, Mariano Eduardo de, and J. J. von Tschudi. *Antigüedades Peruanas*. Vienna: Imprenta Imperial, 1851.

Rivet, Paul. "Les langues de l'ancien diocèse de Trujillo," *Journal de la Société des Américanistes*, XXXVIII (1949).

Rivet, Paul, and Georges de Créqui-Montfort. *Bibliographie des langues aymará et kičua*. Paris: Institut d'Ethnologie, 1951–1956. 4 vols.

Robelo, Cecilio A. "Diccionario de Mitología Nahoa," *Anales del Museo Nacional*, 2ª época, II–V (1905–1908).

Robertson, Donald. Review of *Los antiguos mexicanos a través de sus crónicas y cantares*, in *American Anthropologist*, 63/6 (Dec., 1961).

———. *Mexican Manuscript Painting of the Early Colonial Period: the Metropolitan Schools*. Yale Historical Publications: History of Art, Vol. XII. New Haven: Yale University Press, 1959.

Rocha, Diego Andrés. *Tratado vnico, y singvlar del origen de los Indios Occidentales del Piru*. Lima: Imp. de Manuel de los Olivos, 1681.

Rodríguez, Ignacio. "Instrumentos Musicales en México," *Excelsior*, Sunday Supplement, Dec. 4, 1966.

Rodríguez de León, Antonio. *Relacion delas fiestas qve ala immacvlada concepcion . . . se hizieron en la Real Ciudad de Lima . . . 1617*. Lima: Francisco del Canto, 1618.

Roel Pineda, Josafat. "El Wayno del Cuzco," *Folklore Americano*, VI–VII (Lima, 1959).

———. "Un Instrumento Musical de Paracas y Q'ero," *Boletín del Conservatorio Nacional de Música*, 2ª época, Año II, no. 30 (Lima, Jan.–Sept., 1961).

Rojas, Gabriel de. "Descripción de Cholula," *Revista Mexicana de Estudios Históricos*, I/6 (Nov.–Dec. 1927).

Rojas, Ricardo. *Eurindia* (*Obras*, Tomo V). Buenos Aires: Librería "La Facultad," 1924.

———. *Ollantay. Tragedia de los Andes*. Buenos Aires: Editorial Losada, S.A., 1939.

Rojas Garcidueñas, José. *Bernardo de Balbuena*. México: Instituto de Investigaciones Estéticas, 1958.

———. "Fiestas en México en 1578," *Anales del Instituto de Investigaciones Estéticas*, IX (1942).

Rolón, José. "La música autóctona mexicana y la técnica moderna," *Música* (Aug. 15, 1930).

Romances varios de differentes authores, nuevamente impresos por un curioso. Amsterdam: Ishaq Coen Faro, 1688.

Román Pane, friar. *See* Ramón Pane.

Romero, Carlos A. *Los Orígenes del Periodismo en el Perú*. Lima: Imp. Gil, 1940.

Romero, Jesús C. "Causas que interrumpieron su tradición," *Orientación Musical: Revista Mensual*, II/43 (May, 1943).

———. "¿Existió la Música Precortesiana?" *Boletín de la Sociedad Mexicana de Geografía y Estadística*, LVI/2 (March–April, 1942).

———. *Música precortesiana*. México: Talleres Gráficos de la Editorial Stylo, 1947.

Romero Flores, Jesús. *Iconografía Colonial*. México: Museo Nacional, 1940.

Romero Quiroz, Javier. *El Huéhuetl de Malinalco*. Toluca: Universidad Autónoma del Estado de México, 1958.

———. *El Teponaztli de Malinalco*. Toluca: Universidad Autónoma del Estado de México, 1964.

Rossi y Rubí, José. "Idea de las Congregaciones Públicas de los Negros Bozales," *Mercurio Peruano*, nos. 48, 49 (June 16, 19, 1791).

Rowe, J. H. *An Introduction to the Archaeology of Cuzco*. Cambridge [Mass.]: The Museum, 1944.

———. *Chavín Art*. New York: Museum of Primitive Art, 1962.

———. "Inca Culture at the Time of the Spanish Conquest," *Bulletin 143* (*Handbook of South American Indians*, vol. 2). Washington: Smithsonian Institution, 1946.

Roxo Mexia y Ocón, Juan. *Arte de la lengva general de los indios del Perv*. Lima: Jorge López de Herrera, 1648.

Roys, Ralph L. *The Book of Chilam Balam of Chumayel*. Washington: Carnegie Institution, 1933.

———. *The Indian Background of Colonial Yucatan*. Washington: Carnegie Institution, 1943.

Ruppert, Karl, J. Eric S. Thompson, and Tatiana Proskouriakoff. *Bonampak, Chiapas, Mexico*. Washington: Carnegie Institution, 1955.

Sachs, Curt. *World History of the Dance*. New York: W. W. Norton, 1937.

Safford, William E. "Pan-pipes of Peru," *Journal of the Washington Academy of Sciences*, IV/8 (April 19, 1914).

Sahagún, Bernardino de. *Florentine Codex: General History of the Things of New Spain*, Books 1–5, 7–12. Trans. Arthur J. O. Anderson and Charles E. Dibble. Santa Fe: School of American Research, 1950–1963.

———. *Historia General de las Cosas de Nueva España*. Ed. Wigberto Jiménez Moreno. México: Editorial Pedro Robredo, 1938. 5 vols. Ed. Ángel M. Garibay K. México: Editorial Porrúa, 1956. 4 vols.

———. *Psalmodia Christiana . . . Ordenada en cantares ò Psalmos: paraque canten los Indios en los areytos, que hazen en las Iglesias*. México: Pedro Ocharte, 1583.

———. *Ritos, sacerdotes y atavios de los dioses*. Transcribed from the Códice Matritense [fols. 254v–273] by Miguel León Portilla. Mexico: Universidad Nacional Autónoma, Instituto de Historia, 1958.

Salazar, Adolfo. "El caso de Domenico Zipoli," *Nuestra Música*, I/2 (May, 1946).

———. *La Música en Cervantes*. Madrid: Ograma, 1961.

Salazar de Villasante. "Relación General de las poblaciones españolas del Perú." In *Relaciones Geográficas de Indias*, I (1881). Ed. M. Jiménez de la Espada.

Saldívar, Gabriel. *Historia de la Música en México* (*Épocas Precortesiana y Colonial*). México: Editorial "Cultura," 1934.

———. *El Jarabe, baile popular mexicano*. México: Talleres Gráficos de la Nación, 1937.

Salinas, Francisdo de. *De musica libri septem*. Salamanca: M. Gastius, 1577.

Sánchez de Águilar, Pedro. *Informe contra idolorvm cvltores del obispado de Yvcatan.* Madrid: Vda. de Juan Gonçález, 1639. 3rd ed. Mérida: E. G. Triay, 1937.

Sánchez de Fuentes, Eduardo. *Folklorismo.* Havana: Imp. Molina y Cía., 1928.

Sancho de Melgar, Esteban. *Arte de la lengva general del ynga llamada Qquechhua.* Lima: Diego de Lyra, 1691.

Sandoval, Fernando B. "La Relación de la Conquista de México en la *Historia de Fray Diego Durán.*" In *Estudios de historiografía de la Nueva España* (México: El Colegio de México, 1945).

Santacruz Pachacuti Yamqui, Joan de. "Relacion de Antigüedades deste Reyno del Piru." In *Tres Relaciones de Antigüedades Peruanas.* Madrid: M. Tello, 1879.

Santamaría, Francisco J. *Diccionario de Mejicanismos.* México: Ed. Porrúa, 1959.

Santo Tomás [Navarrete], Domingo de. *Grammatica, o arte de la lengua general de los Indios delos Reynos del Peru.* Valladolid: Francisco Fernández de Córdova, 1560.

———. *Lexicon, o Vocabulario de la lengua general del Perv.* Valladolid: Francisco Fernández de Córdova, 1560.

Sanz, Gaspar. *Instrvccion de mvsica sobre la guitarra española.* Saragossa: Herederos de Diego Dormer, 1674.

Sarmiento de Gamboa, Pedro. *Historia de los Incas.* Buenos Aires: Emecé, 1943.

Sargeant, Winthrop. "Types of Quechua Melody," *Musical Quarterly,* XX/2 (April, 1934).

———. "Music of the Incas Survives in Tribal Melodies of the Andes," *Musical America,* LII/2 (Jan. 25, 1932).

Sartorius, Christian Carl. "Musikalische Leichenfeier und Tänze der Mexico-Indianer," *Caecilia,* VIII/29 (Mainz: B. Schott's Söhnen, 1828).

Sas, Andrés. "Ensayo sobre la música nazca," *Boletín Latino-Americano de Música,* IV/4 (Oct., 1938); also, *Revista del Museo Nacional,* VIII/1 (1939).

———. "La Capilla de Música de Gonzalo Pizarro," *Correo de Insula,* I/3 (Dec., 1946).

———. "Los Primeros Músicos Españoles en Lima," *Anacrusa,* I (June, 1956).

———. "Los Primeros Músicos Indo-peruanos de cultura europea, en el siglo XVI," *Música: Órgano del Grupo Renovación,* I/1 (July, 1957).

———. "Una familia de Músicos Peruanos en el siglo XVII: Los Cervantes del Águila," *Música,* I/2 (Aug., 1957).

Saussure, Henri de. *Antiquités mexicaines.* [*Le manuscrit du Cacique.*] Geneva: Aubert-Schuchardt, 1891.

Saville, Marshall H. "A Primitive Maya Musical Instrument," *American Anthropologist,* X/8 (Aug., 1897).

———. *The Wood-Carver's Art in Ancient Mexico.* New York: Museum of the American Indian, 1925.

———. "The Musical Bow in Ancient Mexico," *American Anthropologist,* XI/9 (Sept., 1898).

———. *Some Unpublished Letters of Pedro de La Gasca Relating to the Conquest of Peru.* Worcester: The Society, 1918.

Schmeckebier, Laurence E. *Modern Mexican Art.* Minneapolis: University of Minnesota Press, 1939.

Schmidt, Er. A., trans. *Peru, nach seinem gegenwärtigen Zustande dargestellt, aus dem Mercurio Peruano.* Zweiter Theil. Weimar: Land. Ind. Comt., 1808.

Schultze Jena, Leonhard. *Alt-Aztekische Gesänge.* Stuttgart: W. Kohlhammer Verlag, 1957.

Seeger, Charles. "Carlos Chávez: Sinfonía India," *Notes of the Music Library Association,* sec. ser., VII/4 (Sept., 1950).

Séjourné, Laurette. *Burning Water: Thought and Religion in Ancient Mexico.* London: Thames & Hudson, 1956.

———. *Supervivencias de un mundo mágico.* México: Fondo de Cultura Económica, 1953.

Seler, Eduard. "Altmexicanischen Knochenrasseln," *Globus,* LXXIV/6 (Aug. 6, 1898).

———. *Comentarios al Códice Borgia.* México: Fondo de Cultura Económica, 1963. 2 vols.

———. "Die holzgeschnitzte Pauke von *Malinalco* und das Zeichen *atl-tlachinolli,*" *Mittheilungen der Anthropologischen Gesellschaft in Wien,* XXXIV/4–5 (Sept. 25, 1904).

———. "Die Tierbilder der mexikanischen und der Maya-Handschriften," *Zeitschrift für Ethnologie,* XLI (1909).

———. *Gesammelte Abhandlungen,* II, III. Berlin: A. Asher, Behrend, 1904, 1908.

———. "Götzendienerei unter den heutigen Indianern Mexikos," *Globus,* LXIX/23 (June, 1896).

———. "Mittelamerikanische Musikinstrumente," *Globus,* LXXVI/7 (Aug. 19, 1899).

Short-Title Catalogue of Books printed in Italy . . . from 1465 to 1600. London: British Museum, 1958.

Sicramio [pseudo. of J. M. Tirado]. "Rasgo Remitido por la Sociedad Poética sobre la Música," *Mercurio Peruano,* no. 101 (Dec. 22, 1791).

Sigüenza y Góngora, Carlos de. *Glorias de Queretaro.* Mexico: Vda. de B. Calderón, 1680.

Siméon, Rémi. *Dictionnaire de la langue nahuatl.* Paris: Imprimerie Nationale, 1885.

Siméon, Rémi, trans. *Annales de Chimalpahin Quauhtlehuanitzin.* Paris: Maisonneuve & Ch. Leclerc, 1889.

Simpson, Lesley B. *The Encomienda in New Spain.* Berkeley and Los Angeles: University of California Press, 1950.

Skinner, Joseph, trans. *The Present State of Peru.* London: R. Phillips, 1805.

Södling, Carl Erik. *Indianska dans-melodier upptecknade i Södra Amerika.* Stockholm: Abr. Hirsch, [1874]. Bound with *Indianska sånger* [1874].

Solís Alcalá, Ermilo. *Diccionario Español-Maya.* Mérida: Editorial Yikal Maya Than, 1950.

Sordo Sodi, María del Carmen. "África en los Orígenes del 'a Go-Go,'" *El Sol de México,* Sección C, Jan. 21, 1967.

———. "La investigación etnomusical en México," *Armonía,* 8–9 (Aug.–Sept., 1966).

———. "Los dioses de la música y de la danza en el Códice Borgia," *Revista del Conservatorio* (Mexico City), 7 (June, 1964).

Soria Lens, Luis. *Notas para el estudio del folklore paceño.* La Paz: n.p., 1954.

Spain. Ministerio de Fomento. *Cartas de Indias.* Madrid: Manuel G. Hernández, 1877.

Spell, Lota M. "Music and Instruments of the Aztecs. The Beginnings of Musical Education in North America," *Papers and Proceedings of the Music Teachers' National Association,* 49th year, 1925 (1926).

————. "Music in the Cathedral of Mexico in the Sixteenth Century," *Hispanic American Historical Review*, XXVI/3 (Aug., 1946).

————. "The First Music-Books Printed in America," *Musical Quarterly*, XV/1 (Jan., 1929).

————. "The First Teacher of European Music in America," *Catholic Historical Review*, n.s., II/3 (Oct., 1922).

Squier, Ephraim George. *Peru: Incidents of Travel and Exploration in the Land of the Incas*. London: Macmillan, 1877.

Staden, Hans. *Warhaftige Historia*. Marburg: Andres Kolben, 1557.

Stanford, E. Thomas. "A Linguistic Analysis of Music and Dance Terms from Three Sixteenth-Century Dictionaries of Mexican Indian Languages," *Yearbook II* of the Inter-American Institute for Musical Research (New Orleans: Tulane University, 1966).

————. "Datos sobre la música y danzas de Jamiltepec, Oaxaca." *Anales del Instituto Nacional de Antropología e Historia*, XV (no. 44 de la Colección), 1962 (1963).

————. "La lírica popular de la costa michoacana," *Anales del Instituto Nacional de Antropología e Historia*, XVI, 1963 (1964).

Starr, Frederick. "Notes on Mexican Musical Instruments—Past and Present: What Was the tecomapiloa?" *American Antiquarian and Oriental Journal*, XXV/5 (Sept.–Oct., 1903).

————. *Notes upon the Ethnography of Southern Mexico*. Davenport: Putnam Memorial Publication Fund, 1900. Reprinted from *Proceedings of the Davenport Academy of Natural Sciences*, VIII.

————. "Popular Celebrations in Mexico," *Journal of American Folk-Lore*, IX/34 (July–Sept., 1896).

Steck, Francis Borgia. *El primer colegio de América: Santa Cruz de Tlatlelolco*. México: Centro de Estudios Franciscanos, 1944.

Steck, Francis Borgia, trans. *Motolinía's History of the Indians of New Spain*. Washington: Academy of American Franciscan History, 1951.

Stols, Alexandre A. M. *Antonio de Espinosa*. México: Biblioteca Nacional, 1962.

Streit, Robert. *Bibliotheca Missionum*. Vols. II, III. Aachen: Xaverius Verlagsbuchhandlung, 1924, 1927.

Strunk, Oliver. *Source Readings in Music History*. New York: W. W. Norton, 1950.

Suárez de Peralta, Juan. *Noticias históricas de la Nueva España*. Madrid: M. G. Hernández, 1878.

Subirá, José. *La Tonadilla escénica*. Barcelona: Ed. Labor, 1933.

Swanton, John R. "The Quipu and Peruvian Civilization." In *Bureau of American Ethnology Bulletin No. 133*. Washington: Smithsonian Institution, 1943.

Tapia Centeno, Carlos de. *Noticia de la lengua huasteca*. México: Imp. de la Bibliotheca Mexicana, 1767.

Tejera, Emiliano. *Palabras indíjenas de la isla de Santo Domingo*. Santo Domingo: Editorial "La Nación," 1935.

Téllez Girón, Roberto. "Informe sobre la investigación folklórico-musical realizada en la región de los Coras, Estado de Nayarit, Enero a Marzo, 1939." In *Investigación Folklórica en México: Materiales*, II. México: Secretaría de Educación Pública, Instituto Nacional de Bellas Artes, Departamento de Música (Sección de Investigaciones Musicales), 1964.

Ternaux-Compans, Henri. *Voyages, relations et mémoires originaux pour servir à l'histoire de la découverte de l'Amérique.* Vols. X, XVI. Paris: Arthus Bertrand, 1838, 1840.

Tezozomoc. *See* Alvarado Tezozomoc.

Thayer Ojeda, Tomás. "Las biografías de los dos 'Cristobales de Molina,'" *Revista Chilena de Historia y Geografía,* XXXVI/40 (1920, 4° Trim.).

Thompson, J. Eric S. *Maya Archaeologist.* Norman: University of Oklahoma Press, 1963.

———. *Maya Hieroglyphic Writing.* Norman: University of Oklahoma Press, 1960.

———. "The Orchestra." In Karl Ruppert, *Bonampak, Chiapas, Mexico* (1955).

———. *The Rise and Fall of Maya Civilization.* Norman: University of Oklahoma Press, 1954.

Tirado, J. M. *See* Sicramio.

Tompkins, John Barr. "Codex Fernandez Leal," *Pacific Art Review,* II/1–2 (Summer, 1942).

Toor, Frances. "Mexican Folk Dances." In Hubert Herring, *Renascent Mexico.*

Torquemada, Juan de. *Veinte i vn libros rituales i Monarchia Indiana.* Madrid: N. Rodríguez Franco, 1723. 3 vols.

Torre, Juan de. *Aclamacion festiva de la mvy noble imperial Villa de Potosi.* Lima: Francisco Sobrino, 1716.

Torre Revello, José. "Algunos libros de música traídos a América en el siglo XVI," *Inter-American Review of Bibliography,* VII/4 (Oct.–Dec., 1957).

Torres, Bernardo de. *Cronica de la Provincia Pervana del Orden de los Ermitaños de S. Agvstin.* Lima: Julián Santos de Saldaña, 1657.

Torres de Mendoza, L. *Colección de Documentos Inéditos relativos al descubrimiento, conquista y organización . . . de América . . . sacados de los archivos del reino y muy especialmente del de Indias.* XX. Madrid: Imp. del Hospicio, 1873.

Torres Rubio, Diego de. *Arte de la lengua Aymara.* Lima: Francisco del Canto, 1616.

———. *Arte de la lengva quichua.* Lima: Francisco Lasso, 1619.

Torres Saldamando, Enrique. *Los Antiguos Jesuitas del Peru.* Lima: Imp. Liberal, 1882.

Tozzer, Alfred M. *A Maya Grammar.* Cambridge, Mass.: Peabody Museum, 1921. (*Papers,* IX.)

Tozzer, Alfred M., ed. *Landa's Relación de las Cosas de Yucatán.* Cambridge, Mass.: Peabody Museum, 1941.

Trend, John B. *The Music of Spanish History.* London: Oxford University Press, 1926.

Tschudi, J. J. von. *Die Kechua-Sprache.* Vienna: Kaiserlich-Koeniglichen Hof- und Staatsdruckerei, 1853. 3 vols.

Tudela, José, and others. *See Relación de las ceremonias.*

Tudela Bueso, Juan Pérez de. "Vida y escritos de Gonzalo Fernández de Oviedo." In *Biblioteca de Autores Españoles,* CXVII. Madrid: Gráficas Orbe, 1959.

Ulloa, Antoine de. *Voyage historique de l'Amérique Méridionale,* I. Amsterdam-Leipzig: Arkste'e & Markus, 1752.

"Un pueblo melódico," *Visión,* XXXI/10 (Sept. 30, 1966).

Urteaga, H. H., ed. *Informaciones acerca de la Religión y Gobierno de los Incas.* Lima: Sanmartí, 1918.

Vaillant, George C. *Aztecs of Mexico.* Garden City: Doubleday, Doran, 1941; Doubleday, 1962.

Vaissière, Pierre de. *Saint-Domingue*. Paris: Perrin, 1909.

Valadés, Diego. *Rhetorica Christiana*. Perusia: Pietro Giacomo Petrucci, 1579.

Valcarcel, Theodoro. "¿Fue exclusivamente de 5 sonidos la escala musical de los Incas?" *Revista del Museo Nacional* (Lima), I/1 (1932).

Valderrama, José. "La Marimba y el Teponaztli como 'Intrusos,'" *Novedades* (Mexico City), Aug. 15, 1966.

Valtón, Emilio. *Impresos Mexicanos del Siglo XVI (Incunables Americanos)*. México: Imp. Universitaria, 1935.

Vargas Machuca, Bernardo. *Milicia y descripción de las Indias*, I. Madrid: Lib. de V. Suárez, 1892.

Vargas Ugarte, Rubén. *Concilios Limenses*, I. Lima: Tip. Peruana, 1951.

———. *De la Conquista a la República (Artículos Históricos)*. Lima: Lib. e Imp. Gil, 1942.

———. *Folklore Musical del Siglo XVIII*. Lima: Empresa Gráfica Scheuch, 1946.

———. "Notas sobre la Música en el Perú," *Cuaderno de Estudio*, III/7. Lima: Pontificia Universidad Católica del Perú [Instituto de Investigaciones Históricas], 1949.

———. *Rosas de Oquendo y otros*. Lima: Tipografía Peruana, 1955.

———. "Un archivo de música colonial en la ciudad del Cuzco," *Mar del Sur*, V/26 (March–April, 1953).

Vásquez, Juan A. "Códice Borgia" (review), *América Indígena*, XXIV/3 (July, 1964).

Vásquez-Machicado, Humberto. "Un códice cultural del siglo XVIII," *Historia* (Buenos Aires), IV/14 (Oct.–Dec. 1958).

Vázquez de Espinosa, Antonio. *Compendio y descripción de las Indias Occidentales*. Washington: Smithsonian Institution, 1948.

Vedia, Enrique de, ed. *Historiadores Primitivos de Indias*, I. Madrid: Sucs. de Hernando, 1918. (*Bibl. de Aut. Esp.*, XXII.)

Vega, Carlos. *Escalas con semitonos en la música de los antiguos peruanos*. Buenos Aires: Imp. y Casa Edit. "Cori," 1934.

———. *La música de un códice colonial del siglo XVII*. Buenos Aires: Imp. de la Universidad, 1931.

———. "La música incaica y el doctor Sivirichi," *Nosotros*, XXIII (vol. 64, no. 239) (April, 1929).

———. *Los instrumentos musicales aborígenes y criollos de la Argentina*. Buenos Aires: Ediciones Centurión, 1946.

———. "Tradiciones Musicales y Aculturación en Sudamérica." In *Music in the Americas*, ed. George List and Juan Orrego-Salas. Bloomington: Indiana University Research Center in Anthropology, Folklore, and Linguistics, 1967.

———. "Un códice peruano colonial del siglo XVII," *Revista Musical Chilena*, XVI/81–82 (July–Dec., 1962).

———. *Música sudamericana*. Buenos Aires: Emecé Editores, 1946.

Vega, Garcilaso de la. *Historia General del Perv*. Córdova: Vda. de Andrés Barrera, 1617.

———. *Les commentaires royaux ou l'histoire des Incas*. Trans. Alain Gheerbrant. Paris: Club des Libraires de France, 1959.

———. *Primera Parte de los Commentarios Reales*. Lisbon: Pedro Crasbeeck, 1609.

Vela, David. *La Marimba. Estudio Sobre el Instrumento Nacional* [Biblioteca Guatemalteca de Cultura Popular, LIV]. Guatemala City: Centro Editorial "José de Pineda Ibarra," 1962.

Vetancurt, Agustín de. *Menologio franciscano*. México: Vda. de Juan de Ribera, 1697, 1698. (*Teatro Mexicano, IV*. Madrid: José Porrúa Turanzas, 1961.)

Vidal Martínez, Leopoldo. *Poesía de los Incas*. Lima: Ed. Amauta, 1947.

Villalba Muñoz, Alberto. "The Tonal System of Incan Music," *Inter-America. A Monthly that links the thought of the New World*, V/4 (April, 1922).

Villa-Lobos, Heitor. *Três Poemas Indígenas* (*Trois Poèmes indiens*). Paris: Éditions Max Eschig, 1929. In three parts: "Canide ioune," "Teirú," and "Iára."

Villareal, Federico, ed. *La Lengua yunga o mochica segun el Arte publicado en Lima en 1644*. Lima: E. Z. Casanova, 1921.

Villareal Vara, Félix. *El "Wayno" de Jesús* (*Departamento de Huanuco*). *Investigación Etnomusicológica*. Lima: Ministerio de Educación Pública, 1957.

Vindel, Francisco. *Apéndice*. Madrid: Talleres tipográficos de Góngora, 1954.

————. *El Primer Libro Impreso en América*. Madrid: n.p., 1953.

————. *En papel de fabricación azteca fue impreso el primer libro en América*. Madrid: n.p., 1956.

Voltaire, François Arouet de. *Essai sur les mœurs et l'esprit des nations*, III in *Œuvres complètes*, XVIII. Kehl: Imp. de la Société littéraire-typographique, 1785.

Wagner, Henry R. "Henri Ternaux-Compans: A Bibliography," *Inter-American Review of Bibliography*, VII/3 (1957).

————. *Nueva Bibliographía Mexicana del Siglo XVI*. México: Editorial Polis, 1940.

————. *The Rise of Fernando Cortés*. Berkeley: The Cortés Society, 1944. (*Documents and Narratives*, n.s., III.)

Weiant, C. W. *An Introduction to the Ceramics of Tres Zapotes̃*. Washington: Government Printing Office, 1943. (Smithsonian Institution, Bureau of American Ethnology, Bulletin 139.)

Weinstock, Herbert. *Mexican Music*. New York: Museum of Modern Art, 1940.

Weitlaner, Roberto. "Cantos otomíes de la Sierra de Puebla." In *Homenaje a Pablo Martínez del Río*. México: Instituto Nacional de Antropología e Historia, 1961.

Welch, Christopher. *Lectures on the Recorder*. London: Oxford University Press, 1961.

Wilson, Charles M. "Open Sesame to the Maya," *Bulletin of the Pan American Union*, LXXXII/7 (July, 1948).

Wisdom, Charles. *The Chorti Indians of Guatemala*. Chicago: University of Chicago Press, 1940.

Wiznitzer, Arnold. "O livro de Atas das Congregações Judaicas 'Zur Israel' em Recife e 'Magen Abraham' em Maurícia, Brasil, 1648–1653," *Anais da Biblioteca Nacional* (Rio de Janeiro), LXXIV (1953).

Xérez, Francisco de. *Libro primo de la conqvista del Perv & prouincia del Cuzco*. Venice: Stephano da Sabio, 1535.

Ximénez, Francisco. *Qvatro Libros. De la Natvraleza, y Virtvdes de las plantas, y animales*. México: Vda. de Diego López Dávalos, 1615.

Yeomans, William. "The Musical Instruments of Pre-Columbian Central America." In *Proceedings of the Thirtieth International Congress of Americanists* (Cambridge, 1952). London: Royal Anthropological Institute, n.d.

Yriarte, Tomás de. "La Música." In *Colección de obras en verso y prosa*, I. Madrid: Benito Cano, 1787.

Yurchenco, Henrietta. "Grabación de música indígena," *Nuestra Música*, I/2 (May, 1946).

———. "La Música Indígena en Chiapas," *América Indígena*," III/4 (Oct., 1943).

———. "La Recopilación de Música Indígena," *América Indígena*, VI/4 (Oct., 1946).

———. "Primitive Music in Indian Mexico: A journey of musical discovery," *HiFi Stereo Review*, IX/4 (Oct., 1962).

———. "Singing Mexico," *American Record Guide*, 25/8 (April, 1959).

———. "Survivals of pre-Hispanic Music in New Mexico," *Journal of the International Folk Music Council*, XV (1963).

———. "Taping History in Guatemala," *American Record Guide*, 25/4 (Dec., 1958).

———. "Taping History in Mexico," *American Record Guide*, 33/1 (Sept., 1966).

Zamacois, Niceto de. *Historia de Méjico*, IV. Barcelona: J. F. Párres, 1877.

Zárate, Agustín de. *Historia del descvbrimiento y conqvista delas Provincias del Peru*. Seville: Alonso Escrivano, 1577.

Zulaica Garate, Ramón. *Los Franciscanos y la imprenta en México en el siglo XVI*. México: Pedro Robredo, 1939.

Zurita, Alonso de. *Historia de la Nueva España*. Madrid: Lib. Gen. de Victoriano Suárez, 1909. (*Colección de Libros y Documentos referentes á la Historia de América*, IX.)